Aberdeen
and the
Enlightenment

AUP titles of related interest

NEW LIGHT ON MEDIEVAL ABERDEEN
edited by John Smith

FROM LAIRDS TO LOUNS
Country and Burgh Life in Aberdeen 1600-1800
edited by David Stevenson

A THOUSAND YEARS OF ABERDEEN
Alexander Keith

SCOTLAND'S NORTH SEA GATEWAY
Aberdeen Harbour 1136-1986
John Turner

WILLIAM ELPHINSTONE AND THE KINGDOM
OF SCOTLAND 1431-1514
Leslie J. Macfarlane

PHILOSOPHY AND FICTION
Essays in Literary Aesthetics
edited by Peter Lamarque

COMMON DENOMINATORS IN ART AND SCIENCE
edited by Martin Pollock

THE MEANING OF FREEDOM
Philip Drew

Aberdeen
and the
Enlightenment

Proceedings of a conference held at the
University of Aberdeen

edited by
Jennifer J. Carter and Joan H. Pittock

ABERDEEN UNIVERSITY PRESS

First published 1987
Aberdeen University Press
A member of the Pergamon Group

© The Contributors 1987

British Library Cataloguing in Publication Data

Aberdeen and the Enlightenment: proceedings
    of a conference held at the University of
    Aberdeen.
    1. Aberdeen (Grampian)—History
    I. Carter, Jennifer   II. Pittock, Joan
    941.2′3507   DA890.A2

ISBN 0-08-034524-7

PRINTED IN GREAT BRITAIN
THE UNIVERSITY PRESS
ABERDEEN

Contents

Section V   Literature of the Enlightenment

Plates

Cover illustration
'Old Aberdeen' by Alexander Nasmyth, by kind permission of Aberdeen District Council.

Abbreviations

AUL   Aberdeen University Library
AUP   Aberdeen University Press
BL   British Library
CUP   Cambridge University Press
DNB   *Dictionary of National Biography*
ESTC *Eighteenth-Century Short Title Catalogue*
HMC   Historical Manuscripts Commission
N & Q Notes & Queries
NLS   National Library of Scotland
OED   *Oxford English Dictionary*
OUP   Oxford University Press
SRO   Scottish Record Office

Introduction

Jennifer J. Carter and Joan H. Pittock
University of Aberdeen

In August 1986 an international conference was held in Aberdeen to celebrate 'Aberdeen and the Enlightenment'. This volume brings together the papers which were presented and discussed at that conference. They relate to philosophy and law, art and music, literature and language, religion and politics, printing and bookselling, the universities and overseas contacts of Aberdeen during the Enlightenment.

A celebration of the Scottish Enlightenment and its flowering in the mid eighteenth century had long been planned by Edinburgh University Institute for Advanced Studies in the Humanities. The plan was realised as IPSE 86, an extended series of lectures, seminars, exhibitions and conferences which took place between April and September 1986, culminating in a group of conferences coinciding with the Edinburgh Festival—a massive and exhilarating exchange on all aspects of the Scottish Enlightenment. The British Society for Eighteenth-Century Studies had been asked to participate in IPSE 86. It seemed that this participation might well be combined also with a conference being organised by the Aberdeen University Quincentenary History Project.[1] The Aberdeen conference was designed to highlight the contribution of the North East of Scotland to the general pattern of Enlightenment activity, and to illuminate the history of Aberdeen University at that time.

If the splendid exhibitions in Edinburgh had demonstrated the truth of Smollett's comment, in *Humphry Clinker* (1771), that Edinburgh was indeed a 'hot-bed of genius', yet there were among the five hundred or so delegates at Edinburgh those who questioned the appropriateness of so exclusive a concentration of interest on such a relatively brief period and on so specific a social group. What of the earlier traditions of late seventeenth-century Scotland, economically poorer but no less committed to practical improvements and the advancement of learning? Is the Scottish Enlightenment still to be seen as the post-Union realisation of a new Scottish identity? Is all Scottish experience, political as well as cultural, to be assimilated to a single pattern, however complex? The concentration on Edinburgh too seems to neglect the achievements, certainly of Glasgow, and perhaps also of Aberdeen.

At Aberdeen, somewhat different perspectives emerged. The deep roots of

1

the Scottish Enlightenment, and the considerable continuity of thought and practical action between the seventeenth and the eighteenth centuries, was one of the keynotes of 'Aberdeen and the Enlightenment'. It was sounded in lively fashion by Mr Donald Withrington, who gave an opening paper at the conference, and equally strongly by one of the two guest speakers, Dr Anand Chitnis. Many other contributors, including Dr Christine Shepherd and Dr David Stevenson, likewise stressed the seventeenth-century inheritance, and elements of continuity rather than discontinuity between pre- and post-Union Scotland. According to the interpretation of the Enlightenment advanced by Chitnis and Withrington, it was the slowly-increasing economic strength of Scotland; its newly-moderate religious stance; its practical involvement with science and technology which formed the basis for the Enlightenment, at least as much as any post-Union craving for national identity. Enlightened attitudes and behaviour were spread well beyond Edinburgh's polite and academic circles.

Though cosmopolitanism was less marked at Aberdeen than in Edinburgh, international connexions were important. The conference heard, for instance, of Aberdeen-educated men who took Enlightened attitudes to India and America, whose activities were evaluated by Professor Kitty Datta and Dr Robert Lawson-Peebles. Dr Paul Dukes found threads of contact between Aberdeen and Russia. The openness of the North East of Scotland to foreign influences was reflected even in minor ways, as shown in Dr William Brogden's comments on Aberdeen architecture, or Dr Roger Williams's account of the work of a Swiss composer being found among the manuscript music at Castle Fraser. The North East of Scotland in the eighteenth century may indeed have been a geographically-isolated community, but it was not inward-looking.

The isolation and political conservatism of the North East has long been taken to be reflected in the strength of its support for Jacobitism. Yet recent interpretations suggest that we should not view Jacobitism as a backward-looking forlorn hope, without significance or popular support. At this conference Dr Murray Pittock discussed the political philosophy of a leading North-East Jacobite, Lord Pitsligo, whose papers have newly been deposited in Aberdeen University Library. Jacobitism was a problem for the University, when following the rebellion of 1715 most of the professors of both King's College and Marischal College were purged. From then onwards, government influence over the University increased, but not necessarily in unhelpful ways, as Professor Roger Emerson's paper demonstrated. Emerson showed how professorial appointments at Marischal were increasingly subject to political influence (the patronage rights of the Earls Marischal having been taken over by the crown when the Earl Marischal was attainted in 1716), and how appointments at King's could also be subject to outside influence, for instance by the strong-minded University Chancellor, Lord Deskford. A politically-influential Chancellor, like Lord Bute, could be most helpful to the University—Bute may have been one of Britain's least successful prime ministers, but he was a good University Chancellor, and presented Marischal College with 1300 medical books, and two telescopes. Government money was increasingly needed too, whether to augment the stipend of a university teacher like Beattie, or to help provide the demonstration equipment used by Copland in his University and his extra-mural lectures. Emerson suggested that political influences, including those of the Aberdeen Town Council as well as of central government, were on the whole beneficial to Marischal College, and were one of the factors that made it more go-ahead than King's in the eighteenth century.

More serious than political influence, with its good and bad effects, was the rivalry of the two colleges in the eighteenth century, and the amount of time and money wasted on inter-college disputes, as well as the litigious intra-mural disputes at King's: these form part of the story told by Mr Colin McLaren's paper—the other part being the necessity of law suits to maintain the income of the University in the eighteenth century. Both colleges were small in the eighteenth century—King's estimated at about 100 students (perhaps only 80 at the end of the century), and Marischal as growing from 190 to 200.[2] Both, however, early absorbed new intellectual influences, as Shepherd showed in her paper on the arts curriculum at the beginning of the eighteenth century. Marischal, later in the century, was keen to take its new learning to a wide public, as Dr John Reid demonstrated in his paper on Professor Patrick Copland, a neglected pioneer of adult education, whose extra-mural lectures on natural philosophy were attended by big audiences (including some women as well as men) and whose colleagues similarly gave evening classes in mathematics and chemistry. Both colleges abandoned the regenting system of teaching in favour of the professorial, Marischal much earlier in the century than King's, though the regenting method had something to recommend it, given the youth of the students attending the university in the eighteenth century, as Dr Paul Wood will argue in a forthcoming study of the eighteenth-century curriculum in the series of Quincentennial Studies in the History of the University of Aberdeen. Both colleges reformed their curricula, Marischal in 1753, and King's nominally in 1754, though the reforms were not fully implemented for two decades.

The earlier reform of the syllabus at Marischal was another factor which tended to make it more attractive to students than was King's in the eighteenth century. Reform developed out of a characteristic Aberdeen concern with the teacher's responsibility for and to his students. The younger Blackwell gave innovative lectures on ancient history at the very time when he was producing his major contribution to what is now recognised as the Aberdeen school of primitivism, his *Enquiry into the Life and Writings of Homer* (1728). The Continental concern with theories of language was reflected in the lectures of Campbell, Gerard, and Beattie. Dr Kirsti Simonsuuri, whose work on Blackwell is already well known,[3] was able to contribute a paper in this area, and Professor Nalini Jain and Dr Christopher Berry looked more closely at theories of language. George Campbell's work on rhetoric was described by Professor Kathleen Holcomb and Dr Lewis Ulman. There was, of course, as these scholars pointed out, cooperation between both colleges in the meetings of the Philosophical Society or Wise Club, which acted as a sounding board not only for some of the most notable publications of the period, Campbell's

Philosophy of Rhetoric, Gerard's *Essay on Taste* and *Essay on Genius* for example, but also for Thomas Reid's celebrated *Common Sense*. It is true that these books were published in London rather than in Aberdeen. The conference heard from Professor Robert Carnie an account of the publishing activities and the chief publishers of the Scottish university towns, which put the work done in Aberdeen in a true perspective, while the papers contributed by Dr Donald Nichol and Mr Iain Beavan showed how current scholarship is establishing more facts about Aberdeen books and the Aberdeen booktrade. In publishing and bookselling, as in so much else, Aberdeen desired to establish an international standing, whilst being constrained and at the same time strengthened by a strong sense of regional separateness and identity.

The literary and written uses of the Scottish language were of major concern to the teachers of the young men from outlying districts: the standards of spoken communication were under attack from teachers like Sheridan whose popularity in Edinburgh in the 1760s illustrates the general desire for improvement in social communication. The preoccupation in Aberdeen was often with intelligibility rather than elegance. The scope of the debate and the issues it raised were explored by Dr David Hewitt in his paper 'James Beattie and the languages of Scotland', while Dr Derrick McClure illuminated the practice of Allan Ramsay in this context. The pragmatism and idealism of the Aberdeen professors is reflected in the early work of David Fordyce, for example, the teacher of Gerard, who was in turn the teacher of Beattie. Among the items of advice to pupils which David Fordyce left in manuscript form at his death in 1753 are the following:

> Remember that the end of all reading & learning is, To be
> Wise, good & useful Creatures,
> That no man can be a good Creature who is not Religious,
> or a lover of God, as well as a friend to men.
>
> In all your reading, search for truth, & seek knowledge,
> not for shew or mere talk; but for use, the improvement
> of your own mind, & the Advantage of others.[4]

Attitudes like these make opposition to the scepticism of Hume, notably by Beattie in his widely popular *Essay on Truth*, not merely provincial inertia or dullness but a matter of personal and religious conviction. It was an aspect of Aberdeen which rejoiced the piety of Dr Johnson himself.

Dr Johnson's concern with Highland culture surfaced among the last of his publications, and was the subject of Professor Thomas Curley's detective work. Some years ago, Professor Donald Greene (an alumnus of the University and a student of that remarkable eighteenth-century bibliophile, Professor John Lothian) announced that Johnson's unrecorded publications included many which had been misleadingly ascribed to other authors. He was then referring to the Vinerian Law Lectures at Oxford, which Johnson had helped his friend Chambers to write. Among the new generation of Johnson scholars Curley, himself a student of Greene, has established that one of the last, if not the last, of Johnson's publications was a pamphlet written for William Shaw, as a final rebuttal of the authenticity of Macpherson's *Ossian*. Macpherson and Ossian attracted a notable number of papers. Professor George McElroy produced an intriguing paper on the Macphersons and India. Macpherson as a student in the tradition of Blackwell was the subject of Dr Maurice Colgan's discussion of Ossian and the Enlightenment. Dr Leah Leneman's description of Ossian's (Macpherson's) influence on the prevailing assumptions about the Highlands and Islands helped to unravel myths and images relating to Scotland. Weaving together the cults of primitivism and imaginative inspiration which the poets of the Enlightenment era seemed (perversely enough) to seek in the Highlands of Scotland, with the demand for scientific approaches to nature and perception, Professor Michel Baridon, the second guest speaker at the conference, synthesised in an imaginative way the appeal of Scottish scenery as a natural extension of the significance of philosophic light.

Aberdeen's most notable contribution to European thought in the eighteenth century is generally considered to be the Common Sense philosophy of Thomas Reid. A Soviet viewpoint on Common Sense philosophy was given by Mr Terence Brotherstone, while Professor Peter Diamond examined Reid's views on civil jurisprudence and the science of man. That these were the only papers on Reid reflects the fact that a whole conference was devoted to his work in 1985.[5] In 1986 as much attention was given to George Campbell and to George Turnbull as to Thomas Reid. Turnbull emerged as something of a polymath, with papers on his 'Common sense jurisprudence' by Mr Kenneth Mackinnon; his ideas on educational reform by Dr M.A. Stewart; and his role as an art historian and critic by Dr Carol Gibson-Wood.

With men such as Thomas Reid, James Beattie, Colin McLaurin, James and John Gregory, George Campbell, Alexander Gerard, Thomas Blackwell, George Turnbull, William Ogilvie, James Dunbar, Patrick Copland and David Skene, Aberdeen was hardly an Enlightenment backwater. There may not have been a 'hotbed of genius' in North-East Scotland, but there were many worthy Enlightenment men. The reputation of Aberdeen University in the eighteenth century, particularly when James Beattie was Professor of Moral Philosophy at Marischal College, attracted not only the would-be clergymen and teachers from country districts, like those afterwards described by George Macdonald in his novels, who studied for six months of the academic year and toiled to earn enough money to continue their studies in the other six, but the sons of professional men and local gentry, as well as some students from England. Students went from Aberdeen to the American and other colonies to export not merely the Scottish system of education but the Aberdeen priorities and standards: an awareness of the community and the individual's responsibilities to it, the mutual respect and responsibilities of family and social life, and a reliance on education for the cultivation of moral worth and enlightened awareness which is the basis of a truly civilised society.

The Editors, and all the contributors to this volume, acknowledge gratefully the help they have received individually from many librarians and archivists, and the permission given to quote from manuscripts in great national and university collections. Most of us owe a particular debt of thanks to the staff of the British Library, the Scottish National Library and the Scottish Record Office, the Edinburgh University Library and the Aberdeen University Library. At Aberdeen we particularly thank Mr C.A. McLaren, the University Archivist, Dr Dorothy Johnston, (now Keeper of the Records at the University of Nottingham), and the librarian in charge of Special Collections, Mrs Myrtle Anderson-Smith.

The Editors are most grateful for the support they received from the Aberdeen University Development Trust, both in paying the travelling expenses of two distinguished guest speakers at the conference, and in subsidising the publication of this volume. We express our gratitude likewise to the Aberdeen University Studies Committee for a further grant in aid of publication. The Aberdeen City Council has kindly allowed us to use for the cover of this book a reproduction of Alexander Nasmyth's painting of Old Aberdeen, which recreates the atmosphere surrounding King's College in the period of the Enlightenment. We have had generous help and advice from the Managing Director of the Aberdeen University Press, Mr Colin MacLean, who himself attended the conference on 'Aberdeen and the Enlightenment' and encouraged the idea of publishing its proceedings. We are grateful too for the expert help of Miss Marjorie Leith, Publishing Manager, in seeing the book through the Press. For skilled and patient secretarial help we are much indebted to Mrs Jenny Albiston, Mrs Lorna Cardno, and Mrs Gill Silver; and for technical advice on wordprocessing to Mr Charles Wilson, Director of the University Printing Service. We are also most grateful to our colleague Dr Alison Saunders for an extra pair of eyes in editing the text.

Notes

1. The QHP is engaged in publishing a series of short scholarly studies of the history of the University of Aberdeen, to celebrate the quincentenary in 1995 of King's College, the older of the two Colleges which came together to form Aberdeen University.
2. Roger L. Emerson, 'Scottish universities in the eighteenth century, 1690-1800', *Studies on Voltaire and the Eighteenth Century*, CLXVII (1977), p.473. Glasgow doubled in size from 400 to 800 students in the course of the century, while Edinburgh grew from 400 to possibly as many as 1600.
3. K. Simonsuuri, *Homer's Original Genius: Eighteenth-century Notions of the Early Greek Epic* (Cambridge, CUP, 1979).
4. AUL, MS M. 184.
5. A selection of papers from the Reid Conference is due to be published by D. Reidel Publishing Co., eds Melvin T. Dalgarno and Eric H. Matthews; and *The Reid Newsletter* was launched in 1985.

SECTION I

The Enlightenment in Scotland and Abroad

1

What was Distinctive about the Scottish Enlightenment?

Donald J. Withrington

University of Aberdeen

Writing about England in a recently published collection of thirteen essays on *The Enlightenment in National Context*, Dr Roy Porter has made a lively attempt to 'diagnose why the English Enlightenment is a scholarly black hole'.[1] Although, as he points out, there is plenty of evidence that the most renowned continental *philosophes* were well aware of English writings on, say, rational religion or moral benevolism, and were much interested in the social harmony that was to be found in England—evidently, or at least by report, based on a populace quietly observing rights of individual liberty under an agreed constitution—where, and in particular characterised by whom, was there a movement that deserved the designation, the English Enlightenment? Where, for instance, were those intellectual giants who could match Scotland's Hume or Reid or Robertson or Smith, figures of undoubted international standing who were, or were assumed to be, so essential to that country's having a 'real' Enlightenment? Porter takes the opportunity, therefore, to question the currently most commonly employed definition of Enlightenment, that now firmly associated with Professor Peter Gay and the legions of his powerful followers. According to this definition, the Enlightenment is a specific, homogeneous movement which had its quintessence in France and, if other countries are properly to be judged as having undergone Enlightenment, then they must be seen to have shared fully in those very characteristics which marked out the French experience—a movement dominated by a group of French-style *philosophes*, with their 'polite' salon-coteries. Porter offers in contrast the situation in eighteenth-century England where, as he discovered, the 'real' intelligentsia were quite different: they were 'not chairbound, but worked in the market-place'; they were not secularists; and they had a striking commitment to empirical and utilitarian ideas.[2] Are they, then, not to be considered as agents of Enlightenment in England?

9

But even before his readers can come to grips with the content of his or other essays, Porter—and his co-editor, Mikuláš Teich—have already faced them with a problem of definition that pervades the whole book. The table of contents declares that we can inform ourselves about the Enlightenment *in* England, *in* France, *in* the Netherlands, *in* Sweden and *in* Switzerland, but we may also puzzle over the *Scottish* Enlightenment, the *Italian* Enlightenment and the *Russian* Enlightenment. It is as if the first group offered local/national versions of what was in essence the same phenomenon (that suggested by Gay *et al?*), while the second group exemplified more distinctive experiences, reflecting national emphases which weakened, submerged or even perhaps denied communality of purpose and effect. It is even more intriguing to find an account of 'Enlightenment in Catholic Germany' alongside one of 'the Protestant Enlightenment in Germany'. We may well be led to wonder if there is a great deal more in these essay titles than just semantic slackness or indifference. There is, unfortunately, no serious attempt to resolve the questions raised by these essay titles in the preface; and in an afterword Teich writes rather unhelpfully about the 'practical application' of Enlightenment in the various countries, this being 'conditioned by local circumstances, national history and social interests'.[3] Yet the essays themselves really do not support a conception of Enlightenment as some kind of magisterial outside force which assuredly affected all countries but which was differentially accepted or rejected, nation by nation. We are left to ponder which particular varieties of some generalised 'Enlightenment experience' could or could not be 'applied', and why that might be so.

It is when we turn to the essays themselves that confusions in definition become quickly and sharply evident. Most remarkably of all, we are told by Professor Owen Chadwick that 'as in every other country, the Italian Enlightenment consisted of a series of small groups—learned marquises, liberal priests, angry anti-clericals, cultured bibliophiles':[4] a presumption which offers no problem at all to the Peter Gay faction but should certainly have been one for the editors, since the claim that this was everywhere the form that Enlightenment took is at once countermanded and overturned in most of the other essays. In both Austria and Sweden, for instance, we find little or no evidence of anti-clericalism, hardly a sign of a liberal priest (or even a liberal Lutheran minister), not even the disappearing tailcoat of a learned marquis. What we discover, in both these countries, is that the mark of Enlightenment there was educational reform, state-led or monarch-led. In Austria it was intended that the reforms should raise the intellectual level of the rural priesthood—and, notably, they included instruction for priests in agriculture and zoology, to enhance their acceptability and usefulness in their parishes.[5] In Sweden meanwhile science teaching was to be introduced into both schools and universities (in the teeth of much opposition from Swedish university teachers, be it noted) as an antidote to or as an alternative to the dominant classical training.[6] Again, in Bohemia, and to some extent in Holland (and, as it has been argued elsewhere, also in Wales) it is suggested that the period of Enlightenment was distinguished by a new or revived nationalism.[7] Here was something very different from that 'civil moralism' which is so often associated with eighteenth-century ideas of *patrie*: here was a crusading interest in revitalising old languages, old literatures, old civilisations, a movement led or confirmed by 'national' institutions such as the church or emphasised in a new modern-style scholarly 'national' history— not, in these instances, fronted by some noble clique, not confined to a group of effete, self-conscious intellectuals, but tending to gain the committed support of widely different social groupings and deeply influenced by popular national agencies. Enlightenment here took a form, and was centred in intellectual endeavours, which appear to be quite remote from that generally taken as characteristic of France.

But let us turn now, more directly, to the Scottish Enlightenment—or is it, indeed, the Enlightenment in Scotland?—about which there has been a considerable amount of writing in the past two decades or so. These studies have, it seems, become dominated by two groups of scholars who, while sharing some common ground and having some common membership, may nonetheless be helpfully distinguished. I should perhaps declare at once, before reviewing both sets of interpretations, that I find both seriously wanting and will not strain to be generous to them; in my view they have proved less than helpful in our trying to reach a better *historical* understanding of the Scottish Enlightenment.

The first group has gathered around, and still feeds off a commentary made as long ago as 1967 by its leader, Professor Hugh Trevor-Roper, Lord Dacre.[8] The Scottish Enlightenment, he then declared, was a 'puzzling phenomenon', a 'mysterious transformation' which seemed to resist attempts to explain it— and so he proceeded in effect, instead, to try to explain it away. How, he argued, could benighted, poverty-stricken, kirk-dominated, inward-looking Scotland of the late seventeenth and early eighteenth centuries have ever been able by itself to bring forth such majestic intellectual development, to lead the western world in such a range of intellectual enquiries? The answer, so runs the argument, must be that Enlightenment was an implant, an importation, and that even then it could only have developed strongly within Scotland through the agency of a group or groups who had distanced themselves, in some clearly marked way, from the debilitating mainstream of Scottish social, political and religious life. And so it is that the Episcopalian and Jacobite gentry of north-east Scotland have had forced on them by the Trevor-Roper brigade a quite extraordinary (and, I would judge, quite unmerited) predominance in the intellectual development of the country. In 1973 Dr Nicholas Phillipson was still claiming that the Scottish Enlightenment was 'one of the most puzzling phenomena of eighteenth-century cultural history', and prefaced his argument in an essay 'Towards the definition of the Scottish Enlightenment' with the disarming statement that 'it was difficult to see why Scotland should have developed so vigorous a cultural life in the eighteenth century'; he then suggested that all scholarly effort could be concentrated, within Scotland, on Edinburgh, on the stupefying assumption that 'the history of the Scottish Enlightenment *is* the history of Edinburgh. Throughout the century the cultural life of the city dominated that of Scotland'. The group's characteristic sleight of hand was at work again: for Phillipson, even more perhaps than for Trevor-Roper, it was the parliamentary union with England in 1707, introducing in due course dramatic economic development (and the social reverberations which that brought) which prompted a new receptiveness to what was happening outside Scotland; for Phillipson the significant intellectual influences were those from Scotland's ancient ally France, the impact of French-style Enlightenment ideas would clearly be concentrated (on a kind of parallel with Paris) in a capital with a special importance in legal, church and educational affairs; and thus we have the emphasis on Edinburgh being allied to a definition of Enlightenment which is, consciously or unconsciously, chosen in order to support the initial assumptions and predilections.[10]

A decade and more later, Trevor-Roper acolytes still follow in the steps of the master—and this despite a wealth of contradictory evidence, appearing since the early 1970s, which undermines his over-simplified and highly prejudiced view of the state of Scotland in the late seventeenth century, but which still seems to underpin the group's interpretation of the period of Enlightenment.[11] Thus we find Dr John Robertson, in his recent book on *The Scottish Enlightenment and the Militia Question*, retaining almost undiluted the central theme of 1967. Robertson, while focussing attention on the militia issue, is still surprised by the intellectual flowering in Scotland in the eighteenth century, and maintains that in all aspects it was stimulated directly from without ('what Scotland could not provide were the intellectual resources with which to pursue the interest: these had to come from the common stock of European political thought') aided by particular and 'alien' groups within.[13] But there has always been a problem for this group: why did dismal Scotland, of all countries in Europe, produce an Enlightenment with so very distinctive an emphasis on matters social (socio-economic, socio-historical, socio-legal, not to say sociological and socio-psychological)? The group's presumption that innovative and 'progressive' impulses necessarily came from outside Scotland forces them to retreat again and again to the fact of the 1707 union—which is then claimed to have initiated such a striking reconstruction of Scottish society that it and it alone could offer a basis for 'take-off' into Enlightenment. Robertson, like Trevor-Roper swallowing whole the writings of Henry Grey Graham,[14] writes of the 'social transformation' of Scotland after 1707—and then, rather puzzlingly, attempts to separate intellectual developments from their indigenous setting in the Scotland of their day, as if intellectual historians need have no truck with the rootedness of ideas, even the quality of responses to new ideas and attitudes, in the society which generated them. He appears to come clean about this particular article of faith in a remarkable passage. He wishes, he says, to:

> escape from the excessive domestication of the Scottish Enlightenment which is likely to result from interpreting it as an episode, however distinguished, in Scottish culture... There is a distinction to be drawn between the enlightening of Scotland and the Scottish Enlightenment...between in Trevor-Roper's phrase, the 'camp-followers' and the 'real intellectual pioneers'—the thinkers of European stature... For it is precisely when the connection between Scottish society and

Enlightenment thought is drawn too close...the wider European context of the Enlightenment is neglected.[15]

But on what historical basis, never mind intellectual or logical basis, is it possible to make this distinction between the 'enlightening of Scotland' (without a capital E) and the 'Scottish Enlightenment' (equipped with its special capital)? What are we to understand in Robertson's statement by 'the European context'? It is clear from the Porter/Teich essays that the context as well as the character of Enlightenment which we might choose to refer to would be strikingly different if we decided to study Russia rather than Switzerland, Sweden rather than France, Holland rather than Austria. We seem to be faced again with that very restrictive definition of Enlightenment, characteristic of the Trevor-Roper and Gay factions, which presumes that only a particular style of Enlightenment is really worthy of being taken into proper consideration. Again, what are we to make of Robertson's warning that we should not draw 'too close' the connexion between Scottish society and Enlightenment? One wonders whether such a thing would ever be said by those seeking a good (and better) understanding of the American Enlightenment or the German Enlightenment or even, particularly in more recent years, the French Enlightenment.[16] What kind of contorted definition of Enlightenment is being employed which judges that there could be no scholarly benefit to historians of Enlightenment anywhere, in our reaching towards a better understanding of it as a *Scottish* phenomenon, since it is so widely accepted that it has a peculiarly Scottish character? Does it not have special strengths which need to be studied in their context, in their inherent relationships to the society in which they have rooted, grown and flourished in their special ways, and from which they have in turn influenced others? We are back, yet again, to the problem of definition and assumptions as to what 'properly' constitutes Enlightenment: the Trevor-Roper group generally follows a highly restrictive definition which then limits the kinds of studies which are 'allowable'. One aspect of this narrowing of focus has been the tendency to define so wide-ranging an intellectual movement in terms of a highly selected and small number of individuals. In 1967, notoriously, Trevor-Roper chose only Hutcheson, Hume, Ferguson, Robertson, Smith and Millar as 'constituting' the Scottish Enlightenment, contriving to cast aside others, including Thomas Reid and Dugald Stewart (for all their vital importance in Scotland and to intellectual movements in other countries) as of little or no consequence. In 1983 Dr Charles Camic limited his list even further, omitting Hutcheson, to 'the five intellectuals who comprise the Enlightenment'. And in 1985, in a distinctly better book, Dr Richard Sher has widened his selection only a little, in number more than in social and intellectual spread: 'I shall define the Scottish Enlightenment quite simply as the culture of the literati of Scotland', he states, but then confines himself to Moderate Churchmen, and especially to a small group of the Moderate Churchmen of Edinburgh, as if they should and could exemplify not only Moderatism but also represent the true flavour of Enlightenment in Scotland as a whole.[18]

The second group of writers, sometimes overlapping with the first, has gathered round another luminary, Professor J.G.A. Pocock.[19] He has discovered in Andrew Fletcher of Saltoun, laird, politician, and controversialist, best known today for his strongly argued federalist views in the Edinburgh debates on parliamentary union with England, an innovative political theorist, whom he has promoted as a major figure in Britain in the revival of Graeco-Roman ideals of 'civic morality'. This in turn has emerged lately among his followers as *the* defining element in Enlightenment in Britain, particularly in Scotland. Some of the Trevor-Roper brigade have been at pains to adopt this definition into their own fabric of argument—even though it has not always been an easy matter for them, since Fletcher was most active as a politician and a writer before 1707, and before there were tangible beneficial results from the incorporating union which he so clearly opposed. Thus, Robertson is to be found arguing that Fletcher, well-known for being determinedly anti-English and vehemently nationalist, 'in effect called upon the Scots to renounce the martial social order and national identity they had inherited... to reconstitute themselves a proper political community on civic principles'.[20] It all seems rather strained, as, once again, are the all but deliberate attempts by this group to maintain a separation between the emergence of intellectual development in, and the historical realities of, the decade of Union and of eighteenth-century developments thereafter. Pocock and company, however, are currently much in vogue: classically-derived ideals of citizenship, of *virtù*, are the now thing in studies of Enlightenment Scotland. Throughout their writings we encounter all the new catch-phrases: civic humanism, civic morality; manners and polite behaviour; polite academies, polite clubs, polite society. And in Scotland, as elsewhere, these are associated with—indeed defined by—an essentially upper-class clientele, urban rather than rural, large town rather than small town (preferably centred in Edinburgh), all tightly knit into a definable social élite.

There is meanwhile hardly a whisper anywhere that contemporary Scotland effectively ignored Fletcher's 1704 proposals to restrict classical training in schools to the gentry and nobility, to promote an expensive and exclusive Renaissance-style education for the well-off and overturn the traditional, cheap and readily available grammar schooling open to all who could take advantage of it;[21] and not a sign that in the early eighteenth century the classics were in any case under severe attack, as no longer being useful or necessary for most school pupils, that Greek had all but disappeared from the schools, and that Latin—save where it was needed for professional training for the law, medicine, the church and in part for teaching—was increasingly at a low ebb.[22] There is little or no attempt to set the theorising about citizenship against the frequent comments, in mid-century and after, that towns and town-life were despised as dirty, immoral, demoralising and debilitating, a view which was even to be extended to newer village settlements: for many, urban living and concepts of community responsibility and of civic moralism (even though this last might not be intended to refer only to a town-based citizenship) were hardly to be spoken of together.[23] Taken against such a background, and with such ready signs of the welcome reception given to other Enlightenment influences—for example, in liberalising school and university curricula, in the vast extension and improvement in public musical life in town and country, in attempting to deal more effectively with dearth and disease and to conceive of means of preventing them—the Pocock group's almost exclusive interest in concepts of civility, at least as it is generally argued, is altogether too lacking in an historical, and in a Scottish, perspective. It is unconvincing because we have here again another attempt to impose something intrinsically alien to the Scottish experience. True, of course, that there were literati of one kind or another who haunted the salons of Edinburgh (and elsewhere), who formed themselves into small and intentionally exclusive so-called polite clubs in the major towns, who—if not in or of the upper classes—yearned to be lionised by them: but if we define the Scottish Enlightenment *only* in terms of that group, of their interests and aspirations, then it seems to me that we seriously misjudge the realities of eighteenth-century Scottish history (including its intellectual history). There is much more to it than some faint imitation of someone else's Enlightenment.[24]

Porter, in writing of the English Enlightenment, astutely comments on the intellectualist fallacy that 'many historians of ideas will hardly raise their hats to thinkers unless they are abstruse, formal and systematic', and goes on to remark that in England much of the most serious writing on Enlightenment themes is to be found in sermons, in manuals of conduct and in periodicals of all kinds.[25] So it is, too, in Scotland: Enlightenment ideas and ideals permeate sermons, periodicals and pamphlets—with these by no means the products only of clubs and societies, and certainly not the writings only of the towering geniuses of the period, or of a few individuals carefully selected for special prominence on some imposed criterion. The really distinctive mark of Enlightenment in Scotland is that its ideas and ideals were very widely diffused, in all areas and among a very wide span of social groups, in what was for the time a remarkably well-educated and highly-literate population, in country as well as in town.[26] Its agents were, undoubtedly, those who taught in the university lecture-room, from the pulpit, and at the dominie's desk, and who reached a still wider audience through the public prints. All of these men, preachers and teachers alike, to be numbered in hundreds upon hundreds, had shared the experience of attending university, not only in the public classes, but also in the many private classes held within and outside the walls of universities, and they in turn passed on what they had been taught. At its height it was, in essence, a self-renewing process.

Professor J.H. Plumb has written, again referring to the enigma of the English Enlightenment: 'Too much attention is paid to the monopoly of ideas among intellectual giants, too little to their social acceptance. Yet ideas acquire dynamism when they become social attitudes.'[27] We can certainly find such dynamism in eighteenth-century Scotland, in the wide acceptance of changes in attitudes which were themselves derived positively from Enlightenment. We will not, and cannot, understand what was happening if we attempt, as Robertson and others do, to distance ourselves from the living society in Scotland which produced those changes; indeed, I believe that we entirely misjudge the Scottish Enlightenment if we try to do so. It is the close relationship of intellectual and social development which, in Scotland, largely accounts for its distinctiveness; its special emphasis on social progress and social development is closely allied to its unique historical origins. In other words, we badly need to put back the history into studies of the Scottish Enlightenment.[28]

We should be sensitive to those concerns which, age by age, characterised eighteenth-century Scottish society, raising consciousness of (and conscience on) this issue and that. We should not be ignoring the impact on writers and thinkers of the fact of famines and food riots; of rising population and anxieties over the loss of the nation's 'good spirits' through emigration; of the impact of disease and poverty, and especially of the successes and failures of attempts to counteract and prevent them. We should not ignore major discussions of central themes of Enlightenment because they do not occur in the productions of 'great men' or even in separately printed treatises. For instance, there is much agonising over political philosophy to be found in debates in General Assemblies, in sharp contributions from Evangelicals as well as from Moderates. In the 1740s and 1750s there were debates over the rights of individuals as against those of corporations, and of local against central governments. Later, it was the rights of colonies against imperial monarchies that were at issue. Nor should we be blind to those periods when sharp confrontations over stipends between clergy and landowners soured relationships which badly hurt old traditions in community identity and upset older ideals of social interdependence. We should not forget, in discussing such topics as the rise of 'polite academies' (very much over-rated in their importance), and other changes affecting schools and universities, that the very practical need to augment salaries (whose value was being ruined by inflation) was a sharper motive for expanding the choices of subjects in curricula than was some abstruse theory of mental development in the young or some received notion of what constituted a 'proper' education. And we clearly should not forget that most remarkable manifestation of Enlightenment idealism at work, the parish returns to Sir John Sinclair's *Statistical Account*. In its very origins and conception; in the willing cooperation he received from over 900 ministers who shared his perception of the special value of the enterprise to society as a whole; in the sheer quality of thoughtfulness and intelligent concern the respondents showed in trying to make their reports both reliable and usable as part of a national survey; and in the intended (and actual) use of the survey in 'analysing the real state of mankind and examining... the internal structure of society' so that a more perfect 'science of government' could be attained in order to 'promote the general happiness of the species'—in all this we see the true spirit of Enlightenment.[29] Indeed, who is to say that an enterprise such as the *Statistical Account*, and the fact of its successful completion,[30] does not exemplify as effectively as any number of philosophical or legal treatises the long-standing inheritance of the Scottish Enlightenment, and at the same time clearly demonstrate its peculiarly Scottish character and achievement?

Notes

1. Roy Porter and Mikuláš Teich, eds, *The Enlightenment in National Context* (Cambridge, CUP, 1981), p.4.
2. *Ibid.*, p.5.
3. *Ibid.*, p.216.
4. *Ibid.*, p.90. Professor Norman Hampson, in the essay on the French Enlightenment (pp.41-53), seems to reject the more extreme forms of Peter Gay's interpretation. Enlightenment, he writes, is to be found 'in a widely disseminated attitude of mind rather than in a specifically literary or philosophical movement. Such attitudes were responsive to social and political, as well as to cultural and intellectual change' (p.43). But he then proceeds to argue within, and not against, that interpretation.
5. *Ibid.*, pp.127-40. The author, Ernst Wangermann, argues that it was the 'free' nations of England and Holland which 'gave birth to the Enlightenment' (p.127).
6. *Ibid.*, pp.164-75. Tore Frängsmyr interestingly begins his essay by offering an apology for the fact that the Enlightenment in Sweden 'never formed a truly coherent current of ideas or became a unified movement', as if only coherence and unity (on a supposed French-style pattern?) would merit the name of Enlightenment.
7. *Ibid.*, pp.54-71 (the Netherlands), pp.145-65 (Bohemia): see also the essay on 'Wales and the Enlightenment' in *Studies on Voltaire and the Eighteenth Century*, XXVII (1963), pp. 1575-91.
8. 'The Scottish Enlightenment' in *ibid.*, LVIII (1967), pp.1635-58.
9. Included in Paul Fritz and David Williams, eds, *City and Society in the Eighteenth Century* (Toronto, Hakkart, 1973), pp.125-47.
10. The same criticism can be levelled at a collection of documents made by Jane Rendall, *The Origins of the Scottish Enlightenment, 1707-1775* (London, Macmillan, 1978), which also greatly overstresses the importance of the Union.
11. For instance, see the great majority of the essays printed in R.H. Campbell and Andrew S. Skinner, eds, *The Origins and Nature of the Scottish Enlightenment* (Edinburgh, John Donald, 1982).
12. John Robertson, *The Scottish Enlightenment and the Militia Question* (Edinburgh, John Donald, 1986). The opening sentence of the book comments on Scotland having produced 'so distinguished a branch of the eighteenth-century European Enlightenment'. But, if we recall the sheer variety of experience noted in the essays in the Porter/Teich book, *which* European Enlightenment was it?
13. *Ibid.*, p.8. The 'interest' referred to here is the question of granting a militia to Scotland.
14. H.G. Graham, *The Social Life of Scotland in the Eighteenth Century* (London, A. & C. Black, 1902, and many subsequent reprintings) is a good read but woefully misinterprets sources and its argument is sometimes distorted by the anti-clericalism of the author—a feature shared with another writer much regarded by the Trevor-Roper group, H.T. Buckle, in the third (and Scottish) volume of his eccentrically-named *Civilization in England* (London, Parker, 1857-61).
15. Robertson, p.17.
16. As early as 1971 Professor Robert Darnton argued powerfully against the too-restricted view of Enlightenment in France taken by Professor Gay : see 'In search of the Enlightenment : recent attempts to create a social history of ideas', *Journal of Modern History*, 43 (1971), pp.113-32.

17. Charles Camic, *Experience and Enlightenment: Socialization for Cultural Change in Eighteenth-century Scotland* (Edinburgh, Edinburgh U.P., 1983), states that he excluded Hutcheson because he wrote 'too early' and was 'too dominated by religion', thus displaying the underlying presumptions of his own definition of Enlightenment. Typically he does not offer much in the way of effective argument for his assertion that David Hume should be taken as the figure who 'inaugurated' the period of Enlightenment in Scotland.

18. Richard B. Sher, *Church and University in the Scottish Enlightenment: the Moderate Literati of Edinburgh* (Edinburgh, Edinburgh U.P., 1985), p.8. Sher concentrates on five figures—Hugh Blair, Alexander Carlyle, Adam Ferguson, John Home, William Robertson—but, much more than other authors, he sees the need to worry about definitions and makes the point that Scottish intellectual historians have too frequently written 'with little concern for local institutions and traditions', so isolating the Scottish Enlightenment 'from the Enlightenment as a whole, which is rarely defined now in terms of intellect alone'. Yet even he falls into the comfortable assumption that those whom we happen now to select as leaders in some era of historical change properly *constitute* that movement, and did so for contemporaries as well as for scholars today. Sher retreats from his relatively open-minded stance (see p.12) and explains that he will exclude from the Scottish Enlightenment such men as Robert Sibbald, Andrew Fletcher of Saltoun, Walter Scott, Frances Jeffrey, Thomas Ruddiman or Robert Burns, 'not because these men lacked "intellectual vitality" but because they stood for different values, spoke different intellectual and ideological languages and inhabited different social and cultural worlds from the literati'—and, regrettably, forces on himself limitations to suit his own purposes and thus devalues a movement which was infinitely more significant than that portrayed by his chosen handful of 'literati'.

19. The most relevant of his writings, for the present purpose, are *The Machiavellian Moment: Florentine Thought and the Atlantic Republican Tradition* (Princeton, Princeton U.P., 1975) and 'Virtues, rights and manners: a model for historians of political thought', *Political Theory*, 9 (1981) reprinted in *Virtue, Commerce, and History* (Cambridge, CUP, 1985).

20. Robertson, pp.15-16.

21. *Proposals for the Reformation of Schools and Universities, in Order to the Better Education of Youth, Humbly Offer'd to the Serious Consideration of the High Court of Parliament* (Edinburgh, 1704): the pamphlet is not signed but there seems to be very little doubt that Fletcher wrote it.

22. See Donald J. Withrington, 'Education and Society' in N.T. Phillipson and Rosalind Mitchison, eds, *Scotland in the Age of Improvement* (Edinburgh, Edinburgh U.P. 1970), pp.169-99.

23. See *ibid.*, especially p.180; also T.C. Smout, 'The landowner and the planned village in Scotland, 1730-1830', *ibid.*, esp. pp.74, 78-79; D.J. Withrington and I.R. Grant, eds, Sir John Sinclair's *Statistical Account of Scotland, 1791-99* (Wakefield, EP Publishing), vol.II (1975): *Pencaitland*, pp.552-53.

24. Professor Andrew Skinner in his introduction to R. H. Campbell and Andrew S. Skinner, eds, *The Origins and Nature of the Scottish Enlightenment* (Edinburgh, John Donald, 1982), p.3, comments on the character of the Pocockian interpretations: 'The light thus thrown on the "nature of Enlightenment" is indirect, rather than direct, and the experience considered is in no wise Scottish.' Dr Anand Chitnis may be distanced from both the Trevor-Roper group and, more particularly, from that surrounding Pocock. He has long considered that the former

limits too severely the spread of intellectual interests which mark out the Scottish Enlightenment. Very recently—in an article which was not published until after this paper was delivered—he has offered a rather gentle but effective critique of the new orthodoxy of the latter grouping: see 'Agricultural improvement, political management and civic virtue in Enlightened Scotland: an historiographical critique', *Studies on Voltaire and the Eighteenth Century*, CCXLV (1986), pp.475-88. Chitnis wishes, he states, 'to draw attention to dangers which must beset any interpretation which rests heavily on the civic humanist tradition because of its potential for underestimating the difficulty of fitting some of the intellectual concepts it stresses to the Scotland of Fletcher, of parliamentary union and eighteenth-century politics' (p.488). Nonetheless, I find Chitnis's own interpretation, as expressed in his recent *The Scottish Enlightement and Early Victorian English Society* (London, Croom Helm, 1986), still rather too élitist, too professional, too urban, too Edinburgh-oriented, indeed, still too concerned with upper-crust literati: but in no way so cripplingly so as, for example, Roger Emerson, who could entitle an essay on the membership of the Select Society 'The social composition of Enlightened Scotland' and end it with this extraordinary statement: 'Such conservative intellectuals made the Scottish enlightenment and made it in their own image', *Studies on Voltaire and the Eighteenth Century*, CXIV (1973), pp.291-329.

25. Porter and Teich, p.5.
26. Be warned against a contrary view taken recently in a poorly-researched and over-ambitious book, with a very mischievous title: R.A. Houston, *Scottish Literacy and the Scottish Identity: Illiteracy and Society in Scotland and Northern England, 1600-1800* (Cambridge, CUP, 1985).
27. Quoted in Porter and Teich, p.6.
28. Compare Ronald G. Cant's comment in his 'Origins of the Enlightenment in Scotland : the Universities' in Campbell and Skinner, pp.42-64: 'What must never be forgotten is that the belief that education and intellectual achievement should have breadth of involvement as well as height of virtuosity was the joint gift to Scotland of the renaissance and the reformation a century before, an inheritance furthermore that would ensure that the Scottish form of the Enlightenment would be protected against the kind of brittle élitism that too often predominated elsewhere.'(p.59).
29. Withrington and Grant, vol.I (1983), p.xv.
30. It may be worth noting here that similar enterprises in other countries, frequently prompted directly by Sinclair's example, came to little or nothing—predominantly because there was no widely-shared belief in the value or importance of the task. It is remarkable, in this respect, that the *Account* was successfully carried through in Scotland because of the willing support it had from ministers, landowners and schoolteachers throughout the country. An English attempt to parallel Sinclair's nation-wide parochial survey failed because of the vehement opposition it aroused among Churchmen and gentry. The *Statistical Account* had an extraordinary impact, as Sinclair had intended, on governments' and others' attitudes to the practical importance of the gathering of data in social surveys, e.g., in the initiation of the censuses, in the setting up of enquiries under select committees of parliament or royal commissions. Yet its place in these developments has been virtually ignored by writers on social statistics and the ideology of improvement who consistently confine their attention to England—e.g., M.J. Cullen, *The Statistical Movement in Early Victorian Britain: the Foundations of Empirical Social Research* (Hassocks, Sussex, Harvester Press, 1975).

2

The Aberdeen Enlightenment and Russia

Paul Dukes

University of Aberdeen

In a brief paper composed about 1747 and entitled 'The Antient History of the Russian Empire', one of the more versatile Aberdeen luminaries, Dr David Skene, wrote about the problems encountered by Peter the Great at his accession:

> He found himself possessed of a vast tract of desert country, thinly inhabited by a Savage, Barbarous and Illiterate People, sprinkled here and there with a few large Cities, surrounded with Potent Neighbours on all Sides who despised and insulted him on all occasions, one only Port in his Dominions [Archangel on the White Sea] known to Strangers. [1]

A local landowner who had actually been in the service of Peter the Great, Major-General Alexander Gordon of Auchintoul near Aberchirder, about forty miles to the North West of Aberdeen, died as late as 1752. Three years after his death, there was published in Aberdeen itself his two-volume work, *The History of Peter the Great, Emperor of Russia*.[2] Another quarter century or so onwards, James Dunbar, Professor of Philosophy at King's College, brought out his *Essays on the History of Mankind in Rude and Cultivated Ages*, in which he described the achievement not only of Peter the Great but also of Catherine the Great, who, he suggested, 'by the protection of arts, by the establishment of her police, and by a well-digested code of internal laws, emulates the honours of her illustrious predecessor; perhaps, in some instances, eclipses his fame'.[3] Certainly, educated Aberdonians in the universities and beyond would have been aware of the achievements of both Peter and Catherine, and could have been kept up to date by the local press, which included at least some notice of events in the wider world. Many of its readers would no doubt have agreed with the sentiment expressed by Lord Fife on 22 February 1779: 'I could not live without the Aberdeen journal'.[4]

A more academic consciousness of Russia was expressed by William

Ogilvie, Professor of Humanity at King's College, in a Memorial of November 1784 lamenting the absence from the Library of the 'Memoirs of the Academies of Sciences of Paris, Berlin, St. Petersburgh, Upsal, Turin etc. etc.', and the acquisition of no more than two volumes of the 'immense publications' of Leonhard Euler, the outstanding mathematician resident in the Russian capital.[5] Dr David Skene, from 1767 Dean of Faculty at Marischal College, made several comments on the work of Peter Simon Pallas, a German scholar who accepted in 1768 the post of Professor of Natural History in the Academy of Sciences in St Petersburg.[6]

The impact made by Aberdeen on Russia was far smaller in the reign of Catherine the Great than in that of Peter. Earlier, the mercenaries Alexander, Thomas and Patrick Gordon, to name but three from one family, and the mathematician from Marischal College, Henry Farquharson, had done much to help Peter solve the problem so graphically described by Dr David Skene.[7] The later decline in Aberdonian influence was partly the consequence of imperial Russia's growing self-confidence, partly the result of a change in north-east Scotland's world outlook. In the late seventeenth century, Aberdonians looked more to the Baltic and its hinterland for fame and fortune than in most other overseas directions. In the early eighteenth century, there was a swing to the West, over the Atlantic, where interest in the Caribbean was already strong. And then, later in the eighteenth century, there was a swing to the East, taking in India in particular. Meanwhile, the view had not been lost of traditional foci of attention such as the Low Countries and Scandinavia, France and Germany.

Although Russia had declined proportionately in the outlook of Aberdonians and other Britons, it still presented opportunities for the energetic and ambitious. For example, in a letter of September 1783, James Beattie described his intercession in St Petersburg on behalf of two nephews anxious to join the Russian Navy. His on the spot intermediary was Dr Matthew Guthrie, whom Beattie had met the previous summer in Edinburgh, and who had told him, or so Beattie claimed, that 'my name was not unknown to his Imperial Mistress'.[8] And the prospect of continuing the Aberdonian tradition of enlightened rather than mercenary service in Russia opened up before a local, non-university savant, James Anderson.

Born near Edinburgh in 1739, James Anderson married the heiress to the estate of Mounie near Old Meldrum in Aberdeenshire in 1768, and soon after leased the estate of Monks Hill in the parish of Udny about a dozen miles to the North West of Aberdeen. His first publication was as early as 1769, and a large number of pieces on a wide variety of subjects followed.[9] One of these, on the uniformity of measures, came in January 1779 to the attention of Jeremy Bentham.[10] In February 1780, Jeremy reminded his brother Samuel, who was now in Russia, not to forget the books of Anderson's *Essays relating to Agriculture and Rural Affairs*, when entering into discussions concerning a Bureau of Agriculture in St Petersburg.[11] In March 1780, Jeremy referred to a long delayed letter sent to Anderson, offering to help arrange for him agricultural correspondence in St Petersburg, and in May, he told Samuel that 'Anderson knows a Scotch Parson who will read a book through and remember it verbatim. Such an animal might be made of use. D'ailleurs he is quite a ninny; as your great-memory-men frequently are'.[12] In another letter of May 1780, Jeremy wrote to Samuel that Anderson was on the point of setting up a weekly newspaper (an ambition that was in fact not to be realised for another fourteen years), and that Anderson had just sent to the Royal Society a paper about potatoes. Anderson had fermented them and distilled 'an ardent spirit' with a flavour like raspberries and fully equal, in its maker's opinion, to French brandy. Jeremy encouraged Samuel to pursue his own idea that the cultivation of potatoes might be advantageous in many parts of the Russian Empire where barley would not grow well. He added: 'Before you give the paper in however inform yourself what use is made of Potatoes there, whether they are in use to distil a spirit from them: lest you should be carrying coals to Newcastle.'[13] Almost certainly, Jeremy's word of warning was appropriate.

At the beginning of June 1780, Jeremy sent Samuel a list of seeds compiled by Anderson, adding the comment:

> He is a solid man—a man who speaks and writes not from imagination but from experience: in point of real knowledge worth a thousand Youngs. Young is like the Alchemists, who, if you would give them a little gold ready made, were generous enough to teach you the art of making as much of it as you had a mind for. According to him a man has nothing to do but turn Farmer, and he may be as rich as Croesus whenever he pleases. If this be the case, then pray, Mr. Young how comes it that you prefer the trade of bookmaking to that of farming?

As if in support of his assertion, Jeremy went on to mention a weighing machine, a barrow and a winnowing machine, all as recommended by Anderson.[14]

In March 1781, Jeremy was in receipt of a long letter from Anderson on the maintenance of the poor in Scotland. Nearly two years later, in May 1783, Jeremy wrote to Anderson with detailed observations on several of Anderson's papers.[15] About this time, Anderson moved back near Edinburgh, taking with him a long experience of farming and an honorary LL.D awarded in 1780 by Marischal College. By now there was talk of Anderson taking his knowledge and fame further afield, to join Samuel Bentham in Russia. After several references by both brothers to such a possibility, Samuel confessed at the beginning of 1784:

> My difficulty in writing, in drawing up any paper, and more particularly in finishing it to my mind, has I fear rather increased upon me ... unless I can get some such man or men as Anderson whose Character would allow me to place the confidence necessary to derive assistance from his abilities I may live here with ease and repute, but shall never make a fortune.[16]

Then in July, Jeremy wrote to Anderson thanking him for his letter of 7 June and stating:

> I am sincerely concerned to hear that times are so bad in Aberdeenshire. I wish

to God some little matter, it can be but little may be got to help them from the Russian employment, if that should be obtainable.

This tells us not only that Bentham was looking into the possibility of sending Aberdeenshire farmworkers to Russia, but also that Anderson had not yet moved permanently from Monks Hill, the lease on which we know he was still trying to sell in 1787.[17]

Jeremy went on in his letter of July 1784 to give Anderson a description of the possibilities held out by his brother Samuel's new employment as assistant to Prince Potemkin in developing an estate at Krichev in the Ukraine:

> Rude as the country is ... an establishment there ... is not to be looked upon as similar to a plan of colonization in America. On the latter place you have no fixed capital ready formed, no moveable capital but what you bring with you, no labour at command but your own, and for sometime your very subsistence is precarious and to seek. On that proposed you have a fixed capital, (such as dwelling-houses, barns, storehouses, mills etc.) ready provided, labour ... without stint, and subsistence assured.

Bentham suggested that Anderson should take with him various craftsmen and their families, and thus help to bring at least a little relief to the distress under which much of Scotland laboured still, adding:

> In particular, some of your own tenants whom you had in view when you said you must turn them out you feared, and so reduce them to beggary, on pain of being reduced to that situation yourself, some of these I say might by means of this plan place themelves in a position probably better than their former one, certainly widely different at any rate from that of beggary.[18]

How the farmworkers of Monks Hill would have fared in the Ukraine is difficult to assess, since in the end the plans of the Benthams and Anderson came to nothing.[19] However, Anderson maintained his connexion with the Benthams until 1793, when he took offence apparently at some critical comments made on one of his works by Jeremy.[20] And his connexions with Russia were strengthened, although at a distance. Several contributions were made from 1791 to 1793 to *The Bee*, his weekly newspaper, by a St Petersburg correspondent, Arcticus, alias Dr Matthew Guthrie, the Scottish physician whose acquaintance Anderson had made probably via the Benthams, possibly via James Beattie.[21] (Guthrie, or perhaps Sir John Sinclair, might have been the author of an original essay entitled 'Some Particulars respecting the Manners and Customs of the Russian Peasants', which appeared in *The Aberdeen Magazine* on 12 February 1789.)[22] Then, in an undated letter of around the same time to George Washington, Anderson offered to act as an intermediary between the American President, Sir William Jones in Calcutta and Professor Peter Simon Pallas in St Petersburg on matters concerning natural history or other useful knowledge.[23] That Anderson's interests were now world-wide was underlined by his December 1793 list of moneys owed him by subscribers to *The Bee*, not only in Russia and America, but also in

Königsberg, Danzig, Elsinore, Gothenburg, Oporto, Jamaica, Calcutta and Madras.[24]

Even wider than the fame of *The Bee* stretched that of the Poems of Ossian, news of which was carried to Russia in particular by some Russian students attending the University of Glasgow in the 1760s.[25] This Conference should at least record the fact that a Soviet scholar, Iurii Davydovich Levin, has not only fully described the impact of Ossian on Russian literature but also added to it by undertaking the formidable task of a full translation of the Poems into the Russian language.[26]

Perhaps it was a measure of the distance that the Russian Empire had travelled from the reign of Peter the Great to that of Catherine the Great that it made less of the utilitarian advice of James Anderson than of the vaporous effusions of James Macpherson.

Notes

I acknowledge with thanks the help given me in preparation of this paper by Mr Colin McLaren and Dr Dorothy Johnston of the Aberdeen University Archives.

1. AUL, MS 37, n.d., ff.108-9. In his paper, Skene referred to the daughter of Peter the Great, the Empress Elizabeth, as being 38 years old. She had been born in December 1709, and so his paper was probably composed in or around the year 1747.
2. *The History of Peter the Great, Emperor of Russia, To which is prefixed, a short General History of the Country, from the Rise of the Monarchy: and an Account of the Author's Life. In two volumes. By Alexander Gordon of Auchintoul, Esq*; several years as Major-General in the Czar's Service (Aberdeen, F. Douglass and W. Murray, 1755).
3. James Dunbar, *Essays on the History of Mankind in Rude and Cultivated Ages*, 2nd edition (London, W. Strachan, 1781), p.271.
4. Lord Fife to Mr Rose, AUL, MS 2226/131/382.
5. Walter Robson Humphries, *William Ogilvie and the Projected Union of the Colleges, 1786-1787* (Aberdeen, AUP, 1940), p.19.
6. AUL, MS 38, ff.148, 149, 152, 156, from 1766 to 1768. See also letters to Skene from John Ellis, MS 38, ff.95, 99, 100, 101, 102, 110, 113, from 1765 to 1770.
7. See Paul Dukes, 'Some Aberdonian influences on the early Russian Enlightenment', *Canadian-American Slavic Studies*, 13 (1979).
8. AUL, MS 30/1/232. Beattie's fame might have been carried to Russia via 'Basilius Nikitin', a Russian gentleman who 'was exceedingly kind during my stay in Oxford and did everything in his power to oblige me' in July 1773. See Ralph S. Walker, ed., *James Beattie's London Diary* (Aberdeen, AUP, 1946), p.67. For further information on Vasilii Nikitich Nikitin, and on Daniil Iakovlevich Pischekov, who received an M.D. from Marischal College in 1784, see A.G. Cross, *'By the Banks of the Thames': Russians in Eighteenth-Century Britain* (Newtonville, Mass., ORP, 1980).
9. See Charles F. Mullett, 'A village Aristotle and the harmony of interests: James Anderson (1739-1808) of Monks Hill', *The Journal of British Studies*, 8 (1968).
10. *The Correspondence of Jeremy Bentham* ed. J.H. Burns (henceforth *BC*), vol.2 (London, Athlone, 1968), p.232.

11. *BC* 2, p.393.
12. *BC* 2, pp.404, 441.
13. *BC* 2, p.444.
14. *BC* 2, p.455. Commenting on some papers of Anderson's in a letter to Jeremy in July 1781, the Earl of Shelburne said that 'they contain'd more usefull matter, tho' not such fine Language as is commonly to be met with among Scotch Writers'. See *BC* 3, 45. In the nineteenth century, Anderson was praised by Karl Marx, and in the twentieth, by Joseph Schumpeter. See Mullett, 'A village Aristotle', p.95.
15. *BC* 3, pp.30-43, 165-69.
16. *BC* 3, p.241.
17. *BC* 3, p.285. AUL, MS 2787/4/1/1/12. James Anderson writes from Colfield near Edinburgh to a Colonel Sim in Aberdeen with details of the proposed sale. There is much evidence of Anderson's close involvement in the agriculture of Aberdeen in his *General View of the Agriculture and Rural Economy of the County of Aberdeen* (Edinburgh, 1794).
18. *BC* 3, pp.287-8.
19. See generally M.S. Anderson, 'Samuel Bentham in Russia, 1779-1791', *American Slavic and East European Review*, 15 (1956). There is no mention of James Anderson.
20. *BC* 4, pp.412-3.
21. See n.8 above.
22. See Paul Dukes, 'An early essay on Russian peasants', *Study Group on Eighteenth-Century Russia Newsletter*, 10 (1982).
23. AUL, MS 2787/4/1/1/13.
24. AUL, MS 2787/4/4/8.
25. See the researches of A.H. Brown as described in Paul Dukes, 'Ossian and Russia', *Scottish Literary News*, 3 (1973).
26. Iu. D. Levin, *Ossian v russkoi literature* (Leningrad, Nanka, 1980).

3

Recent Soviet Views of Scottish Common Sense Philosophy

Terence Brotherstone

University of Aberdeen

There will probably be a fair measure of agreement that, in giving birth to Common Sense philosophy, Aberdeen made its most important single contribution to the Scottish Enlightenment. While interest in Common Sense today in countries where it had direct influence in the nineteenth century—notably France and the United States of America—is unsurprising, the weight given to it in Soviet studies may perhaps provide a more disinterested angle on its significance in the history of modern thought.

The father figure of Scottish Common Sense was Thomas Reid (1710-1796), son of a Kincardineshire manse, minister at New Machar, regent from 1751 to 1764 at King's College, Aberdeen, before his translation to the Chair of Moral Philosophy at Glasgow. Its most vigorous early publicist was James Beattie (1735-1803), schoolmaster of Fordoun, Professor of Moral Philosophy at Marischal College from 1760 to 1794. Of the two, Reid—despite Joshua Reynolds's portrayal of Beattie as *the* scourge of scepticism and infidelity—is generally regarded as pre-eminent. Following the publication of Reid's later works in 1785 and 1788 and, more especially, the appointment of Dugald Stewart (of whom it has recently been said that there were 'few points on which [he] ventured to disagree with Reid'[1]) to the Chair of Moral Philosophy at Edinburgh in 1785, Common Sense arguably became the philosophical underpinning of Scotland's reputation for being a centre of stability in a violently changing world.[2]

Some intellectual historians have recently come to see the question of why eighteenth-century Scotland gave rise to the developments referred to in the term 'Scottish Enlightenment' as a major historiographical problem. It is at least an implication of some of what is written that the Scottishness of the work of the Edinburgh literati—for Edinburgh tends to be the prime focus of this school of interpretation—lay in simultaneously advancing and domesticating the sciences of man and society. The 'civic humanist' school is cogently criticised for underestimating the significance of the progress of the natural sciences while overestimating the discontinuity involved in, and the cultural importance of, the Union of 1707. Yet, whatever the force of these criticisms, the 'civic humanist' argument does draw attention to the problem of the specific intellectual content of the influence exercised by the Scottish Enlightenment on nineteenth-century Britain. That characteristically Scottish intellectual content—it may be inferred—was conditioned as much by the historical circumstance of training 'virtuous citizens' to lead 'the first industrial nation' as it was by the drive to develop new ideas. Seen from this angle, it is the cautious Common Sense philosophy, rather than the sceptical empiricism of Hume, that makes it important to stress the existence of a *Scottish* Enlightenment at all.[3]

The principal Soviet work on Scottish philosophy, Aleksandr F. Griaznov's *Filosofiia Shotlandskoi shkoly*, was first published in Moscow in 1979. Before giving some account of this book, it is necessary briefly to indicate something of the intellectual context in which Griaznov was working on the Scottish school.[4]

The Scottish school of philosophy has been referred to in the general Soviet accounts of the history of philosophy at least since a five-page entry in *Istoriia filosofii*, published in 1941.[5] Short accounts of it characteristically relate its significance to the general conception of common sense as founded in 'the immediate practical relation of human beings to the world', and trace the very different content accorded to common sense by different philosophical schools. The link between the everyday and the philosophical senses of the term is made in one general account with the aid of Engels's statement:

> To the metaphysician, things and their mental images, ideas, are isolated, to be considered one after the other apart from each other, rigid, fixed objects of investigation given once for all... At first sight this mode of thought seems to us extremely plausible, because it is the mode of thought of so-called sound common sense. But sound common sense, respectable fellow as he is within the homely precincts of his own four walls, has most wonderful adventures as soon as he ventures out into the wide world of scientific research.[6]

The different content attributed to common sense within Enlightenment philosophy is characterised as follows:

> The French materialists of the eighteenth century held that man's common sense was incompatible with religion, while representatives of the eighteenth-century Scottish school ... asserted that common sense must inevitably lead to belief in God ... [because] experience itself was possible only to the extent that the human spirit possessed inborn principles of common sense, such as unshakeable faith in God and the surrounding world.[7]

Recent work on French materialism, the blossoming sophistication of work on Reid's philosophy, and, perhaps, a general temperamental antipathy to such bluntness, may lead many Western scholars to recoil at the crudeness of the antithesis. But to demonstrate that one statement is a simplification is not the same thing as replacing it with a more accurate generalisation.[8]

The argument is developed by Theodore Oizerman:

> Whereas French materialists proved that religion was incompatible with reason, the Scottish 'philosophy of common sense' saw its principal mission in proving the opposite. Thomas Reid, the foremost proponent of that school, maintained in his *Enquiry Into the Human Mind on the Principles of Common Sense* (1764) that the admission of the existence of the outside world cannot be based on the evidence supplied by sensory organs because that evidence is valuable only inasmuch as it commands credence. Common sense is the original ability to believe which precedes sense perception and reflection and leads to the admission of the external world and of God. Thus a lack of faith in God is as contrary to reason as the refusal to believe that the objects reported by the senses are real. Therefore, according to Reid, rejecting religious faith is tantamount to refusing to believe that the outside world is real.

Oizerman goes on to indicate that, historically, both materialism and idealism—using the terms in Engels's sense[9]—have claimed to represent common sense:

> Although because of its organic contradictions everyday consciousness obviously sustains opposite philosophies, the everday experience it reflects—the experience shared by all mankind, and constantly enriched and confirmed by social practice—contradicts idealism and serves as one of the starting points of the materialist world view.[10]

Oizerman's remarks—which seem to me to be part of a conception of the tasks of historians of philosophy described in 1974 by E.V. Ilyenkov as the creation of the 'more or less finished blocks' of an intellectual building 'of which we still only dream'[11]—give at least an indication of the body of thought within which Griaznov wrote. His book is claimed as the first critical review in the USSR of the Scottish Common Sense school, 'one of the tendencies in British bourgeois philosophy and ideology in the eighteenth century'.[12] The three aspects of Scottish philosophy which Griaznov identifies as most immediately worthy of study are: its criticism of the theory of ideas; the relationship between the Scottish school and modern realism; and its relationship to linguistic philosophy.[13] He devotes one chapter to the immediate philosophical antecedents of the Scottish school, to discussing how Reid sought to establish first principles, and to the key role of language in Reid's philosophy; a second to the criticism of the theory of ideas and of Hume's scepticism; a third to the theory of direct perception and the concept of natural signs; and a fourth to the importance for Common Sense philosophy of philosophical-psychological research into how the senses provide human beings with knowledge. Here Griaznov concentrates on Reid's theory of vision, making use of Daniels's work.[14] The fifth chapter traces the subsequent history and influence of the Scottish school.[15]

Griaznov argues the case for the importance of studying philosophies which cannot properly be called first-rank or classical philosophies, in that they do not constitute a definite stage in the evolution of Western philosophy, and that they lack systematic erudition, completeness and rigour.[16] He includes the Scottish school amongst such philosophies. He points out that it is considerably referred to, but less often subjected to overall assessment; and that the assessments there are often contradict each other, some speaking of Common Sense as though it were a philosophy of the first rank, others dismissing it as a mere appeal to everyday prejudice; some appealing to it in their attacks on metaphysics, others denouncing it as itself metaphysical.

A recent Western account by Louise Marcil-Lacoste assesses the matter rather more one-sidedly. In her study comparing Reid with his possible predecessor, the Jesuit Claude Buffier, Marcil-Lacoste protests against what, quoting Kant's *Prolegomena*, she takes to be the 'widely-held' and 'standard' view that Common Sense philosophy 'merely states that men believe certain propositions to be true and that they act in accordance with these propositions'.[17] Griaznov's assessment of the perception of the significance of the Common Sense philosophy at the end of the 1970s as confused and contradictory seems more balanced. Marcil-Lacoste is surely right, however, to remark that various scholarly appeals for an overall and 'accurate history of common sense doctrines' have still not been satisfactorily answered.[18]

Griaznov sees the Scottish philosophy as important because, despite its shortcomings, it both provided a body of thought with which more original thinkers had to engage, and because it is also the ground wherein to unearth the roots of modern Anglo-American realist doctrines. He compares the views of the proponents of twentieth-century neo-realism and the Scottish school with regard to the questions of the knowability of objects, the relations of objects to consciousness and the existence of the external world, arguing that, both in their answers to these questions and in their method of describing the epistemological process, there is a close affinity of view.[19]

There is a distinctive quality in the Soviet approach to these problems, but Griaznov's work does not stand in absolute antagonism to Western scholarship, on which, as he acknowledges, he relies at many points. He draws on the work of Daniels, Laudan and others in his assessment of the importance of the Scottish school in the history of science[20]; and of McCosh, Grave, and other standard works in his more general judgments.[21] On Reid's political outlook which, though not a decisive question, is of some relevance to the historiographical task of establishing the relationship between Scottish philosophy and the so-called 'age of revolutions', Griaznov quotes A.C. Fraser's distinction between the speculative and the practical approach to politics—the first concerned with a new type of society as ideally as possible suited to progress, and the second with the adaptation of the existing social order to changing historical circumstances with the minimum of discord.[22] Reid, comments Griaznov, favoured the second approach, finding in the British constitution the possibility of peaceful, evolutionary change, so that he might be said to be, as Engels describes Locke, a 'son of the class compromise of 1688'; but in the case of Reid it would have to be added that he was the son, also, of the Union of 1707 'since he at no time and nowhere stands for the independence of Scotland'.[23]

Griaznov follows Hegel in identifying as leaders of the Scottish school Reid, Beattie, James Oswald and Dugald Stewart, but comments also on George Campbell, Lord Kames, Adam Ferguson and the novelist, Tobias Smollett.[24] He criticises Kant for too easily dismissing the Scottish school (a failing not shared by Hegel), and for placing its criticisms of Hume on a par with those of Priestley, the most vigorous contemporary English critic of Reid, Beattie and Oswald.[25] Kant's priority, of course, was to get to grips with Hume but it may be, as recent research has suggested, that his attitude was also influenced not so much by the insignificance of Reid and his followers in the Germany of the 1770s, but rather by their quite considerable influence.[26]

Griaznov's remarks on Scottish attempts in the nineteenth century to come to terms with the philosophical relationship between Kantianism and Common Sense seem generally in line with the explorations begun by philosophers such as Andrew Seth (Pringle-Pattison) in Scotland in the early 1880s; and they may be seen to be relevant by those who find considerable significance in some of G.E. Davie's historico-philosophical statements today.[27] Indeed, the type of enquiry pioneered by Davie (inspired, at least in part, by Common Sense philosophy and Scottish responses to it) contains some of the possibilites immanent in the approach of the Soviet writers, although the standpoint is of course quite different. Both draw attention to the international significance (or limits to the significance) of Scottish philosophy, and to the possibility of deriving from it insights into the evolution of Scottish social history. Griaznov himself does not pursue this latter line of inquiry, being concerned with the history of philosophy rather than with Scottish history as such; and Davie has been criticised by historians for insufficiently attending to the empirical context in which the philosophers and educationalists he writes about worked.[28] Yet this type of inquiry, if grounded in the developing quantity of research on nineteenth-century Scottish society, will surely result in a much deeper understanding of the transitions in Scottish society from the birth and heyday of the Scottish school to the point at which there was (so one commentator on Hegel claims) 'some strange affinity' between the Scotland of the 1870s and the Germany of the late eighteenth and early nineteenth centuries.[29]

Griaznov briefly traces the course of Common Sense after Dugald Stewart to the point at which John Stuart Mill felt called upon to refute Sir William Hamilton's version of it.[30] He stresses its impact in nineteenth-century France, and in the United States of America. These are familiar enough themes, the basic tendency of Griaznov's particular argument being that the French and American schools made use of the weaknesses of Common Sense to provide bourgeois philosophical establishments with a weapon against materialism.[31]

The overall impact of *The Philosophy of the Scottish School* seems to be to fill out the assessment made by Oizerman of its historically contradictory character. It was of the second rank, but posed important and necessary questions at a particular moment. It must be viewed together with, as well as in opposition to, Hume's scepticism in helping to furnish the historical necessity for the philosophy of Kant and all that was to flow from it. In relationship to Marxism it may be seen as a doctrine which, by criticising the theory of ideas, began to pose the need for consistent materialism, and which anticipated, in the realm of theory, the potential for a new stage in mass consciousness associated with the socio-economic revolutions of the late eighteenth and nineteenth centuries. But it remained, philosophically, rooted in the camp of idealism, and could in no way transcend a conception of the mental processes as the activity of the abstract individual, seen as existing in society to be sure, but in society in general rather than in real class-divided society at a definite and transitory historical moment. Like even the most thoroughgoing eighteenth-century materialism its standpoint was, to adapt Marx, one that could only appear to be that of 'socialised humanity' while in reality being that of 'civil society'; but unlike the materialism of at least some of the *philosophes*, its battles—even those in which it had a good and original case—were all fought (or politely and agreeable argued, at least by Reid) in the name of religion.[32]

What, in conclusion, may be proposed about the relationship between this interpretation of Common Sense philosophy and the efforts of historians to arrive at an overall assessment of the Scottish Enlightenment? Common Sense was only one aspect of the thing as a whole, very far from being its most important contribution to knowledge, and not the aspect of the Enlightenment with which most authors of general accounts of modern Scotland tend to engage. Such accounts in future will have to consider how to incorporate the gains of the current international interest in the Scottish Enlightenment. Yet there might seem to be a danger of celebrating the Scottish moment of 'genius' to the point at which its source could seem almost independent of historical explanation, and the historical limitations of its achievements might be seriously understressed. More attention to the general significance of Common Sense philosophy—whether its progenitor is deemed to be a genius of the first rank or not—may serve as a salutary reminder of the caution advised by Ferguson concerning the significance of the Scottish Enlightenment before it was quite so much in the news.[33]

Secondly, acknowledging that eighteenth-century Scotland was indeed a 'hotbed of genius', is it not necessary to ask those who celebrate the fact to define what line of philosophical continuity (or even what type of discontinuity) connects us today with the literati of that time? Griaznov, Davie, and even Minogue and his 'new enlighteners' of the Right (via their almost atavistic attitude to Smith)[34] provide, from their very different angles, answers to that question.[35] Others perhaps need to do the same if they are not to find themselves, by default, in Minogue's assertive band.

Finally, there is the issue of the relationship between the achievements and limitations of the Scottish Enlightenment and Marxism. It is not argued that whatsoever emanates from the Soviet Union should be accepted, without critical analysis, as an authoritative statement of the 'Marxist view': such a conception would be the antithesis of a Marxist approach. Yet it is also clear that, for some considerable time, it has not been possible automatically to dismiss such work as fatally flawed with Stalinist dogma.[36] The Scottish background to Marxism is not of course a new theme, though it has been neglected of late, and previous discussions have concentrated on history, social science and economics rather than philosophy. But in Marxism and in the *aspirations* of the Enlightenment, these are all connected. Thus Isaac Rubin's comments on the brilliance of Adam Smith, in his lectures on economic theory delivered in the Soviet Union in the 1920s, are balanced by an analysis of the historical constraints on Smith's social philosophy, which can still serve by analogy as a starting point for an all sided analysis of other aspects of the Scottish Enlightenment.[37]

The theme of the Scottish background to Marxism summons another, more familiar echo from the past; an echo from one of the two voices which originally called much of the recent interest in the Scottish inquiry into being. The term appears to have been invented by W.R. Scott, but interest in, initially, the social and historical concerns of the Scots began to flourish a generation or so later, stimulated by those seeking out the historical roots of Western sociology on the one hand and Marxism on the other. Duncan Forbes, a leading exponent since the 1950s of the need to conceptualise and study the Scottish Enlightenment, notes the influence of Marxism on much early research.[38]

A notable feature of this Marxist involvement is that, although it may have assisted the study of the Scottish Enlightenment, it did not lead to any continuing enrichment of Marxism in Britain. When Roy Pascal, writing in the communist *Modern Quarterly* in 1938, introduced the question of the Scottish background to Marx in the form of a still valuable discussion of the Scottish historical school, he was reacting to the neglect of the socio-historical nature of Adam Smith's work at a time when orthodox theory studied Smith as simply the progenitor of capitalist economics. As taken up later, however, this helped towards a neglect of the philosophical aspect of Marxism. As a result, Andrew Skinner was recently able to mount a convincing critique of what, in different circumstances from the 1950s, might have been a seminal article by the Marxist economist Ronald Meek; and was able to base it on a conception of Marx's historical method which seems closer to economic determinism than to historical materialism.[39] One purpose of the present essay is to propose a re-opening of this discussion on a rather broader basis.

When W.R. Scott made his inaugural speculations on the subject of the Scottish Enlightenment, he wrote that to represent it:

> as exclusively Scottish is to cut off all its results from their continuity with past history. A 'kail-yard' school of fiction within reasonable limits is an addition to contemporary literature, but a kailyard philosophy verges perilously close near a contradiction in terms.[40]

One aspect of the current international interest in the Scottish Enlightenment is that it renders all the more unlikely a return of Scottish historical studies to the kailyard in which they have sometimes, needlessly, seemed to languish.

Notes

Youssef-al-Khatib, who studied philosophy at the Department of Philosophy, Moscow State University, from 1967 to 1973, and is now researching in Arabic Studies at the University of Glasgow, made this essay possible for me, a non-Russian speaker, by making translations, particularly of the main book discussed, A.F. Griaznov, *Filosofiia Shotlandskoi shkoly* (Moscow, Moscow State University, 1979). I am very grateful to him not only for the translations but for all his time spent discussing the questions they raised. He has no responsibility for the views expressed on the significance of the Russian works discussed.

1. S.R. Sutherland, 'The Presbyterian inheritance of Hume and Reid', in R.H. Campbell and A.S. Skinner, eds, *The Origins and Nature of the Scottish Enlightenment* (Edinburgh, John Donald, 1982), p.149.
2. Interest in Common Sense was reflected in the cosmopolitan participation at the International Bicentennial Conference on the Philosophy of Thomas Reid held at the University of Aberdeen, 2-4 September 1986, though no reference to Soviet work was made there. Recent general studies include E. Griffin-Collart, *La philosophie écossaise du sens commun: Thomas Reid et Dugald Stewart* (Brussels, Académie Royale de Belgique, 1980); L. Marcil-Lacoste, *Claude Buffier and Thomas Reid* (Kingston and Montreal, McGill-Queen's U.P., 1982); and S.F. Barker and T.L. Beauchamp, *Thomas Reid: Critical Interpretations* (Philadelphia, University City Science Centre, 1976).
3. A.C. Chitnis, *The Scottish Enlightenment and Early Victorian English Society* (Beckenham, Croom Helm, 1986) draws attention to some of these influences. For the current debate on the Scottish Enlightenment, see the essays by A.C. Chitnis and D.J. Withrington in this volume; A.S. Skinner, in Campbell and Skinner, *Origins*, pp.1-6; and R.B. Sher, *Church and University in the Scottish Enlightenment* (Edinburgh, Edinburgh U.P., 1985), pp.3-19. Phillipson's view may be sampled in N. Phillipson, 'Towards a definition of the Scottish Enlightenment', in P. Fritz and D. Williams, eds, *City and Society in the Eighteenth Century* (Toronto, Hakrert, 1973), p.146, and 'Scottish Enlightenment', in D. Daiches, ed., *A Companion Guide to Scottish Culture* (London, Edward Arnold, 1981), p.343.
4. I have found no reference to this work in any periodical I have scanned. The lack of an entry in *The Philosopher's Index* also suggests that it has not been much noticed in the West. An article on Scottish Common Sense in Roumanian, by D. Oprescu, appears in *Revista de Filozofie* (Bucharest), 27 (May-June 1980). The Soviet approach to the history of philosophy is now finding some reflection in the West. J.W. Yolton states, for example, that 'It has become fashionable of late to attempt to mediate what has been perceived as a gulf between philosophy and the history of philosophy', *Journal of the History of Philosophy*, XXIII (1985), p.571. For an attempt by R. Rorty to categorise the different Western approaches to the history of philosophy see R. Rorty, J. Schneewind and Q. Skinner, eds, *Philosophy in History: Essays in the Historiography of Philosophy* (Cambridge, CUP, 1984). This might usefully be compared with, for example, T.I. Oizerman, 'Philosophical trends as a subject of research', *Soviet Studies in Philosophy* (Spring 1972), p.316.
5. *Istoriia filosofii* (Moscow, 1941), vol.II, pp.269-73. Because of its appearance and usefulness, students refer to this work as 'the grey horse'.
6. F. Engels, *Herr Eugen Dühring's Revolution in Science* (Moscow, Co-operative Publishing Society of Foreign Workers in the USSR, 1934), p.28.

7. D.M. Lukanov, 'Common Sense', in *Great Soviet Encyclopaedia* (English translation of the 3rd edition, New York and London, 1975), vol.IX, p.37.

8. For example A.C. Kors in *D'Holbach's Coterie* (Princeton, Princeton U.P., 1976), who rejects the idea that there were many atheists in France, although he stresses that atheism was an issue in France in a way in which it was never allowed to be in Scotland.

9. F. Engels, *Ludwig Feuerbach and the End of Classical German Philosophy* (1886), republished in K. Marx and F. Engels, *Selected Works in One Volume* (London, Lawrence & Wishart, 1968), pp.604-605.

10. T.I. Oizerman, *Dialectical Materialism and the History of Philosophy* (English edition, Moscow, Progress Publishers, 1982), p.110.

11. E.V. Ilyenkov, *Dialectical Logic* (English edition, Progress Publishers, Moscow, 1977), p.5.

12. Griaznov, p.4.

13. Griaznov, p.14. For discussion of linguistic philosophy see pp.116-19.

14. Griaznov, pp.85-95, 99-101; N. Daniels, 'Thomas Reid's discovery of a non-Euclidian geometry', *Philosophy of Science*, XXXIX (1972); Griaznov also refers to N. Daniels, *Thomas Reid's Inquiry* (New York, B. Franklin, 1974).

15. Griaznov's book ends with a section 'In Lieu of a Conclusion' (pp.120-22). Here Griaznov quotes M.A. Abrashnev, *The Problem of Everyday Thinking or Naive Realism* (Russian edition, Gorki, 1971), p.36: 'Everyday thinking should be considered as the rich, rudimentary material which contains implicitly the germ of future theoretical generalisations. Everyday consciousness, for example, can sometimes anticipate tendencies in social life, its direction and contradictions before these can be worked out by theorists.'

16. Griaznov, pp.5-6.

17. Marcil-Lacoste, pp.1-3.

18. Marcil-Lacoste attributes the first such appeal to Etienne Gilson in 1939 and comments that the absence of such a history 'is even more amazing because such philosophies have been quite important and influential in Scotland, France, Spain, Italy and the United States'. She cites works by Gilson, D.F. Norton, E. de Angelis, R.G. Mayor, and H. Pust. D.F. Norton, 'George Turnbull and the furniture of the mind', *Journal of the History of Ideas*, 35 (1975), pp.701-16, stresses the essentially religious basis of Scottish philosophy with a clarity unusual in Western accounts at that time.

19. Griaznov, pp.110 and following.

20. For Daniels, see footnote 14; L.L. Laudan, 'Thomas Reid and the Newtonian turn in British methodological thought', in R.E. Butts and J.W. Davis, eds, *The Methodological Heritage of Newton* (Oxford, Blackwell, 1970), pp.107-31; Griaznov, p.43.

21. S.A. Grave, *Scottish Philosophy of Common Sense* (Oxford, Clarendon Press, 1960) and 'Common Sense', *Encyclopaedia of Philosophy* (New York, 1967), vol.II. James McCosh, *The Scottish Philosophy* (London, Macmillan, 1875).

22. Griaznov, p.9; A.C. Fraser, *Thomas Reid* (Edinburgh, Oliphant, Anderson & Ferrier, 1898), pp.114-16.

23. Griaznov, p.10.

24. G.W.F. Hegel, *Lectures on the History of Philosophy* (translated. E.S. Haldane and F.H. Simson (London, Kegan Paul, Trench, Trübner & Co., 1895), vol.III, pp.375-79.

25. Griaznov, pp.10-11, 12; Joseph Priestley, *An examination of Dr. Reid's Inquiry...*, *Dr. Beattie's Essay...*, *and Dr. Oswald's Appeal* (London, J. Johnson, 1774).

26. M. Kuehn, 'The early reception of Reid, Oswald and Beattie in Germany: 1768-1800', *Journal of the History of Philosophy*, XXI (1983), pp.479-88.

27. A. Seth, *Scottish Philosophy*, 2nd edition (Edinburgh, William Blackwood & Sons, 1890); G.E. Davie, *The Social Significance of the Scottish Philosophy of Common Sense* (Dow Lecture, Dundee, University of Dundee, 1973) and 'Victor Cousin and the Scottish philosophers', *Edinburgh Review*, 74 (1986), pp.108-25.

28. For important beginnings in an empirical critique of Davie, especially his *The Democratic Intellect*, 2nd edition (Edinburgh, Edinburgh U.P., 1964), see D.J. Withrington, 'Raw, pungent spirit', *Universities Quarterly*, 16 (1961-62), pp.94-98, and R.D. Anderson, Appendix II, in his *Education and Opportunity in Victorian Scotland* (Oxford, Clarendon Press, 1983), pp.358-61. For Davie's reply to Anderson, see *Cencrastus*, 16 (Spring 1984), pp.47-48.

29. J.N. Findlay, Foreword to W. Wallace *Hegel's Logic* (Oxford, Clarendon Press, 1975), p.v.

30. This important episode in Anglo-Scottish cultural relations has received short shrift in general accounts of modern Scottish history. Even William Ferguson does not mention it in *Scotland since 1689* (Edinburgh, Oliver & Boyd, 1968). A. Ryan's introduction to *An Examination of Sir William Hamilton's Philosophy* in J.S. Mill, *Collected Works*, eds, F.E.L. Priestley and J.M. Robson (Toronto, Toronto U.P., 1963-), vol.IX, provides a good starting point for the development of this theme.

31. Griaznov, pp.15, 120-21.

32. The reference to Marx is to the tenth thesis on Feuerbach (1845). Marx and Engels, p.30.

33. Ferguson, p.209; for the more ebullient views of some of the class of '86 see, for example, D. Daiches, *The Scottish Enlightenment* (Edinburgh, Saltire Society, 1986); D. Daiches, P. Jones and J. Jones, eds, *A Hotbed of Genius: the Scottish Enlightenment* (Edinburgh, Edinburgh U.P., 1986); N.T. Phillipson, 'A light in the North', *Scotsman*, 26 July 1986, p.1, which was a partial transcript of a talk broadcast by Scottish Television in a ten-part series on the Scottish Enlightenment transmitted at peak viewing times between 11 August and 22 August 1986; Phillipson also delivered an exuberant lecture as part of the Edinburgh International Festival of the Arts, in August 1986.

34. K. Minogue, 'The New Enlightenment', Channel 4 TV, 12 November 1986.

35. Phillipson, 'The Pursuit of virtue in Scottish university education', in N. Phillipson, ed., *Universities, Society and the Future* (Edinburgh, Edinburgh U.P., 1983).

36. For example, T.I. Oizerman, *The Making of Marxist Philosophy* (English edition, Moscow, Progress Publishers, 1981).

37. I.I. Rubin, *A History of Economic Thought*, 2nd edition, 1929; (English edition, London Ink Links, 1979), especially pp.167-76.

38. D. Forbes, *Hume's Philosophical Politics* (Cambridge, CUP, 1975), p.316.

39. R. Pascal, 'Property and society', *Modern Quarterly*, I (1938), pp.167-79; R. Meek, 'The Scottish contribution to Marxist sociology', in J. Saville, ed., *Democracy and the Labour Movement* (London, Lawrence & Wishart, 1954), pp.84-102; A.S. Skinner, 'A Scottish contribution to Marxist sociology?', in I. Bradley and M.E. Howard, *Classical and Marxian Political Economy* (London, Macmillan, 1982), pp.79-114. For a left wing critique of Meek see G. Pilling, 'The law of value in Ricardo and Marx', *Economy and Society*, 1 (1972), pp.281-307. For Meek's reply and Pilling's rejoinder see *Economy and Society*, 2 (1973), pp.499-506.

40. W.R. Scott, *Frances Hutcheson* (Cambridge, CUP, 1900), pp.266-67.

4

The Scottish Origins of Freemasonry

David Stevenson

University of Aberdeen

Freemasonry is a phenomenon that no-one who studies the Enlightenment can ignore. It spread throughout Europe and across the Atlantic in the eighteenth century in the most astonishing way, taking many forms and becoming ever more elaborate, until it sometimes seems that everybody who was anybody was an initiate of 'the Craft', from Burns to Mozart to George Washington. In that the spread of freemasonry took place in the eighteenth century and that it was closely linked to the intellectual, cultural and social developments of that century, it can be seen as an Enlightenment phenomenon. In some of its ideals too, freemasonry can be seen as 'enlightened', stressing brotherhood transcending differences of rank, and a search for truth and morality which played down doctrinal aspects of religion and thus tended towards deism. But in other respects freemasonry seems a movement which sits uneasily in the 'Age of Enlightenment', and indeed even typifies the sort of obscurantism and superstition of the past which those interested in enlightenment and improvement sought to destroy. Elaborate secret rituals of initiation, involving both terrifying and humiliating the candidate, combining solemnity with crude horse-play, performed by men dressed in fancy gloves, aprons and jewels, based on a confused mass of myths and legends. What on earth has all this mumbo-jumbo to do with the Age of Reason?

The success of the movement proves that it somehow met the needs of many eighteenth-century men. What these needs were and how freemasonry satisfied them is a fascinating topic, but the subject of this paper is rather the origins of the movement. The prevailing interpretation is that freemasonry was created in England at the beginning of the eighteenth century, or perhaps in the late seventeenth century, though some influence from earlier movements can be detected. More specifically, the founding of the Grand Lodge of England in 1717 is often cited as the real start of freemasonry, as this was the first of all grand lodges to emerge, exercising authority over ordinary lodges. But this conventional wisdom is contradicted by the vast majority of

36

the surviving sources, for the documentary evidence relates overwhelmingly to Scottish masonry. The evidence has, therefore, frequently been a source of embarrassment to English masonic historians, who have either sought to ignore it, or to explain it away with ingenious special pleading. The foremost masonic historians of this century, Douglas Knoop and G.P. Jones, examined the evidence more dispassionately than their predecessors, and they argued that Scottish influence on early freemasonry was strong—and they even ventured to point out that 1717 was a date of no particular importance to masonic history, as the so called Grand Lodge of England, far from being a national body, at first represented only four London lodges.[1] It would, indeed, have been more accurate to have named it the Grandiose Lodge rather than the Grand Lodge. But even Knoop and Jones tended to seek to interpret the mass of Scottish evidence in an English context, failing to break free from the Anglocentric assumption that freemasonry essentially began in England. So ingrained is this assumption that historians fail even to realise that they are making it.

The full range of the Scottish evidence has never in the past been utilised in trying to understand the origins of freemasonry, and little has been done to interpret that evidence in the context of Scottish rather than English history. I have attempted to remedy this in a forthcoming book, and the research undertaken for the book has demonstrated that most of the essentials of freemasonry emerge first in Scotland, and then subsequently appear in England.[2] The crucial period was the years around 1600, when the master of works to King James VI reorganised the mason craft in Scotland and issued codes of statutes for its conduct. Though much remains obscure, I would argue that if any man deserves the title of founder of freemasonry it is William Schaw. Ironically, in view of later papal condemnations of freemasonry, Schaw was himself a Roman Catholic.

It was Schaw who created the modern lodge system of organisation for freemasonry. Seventeenth-century England can produce only a few scattered references to masonic lodges, the first in 1646. By contrast twenty Scottish masonic lodges are known to have existed in the seventeenth century, and official records of fifteen of them are known. In two cases lodge minutes begin in 1599 and run unbroken throughout the seventeenth and eighteenth centuries. Most of these seventeenth-century lodges still exist today: they are by far the oldest lodges in the world. The two grades or ranks of early freemasonry, entered apprentice and fellow craft master, also appear first in William Schaw's statutes, and though at first his lodges may have been confined to 'operative' masons—that is working stonemasons—in the 1630s lodges began admitting non-operatives of all ranks, from craftsmen to nobles. Schaw's ambition appears to have been to provide the mason craft with an organisation, mythology and ritual which combined medieval craft myths (mainly derived from England) with a number of late Renaissance trends. The evidence is mainly circumstantial rather than direct, but influences present in the emergence of freemasonry include the general craze for secret societies in Europe around 1600; the idea of the occult search for lost knowledge and divine revelation, especially in its Hermetic form; the fashionable idea that craftsmen had, through their practical skills, knowledge the philosopher should seek to learn from; and the placing of mathematics, identified with architecture and therefore with masonry, at the apex of the sciences. In complex ways all these themes contributed to changing perceptions of the mason craft, making men willing to accept that the mason craft had a unique status and valuable secrets. Direct evidence of the influence of one of these late Renaissance themes on freemasonry survives, though it has never been noticed: William Schaw ordered that masons be regularly examined as to their skill in the art of memory. Those who know Frances Yates's book on the subject[3] will recall that the occult art of memory of the period was inextricably involved with the great Hermetic quest.

The origins of the masonic rituals of initiation and recognition are hard to trace, not surprisingly as they formed the secret core of the movement. But again all the early evidence is Scottish. The secrets were known collectively as the Mason Word, and references to the Word appear in Scotland from about 1630. In the 1690s much of the content of the rituals was revealed in the first of the so-called masonic catechisms, and again all the early documents are Scottish in origin or content. Later developments of the rituals of craft freemasonry have been based on these seventeenth-century Scottish originals. To take one example which has recently attracted public attention, the threat in the initiate's oath of secrecy that the masons will cut his throat if he reveals their secrets, abolished in 1986 in English freemasonry, first appears in the Scottish catechisms. Moreover, in the early Scottish lodges evidence can be found of abstract aspects of later freemasonry: brotherhood transcending social status; a morality without reference to specific religious doctrines, supported and illustrated by symbolism based on the tools and practices of stonemasons.

There were of course some English influences in the freemasonry which grew so fast in early eighteenth-century Britain. The medieval English myths which the Scottish masons had absorbed into their freemasonry provided freemasonry with much of its traditional history, and the name 'freemason' itself derives from English usage. But, to use an appropriately architectural metaphor, English freemasons did not construct the edifice of freemasonry; they took over and adapted for their own uses a Scottish structure, and in time came to believe they had built it themselves. The Scottish evidence then came to be played down, one common ploy being to juggle with definitions of the term freemasonry in ways which conveniently disposed of the seventeenth-century Scots masons as interesting perhaps, but not really freemasons. Their lodges, it is argued, were 'operative', essentially composed of stonemasons and concerned with the regulation of their working lives. They may have had rituals, but it is urged that these were too crude to qualify as freemasonry. A study of the Scottish lodges in their own right, and not in the context of freemasonry in England, with the assumption that it began there, reveals that the 'operative' lodges were often mainly concerned with ritual and social functions, trade regulation being secondary. In any case the argument that as most members of early Scottish lodges were working men they could not have had rituals worthy of the name freemasonry rests on the snobbish assumption that people of so humble a social status could not have developed freemasonry, and that it needed gentlemen to refine their rituals to make them respectable. Such assumptions ill become a movement that claims to ignore social differences, by appearing to suggest that masonic ritual only becomes freemasonry when performed by gentlemen: it is not what is done that counts, but who is doing it. This is absurd. Seventeenth-century Scotland saw the birth and development of the lodge system, of the secrets and rituals of the Mason Word and the associated grades of initiate, and of the basic elements of morality and symbolism later associated with freemasonry. If this is not freemasonry, it is hard to know what is.

The processes whereby Scottish masonic organisation and practices were transferred to England in the late seventeenth and early eighteenth centuries are obscure, but one aspect of this development brings Aberdeen into the story. The most influential publication in the history of freemasonry in the eighteenth century was *The Constitutions of the Free-Masons*, which appeared in London in 1723, followed by a very much enlarged edition in 1738. The author of these works was James Anderson, the son of the former secretary of the Lodge of Aberdeen. The only convincing explanation of why he, rather than some prominent English mason, should have been chosen to frame the *Constitutions* which did so much to define freemasonry seems to be that he was regarded, through his contacts with Scottish freemasonry, as more closely in touch with authentic masonic lore than his English colleagues. It may be objected to this that the *Constitutions* give Scotland no prominent place in the development of freemasonry, but the explanation probably lies in what Anderson was trying to do. He was providing constitutions for English masons, and it was therefore natural that he should seek to provide a fabulous history which took the medieval lore of the English masons as its starting point and then placed England at the centre of the supposed growth of the movement. The Scots were not popular in early eighteenth-century England, so stressing how much freemasonry owed to Scotland would have been counterproductive.

To conclude, if eighteenth-century freemasonry contains elements that appear highly incongruous in the Age of Enlightenment, this can be understood by realising that in essence freemasonry is a late Renaissance phenomenon. Its astonishing expansion in the eighteenth century saw it adapt itself, to some extent, to a new age, but in many ways it remained a movement which fits better into the world of the late sixteenth and early seventeenth centuries than into the world of the Enlightenment.

Notes

1. D. Knoop and G.P. Jones, *The Genesis of Freemasonry* (Manchester, Manchester U.P., 1947) p.321.
2. D. Stevenson, *The Origins of Freemasonry. Scotland's Century* (forthcoming, Cambridge, CUP, 1988).
3. F. Yates, *The Art of Memory* (London, Routledge, 1966).

5

James Mackintosh, Learned Societies in India, and Enlightenment Ideas

Kitty Datta

University of Jadavpur, Calcutta

This paper examines the relation between Sir James Mackintosh's approach to his Indian experience, 1804-1811, and his education in late eighteenth-century Scotland, at Aberdeen University from 1780, and from 1784 at Edinburgh where he studied medicine. The printed source for his early years is the account he wrote in Bombay in 1805, published by his son R.J. Mackintosh in 1835. For his Indian years I have used unpublished manuscript material in the National Library of Scotland, the Erskine/Leyden Papers in the British Library, and the manuscript minutes of the Literary Society of Bombay, as well as letters and journals published by his son, and the Literary Society of Bombay's printed *Transactions*.[1]

If one were to believe William Hazlitt, Mackintosh's Indian experience was arid and empty because of deficiencies of mind which, Hazlitt hints, are especially Scottish—a bookish and somewhat inflexible pedantry not sufficiently open to experience:

> Sir James is one of those who see nature through the spectacles of books. He might like to read an account of India; but India itself with its burning shining face would be a mere blank, an endless waste to him. To persons of this class of mind things must be translated into words, visible images into abstract propositions, to meet their refined apprehensions; and they have no more to say to a matter-of-fact staring them in the face without a label in its mouth, than they would to a hippopotamus.[2]

It is true enough, as Mackintosh's correspondence proves, that he 'languished after the friends and society that he had left behind', and did not always in Bombay find the agreeable intellectual company to which he was accustomed in London. It is true also that he went to India to make himself financially independent fairly quickly, and to have more leisure for reading and writing.

But Hazlitt was ignorant of the positive content of Mackintosh's Indian years, which are particularly worth considering in the context of Enlightenment ideas and attitudes.

When Hazlitt noticed that a subject of perennial interest to Mackintosh was 'the progress of the human mind', one recognises the continuation of that concern of Scottish writers of the later eighteenth century with the stages of human culture which befits the pupil at Aberdeen of Professor James Dunbar, author of *Essays on the History of Mankind in Rude and Cultivated Ages* (1780), and the nephew once removed of the Professor of Universal History at Edinburgh, Alexander Fraser Tytler, Lord Woodhouselee. After the publication of William Robertson's *Historical Disquisition concerning the Knowledge which the Ancients had of India* (1791), Fraser Tytler enlarged his own lectures, published as *Elements of History, Ancient and Modern* (1801), to include more Indian material. The tone of sympathetic admiration of ancient Indian civilisation in each is notable, drawing upon the recently published transactions of the Asiatic Society of Bengal, *Asiatick Researches*, and its members' translations—Sir William Jones's *Sákuntalā* and Charles Wilkins's English rendering of the *Bhagavadgītā*—as well as the travels of Sonnerat and Neibuhr and Hodges's prints of antiquities. In 1782, when Fraser Tytler first published the outline of his Edinburgh world history course, there were references to ancient China and Japan, but not to India before the Moghuls. In the 1790s his view widened, no doubt under Robertson's influence.

Yet in the 1780s Fraser Tytler had demonstrated his general interest in the possibilities of Indian experience for Scotsmen, not in widening their cultural horizons, but in establishing a fortune. In the *Lounger* of 1785 appeared an exemplary tale by him on the repair of a decayed Scottish estate by the investment of Indian money, a purified image of oriental acquisition.[3] Was the tale intended as an *exemplum* for his young nephew James Mackintosh who at precisely this time came down from Aberdeen to Edinburgh to study medicine? The youth of the story becomes a surgeon's mate on an East Indiaman, and is placed as a Company surgeon on a nawab's territories, where in twelve years he acquires £25,000, more than enough to buy back his family property, restore the mansion, provide his sister with a dowry sufficient to keep her among the gentry, and to live as a gentleman farmer, giving medical advice *gratis* to the poor. The estate which the fatherless James Mackintosh had inherited was unprofitable, so much so that he sold it off before leaving for India, though it had been his family's since the sixteenth century, and he did not buy it back on his return. His son later wrote with regret of the loss of the estate and thus of the opportunity for exercising the art of improvement as he saw it happening elsewhere:

> All over the Highlands of Scotland may be observed, here and there, the effects of the little stream of East or West Indian gold, running side by side with the mountain torrent, spreading cultivation, fertility, and plenty, along its narrow valley.[4]

The New Statistical Account of 1845 agreed that Sir James Mackintosh's parish of Moy and Dalcrossie lacked 'the fostering hand of a resident landlord', and had decayed, unlike other areas where Mackintoshes had returned from Indian business to invest and enlighten.[5]

Nearer the time of James Mackintosh's departure for India, his uncle, Lord Woodhouselee, was much involved in encouraging the young men of his circle to try what India could do for them. His own son, Alexander, and his son-in-law, James Baillie Fraser, both had Indian careers interesting beyond the ordinary.[6] Those Scots of the Hastings trial generation who had Indian interests and investments were worried by the declining reputation of the East India Company, and conspicuous recruitment from among the promising young Scottish gentry suggests a campaign of conscious reform. Mackintosh himself had few illusions about the past. As he wrote to a friend before departure to India:

> I do not go to India with much expectation of approving the policy recently adopted for our ill-gotten, but well-governed Asiatic empire. That empire, acquired not by any plan of ambition conceived at home, but by the accidents of fortune, the courage, the fears, the vigour, the despair, and the crimes of individual adventurers, is certainly better administered than any other territory in Asia...The conquest arose from the character of the adventurers, and the tempting anarchy of Hindostan.

Throughout his Indian years he was given to acid comment on the system of which he was a part. His former teacher William Ogilvie, Professor of Humanity at King's College Aberdeen and a radical minded admirer of Mackintosh's youthful defence of the French Revolution, interested himself in the problem of Indian land tenure, and in 1808 wrote enquiring whether the produce of the Indian soil could not be distributed between the labourer and the legal owner. In his reply Mackintosh suggested, echoing Adam Smith, that it was against 'the most demonstrated principles of political science' to vest a trade monopoly in an exclusive Company, so the Act which did it should be called 'An Act for Preventing the Progress of Industry in India, in order to hinder the Influx of Wealth into Great Britain'.[7]

There were rumours around 1801, as earlier, that Mackintosh had been invited to superintend the proposed institution of an 'Asiatic College' in Calcutta for young Company recruits to study the Indian vernaculars and widen their knowledge of Indian cultural traditions; so Fraser Tytler wrote to him recommending the services of the Border poet and doctor John Leyden, and enclosing an interesting letter in which Leyden listed his extra-ordinarily wide educational attainments, especially his study in Scotland of several oriental languages.[8] In the end Mackintosh arrived in India, not as principal of a college for oriental studies, but as Recorder of Bombay, a legal appointment which fitted his talents and his later legal studies in London more appropriately. He took the post as an opportunity for bringing about penal reform and improving judicial fairness in a Benthamite spirit. In a letter written soon after his arrival in India in 1804, he described his aims as 'the reformation of the police, of the administration of penal law, and particularly of the prison, which, as I intend, if possible, to return to Europe with a bloodless name, will be my principal instrument of punishment'. Donald Winch has recently shown how, for the pupils and friends of Professor Dugald Stewart of Edinburgh, including Sir James Mackintosh, there was a natural transition from concern with improvements in 'the detail of the municipal code' as central to the modern science of politics, to attention to Bentham's writings. And if, on the issue of parliamentary reform, sceptical Whig in later years disputed with Benthamite, Sir James Mackintosh with James Mill, this was nevertheless a difference between men with a mental kinship traceable to the influence of Scottish university teaching on the history of social progress and the nature of politics, and to Dugald Stewart in particular.[9] Yet, as we shall see, in the matter of fundamental ethical commitments, and in his view of human psychology, Mackintosh stayed closer to Stewart.

Shortly after arriving in Bombay Mackintosh formed, on 26 November 1804, the Literary Society of Bombay, with the Aberdonian merchant-prince, Charles Forbes, as its treasurer; with William Erskine, illegitimate relative of the Erskines of Cardross, as secretary; and other Scots as members. These included Dr John Leyden, Erskine's close friend since their student days in Edinburgh; the Hon. Sir Alexander Anstruther of Balcaskie in Fife, a Company judge; Lieutenant-General Sir John Abercromby of the distinguished Scottish military family; James Calder, Calcutta free merchant, and an active member of the Asiatic Society of Bengal; Captain Basil Hall, son of Sir John Hall, President of the Royal Society of Edinburgh; and Dr Robert Drummond, who had published grammars of the Indian languages, Marathi, Gujarati and Malabari. Alumni of Aberdeen University were Theodore Forbes (whose interesting papers, some relating to his marriage with an Indian woman, are in Aberdeen University archives) and a Mr Skene with scientific interests, whose mathematical proficiency had won praise from the then Professor Hamilton.[10]

This Society, which later took the name 'Asiatic Society of Bombay', if it had its affinities with the Asiatic Society of Bengal, was also a natural formation for men who, like Mackintosh and Erskine, had been members of student societies in the Scottish universities (Mackintosh of the Speculative Society, and Erskine of the Academy of Physics, both at Edinburgh).[11] More than that, as early as 1788, Mackintosh had attended in London a meeting of the Society for Constitutional Information at which the orientalist founder of the Asiatic Society of Bengal, Sir William Jones, was also present. He later became secretary of the radical Association of Friends of the People, though modern discussion of the extent of Mackintosh's radicalism has tended to emphasise its moderation.[12] Before leaving for India he was a member, with others of the *Edinburgh Review* circle, of 'The King of Clubs'. The Whiggish improving progressive note is clearly to be heard in the 'Discourse' with which he opened the proceedings of the Literary Society of Bombay. Though he praises Sir William Jones, his own stress is less purely orientalist, in his proposal that the Society might take up enquiries in the area of natural history, mineralogy, botany, biology, climatology, medicine (including indigenous treatments), and political economy (including economic and population statistics), and provide the kind of information which could be used to influence government, form public opinion, and see that justice is done. The aims of the Society, he claims, were 'perfectly innocent'. If somewhat visionary, they raised the level of its activities above the mere pursuit of amusement. 'With these hopes, they assume the dignity of being part of that discipline under which the race of man is destined to proceed to the highest degree of civilisation, virtue and happiness of which our nature is capable.' This unperturbed assurance about the possession of a true idea of what constitutes 'the highest degree of civilisation' is precisely the western assumption, if innocent, innocently arrogant, which Edward Said and others have recently been drawing to our notice in the orientalist activities of European intellectuals.[13] Of course the central aim here was to raise the intellectual and moral tone of the British community in western India, to civilise the agents of civilisation.

The notion of a Statistical Survey, combining scientific and sociological information, was not new in India. The survey work which followed the annexation of new territories had already begun the process, and in the 1790s especially there was an impressive amount of such work in which Scottish military men were particularly involved.[14] No doubt the broad content of Scottish university education prepared men for such work, not to speak of the example of Sir John Sinclair's great *Statistical Account*. In fact young Henry Brougham had encouraged members of the Academy of Physics, which he had founded at Edinburgh University, to do field work on this model; and in John Leyden, William Erskine and Dr James Hare, Jr, we have a clear case of the Academy's ex-members involved in survey work and in the life of the local learned societies immediately on reaching India.[15] Though Mackintosh saw the Literary Society of Bombay as the hub from which the promotion of the voluntary survey idea would spread out, he had wider ambitions, clearly evident in the Public General Letter of 9 April 1806 from the Court of Directors of the East India Company to the Indian Government, authorising the supply to Sir James Mackintosh of necessary materials for writing 'the History and present State of the British Dominions in India'. Purely antiquarian research and other 'curious' matter were to be excluded; 'a Desideratum in Oriental Literature and Summary of useful information adapted to the present time concerning our possessions and affairs in the East' were to be central. (In the end, of course, it was to be James Mill, and not Mackintosh, who wrote *The History of British India*.) Mackintosh himself referred to his project as 'a Statistical Account of British India', and saw another plan as a necessary preliminary to it.[16]

This was his 'Plan of a Comparative Vocabulary of Indian Languages', which he read to the Literary Society of Bombay on 26 May 1806, and then sent on to the acting Governor-General, who had it circulated to officers in the field, and for comment to the Council of the College of Fort William, now teaching Indian languages to cadets. Mackintosh's inspiration was the Empress Catherine of Russia's 1784 project for linguistic comparison, as well as Sir William Jones's remarks on the affinities among the Indo-European language-group. It is impossible to know how much he had been informed of Dr John Leyden's independent plans for work in comparative philology. In 1807 Lord Minto, the new Governor-General, and Leyden's erstwhile Border neighbour, showed sympathy towards such linguistic plans, and Colebrooke at the College of Fort William rated Leyden's above Mackintosh's.[17] It would be easy to miss the significance of this plan, for Indian vernaculars, especially Hindustani and Bengali, were already being taught to cadets at Fort William College, along with the ancient languages, Persian, Arabic and Sanskrit. But the scope of this survey was to be immensely wider, and, in John Leyden's mind in particular, it was linked both with the idea of comparative philology and cross-cultural history, and with the appreciation of vernacular literatures, of which Leyden did many specimen translations. Though this enterprise has a Herderian flavour, the primary impulse for his own interests, as his friend Erskine noticed, came from his own Scottish Border heritage, his collection and editing of works in the Scottish tongue, and his appreciation of Gaelic. This concern was quite distinct from the classicist concern of Jones and his associates with ancient oriental languages.[18]

When survey work began, Leyden and Mackintosh cooperated, as well as other Scottish contributors in the field, who included the judge Charles Boddam, the administrator Mountstuart Elphinstone, and Francis Irvine.[19] Irvine is a particularly interesting alumnus of Aberdeen University. Son of Alexander Irvine of Drum in Aberdeenshire, he was at Marischal College in 1801-1802, before receiving his Company cadetship. He was proposed for membership of the Bombay Literary Society by Sir James Mackintosh himself in February 1808, and in the same year accompanied Mountstuart Elphinstone on his diplomatic mission to Afghanistan, where his particular allotment of work was the survey of the climate, soil, husbandry and produce of the country. At one time he had thought of publishing a comprehensive account of 'Cabool' on his own, but, as Elphinstone explained in the preface to *An Account of the Kingdom of Caubul* (1814, revised edition 1839), 'it had been from the first less his object to describe a particular people, than to enlarge his acquaintance with the history of human society'—a recognisably Enlightenment preoccupation. Though quite aware of the hypothetical element in 'civil history, which I look upon as half fable', he was deeply attracted by the pursuit of it. But he was also a skilled field worker and observer of detail, so that Elphinstone in the end paid him the tribute of admitting that much of his book's data was Irvine's, so closely had they worked together.[20]

By 1810 Irvine was corresponding familiarly with John Leyden on the Afghan language, commenting on his reading of Herder (who was too rhapsodical for his taste), and writing appreciatively of Leyden's book on African exploration. He was also offering a list of topics for study and discussion, such as the impact of Hinduism on Islam in India; local differences in Hindu belief and practice; Hindu borrowings from other cultures and the spread of Hinduism into south-east Asia; 'mysticism and mystical composition', involving the comparison of Pythagoras and the Eclectics with Islamic Sufis and Hindu devotional writers. He was also enquiring into the rise of castes, and 'how far the system of castes is declining under the English', or whether new castes were then forming. 'Itinerant village bands of natives, with specimens of their poetry', and proverbs, old and new, were other topics which aroused his curiosity. He described a form of grass-roots democracy among the Afghans, comparing it with the Indian village *panchayat*, and wrote a treatise on property holding and rank.[21]

When the Asiatic Society of Bengal had turned down Irvine's essay on resemblances between gipsy language and Hindustani, Mackintosh looked favourably on his speculations (developed quite independently of Marsden's) and they were eventually published by the Literary Society of Bombay. If the modern worldwide association of gipsies looks upon India as their homeland, it is partly due to the insights of early amateur anthropologists like Irvine. He later became much involved in educational work, including the Calcutta School Book Society, and on 21 May 1816 was present at the celebrated foundation meeting of Hindoo College in Calcutta, a landmark in what is now known as the 'Bengal Renaissance', and was appointed its first European Secretary.[22] In the previous decade, Mackintosh had advised Minto that 'knowledge should be imparted to the Natives through Colleges and other Seminaries of instruction and learning and their minds should be gradually enlightened'.[23] This view of education as the primary instrument of change maintains the stress by Scottish writers from Hume through Dunbar to Stewart (arguing against Montesquieu) on moral over environmental causes in forming regional character and effecting social progress.[24] Out of such convictions, Scots were everywhere in the early educational schemes of British India.

So there is a certain family likeness among the interests of this group of Company servants which, if they grew through mutual encouragement and private sharing of ideas on Indian soil, also have links with the kind of education they received in Scotland, with a bias towards comparative cultural studies and 'conjectural' history. The ordinary proceedings of the Literary Society of Bombay during the years of Mackintosh's presidency show the same kind of mixture of the scientific, the cultural-anthropological, and the literary (Dr Drummond on caste, for example, or Sir John Malcolm on the Sunni Muslim sect and the celebration of Dusserah by the Mahrattas), as the proceedings of the Asiatic Society of Bengal, and they included plans for the translation of Indian classics which issued first in a mathematical text, the *Līlāvatī*, and a Sanskrit play, *Probodh Chandradaya*. The translator was a medical man whose investigations into Indian language, literature and philosophy had been encouraged personally by Mackintosh.[25]

It was the special plans of Sir James himself which showed a more directly practical bent towards assisting government with information. Here his own frame of mind probably corresponded nicely with the demands of the Court of Directors. If he was at this period reading Schelling, Fichte, Jacobi and other German philosophical writers, and comparing German with Indian idealism (in a letter to Dugald Stewart), he kept this interest to his private journals and correspondence.[26] In contrast, the books which were ordered for the library of the Literary Society of Bombay soon after he retired, and with his assistance, included all the classics of the Scottish Enlightenment—

Lord Kames, John Millar, Adam Smith, Adam Ferguson, William Robertson, Archibald Alison, Dugald Stewart, Hutton the geologist.[27] Indeed I have discovered in the National Library of India Sir James's personal copy of Hutton's biography, presented to him by its author, Professor Playfair of Edinburgh. (It most probably belonged at one time to the library of Fort William College.)

One special interest of the Literary Society of Bombay which was established during this period, the study of the cave-temples of western India (especially at Elephanta and Ellora) was to develop by the mid century from the descriptions and religio-historical speculations of Erskine to the active promotion of preservation. Mackintosh was a repeated visitor to such temple sites, and encouraged the analysis of different strata, Buddhist, Jaina and Hindu, which is the basis of more elaborate modern studies, though his own attitude was tempered by his belief in the superiority of the Grecian:

> There is nothing reasonable, useful, or beautiful; all is fantastic, massy and monstrous. There are traces of these notions in Greek mythology, sufficient to show its descent; but at last, after Art had been toiling in India, in Persia, and in Egypt, to produce monsters, beauty and grace were discovered in Greece.[28]

William Erskine, in his comments on the caves, in the Literary Society of Bombay's *Transactions* of 1823, was more cautious of any hint at the superiority of western culture.[29]

If all these concerns show Hazlitt wrong when he claimed of Mackintosh that 'he was out of his element among black slaves and sepoys, and nabobs, and cadets, and writers to India. He had no one to exchange ideas with', there may be an element of truth in his further claim that Mackintosh's kind of mind suffered from needing things to be 'translated into words; visible images into abstract propositions'. Too prompt a tendency to fit everything into its place in cultural history, and a cultural history weighted heavily in favour of the West, could indeed be a disadvantage in confronting India. Hazlitt's quarrel with Sir James Mackintosh was part of a wider quarrel with the pundits of his age, with Bentham, Malthus and James Mill, who preferred generalisations to the value of the particular instance, rational theory to the guiding sympathy of the heart. In terms of the inherited ideas of the Enlightenment, which were Hazlitt's as well as Mackintosh's, this was to prefer an outlook focussed primarily upon individual experience and the role of imaginative sympathy in fostering the moral life, to a preoccupation with conjectural history and a utilitarian theory of improvement.[30] Such strains of thought might be found side by side in Adam Smith or Dugald Stewart, but they come here to a confrontation which was significant for the experience and conduct of Empire.

In the appendix to his *Disquisition* on ancient India William Robertson had issued a warning which went more often than not unheeded. In a cunning reference to the stages of civilisation idea, he pointed out its misuse:

> Men in every stage of their career are so satisfied by the progress made by the

community of which they are members, that it becomes to them a standard of perfection, and they are apt to regard people whose condition is not similar with contempt, even aversion.

Nor is this merely a dangerous mental set. It radically distorts human behaviour:

> Happy would it be if any of the four European nations, who have successively acquired extensive territories in India, could altogether vindicate itself from having acted in this manner. Nothing, however, can have a more direct tendency to inspire Europeans, proud of their own superior attainments in policy, science, and arts, with proper sentiments concerning the people of India, and to teach them a due regard for their natural rights as men, than their being accustomed, not only to consider the Hindoos of the present times as a knowing and ingenious race of men, but to view them as descended from ancestors who had attained to a very high degree of improvement, many ages before the least step towards civilisation had been taken in any part of Europe.[31]

That is to say, if the Scottish Enlightenment gave the Western world strong versions of a theory of social progress, its thinkers might also issue warnings about the moral consequences of its misapplication. Mackintosh's early teacher at Aberdeen, James Dunbar, had already done so in a powerful critique of racist theories of civilisation which runs through his *Essays on the History of Mankind in Rude and Cultivated Ages* (1780). The story of Scottish involvement in the imperial process can, I believe, be at least partially written in terms of this clash of attitudes.

Notes

1. *Memoirs of the Life of the Right Honourable Sir James Mackintosh*, ed. Robert Charles Mackintosh, 2 vols (London, E. Moxon, 1835), vol. I, pp.1-80; Asiatic Society of Bombay Minute Book, 1804-1820, inspected by courtesy of the Secretary, Mrs B.K.Seth.
2. William Hazlitt, *The Spirit of the Age, or Contemporary Portraits* (1825, reprinted London, OUP, 1947), pp.155-56.
3. *The Lounger*, 44, 3 December 1785. The attribution to A. Fraser Tytler is in *British Essayists*, ed. James Ferguson (London, J. Richardson, 1823), vol. XXX.
4. *Memoirs*, vol. I, p.169.
5. *The New Statistical Account of Scotland* (1845), vol. XIV, 'Moy and Dalcrossie', p.116, and pp.455, 521-23, on Lachlan Mackintosh of Raigmore, a notable improver, after retirement from his Calcutta agency-house, and Capt. William Mackintosh of Farr.
6. Alexander Fraser Tytler, Jr, *Considerations on the Present Political State of India* (London, Black, Parry & Co., 1815, 2nd edition 1816); James Baillie Fraser, *Journal of a Tour through Part of the Snowy Range of the Himala Mountains, and to the Sources of the Rivers Jumna and Ganges* (London, Rodwell and Martin, 1820), and several other volumes of travel and fiction; also his *Views of the Himala Mountains* (London, Rodwell and Martin, 1820).
7. *Memoirs*, vol. I, pp.194, 385.

8. NLS MS 971, ff.11-13.
9. *Memoirs*, vol. I, p.215; Stefan Collini, Donald Winch and John Burrow, *That Noble Science of Politics. A Study in Nineteenth-Century Intellectual History* (Cambridge, CUP, 1983) chapters 1-3, especially pp.58, 93-95, 97, 111.
10. Asiatic Society of Bombay Minute Book, 1804-1820; *Transactions of the Literary Society of Bombay*, vol. I (1819). William Erskine's legitimation letter of 1830 is in BL, Add. MS 39,945, ff. 64-65. His father may have been James Erskine of Jamaica and his half-brother David of Ceylon (see ff.58-62). The Indian correspondence of the Ogilvie Forbes of Boyndlie family is in AUL: see Roy C. Bridges, 'An Aberdeenshire family and the Indian-African connection in the early nineteenth century', in *An African Miscellany for John Hargreaves*, ed. Roy Bridges (Aberdeen, A.U. African Studies Group, 1983), pp.5-10.
11. NLS MS 756. See also G.N. Cantor, 'The Academy of Physics at Edinburgh, 1797-1800', *Social Studies of Science*, V (1975), pp.109-34.
12. Lionel A. McKenzie, 'The French Revolution and English parliamentary reform: James Mackintosh and the *Vindiciae Gallicae*', *Eighteenth-Century Studies*, XIV (1981), pp.264-82.
13. Edward W. Said, *Orientalism* (New York, Pantheon Books, 1978).
14. Walter A. Hamilton, *A Geographical, Statistical, and Historical Description of Hindostan and the Adjacent Countries*, 2 vols (London, 1820) has several Scottish contributors; Clements R. Markham, *A Memoir of the Indian Surveys*, 2nd edition (London, Allen and Co., 1878).
15. NLS MS 971, ff. 11-13, Hare's membership; NLS MS 756, Leyden as the Academy's correspondent gathering Scottish geological data from 'the statistical accounts'.
16. NLS Minto MS 11726, ff.28-29, Mackintosh to Barlow through Jonathan Duncan, June and July 1806; ff.30-31, Court of Directors' Order; ff.10-11, Mackintosh to Lord Minto, 31 July 1807.
17. *Ibid.*, ff. 12-23, 'Plan of a Comparative Vocabulary... 26 May, 1806', ff.32-35.
18. Sisir Kumar Das, *Sahibs and Munshis. An Account of the College of Fort William* (New Delhi, Orison Publishers, 1978); Kitty Datta, 'John Leyden (1775-1811): local poet, international linguist', *Jadavpur Journal of Comparative Literature*, 20-21 (1982-83), pp.118-36. Hans Aarsleff, *The Study of Language in England 1780-1860* (Princeton, Princeton U.P., 1967) discusses Stewart's and Mackintosh's interest in the philosophy of language, and the contribution of Alexander Murray, also the growing respect for the vernaculars in J.D. Michaelis, Condillac and Herder.
19. Items from Leyden: NLS Minto MS 11327, ff.62-63 (1811); MS 3380, ff.209-10; MS 971, f.41; ff.71-72. Charles Boddam in NLS MS 11726, ff.24-25. The original Charles Boddam in India was born 1680 at Boddam, Aberdeenshire, and became Captain on the China route of the East India Company. See Henry D. Love, *Vestiges of Old Madras*, 4 vols (London, John Murray, 1913). On Boddam's other orientalist interests, see Mildred Archer, *Company Drawings in the India Office Library* (London, H.M.S.O., 1972) pp.119-21.
20. Alistair Tayler and Henrietta Tayler, *The Jacobites of Aberdeenshire and Banffshire in the Forty-Five*, 2nd edition (Aberdeen, Milne and Hutchison, 1928) on the Irvines of Drum. Also information from Mr C.A. McLaren on Francis Irvine in Aberdeen University Archives; from Dr H.J. Bingle, India Office Library; and from Bombay Minute Book, February 1808.
21. Erskine/Leyden Papers, BL, Add. MS 26,579, ff.47, 53-54, 55-62; Irvine to Leyden on Afghaniana and orientalist topics. Irvine rebukes Leyden for using phrases

like 'savage character', since tribes have greater variety than uniformity, so one should not generalise about them, NLS MS 3380, ff.213-14.

22. Erskine/Leyden Papers, BL, Add. MS 26,605, ff.33-34: Irvine to Mackintosh, August 1807; ff.57-58, Kashmiri vocabulary, 1807. 'On the similitude between the gipsy and hindoostanee languages', *Transactions of the Literary Society of Bombay*, vol. I (1819). Elphinstone letter to Irvine on education, 1819, in R.D. Choksey, *Mountstuart Elphinstone, the Indian Years, 1796-1827* (Bombay, Popular Prakashan, 1971), p.237. Association with Hindoo College: P.C. Mittra, *A Biographical Sketch of David Hare* (Calcutta, W. Newman and Co., 1878, reprinted and ed. by G.C. Sengupta, Calcutta, Jijnasa, 1979), pp.7-8.

23. NLS Minto MS 11733 f.62.

24. Clarence J. Glacken, *Traces on the Rhodian Shore. Nature and Culture in Western Thought from Ancient Times to the End of the Eighteenth Century* (Berkeley, California U.P., 1967) Chapter 12, discusses Montesquieu's view of 'the unchanging East', and Scottish criticism of environmental determinism, especially Hume and Dunbar, pp.596-601. David Kopf, *British Orientalism and the Bengal Renaissance. The Dynamics of Indian Modernisation, 1773-1835* (Calcutta, Firma K.L. Mukhopadhyay, 1969) and Michael Laird, *Missionaries and Education in Bengal, 1793-1837* (Oxford, Clarendon Press, 1972), by ending their studies immediately after the Macaulay/Bentinck Minute establishing anglicised higher education, and by confining their attention to Bengal, give an unbalanced picture of the Scottish contribution to Indian general education, and are followed in their emphasis by N.L. Basak, *History of Vernacular Education in Bengal 1800-1854* (Calcutta, Bharati Book Stall, 1974).

25. *Edinburgh Review*, XXII (1813-14), pp.400-409 reviews Dr J. Taylor's translation. The review was probably by the Scottish Sanskritist Alexander Hamilton, from whom Schlegel learned Sanskrit. Scottish geological interests were maintained in India by two outstanding Aberdeen graduates. John Grant Malcolmson (1802-44), born at Forres, studied arts at King's College, Aberdeen, medicine at Edinburgh (1819-22), then immediately joined the Madras Army as an assistant surgeon. His journal written during his first year in India is now in Forres Records, RF 426/1, with other papers. His scientific articles were published in the journals of the Asiatic Society of Bengal, the Royal Asiatic Society of London, the Geological Society, and in the *Calcutta Journal of Natural History*. On leave for his health, he introduced Hugh Miller to Murchison and Agassiz, and became a member of the Royal Asiatic Society's Committee of Agriculture and Commerce. Returned to Bombay in the service of Forbes and Co., he became curator of the Royal Asiatic Society of Bombay (formerly the Literary Society) museum, editor of its journal, and its secretary. He died of jungle fever, 1844. The Malcolmson Medal of the Society was established in his memory. Hugh Falconer (1808-66), born at Forres, educated at King's College, Aberdeen and Edinburgh, was posted as curator of the Saharanpur Botanical Garden, was later at the Calcutta Botanical Garden. He experimented with tea cultivation. He was awarded, with P. Cautley, the Wollaston Medal of the Royal Geological Society for his work on Sivalik fossils, and was a member of the Asiatic Society of Bengal.

26. *Memoirs*, vol. I, p.305.

27. Bombay Minutes, January 1812, October 1813, May 1814.

28. *Memoirs*, vol. II, pp.77-78. Partha Mitter, *Much Maligned Monsters. The History of European Reactions to Indian Art* (Oxford, Clarendon Press, 1977), though not noticing Mackintosh, shows how typical were his reactions.

29. The Aberdeen graduate Dr William Hunter wrote of Elephanta in 'An account

of some artificial caverns in the neighbourhood of Bombay', *Archaeologia* (London, The Society of Antiquaries, 1785); William Erskine, 'Account of the Cave Temple at Elephanta' and 'Observations on the remains of the Boudhists in India', *Transactions of the Literary Society of Bombay* vol. I (1819) and vol. III (1823).

30. See *The Miscellaneous Works of Sir James Mackintosh*, ed. Robert Charles Mackintosh, 3 vols (London, 1846), vol.I, pp.191, 196. Compare 'On the Study of the Law of Nature and of Nations' (1799), vol. I, p.359. Mackintosh's account of the role of the feelings in the moral life is close to Dugald Stewart's. See *The Collected Works of Dugald Stewart*, ed. Sir William Hamilton, 11 vols (Edinburgh, Thomas Constable, 1854), vol.II, pp.452-70. Walter Jackson Bate, 'The sympathetic imagination in eighteenth-century English criticism', *English Literary History*, XII (1945) is still basic, citing several Scottish writers on the topic. Knud Haakonssen has analysed interconnections in several significant recent essays, especially 'The science of a legislator in James Mackintosh's moral philosophy', *History of Political Thought*, V (1984), and 'James Mill and Scottish moral philosophy', *Political Studies*, XXXIII (1985).

31. William Robertson, *An Historical Disquisition concerning the Knowledge which the Ancients had of India*, (London and Edinburgh, A. Strahan, 1791), pp.335-36.

6

The Problem of William Smith: an Aberdonian in Revolutionary America

Robert Lawson-Peebles

University of Aberdeen

William Smith presents a problem to Scottish-American historiography. He has not been conveniently labelled, and in consequence he is often ignored. In this essay I shall try to explain why, and then sketch a model which may help to give him a more adequate place in later eighteenth-century transatlantic history.

The facts of Smith's life are as follows. He was born at Slains, north of Aberdeen, in 1727. He was admitted to King's College in 1743 and graduated in 1747. He then taught for a while at Abernethy. His first publication was an appeal in *The Scots Magazine* for improved pay and conditions for Scottish teachers, a much-vexed question still prominent today. His colleagues asked him to present a petition to Parliament, and on 20 December 1750 he left Abernethy for London.[1] He never returned. Like many ambitious young men, he fell for the siren songs of new opportunities and new lands. In March 1751 he emigrated to New York and within the next year he was publishing, in the colonial press, fabular homilies and proposals for the education of Indians. It was the latter, expanded to include the White Colonists, which initially made his name. His first substantial publication, *A General Idea of the College of Mirania*, appeared in 1753. It was noticed by Benjamin Franklin, who offered Smith the post of Provost at the new Academy of Philadelphia. The Academy became the College of Philadelphia, and then the University of Pennsylvania. Smith was in effect the first Principal of that prestigious institution.[2]

It was normal, of course, for such a position to be held by a clergyman. Smith returned to England in 1753 and took orders in the Anglican Church, on the same day as Samuel Seabury. Back in Pennsylvania, he became active in educating the Colony's large German population, and was instrumental in publishing a translation of *The Life of God in the Soul of Man* by Henry

Scougal, who had preceded him at King's. Smith also became active in Pennsylvania politics. He fretted over the activities of the French and Indians on the Colony's western borders and published two pamphlets attacking the Assembly, then under Quaker control, for failing to protect the Colony. In the process he quarrelled with Franklin and—more seriously—with the Assembly, who imprisoned him for several months in 1758.[3]

Smith's reputation was less controversial in England. He had impressed the leaders of the Anglican Church during his first visit to London in 1751, and by the late 1750s he had become a trusted servant. During a visit to England in 1759 he not only persuaded the Privy Council to quash his conviction, but also obtained Honorary Doctorates from Oxford and Aberdeen. (He would later be awarded a third Doctorate, by Dublin.) In 1762 he was commissioned to prepare a report on the state of the Church in the Colonies. Three years later he published, in Philadelphia, an account of Henry Bouquet's victorious expedition against the Ohio Indians, and in it described new methods of Indian fighting and proposed new schemes for frontier settlement. The book was an immediate success. It was reprinted in 1766 by the Geographer Royal in London, came out in three different editions in Dublin between 1768 and 1770, and appeared in French translations in 1769 and 1778.[4]

As discord grew between Britain and America, Smith attempted to steer a middle path. He denounced British attempts to tax the Colonies but thought that Independence would be disastrous for America. He developed his views in three pamphlets. The first, *A Sermon on the Present Situation of American Affairs*, appeared in mid 1775 and within one year had gone through sixteen editions, published in three American cities and five British. Translations were made into Dutch and Welsh. A second pamphlet followed within nine months. Titled *An Oration in Memory of General Montgomery*, it was like its predecessor immediately popular, and was widely reprinted. A third pamphlet, probably written by others as well as Smith, followed hard on its heels. Called *Plain Truth*, it was designed as an answer to Tom Paine's *Common Sense*. There are at least seven variants of the first Philadelphia edition; it was quickly reprinted in London and Dublin; and it was often bound with *Common Sense* so that, according to the publisher, the public could 'judge ... whether the Americans are, or are not prepared for a state of independence'. These pamphlets did not, understandably, endear Smith to the patriots. He was imprisoned in 1777, and in 1779 was removed from his post as Provost of the College of Philadelphia.[5]

Unlike many who were loyal to the British Crown, Smith did not leave his adopted homeland. Instead, he strove to regain power in the Republic. An early step towards this was a sermon he gave on the day appointed for Thanksgiving after Yorktown. In 1789 he regained his post as Provost. He remained a controversial figure, but on his death in 1803 left a legacy of educational and cultural achievement. He founded Washington College, Maryland. In 1757 he began *The American Magazine* and, in the year that it survived, made it the focus for a rising generation of American writers and artists. In 1769 he founded the American Philosophical Society, which shortly afterwards amalgamated with Franklin's less successful American Society for Promoting and Propagating Useful Knowledge. The list of those whose careers Smith began or fostered is large and impressive. It includes David Rittenhouse, the distinguished astronomer; Francis Hopkinson, the poet who became a signatory to the Declaration of Independence, the designer of the Stars and Stripes, and the composer of the first book of music published in America; Thomas Godfrey, another poet whose play *The Prince of Parthia* became in 1767 the first professionally performed drama in America; and Benjamin West, the painter famous for his history pieces—like 'The Death of Wolfe' (1771)—and who in 1792 succeeded Sir Joshua Reynolds as President of the Royal Academy. As already indicated, Smith himself was a prolific writer whose work was widely read. A check list drawn up in 1950, and incomplete, lists 133 items under his name.[6]

Despite his record Smith is little known today. He is discussed most frequently as an educator. Lawrence Cremin's *American Education*, for instance, deals with Smith's innovative curriculum at Philadelphia, and traces its sources to Aberdeen and to contemporary educational theory. Generally, however, Smith is ignored. The standard histories of the Revolution say little about him. Edmund Morgan's *The Birth of the Republic* (1956) omits him entirely, while Gordon Wood's *The Creation of the American Republic* (1969) gives him only passing mention. One has to consult the Pennsylvania State histories to find out more about him. Similarly, Smith receives scant attention in accounts of Scottish-American relations. Andrew Hook's *Scotland and America* and William Brock's *Scotus Americanus* make only casual references to him. William Lehmann's *Scottish and Scotch-Irish Contributions to Early American Life and Culture* confines its comments to Smith's educational influence. There have been three substantial biographies of him, but each failed to make any impact and disappeared quickly. Otherwise, the most rounded consideration of Smith is to be found in Henry May's *The Enlightenment in America*. It lasts six pages.[7]

How is it that someone who was so well-known, indeed notorious, in the later eighteenth century can drop out of sight so thoroughly? There are, I think, three reasons. The first is the simple, tactical reason of his name. As I have discovered, anyone embarking on research on Smith has to step gingerly through minefields of misdirection. The William Smith I have been discussing should not be confused with his namesake and close contemporary (1728-1793) the New York historian, lawyer and Loyalist who after exile became Chief Justice of Quebec. The catalogues of any substantial library will reveal many William Smiths to be distinguished from the Aberdonian. Perhaps scholars have spent so much time discovering who William Smith was not that they have had little energy remaining to investigate the plenitude of what he was.[8]

The second reason for Smith's disappearance is probably his unpleasant character. His willingness to engage in controversy was part and parcel of a soaring ambition. He wanted, among other things, to be the first bishop in America. Inevitably, he made many enemies. On a visit to Philadelphia John Adams was warned against Smith, and wrote a typically longwinded, carefully nuanced description. Smith was 'soft, polite, insinuating, adulating, sensible, learned, industrious, indefatigable'. Benjamin Rush, Smith's doctor and colleague at the College of Philadelphia, was more direct and more brutal. Indeed, Rush's obituary is a masterpiece of pernicious postmortem prose, competing with Rufus Griswold's obituary of Edgar Allan Poe for the palm of malevolence:

> His person was slovenly, and his manners awkward and often offensive in company ... he early contracted a love for strong drink, and became towards the close of his life an habitual drunkard. He was often seen to reel ... in the streets of Philadelphia. His temper was irritable in the highest degree, and when angry he swore in the most extravagant manner. He seldom paid a debt without being sued or without a quarrel. He was extremely avaricious, and lived, after acquiring an estate of £50,000, in penury and filth ... On his death bed he never spoke upon any subject connected with Religion nor his future state, nor was there a Bible or prayer book ever seen in his room ... He descended to his grave ... without being lamented by a human creature.[9]

Using echoes of Milton's Satan and Marlowe's *Dr Faustus*, Rush surrounds Smith with the calumny of the demonic. The carefully chosen main verb of the closing sentence here seems to provide the natural outcome for such a misspent life. It is doubtless apparent that Rush himself was an ill-tempered man, and his hatred of alcohol was close to being pathological. Nevertheless, his assessment has made its mark. Smith has yet to emerge from the purgatorial odium of obscurity.

The third reason why Smith is ignored is more serious. His life and opinions do not fit the pattern created by the most prestigious analyses of Revolutionary American culture, or of Scottish-American relations. Bernard Bailyn's *The Ideological Origins of the American Revolution*, initially the prefatory essay to a collection of Revolutionary pamphlets and published in its present form in 1967, has become the most influential book on early American political thought. Bailyn regards the Revolution as the expression of a unifying political culture which shrugged off the deferential, hierarchical society of the *ancien régime* in favour of a belief in progress and individualism. It follows from his teleological model that those who dissented from the Patriot cause are dismissed as anachronisms, to be set aside because 'the future lay not with them'. Likewise, Andrew Hook's *Scotland and America* suggests that a milestone in American education occurred with the appointment of John Witherspoon in 1768 to the College of New Jersey, and not with the appointment of Smith to Philadelphia a decade and a half earlier. In this instance no explanation is given but can, I think, be inferred. Witherspoon was a leading figure in the Church of Scotland who travelled directly from Paisley to Princeton. Smith was ordained as an Anglican, and emigrated to America via London. He is disqualified by his cosmopolitanism.[10]

It is possible, however, to put forward a view of Smith's work which grants it higher status and suggests that it became neither outmoded nor diluted. This view is indebted to two recent books, neither of which deals directly with Smith. The first is Jay Fliegelman's *Prodigals and Pilgrims*, published in 1982. Fliegelman regards American society as a family. He suggests that the Revolution was caused by a change in the model of the family from one which was hierarchical and patriarchal to one which was egalitarian, encouraging filial autonomy. For my purposes *Prodigals and Pilgrims* is particularly useful because it traces the source of the familial model not only to Lockeian psychology, but also to Scottish Common Sense Philosophy. It draws attention to the 'innate principle of sociability' which is a central tenet of the Common Sense ideal of moral behaviour.[11]

The second book is Jonathan Clark's *English Society 1688-1832*, published in 1985. Clark, like Fliegelman, suggests that the family is important in eighteenth-century society. His model is more static and more extended. It is centred on the monarch as a father-figure and radiates out through the Anglican Church. Clark attacks Fliegelman—and many other historians—for being too premature in anticipating modern society. Nevertheless, the two books are in many respects complementary. Both help to show how deeply rooted is Smith's work in the concept of the family.[12]

This is apparent from *The General Idea of the College of Mirania*. The pamphlet draws heavily on the ideals of a liberal education, fostering gentility and virtue, which were at that time transforming the Scottish universities and English dissenting academies. But it adapts those ideals to an American context. Smith realises that Pennsylvania, more than most American colonies, is inhabited by a conglomerate of racial and national types. It is vital therefore to unite the family, and this is done by common schooling, lasting three years and intended to discourage prejudice and foster 'indissoluble connections and friendships'. Only at the fourth year are children divided into 'two grand classes'. The 'mechanic class' is then given a utilitarian education to fit it to become 'the hands and strength of every Government'. The other class, naturally, becomes the brains, and is given a broad-based education to prepare it for the responsibilities of a virtuous and patriotic life. Given this vision of a hierarchical yet organically related society, Smith projects it in a poetic preface across the years and the continent:

> Oh! Science! onward thus thy realm extend
> O'er realms yet unexplor'd till time shall end ...
> Not trackless deserts shall thy progress stay,
> Rocks, mountains, floods, before thee shall give way ...
> Where wolves now howl shall polish'd villas rise,
> And towery cities grow into the skies!
> 'Earth's farthest ends our glory shall behold,
> And the new world launch forth to meet the old.'[13]

The poem draws on a complex of ideas and sources. The closing quotation (in fact, a slight misquotation) is drawn from the 1713 addition to Pope's *Windsor Forest*. Much of the preceding imagery is older, drawn from the Bible and rooted deep in the ideology of American settlement, the belief that the wilderness will be transformed into the City of God. The imagery depends, too, on the belief that the transformation will proceed westwards across the continent. This belief, of course, is *translatio emperii*, the movement of civilisation following the transit of the sun. It is to be found in Thomas Sprat's *History of the Royal Society* (1667) and is best known from Bishop Berkeley's *Westward the Course of Empire Takes its Way*, written in 1726 when Berkeley was living in Rhode Island but not printed until 1752, just one year before Smith published *Mirania*. There is, however, one essential difference between Berkeley and Smith. Berkeley suggests that decay and corruption in the Old World is a necessary corollary of the rise of the New. Smith does not make this connexion, hence the quotation from Pope. In all, he presents a potent mixture which asserts that the New World will add lustre to the Old, and which even seems to foresee the City of God as a Garden Suburb and a Corbusian colossus. No wonder it made Benjamin Franklin sit up.[14]

The French and Indian War, followed promptly by Pontiac's Rebellion, caused Smith to augment his model of the family. He now sought not only to unite it but also to protect it against French influence and Indian attack. His proposals included a compulsory oath of allegiance; the suppression of foreign language newspapers; compulsory English lessons for, and the withdrawal of the franchise from, the German community; and a further development of the Protestant ministry. Above all, he believed that 'we must look to our Mother-Country for succour'. Otherwise, the Colony would become victim to 'civil and religious persecution'. His proposals were developed further in his popular book on Bouquet's Expedition. He had now changed his mind about the Indians; they were 'rendered by habit almost insensible to the common feelings of humanity'. They are at the periphery, therefore, of his family; and it is appropriate that they should be kept spatially at the periphery by a system of fortified settlement. This system, moreover, had an additional advantage. Smith had noted with horror that some Whites who had been captured by the Indians preferred to stay with them. Fortified settlements had the advantage not only of keeping Indians out but also keeping Whites in.[15]

The greatest threat to Smith's family, however, was presented not by external threat but by internal dissension. A letter to the Bishop of London reveals how deeply he was troubled by 'the dreadful Calamity in which both Countries are now involved', and how carefully he reformulated his vision of the family to solve that calamity. The three pamphlets written during the early months of the Revolution pay respect both to the rights of the Mother Country and the rights of the Colonists. Smith hopes for a restoration of American liberty within the British Empire. This is particularly apparent in his *Oration in Memory of General Montgomery*. Richard Montgomery had died on 31 December 1775 leading an abortive attack on Quebec during the American invasion of Canada. He immediately became a Revolutionary hero, and was described by Tom Paine as a martyr in the cause of Independence. Smith's portrayal of Montgomery is more sophisticated, resembling the image presented by Burke and Fox in the House of Commons. Smith saw the hero as both a friend to liberty and a loyal subject of the King. Montgomery, in his account, was a successor to James Wolfe, that earlier hero of Quebec so recently immortalised by Benjamin West.[16]

The Declaration of Independence destroyed Smith's careful arguments and isolated him. It was only with the effective end of the War at Yorktown in 1781 that he was able to begin the process of rehabilitation. In his Thanksgiving Sermon he repeated his themes of liberty and family—but the family had, once again, been redefined. The Mother Country and the father-figure of George III had gone the way of all parents and now the family had closed around an elder brother, another George, George Washington. With this new family the way was now open for Smith to assert a new version of *translatio emperii* which took the east coast of America as the baseline for westward expansion. Such images are to be found in his last publications, promoting land companies and canal development.[17]

Smith's flexible model of the family was, I suggest, a result of his particular brand of Scottish Common Sense and Anglican authoritarianism. It enabled him to develop a modernising middle ground between the reactionary Loyalists and the radical Patriots. It was an uncomfortable but certainly not ignoble ground to occupy from 1775 until 1781; and once the dust of conflict had cleared it would provide a useful means of reconciliation with Britain, allowing Americans to look with increasing fondness upon what Nathaniel Hawthorne called 'Our Old Home'. For those two reasons alone we ought, I think, to have a greater regard for William Smith.

Notes

1. William Smith and Thomas Peirson, letter dated Abernethy, 5 November 1750, *The Scots Magazine*, 12 (1750), pp.487-92. Anon. note in *The Scots Magazine*, 12 (1750), p.596. The question of Smith's M.A. degree is problematic. His name does not appear in the degree records of King's. However, the record is known to be incomplete, and the papers concerning his Honorary Doctorate at Oxford clearly indicate that he possessed the degree.
2. [Smith], *Indian Songs of Peace: with a Proposal, in a prefatory Epistle, for Erecting Indian Schools* (New York, J.Parker & W.Wayman, 1752). [Smith], *A General Idea of the College of Mirania* (New York. J.Parker & W.Wayman, 1753).
3. Ordination entry 23 December 1753, Lambeth Palace Library, Fulham Papers, vol.xxxix, f.16. H.Scougal, *Das Leben Gottes in der Seele des Menschen* (Philadelphia, Benjamin Franklin & Anton Armbrüster, 1756). [Smith], *A Brief State of the Province of Pennsylvania* (London, R.Griffiths, 1755); *A Brief View of the Conduct of Pennsylvania* (London, R.Griffiths, 1756).
4. W. Smith, 'A Brief Account of the State of the Church of England in the British Colonies in America', Lambeth Palace Library, S.P.G. Papers, vol.10, ff.140-73; *An Historical Account of the Expedition against the Ohio Indians in the year 1764 under the command of Henry Bouquet* (1765; reprinted London, T.Jefferies, 1766).
5. W.Smith, *A Sermon On the Present Situation of American Affairs* (Philadelphia, James Humphries, Jr, 1775); *An Oration in Memory of General Montgomery* (1776; 2nd edition, London, J.Almon, 1776). [Thomas Paine, William Smith, and others?], *Common Sense, and Plain Truth* (The Third Edition, Corrected, London, J.Almon, 1776), 'Publisher's Advertisement'.

6. Thomas R. Adams, *Trial Check List of the Writings of William Smith* (1950), typescript in the University of Pennsylvania Library, Philadelphia.
7. L. Cremin, *American Education: The Colonial Experience 1607-1783* (New York, Harper & Row, 1970), pp.378-84. G.Wood, *The Creation of the American Republic, 1776-1787*, (1969; reprinted, New York, Norton, 1972), pp.56, 245, 333-34. A. Hook, *Scotland and America: A Study of Cultural Relations 1750-1835* (Glasgow, Blackie, 1975), p.34. W. Brock, *Scotus Americanus: A Survey of the Sources for Links between Scotland and America in the Eighteenth Century* (Edinburgh, Edinburgh U.P., 1982), pp.3, 91-92, 109, 111-12. W. Lehmann, *Scottish and Scotch-Irish Contributions to Early American Life and Culture* (London, Kennikat, 1978), pp.82, 110, 122-23, 136. Horace Wemyss Smith, *Life and Correspondence of the Rev. William Smith, D.D.*, 2 vols (Philadelphia, S.A. George, 1879-1880). Albert F. Gegenheimer, *William Smith: Educator and Churchman* (Philadelphia, Pennsylvania U.P. 1943). Thomas F. Jones, *A Pair of Lawn Sleeves : A Biography of William Smith* (Philadelphia, Chilton, 1972). H. May, *The Enlightenment in America* (New York, OUP, 1976), pp.80-86. Among the State histories which deal with Smith are Theodore Thayer, *Pennsylvania Politics and the Growth of Democracy 1740-1776* (Harrisburg, PA, Pennsylvania Historical and Museum Commission, 1953); and James H. Hutson, *Pennsylvania Politics, 1746-1770: The Movement for Royal Government and Its Consequences* (Princeton, Princeton U.P., 1972). Kenneth Silverman, *A Cultural History of the American Revolution* (New York, Thomas Y.Crowell, 1976), pp.54-59 gives some sense of the group gathered around Smith at the College of Philadelphia.
8. A good biography of the New York William Smith, which suggests some striking similarities of thought and career as well as name with the Philadelphia William Smith, is Leslie F.S. Upton, *The Loyal Whig: William Smith of New York and Quebec* (Toronto, Toronto U.P. 1969).
9. J. Adams, Diary entry 30 August 1774, *Works*, ed. Charles Francis Adams, 10 vols (Boston, Little, Brown, 1856), vol.II, p.358. B. Rush, *The Autobiography*, ed. George W. Corner (1948; reprinted Westport, Greenwood, 1970), pp.263-65.
10. B. Bailyn, *The Ideological Origins of the American Revolution* (Cambridge, Mass., Harvard U.P., 1967), p.311. *Pamphlets of the American Revolution* (Cambridge, Mass., Harvard U.P., 1965), vol.I, p.x. For a clear-eyed assessment of *The Ideological Origins* and its impact, see Thomas P. Slaughter, 'The historian's quest for early American culture(s)', *American Studies International*, 24 (April 1986), pp.30-32. Hook, *Scotland and America*, pp.34-35.
11. J. Fliegelman, *Prodigals and Pilgrims: The American Revolution against Patriarchal Authority, 1750-1800* (Cambridge, CUP, 1982), pp.1-6, 23-26.
12. J.C.D. Clark, *English Society 1688-1832* (Cambridge, CUP, 1985), pp.1-7, 84.
13. W. Smith, *A General Idea of the College of Mirania*, reprinted in his *Works*, 2 vols (Philadelphia, Hugh Maxwell & William Fry, 1803), vol.I, pp.175-76, 180-81. On the liberalisation of Scottish universities, see two essays by Peter Jones, 'The polite academy and the Presbyterians, 1720-1770', *New Perspectives on the Politics and Culture of Early Modern Scotland*, eds John Dwyer, Roger A. Mason and Alexander Murdoch (Edinburgh, John Donald, 1982), pp.167-78; and 'The Scottish professoriate and the polite academy, 1720-46', *Wealth and Virtue: the Shaping of Political Economy in the Scottish Enlightenment*, eds Istvan Hont and Michael Ignatieff (Cambridge, CUP, 1983), pp.89-117. I am grateful to Professor Peter Diamond for drawing my attention to this material.
14. A. Pope, *The Poems*, ed. John Butt (London, Methuen, 1968), p.210. T. Sprat, *The History of the Royal Society*, eds J.I. Cope and H.W. Jones (London,

Routledge and Kegan Paul, 1959), pp.383-85. G. Berkeley, 'Verses on the Prospect of Planting Arts and Learning in America', *Works*, ed. A.A. Luce, 9 vols (London, Nelson, 1955), vol.VII, pp.369-73.

15. [Smith], *A Brief State of the Province of Pennsylvania*, pp.38-42; *An Historical Account of the Expedition*, pp.51, 61.

16. W. Smith to Bishop Terrick, 8 July 1775, Lambeth Palace Library, Fulham Papers, vol.VIII, f.62. W.Smith, *An Oration in Memory of General Montgomery*, pp. iv, 23, 33. [Paine], *Dialogue Between the Ghost of General Montgomery, Just arrived from the Elysian Fields; and An American Delegate* (1776; reprinted New York, Privately Reprinted, 1865), pp.5-6, 12-13. Debate in the Commons, 11 March 1776, W. Cobbett, *Parliamentary History* (London, Longman, 1813), vol.XVIII, Cols 1239-1240. A good brief biography of Montgomery is in DNB, vol.XIII, pp.767-68.

17. W. Smith, Thanksgiving Sermon, 13 December 1781, *Works*, vol.II, pp.148, 152; *An Historical Account of the Rise, Progress and Present State of The Canal Navigation in Pennsylvania* (Philadelphia, Zachariah Poulson, 1795).

7

Kames's *Historical Law Tracts* and the Historiography of the Scottish Enlightenment

James E. Reibman
University of New York

In a letter dated 12 April 1759, David Hume writes to Adam Smith about Lord Kames's recently published *Historical Law Tracts* (1758):

> I am afraid of Lord Kames's Law Tracts. A man might as well think of making a fine Sauce by a Mixture of Wormwood and Aloes as an agreeable Composition by joining Metaphysics & Scotch Law. However, the Book, I believe, has Merit; tho' few People will take the Pains of diving into it.[1]

Despite Hume's tepid reaction, *Historical Law Tracts* became one of the influential books of its period. It should be read less as a legal treatise or a political tract encouraging the British Union, than for what it reveals about the nature of developing Scottish historiography.[2] In eighteenth-century Scotland the genre of history-writing, both as a science and as literature, was the concern of such figures as William Robertson, Adam Ferguson, Hugh Blair, John Millar, Sir John Dalrymple, Lord Hailes, Adam Smith, and most importantly, David Hume. These figures set up two approaches to writing history: conjectural and narrative/philosophical.[3] Of those writing 'conjectural' history, a term initially set out by Dugald Stewart,[4] Kames was an early and influential figure.

Although not an historian, but a lawyer and judge, Kames in *Historical Law Tracts* explores developing legal principles and institutions in an historical context encompassing cultural, social, political, and economic concerns. He sets out his rationale for this approach as follows:

> In tracing the history of law through dark ages, unprovided with records, or so slenderly provided as not to afford any regular historical chain, we must endeavour the best we can to supply the broken links, by hints from poets and historians, by collateral facts and by cautious conjectures drawn from the nature of the

> government, of the people and of the times. If we use all the light that is afforded, and if the conjectural facts correspond to the few facts that are distinctly vouched, and join all in one regular chain, nothing further can be expected from human endeavours. The evidence is compleat so far, at least, as to afford conviction, if it be the best of the kind.[5]

Although this excerpt reveals the habitual caution of the lawyer, it also displays a speculative and theoretical habit of mind.

As a legal treatise *Historical Law Tracts* builds on the intellectual efforts of Stair and Mackenzie in the 1680s, and Montesquieu and Dalrymple in the mid eighteenth century.[6] Although no Scots lawyer of Kames's period could ignore the dominance of Stair's treatise, what Kames as a Scots lawyer could do was to apply his conjectural approach to specific areas of historical development not fully treated by either Stair or Mackenzie. Thus, the essays in *Historical Law Tracts* offer a broader, more sweeping historical examination of the law and legal institutions. Mindful of the hazards and limitations of his historical method, Kames in *Historical Law Tracts* creates a work that is both a fundamental legal study, and a work which embodies the intellectual currents of mid eighteenth-century Scotland.

Kames begins by justifying an enquiry into the history of law and legal institutions. In his preface he distances himself from Bolingbroke's politics yet quotes approvingly his attack on the overly technical profession of law. According to Bolingbroke:

> there have been lawyers that were orators, philosophers, historians; there have been Bacons and Clarendons. There will be none such anymore, till in some better age, true ambition or love of fame prevails over avarice; and till men find leisure and encouragement to prepare themselves for the exercise of this profession, by climbing up to the *vantage ground*, so my Lord Bacon calls it, of science, instead of groveling all their lives below, in a mean, but gainful, application to all the little arts of chicane. Till this happen, the profession of the law will scarce deserve to be ranked among the learned professions: and whenever it happens, one of the vantage grounds to which men must climb, is metaphysical, and the other, historical knowledge.[7]

Accepting the wisdom of this observation, Kames also imitates the structural features of Bolingbroke's *Study of History*: Bolingbroke uses a scheme of letters while Kames uses a system of essays. Both devices allow for discussion of selected topics within an overall theme, and thus differ from the usual historical method of integrated narrative. The Bolingbroke-Kames approach permits maximum speculation on diverse topics and on particular areas. Indeed this approach suggests Samuel Johnson's definition of the essay as 'a loose sally of the mind'. Thus Kames is able to produce a book appealing as much to the general reader as to the lawyer. To achieve this end, he uses a comparative method in each of his essays:

> We must be satisfied with collecting the facts and circumstances as they may be gathered from the laws of different countries: and if these put together make a

regular chain of causes and effects, we may rationally conclude, that the progress has been the same among all nations, in the capital circumstances at least.[8]

Such a methodology in the hands of a master like Kames may prove worthwhile, but can be dangerous in the hands of amateurs, as Kames's biographer Lord Woodhouselee argued.[9] The difference lies in the intellectual vigour and judicious nature that informs Kames's historical speculation and investigation.[10]

Of the fourteen tracts in this volume, the most compelling and least technical is Tract I, 'Criminal Law'. It deals with subjects fundamental to society and which lend themselves to theoretical speculation. The issues of criminality and its effect on the social fabric are central to the Enlightenment. The focus is on the intricacies of punishment and wrong- doing, and in the tradition of Enlightenment thought emphasises the notion of social progress. Kames charts the criminal law by developing a 'class of principles, intended obviously to promote society by restraining men from harming each other'.[11] Implicit in this notion of progress is the insistent blending of cultural and legal patterns. Although Kames in his discussion recognises that competing political, social, legislative and economic interests temporarily influence the course of progress, he does argue that the law has a rational history, one revealed by continuous progress towards a sophisticated society.

This 'blending' of various social values which produce legal institutions explains his evolutionary, historical analysis of the criminal law. Starting from the premise that the criminal law has its origin in resentment and revenge, Kames's analysis relies on a profound understanding of human behaviour:

> The purposes of Nature are never left imperfect. Corresponding to the dread of punishment, is, first, the indignation we have at gross crimes even when we suffer not by them: and next, resentment in the person injured, even for the slightest crimes: by these, ample provision is made for inflicting the punishment that is dreaded. No passion is more keen or fierce than resentment: which, when confined within due bounds, is authorised by conscience. The deliquent is sensible, that he may be justly punished; and if any person, preferable to others, be intitled to inflict the punishment, it must be the person injured. Revenge, therefore, when provoked by injury or voluntary wrong, is a privilege that belongs to every person by the law of Nature; for we have no criterion of right or wrong more illustrious than the approbation or disapprobation of conscience. And thus, the first law of Nature regarding society, that of abstaining from injuring others, is enforced by the most efficacious sanctions.[12]

Thus setting out an appreciation of conscience and morality, Kames quickly indicates how the need for remedy evolves from individual action to institutional response:

> Resentment is raised in different degrees, according to the sense one hath of injury. An injury done to a man himself, provokes resentment in its highest degree. An injury of the same kind done to a friend or relation, raises resentment

in a lower degree; and the passion becomes gradually fainter, in proportion to the slightness of the connection.[13]

With such gradations of personal response, Kames sets out the need for a magistrate to evaluate a crime, to assign a remedy, and to ensure that the response is proportionate to the offence. In this way a social institution emerges, one which must deal with transgressions in a uniform manner; hence, the evolution of the need for judges.[14] Once the concept of judges is accepted, the need arises for jurisdiction which is 'the power of calling a party into court, and the power of making a sentence effectual'.[15] Thus Kames speculates about the organisation of pre-historical society and conjectures from what is known from ancient sources on the progress of civil society.

Kames recognises that the emergence of a neutral public occurs only with certain cultural conditions:

> Revenge, the darling privilege of undisciplined nature, is never tamely given up...The privilege of resenting injuries, was therefore that private right which was the latest of being surrendered, or rather wrested from individuals in society. This revolution was of greatest importance with respect to government, which can never attain its end, where punishment in any measure is trusted in private hands.[16]

From this assumption of the growth of a neutral public, and consequently the creation of those preconditions for a centralised judiciary, Kames proceeds to discuss how the primitive physical practice of retaliation was gradually replaced by punishing crimes by exacting financial compensation:

> I must lay hold of the present opportunity, to bestow a reflection on this singular practice of compounding for crimes. However strange it may appear to us, it was certainly a happy invention. By the temptation of money, men were gradually accustomed to stifle their resentment. This was a fine preparation for transferring the power of punishment to the magistrate, which would have been impracticable without some such intermediate step.[17]

A magistrate working within this growing concept of jurisdiction needs some forum in which to review a case, to ascertain guilt or innocence, and to set an appropriate punishment.

Understanding that in earliest society retribution is the guiding principle of revenge leads Kames to consider the status of the alleged perpetrator. In order to protect one from an avenger, sacred altars or cities of refuge grow up. The purpose of these, like that of a court, was to mitigate *lex talionis* and to provide some sanctuary until guilt or innocence could be established. This evolution from unbridled revenge to a court's authority directed by a magistrate marks progress for the law. Civilisation depends upon an accept-ance of such authority, for Kames argues, 'nothing tends more to support the authority of the magistrate than his power of criminal jurisdiction'.[18] He reaches this conclusion from his review of comparative legal institutions, cultures, legends, accounts, and especially from his study of Mosaic law and

Hebrew narrative. From this reading of history, law, and custom, Kames develops his theory of criminal jurisdiction, courts, and judges.

As these institutions grew in acceptance, power, and complexity, they required sophisticated procedures to deal with the various problems and responsibilities they encountered. As society develops different courts, different jurisdictions, and different writs, different standards for punishment are demanded. Civilisation reaches that point where:

> nothing is reckoned criminal but what encroaches on the safety and peace of society: and such punishment is chosen as may have the effect of repressing the crime in time coming, without much regarding the gratification of the party offended.[19]

Thus, we find the development of the king's peace or the interest of the state superseding that of the individual in righting criminal wrongs.

Kames realises that the progressive nature of civilisation determines the degree and effect of punishment. He points out that historically 'adjusting punishments to crimes' can only occur 'when criminal jurisdiction is totally engrossed by the public'.[20] Political sophistication and authority shape the civil law in criminal matters:

> Though the power of the sword adds great authority to a government, yet this effect is far from being instantaneous and till authority be fully established, great severities are beyond the strength of a legislature. But when public authority is firmly rooted in the minds of the public, punishments more rigorous may be ventured upon, which are rendered necessary by the yet undisciplined temper of the people. At last, when a people have become altogether tame and submissive under a long and steady administration, punishments, being less and less necessary, are commonly mild, and ought always to be so.[21]

Implicit in this evolving relationship between the people and civil authority is an undercurrent of moral scepticism exposing the pessimism in Kames's view of the nature of man.[22] Controlling the rude manners of the people, as evidenced by the Scots legal principle of *vitious intromission*, on the one hand, illustrates the advancing nature of civilisation by its diminished status, and on the other, suggests in its origin the fallen nature of man.[23] By citing this doctrine as an example of advancing civilisation, Kames unwittingly draws attention to a conflict between the idea and the concept of progress, as well as questions of man's morality.[24] Otherwise, why is the criminal law necessary?

Despite this underlying pessimism, Kames believes that society is evolving toward a more perfect state. Thus, in the most enlightened fashion he argues, like Montesquieu and later Beccaria,[25] for proportioning crime to punishment, but also stresses that the severity of the punishment should accord with the needs of society.[26] To Kames social peace and order are the primary elements to be considered in evaluating an appropriate punishment and not the particular gravity of the crime:

> Hence, in regulating the punishment of crimes, two circumstances ought to weigh, viz. the immorality of the action, and its bad tendency; of which the latter appears to be the capital circumstance, as the peace of society is an object of much greater importance, than the peace, or even life of a few individuals.[27]

This regulating of punishments to crimes and its transferring such power of punishment to magistrates advances civilised society, for it keeps revenge 'within the strictest bounds' and 'confines it to its proper objects'.[28]

Having established the presence of magistrates and the authority for determining punishment, Kames discusses who is allowed to prosecute before these judges.[29] Comparing Roman Law with that of Scotland and England, Kames discusses prosecution of both public and private crimes. His argument focuses on the advances that modern governments have made:

> The privilege of prosecuting public crimes belongs to the chief magistrate. The King's Advocate in Scotland is *calumniator publicus*; and there is delegated to him from the crown, the privilege of prosecuting public crimes. In England, personal liberty has, from the beginning, been more sacred than in Scotland; and to prevent the oppression of criminal prosecutions, there is in England a regulation more effectual than that now mentioned. A grand jury is appointed in every county for a previous examination of capital crimes intended to be prosecuted in the name of the crown...With respect to private crimes, where individuals are hurt in their persons, goods, or character, the public, and the person injured, have each of them separately an interest. The King's Advocate may prosecute such crimes alone, as far as the public is concerned in the punishment. The private party is interested to obtain reparation for the wrong done him. Even where this is the end of the prosecution, our forms require the concurrence of the King's Advocate, as a check upon the prosecutor, whose resentment otherwise may carry him beyond proper bounds.[30]

Although society is evolving, civil authority, as Kames warns, must continually guard against an abuse of process that may encourage revenge. Historically Kames notes that when compensation is not sufficient then the existence of the sovereign to punish crimes, as well as the concept of pardon are needed.[31] Yet to prevent an abuse of the prerogative of pardon and thus a possible denial of individual justice the law had to adjust so that:

> by a law of Edward the Confessor (Lambard's collection, law 18), declaring, That the King, by his prerogative, pardon a capital crime; but that the criminal must satisfy the person injured, by a just compensation.[32]

Having established the method of discussion by his reading of historical sources, by conjecture where these sources are silent, and by his rational analysis, Kames concludes by saying:

> But man excels other animals, chiefly by being susceptible of high improvements in a well regulated society. In his original solitary state, he is scarce a rational being. Resentment is a passion, that, in an undisciplined breast, appears to exceed all bounds. But savages are fierce and brutal; and the passion of resentment is

in the savage state the chief protection that a man hath for his life and income. It is therefore wisely ordered, that resentment should be a ruling passion among savages. Happy it is for civilized societies, that the authority of law hath in a good measure rendered unnecessary this impetuous passion; and happy it is for individuals, that early discipline under the restraint of law, by calming the temper and sweetening manners, hath rendered it a less troublesome guest than it is by nature.[33]

The dominant theme of cultural evolution determines for Kames social institutions and how the law operates to inform them.

In his *Historical Law Tracts* Kames by the prominence of his reasoned conjectural method influences the shape and direction of the emerging Scottish historical school. Although there is, as Thomas Warton says in the *History of English Poetry*, the 'triumph of superiority' present in the marking of stages as society progresses from a rude to an advanced culture,[34] there is also legitimate effort to understand how human institutions adapt and how one goes about understanding the institutions of earlier ages and of different cultures. Kames's account of the evolution of Criminal Law powerfully illustrates the experimental and inductive approach to the study of the past so characteristic of the Scottish Enlightenment.

Notes

1. Henry Home, Lord Kames, *Historical Law Tracts*, 3rd edition (Edinburgh, J. Bell and W. Creech, 1776). All citations are taken from this edition, hereafter referred to as *HLT*. David Hume to Adam Smith, 12 April 1759, J.Y.T. Greig, *The Letters of David Hume*, 2 vols (Oxford, Clarendon Press, 1932), vol.I, p.304.
2. See also Kames, *Essays upon British Antiquities* (Edinburgh, A. Kincaid, 1747), especially Essay IV on law and history used in an attack on the feudal system.
3. See Richard B. Sher, *Church and University in the Scottish Enlightenment* (Princeton, Princeton U.P., 1986), pp.316-17.
4. Dugald Stewart, ed., *The Works of Adam Smith*, 5 vols (London, T. Cadell, 1811-12), vol.V, p.452. See also J.W. Burrow, *Evolution and Society* (Cambridge, CUP, 1966), pp.10-23 for an appraisal of this concept.
5. *HLT*, p.25.
6. Sir James Dalrymple, 1st Viscount Stair, *The Institutions of the Law of Scotland, Deduced from its Originals, and Collated with the Civil, Canon, and Feudal Laws, and with the Customs of Neighboring Nations* (Edinburgh, Andrew Anderson, 1681). Sir George Mackenzie...of Rosehaugh, *The Institutions of the Law of Scotland* (Edinburgh, John Reid, 1684), 6th edition revised John Spotisweed (Edinburgh, W. Brown, 1723); Baron de Montesquieu, Charles Louis de Secondat, *L'Esprit des lois* (1748), trans. Thomas Nugent (1873); Sir John Dalrymple, *An Essay towards a General History of Feudal Property in Great Britain* (London, A. Millar, 1757).
7. Henry St John, 1st Viscount Bolingbroke, *Letters on the Use and Study of History* (1735-1738), ed. Isaac Kramnick (Chicago, Chicago U.P., 1972), p.353.
8. *HLT*, p.26.
9. Alexander Fraser Tytler of Woodhouselee, *Memoirs of the Life and Writing of*

the Honourable Henry Home of Kames, 3 vols (Edinburgh, T. Cadell & W. Davies, 1814), pp.305-306; see Appendix X.

10. Thomas Preston Peardon, *The Transition in English Historical Writing* (New York, AMS Press, 1966), pp.18-19.

11. *HLT*, p.1; see also Ian Simpson Ross, *Lord Kames and the Scotland of his Day* (Oxford, Clarendon Press, 1972), pp.202-21.

12. *HLT*, p.4.

13. *HLT*, p.6.

14. *HLT*, pp.20-21.

15. *HLT*, p.21.

16. *HLT*, pp.21-22.

17. *HLT*, p.38.

18. *HLT*, p.39.

19. *HLT*, p.39.

20. *HLT*, p.51.

21. *HLT*, p.51.

22. William C. Lehmann, *Henry Home, Lord Kames and the Scottish Enlightenment: A Study in National Character and in the History of Ideas* (The Hague, Martinus Nijhoff, 1971), p.192.

23. *HLT*, p.52.

24. Lehmann, *Lord Kames*, pp.177-94; Ian Simpson Ross, *Lord Kames*, pp.202-21; Gladys Bryson, *Man and Society: The Scottish Inquiry of the Eighteenth Century* (Princeton, Princeton U.P., 1945), pp.90-96.

25. Cesare Beccaria *Dei dellitti e delle pene* (1764), translated by Henry Paelucci (Indianapolis, Bobbs-Merrill, 1963).

26. *HLT*, p.52.

27. *HLT*, p.53.

28. *HLT*, p.53.

29. *HLT*, pp.45 and following.

30. *HLT*, pp.60-61.

31. *HLT*, p.61.

32. *HLT*, p.62.

33. *HLT*, pp.63-64.

34. Thomas Warton, *History of English Poetry*, Preface.

8

Jacobitism in the North East: the Pitsligo Papers in Aberdeen University Library

Murray G. H. Pittock

Balliol College, Oxford

It is becoming a little less difficult to be a Jacobite to-day. Modern historiography, whether concealed in the seemingly endless, though frequently necessary, production of specialist essays in collections published by John Donald, or in the British-wide context being explored by J.C.D. Clark, is slowly laying to rest the Whig theory of history. It was, of course, buried long ago, except in eighteenth-century studies, where its demise matters most. In a year when so much attention is being paid to the Scottish Enlightenment, and the re-awakening of Scottish identity after the Union, we should perhaps remember that the Scotland of the first half of the eighteenth century at least, was very far from being enlightened in the sense this year is using the term. Half of Scotland's population lived in the Highlands;[1] many of the Lowland lairds, especially in this part of the country, were in resistance, passive or active, to the new scheme of things being evolved in the Central Belt, which was about to begin its long drive to be the powerhouse of Scotland.

My purpose is to appraise one of the more intellectual members of this alternative eighteenth-century Scotland. Alexander Forbes, Lord Pitsligo, was one of the men who can without doubt be identified as an ideological Jacobite, committed unremittingly to the Cause even in extreme old age. Some of his papers, and certain other papers of his family, have been deposited by the Forbeses in Aberdeen University Library.[2] Most of these papers are letters; some are contracts in law; one is an opinion on the validity of the attainder passed against Pitsligo after the '45. It is not my intention to examine these in detail in this paper, although anyone wishing to do so would be well advised to avoid the transcripts, as they are unreliable; the handwriting is not difficult. Instead I wish to concentrate on MSS 14-16 of the first box. Not only are these the most substantial, but they also illuminate a remarkable development in Pitsligo's arguments about and attitude to Jacobitism, which show him as a political apologist for the theory which led the Tory party away from the Stuart cause.[3] The MSS consist of 'A letter on Government' in two versions, the second entitled 'Lord Pitsligo on GOVERNMENT', and two copies of his 'Apologia'. The latter deals with Pitsligo's response to the '45. Before dealing with the issues they raise in detail, let us turn to the noble laird himself.

Born in 1678, Alexander Forbes succeeded to the title in 1691. After going abroad in the 1690s, where he came under French intellectual influences, in particular that of Fénelon, he returned to Scotland to sit for Parliament in 1700. Fiercely opposed to the Act of Union, Pitsligo rejected both the Act of Settlement and that of Abjuration, and as a consequence retired to private life in 1705. A Quietist following his Continental experiences, he nevertheless took arms in the '15, under his first cousin, the Earl of Mar. Although not attainted, Pitsligo spent the years between 1716 and 1720 abroad, frequently with the Court. Some of his tactless attempts to be an honest servant to King James at that time are recorded in *The Jacobite Court at Rome 1719*, edited by Henrietta Tayler in 1938 for the Scottish History Society.[4] A letter, No.1 in the first box, not in the Tayler collection, is from Pitsligo to Lord Nairne, offering to 'make my compliments in the most submissive fashion to both their majestys'. It is dated 8 September 1719. Pitsligo was temporarily out of favour, and returned home.

Hospitable and kindly, the remarkable part of Pitsligo's life begins in 1745, when despite his age he led one hundred and fifty men to join Charles after Prestonpans. Refusing exile after Culloden, he hid in the countryside among his own people till his death in 1762, with many true and apocryphal hairs'-breadth 'scapes from government soldiery. During this life of trial, domesticity, and adventure, he was the author of two published works, *Thoughts Concerning Man's Condition and Duties in This Life* and *Moral and Philosophical Essays*.

Athough this hagiographical account may seem too good to be true, as when we are told elsewhere of Pitsligo drawing his sword as a token of his authority against Fowden, the Manchester constable, or when this other-worldly mystic drives on to cross the Mersey by pontoon in the middle of winter, although nearly seventy years old, the influence of Pitsligo on the image of Jacobitism should not be underestimated.[5] Sir Walter Scott writes that a great prince would immediately have pardoned Pitsligo and restored him his estate, forfeited by an unsuccessfully contested attainder.[6] The laird's character was a model against which to judge the treatment of the Jacobites, a token of their moral superiority.[7] Indeed, Scott is very interested in Pitsligo and it is made fairly clear by the manner in which he writes of him that he is the model for Bradwardine in *Waverley*, not merely in the matter of his being Lowland gentry, nor of hiding on his own estate, nor in the justice of having it returned to him, nor yet in his somewhat antiquated learning. Scott comments on Pitsligo's 'small fortune and embarrassed estate' (we remember Waverley's first impression of Bradwardine's property), and also writes that the 'high-spirited Cavaliers, bred up in Jacobite principles' of the 'north of Scotland', looked to Pitsligo as a leader. This 'gentleman of the old school', as Henrietta Tayler allows him to be, was the one they found.[8] It is remarked that Pitsligo's 'son had the mortification to be indebted to a stranger, now the proprietor of his ancient inheritance by purchase from the Crown'. The pathos of worthy but attainted Jacobites like Pitsligo is passed over by Scott of course, in securing for Bradwardine a happy ending; but he makes use of some of the stories of Pitsligo's escapes, particularly in the matter of the household fool who avoided giving his laird away to the redcoats, just as Bradwardine's does in *Waverley*.[9]

Despite the aid for the family available from the American colonies, particularly from South Carolina and Virginia at this time and just afterwards, (according to the letters), circumstances remained straitened, and Pitsligo was in hiding almost full-time until the mid 1750s.[10] Notwithstanding his hardships, his continual affability and Quietism is apparent from what he writes, as in a letter, dated May 1752, to Mrs Irvine of Drum, one of those who helped in time of trial:

> I find myself at present in more than tolerable Health, and very easy in Mind, every thing considered. We have nothing to depend upon but the Goodness of God every moment, we are sure he can do us no Injustice, and that his Mercys are over all his Works.(MSS 1/6)

Pitsligo looks forward to what for him in those days must have been a rare treat, a meeting with his son John: 'It will even be very agreeable to tryst with you and him at Auchiries', he writes.

But the justifications Pitsligo offers for the Jacobite cause are far more complex than this theology, and often at odds with any mood of resignation or pathos. Just as his threat of military execution to the Manchester constables comes as a surprise after his reputation for kindness and quietness, so his 'Apologia' and 'Letter on Government' after letters like the above to Mrs Irvine, show us a different Pitsligo, an ideological Jacobite with his ideology at work.

The accession of William III has been seen as a conclusive blow to the Divine Right theory in Tory circles. Although theorists like Sir Robert Filmer had come close to making such a right of rule conditional on God's visible approval, and seemed to hold that long possession could justify belief in such approval, the Revolution Settlement was a major jolt even to such 'moderate' theories. The fiction of abdication did not altogether dissolve Tory uneasiness, especially when the Jacobites and non-jurors vociferously continued to hold the theory that Tory supporters of the new Establishment were compromised. High Tories continued to condemn the contract theories of creeping Whiggery till the death of Anne, but the Hanoverian accession knocked the stuffing out of even limited legitimism, and most of its supporters in England kept their practical allegiance to absolutism on the level of election-day white roses, songs, and being on holiday when Jacobite armies sought the exercise of their principles and the support of their tenantry, as Dukinfield of Manchester was when Pitsligo rode in search of him on 30 November 1745.

Those who accepted the new state of things were the heirs of a development implicit in Filmer's own view of political theory: they saw James II's failure to recover his throne as witnessing God's approval of the Revolution. In secular terms, the 'prescriptive right of a well established government' had made great strides during the reign of Anne.[11] Only the Jacobites continued to hold out unconditionally for legitimist ideology, as some were to do right up to the 1890s.[12] Or did they? Pitsligo makes an interesting study in this respect. Despite the fact that he rejected the Act of Abjuration, and was as loyal to the Jacobite cause in the '45 as he had been in the '15, his 'A letter on Government', in both its versions, shows that he was open to precisely those ideological infections from which Jacobites were supposed to be immune.

   'A letter on Government' (undated, except for month and day), seems to have been written in or around 1720. Pitsligo mentions that the Revolution is 'above 30 years past'. He was at this time, as we have seen, somewhat under a cloud with James III, but there is no suggestion that the 'letter' is either pro-George or anti-James on a personal level. Instead the letter, like the one he writes after the '45, seems more akin to an apologia, but this time one for submission rather than revolt. Pitsligo states his intention of 'Submitting to the present Govert', and then goes on to discuss the nature of government as he sees it:

> It is not to be considered a patrimonial esteat or property of the Governor; But as an office or ministry for wch he is accountable to God from whom it flows, and from wch he may be removed entirely or for a time at ye Divine pleasure. And as this is most agreeable to good Sense & Reason in all Constitutions, It is more clearly and unquestionably so in a Limited monarchy, where the most Supreme, that is the Legislative power is shared with the prince by the people he Governs. (MS 1/14)

The first part of this statement is straightforward enough: it merely enunciates Scriptural reservations concerning Divine Right already being voiced in the reign of Charles II.[13] But the second part makes a shift towards an acceptance of the status quo, constitutional monarchy; and therefore a submission, at least implicit, to the Revolution Settlement.

   Pitsligo goes on to discuss usurpation:

> If it shall happen y[t] some members of a Society, contrary to their Duty to God & allegiance to their prince, do wrest the Government out of his hands and confer it on another; we are neither to concur in their Treason, nor tamely to
> * submit to their Lawless force, But if providence shall, for Reasons best known to it self.... If the new prince be acknowledged as such by almost all the Society it Self, and by all the world beside for a Considerable Tract of years... we must Submitt to the Powers that are because they are ordained of God.

Pitsligo appears to have asterisked this passage, which during the last sentence is written very large, as if this were the most important statement, or the author were trying to convince himself of it. The tendency of this section as a whole, however, as we can see, is to drift towards the 'prescriptive right' theory of moderate Toryism. The last sentence puts the doctrine of non-resistance into the context of a new argument; that of *de facto* right. Pitsligo justifies this from history, citing the Wars of the Roses, and accepting that opposition to James VI while Mary was still queen *de jure* was unlawful. In these kinds of examples he goes no further than the state of play accepted by elements of pre-Revolutionary Tory ideology; but the conclusions he draws are in legitimist terms, radical. Accepting that if King James had recovered the throne, those who supported King William would have committed no treason since William was king *de facto*, Pitsligo comes to the position of accepting 'a very strange Shirking oath in opposition to the Title of the Heir of Blood', which he holds as binding only in terms of a 'parliamentary Right'. This seems to imply that Pitsligo accepts King George I only in terms of the parliamentary position on the Acts of Settlement and Union, insofar as these are, in the terms he adopts above, representative of the 'Legislative power' of 'the people'. King George is king, not by Right, but by parliamentary Settlement; a nice distinction which allows Pitsligo to maintain his loyalty to James III as an individual, but not as a co-representative with Parliament of the interests of the people he governs. Almost, it seems, Pitsligo's Jacobitism has become sentimental. His arguments tend towards practical obedience to the Hanoverian regime, and Pitsligo sees himself:

> submitting himself & his aleadgeance to y^t Government wch has been for above 30 years past in full possession of the Supreme Power, has been acknowledged as such by almost the whole society he is a member of... and has vanquist this private man and all oyrs y^t have at any time stood in opposition to it?

Note that Pitsligo does not mention George's right as legitimate; the right is prescriptive, and that of the 'Government' as a whole, both King and Parliament.

The revised 'letter' continues in this vein, although perhaps showing more explicitly how irksome Pitsligo might have found his own rationalisations. For example, he writes that God should be revered 'in the persons he is pleased to set over us even tho they sometimes be for our own punishment'. Using the examples of Julius Caesar's lack of legitimacy as a ruler, and Christ's order to submit fiscally to Tiberius, 'third fro Julius who can hardly be vindicated from usurpation & Rebellion', Pitsligo comes to the conclusion that:

> Therefore when God in his providence Dispossesses a Prince and sets up anoyer in his stead and the people by themselves or representatives revock the Title to Sovereignty they had given and confirm it upon the new set up Prince The Persons Dispossessed may be truly said to have nor right nor title.

This is on the verge of complete acceptance of representative government, and as it stands, might well have annoyed quite a few Whigs. As far as we know, it was the furthest that Pitsligo ever went.

The Memsie apology (MS 16) seems far more typical of the image of the

Lowland Cavalier which has come down to us. It opens with him 'in arms, and on the march into England', rather surprising in view of his age and opinions. Pitsligo reveals that 'the weightiest consideration was on the point of morality', in relation to the question of the justness of civil war. It is clear from the narrative that his attachment to the family which had always claimed his loyalty, played a part in this abandonment of non-resistance:

> When I heard of the Prince's landing in the Highlands, I found an inclination to give him what small assistance was in my power ... These words, 'this is the heir, let us kill him' are often applied, I only repeat them.

Pitsligo also had, however, in the light of the opinions discussed above, more weighty political reasons. These reasons I believe to be of key interest, as they show that an ideological Jacobite could accept evolving eighteenth-century political theory, cast aside the fossilised claims of Divine Right, and still conclude that James III was the rightful king. For reasons dependent neither on Divine Right ideology or MacIvor-like self-interest, Pitsligo arrives at just this conclusion; and as a result led out, at sixty-seven, the largest body of cavalry in Charles's army, confident that God knew his cause was just.[14] He writes of his:

> concern for the good of England ... considering some strong parliament speeches, and the general cry without doors against standing armies, arbitrary government, foreign dominions, to which the blood & treasure of Britain are sacrificed in a shameful manner, and our Condition growing daily more desperate, as the hardships go on in a regular Parliamentary way. To expel this poison, I and others of more Consequence took arms in the year 1745.

This is a very interesting passage of justification. For Pitsligo's complaint is no longer directed at the illegitimacy of the reigning dynasty as such (although he notes it elsewhere in this letter, and it earlier concerned him), but at Parliamentary abuse. It is evident that if the hardships and injustices he mentions are imposed in 'a regular Parliamentary way' against 'the general cry', then Parliament is no longer representative, and its status as the confirming authority for the new dynasty is undermined. Not only that, but Pitsligo, a devout Christian, clearly resents the anti-Popery slogans of the Whig establishment, especially since Pitsligo, Balmerino, and many of the Prince's army were Protestants. Charles himself was far less of a plausible Popish tyrant than his father and grandfather.[15] The Whig attitude, Pitsligo considers, is justified in deceit alone: 'what fitter pretence than religion', he exclaims, 'especially when twisted with liberty and property', could be used to fuel Whig hysteria. Clearly this distresses the laird, who believes that:

> An absolute submission to the divine Will both in ourselves & others is the only thing to be prayed for, as it is the only true essential religion.

Not only is the Whig establishment imposing on the people to oppress them, but it is using religion illegitimately as a political weapon, more ridiculously than ever in the '45. In such a case, Pitsligo decided to go to war without necessarily breaching the adoption of the contractual precepts of government he had made earlier. Here is the spectacle of a devout supporter of the Stuarts preaching Jacobitism as the cure for arbitrary government. A defender of the Stuarts uses the very principles of Whiggery to stand the rallying cries of the Hanoverian establishment on their own heads.

Not that Pitsligo is immune from traditional ideas. He can still write that he does not think the 'government can be counted settled, whilst so many persons nearer in blood than the family of Hanover are ready to put in their claim'. Yet even here he does not stray too far from theories of prescriptive right. If Legitimists are still challenging Hanover in sufficient numbers, then clearly the Parliamentary settlement Pitsligo has conditionally accepted can no longer be accounted fully representative. But Pitsligo makes it clear that the 'poison' he wishes to expel is that of an arbitrary and unrepresentative government as a whole; George II's lack of legitimacy as a monarch is not a sufficient cause. It appears that Pitsligo was shaken by the lack of English recruits to the army: 'I was persuaded too, the English would have taken a part more heartily in design', he writes. So did many, on the basis of the Prince's assurances. Clearly the government's unrepresentative nature was not sufficient to provoke rebellion south of the Border.

The interest in Alexander Forbes, Lord Pitsligo, lies not only in the fact that his character and actions have become a source for apocryphal biography and representative fiction alike, but also that he shows us today, in the important context of a redeveloping appraisal of eighteenth-century history and politics, that not only did Whig attitudes to government permeate senior Jacobite ranks, but that they could be used, once adopted, to undermine the very polity they once excused. Pitsligo is clearly no great thinker: but his acceptance of a representative element in government, and horror at its abuse, were the spurs which led him to resume arms in old age, apparently just as much as did his personal loyalty to the values and persons of the exiled family. Political justice was in his case as legitimate a part of the Cause as legitimism itself. 'Tis plain,' he remarks, 'that K. Saul had no indefeaceable Right.'(MS 15).

Notes

1. William Ferguson, *Scotland: 1689 to the Present* (Edinburgh, Oliver & Boyd, 1968), p.175.
2. AUL, MSS 2740/4/18/1/1-29 and 2740/4/18/2/1-18.
3. H.T. Dickinson, *Liberty and Property* (London, Methuen, 1979), pp.27 and following.
4. Henrietta Tayler, ed., *The Jacobite Court at Rome in 1719* (Edinburgh, Scottish History Society, 1938).
5. F.J. McLynn, *The Jacobite Army in England 1745* (Edinburgh, John Donald, 1983), p.105.
6. Cited in F.J. McLynn, *The Jacobites* (London, Routledge & Kegan Paul, 1985), p.89.

7. *Ibid.*, p.90.
8. Alexander Forbes, Lord Pitsligo, *Thoughts Concerning Man's Condition and Duties in This Life*, ed. Lord Medwyn, 4th edition (Edinburgh and London, William Blackwood, 1854), xv,xvi. Compare Tayler, *The Jacobite Court*, p.39.
9. Pitsligo, p.41.
10. AUL, MS 2740/4/18/1/9, 10, 24, 29.
11. Dickinson, *Liberty and Property*, p.41.
12. Allen Upward, *Treason*, 3rd edition (London, The Tyndale Press, 1904).
13. Dickinson, *Liberty and Property*, p.23.
14. McLynn, *The Jacobite Army*, p.25; *The Jacobites*, p.8.
15. Andrew Lang, *Prince Charles Edward Stuart* (London, Longmans, Green, and Co., 1903), pp.23, 41.

9

The Eighteenth-Century Scottish Intellectual Inquiry: Context and Continuities versus Civic Virtue

Anand C. Chitnis
University of Stirling

I

Two recent articles have levelled charges at historians of eighteenth-century Scotland. The first, by John Lough in the *British Journal for Eighteenth-Century Studies* for Spring 1985, questioned the very use of the term Enlightenment when applied, among others, to the Scottish intellectual inquiry of the eighteenth century.[1] Invariably in that connexion, the term is used vaguely and sometimes its definition can be taken to quite meaningless lengths (as in a recent study of the Moderate Literati).[2] To Lough's charge historians of the intellectual inquiry must, therefore, plead guilty. Consequently, in the absence of a clear and agreed definition as to why certain Scots were indeed *lumières* or why Scotland shared in *Aufklärung*, the present study is content to eschew the term 'The Scottish Enlightenment'.

The second article appeared in the June-August 1986 issue of *Cencrastus*, where Turnbull and Beveridge charged historians of modern Scotland with purveying an official view that perceives Scotland as inferior and culturally subordinate, as disreputable in the century before parliamentary union and as rescued by England thereafter from under-development and barbarism.[3] They have pleaded for a proper elaboration of an alternative view. By no means all Scottish historians are culpable of this second charge. An alternative view has been well served even if it is not well known. Certainly it is less familiar and there has been a reluctance to accept its implications. Publications by economic historians and historical geographers in recent years, for example, have markedly revised stock impressions of the state of Scotland prior to the parliamentary union and, as a result, have questioned established notions of the Treaty of Union as a divide. Furthermore, in 1981 articles by Gordon Donaldson and R.H. Campbell commemorating the Stair Tercentenary effectively argued the case for redressing the traditional bleak portrayal of later seventeenth-century Scotland.[4] Donaldson's trenchant summary was:

> The fashionable concept of 'The Scottish Enlightenment' implies that before 1707 Scotland was an uncultured backwater, with stunted political institutions and dominated by religious bigotry, but that after the Union light and culture flowed in from the south to absorb the vitality of a people who had ceased to be preoccupied with ecclesiastical politics but had not yet found outlets in politics or economic activities. The truth is that too many who babble about 'The Enlightenment' of the eighteenth century have not taken the trouble to find out about Scottish culture in the seventeenth.[5]

Such contributions to an alternative view are not a product of the 1980s alone: Henry Meikle's pamphlet on later seventeenth-century Scotland was published in 1947 and blazed a trail that was for so long neglected.[6] To take the alternative view of another but related period, distinctive Scottish traditions (as exemplified by ideas and the country's university education) were sufficiently strong even a century after the parliamentary union to influence key areas of developing English life.[7]

One group who have wittingly or otherwise served the official view have been those who have isolated intellectual history from the social and economic circumstances in which it thrived. This has resulted in the impoverishment, not to say distortion, of our understanding and appreciation. In both the later seventeenth and in the eighteenth centuries a lively intellectual life was pursued alongside a vigorous economic life in country and town. There may be common underlying causes of the intellectual and economic achievements. Since it has been conventional to emphasise the Union as a watershed so there has been an emphasis on an apparent economic and intellectual revival in Scotland after 1707, without it being fully appreciated that the foundations had been well laid prior to that date.

The subsequent exposition falls into two parts: it will first be argued that the environment in which the intellectual inquiry flourished was developing over a considerable period. Scotsmen were enabled by their social institutions to take advantage of the conditions that favoured not only intellectual inquiry but also economic growth and development. The later seventeenth century in particular was an era of positive transformation. The argument is designed to give expression to at least part of the alternative view. The synthesis it will offer owes much, as will become evident, to the work of several leading students of the period in question, especially R.H. Campbell, T.M. Devine, Ian Whyte and Roger Emerson. Following the demonstration of the pre-union roots of Scottish intellectual as well as social and economic life, attention will be drawn to the shortcomings inherent in a rather different approach. This approach declares that an illuminating way of viewing the Scottish inquiry is as a critique of the classic language of civic morality in the wake of the parliamentary union, and interprets later eighteenth-century Scottish politics as an expression of a provincial aristocracy's need to assert its civic virtue.

II

What picture of later seventeenth-century Scotland emerges if a range of material published by economic, social and intellectual historians in the 1980s is integrated and synthesised? It is a picture of a society improving some three quarters of a century before the purported age of improvement. It is a society with practical schemes and intellectual notions even though the means for implementing them fully had frequently to wait until economic growth became fully established from around the 1740s. Despite limitations, the society depicted is active and enterprising, with a parliament and privy council actively promoting the urban as well as the rural economy and a society at the centre of world trade as the axis moved from the Mediterranean to the Atlantic. Above all it is a religiously-aware society: that is not to say anything very novel, but rather than stressing religion as a disruptive force, the historiography indicates that religion was socially positive and, in areas away from the arts, creative. So many different areas of Scottish life were impregnated by religion that to dissociate it from the origins of the Scottish intellectual inquiry would be curious to say the least.

The inquiries of historical geographers have amply contributed to this rehabilitation of the later seventeenth century. It is they who have pointed out that the perspective of the eighteenth-century improvers, the characterisation of themselves as the first to innovate, valid though it may have been at the time, has necessarily undervalued the century prior to the parliamentary union, and has led to its reputation as an era of rural stagnation. Yet, here was (to quote R.A. Dodgshon) 'a farming system with a capacity for change and adjustment greater than has hitherto been realised'.[8] In addition, concentration on the crop failures of the 1690s has masked the slow development, unobtrusive and sometimes faltering, that preceded the years of scarcity; resumed thereafter and was only checked by the severe but short- lived climatic conditions which caused famine. The development that had taken place was not sufficiently resilient to withstand freak weather and even a more sophisticated agricultural system would have succumbed. Also, the dearth appeared the more disastrous in the wake of thirty-five years or so of good supplies. There were generally agricultural surpluses in the years 1660-1730. Export bounties were intended to encourage grain trading and not protect consumers as in the past.

Consequently, as with so much else, agricultural improvement in the eighteenth century built on the foundations of the seventeenth century.[9] It is, therefore, important to recall the agricultural achievement and assess the extent of structural weakness in the seventeenth-century Scottish economy. The developments to be mentioned were not evident to writers at the time.[10] In summary, the seventeenth-century Scottish agricultural system was in the process of transformation from a primitive to a more dynamic condition. Prior to the Restoration, ideas from other European countries began to penetrate Scotland. The short-lived Act of 1647 which encouraged the division of rough pasture among different proprietors and its conversion to arable in particular parts of Scotland was significant as a pointer for the future.

Landowners clearly perceived the long-term value of agricultural improvement even if they did not yet have the means to realise it fully. They used their position in parliament to pass a series of acts thereafter, between 1661 and 1700, to promote a variety of agricultural innovations, especially the division of runrig and commonty in 1695. The legislation passed about that time consorted with the trend of much earlier agrarian legislation and with legislation in other areas.[11]

The variety of innovatory improvements that were envisaged and implemented locally included the consolidation of property, planting of trees, enclosure, alternation of land between arable and pasture, crop rotation, liming to permit more intensive land use and to bring into cultivation land resistant to traditional fertilisers, the removal of peat to extend arable, the drainage of lochs, and selective livestock breeding.[12] As for improvements affecting tenants, historical geographers have shown the existence of single tenancies much earlier than was assumed. Leases as a vehicle of agricultural change are a more complex issue, not least because the existence of a lease could restrict innovation as well as act as a spur to improvement. It may be sufficient for present purposes to recognise that the lease was seen by many in the seventeenth century as a vehicle of agricultural change and that landowners viewed leases as instruments of modernisation. Furthermore, the commutation of rents from kind to money demonstrates a more commercial outlook.[13]

The number and location of market centres, 346 new non-burghal ones, showed a dramatic increase between 1660 and 1707. By 1707, only 18% of mainland Scotland was fifteen miles distant from a market centre, though it must be recognised that possibly as many as one third of these markets did not function at particular times because of failure or decline.[14] All these developments indicate that agents of seventeenth-century agricultural change desired transformation, were ready to implement it and had a range of ideas for so doing. Improvement may not have been economic in the seventeenth century, but the fact that ideas for it existed means that the antecedents of eighteenth-century improvement must be taken more seriously. Individuals and institutions, be they the local baron courts, privy council or Scottish Parliament, countenanced change. Had they not done so, the much vaunted ethos of eighteenth-century improvement would have proved difficult to establish. The later eighteenth-century improvers were to develop and extend the new agricultural techniques in the more favourable economic conditions of their time when higher prices, for instance, encouraged wider improvement.

If Whyte and others are portraying rural enterprise, T.M. Devine is concerned with urban enterprise as is indicated by a selection of conclusions from two of his many writings, his essay on the merchant class of the larger Scottish towns in the later seventeenth and early eighteenth centuries and his article on the Union of 1707 and Scottish development.[15] The agents of urban enterprise were, of course, the merchants. They were the main organising force behind changing currents of trade. The relaxation of burgess and guild controls permitted non-burgesses, too, to transact business in the burghs. Devine has interpreted the relaxation as showing that this was a period of eager commercial activity: it was evidently futile to try to impose traditional monopolies. The evidence shows a real decline in the number of merchants' apprentices, the opening of alternative avenues to becoming a merchant such as attendance at Dutch commercial schools or similar Scottish institutions founded from the 1690s, and the integration of appropriate subjects for aspiring merchants in the curricula of grammar schools from the late 1720s.

The later seventeenth-century Scottish domestic economy became more flexible: towns grew in size, commodity exchange increased, money rents became common, the post-Restoration Parliament encouraged shipping and there was an active coastal trade. The more sophisticated use of bills of exchange to settle credits and debits indicates that there was a greater velocity of exchange. The privy council took measures to conserve bullion. The commercial sector of the economy was becoming stronger and such features of the structure as outdated protectionist legislation were becoming increasingly inappropriate when, to take an instance, royal burghs, to serve their own interests, exploited unfree towns and villages for trading purposes. Protectionism which encouraged more modern methods (perhaps the Navigation Acts are cases in point) began to be practised.

An increasingly common feature of the investment strategies of the greater merchants in the later seventeenth century was the provision of finance for industry. Between 1660 and 1710, fifty-two industrial ventures were established in towns, concerting with the protectionist policy of the Scottish Parliament. Eighteenth-century public bodies were merely continuing the work of the later seventeenth-century Scottish Parliament and privy council. The later seventeenth-century rise of Glasgow came with the foundation of a variety of industrial enterprises which benefited in their turn from the expansion of trade with the West Indies and America, well established by the 1680s.

At this point, one needs to stand back and ask why efforts to promote the Scottish economy in the seventeenth century have been neglected and why there has been instead an over-emphasis on eighteenth-century developments. It is surely because the measures of the seventeenth century were mercantilist and not liberal, free trading and anti-restrictionist as espoused by the later generations of the eighteenth and nineteenth centuries. Consequently, the neglect of later seventeenth-century economic policy has been due to the belief that it was harmful, even morally wicked. Such an attitude, and not just his Jacobitism, has led to Sir James Steuart being overlooked despite the efforts of Andrew Skinner and others.[16] The mere citing of Steuart surely shows that the mercantilist case had distinguished support in his time.

Devine has also suggested that the Union neither caused nor inhibited economic growth, but rather it provided a context within which the Scots could react. The improvement promoted by landowners, merchants and others after the parliamentary union was not inevitable. It was the result of their ability to take advantage of the opportunities now offered. Before the Union they had already begun to show considerable enterprise which, in the post-union context, could flourish. Post-union economic growth was made possible by the necessary disposition of the agents of economic growth, a disposition which had existed for some considerable time before 1707.

A crucial element in their character was religion. Their theology encouraged those personal qualities that fostered energy and economic enterprise. Here, the contribution of Gordon Marshall's book, *Presbyteries and Profits*, is instructive[17] and also the recent writings of R.H. Campbell. Campbell has argued that, given the lack of distinction drawn by Reformation theology between the religious and the secular, the response to Calvin's call for social action could, on the one hand, be disruptive (as in executions, kirk session discipline and tyranny, and witchcraft trials) but, on the other hand, the response could be constructive. Three elements in the religious outlook had quite positive effects—conscience (how one was viewed by others), predestination (which emphasised the benefits that flowed from justification) and the knowledge that one was an agent or partner of God's will (which had a particularly powerful effect on behaviour and on the cultivation of self-confidence and self-assurance). Campbell has quoted Paul to the Church at Colossae ('Whatever you do, do it heartily in the Lord') alongside an eighteenth-century sermon: 'if, by your abilities, you have gained wealth, and raised yourself to an honourable station among your brethren, so far you have done well...It was heaven bestowed the talents, the industry, the abilities, by which you rose'. The mention of 'talents' here is interesting because the parable of the talents would also have served to encourage the elect to accumulate material goods. Campbell has argued, in addition, that the Scots were directed towards economic effort by a theology that disapproved of the creative arts.[18]

If these recent suggestions are seen alongside two points drawn from the analysis of that great figure of the inquiry itself, John Millar, they are surely strengthened. Millar attributed the intellectual distinction of eighteenth-century Scotland to the social legacy of the Reformation which, in emphasising the cultivation of reason as a contrast to the superstition of pre-Reformation times, bequeathed new or reinvigorated schools and universities to Scotland. Schools and universities were to render minds active as well as to propagate knowledge. Moreover, Millar believed that the Scots' distinction in general culture as opposed to literature in the eighteenth century was due to the removal, in 1603, of the Court, the nation's cultural standard.[19]

Mere mention of these arguments of Millar reinforces an appreciation of the tie between religion, education and economic endeavours in Scotland and serves to connect the economic history of Scotland with the intellectual. Before considering the intellectual, however, it is pertinent to remember that long after the late seventeenth and early eighteenth century the religious temper of the urban trading and mercantile classes continued to dominate Scottish history. Ecclesiastical disputes spilled over into social disruption and political turmoil, from the days of Erskine in Stirling, Richardson in Inverkeithing, the 'Drysdale Bustle' in Edinburgh—the 1730s, 1740s, 1750s, 1760s and beyond, emphasising the continuities in the Scottish preoccupation with religion. To adapt the observation that J.C.D. Clark has made of a neighbouring nation in the same period, it is hard to believe that after 1688 the secular easily came to dictate terms of debate to a society so engrossed by religion and by so distinctive a theological temper.[20]

Given the nature of later seventeenth-century Scottish society, the degree to which religion informed intellectual life is too obvious to deserve remark. It may explain in part the ready acceptance of such powerful extraneous intellectual influences as Grotius, Pufendorf and Newton. The first two were also central to the establishment of the natural law tradition. James Dalrymple, first Viscount Stair, the original systematiser of Scots Law in 1681, sought to harmonise his analysis with scripture and natural theology. He founded Scots Law upon the law of nature which he derived from Grotius and from his personal acquaintance with jurists in Holland in the mid seventeenth century. He gave Scots Law its ethical basis and a capacity to respond and adjust to the evolution of the society it served. In the opinion of one lawyer, it is doubtful if in the wider fields of legal practice Scots Law would have survived the pressures imposed by economic growth and development without Stair's solid and principled foundation.[21] As to the subsequent intellectual inquiry, Stair's work justified property, delineated its relation to civil government and he also gave a sketch, albeit highly compressed, of the stadial theory of the history of society.[22]

Pufendorf's *On the Duty of Man and the Citizen* was introduced in the 1690s as a set text at the University of Glasgow by Gerschom Carmichael who began a substantive reorientation of Pufendorf's work. Carmichael added to Pufendorf's single moral obligation, that every man ought to promote and preserve peaceable sociability with others, two more: 'that all men act in ways which signify their love and veneration of God' and 'that each man cultivate his own happiness and in particular the faculties of his mind'.[23] One of Carmichael's students was Francis Hutcheson. While Hutcheson had views distinctive to himself, and while he expressed reservations about Pufendorf's ethical theory and his position on the natural sociability of man, Carmichael's own approach to natural rights persisted, and was transmitted to the eighteenth century by means of Hutcheson's frequently republished *A Short Introduction to Moral Philosophy* which the author admitted was based on Carmichael's edition of Pufendorf.[24] It has also been remarked by Moore and Silverthorne that Hutcheson considered Carmichael's own notes and supplements rather than the edition of Pufendorf itself to have 'supplied many of the moral and political ideas that lie behind the numerous treatises, tracts and lectures on jurisprudence which were to prove such a fecund source of speculation on human nature and society in eighteenth-century Scotland'.[25]

It is surely worth suggesting that the stress Hutcheson placed on the importance of other men's sense of approval and disapproval in determining the rightness and wrongness of conduct,[26] and Adam Smith's better known and influential views on man's desire for approbation, can be linked to Campbell's suggestion that conscience was an element in the motivation to high economic achievement. Were historians of moral philosophy to accept that both stem from the same theological background, the inter-relationship of society, the economy and intellectual concerns would be even more compelling.

Peter Stein is another who has pointed to numerous features and concerns in eighteenth-century Scottish social philosophy which were derived from

Grotius and Pufendorf, including their belief that universal legal principles had the same certainty and generality as mathematical propositions.[27] This may be of significance in explaining the concern of eighteenth-century thinkers to establish the science of man, morals and society on the same empirical footing as the science of matter. Hutcheson called for a 'more strict philosophical enquiry into the various natural principles or natural dispositions of mankind, in the same way that we enquire into the structure of an animal body, of a plant or of the solar system'.[28] Also Hutcheson considered it to be the will of the supreme being that we study the moral constitution of our nature.

The appeal of Newton in Scotland is a further way in which the intellectual base of the eighteenth-century inquiry was initiated in the climate of the later seventeenth century. As Christine Shepherd has written, Newtonianism was readily accepted because it did not conflict with theological interests, and she has shown how a range of Scottish regents, professors and students pursued experimental science from the 1660s and were familiar with Newtonianism from the 1680s.[29] Religion could stimulate an interest in the philosophy of nature as well as moral questions. Investigations in natural knowledge could imply, as Emerson has recently recalled, the progressive revelation of God's will to those who could read the Book of Nature.[30] At the same time, the pursuit of natural knowledge had more immediately practical and secular benefits, and from the 1680s, the foundation of various institutions and projects, clubs and societies, professional bodies, reinvigorated universities, museums, libraries, botanical gardens, geological, geographical and mineralogical surveys, all served to facilitate the spread of new ideas.

Sir Robert Sibbald was a key figure in the intellectual life of the age but he was by no means alone, his generation including Andrew Balfour, James Halket, Sir George MacKenzie of Rosehaugh, Archibald Pitcairne, James Sutherland and Robert Wodrow to name but a very few of those who comprised the Scottish scholarly community in the later seventeenth and in the earliest part of the eighteenth century. Sibbald's interests were wide and his vision broad. As a physician, he had a rational concern for medicine which in its turn gave him an interest in botany as a means of countering disease. Botany was, however, also of economic interest to him since he was committed to improvement and wished to employ fully all the kingdom's usable resources, be they agricultural, mineral, industrial or commercial. Hence he saw the value of botanical surveys as indicating new sources of food, fodder and raw materials for industry, such as dyestuffs. Botany was related to his geographical interests, too (he was Geographer-Royal for Scotland) and in 1682 he set in train the surveying of Scotland which preoccupied intellectually curious Scots until at least the time of Sir John Sinclair in the 1790s. Natural history surveys assisted the search for ways to improve Scotland: Scots were making inadequate use of their resources because they were ignorant of them. Sibbald sought to locate and identify ore deposits, to extend Scottish fisheries and make them more profitable, and he was also interested in cattle, sheep and goats. In a speech dedicating Andrew Balfour's museum in 1697, he found the words to express how the search for God's

design and purpose, the intellectual curiosity satisfied by experimental science
and sheer utility all converged in his many activities:

> I mean by Nature that Art by which God made preserves and Governeth all the
> Beings in this world, espeacially those which fall under the discovery of our
> Senses, and by the Powers and vertues and Qualities God heth planted in them
> contribute to the use & ornament or pleasing of Human lyfe.[31]

To pursue his interests effectively, Sibbald sought to provide institutional
bases. He was instrumental, with others, in establishing the botanical garden
at Holyrood in 1670, in founding the Royal College of Physicians in 1682, in
compiling the *Edinburgh Pharmacopoeia* from 1682 to 1689 and was
appointed one of the first three professors of medicine in Edinburgh in 1685.
His appointment as Geographer-Royal in 1682 meant that he was in touch
with numerous people engaged in surveys. Between 1688 and 1710, he was
an active participant in many Edinburgh clubs including one in which physicians and other learned men met weekly 'to communicate anything that is
curious or remarkable [and] to keep correspondence abroad and at home'.[32]
Between 1689 and 1702 he twice proposed the chartering of a general purpose
Royal Society of Scotland and the names he had in mind as members were
people connected with the Darien company, distilleries, paper manufacture
and coal, as well as improving landlords and those concerned with developing
education especially in botany, medicine and mathematics. As with others
engaged in agriculture and domestic and foreign trade, Sibbald had conceived
of an ideal in proposing a Royal Society, but the means of realising it fully
did not exist in his time.

The lists of Sibbald's contemporaries drawn up by Emerson and the evidence he has produced on their varied collaborative ventures make it clear
that a community of scholars existed long before the days of Hume and
Ferguson, Smith and Robertson, Black, Cullen and Hutton. The very existence of such a community in Sibbald's time made certain intellectual achievements possible. What is more, Emerson has also made a convincing case for
the persistence of Sibbald's and his contemporaries' interests, techniques and
ideas from the later seventeenth century until the dawn of the nineteenth.
They initiated developments on which a richer intellectual base could build
in the later eighteenth century. Emerson argues that the world of the 1680s
was continuous with that of the 1780s in that both were busy with the same
kinds of activities and differed not in approaches to problems but in style
and sophistication. Sibbald also emerges as a patriotic figure: he sought to
vindicate the honour of Scotland by the ordering of history and antiquities,
the location and collection of manuscripts, the identification of places and
the dating of events. He serves as an alternative patriot to his contemporary,
Andrew Fletcher of Saltoun.

Alongside the actual pursuit of knowledge Sibbald and his contemporaries
were forging a professional ethos as exemplified by the foundation of the
Royal College of Physicians and of the Advocates' Library. Initiatives were
not the sole preserve of the mercantile section of the Scottish middle class.

Both medicine and law owed much to the example and inspiration of the Dutch whose influence was considerably strengthened after 1688/89. Faltering steps ultimately led to the foundation of the medical school (the appointment of professors, the provision of a curriculum, the construction of a hospital) which was modelled particularly on that of Leyden. The example of Holland and the emerging professional ethic in a society already accepting improvement merged with more mundane stimuli to bolster Edinburgh's medical school and university at the end of the seventeenth and beginning of the eighteenth centuries. Two wars discouraged Scottish students from the traditional sojourn in a continental university and the discouragement coincided with the purpose of Edinburgh's town council to save foreign exchange by making continental travel redundant. The town council determined to provide adequate professional education at home (a similar pattern was seen in the education of merchants) and in that way to restore the city, and make it once more a place of resort. George Drummond and his associates determinedly set themselves that task for the eighteenth century, thus serving not only the objectives of the merchants and traders of the city but also those of its growing population of professional men.

The culture of reformed Scotland encouraged the economy and the pursuit of knowledge. By the later seventeenth century ideas and ideals were present in both spheres, but there were constant obstacles to their realisation other than partially and on a small scale. When the context permitted, the Scottish agriculturalists and merchants were equipped and prepared mentally and institutionally to take fuller advantage. So too were the intellectuals. The context enabled them all to thrive together. Religion may underlie key areas of the later eighteenth-century inquiry itself, such as Reid's Common Sense philosophy which accepted that there were some areas of knowledge which were impervious to reason and which recognised fundamental human acceptance of religion and morality,[33] and the immanent wisdom revealed by Hutton in his theory of the earth.

III

It will be seen therefore, how limited appears the interpretation of the social and intellectual history of eighteenth-century Scotland as a reformulation of the civic humanist tradition in the wake of reduction to provincial status. Clearly it is a legitimate exercise for intellectual historians to trace the history of an idea and its development over time and in different countries. In this instance, however, the exercise carries with it two questionable implications that the parliamentary union marks a significant break in continuity and that the Scottish intellectual inquiry was confined to the science of man. For example, Nicholas Phillipson has argued that in accepting the Union of 1707, Scotland was seeking to remedy her backward economy by surrendering her parliament and by purchasing instead access to trade with England and her colonies. Consequently her traditional leaders, confined by poverty to continuing to play on the Scottish stage, were left seeking an ideology:

One way of looking at the Scots inquiry into the Science of Man is to think of it as a critique of the classic language of civic morality undertaken by a group of men living in a sophisticated but provincial community which had been stripped of its political institutions at the time of the Act of Union in 1707 and still hankered after an understanding of present provincial condition...I want to show that the Scots' concern with the principles of virtue can be related to the traumatic effect of the Act of Union on the Scottish political community...By the 1760s the process was complete, and a new language of civic morality had been created which provided the Scots with a new understanding of civic virtue and that 'sociological' understanding of the Science of Man which is the unique contribution of the Scots to the philosophy of the Enlightenment.

Lacking a political forum of their own, the Scots sought:

a language responsive to the economic, social and historical experience of provincial communities and realized that the virtue of a provincial citizen class was more likely to be released by economic and cultural institutions than by a national parliament remote from the provincial citizen's world...I have emphasized the evolution of that discussion of civic morality which derived, so it seems to me, from the peculiar history of their country in the century after the Union and served as a language-system which gave Scotland's intellectuals access to some of the central problems that were to preoccupy them as authors of a new Science of Man.[34]

John Robertson is another who has viewed the Scots' response to the problem of institutions and economic development in 'the terms of the civic tradition' and he too sees the issues and arguments of the Union debate informing later Enlightenment thought.[35] Both authors acknowledge the stimulus they have received from J.G.A. Pocock's writings on civic humanism.

Those who have written about the eighteenth-century Scottish inquiry in terms of civic humanism have shared particular emphases, notably on Andrew Fletcher of Saltoun and on the clubs, societies and universities of eighteenth-century Scotland as nurseries of the reformulated civic virtue.[36] Fletcher is effectively seen as laying down the agenda for the critique: he is 'the ideological father of the Scottish Enlightenment'[37] and 'can be seen to have established the framework for the debate on "the condition of Scotland" in the years preceding the Union'.[38] The preoccupation with Fletcher has led to an emphasis on the aftermath of the parliamentary union as being critical in establishing the intellectual interests and social institutions of enlightened Scotland.

The stress on Fletcher and the debate which he allegedly prompted has also led, effectively, to the limited definition to which reference has been made. It is clearly legitimate to point to the pursuit of natural philosophy and of medicine as essential elements in the philosophic movement that is characteristic of eighteenth-century Scotland. Colin McLaurin, William Cullen, Joseph Black, James Hutton and Alexander Munro are as significant to the Scottish intellectual enterprise as Francis Hutcheson, David Hume, Adam Smith, Adam Ferguson and John Millar. Fletcher was not the ideological father of the natural philosophers. Their part in the network of clubs and societies was as vital in forwarding the inquiry as that of those other philosophers on whom the Fletcherian interpretation concentrates.

To give Fletcher pride of place as the ideological father distorts the origins and nature of the enterprise. However intrinsically interesting Fletcher may be to historians of ideas, and despite his undoubted patriotism, he was nonetheless unable to detect the lasting developments that were at work in his own century, intellectual or practical. Probably for perfectly understandable reasons he did not perceive genuine changes, not least of attitude and outlook, in the economy of his time. Neither does Fletcher serve intellectually as a representative of the currents of his day; he had no followers in his own time nor has he had any since—until recently that is. Stair, Sibbald and Carmichael, on the other hand, and the community of which they were a part, anticipated a broad range of eighteenth-century developments, had a wider influence on the incipient inquiry than Fletcher, and are more representative figures of its prelude.

No one would claim that any single explanation of the Enlightenment in Scotland, whether based on civic humanism, natural jurisprudence, or any other intellectual tradition, is adequate. The phenomenon was too complex to be constricted intellectually. The objective of this criticism has been to draw attention to dangers besetting the Fletcherian interpretation. It neglects the real continuities in Scottish life and takes too narrow a view of the intellectual concerns of the eighteenth-century Scottish intellectual inquiry. What has been offered instead is an explanation that concentrates on the social, economic and intellectual interactions and continuities, on the establishment of the practical and institutional base and on the breadth of interests. If agricultural improvement and mercantile activity which conventionally have been seen as evidence of an eighteenth-century age of improvement are now known to have been developing in the later seventeenth century, then there is equally clear evidence that another feature of eighteenth-century Scotland, its intellectual inquiry, was also emerging then. This is the contextual argument that emphasises the common antecedents of the social, economic and intellectual history of the time. It is misleading to suggest that the Treaty of Union initiated new departures in these areas of modern Scottish history.

The ramifications of civic humanism have been extended from the interpretation of that part of the intellectual inquiry concerned with the science of man to the realm of eighteenth-century Scottish politics, especially in the days of Henry Dundas. Dwyer and Murdoch have argued 'that civil humanist concepts and concerns were essential to the moral culture of the eighteenth-century Scottish community' and 'that the political machinations of Henry Dundas and his enemies' cannot 'be fully understood without reference to the civic humanist critique of an emerging commercial policy based on a foreign empire'. They continue: 'In advancing this we are positing a connection between language and politics which centred on such concepts as public spirit, luxury, corruption, faction and independence'. Henry Dundas exploited the language embodied in these concepts, with the support of fellow politicians, men of letters and their clubs, to establish his political influence especially in opposition to Laurence Dundas. He won the support of the Scottish gentry and nobility by using a language that affirmed their collective rôle and at the same time expressed their fears.

The summary and quotations from Dwyer and Murdoch are drawn from their response to an article in *Studies on Voltaire* in which I have criticised two earlier studies.[39] There I have been concerned to know how the motives that prompted the Scottish political managers and the system of political management that they constructed (as described by Murdoch and Shaw in their books)[40] can be reconciled with the notion of virtue. Consequently, I have contended that the language of virtue is indeed mere rhetoric and bears little relation to reality. In particular, I argue that Henry Dundas was in reality no more virtuous than his opponents and that he was no less a *nouveau* (it is a tenet of the rhetoric of virtue to criticise Laurence Dundas for being *nouveau* and corrupt). I have suggested that the language Henry Dundas used to attack his opponents could equally well be interpreted as propaganda, part of legitimate political in-fighting. I am sceptical of the grandiose interpretation that his arguments are 'peculiarly Scottish variations on the language and concepts of civic humanism'.[41]

Students of eighteenth-century Scotland owe a considerable debt to such scholars as Alexander Murdoch who have resurrected post-union Scottish political history and who have presented episodes from it in so spirited and intriguing a fashion. What is being questioned is whether that presentation is necessarily assisted by its setting in the context of civic humanism. Dwyer and Murdoch admit, in their response, that Henry Dundas 'exploited this language and the concepts it expressed in the establishment of his political influence in Scotland'. Their reply emphasises that their central concern is the language used: 'What is being analysed here is the use of a linguistic network, not the personal morality, however defined, of its exponents' and 'What matters is that Henry Dundas won the support of many of the Scottish gentry and nobility by using a language that affirmed their role collectively and at the same time expressed their fears'. (The link with Nicholas Phillipson's phrase quoted earlier, that the evolution of the discussion of civic morality served as a language system which gave Scotland's intellectuals access to some of the central problems that preoccupied them, will be readily apparent.) It is clear that Dundas did not necessarily need to believe the ideology he so exploited and certainly his conduct of office was not, in another sense, more 'virtuous' than that of his political opponents. That is why I have interpreted Henry Dundas's presentation as rhetoric and legitimate propaganda in the course of political in-fighting. It seems that Dwyer and Murdoch are caught up in the expression of politicians' real or alleged ideals: 'The issue here', they write, 'is one of language. Our argument is not that Buccleuch and Dundas were themselves innocent of corruption, but that they were able to present a picture of themselves as civic heroes and landed exemplars'. I have been concerned to ask what the language may actually be concealing, and my case in *Studies in Voltaire* is that the behaviour of the 'civic heroes' was little different from that of their opponents. The new evidence on later eighteenth-century Scottish politics which Dwyer and

Murdoch adduce will nonetheless continue to shed light on Scottish political life in Dundas's age even though the theoretical framework in which it is established may continue to be debated.

In the view of its different proponents, civic humanism informs Scottish intellectual and political life for a century. Certainly it may be an element worthy of consideration but not at the expense of deeper rooted aspects of Scottish life, which have been my principal concern, and of other intellectual traditions. The Fletcherian interpretation, in particular, sings in unison with that historiography which can perceive little intellectual distinction and economic improvement in Scotland until the parliamentary union of 1707—'then there was light'. The objective here has been to redress the historiographical imbalance, and to propose an alternative approach, an approach which suggests that for Scotland's improvers and intellectuals the Treaty of Union marked no fundamental departure, that many enduring developments were launched in the later seventeenth century and lastly that by relating Scottish intellectual concerns to contemporaneous social and economic developments an appreciation and understanding of these concerns is enhanced.

Notes

1. John Lough, 'Reflections on Enlightenment and Lumières', *British Journal for Eighteenth-Century Studies*, VIII (Spring 1985), pp.1-15.
2. Richard B. Sher, *Church and University in the Scottish Enlightenment: The Moderate Literati of Edinburgh* (Princeton, Princeton U.P., 1985), p.9.
3. Ronald Turnbull and Craig Beveridge, 'The historiography of external control', *Cencrastus* (June-August 1986), pp.41-44.
4. R.H. Campbell, 'Stair's Scotland: the social and economic background', *Juridical Review* (1981), pp.110-27, and Gordon Donaldson, 'Stair's Scotland: the intellectual inheritance', *ibid*, pp.128-45.
5. Donaldson, pp.144-45.
6. H.W. Meikle, *Some Aspects of Later Seventeenth-Century Scotland* (Glasgow, Jackson, Son and Co., 1947).
7. Anand C. Chitnis, *The Scottish Enlightenment and Early Victorian English Society* (London, Croom Helm, 1986).
8. Robert A. Dodgshon, 'Farming in Roxburghshire and Berwickshire on the eve of improvement', *Scottish Historical Review*, LIV (1975), p.154.
9. Ian D. Whyte, *Agriculture and Society in Seventeenth-Century Scotland* (Edinburgh, John Donald, 1979), Chapter 10, and I.D.Whyte, 'The emergence of the new estate structure', in *The Making of the Scottish Countryside*, eds M.L. Parry and T.R. Slater (London, Croom Helm, 1980), pp.117-35. See also I.D. and K.A. Whyte, 'Continuity and change in a seventeenth-century Scottish farming community', *Agricultural History Review*, XXXII (1984), pp.159-69.
10. Whyte, 'The emergence of the new estate structure', p.132 and *Agriculture and Society*, p.259.
11. Whyte, *Agriculture and Society*, pp.110, 99 and 100.
12. *Ibid.*, pp.101, 104, 199, 210, 211-12, 123.
13. I.D. Whyte, 'Written leases and their impact on Scottish agriculture in the seventeenth century', *Agricultural History Review*, XXVII (1979), pp.2-6; M.B..

Sanderson, *Scottish Rural Society in the Sixteenth Century* (Edinburgh, John Donald, 1982),pp.57-60; Whyte, *Agriculture and Society*, pp.192-94; I.D. Whyte, 'Early Modern Scotland: continuity and change', in *An Historical Geography of Scotland*, eds G. Whittington and I.D. Whyte (London, Academic Press, 1983), pp.123-24 and Whyte, 'The emergence of the new estate structure', pp.126 and 128.

14. Whyte, *Agriculture and Society*, pp.183, 185 and 189, and 'The emergence of the new estate structure', pp.128-29.

15. T.M. Devine, 'The merchant class of the larger Scottish towns in the later seventeenth and early eighteenth centuries', in *Scottish Urban History*, eds George Gordon and Brian Dicks (Aberdeen, AUP, 1983), pp.92-111, and T.M. Devine, 'The Union of 1707 and Scottish development', *Scottish Economic and Social History*, V (1985), pp.23-40.

16. Sir James Steuart, *An Inquiry into the Principles of Political Oeconomy*, ed. Andrew S. Skinner, 2 vols (Edinburgh, Oliver and Boyd, 1966).

17. Gordon Marshall, *Presbyteries and Profits: Calvinism and the Development of Capitalism in Scotland 1560-1707* (Oxford, Clarendon Press, 1980).

18. R.H. Campbell, 'The influence of religion on economic growth in Scotland in the eighteenth century', in *Ireland and Scotland 1660-1850*, eds T.M. Devine and D. Dickson (Edinburgh, John Donald, 1983), pp.224-27, and R.H. Campbell, *The Rise and Fall of Scottish Industry 1707-1939* (Edinburgh, John Donald, 1980), pp.27-28.

19. John Millar, *An Historical View of the English Government from the Settlement of the Saxons in Britain to the Revolution in 1688*, 4 vols (London, J. Mawman, 1803),vol. III, pp.84-89.

20. J.C.D. Clark, *English Society 1688-1832: Ideology, Social Structure and Political Practice during the Ancien Regime* (Cambridge, CUP, 1985), p.423.

21. John Cameron, 'James Dalrymple, first Viscount of Stair', *Juridical Review* (1981), p.107.

22. P.G. Stein, 'The theory of law', in *Stair Tercentenary Studies*, ed. David M. Walker (Edinburgh, The Stair Society, 1981), pp.181-82, and Gordon M. Hutton, 'Stair's philosophic precursors', *ibid.*, p.89, and Neil MacCormick, 'Law and Enlightenment', in *The Origins and Nature of the Scottish Enlightenment*, eds R.H. Campbell and A. Skinner (Edinburgh, John Donald, 1982), p.160.

23. James Moore and Michael Silverthorne, 'Natural sociability and natural rights in the moral philosophy of Gerschom Carmichael', in *Philosophers of the Scottish Enlightenment*, ed. V. Hope (Edinburgh, Edinburgh U.P., 1984), pp.2-3.

24. *Ibid.*, p.11.

25. James Moore and Michael Silverthorne, 'Gerschom Carmichael and the natural jurisprudence tradition in eighteenth-century Scotland', in *Wealth and Virtue: The Shaping of Political Economy in the Scottish Enlightenment*, eds Istvan Hont and Michael Ignatieff (Cambridge, CUP, 1983), p.74.

26. Peter Stein, *Legal Evolution* (Cambridge, CUP, 1980), p.12.

27. *Ibid.*, pp.3-4.

28. Quoted from Francis Hutcheson, *System of Moral Philosophy* (1755), *ibid.*, p.9.

29. Christine M. Shepherd, 'Newtonianism in the Scottish universities in the seventeenth century', in *The Origins and Nature of the Scottish Enlightenment*, eds R.H. Campbell and A. Skinner (Edinburgh, John Donald, 1982), p.82.

30. Roger L. Emerson, 'Sir Robert Sibbald, Kt, The Royal Society of Scotland and the origins of the Scottish Enlightenment', paper delivered to the History Department seminar, University of Stirling, 30 April 1986. I an indebted to the author for permission to refer to the typescript of his invaluable paper.

31. Quoted by Emerson from Edinburgh University Library, MS La III, 535, f.1.
32. Quoted by Emerson from John MacQueen Cowan, 'The history of the Royal Botanic Garden Edinburgh—the Prestons', *Notes of the Royal Botanic Garden Edinburgh*, XCII (1935), p.77.
33. Nicholas Phillipson, 'The pursuit of virtue in Scottish university education: Dugald Stewart and Scottish moral philosophy in the Enlightenment', *Universities, Society and the Future*, ed. Nicholas Phillipson (Edinburgh, Edinburgh U.P., 1983), p.86.
34. Nicholas Phillipson, 'The Scottish Enlightenment', in *The Enlightenment in National Context*, eds Roy Porter and Mikuláš Teich (Cambridge, CUP, 1981), pp.22, 26 and 40. The development of Dr Phillipson's ideas to this point can be traced through his earlier articles, 'Towards a definition of the Scottish Enlightenment', in *City and Society in the Eighteenth Century*, eds P. Fritz and D. Williams (Toronto, Hakkert, 1973), pp.125-47; 'Culture and Society in the 18th-century province: the case of Edinburgh and the Scottish Enlightenment', in *The University in Society*, ed. Lawrence Stone, 2 vols (Princeton, Princeton U.P., 1975), vol. II, pp.407-48; 'Lawyers, landowners and the civic leadership of post-union Scotland', *Juridical Review* (1976), pp.97-120 and 'Virtue, commerce and the science of man in early eighteenth-century Scotland', *Studies on Voltaire and the Eighteenth Century*, CLXXXI (1980), pp.750-53.
35. John Robertson, 'The Scottish Enlightenment at the limits of the civic tradition', in *Wealth and Virtue: The Shaping of Political Economy in the Scottish Enlightenment*, eds Istvan Hont and Michael Ignatieff (Cambridge, CUP, 1983), pp.137-78. The quotation is from p.138, and see also p.152.
36. An idiosyncratic essay which contains these emphases is George Davie, *The Scottish Enlightenment* (London, Historical Association, 1981).
37. Phillipson, 'The Scottish Enlightenment', p.22.
38. Robertson, 'The Scottish Enlightenment', p.141.
39. Anand C. Chitnis, 'Agricultural improvement, political management and civic virtue in enlightened Scotland: an historiographical critique', *Studies on Voltaire and the Eighteenth Century*, CCXLV (1986), pp.475-88; John Dwyer and Alexander Murdoch, 'Henry Dundas revisited but not revised', in typescript. The earlier articles were John Dwyer and Alexander Murdoch, 'Paradigms and politics: manners, morals and the rise of Henry Dundas, 1770-1784', in *New Perspectives on the Politics and Culture of Early Modern Scotland*, eds John Dwyer, Roger A. Mason and Alexander Murdoch (Edinburgh, John Donald, n.d. [1982]), pp.210-48 and Alexander Murdoch, 'The Importance of being Edinburgh: management and opposition in Edinburgh politics 1746-1784', *Scottish Historical Review*, LXII (1983), pp.1-16.
40. Alexander Murdoch, *'The People Above': Politics and Administration in Mid-Eighteenth-Century Scotland* (Edinburgh, John Donald, 1980) and John Stuart Shaw, *The Management of Scottish Society 1707-1764: Power, Nobles, Lawyers, Edinburgh Agents and English Influences* (Edinburgh, John Donald, 1983).
41. Dwyer and Murdoch, p.243.

SECTION II

Enlightened Aberdeen

10

George Turnbull and Educational Reform

M.A. Stewart

University of Lancaster

I

George Turnbull was born on 11 July 1698, son of a minister of Alloa of the same name.[1] The family moved to Tyninghame in East Lothian a year later. Entering Edinburgh University in 1711, he spent several sessions in study there but deferred his graduation until April 1721. He was at that time appointed to a vacancy in Aberdeen as one of the Philosophy regents at Marischal College, and is thus one of the succession of young Whig Presbyterians brought in from the South to restock the faculty after 1715.

Given his subsequent career, it is likely that the five or so years unaccounted for here—from c.1716 to 1721—were taken up in studies for the ministry or the law, and perhaps some private tutoring. Turnbull was an early member of the Rankenian Club, founded in Edinburgh in 1716 or 1717, dominated by radical young trainees for those professions and deeply imbued with the philosophical ideas of Shaftesbury.[2] He was certainly in Edinburgh in 1718, when under an assumed name (Philocles) he tried to engage John Toland in London in correspondence—on freethinking, morals and religion, and on some of Toland's utopian ideas. In this period too he prepared a clandestine tract which no publisher would take, in which he limited the state's role in religion to the universal protection of freedom of thought.[3] These facts were probably not known to his sponsors at Aberdeen, where in any case he moved closer to orthodoxy, admitting a place for revealed religion and for religious institutions in the state, though he never showed much tendency to Calvinism.

Turnbull took over the third-year class at Marischal in 1721 and saw them through to graduation in 1723. During this time he corresponded with Robert Molesworth, the Irish peer and leader of the 'Old Whigs', whose highly successful *Account of Denmark as it was in the Year 1692* had once commanded the attention of Locke and Shaftesbury. Molesworth in that work (to which Turnbull pays fulsome tribute) contrasted the 'liberty' of post-Revolution England with the 'slavery' of Denmark, and argued that a liberal educational system—free of clerical authoritarianism, instilling moral values, and offering a broad study of history and literature—was the best guarantee of that liberty. His close intimacy with Shaftesbury became public knowledge through the publication by Toland in 1721 of some of their personal correspondence. Turnbull cashes in on that connexion in his first letter to Molesworth, and then continues:

> My Lord I am setled a Professor of Philosophy in the new College of Aberdeen; & hope now to have Leisure to apply my self to the Study of the Ancients, the Study to which my humor & Genius leads me; And in my publick Profession shal always make it my business to promote the interests of Liberty and Vertue & to reform the taste of the Young Generation. But oh! My Lord, Education in this country is upon a miserable footing; And why should I say in this country, for is it not almost Every where? And must it not be so while Philosophy is a Traffick, and Science is retailed for a peice of bread?[4]

Molesworth acknowledged the letter, and Turnbull's response contains further reflections on the local scene:

> The learned youth of the University of Glascow (with some of whom I have the honour to be acquainted) have indeed given proofs of a free & generous spirit which deserve to be commended. And I am sure they have a very gratefull sense of the Encouragment you have been pleased to give them. Would to heaven, My Lord, I could say our college were as yet in any respect upon a better footing than her sisters. Sure I am I should reckon my Self a happy man if I can contribute any thing in my capacity to promote the interests of Liberty truth & the love of mankind. 'Tis indeed on the Education of y° youth that the Foundation stones of Publick Liberty must be layed. But oh, my Lord, when shal a Formal dogmatical spirit which hath brought true Philosophy & usefull Scholarship into such contempt be seperated from the gown; And our Academies become realy good & Wholesome Nurseries to the Publicke. O when shall all that Idle Pedantick Stuff wh[ich] is now alass the most innocent cargoe our youth can carry with them from our Universities be banished; And that Philosophy which once governed states & Societies & produced Heroes & Patriots take place in it's room. And for this effect when shal the Sprightly arts & Sciences, which are so Essential in the formation of a gentiel & liberal Caracter be again reunited with Philosophy from which by a fatal Error they have been so long severed! But what do I talk of? All this surely is meer Romance & Enthusiasm. For how can it be so while our Colleges are under the Inspection of proud domineering pedantic Priests whose interest it is to train up the youth in a profound veneration to their Senseless metaphysical Creeds & Catechisms, which for this purpose they are daily inured to defend against all Doubters & Enquirers with the greatest bitteness and contempt, in a stiff formal bewildering manner admirably fitted indeed to Enslave young understandings betimes and to beget an early antipathy against all Free thought.[5]

Molesworth, having said it all before, was duly impressed, and offered Turnbull his complete works. In a third letter of 14 May 1723, Turnbull unsuccessfully begged him to look out for a travelling tutorship for him, 'so impatient is my desire of an opportunity of that sort for my own improvement'. In fact, Turnbull stayed put, taking the new class through to graduation in 1726. He has thereby become known to posterity as the teacher of Thomas Reid and so as some kind of father of the Aberdeen Enlightenment.

In March 1725 he was one of a majority of the faculty involved in a fracas with Principal Blackwell. At the end of the summer, after travelling in Scotland with Colin MacLaurin, who was another party to the fracas and on the point of quitting Marischal altogether, Turnbull went off to the continent without leave as a tutor in the Udney family. He left it to Charles Mackie in Edinburgh to fix up with Robert Duncan, a Scots student of Barbeyrac newly returned from Groningen, to be his substitute.[6] But on 12 October the College called him home:

> The facultie Unanimouslie agree's that a letter should be writter to Mr Turnbul by the Prin^l (who is accordinglie appointed so to do) representing to him that the time of ye Colledge Sitting doun now draws Near and y^t in case he should not be present to attend his Class as is Usual his Absence wil be very prejudicial to ye Societie and y^r upon desire y^t he presentlie send an Answer to ye societie as to his final resolution.[7]

This must have crossed in the mail with a letter from Turnbull at Groningen to Mackie, dated 20 October:

> But what are our folks inclinations at Aberdeen I know not. I am afraid the folks I thought would be easiest may be most uneasy. For I have wrote twice or thrice both to Dr Mackail & Mr Varner & have had no answer. If they will make me uneasy I cannot help it: But this winter I neither will nor can come home. Let them do what they please. And indeed I wish heartily I may be so lucky as to have no more to do with that place. But I know I need not put you in mind how much I want to be delivered from Aberdeen; & how much I wish something better would cast up.

However this was resolved, Turnbull was certainly back in Aberdeen by January. His name appears in minutes of 17 January and 1 March.[8] He resigned, though, after one further session, taking with him the first LL.D. degree of Marischal College—of which it was later claimed, by the opponent of a subsequent holder of the same award, that '*Mr. Turnbull* their first Doctor was so conscious that their *Diploma* was good for nothing, that he afterwards applied to the University of *Edinburgh*, and took a fresh one from them in the year 1732'.[9]

II

On leaving Aberdeen Turnbull became tutor for five years to Andrew Wauchope of Niddry, their itinerary taking in Edinburgh, Groningen and Utrecht universities, and tours of the Rhineland and France. He cultivated connexions wherever he could, and wrote to Mackie from London in 1732 and 1733 with grandiose but vague plans for the future. At this time he finally stopped pressuring Mackie and MacLaurin to find him a better job at another Scottish university, and turned his eyes to Oxford. On the advice of Charles Talbot he matriculated in Michaelmas term 1733 at Exeter College and was admitted *ad eundem gradum* to the degree of B.C.L.,[10] with the intention of entering the Anglican church. It must have been about then also that he established contact with the latitudinarian Thomas Rundle and his circle— a customary pattern for ex-Rankenians visiting London. Still in London in August 1735, he was one of the first subscribers to the Society for the Encouragement of Learning, a worthy but financially unstable project to raise capital to publish works of learning without surrendering copyright to the booksellers. He attended the Society's meetings regularly from April 1737 to May 1739, expecting at one time to have their support for his *Treatise on Ancient Painting* and at another time hoping to succeed his fellow-countryman Alexander Gordon as secretary.[11] Between 1735 and 1737 he had spent part of the time in Italy as tutor to Thomas Watson, son of Lord Rockingham, where he conceived the plan for that book. Allan Ramsay, Jr, who was also in Italy, looked after his interest in securing Paderni's illustrations after Turnbull returned home, and reported to a mutual friend on Turnbull's difficulties in meeting the bill.[12]

In 1739 Turnbull used the connexions of Thomas Birch, then treasurer of the Society for the Encouragement of Learning, to obtain ordination by Bishop Hoadly. He used Birch also as a channel to obtain subscribers to several of his books; but Birch's surviving engagement diary shows that the relationship was not a close one. Birch's much closer friend Warburton, responding to pressure to buy *The Principles of Moral Philosophy* (in which Warburton's defence of Pope receives passing commendation), told Birch: 'I never heard of Dr. Turnbull, nor his book, before your account of it'.[13] Turnbull's cultivation of contacts, such as Hoadly and Richard Mead, never-theless brought him close to the Court. He was able to dedicate his annotated translation of Heineccius's *Methodical System of Universal Law* to the Duke of Cumberland in the same year (four years before Culloden) that he became an honorary chaplain to the Duke's rival, the Prince of Wales. He was then living at Kew, taking in a few pupils.[14] In 1742 he obtained only his second, and last, settled job, when Rundle appointed him rector of Drumachose, a scattered Irish parish centred on the small country town of Limavady. Turnbull had already honoured Rundle with the dedication of *Observations upon Liberal Education* in the same year. He died revisiting the Netherlands six years later.

I have here mentioned Turnbull's four best known publications, the out-come of a prodigiously productive period of somewhat undisciplined writing in the late 1730s and early 1740s. He needed the money. But this was only a portion of his output. It is common knowledge that *A Treatise on Ancient Painting* and *Observations upon Liberal Education* belong together, for their emphasis on educational reform and the role of history and the arts in teaching by moral examples; but with them belong also the neglected intro-ductions to his translations of *Three Dissertations* (1740) and Justinus's

History of the World (1742). *The Principles of Moral Philosophy*, though published in 1740, incorporates Turnbull's lectures at Aberdeen, for all that it is now interlarded with later quotations from Hutcheson, Butler and Pope. To see how this is so, it is instructive to compare it with a work which derives from the end of his Aberdeen period, the now little studied *Philosophical Enquiry concerning the Connexion betwixt the Doctrines and Miracles of Jesus Christ.*

Written in 1726 and published in London while Turnbull was abroad in 1731, with two subsequent editions, this is not just the first in a forgotten series of theological tracts, but the first also in a philosophical series. Turnbull throughout his professional career aimed to defend the philosophical (that is, scientific) credentials of morality and religion—the system of morality being based upon an historically informed science of human nature structurally parallel to physical philosophy, and religion being the natural end of any complete science. Not only does he refer constantly to the nature and method of science; but given the belief of all Moral Sense theorists in the mutual independence of morality and religion, he is also still keen to find in the religious belief in immortality a supplementary motive to, and prospect of reward for, virtuous action. These two interests come together in the *Philosophical Enquiry*, in an original use of the concept of 'experiment' which appears to be lacking in his earlier lectures but survives, somewhat inexactly, in his new philosophical writing thereafter: Carol Gibson-Wood documents it for *A Treatise on Ancient Painting* in her contribution to the present volume, and it is found again in *Observations upon Liberal Education* (pp.379-80). An experiment for Turnbull is not just the controlled observation of phenomena, but a 'proper sample' or proof by instantiation of something. So Christ's teaching with regard to a future state was subject to 'experimental proof' in this life, by those miracles which were 'natural proper samples' of the power they confirmed (to raise the dead, promote long-term happiness and well-being, etc.), in the same way that a natural philosopher shows 'certain proper samples' of the qualities he ascribes to the air:

> If therefore certain doctrines of *Jesus Christ* evidently are, or can be, reduced to assertions of his having a certain degree of power or knowledge: his works may be a proper proof of these doctrines; because they may be proper samples or experiments of the power, or knowledge claimed by these assertions. (p.14)

III

The educational reform hinted at in Turnbull's letters to Molesworth, and fully developed in his works on painting and education and in the introduction to Justinus, is one which would abandon an early abstract concentration on language and logic in favour of a solid grounding in history. Civil history was both a natural development out of the history of the world and a necessary precondition for a science of human nature, which would lead in turn into the system of government and morals; and each study, separately or in conjunction, would lead through the examination of final causes into natural religion.

'It is in the histories of mankind that the value of Liberty is best learned, as weel as the ways by which it has been lost & preserved', he wrote to Molesworth, instancing Molesworth's own 'judicious account of Denmark';[15] and it remains to be considered why, apart from youthful opportunism, that correspondence ever arose. Turnbull was not the only correspondent: his Rankenian colleague William Wishart, a young Scots minister and son of the Principal of Edinburgh University, was also implicated. Their ostensible pretext was the common friendship with some of the students of Glasgow shared by Molesworth on the one hand and Turnbull and Wishart on the other. Irish divinity students were particularly restive at Glasgow. There is, for example, a continuous history of events from Francis Hutcheson's involvement as a ringleader in 1717, passing through the expulsion in 1722 of the student who was to become Hutcheson's Dublin publisher and in 1725 of one of Hutcheson's own former Dublin students, to Wishart's move to a Glasgow pulpit in 1724, his active participation in the student clubs, his being brought in as Dean of Faculty in 1728 and his role in Hutcheson's election as a professor in 1729.[16] The civic humanist rhetoric in which the unrest was couched—the restoration of lost liberty, the pursuit of personal and public virtue, the end of ecclesiastical authoritarianism—fits in well enough with the Molesworth line, but obscures the original precise political issue. A majority of the Glasgow faculty sought to break their Principal's irresistible alliance with the Chancellor, the Rector, and the Professor of Divinity, and to restore the running of the university to the whole faculty. To do this they had to break the alliance between the Principal and the Chancellor in the appointment of the Rector. They accordingly organised with the students a revival of the old method of rectorial election and actively encouraged the students to take the university to court for the restoration of their 'liberties'. Molesworth was engaged to present their grievances to parliament, but died before political changes brought victory to the students in 1726-1727.

Turnbull's involvement in university politics at Aberdeen in 1725 was an attempted replay of the Glasgow scenario, except that this time the Rector was in league with the majority of the faculty against the Principal; but this time it was the Principal who successfully sought redress in the courts. The immediate occasion for the troubles was again the right of the students to elect their Rector. At Marischal College this right had never been lost; but in 1725 the Principal refused to proceed with the election, because of some alleged irregularities in the electoral process and because some of the procurators (the students' electoral college) were 'Severall of them notourly disaffected To our present Church Establishment'. The Principal's party was outvoted by the rest of the faculty, who proceeded to run the election. The Principal refused to recognise this, was summoned before the rectorial court, refused to appear, and secured a Sist of Advocation from the Court of Session.[17] Recent events only added to the faculty's long list of complaints against the Principal, who had 'by many ... oppressions overturned the peace, order & Rights of the Society and prostituted it's Honour and Independency after great pains had been taken to bring him to Temper and Divert from these proceedings'. The masters accordingly pleaded for an end to the 'encroachments on the liberties & immunities of the rights of the Colledge'. But, reading between the lines, this appears to have been largely an act of retaliation by Colin MacLaurin and his friends for the Principal's perceived collusion with the town council in 1724 in having MacLaurin censured for absenteeism.[18]

Was this enough to turn an impassioned Turnbull off Aberdeen? No doubt the politics, both academic and theological, were tense; and the pay was poor—£417. 13s. 8d. Scots was less than £35 sterling.[19] Turnbull was academically ambitious and something of a social climber, and his self-image did not in the long run do him a lot of good: it is unfortunate for his reputation that so much of his surviving correspondence should be seeking favours. But there is little evidence—either in *The Principles of Moral Philosophy*, or in the 1723 and 1726 graduation theses, which Turnbull referred back to in the introduction to the *Principles* as 'indicating the importance of this philosophy'—that he was seriously constrained in what he could teach. He was not even the first to teach Shaftesbury's ideas sympathetically at Marischal— David Verner had introduced Shaftesbury in the 1721 class.[20]

One thing Turnbull clearly could not do on his own was reform the *order* of the curriculum—languages still dominated the first year; moral and natural philosophy were for him the wrong way round, and moral philosophy was taught independently of history. Marischal College had to wait until the 1750s for many of these reforms to take effect, and for the institution of the Chair in Natural and Civil History. But Alexander Gerard's 1755 manifesto harks back not to Molesworth and Turnbull as his authorities, but to the ancient Stoics and Bacon. Where Turnbull was more directly effective was in the education of his private pupils: the first thing he did with Udney at Groningen in 1725 and Wauchope at Edinburgh in 1727 was to enrol them in the history classes.

In spite of his bombastic style and shifting theological allegiances, Turnbull's writing is a 'proper sample' of the main current of thought among the new generation of Scottish-Irish Presbyterians in the 1720s and 1730s.[21] The current itself can hardly be ignored by those who wish to understand properly the intellectual history of the later part of the century, and Turnbull's place in this tradition deserves the attention which it has recently started to attract.

Notes

This paper was prepared during tenure of a visiting fellowship at the Institute for Advanced Studies in the Humanities, University of Edinburgh, as part of the 1986 IPSE programme.

1. *The Diary of the Rev. George Turnbull*, ed. R. Paul (Edinburgh, Scottish History Society Publications, 1893), p.376. The biographical information in this paper is

derived mostly from the University Archives at Aberdeen and Edinburgh and from Turnbull's surviving correspondence—to Lord Molesworth (National Library of Ireland microfilm n.4082, verbatim citations being made by permission of Mr Martin Townsend, the present owner of the originals); Charles Mackie (Edinburgh University Library, La. II. 91, verbatim citation by permission of Dr J.T.D. Hall); and John Toland, Thomas Birch and Alexander Gordon (BL, Add. MSS 4465, 4319, 6190). I am also grateful to the Registrar of the Royal Archives at Windsor and to the Rev. F.W. Fawcett for information.

2. M.A. Stewart, 'Berkeley and the Rankenian Club', *Hermathena*, 139 (1985), pp.25-45.

3. This lost document was recently discovered by Paul Wood and is to be included in a collection of the letters, manuscripts and other minor writings of Turnbull which he and I intend to publish together in due course.

4. Turnbull to Molesworth, 3 August 1722.

5. Turnbull to Molesworth, 5 November 1722. Turnbull is aping a footnote in Shaftesbury's 'Soliloquy, or Advice to an Author', III.iii.

6. Turnbull to Mackie, 3 September and 20 October 1725; R. Wodrow, *Analecta: or Materials for a History of Remarkable Providences; mostly relating to Scotch Ministers and Christians*, 4 vols (Edinburgh, for the Maitland Club, 1842-43), vol.3, pp.303-5.

7. AUL, M. 387/11/2/17/2, cited by permission.

8. AUL, M. 387/11/3/17/1; M. 104.

9. AUL, K. 144, p.275.

10. J. Foster, *Alumni Oxonienses*, 4 vols (Oxford, Parker, 1888), vol. 4, p.1448. Turnbull spent long enough in Oxford to be able to say to Birch as late as 1739 that that was where most of his clerical contacts were.

11. Besides the BL holdings cited in note 1, see the minute books and other papers of the Society for the Encouragement of Learning, BL, Add. MSS 6184, 6185, 6187, 6191.

12. See Alexander Cunningham's diary cited in Margaret Alice Forbes, *Curiosities of a Scots Charta Chest* (Edinburgh, W. Brown, 1897), p.114; Ramsay to Cunningham, 2 August 1737, 5 November 1738, 14 August 1740, SRO, GD 331/24/2, 331/24/4, 331/5/15; I.G. Brown, 'Allan Ramsay's rise and reputation', *Walpole Society*, 50 (1984), pp.209-47.

13. Besides Turnbull's letters to Birch, see Birch's diary, BL, Add. MS 4478C, and J. Nichols, *Illustrations of the Literary History of the Eighteenth Century*, 8 vols (London, Nicholas, Son & Bentley, 1817), vol.II, p.119.

14. Turnbull to Birch, 24 April 1741.

15. Turnbull to Molesworth, 5 November 1722.

16. I discussed this more thoroughly and with extensive documentation in 'Warmth in the cause of virtue', a paper presented to the Conference for the Study of Political Thought at Edinburgh in 1986.

17. AUL, M. 104; M. 387/9/1/5/1; M. 387/9/1/6.

18. MacLaurin had been a friend of Hutcheson from Glasgow days. See MacLaurin to Hutcheson, 22 October 1728 (copy of unknown provenance), SRO, RH 1/2/497. On his conflict with the Principal and the town council at Aberdeen, see the sources cited in note 17 (where there is some evidence that the Principal's son may actually have argued that MacLaurin's travels had done Marischal College's reputation some good) and Aberdeen Council Register vol. 59, pp.151-2, 159-60, 180, 225. There is a relevant 1724 letter from MacLaurin to the Lord Provost in the Town House archives (Aberdeen Letter Book, vol. 9).

19. AUL, M. 361/10/8 lists the salaries of all the faculty in 1726. There were great disparities between individuals.
20. Copies of Verner's and Turnbull's graduation theses are held in AUL.
21. I have had no room to go into detail here on Turnbull's philosophy, on which there is still a very meagre secondary literature. See however J. McCosh, *The Scottish Philosophy* (London, Macmillan, 1875), article 12; D.F. Norton, *David Hume, Common-Sense Moralist, Sceptical Metaphysician* (Princeton, Princeton U.P., 1982), chap. 4; my own paper cited in note 2 above; and some recent papers by J.C. Stewart-Robertson, especially 'The well-principled savage, or the child of the Scottish Enlightenment', *Journal of the History of Ideas*, 42 (1981), pp.503-25.

11

George Turnbull's Common Sense Jurisprudence

K.A.B. Mackinnon
University of Aberdeen

History has treated Francis Hutcheson (1694-1746) and George Turnbull (1698-1748) very differently: Hutcheson is perceived as the father of the Scottish Enlightenment, while Turnbull is only mentioned as the teacher of Thomas Reid, merely passing on to Reid the ideas of Hutcheson.[1] Although it would indeed be more unjust to view Hutcheson merely as Adam Smith's teacher, and Turnbull as the founder of Scottish Common Sense Philosophy, history has done Turnbull a disservice in concentrating too intensively on his no doubt more important contemporary.

In fact there were some notable parallels in the lives of these two early Enlightenment figures. Both were sons of the manse born in the closing decade of the seventeenth century; both were educated in Scotland, but had Irish connexions and came under the patronage of Lord Molesworth; both published extensively, primarily on moral philosophy, taught in Scottish universities and included amongst their students several who would later make significant contributions to Enlightenment thought; but dying while still fairly young, neither lived long enough to see the Scottish Enlightenment come into full flower.

Strictly speaking the first to publish was Turnbull, but what he published was the graduation thesis he presented at Marischal College in 1723. This was a brief piece in Latin whose message he was to reiterate throughout his life, namely, that moral philosophy should adopt the same empirical methods which Newton had shown to be so fruitful in natural philosophy.[2] Although hardly influential, this and the 1726 thesis[3] indicate that at the time of Hutcheson's important *Inquiry* in 1725 and *Illustrations* in 1728,[4] Turnbull was already pursuing the inductive method of moral sense philosophy associated with Hutcheson. The theses tend to confirm Turnbull's claim in the preface of his *Principles of Moral Philosophy* published in 1740:

> this enquiry...is...the substance of several pneumatological discourses...read

above a dozen years ago to students of Moral Philosophy, by way of preparative to a course of lectures, on the rights and duties of mankind.[5]

After only six years at Aberdeen, Turnbull resigned in 1727. During the next twelve years, Turnbull travelled, publishing works on theology and on painting,[6] while from 1730 Hutcheson taught at Glasgow. In 1740, Turnbull published both *The Principles of Moral Philosophy* and *Christian Philosophy*,[7] and wrote *A Discourse upon the Nature and Origine of Moral and Civil Laws* which he appended to his translation and annotation of Johann Gottlieb Heineccius's *Elementa Juris Naturae et Gentium* (1737) for publication the following year as *A Methodical System of Universal Law*.[8] Although Hutcheson, like Turnbull, lectured on jurisprudence, there was little discussion of legal theory in his early works, while the first of his later works did not appear until 1742.[9] Thus Turnbull's contribution to legal theory was in print in advance of Hutcheson's. On the other hand, Turnbull freely admitted that much of his moral theory (of which his legal thought was an extension) was derived from Hutcheson's early works.[10] But Turnbull's claim for a place in the history of ideas does not rest on the chronology of publications, especially since he admitted so much was derivative, notably from 'the better ancients', from Clark, Berkeley, Butler, Shaftesbury, Hutcheson and Pope.[11] The method and substance of his work has intrinsic interest.

The analogy between physical science and moral science remained the starting point in all Turnbull's major writings. Being pre-Humean, he took it that the former was well established. 'Natural Philosophy is defined to be the science of the laws, according to which nature operates in producing its effects, and to which human art must conform in order to produce certain effects.'[12] But his concern was moral philosophy which:

> will naturally divide itself into the same parts as natural philosophy does; i.e. into the part which investigates the connexions or laws of nature, and the part which shows how certain ends may be obtained by human art or action, in consequence of the settled laws of nature; the first of which is justly denominated a theoretical, and the other a practical science.[13]

To commence the theoretical science, 'we must enquire into moral phenomena, in the same manner as we do into physical ones: that is, we must endeavour to find out by experience the good general laws to which they are reducible'.[14] Experience—here the self-analysis of the human nature—reveals in man's constitution a variety of appetites, affections, senses and powers, among which is 'a moral sense, or a sense of right and wrong'.[15] These all by their nature seek gratification but are not necessarily self-interested, for there are social and altruistic appetites amongst them. Experience (or 'common sense') shows that total submission to one appetite means that other appetites cannot be gratified, but it also shows that man has the ability to regulate his appetites in such a way that maximises their gratification and produces happiness. That ability is reason:

and we have a power of reason and reflexion by which we may discern what course of acting will naturally tend to procure us the most valuable sort of gratifications of all our desires, and prevent all intolerable or unnecessary pains... Now as to take away our passions and affections would be to deprive us of all the springs and motives, all the principles necessary to action, and to leave nothing to our reason to govern and guide, so, on the other hand, to rob us of our reason, would be to deprive us of a guiding principle, and to reduce us to the lowest condition of animals impelled and driven by instinct and appetites, without any foresight, without any capacity of chusing, and consequently without all capacity of virtue or merit.[16]

But Turnbull was concerned to make clear that he rejected the self- interested egoism of Hobbes where the gratification of one's desires was *the* motive for action. Turnbull's solution was to claim that in regulating the appetites, reason acted in conjunction with the moral sense: any gratification of an appetite had also to be approved as virtuous. His belief was that man is so well designed that his true self-interest coincides with virtue: 'These two, happiness or interest, and becoming or virtue, are the same, or at least inseparably connected.'[17] This led him to equate man's moral perfection, and man's happiness[18] and on several occasions even to equate reason and moral sense,[19] something Hutcheson would have deplored in his mission to refute not only egoism but also ethical rationalism. Indeed the image of the moral sense presented by Turnbull is more akin to Reid's 'conscience' than to Hutcheson's moral sense: it is indubitably both affective *and* cognitive[20] and is capable of self-conscious improvement through culture and care.[21] In Turnbull's *Discourse*, the moral sense is almost completely subsumed under 'reason', though reason is then not to be understood as a purely intellectual power.

Having identified the end (i.e. the promotion of happiness through virtue) and, in a general way, the means ('the regulation of our affections and actions')[22] the task of Turnbull's moral scientist is to discover more specific connexions which determine the means by which the end can be achieved. Human nature itself indicates certain internal connexions or rules which reason has to comply with in its regulation of man's appetites and affections, if, that is, happiness is to be achieved. These are laws of human nature analogous to Newton's laws of physical or mechanical nature. At the most general level, then, the 'first law of nature with regard to our conduct, is to maintain reason in our mind as our governing principle over all our affections and pursuits'.[23] It is not to become a 'slave to our headstrong passions'.[24] But 'the first particular law' for the harmonious gratification of man's sensitive, intellectual and social appetites is the 'law of industry; or the necessity of our activity, application or industry, in order to attain to any goods'.[25] The second particular law is 'the law of sociality'[26] which holds that men are interdependent and their happiness depends on social co-operation, communication and assistances. In both cases these laws are as morally 'agreeable' as they are necessary as a means to man's ends, and they are 'common sense' in that 'They stare at everyone, who considers human nature with any attention, so to speak, in the face'.[27] These are laws in that they are necessary and universal means to desired ends:

> in the sense, that the laws of motion are laws to human arts for the attainment of their ends...We can no more alter these connexions than we can change the laws of motion and gravity.[28]

However Turnbull claimed that they are laws in a second, stricter sense: they are 'The will of a superior who hath a just title to command, and sufficient power to enforce conformity to his commands'.[29]

If, as appears at first sight to be the case, Turnbull was giving this as a general definition of law in the juridical sense, then his position was noticeably at variance with those of Hutcheson and of Reid. They, as did most of the writers Turnbull quoted with approval, held a natural law view. Turnbull's definition, in contrast, seems to allow a sovereign to pass any law he can enforce regardless of its moral content. However a wider reading of Turnbull's work (especially his remarks on Heineccius's theory) provides grounds for believing that he did not intend to adhere to this 'command theory' version of legal positivism.

Heineccius argued that since even the most well-intentioned individual may mistake evil for good, man needs guidance in the form of rules of good conduct. Man may be motivated to obey these rules by an obligation either internal or external to the rules: the obligation, that is, must:

> consist either in the intrinsic goodness and pravity of actions themselves, or arise from the will of some being whose authority we acknowledge, commanding and forbidding certain actions under a penalty.[30]

To constitute a law, a rule must have external obligation: it must be commanded by a superior. Consequently a person doing good simply because it is good may be thought of as acting morally, but is not acting 'justly'—i.e. in conformity with a law—unless he is acting in response to a command of a superior. The conclusion Heineccius wished to establish was—contrary to what Grotius had argued—that there can be no natural law without God.

Turnbull disagreed. Accepting that 'it is the will of God which constituted external or legal obligation',[31] he pointed out that 'conformity to reason is the mean by which agreeableness to the divine will may be known'.[32] Thus it *is* sufficient to create legal obligation if reason dictates and approves a course of action: 'reason...talks to us (if I may so speak) with the authority of a lawgiver or ruler'.[33] Turnbull realised that his identification of external with internal obligation meant that the certainty which an externally imposed rule offers would disappear. His equanimity over this was perhaps due to his conviction that for an action to carry internal obligation, it must have already satisfied two criteria: approval by the moral sense and identification by reason as tending to promote happiness. Nevertheless the detailing of man's legal duties and obligations, that is, the practical part of morals and law, is less easy than the theoretical, though it is facilitated by the drawing up of civil laws in individual political states.[34]

Turnbull maintained that the civil state is a natural phenomenon which evolves, or, to use his words, undergoes a 'natural generation'.[35] Man is fitted and designed, in part by the natural law of sociality in his constitution, for achieving his greatest perfection and happiness 'in a rightly constituted civil state'.[36] In contrast to Hutcheson and Heineccius, Turnbull denied that the state is based on a social contract. Instead experience shows that men are unequal in their powers and abilities: 'The Author of nature hath spread over mankind a natural aristocracy, which appears in every assembly of mankind.'[37] This 'gives authority to men of superior wisdom',[38] and makes others dependent on them. Natural disparities in the accumulation of property also lead to relations of dependence and hence to political power and dominion. The form of government best suited to a particular society will be discovered through historical experience. But, whatever its form, the authority thus acquired is a subordinate to the laws of nature:

> natural law ought to be the substance of the civil law; and the regulations it adds about things which the law of nature prescribes only in general and indefinite manner, ought to be conformable to the spirit and scope of the law of nature.[39]

A legislator who goes against the law of nature, who fails to identify the best means of achieving nature's ends, can and should be replaced. It is in this context that Turnbull's definition of law should be viewed. The legislator's command backed by sanction does not in itself provide a sufficient motive or obligation for following a particular course of action, but merely makes more specific and reinforces the existing obligation. Civil society, political authority and civil laws are all means to the same end, namely the happiness and perfection of man.

Turnbull was not concerned to set out the details of the laws of nature or of the civil state himself and was content to accept, by and large, Heineccius's account of them:

> And indeed the reason why I choose to translate this Author into our language, is because there is seldom any occasion to add to what he says, and almost never any ground of disputing against him.[40]

He felt that in the *Principles of Moral Philosophy* and the *Discourse upon the Nature and Origin of Moral and Civil Laws*, he had achieved his aim:

> to deduce the laws of nature, and the end of civil society and its laws, by an analysis of the human mind, from our internal principles and dispositions.[41]

The search for the laws of human nature is the core of Turnbull's work. He claimed that the methods of searching are exactly analogous to the methods of the natural sciences. Although not rigorous in his pursuit of experimental investigation, relying too often on teleological assumptions, the argument from design and quotations from like-minded moralists (thereby making his work less distinctive), Turnbull did apply the empirical method further than, and at least as consistently as, his sources such as Hutcheson had, so as to infer a system of part-psychological, part-moral laws of human nature. In this there are similarities with Hume's *Treatise of Human Nature, an Attempt to Introduce the Experimental Method of Reasoning into Moral Subjects*, published at the same time as Turnbull's main works. The vital difference between the two lay in Turnbull's complacency, his eagerness to go beyond the empirical data, his faith in Providence, or, indeed, his unsupported reliance on common sense. It took Hume's challenge to such complacency before Reid was to realise that his old teacher's reliance on common sense needed rigorous justification. So it came about that the work of Turnbull was considered too old-fashioned to be of use to the new Common Sense school of Scottish philosophy in their efforts to refute Hume. Nevertheless a study of his work, either as a point of comparison with other philosophers of the time, or as a serviceable model for a natural science of morals, may well prove to be a profitable exercise for the modern reader.

Notes

1. A chapter on Turnbull appears in J.McCosh, *The Scottish Philosophy* (London, Macmillan, 1875), pp.95-106. J. Laird was more critical in *Aberdeen University Review*, 14 (1926-27), pp.123-35. Turnbull's writing is put in its historical context in G.E. Davie, *Philosophy*, 40 (1965), pp.222-34 and C. Robbins, *The Eighteenth-Century Commonwealthman* (Cambridge, Mass., Harvard U.P., 1959), chapter 6. The fullest discussion of his philosophy is by D.F. Norton, *Journal of the History of Ideas*, 36 (1975), pp.701-16 and *David Hume—Common Sense Moralist, Sceptical Metaphysician* (Princeton, Princeton U.P., 1982), chapter 4, which includes an assessment of Turnbull's place in the Common Sense tradition. Turnbull's experimental method is considered in chapter 1 of D. Forbes, *Hume's Philosophical Politics* (Cambridge, CUP, 1975).
2. George Turnbull, *Theses Philosophicae de Scientiae Naturalis cum Philosophia Morali Conjunctione* (Aberdeen, J. Nicol, 1723).
3. George Turnbull, *Theses Academicae de Pulcherrima Mundi* (Aberdeen, J. Nicol, 1726).
4. Francis Hutcheson, *An Inquiry into the Original of our Ideas of Beauty and Virtue* (London, J. Darby, 1725), and *An Essay on the Nature and Conduct of the Passions, with Illustrations upon the Moral Sense* (London, J. Darby & T. Browne, 1728).
5. George Turnbull, *The Principles of Moral Philosophy* (London, John Noon, 1740), p.xii.
6. George Turnbull, *A Philosophical Inquiry Concerning the Connexion between the Doctrines and Miracles of Jesus Christ* (London, R. Willock, 1726); *Christianity neither False nor Useless* (London, R. Willock, 1732); *A Treatise on Ancient Painting* (London, A. Millar, 1740).
7. George Turnbull, *Christian Philosophy* (London, John Noon, 1740), published as vol.II of *Principles*.
8. J.G. Heineccius, *A Methodical System of Universal Law: or the Laws of Nature*

and Nations deduced from Certain Principles and applied to Proper Cases. Translated and illustrated with notes and supplements by George Turnbull. To which is added A Discourse upon the Nature and Origine of Moral and Civil Laws, 2 vols (London, G. Keith, 1741).

9. F. Hutcheson, *A Short Introduction to Moral Philosophy* (Glasgow, R. Foulis, 1747)—originally published in Latin in 1742. *A System of Moral Philosophy* (London, A. Millar, T. Longman, 1755).

10. Turnbull, *Principles*, pp.xv-xvi.

11. *Ibid.*, pp.iii, vii-x.

12. Turnbull, *Discourse*, p.247.

13. *Ibid.*, p.249.

14. Turnbull, *Principles*, p.12.

15. *Ibid.*, p.110. Turnbull spent the next dozen pages 'proving' the reality of the moral sense by reference to its being experienced by everyone as a fact.

16. *Ibid.*, pp.181-82.

17. *Ibid.*, p.97.

18. E.g. *ibid.*, p.202.

19. E.g. *ibid.*, pp.218, 125.

20. On whether Hutcheson viewed the moral sense as cognitive, compare W.K. Frankena, *Journal of the History of Ideas*, 16 (1955), pp.356-65, and D.F. Norton, *Dialogue*, 13 (1974), pp.3-23.

21. Turnbull, *Principles*, p.139, and *Discourse*, p.266. He discussed good education in many parts of his work, and published *Observations upon Liberal Education* (London, A. Millar, 1742).

22. Turnbull, *Discourse*, p.250.

23. *Ibid.*, p.262.

24. *Ibid.* Contrast Hume, *Treatise*, Book II, part iii, section 3, 'Reason is, and ought only to be the slave of the passions, and can never pretend to any other office than to serve and obey them', David Hume, *A Treatise of Human Nature* (1739) ed. L.A. Selby-Bigge (Oxford, Clarendon Press, 1888).

25. Turnbull, *Discourse*, p.269. This law helps to justify private property.

26. *Ibid.*, p.273.

27. *Ibid.*, p.290.

28. *Ibid.*, p.293.

29. *Ibid.*, p.315, a definition repeated almost exactly in Turnbull's remarks on the first chapter of Heineccius, *Methodical System*, vol.I, p.17.

30. Heineccius, *Methodical System*, vol.I, p.4.

31. *Ibid.*, p.62 (Turnbull's 'Remarks').

32. *Ibid.*

33. Turnbull, *Discourse*, p.261.

34. Heineccius, *Methodical System*, vol.II, p.223 (Turnbull's 'Supplement Concerning the Duties of Subjects and Magistrates').

35. *Ibid.*, p.117. (Turnbull's 'Remarks').

36. *Ibid.*, p.109.

37. Turnbull, *Discourse*, p.282; a view expressly rejected by Hutcheson, *Short Introduction*, Book II, chapter iv, section 4, p.143.

38. Turnbull, *Discourse*, p.283.

39. *Ibid.*, p.323. See also Heineccius, *Methodical System*, vol.II, p.156 (Turnbull's 'Remarks').

40. Heineccius, *Methodical System*, vol.I, p.243 (Turnbull's 'Remarks').

41. Turnbull, *Discourse*, p.325.

12

Reid, Natural Law and the Science of Man

Peter J. Diamond

University of Utah

Thomas Reid will no doubt always be known to students of eighteenth-century thought as a philosopher of the human mind who, with remarkable single-mindedness, attempted to refute the scepticism issuing from what he called 'the common theory of ideas'. Reid himself, with characteristic though unwarranted modesty, foretold as much toward the end of his long career when he insisted that the merit of his philosophy lay chiefly in having questioned the erroneous hypothesis that we do not really perceive things that are external, but only certain images and pictures of them imprinted upon the mind, which are called impressions and ideas.[1] Now, the merest acquaintance with Reid's published writing will suggest that it is difficult to underestimate his concern with the theory of ideas. But it is a mistake to take Reid entirely at his word or to envisage him as a one-dimensional anti-sceptic.[2] To do so is to risk losing sight of his participation in the contemporary Scottish debate over the nature and limits of the science of man. For the very point of Reid's investigations was to help depict such a science, which he believed would contribute to human improvement.

In this paper I shall attempt to shed some light on Reid's efforts to advance a science of man by examining the extent of his reliance upon the texts of seventeenth-century natural law. For eighteenth-century Scots such as Francis Hutcheson, George Turnbull, David Hume, Lord Kames and Adam Smith, the natural law writings of Grotius, Pufendorf and others were the primary sources of debate over the principles of human nature and of social living. Yet Reid had little to say about natural law in his published writing.[3] Concerned as he was with theories rather than systems of morals—the former, he explained, concern the structure of man's moral powers and have little connexion with the rules of moral conduct; the latter are intended to teach young men morals—he devoted but one chapter of his *Essays on the Active Powers of the Human Mind* to 'Systems of Natural Jurisprudence'. Although Reid published little about natural jurisprudence, I wish to argue

111

that the seventeenth-century natural jurists offered Reid a framework for his discussion of active power and moral liberty, a discussion which should be viewed in terms of his larger project of pursuing an improvement oriented science of human nature. For Reid believed that every man of sound mind is a moral agent, that he possesses 'a power over the determinations of his own will'. Only on these terms, he believed, can we make sense of the fact that man is an accountable being, capable of effecting moral improvement in himself and in others. Without the concept of moral liberty, he implied, we lose the very point of a science of man.

Reid's doctrine of moral liberty is based on what may be termed a reassertion of the notion of 'active power'. Here is a term the vulgar understand perfectly and employ daily in ordinary discourse, Reid declared, which philosophers have beclouded. They fail to realise that power 'is a thing so much of its own kind, and so simple in its nature, as not to admit of a logical definition'. As the *Active Powers* unfold, it becomes clear that Reid directed his criticism against all who failed to allow what every man knows by 'the light of his mind', that God and to a lesser degree man, possess active power. Reid was acutely aware that his common-sense defence of active power appears, at best, otiose. For if all men understand and use the concept of power, then no defence should be necessary. From a practical standpoint, Hume's contention that we have no idea of power is refuted by its patent absurdity. Moreover, to refute Hume's conclusions, which are 'deduced with great acuteness and ingenuity from principles commonly received by philosophers', Reid admitted, 'is difficult and appears ridiculous'. Why, then bother? Reid's answer is contained in the regard, both philosophical and practical, he paid to first principles. 'It is difficult', he responded, 'because we can hardly find principles to reason from, more evident than those we wish to prove; and it appears ridiculous, because as this author justly observes, next to the ridicule of denying an evident truth, is that of taking much pains to prove it'.[4] But the effort must be made because it is upon first principles that the extended reasoning of a science of man is founded.

Reid's doctrine of moral liberty was informed by the wide array of seventeenth-century theories of 'active virtue' which, in part, arose in reply to Hobbes's system of materialism. The notion of 'active virtue' is drawn from Cicero, and refers to the belief that 'the whole glory of virtue is in activity'. It reflects the resolve, which was shared by Turnbull and Reid, that 'all our thought and mental activity will be devoted either to planning for things that are morally right and that conduce to a good and happy life, or to the pursuits of science and learning'.[5] It was Reid's student, Dugald Stewart, who described the 'practical doctrines' of the modern natural law writers, Grotius, Pufendorf and Gershom Carmichael, as 'favourable to active virtue'. He meant that they had remained faithful to classical expositions of moral liberty, while opposing 'the absurd and illiberal systems which they supplanted'.[6] I shall keep to Stewart's usage, which was not unfamiliar to Reid, though its signification may be broadened to include such ethical rationalists as Ralph Cudworth, Samuel Clarke and William Wollaston, all of whom manifested much the same awareness of the practical importance of accounting for moral liberty. Reid directed his efforts along similarly Ciceronian lines, which he complemented by a scrupulous adherence to an inductive science of the human mind. His doctrine of moral liberty was an attempt—as Locke might have put it—to 'bottom' his study of man upon a common-sense under-standing of the limits of human agency. His accomplishment was remarkable because he managed to avoid the necessitarianism which threatened to over-whelm the unrestrained naturalism of Turnbull's moral philosophy[7] and which was manifest in the writings of Lord Kames—both of whom were heirs to the previous century's philosophies of active virtue.

In the course of propounding his doctrine of moral liberty, Reid paused to note that Hobbes was the first philosopher to maintain 'that liberty does not extend to the determinations of the will, but only to the actions consequent to its determination'.[8] Reid did not again refer explicitly to Hobbes's theory of liberty and so chose not to exploit the rhetorical opportunity of linking Hume and Joseph Priestley with Hobbes. There was little need for Reid to belabour what was obvious to contemporaries, for Hobbes's position, expressed in the 1650s in his debate with John Bramhall, Bishop of Derry, was the *locus classicus* for theories of philosophical necessity during the next one hundred and fifty years. As Stewart remarked in his *Dissertation Exhibiting the Progress of Metaphysical, Ethical, and Political Philosophy*, 'the most eminent moralists and politicians of the eighteenth century may be valued in the number of [Hobbes's] antagonists...It is from the works of Hobbes..that our later Necessitarians have borrowed the most formidable of those weapons with which they have combatted the doctrine of moral liberty'.[9] Had Reid wished to devote himself to discrediting Humean scepticism, *tout court*, the task could not have been better served than by drawing attention to the Hobbesian aspects of Hume's theory of necessity. For Hobbes's treat-ment of human necessity had effectively tainted what had hitherto been a theologically respectable aspect of Christian doctrine. 'Let this opinion be once radicated in the minds of men', Bramhall concluded, 'that there is no true liberty, and that all things come to pass inevitably, and it will utterly destroy the study of piety'. God will be deemed responsible for evil and sin; prayer will be rendered useless. 'Either allow liberty, or destroy Church as well as commonwealth, religion as well as policy.'[10] Subsequent commentators, Cudworth and Clarke among them, understood Hobbes's theory of necessity as a function of his materialism and, consequently, as wedded to atheism.

Yet there is reason to suggest that there was method in Reid's reluctance to develop the connexion between Hobbes and his successors. Unlike James Beattie, for example, Reid did not believe that necessitarianism was a serious threat to public morals. For our speculative and practical faculties of percep-tion, as Bishop Butler explained, are 'intended by nature, to inform us in the theory of things, and instruct us how we are to behave, and what we are to expect in consequence of our behaviour'.[11] Consequently, there is little reason to fear, added Reid, 'that the conduct of men, with regard to the concerns of the present life, will ever be much affected, either by the doctrine of necessity, or by scepticism'.[12] Beattie, on the other hand, who was never unwilling to seize a perceived rhetorical advantage, declared that Hobbes and Hume were alike 'enemies to our faith' whose respective theories of necessity—Beattie in fact comes close to calling the two men 'Fatalists'—were the ground of infidelity and atheism.[13] A rhetoric of piety such as Beattie's had little bearing upon Reid's concern with describing the limits of human agency. It remains the case, of course, that Hobbes, Hume and Priestley each espoused an essentially naturalist approach to the study of man insofar as they attempted to account for all mental phenomena by a method appropriate as well to natural philosophy. Despite the fact that their naturalism now appears an obvious source of comparison, it should be recalled that Reid was preoccupied with the theory of ideas as the source of contemporary philosophical confusion; Hobbes's system of materialism, unlike the quite different theories of Hume and Priestley, had basically metaphysical, not empirical, foundations. For this reason Reid may have regarded Hobbes's doctrine as belonging to the different philosophical interests of an earlier generation. Reid objected to Humean scepticism less because he thought it imperilled Christian faith than because he believed it failed according to the one criterion according to which a science of man must be measured: it failed to provide an account of human action grounded in deliberation and choice, an account upon which a useful, improvement-oriented science of human nature could be based.

Reid's lack of apparent interest in either Hobbes's theory of necessity or his moral scepticism should historically thwart an attempt to argue that Reid regarded Hume, or, for that matter, Priestley,[14] as the reincarnated Hobbes. Reid should not be grouped with Beattie and the other common-sense philosophers as having been as alarmed by Hume's epistemological and metaphysical scepticism as Shaftesbury, Hutcheson and Turnbull were by the moral scepticism of Hobbes and Mandeville.[15] Nevertheless, it is impossible to make historical sense of Reid's discussion of moral liberty or his rejection of necessitarianism without taking account of the arguments raised in the Hobbes-Bramhall debate and the subsequent attempts by Hobbes's natural law and latitudinarian opponents to describe man's moral agency.

It is important to notice that Reid addressed the question of free-will in the course of providing an account of man's moral agency. Indeed, the threat posed by Hobbes's system of materialism, which surfaced in the Hobbes-Bramhall debate, may be described succinctly as the loss of the concept of moral agency. By defining deliberation as the succession of contending appetites and aversions, and will as merely the last appetite in the process of deliberation, Hobbes had eliminated the notion that our actions in some sense depend upon ourselves, and are not the result of physical laws which cannot be resisted. Although Hobbes's account of authority and obligation was based upon consent—'wills...make the essence of all covenants'—his theory of the will was incompatible with his own requirement that there is 'no obligation on any man, which ariseth not from some act of his own'.[16] For Hobbes insisted that the will is unfree and is causally determined by appetites to which animals, no less than persons, are subject. Although the Hobbes-Bramhall debate was an important source for subsequent discussion of the free-will question, Reid was less interested in that debate and in seventeenth-century responses to Hobbes's materialism, *per se*, than in the extent to which the available replies to Hobbes helped restore to philosophical discussion the notion of moral agency which had been eliminated by Hume's science of man and Priestley's 'modern system of materialism'. To view the matter from Reid's perspective: Hobbes's science promised a measure of social control which derived from an ability to deduce, from an etiology of entirely material stimuli, what men set out to do. Such control was purchased by discounting man's common-sense awareness of a power to know and obtain what is good. Hobbes in effect denied man's ability to act as an autonomous agent of the Deity, thus precluding the possibility of his incurring and creating obligations in the course of social existence. Reid would understand himself to be faced with much the same problem in confronting Hume and Priestley; their theories as well effectively denied man's ability to perform 'the manly duties of social life'.[17] From Reid's standpoint, Hobbes, Hume and Priestley each emasculated the notion of human action by denying man the capability of acting morally.

Reid, I believe, consequently understood Hobbes's critics to be confronted with the task of providing an account of man's capacity for moral action. Bramhall had attempted to provide a theory of moral agency in the course of answering the moral 'inconveniences' of Hobbes's system, by endowing the will with the power to begin motion. But his account was ensconced in a language of occult faculties and powers. Bramhall's reply was succeeded by a wealth of responses concerned with rebutting Hobbes's so-called atheism without recourse to a scholastic idiom. As we have noted, one such response of importance to Reid was made by the natural law writers, another by the Cambridge Platonists, particularly by Cudworth and his latitudinarian follower, Samuel Clarke. Although natural law philosophy and Cambridge Platonism are species of ethical intuitionism (both hold that man has an immediate awareness of moral values), they have very different foundations. For example, Pufendorf and Richard Cumberland held that natural law is evident in the constitution of the external world, and knowable through the senses.[18] Cudworth supplanted Hobbes's materialism with an autonomously existing 'intellectual' world in which moral truths are apprehended directly by the human mind. Nevertheless, both were congenial to Reid because they offered an account of the human mind which expressed a commitment to Cicero's notion of 'active virtue'. In other words, both concentrated upon man's power to act according to the rational determinations of his conscience or moral sense.

Their reliance on ancient philosophy appeared in their restoration, in light of Hobbes's materialism, of the Aristotelian division of the faculties of the human mind into understanding and will. The powers attributed to the two faculties varied according to the demands of their respective theories of knowledge, as did the precise relationship between them. But the kernel of the argument remained constant: moral agency, it was asserted, by empiricists and rationalists alike, depends upon freedom of the will, which in turn is related to the agent's rational power of judgment and choice. Hobbes, in effect, had denied an active role to both faculties. Reid adopted the distinction in response to Hume's theory of ideas. Although I shall not consider the problem Hume's theory of ideas posed to the notion of active power and to freedom of the will, we should note that Reid faced two difficulties in light of Hume's undeniable assertion that our conception of active power is not acquired by sensation or reflection. Since Reid could not agree with Hume that we never therefore have any idea of power, he had, firstly, to restore the notion of active power to moral discourse and, secondly, in view of Hume's naturalism, to describe its nature so as to ensure man's agency. Reid resolved the first problem by claiming that we infer the existence of an active power in ourselves from a conviction or belief, arising from our constitution, of such power. In treating the second problem, Reid took the relationship between understanding and will as his starting-point. It is evident, he declared, 'that, as reason without active power can do nothing, so active power without reason has no guide to direct it to any end'. Beyond that, he acknowledged, we do not know what connexion there may be between reason and power.[19] Although Reid claimed that the evidence of our minds is sufficient to establish the belief that we are the efficient causes of our voluntary actions, he professed ignorance of the precise nature of efficient causality.

Hobbes's critics also marshalled the Stoics' design argument in order to warrant their own efforts to depict human agency. Hobbes had promised to 'leave men but as they are, in doubt and dispute',[20] and had, indeed, challenged the teleological conception of nature which had so prominently been a part of natural law from the Stoics to the time of Richard Hooker. Hooker had insisted that all the acts of God and man necessarily work toward some fore-ordained end. Further, 'no certain end could ever be attained, unless the actions whereby it is attained were regular; that is to say, made suitable, fit and correspondent unto their end, by some canon, rule or law'. Hooker had found that 'the wise and learned among the very heathens' all acknowledged the existence of a first cause wherein '*counsel* is used, *reason* followed, a *way* observed; that is to say, constant *order* and *law* is kept'.[21] But Hobbes cut the laws of nature off from their divine source by arguing that the universe and man are nothing more than matter in motion. 'But for an *utmost* end', he argued 'in which the ancient *philosophers* have placed felicity, and disputed much concerning the way thereto, there is no such thing in this world, nor way to it, more than to Utopia: for while we live, we have desired, and desire presupposeth a further end.' The laws of nature concern the means by which man may preserve his life on earth; they supply 'no natural knowledge of man's estate after death'.[22] Confronted by Hobbes's materialist system and its fundamental moral scepticism, his critics argued that man's faculties are providentially ordered for his well being; that, to recall Cicero, he is 'designed by nature for activity'.[23] Thus Jean Barbeyrac, summarising the groundwork laid, not only by Cicero but by the modern natural jurists from Grotius onwards, observed that the idea of a Creator, 'boundless in Power, Wisdom, and Goodness' and the 'Idea of ourselves, as intelligent, reasonable, and sociable Creatures' would 'if well looked into, and compared together in their whole Extent ... always furnish us with steady Grounds of Duty, and sure Rules of Conduct'.[24] And Cudworth, responding some five decades earlier to Hobbes's materialism, grounded his belief that men (unlike brutes) are endowed with an inward active principle enabling them to act morally upon the observation of 'how all things in this great mundane machine or animal (as the ancients would have it) are contrived not only for the beauty of the whole, but also for the good of every part in it, that is endued with life and sense'.[25]

So far so good. But neither position was entirely satisfactory to Reid. He followed the natural jurists in arguing that moral agency must be conceived in terms that reflect man's natural sociability: that man's conception of particular moral obligations and duties reflects the manifold circumstances of his social existence. In this he joined Pufendorf, who held that human action consists of 'that motion only which proceeds from and is directed by those faculties which the Creator has given mankind above the brutes,—I mean that which is undertaken with intellect lighting the way, and at the bidding of the will'.[26] Pufendorf endowed the understanding and the will each with two powers: one of necessary apprehension and approbation by which man grasps the necessary principles of the law of nature, another of judgment and choice which is free and responsible for the examination and implementation of particular actions.[27] It should be noted, however, that Pufendorf and other pre-Lockian natural jurists did not recognise a problem of knowledge. In detailing the first set of powers, he never doubted that man can attain certain knowledge of the general precepts of natural law. Reid, of course, began his account of moral action by examining the ideal theorists' attempts to solve the problem of knowledge; in this respect Reid's intentions were quite dissimilar from those of Pufendorf and other seventeenth-century natural jurists. Their interests were allied, however, insofar as they concerned themselves with describing the nature and circumstances of moral judgment. While Pufendorf presumed that man is capable of attaining certain knowledge of general moral precepts, he recognised that knowledge derived from man's second set of powers, from judgments of 'the human tribunal' (forum humanum), are subject to the vagaries of an often confused understanding, and to the contingencies of social existence. Hence the importance of improving man's judgment through education and the sanction of law.[28]

It was to this conception of moral action, the conjunction of the understanding as a deliberative, improveable, judging faculty and the will, that Reid was indebted. For Reid, as for the natural jurists, the first principles of moral action are available to all men of ordinary understanding; their judgments concerning particular moral actions, where specific facts come before 'the human tribunal', require that:

> we learn to observe the connections of things, and the consequences of our actions; and, taking an extended view of our existence, past, present, and future, we correct our first notions of good and ill, and form the conception of what is good or ill upon the whole; which must be estimated, not from the present feeling, or from the present animal desire or aversion, but from a due consideration of its consequences, certain or probable, during the whole of our existence.[29]

Moral judgments are in part informed by man's experience of what constitutes *honestum*, the 'right and honourable in human conduct'.[30] Reid and the natural jurists shared a commitment to describing and—as moral educators—to generalising about human conduct and the circumstances in which it ought to be judged right or wrong. The problem, in other words, posed for modern natural law philosophers by Epictetus, of discerning things put by nature *eph'hemin* (within our power), was resolved by supplying the intellect with experience; only thus, they believed, can man cultivate his ability to judge the parameters of his own and others' moral responsibility. Reid accepted the natural law argument in holding that man's conception of duty or moral obligation is not purely some 'real quality of the action considered by itself, nor of the agent considered without respect to the action', but is formed by deliberating upon the relationship between the one and the other as it unfolds in the course of man's social existence.[31]

But Reid could not agree with the jurisprudential systems of either Hutcheson or Turnbull, for whom the first principles of morals depend upon the very structure of the human constitution—from our desires and appetites and the moral sense. To argue that taste or feeling, not reason, determines the ends of human action, was, to Reid's mind, to err on two counts. First, to argue thus is to deny that the principles of morals are necessary truths, which contradicts the way we ordinarily regard our ethical determinations.[32] Second, it is to neglect the fact that we determine the ends of human action by *reasoning*, and this involves learning to 'extend our view both forward and backward...reflect[ing] upon what is past, and, by the lamp of experience, discern[ing] what will probably happen in time to come'. By these means we 'find that many things which we eagerly desired, were too dearly purchased, and that things grievous for the present, like nauseous medicines, may be salutary in the issue'.[33]

But neither could Reid approve of either Cudworth's claim that there are objective ethical qualities in actions, or Clarke's belief that there are eternal and necessary differences and relations between acts and circumstances. These amounted to misguided attempts to define what is incapable of definition. Yet Reid also sought to reject the subjectivist theories of Hutcheson and Turnbull by capturing the force of referring to a proposition's 'truth-in-itself' or to an action as 'good-in-its-nature.'[34] Accordingly Reid held that the evidence of our moral first principles is intuitive; no sooner are they understood than they are believed by every man whose 'understanding and moral faculty are ripe'. 'The judgement', he explained, 'follows the apprehension of them necessarily, and both are equally the work of nature, and the result of our original powers. There is no searching for evidence; no weighing of arguments; the proposition is not deduced or inferred from another; it has the *light of truth in itself*'.

D.D. Raphael suggests that Reid's attack on Hutcheson was half-hearted because Reid purportedly was not convinced that Hutcheson was wrong. Moreover, Reid himself often spoke as if first principles depend upon a man's constitution. To rebut Hutcheson, Raphael argues, Reid would have had to show that there exist *a priori* moral axioms which are known to be necessarily and universally true. Raphael believes that not only did Reid fail to do this, but that he missed the point of the rationalist position.[35] But Reid not only understood the rationalists' intention to establish the objectivity of moral facts—indeed, (as I shall point out) he attempted to salvage something from Hume's attack on the argument—but, as we have observed, he employed its language to counter Hutcheson's feeling theory of ethics. In Book III of the *Treatise*, Hume had objected that if an action is presumed to be good in its nature, the judgment of the agent cannot make it bad. 'To suppose that the mere regard to the virtue of the action is that which rendered it virtuous, is to reason in a circle.'[36] Reid countered by recalling the scholastic distinction between actions that are 'materially' good, that is, good in their own nature, and those that are 'formally' good, that is, performed with a good intention. Reid was not willing to dispense with the notion of material goodness, which was established in ordinary language, because it serves to designate those actions 'which ought to be done by those who have the power and opportunity, and the capacity of perceiving their obligation to it'.[37] Reid viewed the distinction, in other words, as having a basis in practical morality. At the same time, Reid insisted that we must have the idea of formal goodness in order to preserve the concept of moral agency. 'The abstract notion of moral good and ill', Reid added, 'would be of no use to direct our life, if we had not the power of applying it to particular actions, and determining what is morally good, and what is morally ill'.[38] To put the matter starkly, Reid realised that the tendency of any theory of eternal and immutable morality is antinomian, for it neglects the circumstances of human action. At the very least, he was well aware that the extreme rationalism advanced by Cudworth and Clarke had the effect of beclouding man's understanding of moral agency. Hume's rhetorical argument was ample proof of that. Reid's distinction between material and formal goodness was thus a *tertium quid* between ethical rationalism and Hutcheson's subjectivism.[39]

To summarise: Reid believed that the doctrine of moral liberty is attested to by experience and is supported by the common sense of mankind. Men unfailingly act upon their belief that they are responsible for those acts which depend upon their will. They feel remorse and guilt when they fail to act according to their better nature. And they excuse all those who, though they act voluntarily, have little or no power of self-government. Children, idiots, those subject to a fit of passion or to the rage of madness, are deemed more or less innocent of the ill which may result from their actions. These facts of common sense are perfectly compatible with the system of liberty. The burden of proof, Reid argued, must consequently rest with the advocates of necessity. 'If it cannot be proved that we always act from necessity, there is no need of arguments on the other side, to convince us that we are free agents.'[40] Nor is there any reason to fear that the doctrine of necessity will influence men's conduct.

Appearances to the contrary notwithstanding, Reid did not regard his account of human agency to be without practical importance. For Reid was convinced that theories of necessity, which, after all, are merely by-products of theories which view every aspect of human life as naturalistically explicable, are impediments to the proper understanding of human conduct. Just as

Hume and Priestley believed that it is impossible to devise a science of human nature without acknowledging the doctrine of necessity, so Reid believed that the human improvement such a science would facilitate could not take place according to theories which contradict the facts of common sense.

Notes

1. Reid's self-assessment appears in a letter to James Gregory, quoted in Dugald Stewart's *Dissertation: Exhibiting the Progress of Metaphysical, Ethical, and Political Philosophy*, in the *Collected Works of Dugald Stewart*, ed. Sir William Hamilton, 11 vols (Edinburgh, Thomas Constable, 1854), vol.I, p.457.
2. Reid is so envisaged by Norman Kemp Smith, *The Philosophy of David Hume* (London, Macmillan, 1941), pp. 3-14.
3. For an excellent discussion of Reid's unpublished lectures on natural juris-prudence, see Knud Haakonssen, 'Reid's politics: a natural law theory', *Reid Studies*, 1 (1986-87), pp.10-27.
4. *Essays on the Active Powers of the Human Mind*, Essay I, chapter ii (hereinafter *AP*, I, ii) in *The Works of Thomas Reid, D.D.*, ed. Sir William Hamilton, 8th edition (Edinburgh, J. Thin, 1895), p.518.
5. See Cicero, *De Officiis*, trans. Walter Miller (Cambridge, Mass., Harvard U.P., 1913), vol. I. vi. 19, p.21 and *De Finibus*, trans. H. Rackham (Cambridge, Mass., Harvard U.P., 1914), vol.V, xiv. 38, p.437.
6. Stewart, *Collected Works*, vol.I, p.79.
7. Reid differed at length with Kames over the latter's necessitarian views. Nothing specific is known of Reid's opinion of Turnbull's position, but it may be surmised that he found Turnbull's naturalism inconsistent with his assertion of moral liberty.
8. Reid, *AP*, IV, i, p.601.
9. Stewart, *Collected Works*, vol.I, pp.80, 84.
10. Thomas Hobbes, *The English Works of Thomas Hobbes*, ed. Sir William Mole-sworth, 11 vols (London, John Bohn, 1839-45), vol.V, pp.197-98.
11. *The Works of Joseph Butler*, ed. W.E. Gladstone, 2 vols (Oxford, Clarendon Press, 1897), vol.I, pp.156, 138-60.
12. Reid, *AP*, IV, xi, p.636.
13. James Beattie, *Elements of Moral Science*, 2nd edition, 2 vols (Edinburgh, Creed, 1817), pp.207-9 and *An Essay on the Nature and Immutability of Truth in Opposition to Sophistry and Scepticism* in *Essays* (Edinburgh, William Creech, 1776), pp.191-238.
14. It is clear, however, that Reid was willing to allow the comparison, from the standpoint of natural philosophy, in the case of Priestley. See Reid's unpublished manuscript, 'Some Observations on the Modern System of Materialism', AUL, MS 3061/1/4.
15. See David Fate Norton, *David Hume: Common-Sense Moralist* (Princeton, Princeton U.P., 1982), pp.196-97.
16. Thomas Hobbes, *Leviathan*, ed. Michel Oakeshott (Oxford, Blackwell, 1946), p.141.
17. 'Manly duties of social life' belongs to the eighteenth-century idiom of active virtue. See Stewart, *Collected Works*, vol.I, p.179.

18. See Murray Forsyth, 'The place of Richard Cumberland in the history of natural law doctrine', *Journal of the History of Philosophy*, XX (1982), pp.25-26.

19. Reid, *AP*, IV, v, p.615. Jerome Weinstock accuses Reid of equivocating over the precise connexion between the will and faculty of judgment, but Reid intentionally avoided defining a relationship of which he believed man ignorant. See J. Weinstock, 'Reid's definition of freedom', in Stephen F. Barker and Tom L. Beauchamp, eds, *Thomas Reid: Critical Interpretations* (Philadelphia, University City Science Centre, 1976), p.97.

20. Hobbes, *English Works*, vol. IV, p.1.

21. Richard Hooker, *The Works of That Learned and Judicious Divine, Mr Richard Hooker, with an Account of His Life and Death, by Isaac Walton*, 2 vols (Oxford, OUP, 1845), vol.I, pp.148-50.

22. Hobbes, *English Works*, vol.IV, p.33 and *Leviathan*, p.96.

23. Cicero, *De Finibus*, vol.V, xxi. 58, p.459.

24. Jean Barbeyrac, *An Historical and Critical Account of the Science of Morality* in Samuel Pufendorf, *The Law of Nature and Nations*, trans. Basil Kennet, 5th edition (London, J. & J. Bonwick, 1749), p.10.

25. Ralph Cudworth, *The True Intellectual System of the Universe: wherein all the Reason of Atheism is Confuted, and its Impossibility Demonstrated, with a Treatise concerning Eternal and Immutable Morality*, ed. J.L. Mosheim, trans. J. Harrison, 3 vols (London, T. Tegg, 1845), vol.III, pp.597-99.

26. See Barbeyrac's notes to Hugo Grotius, *The Rights of War and Peace*, trans. Basil Kennet with the notes of Jean Barbeyrac (London, W. Innys, 1738), pp.10-11; Jo.Got. Heineccius, *A Methodical System of Universal Law*, trans. George Turnbull, 2 vols (London, G. Keith, 1763), vol.I, p.10.

27. Samuel Pufendorf, *De Officio Hominis et Civis Juxta Legem Naturalem Libri Duo*, trans. Frank Gardner Moore, 2 vols (New York, OUP, 1927), vol. II, p.3.

28. Pufendorf, *Law of Nature and Nations*, pp.19-20, 27-28. I am indebted to Leonard Krieger (*The Politics of Discretion* (Chicago, 1965), pp.68-73) for the following summary of Pufendorf's theory of knowledge. See Richard Cumberland, *A Treatise on the Laws of Nature* (London, R. Phillips, 1727), p.94 and Heineccius, *Methodical System*, vol.I, pp.22-24.

29. See Pufendorf, *Law of Nature and Nations*, p.20.

30. Reid, *AP*, vol.III, ii, pp.580-81.

31. *Ibid*, vol. III, v., p.588.

32. Reid, *Essays on the Intellectual Powers of Man* (hereafter *IP*), VI, iv, in *Works of Thomas Reid*, p.455. Raphael's analysis (see David D. Raphael, *The Moral Sense* (London, OUP, 1947), pp.158-60) of Reid's argument is shrewd, but compare note 35.

33. Reid, *AP*, vol.III, ii, p.580.

34. Reid, *AP*, vol.VI, iv, p.434.

35. Raphael, *Moral Sense*, pp.160, 167. Raphael maintains that Reid misunderstood Clarke's motives because Reid believed 'right' and 'wrong' 'virtuous' and 'vicious', are indefinable. Clearly Reid objected to Clarke's Cartesian belief that the criterion of truth is to have a clear and distinct idea of moral propositions. But Reid did not fail to understand that Clarke sought to emphasise the objectivity of moral facts. On the contrary, he believed that such an abstract notion of moral goodness contributes little to our understanding of moral relations.

36. David Hume, *A Treatise of Human Nature*, ed. L.A. Selby-Bigge (Oxford, Clarendon Press, 1888), p.478.

37. Reid, *AP*, vol.V, iv, p.649.

38. *Ibid.*, vol.III, p.589.
39. Reid's position is most clearly expressed in the following passage: 'Every judgment is, in its own nature, true or false; and though it depends upon the fabric of the mind, whether it have such a judgment or not, it depends not upon that fabric whether the judgment be true or not. A true judgment will be true, whatever be the fabric of the mind; but a particular structure and fabric is necessary in order to our perceiving that truth. Nothing can be said of mere feelings, because the attributes of true or false do not belong to them.' See *ibid*, vol.V, vii, p.676.
40. Reid, *ibid.*, vol.III, v, pp.588-89; vol.III, iii, p.583; vol.III, viii, p.595.

13

David Hume and Principal George Campbell

Henry Sefton

University of Aberdeen

William Law Mathieson asserted that 'the England of that day produced no such philosopher as Hume; no such opponent of his scepticism as Campbell'.[1] Some fifty years later Lloyd F. Bitzer described Campbell as a 'pupil' of Hume, at least insofar as his *Philosophy of Rhetoric* was concerned.[2] In a recent article Dennis R. Bormann dealt ably with Campbell, Hume and the *Philosophy of Rhetoric*, so this paper will be concerned only with Principal Campbell's *Dissertation on Miracles*, considered as a reply to David Hume.[3]

In a letter to Campbell dated 7 June 1762 Hume explains how he first became interested in the question of miracles:

> I was walking in the cloisters of the Jesuits' College of La Fleche (a town in which I passed two years of my youth) and was engaged in conversation with a Jesuit of some parts and learning, who was relating to me and urging some nonsensical miracle performed lately in their Convent—when I was tempted to dispute against him.

This incident took place at some time during the two years 1735 to 1737 while he was writing his *Treatise of Human Nature*, and naturally Hume's mind was very much upon that at the time of the conversation. An argument occurred to him which, he tells Campbell, 'very much gravelled my companion'. The Jesuit had then recovered somewhat and had observed 'that it was impossible for the argument to have any solidity, because it operated equally against the Gospel as the Catholic Miracles'.[4] Hume politely admitted that this was a sufficient answer, but clearly he was not convinced. However, when he was preparing the *Treatise* for publication, he decided to omit 'Reasonings concerning Miracles'. He tells his kinsman, Lord Kames, that the piece 'will give too much offence, even as the world is disposed at present', but he sends Kames a copy and asks for his opinion on the argument and the style.[5]

To say that Hume was disappointed at the reception accorded to the *Treatise* when it was published in 1739 would be an understatement. He had attempted to avoid religious controversy in the hope that his philosophy would receive serious consideration. 'My Principles', he informed Kames, 'are ... so remote from all the vulgar sentiments on this subject, that were they to take place, they wou'd produce almost a total Alteration in Philosophy'.[6] In an account of his own life Hume ruefully recalls: 'Never literary attempt was more unfortunate than my Treatise of Human Nature. It fell dead-born from the press'. He was, however, convinced that this cold response arose 'more from the manner than the matter'.[7] He therefore 'cast the first part of that work anew in the Enquiry concerning Human Understanding'. This was published in 1748 as *Philosophical Essays Concerning Human Understanding.*

Hume's thoughts on miracles now appeared as Section X of the *Philosophical Essays* and soon brought him as much attention as he could have wished. This and the later *Enquiry Concerning the Principles of Morals* (1751) led to an attempt to have Hume censured and disciplined by the General Assembly of the Church of Scotland in 1755. But the General Assembly contented themselves with a general condemnation of the principles of infidelity and immorality avowed in lately published books. This did not satisfy Hume's opponents and a pamphlet entitled *Infidelity a Proper Object of Censure* was published immediately before the opening of the General Assembly of 1756 by a retired army chaplain called George Anderson. Anderson argued that the Church was obliged to censure avowed infidels who were baptised persons and to cast them out of the Church if they were irreclaimable.[8] The matter was raised in the Committee on Overtures and an overture was proposed calling for an inquiry into Hume's writings. For two days the debate raged. The point at issue was the necessity or expediency of inquiry, not whether Hume's works were free from error. His errors were assumed, but was he accountable to the Church? It was urged that Hume was not a Christian and therefore the Church had no authority over him. To this it was replied that he had been baptised and had never repudiated his baptism. Eventually it was decided by 50 votes to 17 not to transmit the overture to the General Assembly and accordingly no official Church inquiry was made into Hume's work.[9]

However much Hume's opinions were disliked, he himself was remarkably popular, and included among his friends and associates several ministers of the Church of Scotland, as is shown by a letter written to Hume by Thomas Reid:

> Your friendly adversaries Drs. Campbell and Gerard return their compliments to you respectfully. A Little Philosophical Society here of which all three are members is much indebted to you for its entertainment. Your company would, although we are all good Christians be more acceptable than that of St. Athanasius. And since we cannot have you upon the bench you are brought oftener than any other man to the bar, accused and defended with great zeal but without bitterness. If you write no more in morals, politicks, or metaphysicks, I am affraid we shall be at a loss for subjects.[10]

The Philosophical Society of Aberdeen had been formed in 1758, and Hume was probably in the founders' minds when they drew up Rule 17 which states that one aim is 'the examination of false schemes of Philosophy and false methods of Philosophizing'.[11] Despite Reid's letter it would appear from the minutes, and indeed from the works of the members of the Club, that Hume was more often accused than defended.

The minutes of the Philosophical Club for 14 July 1761 record:

> There was no discourse from Principal Campbel who being engaged in a work for the public, the meeting dispensed with his discoursing untill the month of January next when he will be liable for two discourses if he does not deliver a discourse betwixt & that time.[12]

The work on which Principal Campbell was engaged had originally been a sermon delivered before the Synod of Aberdeen on 9 October 1760. Synod sermons in the eighteenth century were regarded as an appropriate vehicle for comment on matters of recent or current controversy, and often gave rise to further controversy when published. Campbell informs us that he had been desired to publish the sermon but had judged it necessary 'to new-model the discourse'.[13] Its remodelled form is the *Dissertation on Miracles* first published in 1762.

In the Advertisement to the *Dissertation* Campbell is at pains to point out that it is not his only, nor even his chief design 'to refute the reasoning and objections of Mr. Hume with regard to miracles: the chief design ... is to set the principal argument for Christianity in its proper light'. Nonetheless he asserts that the *Essay on Miracles* 'deserves to be considered as one of the most dangerous attacks that have been made on our religion'. He pays tribute in several places to his adversary, describing him as ingenious, subtle and powerful, and comments: 'with such an adversary I should on very unequal terms enter the lists, had I not the advantage of being on the side of truth'.[14]

Hume had written:

> A miracle is a violation of the laws of nature; and as a firm and unalterable experience has established these laws, the proof against a miracle from the very nature of the fact, is as entire as any argument from experience can possibly be imagined.[15]

To this Campbell replied:

> In the Essay there is frequent mention of the word *experience* and much use made of it. It is strange that the author has not favoured us with the definition of a term of so much moment to his argument.[16]

Campbell said that Hume had used the word in two very different senses, and so he distinguished two kinds of experience: our own personal experience founded in memory, and our derived experience founded in testimony. Hume's argument had depended on the first of these meanings when he spoke of miracles being 'contrary to experience'. This had meant something which we had not yet personally experienced, and so Hume was able to beg the question by arguing as to what could not be, without determining whether it actually had been. The evidence for the Gospel miracles, said Campbell, was not restricted to the writers of the four Gospels but was determined by the very existence of the Church. There was no reason to associate either fraud or credulity with the first converts. Yet there existed no evidence from either friend or foe which did not associate Jesus with miracles. Any man who argued that miracles were essentially impossible should have dealt with the evidence which plainly stated that they had been witnessed.[17]

Hume had concluded his essay with an ironical paragraph:

> We may conclude that the Christian Religion not only was at first attended with miracles, but even at this day cannot be believed by any reasonable person without one. Mere reason is insufficient to convince us of its veracity: And whoever is moved by Faith to assent to it, is conscious of a continued miracle in his own person, which subverts all the principles of his understanding and gives him a determination to believe what is more contrary to custom and experience.[18]

To this Campbell replied: 'An author is never so sure of writing unanswerably as when he writes altogether unintelligibly'. If any meaning can be gathered from 'that strange assemblage of words' it must be either that there are none in the world who believe the Gospel, or that there is no want of miracles in our time. If the second is true, experience can hardly be urged as a reason for not believing in miracles. If the first is true, why all this ado to refute opinions which nobody entertains?[19]

There were many replies to Hume. E.C. Mossner has counted two published in 1751, four in 1752, five in 1753, three in 1754 and two in 1755.[20] Campbell's reply was therefore rather late but it is also unique because it is the only one on which Hume commented. His normal practice was to refuse to enter into controversy and to leave his writings to speak for themslves. But even in this case Hume's comments were not made publicly, but were made in a private letter to a friend of Campbell, Dr Hugh Blair, one of the ministers of Edinburgh. Campbell had submitted his manuscript before publication to Blair and readily consented to Blair's suggestion that it be shown to Hume. Hume's comments on the *Dissertation* are made in a letter to Blair which was, with his permission, transmitted to Campbell. The letter is printed as part of the preface to the enlarged third edition of the *Dissertation* which was published in 1797, twenty-one years after Hume's death.

In the Preface to the edition of 1797 Campbell makes this comment on Hume's letter:

> I was not a little surprised, that I could find nothing in reply to my refutation of his abstract and metaphysical argument on the evidence of testimony, displayed with so much ostentation in the first part of his Essay, the production of which argument, to the public seems to have been his principal motive for writing on the subject. All his observations of any moment were levelled against the answers which had been given to his more familiar and popular topics, employed in the second part.[21]

In this Campbell seems to have taken a more sanguine view of his own performance than was really justified, for Hume does not really seem to have accepted Campbell's argument about the two kinds of experience. Certainly he did not modify his argument in subsequent editions of the *Essay* and the changes made were merely on small points of detail.[22]

In his letter to Blair, Hume had complained a little about the tone of Campbell's *Dissertation*. Some passages in it seem to him to be more worthy of Warburton and his followers than of so ingenious an author. It would appear, however, that before publication Campbell had been able to make some alterations, for in his letter to Campbell dated 7 June 1762 from Edinburgh Hume tells him:

> Any little symptoms of vehemence, of which I formerly used the freedom to complain, when you favoured me with a sight of the manuscript, are either removed, or explained away, or atoned for by civilities, which are far beyond what I have any title to pretend to.[23]

It was for this reason that he thanked Campbell for 'the civil and obliging manner' in which he had conducted the dispute against him.

Amidst all this civility perhaps the most sincere tribute Hume could pay to Campbell is the somewhat oblique one of remarking: 'I own to you that I never felt so violent an inclination to defend myself as at present, when I am thus fairly challenged by you.'[24] Hume had little or no time for his other opponents.[25] Campbell at least had earned his respect.

Notes

1. W. Law Mathieson, *The Awakening of Scotland* (Glasgow, James MacLehose & Sons, 1910), p.203. George Campbell (1719-1796) M.A. (King's College, Aberdeen) 1738; Minister at Banchory-Ternan 1748-1757; one of the Ministers of Aberdeen 1757-1771; Principal of Marischal College 1759-1796; D.D. (King's College, Aberdeen) 1764; Professor of Divinity at Marischal College and Minister at Greyfriars' Aberdeen 1771-1795.
2. Lloyd F. Bitzer, ed., *The Philosophy of Rhetoric* (Carbondale, Southern Illinois, 1963), Introduction.
3. D.R. Bormann, 'Some 'Common Sense' about Campbell, Hume and Reid: the extrinsic evidence', *The Quarterly Journal of Speech*, 71 (1985), pp.395- 421. I am grateful to Professor Bormann for a copy of his article and for helpful conversation on the topic.
4. AUL, MS 651 contains a transcription by Campbell of this letter. It is printed in the 3rd and later editions of the *Dissertation*.
5. T.H. Green and T.H. Grose, eds, *The Philosophical Works of David Hume* (London, Longmans & Co., 1875), vol.III, p.51. Cited hereafter as *Phil. Wks*.
6. R. Klibansky and E.C. Mossner, eds, *New Letters of David Hume* (Oxford, Clarendon Press, 1954), p.3.
7. *Phil. Wks*, pp.2 and following.
8. George Anderson, *Infidelity a Proper Object of Censure* (Glasgow, 1756).
9. *The Scots Magazine* (1756), 18, pp.280-84; N. Morren, *Annals of the General*

Assembly of the Church of Scotland 1752-66 (Edinburgh, J. Johnstone, 1840), pp.54-61, 86-92.

10. J.Y.T. Greig, ed., *The Letters of David Hume*, 2 vols (Oxford, Clarendon Press, 1932), vol.I, pp.376 and following.
11. E.H. King, 'A Scottish philosophical club in the eighteenth century', *Dalhousie Review*, 50 (1970), p.211.
12. AUL, MS 539.
13. *The Works of George Campbell, D.D., F.R.S.*, 6 vols (London, Thomas Tegg, 1840), vol.I, p.iv. Cited hereafter as *Works*.
14. *Works*, vol.I, p.13.
15. *Phil. Wks*, vol.IV, p.93.
16. *Works*, vol.I, p.29.
17. *Ibid.*, pp.56-63.
18. *Phil. Wks*, vol.IV, p.108.
19. *Works*, vol.I, pp.133 and following.
20. E.C. Mossner, *The Life of David Hume* (Oxford, Clarendon Press, 1970), p.286.
21. George Campbell, *A Dissertation on Miracles*, 3rd edition, 2 vols (Edinburgh, Bell & Bradfute, William Creech, 1797), vol.I, pp.12 and following. Cited hereafter as *Dissertation*.
22. See *Phil. Wks*, vol.IV, p.100 where there are minor amendments to the story of a miracle related by Cardinal de Retz.
23. *Dissertation*, vol.I, pp.14, 5-7.
24. *Ibid.*
25. For instance, Hume commented on James Beattie's *Essay on Truth*, 'Truth!, there is no truth in it; it is a horrible large lie in octavo', Mossner, *Life of Hume*, p.581.

14

Enlightened Men at Law: Litigation at King's College in the Eighteenth Century

C.A. McLaren

University of Aberdeen

College lawsuits in the eighteenth century were sometimes lengthy, often inconvenient and always expensive. They were in short 'vexatious', as the masters on more than one occasion described them. They were nonetheless inescapable, for it was through litigation that the college protected its rights and, when other means failed, resolved disputes among its members. The subject deserves more consideration than it has hitherto received, since it elucidates the processes of college government and the varying degrees of enthusiasm and aptitude with which men of learning doubled as men of affairs. This paper describes one of the sources on which further study might be based.

The principal sources are the minutes of college meetings; procuration accounts and rentals; legal instruments preserved for the most part in the college charter chest; and the archives of the courts themselves. Court records in the age of Peebles versus Planestanes are notoriously complex but the college archives themselves present problems. The minuting of legal business is at best irregular and the series of surviving legal instruments, though extensive, is far from comprehensive. Deposit in the charter chest was no guarantee that documents would remain there. In 1762 the masters were unable to deliver up a promissory note of Lord Lovat, 'the agent for the college having lost or mislaid the same so that it cannot at present be recovered'.[1]

An additional source, which has only recently become readily accessible for research, is a collection of miscellaneous legal papers formerly kept in the Crown Tower of King's College. The papers were stored in empty shuttles of the charter chest, having been examined and annotated, but not inventoried, by P.J. Anderson. They have now been arranged and are held in the university library. They comprise letters, drafts of letters, notes and calculations, covering letters without enclosures, enclosures without covering letters, ephemeral legal instruments, and draft memorials and opinions. Of particular interest are three series of correspondence from the college's law agents: from James Hay, in the 1730s; Roderick Macleod, in the 1760s; and Richard Hotchkiss, in the 1790s. Of even greater value are memorials and submissions composed during the college disputes of the 1700s and 1760s, hitherto known only from citations in the minutes of college meetings. It is from this collection that the illustrations to the paper have been drawn.[2]

The scope of college litigation was succinctly described by Principal John Chalmers, Sub-Principal Roderick Macleod and Regent Thomas Gordon in 1770, when they sat as a committee to consider the expense of it. They divided lawsuits into two categories: for the defence of the college's rights; and the defence of its revenue. They then subdivided the second category into cases for augmenting the revenue, and cases for defending it.[3]

Litigation in defence of college rights includes proceedings in which the college as a whole responded to an external threat: for example, from the rival institution in the New Town. The college lawyers, wrote its agent in 1735, 'are both of the opinion that you would prevaill in the process anent the Stationers hall books if the subject be only worth the expences of a pursuit'. The masters decided that it was; they opposed Marischal College's claim to the receipt of new publications and retained their right of custody.[4]

The same category embraces lawsuits in which the identification of the college, its rights and their defenders, is not so straightforward. These are the suits that arose from the bitter internecine battles of the 1700s, the 1760s and the 1780s. 'It will not be deny'd', wrote Regent Alexander Burnet in 1714, 'that the privilege of any member is the privilege of the Society'. Adhering to this principle, both sides in the disputes represented themselves as champions of the college and its rights. The 'schemes of our antagonists', declared Principal John Chalmers in 1763, 'have tended to subvert order, to infringe the rights and privileges both of the masters and students, to defeat the purposes of a free and a liberal education, and to overturn the foundation charter'. 'We... want only... to preserve every one in the possession of their accustomed rights and privileges', replied Thomas Gordon, then Humanist, 'against those who seem inclinable to do everything in their power to breed confusion'.[5]

Litigation to augment college revenues includes proceedings brought to secure mortifications to the college and—more important—suits for the valuation of teinds. The college drew teinds from nine parishes: they were, indeed, its principal source of revenue. Valuation was a process by which this revenue could be maximised and regularised. Most of the teinds had been valued in the seventeenth century. Valuation of the remainder, together with the sale of superiorities and the patronage of college kirks, was the means by which John Chalmers, on assuming the principalship, sought to boost the college's income. They began the valuation, he wrote some fifty years afterwards, in 1747 and completed it in 1755. 'The expense of these cost us above £500 sterling but added £150 a year to the revenue.'[6]

In court the college was confronted by opponents whose litigiousness was at best resolute, at worst rampant. A particularly formidable adversary was Margaret Forbes, wife of Alexander Skene of Lethenty. 'She is really a very keen antagonist', remarked the college agent, adding—his admiration turning to glee—'I really expect she'll be soused in expences'. Surviving letters from the lady herself reveal her steely nature. 'I owe thee thanks for thy civility', she told Regent Alexander Rait. 'Had your whole society shown as little ill nature and letigiousness, all questions... might have been decided some time ago.'[7]

Litigation undertaken to defend college revenues included suits brought against land owners who encroached on college lands, and tenants or tacksmen who defaulted. Of more significance, however, were the cases which arose when ministers in the college parishes applied to the Teind Court for an augmentation of their stipend from the college teinds. The college had a responsibility to provide for them but, in the course of increasing its revenue by process of valuation, was reluctant to see it reduced in this way. The masters were relieved, therefore, when the applications of the second minister of Old Machar and the incumbents of Slains and Marykirk were unsuccessful. 'All of them', wrote Principal John Chalmers, 'were refused by the Court of Teinds on the ground that the ministers being provided in legal stipends the superplus tithes were the patrimony of the college. In consequence whereof in 1756 the college are... declared free therefrom in all time coming. And this was firmly understood to be the law till 1789.'[8]

That date marked a dramatic change of policy in the court, which for most of the century had shown little sympathy to the Church: 'the clergy', said Alexander Carlyle, an energetic advocate of change, 'were allowed almost to starve'.[9] Now decisions went in their favour. When John Brymer, minister of Marykirk, applied for an augmentation in 1788, having been, he told the masters, 'long deterred from this measure from a fear of contending with so powerful a body of men', he successfully challenged the ruling of 1756. He was followed by the second minister of Old Machar: 'the other four will undoubtedly follow as fast as they can', prophesied the principal, 'and in the present mania of the court we shall in all appearance be undone'.[10]

Chalmers had by that time settled contentedly—between attacks of gout— on his farm at Sclattie. He roused himself and fired off a series of letters and memoranda criticising the tactics of the lawyers who were handling the college's defence and the dilatoriness of the masters. 'The principal was here yesterday', wrote William Ogilvie, his old opponent, 'in admirable spirits but rather angry that nothing had been done relative to his memorial. [He] says it is just one month wanting a day since it was finished by him and delivered to the society.' Chalmers believed that the lawyers' arguments before the court 'were rather sophistical than solid'. His own arguments were based partly on the invalidity of the proceedings of the Teind Court, partly upon the special nature and needs of the college, as established in its foundation charters. 'We are not ecclesiastical, I am wel persuaded but betwixt purely ecclesiastical and purely lay, is there no medium.' His strategy did not impress another old—but still vigorous—opponent, Thomas Gordon: 'It is not showing and pointing out what we wish and what would be good for the college that can be considered as an argument, but showing and pointing out what our original rights have actually and expressly given us.'[11]

By 1795 masters and lawyers had resolved to appeal against the court's decision to the House of Lords. It would not have been the first time that the fate of the college had been decided by an appeal there: the status of the professors of mathematics, Hebrew, law, and divinity, and the case of the errant ex-Principal Middleton had all been reviewed by the peers.[12] 'On this occasion', said Chalmers, 'it is the only thing that can be done for the salvation of the college and if we are not supported we must be suppressed'. In the following year the groundwork was prepared. 'We all see with pleasure that our affairs are *en train*', wrote Gilbert Gerard, Professor of Divinity, to Alexander Daunay, the Civilist, who was then in London on the college's behalf, 'and are satisfied that no exertions will be wanting on your part'.[13] But the appeal does not seem to have been taken further. Instead, the principal's forebodings were confirmed and the teinds were almost exhausted by the succession of augmentations. A royal grant-in-aid of 1807, however, ensured that his worst fears were not realised.[14]

Although some college litigation took place locally in the sheriff court and elsewhere, most of the loose legal papers derive from litigation in Edinburgh, at the Court of Session, the judges of which had assumed the powers of the seventeenth-century commissioners of teinds. Here it was essential to have an efficient and experienced agent, through whom business could be despatched at a distance.

The letters of James Hay, law agent to the college in the 1730s, show him discharging his duties conscientiously, calling for documents from the charter chest; sending back documents promulgated by the court; convening meetings with the college lawyers; and summarising the progress of each case. He had the pleasure of reporting successes and the problem of explaining failures: 'It happened unluckyly that David Caw [Counsel] was taken ill of the gravell... for if he had been present he would have pointed out the decisions which have gone on our side of the question.' Hay scrupulously followed the masters' instructions but occasionally, to their dismay, backed his own judgment: 'I am heartyly sorry that you or your colleagues should be offended at my indulgence... I can assure you it will be a lesson to me for the future never to consent to a delay without a special commission from my imployers.' On that occasion, in 1740, his decision was vindicated. 'I hope', he wrote triumphantly, 'the principall will now take ane honest lawiers's word again.' Nevertheless the college treated him sometimes with little consideration. '[My] account has not been paid now for two sessions', he wrote reproachfully in October 1739. The following month, however, he apologised for the solecism. 'I was a little straitn'd for money... or else I would not have called [for] it till it had been convenient for you to pay it.'[15]

It was also an agent's task to use his knowledge of the working of the court and of its personalities to the college's advantage. Roderick Macleod, the agent in the 1750s, had hopes, he wrote to the principal, of getting a case heard before Lord Prestongrange, 'which I would like, as he is already well known to the affairs of your college'. The case, arising from the disputed appointment of the civilist in 1761, went badly for the principal, and Macleod had to break the news: 'the whole court were unanimous, as there was not one spoke for you and the lord president was particularly hard upon you.' Macleod also counselled the principal against seeming to be offended by the victors: 'appearing to be so will but furnish them with a handle for clatters'. As conscientious as James Hay, he 'sollicited and indeed importuned' Counsel to attend to college business, but had sometimes to admit defeat, as when Counsel was 'so hurryed with the Douglas affair, which has ingrossed a great part of the time both of lawiers and judges this session that it was within two dayes of the end of the session before he returned'.[16]

From the 1790s survive not only the letters of the agent Richard Hotchkiss but copies of letters to him, together with letters between the principal and the masters, commenting on his handling of their business. Hotchkiss had been the partner of William Tytler, college agent until his death in 1792. A year later, Hotchkiss broached a delicate subject: 'a remittance could never be made more seasonably for me than at present, when money is so scarce... and as I am winding up Mr Tytler's affairs as fast as possible... a final settlement of *his* accompt would be more particularly aggreeable'. The principal was not convinced, however, that the college was getting value for the money it was neglecting to pay. 'Our lawiers', he complained, 'have more business on hand than they are fit to manage and ours is only a sort of bye job'. He described their presentation of the college's case against the augmentations of stipend as 'overloaded and in my opinion almost buried' in a 'load of rubbish'. Hotchkiss responded with dignified contrition when these criticisms were forwarded by Alexander Daunay:

> I can assure you I feel very sensibly the accusations of neglect to the college's business... and do acknowledge that in the article of *correspondence* I may have been to blame.... At the same time nothing has been left undone on my part in attending with the greatest care to all the proceedings in the different processes before the Teind Court in which the college is interested.

But he evidently felt, like Thomas Gordon, that the principal's line of defence was unrealistic: 'The court in every former instance have paid very little attention to the particular situation of the college's revenue arising almost solely from teinds.'[17]

Stubborn adherence to a position, realistic or not, characterised Chalmers's role during the fifty years of his principalship. It is illustrated in the memorials and submissions that survive from the conflict of the 1760s and are, perhaps, the most valuable items among the loose legal papers. The gravity of the dispute between the principal and his opponents is apparent in the list of grievances which they submitted to the rector in 1763. They complained of his unconstitutional practice of influencing elections; his conception of a 'philosophy college' and the decisions affecting education and discipline that he took in its name; irregularities in his administration of the college finances and bursaries; his refusal to grant the professors of divinity and Hebrew a role in college meetings and a share of college revenues; and his disregard for the authority of the rector. The inevitability of the dispute is clear from Chalmers's own view of his authority. 'The principal by the Foundation is not like the praeses of a meeting, or the moderator of a presbytery. The whole government of the university is committed to [him] with more ample powers than the praeses of any court.'[18]

It is not unreasonable, perhaps, to look for some sign of Thomas Reid as a moderating influence in the conflict. Certainly, he told Chalmers that 'he desired nothing so much as peace and chose to be directed in all things by the majority'.[19] Among the loose papers is the copy of a document which confirms this. 'The following paper', runs the heading, 'entitled Proposals for Accommodation, was drawn up by Mr Reid in name of himself and the other four professors about February 1760'.[20] It proposes solutions for specific grievances and, briefly, suggests how the college should be governed in future. The solutions include recourse to the Court of Session to decide, by an amicable case at the college's expense, the legality of uniting bursaries. Reid's view of college government is founded upon the pre-eminent authority of the college meeting. It should be 'the last resort in all college business; and no person or part of the society shall claim any authority in college matters, whether of discipline, revenue or application of the college funds, which is not subordinate to it'. The principal's claim to 'whole government' is thus rejected; the emphasis is upon majority rule—'the proposers', according to the heading of the document, 'made an undoubted majority' at the time; and there is no reference to the inquisitory role of the rector or the mediating role of the chancellor. Reid was advocating, in short, a form of government that had already proved defective. The attempt at conciliation seems, nevertheless, to have been sincere. Sadly, nothing came of it. The copy has a postscript: 'The answer of Principal Chalmers to the above proposals was—that they deserved no answer.'

Notes

1. AUL, MS K.45, Minutes of college meetings, p.66. All manuscripts cited hereafter are from the same source.
2. K.281/1-37.
3. K.47, pp.14-15.
4. K.281/14/31; P.J. Anderson, ed., *Fasti Academiae Mariscallanae Aberdonensis*, 3 vols (Aberdeen, New Spalding Club, 1898), vol.I, pp.387-90.
5. K.281/12/9/10; 28/4, p.73; 24/1, f.2v.
6. K.281/33/15.
7. K.281/19/2; 17/6.
8. K.281/33/15.
9. John Connell, *Treatise of the Law of Scotland Respecting Tithes*, 3 vols (Edinburgh, P. Hill, 1815), vol.II, pp.107, 112; Alexander Carlyle, *Autobiography* (Edinburgh and London, W. Blackwood, 1860), p.502.
10. K.281/30/9; 33/15.
11. K.281/32/23/11; 33/21; 33/23/1.
12. P.J. Anderson, *Officers and Graduates of the University and King's College*

(Aberdeen, New Spalding Club, 1893), pp.61, 71, 75-76; *Journals of the House of Lords*, vol.XXI (1718-21), pp.476, 540.

13. K.281/33/15; 35/7.

14. K.49, pp.174-5; Scottish Universities Commission, *Supplementary appendix to returns by the University and King's College* (Printed by the commissioners, 1827), pp.3, 8.

15. K.281/16/5; 19/6, 9; 17/15, 16A.

16. K.281/25/5; 27/7, 8, 15. 'Clatters' i.e. gossip.

17. K.281/32/14, 17; 33/22; 32/18; 34/8, 11.

18. K.281/26/13; 28/4, p.69.

19. K.281/28/4, p.36.

20. K.281/23/2.

15

All Honourable Men? The Award of Irregular Degrees in King's College and Marischal College in the Eighteenth Century

Dorothy B. Johnston
University of Nottingham

It is difficult to define the character of irregular degrees awarded by the Aberdeen Colleges in the eighteenth century. They tend to be referred to as 'unearned' or 'honorary' awards, but these phrases encourage anachronistic interpretations and comparisons with the modern system of honorary degrees. Neither of the Aberdeen institutions apparently employed the *honoris causa* formula of eighteenth-century Oxford, and the contemporary records yield ambiguous results. There is indeed a formidable quantity of evidence for a study of these awards. The lists of recorded graduates alone comprise some 62 D.D.s, 58 LL.D.s and 366 M.D.s from Marischal College and 92 D.D.s, 39 LL.D.s and 320 M.D.s from King's. In addition we know of approximately 50 A.M.s from each university who graduated in exceptional circumstances, and of a small number of B.D.s from King's College and one Bachelor of Law from Marischal. In this paper I shall indicate some of the difficulties in the data and illustrate the general issues from data about particular awards. My scope is necessarily limited. I shall not, for a start, compare the system in Aberdeen with that of other Scottish universities,[1] or consider the relationships between universities which might be revealed in an examination of *ad eundem* awards.[2] I shall also leave aside the specific constitutional issue as to whether Marischal College had a right to grant any award other than a regular arts degree.[3] In practice Marischal did exercise such a right. Although specific regulations governing eligibility did vary, the two colleges appear to have followed a broadly similar system, and my illustrations are drawn from the records of both institutions, without distinction.

The patchy and inconsistent quality of the data presents more of a problem than its volume. The register which was begun for King's College graduates in the 1720s was only intermittently used until the 1750s.[4] In the case of

136

Marischal College the authoritative album is in the hand of Professor William Knight, who began its compilation in 1825, and whose retrospective lists are incomplete and misleading in, for instance, their use of the expression 'Honorary'.[5] For both colleges, therefore, it is necessary to look to ancillary sources. The college accounts are helpful, supplying details of names, dates and fees, but the information was erratically entered, and its form is sometimes terse to the point of obscurity.[6] Fuller records tend to be found in the college minutes, but the series is incomplete and the surviving entries are sometimes very brief.[7] Our register must therefore be amplified by non-archival sources, such as the *Aberdeen Journal* with its contemporary records of a number of degrees.[8]

Assessing the evidential value of these various sources would be a study in itself. The following examination relies primarily upon the printed lists of graduates, as edited by P.J. Anderson in the 1890s.[9] This cannot be done entirely without reservation. Although their literal accuracy can rarely be faulted,[10] Anderson's lists inevitably compress the records. They also give little guidance about the fluctuations which can be seen in the course of the century. Only from the original albums can one relate these patterns to gaps or inconsistencies in the records rather than to institutional policies or external pressures. Furthermore, although Anderson drew on the principal college records, he did not exhaust all the archival series. King's College Library Accounts, for instance, add the name of 'Mr Dungworth' in 1714 to our D.D. register, and it is likely that further examination of all the subsidiary financial vouchers would contribute other additions.[11]

Before considering any general issues, I shall look in turn at the various degrees, beginning with the irregular A.M. awards. Regulations governed the eligibility of matriculated students for graduation, but both colleges exercised the right to grant the degree on other occasions.[12] Such candidates might be examined orally, and some were rejected.[13] The applicants were usually either men who had completed part of their study elsewhere, alumni from Aberdeen who had for some reason not taken their degree when they finished their magistrand year, or men who were simply known to be worthy by their 'merit and estimation in the Republic of Letters'.[14]

A principal difficulty with these A.M. awards is distinguishing between the categories of applicants. This can be shown through analysis of two notebooks kept by Professor James Beattie, in which he recorded the fees he received as promotor from a number of 'incidental' graduates.[15] Most of these men are not shown as graduates in the official lists, though it could be argued, from coincidence of names, that some had attended Beattie's classes in earlier years. The notebooks give us information about 29 arts degrees which are either omitted from the college records or imperfectly described there.

Perhaps the most interesting question prompted by such lists is the motivation behind A.M. applications. Students of divinity were supposed to have an arts degree, and many of the candidates were ministers or hoped to enter the church.[16] Applications from medical students are found in increasing numbers in the second half of the century, and the move towards viewing the

A.M. as a preliminary to medical qualification was sufficiently advanced by 1761 that it became an issue between Principal Chalmers and the rest of the masters of King's College, prompting the latter to protest that 'it has not been the practice of this university to require any such certificate previous to the conferring the degree of Dr in any of the Faculties of Divinity, Law or Medicine'.[17]

As far as medical degrees are concerned, I do not propose here to comment either on the cases where the colleges gave degrees to men who subsequently were exposed as quacks,[18] or upon the wider professional issues concerning medical qualification which caused an increase in the number of candidates for university degrees. The procedures governing awards varied considerably. References to theses and oral or written examinations can all be found.[19] With local candidates the word of the Professor of Medicine or the doctor to whom a student had been apprenticed was often judged sufficient, leaving us with implicit evidence about the provision of medical education in Aberdeen before the formal establishment of any medical school.[20] In practice, as so many degrees were awarded *in absentia*, the mediciner could not normally vouch for candidates himself.[21] It was therefore usual for the college to accept the attestation of two or more doctors, supported by what amounted to a character reference. A few such attestations survive, and for many other candidates we know at least the names of their professional referees.[22] The lists of these recommendations would repay further study. Even a superficial examination shows that many doctors had long-term associations with Aberdeen, received their own degrees from one of its colleges and continued over the years to recommend colleagues. Occasionally the men who attested that the candidates were worthy gentlemen can be identified as members of the dissenting community in London with which the Aberdeen colleges apparently had strong links.

With doctorates in divinity, one finds the same research potential in the lists of attestations which were submitted with applications, with dissenting ministers and educationalists featuring prominently.[23] For King's College, theses on theological subjects were still occasionally mentioned in the early years of the century.[24] Marischal's first recorded D.D. is in 1724, but the contemporary records are very thin and earlier ones may have been granted.[25] Looking at the identity of the individual graduates, it is clear that the D.D. was frequently conferred upon men in the church for their general literary or philosophical abilities rather than for any contribution to theology or eminence as divines.[26]

In the case of LL.D.s, the association between the degree and the professional status of men of law is even more remote. It is, however, never entirely absent. The promotor for the degree was the civilist in King's and David Verner, who is said to have given lectures on law as regent, apparently acted as dean and promotor for candidates in law in Marischal.[27] That the LL.D. was supposed to confer professional status was most notoriously demonstrated by the litigation concerning James Catanach, whose claim to the civilist's office in King's College was linked to his LL.D. degree from Marischal.[28] Thomas Gray's refusal to accept an LL.D. from Marischal in

1765 makes it clear that he viewed the award as a professional privilege,[29] and King's College in 1786 showed in its diploma to Duncan McDonald, whose studies in jurisprudence and law were attested by eminent colleagues, that their doctorates in law were still being awarded on professional grounds.[30] Such cases were, however, exceptional. The majority of LL.D.s in the eighteenth century were granted to teachers and men of letters who had no immediate association with the law.[31]

Although patterns do thus emerge about the different degrees, it is not easy to draw any brief conclusions. Until we know why individual degrees were sought or granted we cannot generalise about the system. On investigating the reason for particular degrees, it is clear that in many cases the application came from the individual himself. This was particularly true of arts and medical degrees, but men also applied for D.D.s and LL.D.s.[32] Degrees were also obtained on the initiative of a third party, who probably but not necessarily had some association with the university, and who may have been acting without the knowledge of the prospective graduate.[33] Such degrees are comparable with the most common form of degree arising from action within the university, when an individual professor recommended somebody for an award.[34] Finally there are the instances where the university took the initiative for institutional reasons, most typically in expressing gratitude to a benefactor by conferring on him an honorary degree.[35] Deciding which category a degree fits into can be difficult and our findings will change as additional evidence is discovered.

There seems, unfortunately, to be no clear correlation between these different categories and the possibly honorary quality of a degree. It is tempting to assume that those who sought honours for themselves would have to pay for them, but this was certainly not invariably true.[36] As far as fee payment was concerned, the system was complex. At the most basic level, some men paid the full dues themselves, that is to say the fees to the promotor and to the library and the incidental college expenses to cover the writing of the diploma.[37] In some cases, however, it appears that a third party might settle with the college, giving the recipient the impression that it was an honorary award.[38] Such cases are difficult to identify unless correspondence to that effect survives, as individuals with no known personal connexions were often involved in the transactions, settling the fees as agents for the graduates or their patrons.[39] It was also possible for portions of the fees to be remitted. The mediciner for instance occasionally 'passed his fees'.[40] With A.M. awards it is difficult to detect this difference between regular and incidental graduates in the promotor's accounts with the college procurator for the library dues.[41] Sometimes the award itself is described in the minutes as *gratis*.[42] In such cases no library fees would be in question, though the college itself would still account for the expenses of the diploma.[43] It is by and large these *gratis* diplomas which Knight identified as honorary degrees. If this were not all complicated enough, even greater confusion is caused by the evidence that the college accepted money in kind for fees. There is a clear relation between lists of subscribers for college buildings and recipients of *gratis* awards, and it can also be shown that the awards did not always follow a benefaction but were made in expectation of it.[44]

In the circumstances, there is great value in private papers which contain references to the award of Aberdeen degrees. Thomas Birch, the antiquarian divine and secretary of the Royal Society, provides a good example. In 1753 he was awarded a D.D. from Marischal College. He was recommended by Principal Thomas Blackwell and no fees seem to have been charged.[45] The background to the award can be found in the British Library where correspondence between Blackwell and Birch survives. Birch was one of a group of men whom Blackwell knew when he was in London, and whose patronage helped him to achieve the principalship in 1748. In 1751 Birch wrote to Blackwell, referring to an A.M. degree which Marischal had evidently bestowed on him. He goes on to excuse himself from any further honour, 'for which I assure you with the utmost Sincerity I have no relish nor ambition and which will probably give umbrage to and excite the envy of many of my Brethren of the Clergy'. The initiative in the affair had clearly come from Blackwell himself. When his colleagues were told of Birch's diffidence, they answered, Blackwell explains, 'with one Voice, that such Modesty ought to be one of the chief Reasons for immediate dispatch, to which I cou'd not chuse but assent'. Birch was left with little option but to write with a graceful acceptance of the honour.[46]

Such personal insights are all too rare, but the papers of James Beattie from the 1770s to 1790s provide a rich source. The scope of the evidence can be seen in the correspondence from Edward Dilly, the London publisher and bookseller, to Beattie concerning a medical degree for Mr Abraham Ludlow of Bristol, and an LL.D. for Henry Mayo, the dissenter. The letters highlight several themes which recur in the literature about irregular degrees; notably the distinction which contemporaries made between purchased higher degrees and those which were not solicited, and the wide circle of friends and interests which the Aberdeen colleges maintained in London. It is also worth noting Dilly's hint that Beattie's publications would increase their sales if he procured the degree for Mayo.[47]

Dilly's letter gives the flavour of many other degree transactions which are described in the Beattie correspondence. I have found references to some twenty individuals. Some, like Thomas Blacklock, the blind poet, who applied to Beattie for his D.D. in 1767, were already personal friends.[48] Blacklock in turn recommended for an arts degree George Chapman,[49] and for a medical degree Hugh Downman of Exeter.[50] His recommendation of a 'Mr Tarpley' failed because, apparently, of new regulations in Marischal College in 1770.[51]

Among the various categories of applicants to Beattie must be mentioned the alumni who had made their careers abroad. For instance, Professor John Kemp of Columbia University, himself a Marischal graduate, applied for an A.M. on behalf of John Urquhart, who had been too poor to take his degree when he left college.[52] Professor Peter Wilson, also of Columbia, reported an honorary award from Union College, Schenectady, and hinted that an LL.D. from his *alma mater* would have been more acceptable.[53] Nearer home, Beattie was involved in the award of several medical degrees, and his correspondence with the mediciner and other interested parties helps to explain how the system worked.[54] The case of Thomas Gordon of Speymouth shows that Beattie's recommendations were not always sustained.[55] On other occasions men like John Seally, who wrote applying for *gratis* awards, became the subject of informal investigation before being duly honoured.[56] Sometimes there are references to patrons of candidates, like the Earl of Erroll, who promised his future favours in return for the D.D. diploma granted to his protégé Robert Cramond.[57] Occasionally we can see that the initiative lay with the applicant rather than the recommender, as in the case of Nicholas Wanostrocht, who asked Dr Thomas Morison of London to approach his brother-in-law Professor Robert Hamilton about an LL.D.[58] Evidence does not record whether this was also true of Thomas Newte, recommended in 1795 by John Lorimer.[59] In contrast, the degree granted to William Dickson, the abolitionist, was quite unsolicited.[60]

Beattie's involvement in these awards was often quite peripheral. His fellow professors would have had similar contacts and their personal correspondence, if it survived or could be traced, would yield comparable riches. A letter from Professor George Skene to Lord Buchan in 1797 illustrates the point. It concerns an M.D. degree for Benjamin Worship. Skene explained that the behaviour of the mediciner, Dr Livingston, was responsible for the delay and used the opportunity to fulminate against Livingston's appointment 'by parliamentary influence'. He explained this privately to Buchan rather than to his protégé Worship, 'that I might not expose the defects of Scots Universities particularly the one from which a Gentleman of such Merit wished to have a Degree'. In the event Mr Worship did not wait, but received an M.D. six weeks later from King's College.[61]

The evidence of these letters suggests that we should be cautious in making judgments about Aberdeen's academic awards. Though contemporaries did express criticisms of the ease with which awards were granted, venality was not, apparently, in question, and charges to that effect, made in the heat of the university union debate of the 1770s by men like William Ogilvie, were frankly polemical.[62] As the papers of Blackwell and Beattie show, the awards are very inadequately explained by the minuted applications or receipted vouchers which we find in the archives. The subject, it seems, represents an area of university history where illumination is likely to be found in the private papers of professors and the graduates themselves, and where a definitive study would, incidentally, demonstrate links between Aberdeen and scholars or literary figures throughout the country and between the universities and their most ambitious alumni.

Appendix

1. Edward Dilly to James Beattie, 31 October 1771 (AUL, MS 30/2/67):
   Now I mention the above Diploma, it reminds me of what I intended to speak to you about when in Town, if you remember, one Day that you dined at my

House I had the pleasure of the Rev Mr. Henry Mayo's Company at the same Time. This Gentleman is one of the chief Persons among the Body of Dissenting Ministers in this City, a very intimate friend of Dr. Price, Dr. Amory, Dr. Furneaux, Dr. Harris, Dr. Calder and other eminent Divines. He is a Person of great Erudition, many years Pastor of a considerable Church in London, and consulted almost upon all occasions relative to the Dissenting Interest in England, but at the same Time a Person of great Modesty in every thing which regards himself. He is now a Master of Arts and I believe would have no objection to the Degree of Doctor of Laws, if it was on the footing of a Complimentary Degree, without the least Idea of a purchase in any Shape, either by himself or by a friend. What I mention to you on this Head is entirely in Confidence, for Mr. Mayo does not know a tittle about my writing to you on the subject, and therefore I submit to your opinion in regard to the Propriety of the thing. If it is not proper, I beg you will not mention it to any Soul living, but if you have Interest to procure it on the genteel footing as you did Dr. Calder's, I am perswaded it will be esteemed a very great favour, and it will be no disservice to any of your future Publications, for this Gentleman has it greatly in his power to promote the Interest of a New Work. As he has the management of a Literary Society and frequently writes in the Papers upon the Subject of a New Publication, his opinion is often asked in regard to the merit of a Work, and what he says has great weight.

2. Dilly to Beattie, 6 January 1772 (AUL, MS 30/2/71):
    I do not know of one that is more deserving of the Title, and I had at the time reason for my Application, and though I am sensible Mr Mayo would not accept of it, if he imagined it was upon the footing of a purchase from any Person, but as the application comes from me, I could not think of Soliciting such a favour of you, without making a proper Compliment to the College. I intended at my first mentioning the affair, if I had rec'd the Diploma, to have sent a Present to the College of a number of valuable Books, fully adequate to [sd.] purchase and have accordingly Band them up very neat and uniform Calf Gilt and Letter'd which I leave to you either to Present to the College, or to such of the Professors you think proper.

Notes: Dr Henry Mayo, LL.D. 1772
Dr John Calder, D.D. 1771, 'on motion of Principal Campbell'.

The books in question were all publications by Dilly. They were indeed sent and most of them can today be identified in Aberdeen University Library.

Notes

1. The system seems to have been broadly similar. For a retrospective view of the different colleges see British Parliamentary Papers, *Report to His Majesty by a Royal Commission of Inquiry into the State of the Universities of Scotland*, Sess. 1831 (310) XII, pp.275-77, 387-88, 440-41, 470, 521-23.
2. E.g. in 1726 the masters of King's College noted that Sir Nicholas Trott had been created LL.D. by Oxford and agreed to send him a diploma *ad eundem gradum* from Aberdeen; College Minutes, AUL MS K.42, f.33. Unless otherwise indicated, all manuscript references in this paper come from Aberdeen University Library.
3. The controversy reached a peak in the 1850s. See *Has Marischal College, in New Aberdeen, the Power of Conferring Degrees in Divinity, Law and Medicine?*

(Aberdeen, Wyllie, 1850), and *The Right of Marischal College and University, Aberdeen to Confer Degrees ... Vindicated ....*(Aberdeen, Smith, 1853).

4. Register of Graduates, MS K.13. It was begun after the loss of an earlier volume; College Minutes, MS K.41, ff.36v, 52v. In 1726 the newly drafted forms of diplomas for divinity, law and medicine were entered; MS K.42, f.34 and K.13, ff.lv, 2v, 93-94.

5. MS M.21. Knight's lists are also occasionally inaccurate; e.g. Andrew Mackay is credited in 1786 with an LL.D. In fact, the accounts from which Knight quotes refer to an A.M. award; College Accounts, MS M.60, f.36 and Vouchers subsidiary to Honorary Degrees, MS M.397/7/33.

6. Confusion sometimes arises as to which degree is in question. See, for example, Anderson's note to LL.D. entries for S. Gough and J. Entick; P.J. Anderson, ed., *Fasti Academiae Mariscallanae Aberdonensis*, 3 vols (Aberdeen, New Spalding Club, 1898), vol. II, p.95, hereafter cited as *Fasti*.

7. Typical of the bald uninformative entries is that for James Paton, who received a D.D. from King's College in 1792, the college minutes merely stating that he was 'a gentleman of very respectable character'; MS K.48, f.24.

8. Degrees were not normally inserted in the newspaper. James Beattie, for instance, made a special point of sending a notice to the *Aberdeen Journal* when he procured a D.D. award for his friend Thomas Blacklock; Beattie Collection, MS 30/1/11.

9. P.J. Anderson, *Roll of Alumni in Arts of the University and King's College of Aberdeen, 1596-1860* (Aberdeen, Aberdeen University, 1900); *Officers and Graduates of the University and King's College, Aberdeen, 1495-1860* (Aberdeen, New Spalding Club, 1893) hereafter cited as *Officers*. *Fasti*, vol. II.

10. But see *Fasti*, vol. II, pp.360-61, which omits five names from the list of magistrands in 1786-7, as given in *Album Studiosorum*, MS M.3, f.98v; *Officers*, p.127 records an M.D. in 1729 to Benjamin Godspree instead of Godfrey, as in MS K.13, f.85. 11. MS K. 257/21/4. Anderson did use the Library accounts in his *Roll of Alumni*, and thus adds a number of arts degrees to the record of *Officers*, but he did not correct the graduation record in other faculties.

12. See, for example, Marischal College Minutes, 25 January 1781, MS M.41,f. 84v.

13. E.g. in 1750 Henry Caldwell and Andrew Young failed their trial in Marischal College, despite certificates from professors in Edinburgh; MS M.41, f.34.

14. So expressed in the King's College regulations of 1819; MS K.50, p.40.

15. MS 30/14,15. As Professor of Moral Philosophy in Marischal College Beattie taught the final-year students and acted as promotor at all arts graduations. His notebooks also preserve the names of an unidentified Thomas Warton (1773) and James Hay (1773) as D.D. graduates and George Skene (1772) and Robert Honyman (1772) as M.D.s (*ibid.*, ff.30-35).

16. In 1737 Principal Chalmers of King's College asked the Professor of Divinity to conform to the Acts of General Assembly in this respect; College Minutes, MS K.43, f.27.

17. College Minutes, MS K.44, p.216.

18. See, for example, William Brodum [Boddum], who sustained his right to a Marischal College M.D. despite efforts to expel him from College membership; Anderson, *Fasti*, vol. II, pp.133-34.

19. See Anderson, *Officers*, pp.120-45 and *Fasti*, vol. II, pp.111-38.

20. The lists of graduates kept by the Professors of Medicine in Marischal College show that many of the local candidates were thus recommended; MS M.27-8.

21. The mediciner did on occasion examine candidates in other places. In 1762 [John] Hammond passed his trials when Professor Donaldson 'happened to be in London'; MS M.28.

22. See, for example, the attestation for Alexander Houston, M.D., King's College, in 1750; MS K.236. Anderson includes the names of referees in his lists of graduates in *Fasti* and *Officers*.

23. Anderson, *Fasti*, vol. II, pp.81-86 and *Officers*, pp.98-105.

24. E.g. John Sharp in 1714 gave a public discourse after the ceremony of graduation for his D.D.; College Minutes, MS K.40 f.26v and J. Sharp, *De Rebus Liturgicis* (Aberdeen, Forbes, 1714).

25. Among early D.D.s not listed in *Fasti* is the 1732 award to James Anderson, dissenting minister of London; A.L. Miller, 'The connection of Dr James Anderson of the "Constitutions" with Aberdeen and Aberdeen University', *Ars Quatuor Coronatorum*, xxxvi (1923), pp.86, 98-101. I am indebted to Dr David Stevenson for this reference.

26. E.g. Thomas Reid, the philosopher, was awarded a D.D. by Marischal College in 1762; *Aberdeen Journal*, 18 January 1762.

27. Verner's position is obscure. In 1749 he received as promotor half the fee for the LL.D. award to Theophilus Hibbins; MS M.60, f.83v. In 1760 the Principal acted as dean and promotor in law until Verner should be replaced; MS M.41, f.61.

28. The case is summarised in *Fasti*, vol. I, pp.70-71.

29. *Fasti*, vol. II, pp.97-98.

30. MS K.47, p.212.

31. E.g. James Anderson of Mounie, who wrote on agriculture and rural economy; *Aberdeen Journal*, 2 December 1782.

32. E.g. William Kenrick, LL.D., 27 February 1772; *Fasti*, vol. II, p.98. Personal solicitations for degrees continue to be found until the 1860 'Fusion' of the universities. See, for example, James Robertson of Nova Scotia who in 1856 wrote enquiring 'if it were at all practicable to obtain the Degree of LL.D. from my old Alma Mater without crossing the Atlantic'; Papers concerning Honorary Degrees, MS K.277/3.

33. E.g. Abraham Taylor, D.D., 1736; Letter from A. Cruden to Principal Osborn quoted in *Fasti*, vol. II, p.82, from MS M.387/12/1/8.

34. E.g. Nicholas Wanostrocht, recommended for a LL.D. by Professor Robert Hamilton in 1795; NLS, Fettercairn Papers, MS Acc. 4796, Box 99, Hamilton to Beattie, 23 October [1795].

35. E.g. James Fraser was awarded an LL.D. from King's College in 1715 'as an expression of their gratitude'; *Officers*, p.110.

36. E.g. John Seally, Marischal College LL.D., 1784; MS 30/2/451. MS M.21 records Seally as an 'Honorary' (i.e. *gratis*) graduate.

37. References to scales of fees appear in college minutes and accounts and some are cited by Anderson in *Officers* and *Fasti*. The role of the promotor can be illustrated from James Beattie's Daybooks, MS 30/14, 15.

38. E.g. in the case of Henry Mayo, Edward Dilly applied in confidence and gave a donation of books in lieu of fees; see Appendix above.

39. E.g. Beattie received 12 guineas for Thomas Warton's D.D. in 1773 from Alexander Angus, the Aberdeen bookseller whose involvement was probably limited to the question of a convenient method of payment; MS 30/14, p.34.

40. E.g. Dr Gregory did not claim his promotor's fee in the case of Thomas Garden, M.D. 1728; MS K.42, f.56.

41. See, for example, payment for 12 graduates in College Accounts for 1768-9. Of these five were in fact among Beattie's 'incidental' graduates; MS M.60, f.6r; compare MS 30/14, ff.14-15, 18-19.

42. E.g. David William Morgan's D.D. in 1762 was awarded *gratis* 'in consideration that Mr Morgan is patronized by the Earl of Bute'; MS M.41, ff.62-3.

43. See MS M.397/7/1-36, *passim*.
44. E.g. Alexander Garden of South Carolina, who 'designs some benefactions', received a D.D. award from King's College in 1726; MS K.42, f.33. John Turner's fees for his M.D. in 1738 were likewise excused, 'he having given 20 Gs. to the N. Buildings and promised to be otherways a benefactor to the college'; MS M.27.
45. MS M.41, f.43.
46. BL, Add. MS 4301, ff.141-45. No record of Birch's A.M. award survives in Aberdeen.
47. MS 30/2/67, 71; see Appendix, above, for section concerning Mayo.
48. MS 30/1/11.
49. Marischal alumnus of the 1750s and LL.D., 1786; MS 30/1/30.
50. NLS, MS Acc.4796, Box 91, Beattie to Blacklock, 23 May, 18 June 1772.
51. MS 30/2/31, 30/1/22; NLS, MS Acc.4796 Box 91, Beattie to Blacklock, 27 May 1770. The regulations do not survive in the college minutes.
52. MS 30/2/728.
53. MS 30/2/774.
54. E.g. William Laing, 1782, MS 30/1/213, 216; Robert Prower, 1786, MS 30/1/256; John Laurence, 1789, MS 30/1/302; and William Wilson, 1790, MS 30/2/639.
55. D.D. applicant, 1776, MS 30/2/256; NLS, MS Acc.4796, Box 92 Beattie to Duchess of Gordon, 17 October 1784.
56. MS 30/2/451, 454, 458.
57. MS 30/2/63.
58. NLS, MS Acc.4796, Box 99, Hamilton to Beattie, 23 October [1795].
59. MS 30/2/688.
60. MS 30/2/676.
61. NLS, Miscellaneous Autographs, MS 3873, ff.253-4; *Officers*, p.142.
62. His charges are summarised in W.R. Humphries, *William Ogilvie and the Projected Union of the Colleges* (Aberdeen, AUP, 1940), pp.19, 25, 53.

16

The Arts Curriculum at Aberdeen at the Beginning of the Eighteenth Century

Christine Shepherd
Edinburgh

The arts curriculum at Aberdeen at the beginning of the eighteenth century has not been given much attention, but it does repay investigation. It was around 1690 that new ideas began to make a significant impact on the arts teaching. There are three main contemporary sources of information for this period—student notebooks, graduation theses, and official university and commission reports and minutes. Between 1690 and 1720 there are fourteen manuscript student notebooks for King's College and eleven for Marischal (see Appendix 1). After this date there is a considerable gap—we know of no further notebooks for King's until 1757 and for Marischal until 1743. These notebooks may be dictates, that is to say that they may record the regent's actual dictated words. Whether they were dictated or not, though, they are a fairly reliable reflection of what was taught. Complementary to the dictates are the graduation theses (see Appendix 2). These are in printed form, and were produced for the annual graduation ceremony at the end of the four-year arts course. They consist of a list of theses, probably composed by the regent in charge of the current magistrand class; the theses relate to the subject matter of his course, and were to be defended by the candidates at their laureation ceremony. The dictates and theses are the primary sources of evidence for the content of seventeenth- and eighteenth-century philosophy courses. But for contemporary theories about what the courses should contain, and how they should be taught, the reports of various commissions appointed to visit the universities, faculty minutes and other college records are invaluable.

Official university records reveal that for all the universities in Scotland the sequence of subjects taught was more or less the same. The first year was spent on Greek, which was regarded merely as an introductory subject to the study of philosophy. The second year was devoted to logic, the third to ethics and the fourth to physics or natural philosophy. Teaching was by the regent system; instead of having one teacher allotted to each subject, as in the professorial system, the regent took his class right through the philosophy course, teaching every subject in turn. Various objections to this system were raised during the seventeenth century, and indeed the changeover from the regenting to the professorial system took place early in the eighteenth century in both Edinburgh and Glasgow. Aberdeen, however, was the last of the Scottish universities to make the transition, with Marischal effecting the change in 1753 and King's not until 1799.

Logic and metaphysics were the first philosophy subjects encountered by the student. In both, the content of the lectures is mainly scholastic, despite a nodding acknowledgement of Cartesianism. The theses are more unreservedly Cartesian, and by 1696 Locke's theories had won acceptance with some regents, though this acceptance was not universal. For instance, George Peacock (Marischal, 1711) and William Smith (Marischal, 1712) are strongly opposed to the *tabula rasa* theory. The logic and metaphysics lecture notes show that the same lectures were used within the one college over a number of years. For instance, there are four sets of logic notes taken from the lectures of George Peacock at Marischal. Their dates are 1690, 1694, 1695 and 1699 (this set was probably begun in 1699 and completed in 1707) and the earlier three are duplicates. This may indicate that Peacock actually used the same lectures over a period of years, though the system of regent rotation meant that he could not have been teaching logic in both 1694 and 1695, so a more likely explanation is that his lecture notes were copies—there is evidence that there was quite a trade in the copying of lecture notes and their sale to students.[1] A third alternative is the existence of some sort of standard course around this time. At King's College there are indications of the same lectures being given over a much longer period of time. There is a set of notes for 1691, possibly delivered by William Black, which contains too many verbal similarities to James Urquhart's lectures of 1717 for there not to be a connexion between them. The earlier lectures probably served as a model for the later ones, though Urquhart cuts out a lot of material as being superfluous to logic.

Not only are the same lectures used within the one college, but we have evidence of an identical set of lecture notes being used at Marischal and King's. George Skene's *Cursus logicus* of 1702 is duplicated by Peacock's lectures at Marischal in 1699 and 1707. This practice is confirmed by a comment on behalf of Marischal College on the recommendations of a parliamentary commission in 1695 concerning a uniform course to be taught throughout the Scottish universities. Their representatives noted that a uniform course had already been adopted by them:

> For the preventing the inconveniency of the students spending their time in writing, we have all agreed upon, and teach the same courses, by which there is such abundance of copies to be had that few are obliged to write, except some small tractats, which every particular master dictats at his pleasure.[2]

Possibly the idea of uniformity was extended to the two colleges.

Ethics was taught in the third year of the arts course. It was considered a very important part of philosophy by most of the regents, and by some the most important part, since it taught a man how to live well and happily. The King's College notebook which contains the standard metaphysics course also includes a moral philosophy course. This is dated 1692 and was probably taken down from the lectures of William Black, but in fact the text is identical to that contained in Henry Scougal's lectures of 1682. Scougal starts out with a statement of the practical nature of moral philosophy: the aim of ethics is to enable us to live well, and because of this practical aim, we should not get bogged down in arid debating. In this he is typical of Scottish regents. The lectures are divided into five parts. The first part deals with the nature of happiness in general, and after rejecting the usual categories of goods of fortune, the body and the mind, Scougal gives the traditional Christian verdict that true happiness consists in contemplation of God. He then moves on to discuss virtue. Hobbes's view that the natural human condition is a state of war is disputed, and Scougal also dislikes the belief that morality depends on God's will; if this were so we could be certain of nothing; the goodness or badness of an action must be intrinsic and unvarying. The first rule of moral action is the 'governing of right reason' and only spontaneous actions can be judged moral or immoral. The third section deals with the passions, for which Scougal follows Descartes's classification. Henry More and Robert Boyle are spoken of with approval. Next Scougal deals with the virtues. He thinks that the Aristotelian division of the virtues is not entirely accurate, but it is commonly followed, and everything can more or less be reduced to his scheme; accordingly he proposes to adopt it. Under the chapter on *fortitudo* Scougal discusses at some length the question of whether a Christian can engage in war and under what circumstances—a question which looms large in seventeenth-century ethics dictates. As in many of the other dictates, the chapters on justice take up far more space than those on the other cardinal virtues. The final chapter deals with the acquisition of virtue and borders very much on theology. And as a coda Scougal has a short section on the nature of society and government, in which he claims that the best type of government is an enlightened monarchy, and that it is unlawful ever to resist the supreme magistrate.

In 1702 George Skene provided his students with *A Manual of Moral Philosophy* in which he follows Henry More. Skene favours More's definition of good, virtue and the passions (where More adopts the Cartesian classification); More's *Tractatus de Animae Mortalitate* is cited, and Skene ends with a section on the nature of government similar to that in Scougal's notes.[3]

We have two sets of ethics lectures for Marischal, delivered by George Peacock in 1688, and by Alexander Moir in 1701, the second of which is probably a duplicate of the first—further evidence for the existence of a uniform course in the Aberdeen colleges. The lectures are divided into three parts, part one dealing with the *summum bonum*, part two with the passions (for which the Cartesian division is adopted) and the virtues (basically Aristotelian) and part three with free will. As with the King's College lectures there is a final section on the nature of society, and in fact the arguments and conclusions are virtually identical. It is interesting to note that Aberdeen seems to have been the only university which consistently included sections on politics in its ethics teaching. The graduation theses fill out this picture of ethics teaching. The regents of the 1690s and the early eighteenth century support Descartes and also Henry More. They tend to devote most of their theses to natural philosophy, but they nearly all list some rules of moral conduct, obviously considering this to be the essential part of ethics.

The natural philosophy part of the arts course is perhaps the most interesting in relation to Aberdeen, since the Parliamentary Commission set up in 1690 to reform the universities allotted special physics to King's and general physics to Marischal in its scheme for a uniform course.

There is only one set of natural philosophy lecture notes for King's, dated 1702, and possibly delivered by George Skene. It may have been a standard course for Aberdeen—though not that produced by Marischal for the 1695 Commission, of which an outline survives.[4] The lectures are basically Cartesian, but the student is also referred to Robert Boyle's treatises *On the Origin of Forms and Qualities*,[5] and to his air pump experiments. Under the section on light there is a description of the Newtonian theory of light and colours; this is in different handwriting, and fills a complete gathering, so may have been inserted later. At any rate, no view is offered as to whether the Newtonian or the Cartesian theory is nearer the truth. The notes say that while Descartes's theory is clever and consistent with reason, it is contradicted by many things in Newton's theory; however, the decision as to which is most probable is left to the student. There are three sets of physics lectures for Marsichal College, dated 1688, 1691 and 1693. Like the King's College lectures they are Cartesian, with references to contemporary or recent scientific experiments. The lectures of 1693, delivered by Alexander Moir, are based on those of William Seton, regent in 1674 and 1675, and repeat those of 1691, pointing yet again to the existence of a standard course at Aberdeen.

To give a clearer idea of the progress of ideas at Aberdeen it would be best, before considering the evidence of the theses which go up to 1712, to turn now to the evidence of the uniform courses. A plan of Marischal College's general physics course survives. It is divided into two parts, of which one contains introductory matter and the *principia* of natural body, and the other deals with movement, rest, continuity, divisibility and other properties of body. It is mainly Cartesian, but does set out Newton's theory of light. The special physics course, which survives in its entirety, was written by William Black, regent at King's College. Black begins with a discussion of the different world systems and pronounces in favour of the Copernican hypothesis. He then proceeds to divide special physics into two sections, corresponding to terrestrial and celestial matter. The introductory account of the origin of the world would seem to be based on scriptural premises rather than on those of natural philosophy. Certainly he does later refer to the experiments of contemporary scientists, for example Boyle, Wren, Hooke and other members of the Royal Society (the *Philosophical Transactions* are cited several times), and he actually describes a number of experiments which can be carried out to prove various statements, for example in the sections on the magnet and on hydrostatics. However, in the section on light there is no mention of Newton, and although Black does refer to Newton's theories about planetary movement, he sees no reason to reject the Cartesian vortex theory.

The course was circulated to the other universities, and their comments are preserved in a manuscript volume in Edinburgh University Library.[6] The bulk of the comments came from the regents of St Andrews, and they are both lengthy and critical in the extreme. Their main objections are as follows:

1. Black does not show a truly scientific spirit in his approach.
2. He strays beyond the bounds of philosophy into theology.
3. He poaches on medicine's preserves in giving a table of the healing properties of plants.
4. He neglects optics, dioptrics and catoptrics.
5. He is disrespectful to philosophers whose opinions differ from his, in particular Newton, whose findings Black rejects on insufficient grounds.

There are two replies to the St Andrews' criticisms, one from Aberdeen and one from a meeting of all the university delegates.

Aberdeen begins by pointing out that in the vast field covered by special physics there is bound to be a certain amount of error. St Andrews' animadversions are thought to be vindictive and unnecessary. What is more, the Aberdeen masters think it unpardonable that not only the work should be attacked, but its author too. The charge that Black strays into the realms of theology and medicine is rejected. As for the omission of optics etcetera, it was agreed that they should be dealt with by Marischal College in their course on general physics. Black does not detract from those whose views are contrary to his own and he considers himself justified in sometimes disagreeing with Newton, since he does not always deem Newton's theories to be well founded. For instance, in the section on the ebbing and flowing of tides, Black does not promise to discuss all the hypotheses which are worthy of note (as his critics imagine), but only those of Descartes and Galileo. He passes over the Newtonian theory because it is too difficult for the students at whom the course is aimed. After dealing with all thirty-five of St Andrews' criticisms, the masters of Aberdeen conclude by stating that it is obvious that St Andrews have not followed the rules they laid down in their own course of logic, 'that we should take care not to make it our first aim to criticise others, or falsify their opinions, for nothing is more absurd than to try to persuade another of the truth before we ourselves have grasped it'.

The delegates of all the universities shared Aberdeen's opinion that the personal attacks on Black were unwarranted. They disagreed that a table of the healing properties of plants was out of place in a treatise on special physics. Some of St Andrews' criticisms were accepted and referred to Black for alteration, which in several cases he refused to undertake. On some points the delegates were split, for example, on the treatment of comets, tides and the vortex theory, with Newtonians arguing against Cartesians.

Turning now to the theses, Cartesian physics predominate in the 1690s, but there are an increasing number of references to the theories of other scientific writers, such as Boyle, Huygens, Wallis and Newton. There is even speculation about the possibility of aeroplanes:

> The art of aeronautics is not entirely impossible; for a little ship can be fashioned to carry a given number of men into the air; they can use its oars or wings to steer in the fluid air through regions far above the highest mountains.[7]

The first rejection of Cartesian physics appears in Alexander Fraser's theses (Kings, 1693). He does not accept Descartes's explanation of movement, because it has been proved false by experiments. Descartes's ideas about colour are ingenious, but they have been superseded by Newton's. Fraser does not know what to think about gravity, but states that the Cartesian theory will do for want of a better one. However, Cartesianism was not fully superseded until the 1700s. Thus, in 1708 William Smith of Marischal maintains that experiments and mathematical calculations are essential for physics, and he praises Newton's use of analytic and synthetic methods. Newton, he says, worked from the particular to the universal, experimenting and observing; his experiments and mathematical calculations are extremely accurate. Keill is recommended and Huygens's theories about light are cited.

Although Black's special physics were Cartesian, he had abandoned Cartesian ideas by 1705, and seems to favour Keill's mathematical method. George Fraser too, whose 1691 theses were completely Cartesian, now admits that many of Descartes's physical theories have been superseded (though he still upholds the Cartesian method in the logic part of his theses, and his metaphysics are Cartesian). The three last Aberdeen theses we possess within the period under discussion—those of James Urquhart (King's, 1710), George Peacock (Marischal, 1711) and William Smith (Marischal, 1712)— are all thoroughly Newtonian.

What conclusions can we draw from this survey of arts teaching at Aberdeen? One interesting factor to emerge is the probability of a standard course being taught at both King's and Marischal. This curricular agreement is the more surprising when one considers the rivalry that existed between the two colleges. For instance, there were always religious tensions, stemming from the fact that Marischal was originally a Presbyterian foundation, while King's was Episcopalian. The rivalry extended to student poaching; regents from both colleges went round the countryside in the summer vacation trying to attract students from the other college; this was the cause of frequent complaint, and acts were passed prohibiting the practice. Other factors beside religious ones entered into the Kings-Marischal antagonism; for instance King's resented the establishment of a second rival, university at Aberdeen, especially when Marischal's library soon became far superior as a result of Duncan Liddel's and Thomas Reid's benefactions; likewise Marischal, as the younger college, was constantly on the defensive, especially so in 1707 when the Copyright privilege went to King's. Nevertheless, the two colleges were aware of the advantages of a uniform course.

Another point of interest is the fact that we have no evidence that Marischal's general physics and Black's special physics did become the standard course either for all the Scottish universities or even for Marischal and King's. This is particularly surprising since standard courses *were* being taught at the two colleges during the 1690s and early 1700s, and the content of the courses produced for the Commission was not so very different from the content of contemporary physics lectures. One suspects that the universities resented the interference of the Parliamentary Commission with their right to teach what they pleased. So, while it was politically inadvisable to refuse to comply with the Commission's requests and not produce the requested standard courses, the policy of inaction was still an effective obstructing tactic. After 1699 the Commission seems to have given up trying to get the universities to adopt a uniform course.

However, the most obvious factor to emerge is that, even though many aspects of the curriculum still owed much to scholastic influence, and there was not always wholehearted acceptance of new ideas, nevertheless these ideas *were* being mooted. Contemporary library lists show that many of the works of recent authorities referred to in the lectures and theses were available for consultation. The ground was being prepared for later developments in the eighteenth century. Just as the Renaissance did not suddenly erupt from the dark Middle Ages, so the Scottish Enlightenment had firm roots in what has often wrongly been considered the benighted seventeenth century.

Appendix 1
Student notebooks 1690-1720

Date	Regent	Student/Owner	Location	Notes
1690	?George Peacock (M)	John Arbuthnott	NLS,MS 9387	Logic
1691	?George Peacock (M)	John Stewart Ludovick Reid	AUL,M. 183	General physics
1691	?William Black (K)	—	AUL,K. 152	Logic
	This is very similar to K.158—not an exact duplicate, but too many verbal similarities to be merely coincidence. Probably K.158 used the earlier one as its model.			
1692	?William Black (K)	—	AUL,K. 153	Metaphysics (Text as in K.159) Ethics Cosmography Geography (Text as in K.159, K.155 and MS 1026)
1693	Alexander Moir (M) based on lectures of William Seton (M)	Alexander Irvine	AUL,M. 180	Physics
	Very similar to M.183—not an exact duplicate, but the only differences are slight differences in word order, and this has an introductory note, absent from M.183, on Cartesian laws of movement.			
1694	?George Peacock (M) Duplicate of notes dictated by Peacock 1688-89	Thomas Paull	St Andrews, MS 1503	Logic
1694	?William Black (K)		NLS,Adv. MS 22.7.15	Metaphysics
1694	George Skene (K)	William Gordon	AUL,K. 204	Geometry Trigonometry (Text as in K.109)
1694	?George Skene (K)	Alexander Abercrombie	AUL,K. 109	Logic
1694-5	Alexander Fraser (K)	Kenneth Sutherland Daniel MacKenzie Colin Campbell Andrew Henderson	AUL,3084	Logic
1695	George Peacock (M) Duplicate of NLS, MS 9387	John Douglas	NLS, MS 9388	Logic

1699	George Peacock (M)	Patrick Forbes John Forbes Alexander Forbes	AUL, M.175	Logic Metaphysics

Begun in 1699, probably completed in 1707.
Duplicate of K.154 and 2859.
Text as in 3166.

1701	Alexander Moir (M)	Patrick Simpson	AUL, 3166	Metaphysics
1701	Alexander Moir (M)	William Watt	NLS, MS 9389	Ethics
1701-4	?George Skene (K)	?Alexander MacLennan	AUL, 2092	Geography Metaphysics

Text as in K.153.

1702	George Skene (K)	William Stewart	Edinburgh University Library, Dc.5.33	Ethics
1702	George Skene (K)	Thomas Ogilvie	AUL,K.154	Logic

Part of text as in M.175 and 2859

1702	?George Skene (K)	Thomas Ogilvie and unidentified writer	AUL, 141	Physics
1702	?William Black (K)	David Kinloch	AUL, 2859	Logic

Text in part similar to K.154 and M.175

1707-8	? (M)	Philip Lyon	St Andrews 30313	Metaphysics
1708-9	? (M)	Patrick Lyon	St Andrews 30312	Metaphysics
1708-9	? George Skene (K)	Alexander Stewart	AUL, K.155	Ethics

First part of text as in K.153, K.159, 1026 and James
Urquhart (K)

1717	? James Urquhart (K)	John Ogilvie	AUL, K.158	Logic
1717-18	John Anderson (M)	James Brodie John Tyler	Photocopy AUL,3105	Logic
1719-20	Henry Scougal (K) ? Alexander Burnet	Francis Skene James Troup	AUL, 1026	Ethics

Text as in K.153, K.159, K.155

Appendix 2
Graduation theses 1690-1712

Date	Prases	Location	Title
1691	George Fraser (K)	AUL, The.K.691	Positiones aliquot philosophicae
1691	Alexander Moir (M)	AUL, The.M.691	Theses philosophicae
1693	Alexander Fraser (K)	AUL, The.K.693	Determinationes philosophicae
1693	George Peacock (M)	AUL, The.M.693	Theses philosophicae
1695	George Fraser (K)	AUL, The.K.695	Theses philosophicae
1696	George Skene (K)	AUL, The.K.696	Theses philosophicae
1697	Alexander Fraser (K)	AUL, The.K.697	Theses philosophicae
1700	William Smith (M)	NLS, 1.207(3a)	Theses philosophicae
1704	William Smith (M)	AUL, The.M.704	Theses philosophicae
1705	William Black (K)	AUL, The.K.705	Theses philosophicae
1706	George Fraser (K)	AUL, The.K.706	Theses philosophicae
1708	William Smith (M)	AUL, The.M.708	Theses philosophicae
1710	James Urquhart (K)	AUL, The.K.710	Placita nonnulla philosophica de rerum cognitione
1711	George Peacock (M)	NLS, Jolly.532(5)	Theses philosophicae
1712	William Smith (M)	NLS, Jolly.532(6)	Theses philosophicae

Notes

1. *Two Students at St Andrews, 1711-1716*, ed. from the Delvine papers by William Croft Dickinson, St Andrews University Publications, No. 50 (Edinburgh, Oliver and Boyd, 1952). This shows that Alexander and Kenneth Mackenzie both purchased sets of lecture notes (e.g. Gregory's dictates on astronomy were copied out for Alexander at four shillings a sheet). The casual way in which these transactions are recorded in the Accounts suggests that the selling of dictates was more or less standard practice.

2. *Evidence Oral and Documentary taken and received by the Commissioners appointed by His Majesty George IV, July 23, 1826...for Visiting the Universities of Scotland* (London, 1837), vol.4, p.312.

3. This is a slightly misquoted reference to Henry More's *The Immortality of the Soul, so farre forth as it is demonstrable from the Knowledge of Nature and the Light of Reason* (London, by J. Flesher for William Morden in Cambridge, 1659).

4. AUL, K.219 (Box A).

5. Robert Boyle, *The Origine of Formes and Qualites according to the corpuscular philosophy, illustrated by considerations and experiments* (Oxford, H. Hall for Ric. Davis, 1666).

6. Edinburgh University Library, Dc.1.4.

7. George Peacock, *Theses Philosophicae* (Marischal, 1693).

17

Aberdeen Professors 1690-1800: Two Structures, Two Professoriates, Two Careers

Roger L. Emerson

University of Western Ontario

Towards the end of the eighteenth century Aberdeen had two quite different universities. Relatively similar in 1690, they followed divergent careers during the 1700s, as this paper will show.

In 1690 Marischal and King's College had been about the same size and not markedly different, but by 1790 the former had surpassed its older sister in almost every way. It had more students and more educational assets, although it was meanly housed.[1] It shared the books deposited by the Stationers' Company in the King's College Library, litigation having established this right in the 1730s. Its own library in 1783 had received from the University Chancellor, Lord Bute, a handsome present of 1300 medical books which were to become the nucleus of a collection for the teaching of medicine which the University hoped soon to commence.[2] The College had many fine mathematical and scientific instruments. During the 1780s Patrick Copland, who taught natural philosophy, added to these a large collection of model machines and other teaching toys which were specially made for him but subsidised by the government.[3] In 1780 Professor Copland had raised funds for a new observatory which had been completed in the autumn of 1781, again with funds made available by the government and the Aberdeen Town Council.[4] It was well furnished with money raised by subscription and possessed two telescopes given by Lord Bute. One of these was an equatorial telescope made by Ramsden and worth about £500. Copland's colleague, the Professor of Natural and Civil History, James Beattie II, possessed a museum of natural curiosities worth about £500 which included a chemical laboratory.[5] Another in the College buildings belonged to George French who in 1793 would join the faculty as the first Professor of Chemistry.[6] A small botanical garden had recently been started and it was known that agriculture as well as medicine would be taught in the future.[7] Four of the eight men then teaching were vigorous and already had or were to make reputations, three of them in science. Two of the four other instructors were distinguished and still active.[8] The place was prosperous, confident, well connected with local politicians in Henry Dundas's camp and had aggressively tried to swallow its Old Aberdeen rival as recently as 1787.[9] Marischal College's faculty was without serious internal divisions, and its students were generally satisfied with the instruction they received from specialist professors who taught only one subject but often to some depth.[10]

The scene at King's College was not as bright. The College fabric had somewhat decayed over the century and the buildings were not all in good repair. They were also no longer ornamented by the bells which along with feudal superiorities and lands had been alienated to sustain professors whose salaries and fees had not kept pace with price rises and heightened expectations. The College Library had not been well maintained and no benefactor had been as generous as Lord Bute.[11] The instrument room does not seem to have been notable.[12] There were few or no model machines and probably no chemical laboratory.[13] There was not much in the way of a botanical garden and no one was soon to give botany lectures at King's as they were to do at Marischal College in 1792-1793.[14] The museum was impressive but it was kept by William Ogilvie, a man harassed by the majority of his colleagues and who in turn tormented at least seven of them.[15] Enrolments had not grown as they should have done and the place had probably never recovered from the doldrums which came after the failure of the Jacobite uprising of 1715. King's, an institution suspected by Whigs of being Jacobite and Episcopalian in sympathy, had not been blessed with government grants, and since the 1730s had found little private aid. In 1790 its faculty ranged in age from 20 to 76 with the average member 56 years of age.[16] Only three of the ten professors had reputations of any note. Students were still taught by regents whose classes covered every subject the student studied in his years at the College. The boys received an education which was probably poorer than that given anywhere else in Scotland where specialised professors had long been the rule. King's graduated students deficient in mathematics and science but perhaps as well schooled in history, classics and moral philosophy as those in New Aberdeen. If the students had reasons to be unhappy, so too did the teachers who continued to squabble among themselves as they had done throughout the century.

The contrasting conditions and achievements of the two institutions are mostly explained by the differences in their constitutions and the implications which these had in the recruitment of new professors. After 1690 and the abolition of Episcopacy, King's became in effect a closed corporation. Active, resident and concerned bishops no longer sat as Chancellors able to influence appointments or to arbitrate and settle disputes. They were replaced by the Earls of Erroll who favoured a Jacobite faction within the College. From 1716 to 1761 King's actually had no Chancellor, a condition into which it again relapsed from 1770 until 1793. One normal connexion with the political world was lacking. In its absence the Masters were freer to co-opt new professors than they would otherwise have been. The Rectorship of the

University was also often vacant and when filled it was usually supplied by men who were mostly absentees who seem not always to have appointed *vices*. Since the King's Rector usually did not help to elect new professors as did his Glasgow counterpart, the Rector's influence upon collegiate matters was less than it might have been. Local gentlemen were called upon to serve as Procurators of the Four Nations and thus to form part of the *ad hoc* bodies which chose the Principal, Sub-Principal, Civilist, Mediciner and Humanist. Others also served as Assessors to a Rector. In each case they almost invariably represented a dominant faculty clique since they were elected or indirectly chosen by the Masters. The Synod of Aberdeen chose the Professor of Divinity and after 1698 the Crown picked the Regius Professor of Oriental Language. The other three livings were really in the gift of the installed Masters who could and did disregard the wishes of outsiders whenever periods of peace and stability allowed them to pursue their inclinations.[17] During the earlier seventeenth century the College had felt outside pressures, but after 1660 the King's faculty behaved as one expects a closed corporation of that time to behave. Its members looked after their own and not even the Visitation Commission of 1690 much affected the institution. St Andrews in 1690 had all but one of its professors purged but the Aberdeen colleges were not touched. From c.1670 to 1717, when these colleges were purged of Jacobites after the 1715 Rebellion, King's College was run increasingly as a family affair by Principal George Middleton who was himself the son of Principal Alexander Middleton. In 1690 Principal Middleton could point to four relatives on the staff (George and Alexander Fraser, James Garden, Patrick Gordon); it is likely that two other Masters were related to each other and perhaps to this dominant family connexion. In 1717 Principal Middleton, still in office, could point to five relatives, three of them Gordons. Such inbreeding the 1717 Visitation Commission may have tried to end when it appointed five apparently unrelated men to livings held by the Jacobite Masters whom it had deposed. This resulted in the formation within the College of a new political faction loyal to the Squadrone whose influence had secured the places. By 1726 or so this political connexion had also begun to look like a family alliance. Principal Chalmers and the Gordons and Gregories had begun to vote together against the Squadrone men. By the 1740s both factions had consolidated. Sub-Principal Alexander Burnet, his brother-in-law (John Chalmers), two nephews (Daniel Bradfute and Alexander Rait), and a more distant relative (James Catanach), were all generally voting together in College meetings in opposition to Principal Chalmers who by now was related by marriage to the Gregory and Gordon families. Even in 1790 Principal John Chalmers would be sitting in meetings with a brother-in-law (William Thom), a cousin (Thomas Gordon), and the cousin's assistant, successor and grandson (Robert Eden Scott). Voting often with these men was Alexander Gerard whose son, Gilbert, joined the faculty in 1790. The closed corporation perpetuated family interests but it had brought into the College few men from outside the Aberdeen area, few men of distinction and few whose perspective on things was different. Nepotism had led to a conservatism which by the 1780s had become as sclerotic as the elderly men who then presided over the College. Nepotism had also produced conflicts which had soured tempers and used up in litigation resources which could have been better spent.

The families installed at King's prior to 1717 had been Jacobite and Episcopalian in outlook but not greatly at odds with one another. After 1717 the old unity of sentiment was gone. Jacobites, Squadrone supporters and Argathelians loyal to the Duke of Argyll wrangled endlessly over issues which could not be resolved intra-murally without a Chancellor or a strong Rector. Disputes were carried to the law courts not only to settle matters of principle but also to show the strength and support of political factions. Happy enough to foment or use College disputes to their own advantage, politicians did not intervene at King's in constructive ways.[18] Only with the appointment of James Ogilvie, Lord Deskford, to the Chancellorship in 1761 did this stop. Deskford, an assertive man, demanded that new proposals, methods and ideas be accepted and acted upon. He also wanted appointed men who believed in them and were loyal to him. When this happened, King's began a museum, the teaching of ancient history, drawing and other polite skills. The reformed curriculum adopted in 1754 and constantly questioned was now put beyond repeal.[19] It is also worth noting that it was Deskford's protégés and appointees (William Ogilvie, James Dunbar and John Ross), who favoured the union with Marischal College in 1785-1787. Had King's College and University been less insulated from the outside world it would have done better during the eighteenth century.

Marischal College found its Chancellors in the patrons of the University, the Earls Marischal to whom the founder had reserved the right to appoint five of the seven men teaching in 1715.[20] Because the tenth Earl had joined the Jacobites in the Rebellion of 1715, these rights had been forfeited to the Crown and the chairs converted to Regius Chairs in that year. Both the Earls' and the King's political managers tended to use their patronage powers to maximise their influence in and around Aberdeen. This helped to keep the corporation open to outside influences as did the involvement of the Aberdeen Town Council in Marischal College affairs. The Town Fathers served as trustees of many College funds and held rights to appoint to the Chairs of Divinity and Mathematics as well as to the church living normally held by the College Principal whose income was largely derived from this parish.[21] The degree to which this openness to outside influences mattered is easily and clearly to be seen.

In 1690 the seven Marischal College Masters seem to have included only two men who were related—Alexander and James Moir. In 1715 Principal Robert Paterson could point to a son-in-law (William Smith), but none of the other professors are known to have been related. Indeed, throughout the period 1690 to 1800 only 34% of the faculty members seem to have been related to anyone concurrently belonging to the corporations. At King's, on the other hand, at least 38 of the 67 men who taught there during this period (57%) could point to one or more relatives on the faculty during their tenure of office. Over 70% could find a relative by blood or marriage who had preceded or would succeed them. The Marischal College figure was 40%.

What replaced familial relationships at Marischal College were political patronage ties. Between c.1675 and 1716 the Earls Marischal appointed at least one family tutor (William Meston), a distant relative (George Keith) and several men recommended to them by friends. Among these were Dr Thomas Bower (recommended by the Earl of Erroll) and William Smith, a protégé of Lord Pittmeddan and Lord Charles Hay.[22] Other appointees probably had the endorsement of the Town Council since they were themselves burgesses (Patrick Chalmers) or the sons of burgesses (George Peacock).[23] The Town Fathers continued to be interested in appointments and after 1715 they came to enjoy more power over them, since granting their wishes helped politicians to manage the town and to secure its vote for their parliamentary interest group.[24] The consequence of this was that jobs went to the brighter sons of relatives of town councillors, to city ministers and to men with London connexions who stood well with the political managers of Scotland. Before 1715 the Town Council had been most concerned with its own chairs; after that date it sought with some success to fill others.

In 1716-1717 the councillors lobbied the Visitors concerning the seven appointments to be made in those years.[25] The results were rather impressive. Thomas Blackwell was picked to be Principal in 1717 as the Council had asked. The livings which had reverted to the Crown were not filled by time-serving hacks but by the 'good Masters' whom they had requested. Among them were Colin MacLaurin, Provost Cruden's son, George, and two other men (John Anderson and Patrick Hardie) who probably had local connexions. None of these men appear to have been related but they were all clearly in debt to the Squadrone politicians who secured their election or the royal warrants for their chairs. In the period with which we are concerned, ten men named Gordon taught at King's. At Marischal, politics prevented such nepotism. There were three Beatties but no other surname occurs more than twice. Moreover, while King's had almost no one teaching at it from outside the area, Marischal throughout the period benefited from an infusion of talented men educated elsewhere. Among those who brought along with them new ideas and attitudes are to be counted Thomas Blackwell, Sr, George Turnbull, Robert Pollock, Robert Hamilton, William Morgan, James Kidd and William Laurence Brown—all of whom owed their jobs to politicians in Edinburgh and London as well as to men in Aberdeen.

The political upheaval caused by the 1715 Rebellion also seems to have benefited Marischal College in other ways. Both King's and Marischal lost Chancellors as a result of it. Because of bungling and shifts of power in London, King's was not to know a Chancellor's authority again until 1761.[26] It was thus without a head and without the usual connexion to the political system. Marischal College did not elect a Chancellor, but from c.1725 to 1761 this role was effectively played for the corporation by Lord Ilay, after 1743 the third Duke of Argyll.[27] He and the town council acted as protectors and benefactors of an institution which they kept open to outside influences and which they expected to be responsive to the felt needs of the area from which it recruited its students. Ilay might not have wanted to be Chancellor but his role as the political patronage manager of Scotland during successive administrations more or less involved him in the usual duties of a Chancellor—approving appointments, negotiating with the government and securing favours for the College. The College could have had no better patron. He was followed in these functions by his nephew, the third Earl of Bute, who was elected Chancellor in 1761. Bute paid little attention to the Aberdeen town councillors but he too kept the institution open and responsive to changes. Indeed, by recommending to the Crown for appointments men versed in science, he may have encouraged the development of a school whose alumni graduated with more exposure to and training in science than was the case elsewhere in Scotland. Both Ilay and Bute paid a decent regard to the wishes of professors but both also had an input into the process by which professors were chosen.

Finally, the 1715 Rebellion led at Marischal to a more thorough purge of Jacobite professors.[28] This allowed for the creation of a faculty thoroughly Whiggish (and Squadrone) in outlook. Unrelated men tied to political sponsors in the same camp neither quarrelled so much nor as bitterly as did members of competing families and political parties ensconced at King's. Marischal College professors were forced to look outside their corporation for favours which, if they found them, had to be approved by men holding political power. As it happened, the men who generally dispensed patronage in eighteenth-century Scotland were quite enlightened.[29] Most were improvers; many were intellectuals. Some were also keen to see merit rewarded and recognised it in polite, secular pursuits tinged neither with fanatic religious enthusiasm nor Jacobitism. It is hardly surprising that Marischal was a more dynamic and fast changing institution. It well served the classes from which its students and professors came just as King's better reflected the outlook of the more conservative landed gentry.

At both colleges the professors were recruited from the professional class, from the gentry and from the affluent business families of the city of Aberdeen. There are few clear and obvious differences shown by statistics concerning the social origins of either set of professors. More of the King's men came from landed families (17%) and fewer had tradesmen for fathers (3%), than was true at Marischal (9%, 10%). While there were more lawyers, doctors, physicians and professors among the parents of King's men (49%) than among those of the Aberdeen College (36%), they were very close in the number of clerics (21% and 30% respectively). The mothers' backgrounds were similar although they tended as younger daughters to marry down a bit. The statistics, however, do not tell the whole story. The landed families whose sons became Marischal college professors seem usually to have been connected with trade and small estates rather than to the greater gentry or nobility. At least five of the King's professors descended from fathers or grandfathers with titles. Only one Marischal man seems to have done so. The professors there could point back to provosts and baillies of Aberdeen or elsewhere but not to substantial landed estates. The same pattern is shown by their marriages. Three King's professors married titled ladies or the daughters of titled aristocrats; one professor at Marischal could claim that honour. There seems also to have been a difference in the numbers marrying into landed families. Nineteen men in Old Aberdeen did so but only eleven in the New Town (33%, 21%). At least 78% of the professors at King's married (7% did not). The Marischal College figures are slightly different: 70% and 9%. The average age of marriage of these men declined from 33+ years in the seventeenth century to below 30 around 1800. The age declined as incomes rose and patriarchalism diminished. It is not surprising that Marischal College men should have been marrying at about 28 near the end of the period. What is a bit surprising is the professors' ability to preserve or better the status of their fathers even though many were younger sons.

The birth order of 26 (45%) of King's College professors is known, as is that of 33 (62%) of the men at Marischal. At King's 58% of those known were eldest or first surviving sons; only slightly more than a third (36%) of the Marischal sample falls in that category. One would therefore expect King's to have a higher rate of men maintaining or advancing over their fathers' status in life but this may not have been the case. Only 43% of the King's professors bettered their condition; 24% remained the same while 9% lost ground. At Marischal where the proportion of younger sons was much higher more of them did better, and better than their fathers. At least 54% advanced beyond their fathers, while 12% stayed even, and 17% declined in status. Marischal College men seem, then, to have been a bit brighter, more aggressive and higher achievers. Certainly the greater representation of upwardly mobile men in the New Town College would have made it a more dynamic place. It may also in part account for their promotion of an education which was practical, useful and more demanding than that given at King's. This seems to be borne out by the educational experiences of men at each place.

Most men at both colleges were educated locally at least as undergraduates.[30] This is known to be true of 86% of the King's professors of whom no more than eight could have pursued an arts course outside Aberdeen. A quarter of the men who taught at Marischal may have done so, and 19% are known to have studied elsewhere before taking an M.A.: Marischal College is known to have employed more of its own alumni than did King's. It also educated more men who taught at King's than that college sent to Marischal, a fact which suggests the city's college was better than the one in the Old Town. Both colleges generally employed men who had some education beyond the arts course—80% of the faculty at King's, 89% at Marischal. These figures meant, however, quite different things for the students in the two institutions. The King's figure is inflated by fifteen sinecure professors, Civilists and Mediciners, who did not teach. At Marischal most of those who possessed medical or legal training did indeed conduct classes although not necessarily in law and physick. When allowance is made for the sinecurists at both schools, Marischal College still ends up with 85% of its teaching faculty having pursued some form of further education while only 53% of the teachers at King's are known to have done so. This experience is clearly reflected in the professors' initial occupations and careers prior to appointment. About equal numbers tutored or taught at grammar school before appointment to a faculty—6 in each case. Another 7 at each college began as assistants to sitting professors. Twice as many (12, 21%), found in a King's College professorship their first significant adult job. At Marischal about half (49%) of the effective teaching staff had qualified for or pursued some profession prior to appointment to the faculty. At King's the figure was closer to a third (34%).

The experiences which each set of men brought to bear upon their teaching was also affected by the places in which they had received their education. Before 1746 the King's men had a clear statistical edge in those educated abroad. But, since these were mostly M.D.s and advocates who did not lecture, this figure is not very meaningful. There was probably little difference on this score between the men teaching arts up to c.1750 when the balance shifted in favour of Marischal College. This is perhaps more easily seen in the figure for those who travelled abroad, where the decline in the King's travellers is very sharp. While generally true in other universities, this trend affected Marischal less, for it could point to four men teaching after 1770 who had been partially educated abroad.

Marischal College professors seem to have been somewhat better educated and more accomplished men by the time they were appointed. That judgment is also borne out by the age at which they generally qualified for professions. At Marischal the median figure ranged between 21 and 22/23 for cohorts entering or in academic life before 1690, 1690-1719, 1720-1749, 1750-1799. At King's the range was between 22 and 27 with only one median (1720-1749) below that at Marischal. The average ages of entry into a career were nearly the same, 22.8 at King's and 22.7 at Marischal. The average age of appointment to their university posts was about the same: 32 at King's, 31 at Marischal. The differences are marginal but suggest that the more vigorous school appointed men who were just a bit better all along the way. This is supported by the fact that towards the end of the period the average age of appointment at Aberdeen's college had actually dropped to 28 while that at King's continued to be very close to 30. These figures have to be seen in relation to others concerning the average tenure of the faculty members at both universities.

The average tenure of a Marischal College chair (the time a man held a particular appointment), was 17.9 years in arts, 22.7 years for divinity and 26.7 years for medical men. That works out at about 20 years for the average university appointment. At King's the figures were about the same with the average also 20 years. Another set of figures is very different. Marischal had a steady intake of new men in every decade except two: 1700-1709 and 1710-1719. On average between 1690 and 1799 a new professor was added to the King's faculty every three years and to the Marischal College faculty every 3.8 years. Because of the size of the faculties and their effective teaching staffs this replacement (and expansion) rate meant that there was usually greater change per decade at Marischal than at King's. In six of the eleven decades studied, the change in teaching professorships was usually more marked, averaging about 49% at Marischal and only 37% at King's. For the faculties generally, the rates were 43.7% and 30.5%. There was consequently a much greater inflow of new ideas at the burgh's college than in the Old Town. It is

TABLE I
EDUCATIONAL RECORD OF PROFESSORS

	King's College		Marischal College	
	Numbers	%	Numbers	%
Educated locally	50	86	40	75
Elsewhere	4	7	10	19
Unknown	4	7	3	6
Total	58	100	53	100
Alumni	39	67	39	79
Educated at M.C./K.C.	11	19	5	9
MAs	30	51	29	55
Some Divinity School	18	31	27	51
Divinity Hall K.C./M.C.	7	12	13	25
Divinity School not in Aberdeen	0	0	10	19
Law (teachers)	9 (0)	16	3 (3)	6
Medicine (teachers)	12	21	9 (7)	17
Some further education (T = teachers)	46 (31T)	80 (53)	47 (45T)	89 (55)
Studied outside Scotland	10	17	8	15

	King's College			Marischal College		
	(bef. '46)	(aft. '45)		(bef. '46)	(aft. '45)	
Travel in Europe before appoint.	11 |19%	12 21%	| 2 3%	7 |13%	5 9%	| 6 11%
after appoint.	2 | 3%	1 unknown		6 12%		
Totals	13 |22%	13 22%	|	11 |21%	11	|21%
Tutored or taught before appoint.	13	|22		13	|25	

also interesting that the longest period between King's appointments was ten years; at Marischal it was six. If sinecure chairs are disregarded, then the periods lengthen at King's to 12.1 years but only to 8.4 at the neighbouring institution. There was also a greater opportunity at King's for men to be advanced from one chair to another. Because of that, the average length of service in the institution was greater: 26.1 years at King's but only 22.2 at Marischal. The longevity of staff members at King's also worked to increase the conservatism of a professoriate which was composed of men who came to their jobs seeking security and not intending to change much. Those who did not fit this mould tended to leave if they could do so.[31]

Were this paper not restricted in length, it would be interesting to discuss the achievements of the 111 men who taught in Old and New Aberdeen between 1690 and 1800. Since there is not space to do this, let me summarise my findings. The structures of the two universities determined their processes of recruitment. These gave to each college a set of professors differing in origin, outlook and vigour. They in turn set the courses which each institution followed during this period. King's men were contentious, litigious and conservative in outlook; those at Marischal pursued the interests of their patrons which they shared and were useful to the thriving industrialising port of Aberdeen. King's somewhat consciously catered to the educational needs of landed families, often Highland families, who expected their sons to make careers in fields in which science was not too important, but to which history, the classics and moral philosophy with a didactic emphasis were seen as guides to the understanding and leadership of men. King's stagnated throughout much of the eighteenth century, unable to rise above the mediocrity to which its recruitment policies confined it. When good men did turn up, they did so in families which were for the moment dominant; their appearance was somewhat accidental. Marischal's men were no less nepotistically inclined but they could not exclude outside influence upon appointments. Town councillors, politicians, gentlemen, clerics and many men not in Aberdeen all helped to pick the teachers at Marischal. Because they hoped to place those they recommended, the recommendations had to be of fairly good men. The recruitment process at Marischal College was rather typical of that at Edinburgh and Glasgow Universities. It shows us why those institutions also flourished, and why King's, and the St Andrews arts colleges which resembled it, did not.

Notes

1. As early as 1759 Marischal College was said to be enrolling double the number of students then attending King's; Minutes of King's College, vol.9, 31 October 1759, AUL, MS K. 44.
2. William Knight, 'Marischal College Collection', AUL, MS M. 111: 1107; 'Catalogue of Medical Books presented to the Library of Marischal College by John Earl of Bute 1783', AUL, MS M. 362.
3. These, and his use of them, are described by John S. Reid, 'Patrick Copland 1748-1822: aspects of his life and times at Marischal College', *Aberdeen University Review*, 172 (1984), pp.355-79.
4. John S. Reid, 'The Castlehill Observatory, Aberdeen', *Journal of the History of Astronomy*, 13 (1982), pp.84-96, 88.
5. The value of this collection can be inferred from letters of Professor James Beattie who arranged for a loan which allowed his nephew of the same name to purchase the collection and in a sense the Chair of Natural and Civil History which was valueless without its teaching materials. James Beattie to Sir William Forbes, 20 October 1788, NLS, Fettercairn MSS, MS 4796 Box 94; James Beattie to James Hay Beattie, 19 October 1787 and 3 August 1788; Cosmo Gordon to James Beattie, 24 September 1788, 12 November 1791, Beattie Correspondence, AUL, MS 30/1 275, 288; 30/2 575, 659. The collection James Beattie II purchased combined those of Professors George Skene and William Morgan.
6. French seems to have taught chemistry in Marischal College after October 1783 but he was formally admitted as a professor only in December 1793 when the deed of settlement establishing the chair came into effect, Alexander Findlay, *The*

Teaching of Chemistry in the Universities of Aberdeen (Aberdeen, AUP, 1935) pp.4-7.

7. The botanical garden is mentioned in Marischal College Minutes, 6 May 1780, AUL, MS 41. A Chair of Agriculture had been established in 1790 by the testament of Sir William Fordyce, but the bequest did not take effect until 1840, P.J. Anderson, *Fasti Academiae Mariscallanae Aberdonensis* (Aberdeen, New Spalding Club, 1889-98), vol. I, pp. 452-54, vol. II, p.73. University medical teaching can be said to date from 1789 when the Aberdeen Medical Society was founded and given a meeting place in Marischal College.

8. James Beattie II, John Stuart, Patrick Copland, Robert Hamilton; Principal George Campbell, James Hay Beattie, James Beattie I and Alexander Donaldson. Principal Campbell and Professor Donaldson each held two chairs.

9. W.R. Humphries, *William Ogilvie and the Projected Union of the Colleges 1786-1787* (Aberdeen, AUP, 1940).

10. There is much evidence to support this claim, some of it cited by Reid (see note 4 above).

11. These charges were all made by William Ogilvie and were generally true; Humphries, *William Ogilvie*, pp.4-23.

12. King's College had had an instrument room since at least c.1710 but few additions to it are recorded in the King's College Minutes save in 1743 and 1754.

13. Chemistry had been taught at King's as early as 1754 but it had probably ceased to be a serious academic subject by c.1760 when it became clear that a plan to begin the university teaching of medicine in Aberdeen had failed; Findlay, *The Teaching of Chemistry*, p.43.

14. Alexander Smith had taught botany in Aberdeen 1792-1793. In 1794 he petitioned the Town Council for an annual salary of £10.00. The Council, had it granted this request, would, in effect, have created a Chair of Botany in Marischal College since that is where the garden existed, and the Town enjoyed influence and patronage which it was always eager to increase. Aberdeen City Archives, Town Council Letter Book 13, Alexander Smith to Provost Abercrombie, 10 November 1794.

15. Ogilvie enjoyed some celebrity as a naturalist and was praised by others to whom he had been useful—the eleventh Earl of Buchan, the Comte de Lauraguais. 'Extracts from the Diaries and Letter books of the Earl of Buchan, No. 9', Glasgow University Library, Murray MS 201/65; Mr McLeod to Dr David Skene, n.d. AUL, David Skene MSS, MS 38.

16. King's College appointments made during 1790 had reduced the average age to 49 by the end of the year. At Marischal College the average age was around 44 with the range running from 22 to 71. The median at King's was 55 and 48; at Marischal it was 41.

17. After the Revolution of 1688/89 a Visitation Commission had mandated open, competitive trials for candidates seeking regencies. The rule was ignored at Marischal College and fell into disuse at King's after 1711.

18. The different sides in college disputes were usually represented in courts by counsel belonging to opposed political factions. These groups could also rely upon the loyalties of professors in the short run but not generally during a long period of opposition. At King's such loyalties allowed the elections of university professors, particularly the Civilists, to become complicated contests which helped to show the local political strength of competing groups.

19. The printed 'Abstract of some Statutes and Orders of King's College in Old Aberdeen' (1753) provided for 'those Parts of Education, which are not commonly

reckoned Academical, such as Dancing, Writing, Book-keeping, French, & c' (p.11) but there is little evidence of these additions until the 1760s. A drawing master came c.1760 but other items on this list were probably only taught after that date. Marischal College enacted similar reforms in 1753. These are described in [Alexander Gerard], *Plan of Education in the Marischal College* (Aberdeen, James Chalmers, 1755) and in the Minutes of Marischal College for 11 January 1753, AUL, MS M. 41.

20. The College had been founded in 1593 by George Keith, fifth Earl Marischal, who had reserved to his successors these patronage rights.

21. The Mathematics Chair had been endowed by its founder Duncan Liddel in 1613 with the Town Council as the trustee. Gradually the Council squeezed the Liddel family out of its right to help pick the professors. The Town had endowed the Chair of Divinity in 1616 and retained the right to fill it. The patronage of the burgh churches was also vested in the corporation.

22. Bower belonged to the circle of Edinburgh medical Newtonians gathered about Dr Archibald Pitcairne. See R.L. Emerson, 'Science and the origins and concerns of the Scottish Enlightenment', forthcoming; AUL Thomas Gordon Papers, MS K. 34: 72; P.J. Anderson, *Fasti*, vol. II, p.39; AUL, MS M. 93.

23. I am grateful to Mr Gordon Des Brisay for supplying this information.

24. After the Union of 1707 Aberdeen joined with three smaller burghs, which it could often control, to elect a single M.P.

25. Aberdeen City Archives, Aberdeen Council Register, vol. 58: 2 May 1711; 6, 24 September 1716, 3 October 1716; 30 January, 10 April, 1 May, 16, 28 August, 11 September 1717; Letter Book 8.

26. Neither the Duke of Roxburgh nor Lord Ilay became Chancellor after the '15. The story is best told by Thomas Gordon. Ilay refused to accept the office given 'in compliment to the Argathelian party' because it had, in 1716 'lost much of its influence ... he declining to accept, the Duke of Roxburgh was chosen 1st Sept 1718 during the power & influence of what was called the Squadroni Party of which he was the head. But he also politely excused himself on account of the E. of Ilay having a subsisting nomination & patent of election under the College seal'. AUL, MS K. 34, p.5.

27. Thomas Gordon went on to say that Marischal College lacked the power to elect a Chancellor since that had reverted to the Crown along with the patronage rights of the Earl Marischal, *ibid*. This is partially borne out by a petition to the Crown drafted in 1727 and signed by those professors who sided with Ilay. This notes the College and University's want of a Chancellor and asks the King to name as Chancellor the six year old Duke of Cumberland, William August. AUL, MS M. 387/9/7/2.

28. At Marischal College only Thomas Blackwell, Sr survived the purge of 1717 which ousted six of the seven other members of the corporation. Blackwell became Principal, as did his better known son Thomas, Jr in 1748. King's in 1717 replaced only half of its ten professors.

29. Lord Ilay's importance as a university patron ought not to be under-estimated. He brokered or had some involvement in at least sixty of the 123 appointments made during his 31 years of service to London ministries. His influence was greatest at Glasgow but in Aberdeen he also counted. Between 1730 and 1760 four of eighteen appointments made at King's were probably his (22%). At Marischal from 1727 to 1760 fifteen of twenty-two were (68%). Between 1761 and 1788 Lord Bute brokered six of thirteen placements (46%). Both men were intellectuals eager to reward merit.

30. See Table I.
31. Marischal College lost only five men during the period, who left voluntarily. Two, Colin MacLaurin and William Duff, had been censured for misconduct and a third, George Skene, seems to have been informally admonished. Another, George Turnbull, left to secure a higher income and more pleasant life. The fifth, Alexander Gerard, went to King's College for reasons unknown. At King's there were eight resignations. Six of the men left their position for greener pastures (Thomas Bower, David Dalrymple, Alexander Garden of Troup, John Gregory, John Ker, Thomas Reid). Two others retired to live upon their estates, John Ross and James Dunbar.

18

Late Eighteenth-Century Adult Education in the Sciences at Aberdeen: the Natural Philosophy Classes of Professor Patrick Copland

John S. Reid

University of Aberdeen

I

Beginning in 1785, fifteen years before George Birkbeck, Patrick Copland delivered an evening course of some seventy lectures a year, aimed specifically at those involved in the mechanical and other professions. The course was repeated roughly once every two years over the next twenty-seven years, representing a greater and more sustained effort than any of his contemporaries in the field. This was an impressive venture, rightly deserving the tag of 'pioneering'.[1]

Even without the introduction of evening classes, there was already provision at Marischal College (as at Glasgow and Edinburgh) for citizens to attend the regular academic course in natural philosophy. At Marischal this consisted of about 300 lectures given by Copland and called the 'public' course. Any man could simply enrol along with the official university students. There was no entrance examination, and expenses totalling about £4 for the entire course were within reach of the savings of many. Quite a number made use of this opportunity, as can be seen from the accompanying Table 1; they were known as 'ungowned' students and generally fell in with the discipline of the gowned class. Admirable though the arrangement was, it required a commitment on the part of the ungowned student to attend during the daytime sixteen hours of teaching each week, continuously for five months from November until April. In addition, the lectures did have the unwritten prerequisite of a modest mathematical knowledge. On both these counts they were therefore unsuitable for most artisans.

The teaching and practice of natural philosophy had radically changed at the beginning of the eighteenth century, with the introduction into teaching of apparatus specially designed to demonstrate principles which had pre-

TABLE I

Year	ug	tot	Year	ug	tot	Year	ug	tot	Year	ug	tot	Year	ug	tot	Year	ug	tot
			1780	1	13	1790	1	19	1800	4	26	1810	10	52	1820	14	72
			1781	2	28	1791	2	21	1801	7	48	1811	11	58	1821	21	73
			1782	3	30	1792	7	39	1802	6	37	1812	8	49			
			1783	2	26	1793	1	27	1803	11	30	1813	9	44			
			1784	7	39	1794	4	27	1804	10	34	1814	9	66			
1775	7	36	1785	6	39	1795	6	30	1805	13	50	1815	15	58			
1776	7	25	1786	3	32	1796	3	34	1806	10	47	1816	6	60			
1777	4	37	1787	4	28	1797	4	31	1807	8	57	1817	8	64			
1778	4	26	1788	(3	28)	1798	6	41	1808	6	43	1818	13	60			
1779	7	34	1789	2	38	1799	8	34	1809	10	43	1819	11	84			

For the academic session beginning in the years shown, the table shows the number of ungowned students (ug) taking classes in Copland's year, and the total number of students in that year (tot). The expression 'ungowned' is that used by Knight in AUL, MS M 114, p.2325. As ungowned students the table counts those who appear in the college records only for the tertian year. This is probably unduly strict for there were also an appreciable number of students taking only two years study out of four, one being Copland's year. The years cover Copland's tenure, though in 1779 Robert Hamilton took the natural philosophy class and Copland the mathematics class. In 1788 the roll was not recorded, for some reason, but that year 26 students took the second mathematics class and hence likely figures for 1788 are as shown. For the 47 years there were a total of 2238 students of whom 324 were ungowned. The figures are not absolutely precise because in addition to the students of 1788 some other students are known to have attended the course without appearing on the register. See the evidence of Professor Knight, 19 September 1827, in *Evidence, Oral and Documentary, taken and received by the Commissioners Appointed by His Majesty George IV, July 23rd, 1826; and Reappointed by His Majesty William IV, October 12th, 1830 for visiting the Universities of Scotland*, vol. IV, *University of Aberdeen*, pp.93 and 291 (HMSO, London, 1837), and P.J. Anderson, *Fasti Academiae Mariscallanae Aberdonensis* (Aberdeen, New Spalding Club, 1908), vol. II, pp.345-442. The 1788 figures are from AUL, MS M. 388/1.

viously been explained by philosophical and mathematical argument. In 1783 Copland obtained a three-year grant to employ an instrument maker, John King, to furnish him with a set of working models to illustrate the application of mechanical principles to industrial and agricultural practice.[2] These models were to be additional to Copland's own demonstration apparatus. By the autumn of 1785 the project was sufficiently well advanced for Copland to place an advertisement in the *Aberdeen Journal* announcing that he would begin a private evening class directed towards those 'engaged in the mechanical professions, or to such gentlemen as are inclined to renew their acquaintance with those studies'. He continued:

> In this course, the Principles of *Mechanics, Hydrostatics, Electricity, Magnetism and Astronomy*, together with the late discoveries on the different kinds of *air* will be illustrated, chiefly by experiments, and reasonings deduced from them.[3]

The spirit of this advertisement echoes the unsuccessful 1726 proposals of Marischal College to establish a formal course on 'Experimental Philosophy'.[4]

Copland's course was to be given on Tuesdays, Thursdays and Saturdays at 7 o'clock, days used the previous year for Mr French's private chemistry course. French changed his days to alternate with Copland's. The price of the course was one guinea, a substantial sum in 1785, representing about a week and a half's pay for a journeyman. Nonetheless it was a pretty good bargain for a course of 70 lectures illustrated by a range of models and apparatus that far exceeded the stock in trade of an itinerant lecturer. The typical charge of an itinerant giving a few lectures (aimed at the middle classes) was one to two shillings a lecture. By comparison the local newspaper cost 6d in 1800; a seat at the theatre, one or two shillings. Copland's charge remained at one guinea until 1806/1807 when it was increased to two guineas. He seems to have given the course on fourteen occasions over a twenty-seven year period. Once it had become established, the advertisements shrank to a few lines of intimation, always emphasising the mechanical content and occasionally suggesting a change in the supporting topics.[5]

Although Copland can rightly be considered one of the real pioneers of serious scientific education for tradesmen, he was by no means operating in a vacuum. Professor Hamilton of Marischal College advertised mathematics classes in 1781, 1782 and 1783 aimed at 'those Subjects which are useful in different Departments of Life; Geography, Navigation, Fortification, Perspective, Astronomy and the like'.[6] French's evening class begun in 1782 was directed at 'the application of Chemistry to Manufactures, Arts and Agriculture', with lectures also on the preparation of medicines.[7] It was given on at least thirty occasions and probably every year over a thirty-six year period, and continued thereafter by his assistant Dr William Henderson. French was appointed the first Professor of Chemistry at Marischal College in 1793 and his evening course, although open to the public, became the official chemistry course of the college.[8] It never acquired the astonishing popularity achieved by Thomas Hope's chemistry course in Edinburgh.[9] Dr Livingstone, Professor of Medicine at Marischal College, offered an early evening class on tropical and military diseases as one of several medical classes available; Professor Kidd offered classes in Latin and elementary Arabic. In the 1790s in particular, there was a remarkable enthusiasm among the Marischal College professors for extra-mural teaching.

Outside the college Andrew Mackay, whom Copland had appointed as Superintendent of the Castlehill Observatory, gave lessons on navigation and surveying, astronomy and geography.[10] As David Gavine has discovered, private tuition in these subjects and in mathematics was widely available in Scotland in the second half of the eighteenth century.[11] In Aberdeen in the late eighteenth century, private classes could be found with relative ease on several modern languages, the classics, dancing, music making and other social accomplishments. Aberdonians were not content to have two universities about a mile apart; there was a belief, which seemed to take root in the population at large in the eighteenth century, that further education was a valuable investment. Indeed, the spirit of self-help so essential to the spread of education in the nineteenth century was clearly present in late eighteenth-century Aberdeen.

Aberdeen was unusual in that it had to provide this education almost entirely from its own ranks, for its geographical isolation in all but the last decade of the eighteenth century discouraged itinerant lecturers. In the year after Copland started, a Mr Clarke (probably Cuthbert Clarke) did make the trip north through the east coast towns, giving his course of lectures on natural and experimental philosophy at various stops.[12] Upon reaching Aberdeen, and hearing of Copland's course, he gave only one lecture there. Two other itinerants appeared during Copland's time: J. Fleming, a member of the London Philosophical Society whose ten lectures on the Elements of Natural Philosophy in 1812 were more concerned with metaphysics and morals; and T. Longstaffe, who gave in 1815 a course of popular lectures on astronomy, illustrated by appropriate apparatus and the phantasmagoria.[13] This was nothing compared with the itinerant and private activity in Edinburgh, for example, where in 1802 a friend of Copland's remarked in a letter 'the Professors are very much alarmed at the increase of private classes'.[14] The relative lack of itinerant activity in Aberdeen is confirmed by John Cable, whose survey of eighteenth-century itinerant lectures in science in Scotland finds virtually nothing in Aberdeen.[15]

II

In a letter to the Danish scholar Grimur Thorkelin, Copland remarked in 1790 that his course:

> has been attended by a much greater number of Mechanics (such as Millwrights, Watchmakers, Carpenters, Joiners, Smiths &c) besides Merchants and private Gentlemen in Town, than I could have hoped for.[16]

However, if Copland kept a record of his attendees, it has not come to light. Professor Knight, Copland's successor to the chair at Marischal College, implies in his evidence to the Royal Commission which investigated Marischal College in 1827 that a typical attendance at Copland's course was about sixty.[17] Knight himself ran a private class on chemistry and natural history for five years between 1811 and 1816.[18] A meticulous man, he has left us a list of the participants and, in many instances, their professions. In the absence of direct information on Copland's audience, it is worth looking briefly at Knight's list. In his first year he attracted 95 paying participants, including 20 clergymen, physicians and lawyers; 42 gentlemen, manufacturers and merchants; and 33 college students. In addition 7 free tickets were given as a courtesy to friends. In 1812/1813, the year that Copland gave his last course on alternate days with Knight, there were 37 gentlemen, merchants, etc; 27 college students; and 2 free tickets, including one to Copland's eldest son, Alexander. In 1813/1814, 58 paid and 2 were free, including Copland himself; in 1814/1815, 50 paid and 2 were free; in 1815/1816, 48 paid and 6 were free. Knight's lists are a cross-section of early nineteenth-century middle-class Aberdonians, with many trades represented. Copland's own audience would have contained artisans particularly interested in the applications of mechanics, plus a good number from Knight's list or its equivalent in earlier years.

The only known documented case of a student at Copland's class gives us some further insight into private classes in Aberdeen. The student was Joseph Clement (1779-1844), one of the best mechanical engineers of his day, noted for his development of the lathe and other tools, and his work as the engineer in charge of Babbage's calculating machine.[19] Among the papers in Clement's effects was found a ticket for Copland's lectures in the session 1812/1813. In 1812 Clement had been employed as a designer and maker of power looms by Leys, Masson & Co. in Aberdeen, at a wage of three guineas a week (a good wage for a mechanic). What Clement's biographer does not relate is that in the winter of 1812 Clement set himself up as a teacher of 'Geometrical and Perspective drawing; the principles of Mechanics and Architecture; the method of Drawing ornaments for friezes and capitals; and the method of shading them by Geometrical Principles'. He must have left Leys, Masson & Co., for he offered a day class at hours suited to clients and an evening class 'for young mechanics' on Mondays, Wednesdays and Fridays from seven to nine.[20] He was therefore going to Copland's lectures on Tuesdays, Thursdays and Saturdays, while giving his own on the alternate days. In 1813 he left Aberdeen for London, where he made his reputation. The fact that Clement kept his ticket for thirty years suggests that he had some regard for Copland's lectures.

III

Copland's course usually began in the second week of November and continued uninterrupted at the rate of three lectures a week until towards the end of April, a little longer than the academic session. This made it just over 70 lectures. In his letter to Thorkelin in 1790, he confirms this figure with the comment:

> The Course consists of about seventy Lectures from one and a half to two hours each, according as I see the attention of my hearers continue.[21]

Two volumes of Copland's manuscript notes have recently come to light, put together by one of his grandsons, Charles Murchison (1830-1879).[22] Volume 1 has been labelled by Murchison as Copland's private course notes and though there is internal evidence that some are so, it is not clear that the division of notes between academic and private courses is as simple as Murchison implies. Unfortunately, identification can now be made with less certainty than might be expected, for the notes confirm that Copland did not follow the custom of his day and deliver his course from written lectures but spoke, for the most part, *extempore*. His academic course was likewise presented.

Although the lure to tempt the practical man into the audience was utilitarian, the lectures were not merely maxims for mechanics. Their aims were to broaden the mind of the listener and to provide him with the principles, concepts and applications of physics. In the opening lecture, Copland outlined the reasons why his audience should listen: natural philosophy is 'a pursuit of the highest utility', but in addition it produces leisure and independence, augments the stock of human knowledge, gratifies curiosity, improves our reasoning powers and 'leads us to a knowledge of the wisdom of the Supreme Being in the construction of the Universe; and thus lays the best foundations for Natural Religion'.[23] It was with similar broad motives that scientific and technical education was promulgated in the nineteenth century.[24]

The time spent on each subject cannot be reconstructed from the notes with certainty but the following table is an attempt:

Mechanics	—23 lectures
Kepler, Galileo and Newton	— 1 lecture
Hydrostatics and Hydraulics	— 6 lectures
The Earth	— 2 lectures
Pneumatics	— 9 lectures
On Various Airs	— 9 lectures
Magnetism	— 2 lectures
Electricity	—12 lectures
Optics	— 7 lectures
Optics first appeared in the advertisement in 1798	

What is clear from the notes is the sheer effort put into the course by Copland, involving hundreds of demonstrations of the principles and applications of physics, using a collection of working models, scientific apparatus and diagrams that were the development of a lifelong interest. An inventory of his stock made at his death numbered over 500 items.[25] On the whole he avoided the purely entertaining demonstrations such as had been developed by Guyot, and popularly described by Hooper, and concentrated on the now classic demonstrations of phenomena that were developed by Desaguliers, Ferguson, Adams and others in the eighteenth century.[26] However, he obviously enjoyed shocking his audience with his electrostatic generator, discharging the college electrical cannon, filling the room with pungent blue smoke to exhibit the properties of oxygen, baffling the audience with magnetic deceptions and such like diversions. It was clearly no less important two hundred years ago than nowadays to leaven a serious public lecture with entertainment. Perhaps not wishing to admit this aspect, Copland's own justification was:

> let us not then despise what can at present, only gratify curiosity, seeing as...someone may afterwards arise who shall turn it to a *usefull* purpose.[27]

On a more serious note, the scientific methodology advocated by Copland represented a mature evolution of the Newtonian principles so widely broadcast at the beginning of the eighteenth century. Strong emphasis was placed on the value of experiment as a driving force for innovation and generalisation, and as an arbiter between theories. The application of Newton's edict 'hypothesis non fingo', embodying an unwillingness to speculate on unproven concepts, is evident throughout the course. The debt to Newton is freely acknowledged for he receives several panegyrics:

> His inimitable work, the Mathematical Principles of Natural Philosophy, contains the true philosophical faith, and those who reject its principles are worse than heretics, as they shut their eyes against the clearest of all lights, Demonstration.[28]

Such language is not typical of the lecture notes as a whole, which concentrate on the exposition of purely physical ideas.

It is salutary to be reminded by Copland of the social hopes which were entertained for the mechanical sciences two hundred years ago, hopes which are today proffered for different technologies on the strength of similar ideals. Apparently following Adam Smith's arguments, he developed the themes that both mechanisation and specialisation of labour improve the competitiveness of the country's economy. The discussion concluded with an optimism verging on the romantic:

> Scarce any Man, and rarely any Nation is permitted to be sufficient for itself, or to be able to supply all its own wants: and the innumerable infirmities, diseases, and wants to which human nature is subjected, require innumerable supplies from the various Arts, Sciences, Manufactories, and occupations exercised throughout the Earth—for from these alone arises the Wealth of the World— whatever is necessary, usefull, commodious—whatever conduces to the convenience;—delight,—or happiness of mankind. Hence the burr of Reels, Wheels and Looms; the sound of Hammers, Files and Forges; the shouts of Vintage and the songs of Harvest.[29]

In the largely rural Scotland of Copland's youth (the 1750s), most families did live close to the poverty level. In his lifetime he witnessed how industrialisation brought diversity and specialisation, a skill for many men and respect for their abilities, merchandise in every household undreamt of by previous generations. Copland certainly aimed to promote such a trend. Whether he was aware of the dangers some of his contemporaries had foreseen is not clear. With hindsight, we can see that this recipe for improving the 'delight and happiness of mankind' was ingenuous, though utterly sincere. His unpolished lecture notes convey this sincerity with a revealing freshness.

IV

There is no question that Copland's lectures made an outstanding impression locally. Not only does the period over which he gave such a substantial course bear witness to this, but in 1803, upon the death of the poet and philosopher James Beattie, half of Beattie's royal pension of £200 was obtained through Lord Sidmouth for Copland 'as a reward for the great service he had been in that part of the Country to Tradesmen and to the public by his lectures and his skill in forwarding the public improvement of the Town'.[30] Upon Copland's death in 1823, the *Aberdeen Journal* gave him an unusually lengthy obituary, noting of his private classes that 'these were always numerously attended, and served to diffuse a knowledge of true philosophical principles among all ranks'.[31]

It is also possible that, in spite of their lack of recognition by historians, Copland's lectures did leave their mark. He showed how such lectures could be given successfully. His ingredients were motivation, a good set of models, demonstrations and diagrams, a clear lecturing manner in language intelligible to the audience, regularity of time and place, and a moderate fee for an extensive course. He must also have demonstrated that the gains far outweighed the political misgivings of some in the 1790s who feared that educating any of the lower classes might cause Britain to follow the revolutionary path of France. It is quite likely that these political fears helped to delay the introduction of similar educational programmes in England. Thomas Webster (1722-1844) claimed to be the first in England to provide a 'school for mechanics', sometime in the late 1790s.[32] Webster was by then a trained architect working in London and his school contained about a dozen students, 'chiefly of the building class'. He is worthy of mention here because he was an undergraduate pupil of Copland's in the late 1780s and was intimately involved with the Royal Institution in its formative years. Webster relates: 'At Marischal College, I was a favourite pupil of Professor Copland, the well known and justly celebrated Professor of Natural Philosophy—I made many drawings for his lectures'.[33] Webster joined Count Rumford in 1799 in the project to establish the Royal Institution, because he was persuaded that it would provide an effective forum for educating working mechanics, 'a class of men whose deficiency in knowledge proves one of the greatest drawbacks to the progress of art'.[34] Webster was influenced because, in his own words, he knew 'from previous experience what it was possible to effect in their improvement'.[35] This remark could at least in part refer to his knowledge of Copland's evening class.

Webster claimed to have designed the Royal Institution's famous lecture theatre, the chemical laboratory later used by Davy and an artisans' gallery served by a separate stairway (subsequently removed). He stayed until a few months after Thomas Young was appointed as Professor at the Royal Institution. Young himself had visited Copland in 1795 and been much impressed by Copland and his apparatus.[36] He wrote to him in May 1802 remarking how he aimed to follow Copland's precedent in trying:

> to form a connecting link between abstract science and mechanical practice, and to direct the efforts of speculative men to the improvement of the inconveniences of life.[37]

Webster and Young form an interesting link between Copland and developments at the forefront of popular lecturing in London. Locally, there is no doubt that Copland's contribution was timely and relevant. He and French were lecturing during a period of immense improvement to the City of Aberdeen and the County of Aberdeenshire. In the town there were major projects to improve the water supply, sanitation, roads, paving, street-lighting, harbour buildings and other public amenities; in the countryside, land drainage, stone clearance and cultivation developed Aberdeenshire into the premier cattle breeding county and raised the living standard considerably above the poverty level of the mid-eighteenth century. These social changes rested on the application of science to technological development. To accelerate the process there was a need for educated people who could apply scientific principles to the design and construction of machinery that would improve the effectiveness of human effort. Copland in particular, and also French and Knight, provided in Aberdeen an education for the expanding class of skilled workers, both manual and professional.

All these social improvements were paid for by the successful commerce of the town, based in the early nineteenth century on the well established woollen manufacturers, the introduction of linen and cotton manufacture, the rise in the granite trade and papermaking, the expansion of the fishing fleet and various smaller enterprises. These industries, too, developed because scientific principles were intelligently applied to create machinery that was much superior to any previously available. These industries created a large pool of skilled and semi-skilled workers in a part of the country where education was considered a desirable social pursuit, even among the genuinely poor sections of the community. A Trades School was founded in 1808, and the Aberdeen Academy, which taught technical subjects, ten years later. For self-improvement, Aberdeen could boast a public library with 'a collection of books superior to that of any Provincial Institution of a similar nature in the Kingdom' by the time Copland stopped lecturing.[38] It is not at all surprising that upon the foundations laid by Copland and his contemporary adult education lecturers in science, Aberdeen was one of the earliest towns to establish a Mechanics Institute—inaugurated in April 1824, after preliminary meetings in 1823.[39] Unlike the fate of Mechanics Institutes in some cities, Aberdeen's survived the depression of the 1830s, making a notable contribution during the nineteenth century to adult education in the town.

For their local importance alone, Copland's natural philosophy classes must be considered a significant feature of Scotland's social history, bringing Enlightenment from the elite to the people in a manner that was characteristic of the best Scottish educational practice.

Notes

1. For Birkbeck see Thomas Kelly, *George Birkbeck: Pioneer of Adult Education* (Liverpool, Liverpool U.P., 1957), chapter 2. Copland is not mentioned even in such well researched works as Kelly's *A History of Adult Education in Great Britain* (Liverpool, Liverpool U.P., 1970). Many semi-entertaining lectures, mostly aimed at a middle-class audience, were given by itinerant lecturers like Benjamin Martin, for whom see John R. Millburn, *Benjamin Martin: Author, Instrument-Maker and Country Showman* (Leyden, Noordhoff, 1976), pp.35-64, and *Benjamin Martin: Supplement* (London, Vade-Mecum, 1986). Ian Inkster, 'Scientific culture and scientific education in Liverpool prior to 1812—a case study in the social history of education', in M.D. Stevens and G.W. Roderick, eds, *Scientific and Technical Education in Early Industrial Britain* (Nottingham, Nottingham U.P.,

1981),pp.28-47, shows that public lectures by peripatetics and local teachers thrived from the 1720s onwards. No lectures of these kinds were primarily vocational, except perhaps those of Professor John Anderson of Glasgow; see James Muir, *John Anderson Pioneer of Technical Education and the College He Founded* (Glasgow, John Smith & Son, 1950).

2. John S. Reid, 'The Apparatus of Professor Patrick Copland at Marischal College, Aberdeen' in preparation for *Annals of Science*.

3. *Aberdeen Journal*, 17 October 1785, p.3, cols 2-3.

4. AUL, MS 3017/10/18.

5. Advertisements in the *Aberdeen Journal*: 17 October 1785, p.3, cols 2-3; 14 November 1785, p.3, col.3; 9 October 1786, p.2, col.4; 9 October 1787, p.3, col.1; 13 October 1788, p.3, col.3; 4 October 1790, p.3, col.1; 25 October 1790, p.3, col.3; 14 October 1793, p.3, col.3; 4 October 1796, p.4, col.2; 15 October 1798, p.4, col.2; 13 October 1800, p.4, col.2; 29 September 1802, p.4, col.1 (★); 13 October 1802, p.4, col.3 (★); 3 November 1802, p.4, col.1; 3 October 1804, p.4, col.1 (★); 10 October 1804, p.1, col.2 (★); 17 October 1804, p.1, col.1 (★); 24 October 1804, p.4, col.1 (★); 8 October 1806, p.4, col.2; 27 September 1809, p.1, col.5 (★); 4 October 1809, p.1, col.1 (★); 11 October 1809, p.1, col.2 (★); 1 November 1809, p.1, col.2; 7 October 1812, p.1, col.4; 4 November 1812, p.1, col.1. Dates marked (★) are only two-line intimations.

6. *Aberdeen Journal*, 15 October 1781, p.4, col.1; 7 October 1782, p.4, col.2 and 6 October 1783, p.3, col.2.

7. From advertisements in the *Aberdeen Journal*, French gave his chemistry course in at least thirty winters, between 1783 and 1819. His course was about 60 lectures. The advertisement on 18 October 1784, p.3., col.1 gives a synopsis of the course; that of 29 September 1795, p.1, col.4 a slightly different flavour. As Professor of Chemistry, he was obliged to keep going in the five winters of 1811-1815 in spite of the appearance of Mr Knight (later Professor Knight, Copland's successor in 1822) offering an evening chemistry course, with natural history, covering the same topics, to be delivered at clashing times in a public room above the Athenaeum that could hold considerably more than the small Marischal College room used by French.

8. Alexander Findlay, *The Teaching of Chemistry in the Universities of Aberdeen* (Aberdeen, AUP, 1935).

9. Anand C. Chitnis, *The Scottish Enlightenment: A Social History* (London, Croom Helm, 1976),p.142.

10. John S. Reid, 'The Castlehill Observatory, Aberdeen' *Journal for the History of Astronomy*, XIII (1982), pp.84-96.

11. David M. Gavine, 'Astronomy in Scotland 1745-1900' (Open University, Ph.D.thesis, 1982).

12. *Aberdeen Journal*, 2 October 1786, p.3, col.3, and 16 October 1786, p.3, col.3. The second mention corrects the name to Clarke and details that his Aberdeen lecture will be on vegetation, ploughs and wheel-carriages, 'for each of which subjects, he has been honoured with premiums from the SOCIETY of ARTS in London'. The description of two improved ploughs by Cuthbert Clarke, at least one of which was awarded a premium in 1766, are given in William Bailey, *The Advancement of Arts, Manufactures, and Commerce; Descriptions of the Useful Machines and Models contained in the Repository of the Society for the Encouragement of Arts, Manufactures, and Commerce: &c* (London, Privately printed, 1772).

13. *Aberdeen Journal*, 14 October 1812, p.4, col.2, and *Aberdeen Journal*, 25 October 1815, p.2, col.5; 8 November 1815, p.3, col.3; 15 November 1815, p.3. col.1.

14. James Clarke to Patrick Copland, 28 October 1802, in the private collection of P.A. Copland (North Waltham). The author is most grateful to Patrick Alexander Copland, a direct descendant of Professor Copland, for the access given to his family's archives.

15. John A. Cable, 'Popular lectures and classes on science in the eighteenth century' (Glasgow University, M.Ed. thesis, 1971), chapter 4, pp.34-73. Cable fails to mention Copland.

16. Patrick Copland to G.J. Thorkelin, 2 August 1790, Edinburgh University Library, La III, 379.167.

17. See Table 1.

18. Knight advertised his chemistry course twice before beginning each year. The first advertisements occur in the *Aberdeen Journal*, 23 October 1811, p.1, col.5; 30 September 1812, p.4, col.3; 20 October 1813, p.3, col.2; 26 October 1814, p.3, col.2; and 25 October 1815, p.2, col.4. They give some detail of his intentions. He planned to continue in 1816 (*Aberdeen Journal*, 9 October 1816, p.3, col.3) but cancelled the classes upon being appointed Professor of Natural Philosophy at Belfast (*Aberdeen Journal*, 6 November 1816, p.1, col.1). Knight records (AUL, Knight MS M. 118, section IV) that the first two years' classes contained respectively 63 and 61 lectures on chemistry, and natural history. He subsequently divided his material into two courses of about 35 chemistry lectures and 30 natural history lectures. Knight also gave classes on 'popular chemistry' in the late winter and early spring which were well attended by ladies (including Mrs Copland and her daughter in 1813). He lists these as being given in 1813, 1815, 1818, 1819, 1820 and 1822. Presumably the last four were given in Belfast. The Aberdeen course was 20 lectures and was attended by about 70 people in the first year and 35 in 1815.

19. Samuel Smiles, *Industrial Biography: Iron Workers and Tool Makers* (London, John Murray, 1863), p.240.

20. *Aberdeen Journal*, 11 November 1812, p.4, col.2, where his name appears as 'Joseph Clemmet'.

21. See note 16 above.

22. 'Manuscript Notes of Popular Course on Natural Philosophy delivered at Aberdeen by Professor Patrick Copland of Marischal College 1807? collected and arranged by his grandson Dr Charles Murchison 1856', AUL, MS 3123/1. It is possible that Murchison came by his grandfather's notes upon the death of Copland's wife in 1852. He settled in London late in 1855 after having spent two and a half years in the East India Company. Although Murchison attended University at Aberdeen from 1845 to 1847 he did not stay to take the third-year natural philosophy course himself but left to obtain a medical education at Edinburgh. He therefore had no first-hand experience of the teaching of natural philosophy at Aberdeen. There is no record in the rolls of alumni of either Marischal College or King's College of Murchison's enrolment, only that of his brother John attending Marischal College eight years earlier. The notes are bound together in one volume of 439 folio pages, a full page containing about 20 lines at approximately seven words per line.

23. *Ibid.*, ff.8-30. Lecture 1 is fairly fully written out. In one paragraph Copland says that in the last two courses astronomy has been dropped. Knight in AUL, MS. M 111, pp.1215-1217 mentions that astronomy was dropped after the first course, which would date this lecture to 1788 or 1790.

24. See, for example, J.V. Smith, 'Manners, morals and mentalities: reflections on the popular enlightenment of early nineteenth-century Scotland', in *Scottish*

Culture and Scottish Education 1800-1980, eds W.M. Humes and H.M. Paterson (Edinburgh, John Donald, 1983), pp.25-54.

25. See note 2 above.
26. Gilles Edmé Guyot, *Nouvelles récréations physiques et mathématiques*, 4 vols (Paris, Gueffier, 1769); W. Hooper, *Rational Recreations, in which the Principles of Numbers and Natural Philosophy are Clearly and Copiously elucidated, by a series of Easy, Entertaining, Interesting Experiments*, 4 vols (2nd edition, London, L. Davis, 1783).
27. AUL, MS 3213/1, f.15.
28. *Ibid.*, f.158r.
29. *Ibid.*, f.136v.
30. According to a note by his son Charles in the private collection of P.A. Copland (North Waltham).
31. *Aberdeen Journal*, 20 November 1822, p.3, col.4.
32. Autobiography by T. Webster, signed and dated 6 July 1837, bound in the Webster MSS, cat.no. 121A-121B, p.4 in the Archives of the Royal Institution.
33. *Ibid.*, p.3.
34. Thomas Webster to Thomas Garnett, presumed August or September 1800, quoted by Nicholas Edwards, 'Some correspondence of Thomas Webster (circa 1772-1844), concerning the Royal Institution', *Annals of Science*, 28 (1972), p.51.
35. H. Bence Jones, *The Royal Institution: its Founder and its First Professors* (London, Longmans, Green & Co., 1871), p.3.
36. George Peacock, *Life of Thomas Young, M.D., F.R.S., &c* (London, John Murray, 1855), p.67. Although barely 22 when he visited Aberdeen, Young was already a Fellow of the Royal Society.
37. Thomas Young to Patrick Copland, 17 May 1802, in the private collection of P.A. Copland (North Waltham).
38. *Aberdeen Journal*, 13 October 1813, p.3, col.5.
39. AUL, Knight MS M. 167 'Original Papers' contains 11 rules and objectives of the proposed Aberdeen Mechanics' Society dated 5 December 1823. It also contains a 6-page account of the early history of the Aberdeen Mechanics Institution (as it was called upon being formally inaugurated in 1824) from 1824 to 1832, including mention of the formation of a dissenting rival body, the 'Aberdeen School of Arts', in 1824.

SECTION III

Music and Art in the Enlightenment

19

A Lost Sonata Reconstructed: Scherrer's Opus 7 from Castle Fraser

Roger Williams

University of Aberdeen

When invited to produce a handlist and a subsequent catalogue of the music of Castle Fraser I approached the task of examining some 200 volumes with a certain apprehension.[1] This apprehension was sharply dispelled one day when, examining a volume collected sometime before the close of the eighteenth century, which originally belonged to the Hon. Mary Hay, I came across a work to which I could find no reference in any of the standard catalogues of the period. Granted, the composer Scherrer was hardly a household name, nor, evidently had he been prolific. The edge of excitement was however somewhat blunted when I discovered that of the two parts to make the work whole, only one was present. Two questions presented themselves. Why is it that these sonatas by an obscure Swiss composer are held in a relatively remote corner of north-east Scotland? What has this got to do with a conference devoted to Aberdeen and the Enlightenment? These two questions quickly become intertwined.

To answer the second question first. The Enlightenment was concerned with an expansion of knowledge and a sharing of thoughts both national and international. As with the world of science, so in the world of the arts there was a feeling of extension of what could be expressed—irrespective of genre, country, creed or fashion.

Music in domestic situations underwent considerable development not only in the courts of the rich and celebrated, but also in more modest establishments. At Castle Fraser, the spinster heir to the Castle—Elyza—and her lifelong companion, Miss Bristow, were vitally interested in all manner of subjects including music. It was they who began the collection of music in the middle of the eighteenth century and acquired the works of Corelli, Handel, Scarlatti and their contemporaries. The collection was continued well into the nineteenth century by Elyza's successor, her great nephew

Charles. He married Jane Hay in 1817—herself from a musical family—and they had a family of some fourteen children, many of whom played instruments and sang. We learn from letters in the Castle Fraser collection that this generation was fortunate to count amongst its friends the Cramers. J.B. Cramer was a celebrated pianist, well thought of by no less a figure than Beethoven, and his younger brother Francis became Master of the King's Music in 1834. These then were no ordinary amateur musicians, but men at the top of their profession, and it seems unlikely that they would have bothered with friends who were of a much lower standard than themselves. Numerous copies of music in the Castle Fraser collection testify to the thorough nature of the family's musical interests. The children were not allowed to play the piano in the Hall until their lessons had been perfected on the pianos in the schoolroom. And in many copies ornaments, breath-marks and corrections are added with obvious professional expertise.

The collection consists of both printed and manuscript copies, with the former in a majority. Amongst delightful and valuable rarities is a manuscript book, copied by Jane Fraser in July 1818. In addition to well-known pieces for piano, and operatic excerpts, there are anonymous piano duets and Scottish songs in historically valuable versions from the turn of the nineteenth century. Collections of traditional Scottish music remind us of the necessity of home-produced music for balls and social events.

Who then was Scherrer? The *New Grove Dictionary of Music and Musicians* is unhelpful in what must be one of the least informative of articles in any encyclopaedia.[2] Dieter Härtwig suggests the initial of Scherrer's forename 'N' might stand for Theophil! The article suggests neither date of birth (nor place) nor date of death. In *MGG* the same author tells us Scherrer worked in Geneva in the 1770s and 1780s, and that he taught piano to Prince Friedrich Franz of Mecklenburg-Schwerin—who became Grand Duke in 1785.[3] We also learn that Scherrer's Opus 1 Trios were dedicated to that patron. In Refardt, Scherrer's forename is given as Nicolas.[4] A Jean-Jacques Scherer, an organ builder in Lausanne in 1756, built the organ in St Peter's in Geneva. At the same time Nicolas Scherrer was the organist at this church and he was subsequently recorded as being a citizen of Geneva in 1791. On 15 May 1789 a programme given at St Peter's in Geneva contained two cantatas on sacred subjects 'put into music by Mr. Scherer'. It seems that this Scherrer is the same as our composer.

All three sources agree with the *RISM* catalogue in assigning to Scherrer the following compositions:

Op.1 Six Sonatas put into Trios for Harpsichord, Violin and Violoncello. Published by the author in Geneva.
Op.3 Three Sonatas for Harpsichord with accompaniment for violin ad libitum, the same could be played on cello. Again published by the author in Geneva.
Op.4 Three Sonatas for Harpsichord with accompaniment for a violin ad libitum, the same could be played on cello.
Op.5 Six Sonatas for cello with accompaniment on a bass.

Op.6 Six Symphonies in 8 obbligato parts.
Op.8 Three Sonatas for Harpsichord with accompaniment for violin ad libitum, which could be played on a cello.
Op.9 Six Sonatas for the cello with accompaniment for a bass.
       A Periodic Symphony in eight parts.
       Sonata for piano forte and flute obbligato published in Naples.[5]

Thus there is no reference to any cantatas, nor to Opus 2 or Opus 7. In *RISM* it is also worth noting that the entry reads 'Scherrer, N (le cadet)' i.e. a younger member of the same family, but the same as what? This description—which is also present on the title pages of at least two sets of works—would substantiate the entry in Refardt, and perhaps an assumption may be made that the Jean-Jacques Scherrer who built the organ was either father, uncle or elder brother to the composer Nicolas. Although these works were all published in Geneva—Opus 8 and Opus 9 in manuscript—the works only remain complete today in Rostock Universitätsbibliothek, and in the library at Schwerin. The British Library in London has only Opus 1 and that is without its cello part.

It was thus a surprise to find bound in the same volume as the Opus 1 set, Opus 7, of which I have been able to discover no other extant copy. What has survived is the keyboard part. When the violin has the main melodic material however it is 'cued in' in smaller notes in the right-hand part and the bass is figured for that section. There is no reason why the violin part that exists should not be played exactly as printed, and as a succession of musical ideas comprising a sonata, such a version has much to commend it. There is a commanding opening phrase—one of the 'calls to attention' frequently used as openings to operatic overtures, symphonies, and sonatas throughout the latter part of the eighteenth century. After a suitably contrasting melodic theme, over repeated chords in the bass, and a short increase of rhythmic activity for the cadence, the violin enters with new material—transition, or second subject—of a contrasting nature. The word 'contrast' is a vital component of the new classical sonata structure. However, as a typical 'Sonata for the Clavecin ou forte piano/avec acompagement (sic) de Violon/Obligé' it just will not do.

By comparing with other eighteenth-century compositions and by analogy with other extant works by Scherrer—the use of a violin, as designated on the title page, would have been much more prevalent. However strange it may appear to us today, the word 'accompaniment' meant exactly what it said. The problem is what would the violin have played?

When I first sought a solution, I fancied that the violin would have probably shared in the arresting opening material—in the 'call to attention' to reinforce the clavecin. However, after examining the violin parts of Opus 1 and Opus 3, I have not found anywhere else any similarly strong sharing of the melodic material. In fact, far from the violin sharing anything dynamic with the keyboard, it takes very much a secondary role. Much of the violin writing by this composer is simple and relatively easy to play. When the keyboard has the main melodic material, the violin merely adds notes common to the harmonic progressions and has very little musical interest *per se*. Apart from the solos—indicated in the keyboard score—the violin part is really rather boring and utilitarian. I therefore rethought a projected violin part, and have made it as modest as those others which we have from this composer. It may seem less interesting to play, it may seem less forceful to the listener, but hopefully it is more authentic.

In trying to assess the musical value of such a reconstruction we do well to bear certain aspects of eighteenth-century music-making in mind. Firstly, the description of the work on the title page. Granted, many title pages read rather like formulae, and, it must be admitted, commercial reasons were certainly to the fore in the mind of many a publisher in the eighteenth century. A publisher survived by the number of copies of his catalogue that he sold and if a work were able to appeal to violinists, cellists and keyboard players there was the possibility of trebling potential sales. However when we examine Scherrer's title pages, we find many differences in the various descriptions. The conclusion is that Scherrer and his publisher—whoever he was—described exactly what the composer intended. Thus a description on the title page commands obedience.

Secondly, the conditions of performance in the eighteenth century were not as they now are, when performing professional concerts, recording, or broadcasting—where if a work demands certain performers they can be guaranteed. In the eighteenth century there was a great deal of amateur music making often of the highest calibre—the word 'amateur' did not have attached to it the faint stigma of 'worthiness' that is so often applied today. Many performances must have taken place with whatever instruments and players were to hand. What was obligatory in all but unaccompanied works was a keyboard, or at least a continuo instrument capable not only of supplying a bass to the ensemble, but of adding the harmonies as well. Thus it is that many eighteenth-century compositions and arrangements are able to be played quite satisfactorily on the keyboard alone.

Thirdly, the violin which we hear in our concert halls today is essentially the nineteenth-century instrument developed in Paganini's day, then later in the nineteenth century—so that it could compete in dynamic and technical terms with the romantic symphony orchestra. The classical violin was essentially a softer, more mellow instrument, strung with gut, with a lower bridge, a smaller fingerboard and played with a slacker bow. The quality and not the volume of tone was the important factor. Thus it was much more suitable to blend with the keyboard instrument which would have to 'give way' before the violin could be heard as a soloist. Even the method of expression was different. Instead of contrasting dynamic ranges—something we take for granted—more attention was paid to articulation—the way a phrase can be presented through a mix of long or short notes.

Fourthly, what sort of keyboard instrument did the composer intend? 'Clavecin' is the French word for harpsichord while 'Forte piano' refers to the pianoforte. In the late eighteenth century, however, the piano was a rather different instrument from that to which we are accustomed today. Pianos of two types were made—the large 'grand', the shape of which remains today.

But the eighteenth-century instrument would have been lighter in construction and made with a wooden frame—it would also have had lighter hammers. The touch would therefore have been less deep and more responsive to the light, integrated ornaments of the time. The tone would have been quieter with a greater emphasis on the upper harmonics than in present-day instruments. The other type of 'piano' would have been the 'square piano'. As with the grand, this would have been constructed on a wooden frame, with lighter hammers, and with thinner strings at a lower tension than today. Again the touch would have been shallower and lighter, the dynamic contrast smaller, and the whole instrument much brighter in sound. In other words, although we recognise the name and the description of the instruments on the title page, they were very different from their modern counterparts.

How would one describe Scherrer's musical character? We know that he was essentially a keyboard player and teacher, and from his keyboard parts we can guess he was highly competent and there is much that is positively virtuosic about his keyboard writing. The left hand part of the first of Opus 7 number 1 is not for a faint heart—nor for tentative hands. Not for Scherrer the rather delicate keyboard textures of Haydn and Mozart. Rather, he inclines towards the thicker textures of Clementi and Dussek—from whom the young Beethoven learned so much. It is a pity that so little is known of the young Scherrer's own musical apprenticeship, for it might be interesting to see whether he himself pioneered this rather heavier style of writing or picked it up from someone else.

Scherrer's musical gifts also include a typically classical concern for the overall structure of a piece. So much so, that one occasionally feels his musical material is subject to rather more repetition than it ought to be. He has a gift for well-turned melodies—as in the transition in the first movement of Opus 7 number 1. His ability to create a sort of 'jolly' rustic dance mood is also exemplified in this sonata in the last movement whose main theme is utterly unpretentious. Another side of his character is shown in the dark-hewn opening movement of the second sonata of Opus 7—in F minor—a movement where tragedy and pathos are never very far away.

Scherrer, then, is not in the same league as Haydn or Mozart, as C.P.E. Bach or J.C. Bach, all composers who, through the power of their individual personalities, forged new paths for subsequent generations. He was rather more like our own Thomas Arne, someone who wrote music which was well crafted and highly effective for its designedly limited scope.

What is the value of this reconstruction? First, the composer Scherrer is little known today. There are few extant compositions. Although a reconstruction of his complete *oeuvre* is hardly likely to revolutionise our view of music in the classical period, Scherrer nonetheless was an important, though perhaps a rather run-of-the-mill composer. Inevitably his compositions add another piece to the jigsaw of his age. The music may not be world-shattering in emotional range, it may be inhibited in dramatic scope, but it has value as background against which we appreciate and evaluate the genius of Haydn, Mozart and Beethoven.

Secondly, it is worthwhile recalling that this work was actually published.

The composer and a publishing house evidently felt that this set of compositions was worth publishing—that it would make some money for someone.

Thirdly, these pieces by Scherrer exist in a collection that was obviously built up with care and discernment—and at a time when music was relatively expensive. It was bought by a family that actually played music, who evidently felt it was a worthwhile composition.

Finally, here in the North East of Scotland, and at Castle Fraser in particular, we learn more about music and its importance in the domestic scene. As a social accomplishment or an 'innocent diversion' music had a valuable place in the home.[6] Music made its contribution to the Enlightenment ideal of the civilised, rational and feeling human being. Even in relatively remote Aberdeenshire, we observe a private family entering into the spirit of the age, sharing intellectual pursuits and experiences. Neither Elyza Fraser nor her companion may have qualified for membership as Royal Academicians, but their contribution—as that of many others similarly placed—was no less valuable and no less demonstrative of the Enlightenment in Scotland, albeit in a modest and charmingly human way.

Notes

The author wishes to thank the following people. Mrs Lavinia Smiley for her generosity in allowing free access to her private property; the representatives of the National Trust for Scotland at Castle Fraser—Mrs Catriona Webster and her husband Comyn—and Petrina Miller.

1. R.B. Williams, *Catalogue of Music Holdings at Castle Fraser* (forthcoming).
2. D. Härtwig, 'Scherrer' in *New Grove Dictionary of Music and Musicians*.
3. D. Härtwig, 'Scherrer' in *Die Musik in Gesichte und Gegenwart*.
4. E. Refardt, 'Scherrer' in *Historisch—Biographisches Musiker—Lexicon der Schweiz*.
5. *Répertoire international des sources musicales* (*RISM*) *Catalogue*.
6. P. Piggott, *The Innocent Diversion*, (London, Clevedon Press, 1979).

20

Painting as Philosophy: George Turnbull's *Treatise on Ancient Painting*

Carol Gibson-Wood

Queen's University, Kingston, Ontario

It is an interesting paradox that George Turnbull's *Treatise on Ancient Painting*[1] of 1740 was dismissed as worthless by major art theorists on both sides of the ancients versus moderns debate, Hogarth and Winckelmann. In his print 'Beer Street' (plate 1), executed in 1750, William Hogarth included Turnbull's *Treatise* among the useless books shown bundled up ready for recycling by the trunkmaker. More surprisingly, perhaps, J.J. Winckelmann, champion of antique art, wrote in 1755 that it was the plates alone which gave 'some value to the magnificent and abused paper' of Turnbull's work.[2]

Magnificent indeed was Turnbull's tome—a large folio, beautifully bound and including fifty-four finely engraved plates after drawings by Camillo Paderni.[3] It was evidently not just Winckelmann who found these plates the most valuable part of the book, for in 1741 they were reissued as *A curious Collection of Ancient Painting, Accurately Engraved from Excellent Drawings*, with only a brief introduction in place of the *Treatise*'s lengthy text. Modern commentators, too, have paid little attention to Turnbull's text, which is admittedly turgid and verbose.[4]

It is not my intention here to analyse fully the *Treatise*, although several aspects of it do merit further discussion. Rather, I wish only to consider certain parts of Turnbull's argument from the point of view of their relationship to established art theory in Britain in the early eighteenth century, and to suggest that the *Treatise* can in some respects be seen as quite revolutionary, even anti-classical. Seen in this light, it is perhaps easier to understand both Winckelmann's rejection of the text of the *Treatise* and its apparent lack of influence on writers like Joshua Reynolds.

As the full title of the *Treatise* indicates, and as Turnbull's own preface and very detailed table of contents make explicit, the work consists of several

Plate 1. *Beer Street* (detail) by William Hogarth, 1750, by kind permission of the Trustees of the British Museum.

parts. We might most usefully consider the book in terms of four interrelated subdivisions.

The lengthiest part of the book, comprising the first six chapters, consists of Turnbull's discussion of ancient painting. Here he brings together and organises into a coherent discussion a vast number of observations on painting as found in the writings of ancient authors. He acknowledges his debt to Franciscus Junius's *De Pictura Veterum* (1637) for much of his information, but the questions he poses reflect his own priorities. In what esteem was painting held by the ancients? What distinguished the styles of the most renowned masters? How did the Greeks include painting in their system of education? How did they perceive its relationship to poetry and philosophy? To what extent were political factors responsible for the rise and decline of art among the Greeks and Romans? Throughout these chapters Turnbull introduces references to modern painting—relating, for example, the characteristics of the ancient masters to those of more recent painters like Raphael or Correggio. But the whole point of Turnbull's lengthy discourse on ancient painting is, he points out, 'to prepare the way for a philosophical Consideration of the Fine Arts' or, more specifically, 'to prepare the way for shewing [painting's] Usefulness in Education'. This is the concern of his seventh chapter, which contains the central arguments of the book.

The seventh chapter is followed by 'Some Observations on the particular Genius, Characters, Talents and Abilities of the more considerable modern Painters, and the commendable Use they made of the antient Remains in Painting as well as Sculpture'.[5] Apart from an interesting little section that concludes this discussion (which I will describe at a later point), these observations derive largely from the writings of Lomazzo, De Piles, and Félibien.

The final section of Turnbull's book consists of the series of plates, whose relationship to the rest of the text is rather tenuous. Engraved by Mynde after drawings by Paderni, the plates reproduce fifty examples of ancient painting preserved in eighteenth-century collections—mainly in Rome, but also including pieces owned by Dr Richard Mead in London (plate 2). They do not form the basis of Turnbull's discussion in any extended way, being neither the examples by which he demonstrates the historical development of painting, nor concrete instances of the principles of art he is defending. Occasionally he refers to one of them in his account of ancient painting as exemplifying qualities he is referring to more generally, but his discussion there relies above all on descriptions of lost paintings, not the examples reproduced. The plates essentially form a separate visual appendix; at the very end of his text Turnbull includes a list of the illustrations, giving the subjects, size, and whereabouts of the original paintings.

The title of the *Treatise* is therefore rather misleading, for the discourse on ancient painting serves mainly as historical background, demonstrating by great past examples the principles and practices for which Turnbull wants to argue in the present. Turnbull's primary aim in writing the *Treatise* was, as he often reiterates, 'to set the Arts of Design in a just Light; and to point out in particular the excellent Use that may be made of them in Education' (p.xx).

The purpose of education was, according to Turnbull, to 'cultivate and improve the rational Faculties and Dispositions in our natures' (p.179), these being 'our Understanding or Reason, our Imagination, and our moral Temper' (p.181).[6] For education to be most effective, he insists, 'all the liberal Arts and Sciences' should be united in it. 'Nature being one, all the Sciences which inquire into Nature as one Whole must be One, or strictly and intimately related' (p.180). Elsewhere in the *Treatise* he expresses his belief in the unity of the arts and sciences by maintaining that it is philosophy alone

Plate 2. 'Augustus giving a crown' after a fragment of a Roman wall painting owned by Dr Richard Mead, one of the plates in Turnbull's *Treatise on Ancient Painting* (1740).

which must be taught, philosophy being 'the Knowledge of Nature' (p.x), but that this must be constantly accompanied by demonstration through the arts of the ways in which truths are exhibited or enforced. Turnbull states that the major errors in the modern educational system consist of teaching moral and natural philosophy separately, and the liberal arts independently of both (p.x). 'There can be but two Objects of human Speculation and inquiry', he writes, 'Truths themselves, and Languages, that is the various Ways of expressing, embellishing, or enforcing Truths on our Minds' (p.179). Philosophy representing the 'truths themselves', the arts of oratory, poetry, sculpture and painting are characterised as the corresponding 'languages'. Turnbull defines this interrelationship in another way by maintaining that artistic examples which express or enforce a philosophical truth on our minds should rightly be called philosophical 'experiments'.[7] Painting being one of these instructive 'languages', it follows that all pictures convey to the mind either 'Ideas of sensible Laws, and their Effects and Appearances', or moral truths. The former can be considered to be experiments in natural philosophy, the latter experiments in moral philosophy (p.145).

In arguing that painting had instructive value, Turnbull was following a well established line of defence for the status of the art. Since the fifteenth century, writers on art had argued that painting, like poetry, had intellectual value and offered more than sensual pleasure, due to its ability to portray morally uplifting or thought provoking subjects. This argument, depending as it did on the nature of the subject matter chosen for representation, necessarily gave to history painting alone this full instructive potential. As long as this was the accepted theoretical position, its consequences for the classification of different types of painting as more or less admirable were inescapable. By the beginning of the eighteenth century, the hierarchy of genres was well established: history painting was pre-eminent, with the less edifying branches of the art (portraiture, landscape, genre and still life) trailing behind.

A second, related theoretical argument which did not alter this basic hierarchy but introduced to it modifications and further distinctions, was the question of idealisation. A painter who did not just copy natural appearances, but who improved upon them by imagining and portraying more perfect forms, demonstrated greater intellectual powers, and thereby imparted to his works greater instructive value for the viewer by revealing to him a higher level of reality in the neoplatonic sense. Most highly regarded was idealised history painting in which the artist improved an already edifying subject, both by giving idealised forms to the figures and setting, and by using his powers of invention to present visually a described scene in an effective way. But even among the lower orders of painting, this distinction existed between idealised and unidealised renderings. A landscape by Claude Lorrain, for example, with its idealised, classicised forms, was theoretically more admirable than a 'common' landscape by a Dutch master. Landscapes by Claude and Poussin also often managed to creep further up the hierarchy by including historical subject matter on a minute scale or in the background of the picture.

The two foremost art theorists of early eighteenth-century Britain, the third Earl of Shaftesbury and Jonathan Richardson, Sr (whose writings were well known to Turnbull and referred to in the *Treatise*), had laid particular stress on painting's potential to be morally improving, but essentially within the limitations of these neoclassical doctrines. Shaftesbury, notably in 'An Historical Draught of Hercules' (1711) restricts his discussion of the lofty aims of painting to history painting alone. Richardson, in his *Essay on the Theory of Painting* (1715) and *Two Discourses* (1719), himself a portrait painter, is much readier to see value in all branches of painting, but nonetheless remains steadfast in the view that instruction is a nobler aim than pleasure and those parts of painting which exercise the artist's intellect, namely invention, expression and the ability to idealise, are most important. Consequently, although Richardson argues that portrait painting deserves a status nearly equal to that of history painting, landscape and still-life continued to have little instructive value within his critical system.

In most respects Turnbull, too, seems to be adhering to conventional neoclassical art theory in his *Treatise*. He constantly cites the views of writers like Du Fresnoy, Shaftesbury, and Richardson, as well as those of ancient writers, on issues like the artist's proper goal of idealisation, or the ennobling effects of heroic subject matter. And after all, it is chiefly the principles of ancient classical art which he is championing throughout this book. But it is noteworthy that he never once refers to the traditional hierarchy of painting types; nor does he specify that his observations relate to history painting alone. Indeed, his philosophical premises prohibit such exclusiveness.

Because Turnbull conceives of painting as a language which provides examples of philosophical truths, and because he maintains that all such examples contribute to improving the faculties of the mind, *all* kinds of paintings are instructive in his view. In place of the conventional distinction made between the instructive aim of painting and the merely pleasurable one, he posits solely the instructive role, but is willing to see instruction arising from a variety of different types of subject matter and different treatments. Turnbull does not carry these premises to their logical art-theoretical conclusions in the *Treatise*, but he does put forward, in his seventh chapter, a resulting view of landscape painting which is radically different from the conventional view at this time. Having pointed out that 'Pictures are of two Sorts, natural and moral', and that 'the former belong to natural, and the other to moral philosophy' (p.145), Turnbull maintains that:

> Pictures which represent visible Beauties, or the Effects of Nature in the visible World, by the different Modifications of Light and Colours, in Consequence of the Laws which relate to Light, are Samples of what these Laws do or may produce. And therefore they are as proper Samples and Experiments to help and assist us in the Study of those Laws, as any Samples or Experiments are in the Study of the Laws of Gravity, Elasticity, or of any other Quality in the natural World. They are then Samples or Experiments in natural Philosophy. (p.146)

He also argues that looking at pictures of the natural world has certain advantages over looking at nature itself. 'For not only does the double Employment of the Mind, in comparing a Copy with the Original, yield a double Satisfaction to the Mind' he notes (a standard Aristotelian idea about representation), 'but by this comparing Exercise, the Original is brought, as it were, nearer to our View, and kept more steadily before us, till both Original and Copy are fully examined and comprehended: The Mind...is excited narrowly to canvass the Resemblance; and thus it is led to give a closer and more accurate Attention to the Original itself' (p.145).

He continues in a vein that anticipates writings on the Picturesque later in the century:

[one] may easily comprehend what superior Pleasures one must have, who hath an Eye formed by comparing Landscapes with Nature, in the Contemplation of Nature itself, in his Morning or Evening Walks, to one who is not at all conversant in Painting. Such a one will be more attentive to Nature, he will let nothing escape his Observations; because he will feel a vast Pleasure in observing and chusing picturesque Skies, Scenes, and other Appearances, that would be really beautiful in Pictures. He will delight in observing what is really worthy of being painted; what Circumstances a good Genius would take hold of; what Parts he would leave out, and what he would add, and for what Reasons. The Laws of Light and Colours, which, properly speaking, produce all the various Phaenomena of the visible World, would afford to such an inexhaustible Fund of the most agreable Entertainment. (p.146)

Both pictures which are 'exact Copies of some particular Parts of Nature, or done after them' and 'imaginary' landscapes which are nonetheless 'conformable to Nature's Appearances and Laws' are, according to Turnbull, 'experiments in natural Philosophy' because 'they serve to fix before our Eyes beautiful Effects of Nature's Laws, till we have fully admired them, and accurately considered the Laws from which such visible Beauties and Harmonies result' (p.146).

Some of these points concerning the merits of landscape painting had already been made by Jonathan Richardson. He had argued, for example, that the connoisseur learns by looking at pictures to appreciate beauties in nature to which he otherwise would have remained blind.[8] But Richardson was not willing to accept idealised and unidealised landscape on equal terms as both contributing to the same instructive end, nor was he ready to relinquish the view that other kinds of subject matter were much more edifying than views of nature. The following passage from Richardson's *Theory of Painting* neatly summarises the standard neoclassical view of how landscape painting was estimated within the general scheme of things:[9]

There is some Degree of Merit in a Picture where Nature is Exactly copy'd, though in a Low Subject; Such as Drolls, Countrey Wakes, Flowers, Landscapes, &c. and More in proportion as the Subject rises...Herein the *Dutch*, and *Flemish* Masters have been equal to the *Italians*, if not Superior to them in general. What gives the *Italians*, and Their Masters the Ancients the Preference, is, that they have not Servilely follow'd Common Nature, but Rais'd, and Improv'd it...This gives a Dignity to a Low Subject, and is the reason of the Esteem we have for the Landscapes of *Salvator Rosa*, *Filippo Laura*, *Claude Lorrain*, the *Poussins*; ...and This, when the Subject it self is Noble, is the Perfection of Painting: As in the Histories of the best *Italian* Masters.[10]

In contrast to this theoretical position, it is clear that Turnbull's view of landscape painting is radically different. He does not maintain that pictures which are 'experiments in moral Philosophy' (that is to say history paintings) should in any way be regarded as superior to those which are 'experiments in natural Philosophy', for both contribute to our knowledge of Nature and are truly educational. He argues that painting is of great use 'in whatever View Education is considered, whether as it is designed to improve the Senses and Imagination, or...to improve our reasoning Powers, and our inward Sense of Beauty natural and moral, or...to form a benevolent, generous, and great Temper of Mind' (p.150). Turnbull's philosophical system thus provided the theoretical underpinning which made it possible for landscape painting to be regarded as no more lowly an art form than history painting. His line of reasoning, however, does not seem to have been taken up by any of those many British writers on the Picturesque who, although warm indeed in their admiration of landscape, and able to demonstrate all kinds of pleasures arising from its contemplation, never really posited an alternative theory in place of the neoclassical one which justified their enthusiasm.

The potential which Turnbull's system carried for revolutionising art theory was seized neither by Turnbull himself nor by those who would have liked to have ended the tyranny of neoclassical doctrines. This potential was probably not even noticed by the latter, hidden as it was in a book which superficially bore all the marks of maintaining the exalted position of the principles of classical art. If Hogarth, for example, had been aware of the full implications of Turnbull's theoretical position, he might well have been less ready to portray the *Treatise* as rubbish. For it was not just landscape painting whose intellectual status could have been raised by using Turnbull's theoretical premises; *all* of the so-called lower orders of painting could be seen as samples of moral or natural philosophy. Much of Hogarth's own art, satirising as it did the foibles of human nature and conduct, could have qualified as 'experiments in moral philosophy'.

Turnbull's purposes in writing the *Treatise* had been mainly to develop a theory of education, not a new theory of art; that he therein laid the philosophical foundations for the latter was more of a side effect than anything else. Admirer of ancient art that he was, he would hardly set out to propose an art theory which could undermine its authority. Moreover, it is evident throughout the *Treatise* that Turnbull in most respects accepted uncritically the views of established writers on art. But an awareness that he had in fact made some rather radical revisions seems to dawn on him at the very end of his text. In what is probably the most original section of his book with respect to its observations on modern painters, Turnbull proposes a list of the subjects that he hypothetically would have liked each of the masters to have painted for him, according to their respective talents. From Michelangelo, for example, he desires the Labours of Hercules, from Tempesta 'a Hurricane at Sea, frightened Mariners, and the Ship ready to be shatter'd into Pieces, or sink to the Bottom', and from Caravaggio 'a few Pictures of common ordinary Nature' (p.169). At the end of this list Turnbull declares that:

> And thus I should have had Pictures for all the noble Uses of Painting; to preserve the Memory of Friends; to represent the Characters of antient great Men; to raise my Imagination, move my Passions and Affections of every kind, in a truly wholsome and moral Manner; and to instruct me in the profoundest Secrets of the Human Heart, in all its various and complicated Workings and Motions; to convey agreable Images, and sooth my mind; or to rouze it, and awaken great and strong Thoughts: Pictures to compose me into Meditation, or

to refresh and chear me after Study and Labour: Pictures to compare with the finest Descriptions of the best Poets of every kind; and Pictures to inforce the sublimest purest Doctrines of moral Philosophy, and true Religion: Pictures wherein to study the visible Beauties of Nature, and all the charming Effects of variously modified Light and Colours: and Pictures in which I might view myself, and contemplate human Nature as in a moral Mirror. (p.169)

In maintaining that these were all 'noble uses of painting', Turnbull was indeed taking an unconventional stand. And it is immediately after this passage that he reveals both his awareness of the fact that his ideas challenged contemporary art theory, and his disdain for unreflective amateurs of art. 'I have been all this while venturing, perhaps, too far', he suggests, 'and taking too much upon me; but wherein I am wrong or mistaken, I shall be glad to be set right. And if I, by my Boldness, shall put others upon considering Pictures in another more profitable Way than the greater Part of those who are called, or love to be called *Virtuosi*, do; without any prepossession, or blind Attachment to great Names and Authorities, I shall gain one of the main Points I have in view in this Essay' (p.170).

Notes

I am grateful to the Social Sciences and Humanities Research Council of Canada for a post-doctoral fellowship during the tenure of which this paper was prepared, and to the Office of Research Services of Queen's University for financial support enabling me to attend the conference at which it was presented.

1. George Turnbull, *A Treatise on Ancient Painting, containing Observations on the Rise, Progress, and Decline of that Art amongst the Greeks and Romans; The High Opinion which the Great Men of Antiquity had of it; its Connexion with Poetry and Philosophy; and the Use that may be made of it in Education: To which are added Some Remarks on the peculiar Genius, Character, and Talents of Raphael, Michael Angelo, Nicholas Poussin, and other Celebrated Modern Masters; and the commendable Use they made of the exquisite Remains of Antiquity in Painting as well as Sculpture* (London, A. Millar, 1740).
2. J.J. Winckelmann, *Gedanken über die Nachamung der griechischen Werke in der Malerei und Bildauerkunst* (Dresden, C.. Hazenmüller, 1755); English translation by Henry Fusseli, *Reflections on the Painting and Sculpture of the Greeks* (London, A. Millar, 1765), p.53.
3. Publication of the volume was financed through subscription. In 1737 the Society for the Encouragement of Learning (of which Turnbull was a member) had agreed to assist in printing the work, but this offer was withdrawn when Turnbull sought subscribers as well. This information is contained in the Minutes of the Society for the Encouragement of Learning (BL, Add. MS 6187); I am grateful to P.B. Wood for this reference. The 1741 reissue of the plates was probably an effort further to cover the costs of having the drawings and engravings made, for despite the subscription list, Turnbull still complained of 'the Author's Expence' (*Treatise*, p.xxvi).
4. The best discussion of Turnbull's *Treatise*, notably with respect to its philosophical aims and context, is Vincent Bevilacqua's introduction to his edition of

the text (without the plates) (Munich, W. Fink, 1971). Johannes Dobai's discussion of the *Treatise* in *Die Kunstliteratur des Klassizismus und der Romantik in England*, 3 vols (Munich, Benteli, 1974), vol.I, pp.669-80, is general but accurate; it is particularly informative regarding the commissioning of the drawings and plates, and Allan Ramsay's role in this. The only other extended treatment of the *Treatise* is Lawrence Lipking's rather inaccurate one in *The Ordering of the Arts in Eighteenth-Century England* (Princeton, Princeton U.P., 1970), pp.31-37. On Turnbull's history of art as an example of conjectural history, see Roger L. Emerson, 'Conjectural history and Scottish philosophers', in the Canadian Historical Association's *Historical Papers* (1984), pp.63-90.

5. *Treatise*, p.xxiii and p.129. All following page references to the *Treatise* are cited at the end of the relevant quotation rather than in notes.

6. My brief synopsis of Turnbull's views on education is based solely on his remarks in the *Treatise*, but the purposes and principles of education are also discussed in his other major writings, *Principles of Moral Philosophy* (London, John Noon, 1740) and *Observations upon Liberal Education* (London, A. Millar, 1742). At the practical level, Turnbull's involvement with teaching consisted of six years as a regent of Marischal College, Aberdeen (1721-27), and a period as a travelling tutor in the late 1720s and 1730s.

7. Turnbull uses the term 'experiment' synonymously with 'sample', 'example' and 'instance'. Dr M.A. Stewart has pointed out to me the fact that Turnbull had also used 'experiment' in this sense in a rather unusual way in his *A Philosophical Enquiry concerning the Connexion betwixt the Doctrines and Miracles of Jesus Christ* (London, R. Willock, 1731), in which he argues that Christ's miracles were 'experiments' indicating that he had the powers he claimed.

8. Jonathan Richardson, *Two Discourses* (London, W. Churchill, 1719), part 2, pp.202-204.

9. An exceptional view of landscape painting had earlier been expressed by the French art theorist Roger de Piles who, in his *Abrégé de la vie des peintres* (Paris, 1699), wrote that 'If Painting be a sort of creation, 'tis more sensibly so in Landskips than in any other kind of pictures. We see there nature rising out of her Chaos, the elements separated, the earth adorn'd with her various productions, and the heavens with their stars. This sort of Painting contains all the others in little, and therefore the Painter, who exercises it, ought to have an universal knowledge of the parts of his art; if not in so particular manner as those that are us'd to paint history, yet, at least, speculatively, and in general', *The Art of Painting with the Lives and Characters...of the most Eminent Painters* (London, C. March, 1744), p.32.

10. Jonathan Richardson, *An Essay on the Theory of Painting*, 2nd edition (London, A.C. & A. Bettesworth, 1725), pp.171-72.

21

Blackwell and the Myth of Orpheus

Kirsti Simonsuuri

Academy of Finland & Harvard University

Orpheus was a central figure in Blackwell's thought, possibly, it may be suggested, as important as Homer, despite the fact that the latter was the subject of a whole treatise, namely the *Enquiry into the Life and Writings of Homer* (1735).[1] My argument in this essay is that Blackwell was primarily interested in Orpheus and the Orphic poems, because they provided substantial proof for his theory of the origin of the Homeric epic and for his view of myth and poetry, and not because he had a desire to establish the nature of the Orphic poems as such. The time was too early for that. Blackwell was aware of the fact, as he noted in passing, that the Orphic hymns were not composed by Orpheus, but only attributed to that name much later.[2] Thus the advancement of classical philology was not primarily in his mind, but rather the understanding and interpretation of the causes and origins of poetry.

As mythologist Blackwell was a *philosophe* rather than an *érudit*, to use Arnaldo Momigliano's distinction in his *Studies in Historiography* (1966). Or rather, Blackwell's erudition was combined with an imaginative frame of mind, particularly when one compares his work with those contemporaries who used their learning purely for pedestrian aims—like Fourmont or Banier, or any of the scholars who held reductionist notions of history and myth.

It is interesting to observe, in the first place, that the problem of authentication as perceived by Blackwell related to Homer and not to Orpheus. He treated Orpheus as an historical character, as an individual poet who had lived a few generations before Homer, so that Orpheus's grandson, Eumolpus, son of Musaeus, was more or less a contemporary of Homer whose historicity was without question in Blackwell's thesis. Blackwell's problem then was how to establish a poetic genealogy for Homer and thereby authenticate an entire poetic tradition. The analytical framework was not historical relativism, but poetics. It was an inquiry concerning the conditions of poetic authenticity, thus constituting a central theme for Scottish Enlightenment.

Orpheus was one of the most evocative figures of Greek mythology, as well as one of the most complex.[3] On the one hand there is the founder of a religion or a sect, in the guise of the poet and the singer. As Walter Burkert has remarked, Orphism, because it indicates a radical transformation that took place in Greek religion in pre-classical times, has become one of the most disputed areas in the study of Greek intellectual and religious life.[4] Modern scholarship has profited from recent discoveries such as the Derveni papyrus which contains a presocratic commentary on the theogony of Orpheus, and the graffiti from Olbia (in Sardinia) attesting to the existence of Orphic literature in the fifth century B.C. All these pieces of evidence have for the most part diminished the element of conjecture regarding Orpheus as an historical figure; the speculative nature of Blackwell's discussion stands in sharp contrast to the present state of Greek studies.[5]

On the other hand, there is the myth of Orpheus in which the Thracian singer casts a spell on animals and trees, goes to the Underworld to bring back Eurydice, and is eventually torn asunder by raving Thracian maenads. The stories relating to Orpheus were spread throughout the ancient world, and we find references to him in Ibycus, in Simonides, in Pindar, in Euripides, in Aristophanes and in Plato; the *Odyssey* refers to the story of the Argonauts without revealing whether Orpheus was on board the Argo as presumed in antiquity.[6]

What is interesting is that we have a figure that has survived in tradition, a figure which is neither completely a symbol nor an historical person but is, rather, a complex of ideas around a name. Martin West has in a recent study reinstated the view that Orpheus is to be seen in the context of northern shamanism which left its traces in Greek myth and legend.[7] Orpheus, together with various other legendary singers and poets, such as Musaeus, Linus, Eumolpus, Melampus (all of which were known to Blackwell), both became the subject of mythical tales and had a large corpus of poems attributed to their authorship. The less familiar material was absorbed into the better-known by the principle of association. By and large from the late sixth century onwards, the figure and name of Orpheus predominated over the others. Also an influential *Rhapsodic Theogony* was ascribed to him which has survived in fragments. The Orphic poems that have remained do not distinguish themselves in any remarkable way from any other fragmentary or even mediocre Greek poetry. This is interesting, since the reverse is true of the Homeric poems. The Homeric epics and hymns are immediately strikingly powerful, even in fragments. This fact was noticed by Blackwell, who made it one of the main critical tenets of his study on the origin of the Homeric epic.[8]

But a more trenchant point than the quality of the Orphic verse is the strong tradition that has survived for an extremely long time, even to our days, of Orpheus as a magician and an artist with unique musical gifts and with extraordinary powers of persuasion. With numerous variations, the legend has been told in different cultural contexts for over two millenia.[9]

In the original versions which have survived to us in Greek poetry and drama, we can distinguish the following separate and interconnected motifs

Plate 3. 'Orpheus with his lute' attributed to Gravelot (Hubert François Bourguignon d'Anville) prefixed to Chapter VII of Blackwell's *An Enquiry into the Life and Writings of Homer* (1735), by kind permission of the Houghton Library, Harvard University.

of the legend. Firstly, birds, animals and all creatures came to hear Orpheus perform; rivers and waters were stayed in their courses, and rocks and stones came rolling down the mountain slopes. Secondly, Orpheus took part in the Argonautic expedition and saved the Argonauts from the peril posed by the fatal Sirens by outsinging them. Thirdly, Orpheus prevailed upon the powers of death by trying to release his wife Eurydice from the Underworld. And fourthly, Orpheus was killed by a group of Thracian women (while men sat enchanted by his music). The women tore off his head, and as it was carried down the river, it continued singing.

When we examine this early evidence, we can see that originally there was nothing to suggest that Orpheus might have been a predecessor of Homer, but all the evidence, on the contrary, suggests that he was a poet and a singer of a completely different type, a shaman and a magician from Thrace, and maybe a seer who could exercise power over the natural world. Of these characters Greek history and folklore knows a legion; but we are also reminded of characters belonging more firmly to the world of the fairytale, such as appear in the folktale sequence of the *Odyssey*. Modern research indicates that the composite figure of Orpheus began to emerge in early classical times, in the late sixth and the early fifth centuries B.C. This figure combined traits derived from characteristically Greek myths, such as Apollo and the Muses (whose son he was thought to be) as well as features belonging to the later epic poets, such as Homer and Hesiod. The process of story-telling helped to rationalise and synthesise the various elements, and then the early magical and shamanistic elements began to be regarded merely as signs of poetic and musical powers. And gradually the figure of Orpheus could be regarded as a kind of mythical symbol, such as we frequently encounter in modern times, sufficiently distanced from the original context. It is no coincidence, to take one example from recent intellectual history, that George Steiner calls an early essay on Lévi-Strauss 'Orpheus with his myths' (1965), detecting a degree of 'super-rationalism' in Lévi-Strauss's *science humaine*, an interest in aetiological pursuits of modern science and thought—an interest which may be said to agree with Orphic theogony.[10]

These shores are not too distant from Blackwell and the problems of his day. Re-reading the *Enquiry into the Life and Writings of Homer* (1735) and *Letters concerning Mythology* (1748), the two works where Orpheus is discussed, one is acutely aware that the theme of Orpheus, too, must be seen in the context of the literary and philosophical disputes of the time.[11] In the first place, it illustrates Blackwell's methods of literary criticism which are analytical and rationalist. They seek to establish historical causes and antecedents and provide a kind of theory of origins. These are offered as interpretative and explanatory measures in the case of Homer, for instance. Homer needed to have predecessors; if none were available, they had to be created. The difficulty came from the discrepancy of the information, since Blackwell had to work without the results of modern scholarship which have made it possible to detect the different layers of composition. The question of the authorship of the Orphic poems therefore has a more realistic basis than it had in Blackwell's time. It would be inconceivable to discuss Homer, Hesiod, Orpheus, Virgil, and the Eastern oral traditions as literatures based on the same foundations. Yet Blackwell's analysis illuminates some contemporary notions of poetic creation:

the Turks, Arabs, Indians, and in general most of the Inhabitants of the East, are a solitary kind of People: They speak but seldom, and never long without Emotion: But when, in their own Phrase, they open their Mouth, and give loose to a fiery Imagination, they are poetical, and full of Metaphor. Speaking, among such People, is a matter of such Moment, as we may gather from their usual

Introductions; for before they begin to deliver Thoughts, they give notice, that they will open their Mouth; that they will unloose their Tongue; that they will utter their Voice, and pronounce with their Lips. These Preambles bear a great Resemblance to the Forms of Introduction in Homer, Hesiod, and Orpheus, in which they are sometimes followed by Virgil.[12]

In the second place, it seems to me that Blackwell was riding a hobby horse. The Thracian connexion did not remain unnoticed by him for he was well aware of the Celtic elements of Scottish culture. One of his central arguments is the role of cultural exchange in shaping the literature and arts of peoples. The interest in the origin of the Celts was topical.[13] Moreover, the presence of a kind of Orphic figure in Celtic folktales is beyond doubt: there is a fourteenth-century ballad called *Sir Orfeo*, based on older Breton lays, where the main figure is like a fairy-king and not very much like the sha- manistic or even classical Orpheus. It is a matter of dispute, however, whether the fact that the Celts originated in locations near to the regions of the Thracians would explain the appearance of this figure, present also in some Shetland songs and in Henryson's poem *Orpheus and Eurydice* from the fifteenth century.[14] For Blackwell, the birthplace of Orpheus was a matter of importance:

This intercourse between the Nations, and Affinity of their Dialect, will appear still stronger, if we call to mind who were the masters of the ancient Musick and Poetry, and the first famed for these Arts among the Greeks? It was Orpheus, Musaeus, Thamyris, and Eumolpus, all Thracians; who were not only understood by the then Greeks, but able to charm them with their Eloquence and Melody, and persuade them to exchange their Fierceness for a social Life and peaceful Manner.[15]

It may not be inapposite to suggest that Blackwell had the analogy of his own country in mind. The political and religious disputes of early eighteenth- century Scotland were a subject of concern to him, as we read from the barely veiled references to contemporary issues in the pages of the *Enquiry*: 'the happy Change that has been since wrought upon the face of religious Affairs.' (p.3). The classics of Greece and Rome have throughout the ages been read for the purposes of even greater self-interest than Blackwell's enlightened nationalist cause.

In the third place, Blackwell's interpretation of the myth of Orpheus illus- trates his conception of myth as a living entity in cultural processes. When speaking about Orpheus, he refers to contemporary musical performances as specimens of Orphic song and poetry. Orpheus was a popular musical theme. In England and Scotland alone, we have song collections with Orpheus in the title: Purcell's collection *Orpheus Britannicus* (1706), John Hill's opera *Orpheus* (1740), and numerous imitations of Orphic hymns, such as John Hughes's *An Ode to the Creator of the World* (1713).[16] In Blackwell's view, the meaning of the myth of Orpheus related primarily to the power of music and of the creative act. He wrote: 'There are few Things in ancient Poetry, more moving than the story of Orpheus and Eurydice', and added that the meaning of the myth can be found in the performance of music as well as in philosophical discourse. This should not be read as an expression of anti-intellectualism, which it was not, but as a view that sometimes the allegorical elements of myth lend themselves to dramatic representation better than to analysis—particularly Orpheus which in the form of a myth illustrated the musical foundations of poetry.[17]

Most clearly illuminated, however, in Blackwell's discussion of the myth of Orpheus is the idea of the social and public roles of the poet. First of all, the Orphic theogony, Blackwell thought, provided a plan for 'the Government of the World'. It supplied an allegorical framework for the interpretation of the world of phenomena, just as the Homeric mythology did. All true poets, Blackwell maintained, were the teachers of mankind and 'the Great Masters of Science'. (One can almost hear the Poundian idea of the poet as the mathematician of the world.) Such was Orpheus, the artist, poet, musician, lawgiver, and the civiliser of the Greeks. And moreover, he was the prerequisite and matrix of Homer.

Far from deprecating the mentality that produced mythology, as Fontenelle or Banier did, Blackwell introduced to the thought of the Enlightenment the true appreciation of the mythopoeic mind, which had a lasting impact and far-reaching consequences as it emerged again in Herder and in Karl Ottfried Müller and even later in modern anthropological thought.[18]

Though Blackwell fully understood the social context of myth and the evolution of nations in history, he emphasised that mythological thinking was the instrument of civilisation. He believed that myth would create functions for itself in civilised societies, too. The myth and figure of Orpheus was to Blackwell evidence of that.

I regret that my discussion has been far from complete, and I am aware that it is only a beginning. And while I hope that my paper has pointed out some possible new lines of inquiry, I end by quoting John Ashbery's poem 'Orpheus' (1975):

> To which Orpheus, a bluish cloud with white contours,
> Replies that those are of course not regrets at all,
> Merely a careful, scholarly setting down of
> Unquestioned facts, a record of pebbles along the way.

Notes

1. See my 'Blackwell et la mythologie classique', *L'Européen et la découverte de l'autre*, eds D. Droixhe and P.-P.Gossiaux (Brussels, Editions de L'Université de Bruxelles, 1985), pp.95-106; and *The Rise of Modern Mythology 1680-1860*, eds Burton Feldman and Robert D. Richardson (Bloomington, Indiana U.P., 1972),

pp.5-6; Gustavo Costa, *La critica omerica di Thomas Blackwell* (Rome, Institute of Philosophy, 1959), pp.41-42. An engraving of 'Orpheus with his lute' is prefixed to Chapter VII of Blackwell's *Enquiry* (Plate 3).

2. J.G. Schneider, *Analectica critica*, vol.I (Jena, 1779); Thomas Tyrwhitt, *De Lapidibus* (Oxford, 1781).

3. Robert Böhme, *Orpheus: der Sänger und seine Zeit* (Berne, Francke, 1970); Gianni Carchia, *Orfismo e tragedia: il mito trasfigurato* (Milan, Celuc libri, 1979); Fritz Graf, *Eleusis und die orphische Dichtung Athens in vorhellenistischer Zeit* (Berlin, De Gruyter, 1974); W.K.C. Guthrie, *Orpheus and Greek Religion* (London, Methuen, 1935); I.M. Linforth, *The Arts of Orpheus* (Berkeley, California U.P., 1941).

4. Walter Burkert, *Greek Religion* (Oxford, Blackwell, 1985), p.296.

5. The texts have been published in Otto Kern, *Orphicorum Fragmenta* (Berlin, Weidmann, 1922); see also Burkert, pp.1-7.

6. *Od.* 12, lines 57-72; Simonides, from l.62; Pindar, *Pyth.* 4, lines 171-7; Aristoph. *Frogs*, line 1032 ff.; Plato *Apol.* 41.a; Euripides, *Alc.*, lines 357-362, and elsewhere.

7. M.L. West, *The Orphic Poems* (Oxford, OUP, 1983), pp.5-7; see also E.R. Dodds, *The Greeks and the Irrational* (Berkeley, California U.P., 1951); K. Meuli, 'Scythica', *Hermes*, 70 (1935), pp.121-76.

8. *Enquiry*, p.72; pp.169-73; a recent appreciation of the Homeric verse, J. Griffin, *Homer on Life and Death* (Oxford, OUP, 1980), pp.xiii-xvi.

9. *Orpheus. The Metamorphoses of a Myth*, ed. John Warden (Toronto, Toronto U.P., 1982); Walter A. Strauss, *Descent and Return: the Orphic Theme in Modern Literature* (Cambridge, Mass., Harvard U.P., 1971); W.H. Cohen, *A Rilkean Aesthetics of poetry: a New Interpretation of Rilke's Sonnets to Orpheus* (Edwardsville, Ill., Southern Illinois University, University Microfilms, 1969); Hans Knoch, *Orpheus und Eurydike: der Antike Sagenstoff in den Opern von Darius Milhaud* (Regensburg, Bosse, 1977).

10. George Steiner, *Language and Silence* (London, Harmondsworth, 1967), pp.248-60.

11. See Jean Starobinski, 'Le mythe au XVIIIe siècle', *Critique*, 366 (1977), pp.975-97; Frank Manuel, *The Eighteenth Century Confronts the Gods* (Cambridge, Mass., Harvard U.P., 1959); and my *Homer's Original Genius: Eighteenth-century Notions of the Early Greek Epic* (Cambridge, CUP, 1979).

12. *Enquiry*, pp.43-44.

13. E.g. John Toland, *A Critical History of the Celtic Religion and Learning* (London, Lackington, Hughes, Harding & Co., 1740); see also R.F. Sullivan, *John Toland and the Deist Controversy* (Cambridge, Mass., Harvard U.P., 1982).

14. John B. Friedman, *Orpheus in the Middle Ages* (Cambridge, Mass., Harvard U.P., 1970); Patricia Vicari, '*Sparagmos*: Orpheus among the Christians', in J. Warden ed., *Orpheus. The Metamorphoses of a Myth*, pp.63-83.

15. *Enquiry*, p.295. Blackwell quotes Eusthatius's commentary to *Iliad 2*, as proof of the first poets—not a very fortunate choice since it was a twelfth-century source.

16. On the Continent, Orpheus had also been a popular subject: Claudio Monteverdi, 'Orfeo' (1607); O. Rinuccini and J. Peri, 'Eurydice' (1600), as well as later in the century C.W. Glück, 'Orfeo e Eurydice' (1762); and Mozart's 'The Magic Flute' (1791) with its figure of Tamino. The most recent opera on Orpheus is Harrison Birtwistle's 'The Masks of Orpheus' (1986).

17. *Enquiry*, pp.216-17.

18. J.G. Herder, *über die neuere deutsche Literatur* (1766-), and in other writings; Isaiah Berlin, *Vico and Herder* (London, Viking Press, 1976); Jan de Vries,

Forschungsgeschichte der Mythologie (Freiburg, K. Alber, 1961); Walter Burkert, 'Griechische Mythologie und die Geistesgeschichte der Moderne', in *Les études classiques aux XIXe et XXe siècles: leur place dans l'histoire des idées*, ed. Willem den Boer (Geneva, Fondation Hardt, 1980); Hans-Georg Gadamer, *Wahrheit und Methode* (Tübingen, Möhr, 1960).

22

The Architecture of Eighteenth-Century Aberdeen

W.A. Brogden

Scott Sutherland School of Architecture, Robert Gordon's Institute of Technology, Aberdeen

In the eighteenth century Aberdeen was a small town not only remote from London, but also remote from Edinburgh. Aberdeen's customary links with the Baltic and the Low Countries continued to be important in trade and commerce, and perhaps in architectural style also. At the beginning of the century there was little architectural activity but from the mid century there is a quickening pace in building projects, and the somewhat vernacular style enlivened by remote references to foreign features gives way to rational, sober, almost Palladian propriety in common with the rest of Britain and Europe. In the last quarter of the eighteenth century there grew up a general dissatisfaction with the form and nature of the town, and in a series of extraordinary public meetings very grand plans for expansion were accepted.

Aberdeen's architectural heritage was far from inconsiderable: the venerable Brig o'Balgownie over the Don (twelfth-century by Richard Cementaries, the first Provost of Aberdeen); and Elphinstone's and Dunbar's handsome Bridge of Dee—considerably remodelled and thoroughly repaired during the eighteenth century. However, major buildings were ruinous. Indeed, an eighteenth-century Lady Aberdeen, when wakened in her coach for her first glimpse of Rome, is supposed to have remarked: 'Och, it does have the look of Aberdeen about it'. St Machar's Cathedral, incomplete at the Reformation, and neglected and abused in the ensuing century, had finally lost its crossing and transepts in a storm in 1688. Bishop Leighton's fifteenth-century nave had been repaired and turned into the galleried preaching box it remained throughout the eighteenth century. The other twelfth-century foundation, St Nicholas' Kirk, kept its choir crossing and transepts; but its nave, deserted by its congregation and minister, and used as stables by Cumberland's army in 1746, mouldered in ruins until 1750 when James Gibbs's scheme for rebuilding was realised by James Wylie. As far as their buildings were concerned, neither of the two colleges was flourishing or great. King's College, especially the famous Chapel, was 'very ruinous', according to Pennant. A few years earlier Alexander Carlyle reported that Marischal College was:

> a very ordinary building in bad order. They have a shabby church, a hall and a library that are merely decent, some lodging rooms for students, the schools, and two or three houses for Professors. But they are all in very bad order. The stairs are not so much as plastered.

In spite of all this Aberdeen remained a handsome and rich burgh admired for its leafy gardens, its cleanliness and its busy streets. Built on a pattern established in the Middle Ages the compact burgh was of two parts—the larger, to the south, built on three hills (Castlehill, St Katherine's and Gallowhill) and overlooking the Dee estuary to the south and the Denburn (from whence it derived its name) to the west. To the north was the Aultoun, a long, straggling street from Mounthooley to St Machar's. Aberdeen had two natural advantages, its harbour and the rich farmlands of the Mearns, Marr, Formatine and Buchan, which lay beyond the semi-circle of hills which define modern Aberdeen: in the eighteenth century much of this ground was stony and unproductive.

The landward entry was by way of the Bridge of Dee, Hardgate and then Windmill Brae and the tiny Bow Brig to the Green, the ancient market place. From here were two narrow ways into the town proper—either to the south, by the harbour and the Shiprow, or to the north by Carnegie's Brae and Benholm's Lodging, of which J.C. Nattes remarked in 1799:

> the view is extremely picturesque and not unlike some of the towns in Italy, in which the style and masses of the building to the north are often very similar.

From the twelfth century the market place was the spacious Castlegate, the site also of municipal government, and of the houses of rural grandees as well as the principal citizens. According to Daniel Defoe the Castlegate was:

> very beautiful and spacious...the Houses are lofty and high; built not so as to be inconvenient, as in Edinburgh, or low, to be contemptable, as in most other places. But the generality of the citizens Houses are built of stone four storey high, handsome sash windows and are very well furnished within.

It should be noted that the word *house* in eighteenth-century Aberdeen did not necessarily imply the full building, but referred to the chambers occupied by a family, usually one floor (or in Scottish terminology a *flat*) and in legal terms an apartment still known as a flatted dwelling house. Apparently the first building put up on purpose to accommodate several families in comfort was the seventeenth-century Rolland's lodging on the south side of the Castlegate. During the eighteenth century, the type was improved and great numbers were constructed.

The improving spirit was not confined to common dwelling houses. A handsome, even splendid new Record Office was designed by Robert Adam to stand at the eastern end of the Castlegate, but a much plainer building, ornamented by a central pediment only, was built instead. Adam's father, William, had worked in the city in the 1730s, most notably to build Robert Gordon's Hospital, a rather tall building with bell-shaped pediments over the end bays. This was founded by a Danzig merchant to educate poor boys of the burgh and was built on the north-west edge of the town. Although complete by 1738 it lay empty for a further decade while Gordon's capital built up again—in 1746 it became, briefly, Fort Cumberland. Not to be outdone, a new Grammar School building (low, somewhat plain, but agreeably Palladian) soon followed nearby, and continued in use until the 1860s. Lord Byron was briefly a pupil there in the 1790s. In the Aultoun (a separate burgh until 1890) a new Town House was built in 1788 by Alexander Jaffray at the junction of Don Street and the Chanonry. This sober cube is the best of our eighteenth-century buildings.

Even the colleges were improved, although William Adam's work at Marischal was not universally admired. It may have been the same architect who rebuilt the south wing of King's College, forming lodgings above an open arcade known as the piazza. Later in the century a fire destroyed the libary, a lean-to affair against the south wall of the Chapel, and for nearly a hundred years the nave end of the Chapel was employed as the library—a fine example of the Enlightenment in anti-clerical mood. In the 1770s the west front of the college, which had housed a Grammar School and the Principal's Lodging, was torn down, and slightly further south in College Bounds a short regular terrace of houses was built using the old materials.

At the same time as Lord Provost Drummond of Edinburgh was building the North Bridge, and holding the competition for the design of a New Town, Aberdeen began Marischal Street. The purpose in both cases was to break the mediaeval mould of the town, and introduce a convenient, broad and rational street of entry. Marischal Street runs from the Castlegate site of the Earl Marischal's Hall southwards to the harbour. Not only was the ancient and venerable Hall removed, but there was a great deal of underbuilding and a handsome stone bridge (itself destroyed in the 1970s) required to get the slope sufficiently easy. To either side regular and identical Georgian houses were built.

This experiment in urban improvement encouraged the Aberdonians to further efforts. The quayside was consolidated and extended to a sort of terrace-walk, soon to be built up with substantial houses. Thomas Smeaton was consulted about further improvements to the harbour. Other engineers were at work improving the roads in Aberdeenshire and Kincardineshire, and the Aberdeenshire Canal was constructed to link the harbour with the River Don and the hinterland to the north west.

All these improvements simply confirmed the obvious: Aberdeen was awkward to get into. However, there was no apparent solution. In 1794 a Town Meeting agreed to seek proposals from Charles Abercrombie, and in due course he proposed three alternatives: a new bridge across the Dee at the foot of Marischal Street; a new road along the north shore of the Dee linking the Old Bridge of Dee to Marischal Street (two proposals which were doubtful for purely engineering reasons); or a new road to come from the west, a grand bridge across the broad Denburn valley, and a new street to run *through* St Katherine's Hill to the Castlegate. Aberdeen was amazed by Abercrombie's plans, but little by little they grew to like them and in 1799 the Trustees advertised for architectural designs to realise Abercrombie's scheme. In 1801 seven entries were exhibited in the Town House and David Hamilton's was selected. The only design to survive, however, is James Young's. This shows a truly monumental proposal: two enormous terraces, composed palace fashion, with centrepieces, wings, and balanced terminal pavilions, were to stretch from the Castlegate to the new bridge. Had they been built, Union Street would have closely resembled the contemporary Rue de Rivoli in Paris. Whatever Hamilton himself may have proposed he became preoccupied by the bridge itself. At the same time a shorter, more typically eighteenth-century terrace was proposed by James Burn and Thomas Fletcher for the other new street—to be called King Street. Although begun in 1803, only a fragment at the south end was built immediately.

The pattern for Aberdeen's great civic improvements was undoubtedly eighteenth-century—rational, ingenious, and unconcerned with architectural form except for decent propriety. But over a decade was spent in building the bridge, the great causeway, and in clearing the ground. When it came, the architectural realisation was characteristically nineteenth-century, and it is the subject of another story.

Notes

An account of Aberdeen's architecture may be found in W.A. Brogden, *Aberdeen, an Illustrated Architectural Guide* (Edinburgh, Scottish Academic Press, 1986).

23

'All Delicacy': the Concept of Female Beauty in Mid Eighteenth-Century British Painting

David Mannings

University of Aberdeen

In 1759 Horace Walpole wrote to Sir David Dalrymple, 'Mr Reynolds and Mr Ramsay can scarce be rivals; their manners are so different. The former is bold, and has a kind of tempestuous colouring, yet with dignity and grace; the latter is all delicacy. Mr Reynolds seldom succeeds in women: Mr Ramsay is formed to paint them'.[1] Walpole, so often a barometer of progressive eighteenth-century taste, is contrasting the two painters along fashionable Burkean lines: Reynolds, bold and tempestuous, is a painter of the Sublime; Ramsay, 'all delicacy', of the Beautiful.[2]

Yet in earlier periods Ramsay's delicate manner would have qualified him perfectly well to paint men as well as women. As an American scholar, Dr Judith F. Hodgson, reminds us in a recent study:

> Renaissance art and literature admires the beauty not only of the young Adonis, but also of Hercules and Christ, Venus, the Madonna, and Juliet. Young as well as mature figures of both sexes, and symbols of secular as well as religious love were all included as types of beauty in the human form, while modern concepts of human beauty have become almost exclusively limited to the objects of a man's love.[3]

We can see this as part of a wider movement. In the eighteenth century the concept of beauty withered and was gradually pushed aside by other concepts, most notably the Sublime and, slightly later, the Picturesque. The adjective 'beautiful' came more and more to be restricted to young women and children, a convention which still, of course, prevails. Sir Joshua Reynolds's portrait of Mrs Lloyd, shown at the Royal Academy in 1776, represents the lady writing her husband's name on a tree, her pose taken from Raphael's drawing of *Adam Tempted* which had been etched in reverse, that is to say in the same direction as *Mrs Lloyd*, a few years earlier. The resulting portrait exactly mirrors, therefore, the process whereby the beautiful Adam of the Renaissance was transformed into the type of graceful young woman admired by the eighteenth century. The increasing emphasis in male portraiture on the expression of character, on qualities of intellect and moral greatness, illustrates very clearly what happened to the concept of masculine beauty. It was replaced by a new category which stressed moral rather than physical qualities, appropriate to the higher dignity and intellectual superiority of men. Thus, as Dr Hodgson puts it:

> the active male is more beautiful than the passive female ... Feminine beauty is merely a perception of the masculine observer, who becomes the man of taste by learning to perceive morality in beauty. Sensual beauty itself is on the lowest level of the moral hierarchy which is raised by art to a safe and morally respectable position through the agency of the man of taste.[4]

I have no time fully to explore this concept of passive femininity, which reached a kind of climax in the art and literature of the nineteenth century, and has been the subject of a great many studies in recent years.[5] Instead I shall simply suggest some ways in which this movement was reflected in mid eighteenth-century British portraiture. In that narrow field painters refined and perfected a certain type of image and thereby made their own subtle contribution to what is nowadays called the construct of femininity. And no painter showed a greater refinement of skill in this respect than Allan Ramsay.

In the well known half-length portrait of Margaret Lindsay, his second wife, arranging roses in an oriental vase (Plate 4), Ramsay employs the device of an action interrupted, while in the equally fine but less well-known three-quarter-length portrait of Mrs Montagu of 1762 he turns the sitter's gaze away from the spectator. This apparent unconcern with the fact of being seen, eyes turned away as if unaware of our presence, or meeting our gaze, surprised in the performance of some simple action, is intended to instil that ease of manner which Castiglione had called *sprezzatura*, and which had by the eighteenth century, and more particularly since Pope's *Essay on Criticism* of 1711, become the highly desirable quality of *grace*.[6] Most eighteenth-century writers who discussed this particular quality connected it with movement or action. Daniel Webb, for instance, referred back to Milton—'Grace was in all her steps, heaven in her eye'[7]—while Archibald Alison stressed its connexion with good breeding, with high social rank. Grace is rare, he pointed out, and by no means synonymous with anything so common as 'mere beauty' (a significant phrase). It is, he declared—quoting Adam Smith with approval—a 'noble propriety', and when we do encounter it in pose or gesture we always feel some sentiment of respect or admiration for the person concerned. We are struck by an air of superiority and dignity. Not surprisingly it is seldom found 'in the attitudes or gestures of the lower orders of mankind'.[8]

Grace is achieved, therefore, through movement, but also to some extent through facial expression, which both painters and their clients agreed should be serious. Lomazzo, widely read in the eighteenth century in Haydocke's

Plate 4. *The Artist's Wife* by Allan Ramsay, c. 1760, by kind permission of the National Gallery of Scotland, Edinburgh.

translation, had written that total lack of expression was most in keeping with the virtue of female modesty.[9] This convention still held in the mid eighteenth century, as we can tell from a number of descriptions of female beauty in both fiction and criticism. The Swiss writer André Rouquet, for instance, writing about 1750, or shortly afterwards, explained that a lady's mouth in a portrait should be 'graceful, without a smile, but rather of a pouting turn, which gives it at once both grace and dignity'.[10] In keeping with this convention, Margaret Lindsay, like most of Ramsay's sitters, does not smile. In fact Ramsay normally avoided an over-solemn effect, especially in his later pictures, by turning the corners of the mouth very slightly upwards.

It might be objected that Hogarth, for one, employed a greater variety of facial expressions, as in the *Shrimp Girl* in the National Gallery, London, who—like Lady Hamilton in some of George Romney's pictures of her— smiles broadly enough to show her teeth. The answer of course is that these pictures are not portraits; they are what the eighteenth century called Fancy Pictures. Toothy smiles are as conventional in that type of picture as they are in modern snapshots. A more interesting case is that of Mrs John Elliott in Thomas Gainsborough's portrait of her exhibited (probably) in 1782 and now in the Frick Collection. This is certainly a portrait and allows the beholder a rare glimpse of her teeth. I am not suggesting that this is unique in Gainsborough's work—to take just one more example, the Hon. Frances Duncombe, also in the Frick, smiles through similarly parted lips—but it is in contrast to the usual convention followed by Gainsborough's fellow painters. On the whole, ladies preferred to keep their lips together, affecting a faint, placid smile not unlike that found on certain Imperial Roman busts[11]— a point to which I shall return.

It is hard to say to what extent the serious faces in mid eighteenth-century portraits reflect artistic as opposed to social conventions, but it is easy to see why many people concerned about their appearance would, in general, have kept their mouths shut. 'The art of pleasing in conversation and social life', is, as the royal dentist, Thomas Berdmore declared in 1768, badly affected by loss of teeth, rotten stumps, fallen lips and hollow cheeks, and of course bad breath.[12] No wonder Lord Chesterfield, whose own teeth, we are assured by Lord Hervey, were quite black,[13] thought a gentleman should never laugh. In general, British ideas of gentility found it impossible to cope with the obtrusive physicality of teeth. Even healthy teeth are all too obviously associated with the basest animal appetites, and I need only remind you of Tom Jones's justly famous meal with Mrs Waters in the Inn at Upton to indicate how well the eighteenth century appreciated the connexion between eating and sex. A more decorous ideal is evoked by Joseph Spence in 1752 when he wrote that in a very graceful face we look for 'something not quite enough to be called a smile, but rather an approach toward one'. This, he declared, is 'one of the most pleasing sorts of grace'.[14]

This particular sort of grace was given the final seal of approval by being associated with classical antiquity. Indeed, Alison considered it to be *the* special quality of the art of classical times.[15] By means of this rare quality female portraiture could, therefore, share something of the grandeur and status of the Antique. Some painters tried to achieve this enhanced grandeur through a studiedly graceful pose, combined with accessories such as relief carvings, or by swathing the lady in some sort of 'classicising' drapery. But that approach always ran the risk of looking just plain silly, a risk which was seized upon with delight by contemporary caricaturists, novelists and playwrights. How could any painter hope to bridge the gap between ancient and modern, between the marble statue and the flesh and blood woman? Miss Betsy Thoughtless, in Eliza Haywood's novel published in 1751, finds herself compared, by a would-be seducer, to a Grecian Venus. She replies briskly: 'If you mean the compliment to me, sir, the Grecian Venuses are all painted fat, and I have no resemblance of that perfection'.[16] In *Polymetis* (1747), Joseph Spence tries to describe the Medici Venus but in terms that could only really be applied to Boucher or Fragonard. Her breasts, he says, 'are small, distinct, and delicate to the highest degree ... There is a tenderness and elegance in all the rest of her form, as well as in the parts I have mentioned. Her legs are neat and slender ... and her very feet are little, white and pretty'.[17] He seems to be confusing the sculpture itself with half-remembered paintings, and thereby transforms the goddess of fertility into a dainty mid eighteenth-century lady of fashion.

With certain perhaps slightly notorious exceptions painters avoided taking the Medici or any other Venus as their model when a lady sat for her portrait. Most were, like Ramsay and Gainsborough, content to follow 'fashion' and this seems especially true of an artist like Francis Cotes, to whose female images the words 'tender', 'neat', 'little' and 'pretty' seem particularly apt. 'His basic intention', writes Edward Mead Johnson in his standard monograph, 'in painting the face was to make it the most fitting complement possible to the fashionable and beautifully coloured clothes of the sitter and an integral part of an essentially decorative composition'.[18] I think Cotes intended slightly more. Like other portraitists in this period he hoped to imbue his subjects— both male and female—with the spiritual qualities I have been discussing, especially grace. That at least partly explains his emphasis on the eyes. What he sought to avoid, above all in his female portraits, was too much emphasis on the body.

I have already commented on the reservations people had about displaying their teeth; a similar problem arose through the depiction of hair. There is no need for me to recapitulate the ancient symbolism of long hair. Sufficient to stress that hair is, like teeth, an unavoidably physical feature and has since biblical times been associated with (in men) physical strength and (in women) sexual attraction. All very much in contrast to the purely spiritual qualities associated with the eyes, or with certain movements or hand gestures. Hogarth was well aware of all this. Hair was, for him, an instance of the beauty of waving and serpentine lines. It is surprising how rarely he painted a lady with her hair uncovered. He was especially fond of flowing curls, and in a passage which looks forward to Rossetti he praised 'the many waving and contrasted turns of naturally intermingling locks [which] ravish the eye with the pleasure of the pursuit, especially when they are put in motion by a gentle breeze'. But he warned his readers that 'a lock of hair falling ... cross the temples, and by that means breaking the regularity of the oval, has an effect too alluring to be strictly decent, as is very well known to the loose and lowest class of women'.[19] There was, in fact, during the 1750s and 1760s, a definite tendency to suppress this aspect of female appearance. Whereas in the 30s and 40s the fashionable 'Dutch coiffure' allowed a certain display of female hair—Richardson's Clarissa is praised for 'the wavy ringlets of her shining hair'[20]—the style of the later 50s and 60s was tighter and more austere. For about twenty years women, like Margaret Lindsay, scraped their hair tightly back or concealed it under their caps until, in the 1770s it rose to fantastic heights before exploding in the 1780s into a riot of curls.

Even the tight styles of around 1760 could be enriched by plaiting or braiding. Braided hair had a secret grace of a particularly potent sort. Hogarth described it as looking 'like intertwisted serpents', and 'extremely picturesque'.[21] The same word was used by Romney when, travelling in Italy in the early summer of 1773, he noted how charming were the women of Genoa, with 'the most picturesque and elegant hair ... braided up the back of the head and twisted round several times and beautifully varied'.[22] Plaits are worn by Margaret Lindsay and by the Muse of Tragedy who sternly confronts David Garrick in Reynolds's well known picture exhibited in 1762.

I have quoted Spence's description of the goddess Venus; I shall finish with his description of Minerva—which could be applied, almost word for word, to Reynolds's Muse of Tragedy—taken from the same text. Notice the extent to which the writer stresses her masculine appearance:

> Minerva, you see, is a beauty; but a beauty of the severer kind. She has not any thing of the little graces, or of the softness and prettiness of Venus. It is that dignity; that becoming air; that firmness and composure; with such just features, and a certain sternness that has much more of masculine than female in it; which makes the distinguishing character of her face. This goddess, as the ancients used to represent her, is more apt to strike one with awe and terror, than to charm one, at first sight.[23]

And in Garrick's half-apologetic choice of Comedy we may see symbolised the conceptual shift discussed by Dr Hodgson in the study from which I quoted at the beginning of this paper. Beauty loses its claim to determinate moral choice and is reduced to the object of male regard; dignity, firmness and composure, more apt to strike one with awe, become the prerogative of the man of action. Minerva, in possessing these qualities, loses her femininity.

It is easy to think of exceptions to what I have been saying. Reynolds, for instance, not infrequently imbues his female subjects with great force of character; but my point would be that he does this by devices—assertive poses, for instance, and strong textures—normally and traditionally associated with male portraiture.[24] I have been talking about the background of normal expectation against which exceptional images can be identified and correctly analysed.

Notes

1. Horace Walpole to Sir David Dalrymple, 25 February 1759, Horace Walpole, *Correspondence*, eds W.S. Lewis, Charles H. Bennett and Andrew G. Hoover (New Haven, Yale U.P. 1951), vol. XV, p.47.
2. Edmund Burke, *A Philosophical Enquiry into the Origin of our Ideas of the Sublime and Beautiful* (London, 1757).

3. Judith Feyertag Hodgson, *Human Beauty in Eighteenth-Century Aesthetics* (University of Pennsylvania, Ph.D., 1973), pp.1-2.

4. *Ibid.*, p.11, note 3.

5. Katharine M. Rogers, *Feminism in Eighteenth-Century England* (Brighton, Harvester Press, 1982).

6. Samuel H. Monk, 'A grace beyond the reach of art', *Journal of the History of Ideas*, 5 (1944), pp.131-50.

7. Daniel Webb, *An Inquiry into the Beauties of Painting*, 2nd edition (London, R. & J. Dodsley, 1761), pp.55-56; quoting *Paradise Lost*, VIII, 488.

8. Archibald Alison, *Essays on the Nature and Principles of Taste*, 6th edition (Edinburgh, Constable, 1825), vol. II, quoting the *Theory of Moral Sentiments*, pp.401-402; referring to 'mere beauty', p.381; and to the 'lower orders', p.393. The whole of chapter 6, section 5, deals with *Grace*.

9. Paolo Giovanni Lomazzo, *A Tracte Containing the Artes of Curious Paintings* (Oxford, J. Barnes, 1598), Book II, chapter 14.

10. J. André Rouquet, *The Present State of the Arts in England* (1755, reprinted London, Cornmarket Press, 1970), p.47.

11. Compare, for example, the head of an unknown lady of the time of Commodus, at Wilton House, illustrated in F. Poulsen, *Greek and Roman Portraits in English Country Houses* (Oxford, Clarendon Press, 1923), no.93.

12. Thomas Berdmore, *A Treatise on the Disorders and Deformities of the Teeth and Gums* (London, The Author, 1768), p.4.

13. *Memoirs of the Reign of George II*, ed. J.W. Croker, 2 vols (London, 1855), vol. I, p.96.

14. 'Sir Harry Beaumont' (pseudonym of Joseph Spence), *Crito: or, a Dialogue on Beauty*, ed. E. Goldsmid (Edinburgh, Privately Printed, 1885), p.35.

15. Alison, *Essays*, vol. II, p.385.

16. *The History of Miss Betsy Thoughtless*, [by Eliza Haywood], 4 vols (London, T. Gardner, 1751), vol. II, pp.283-84.

17. Joseph Spence, *Polymetis*, 2nd edition (London, R. & J. Dodsley, 1755), pp.66-67.

18. Edward Mead Johnson, *Francis Cotes* (Oxford, Phaidon, 1976), pp.6-7.

19. William Hogarth, *The Analysis of Beauty*, ed. J. Burke (Oxford, Clarendon Press, 1955), p.52.

20. Samuel Richardson, *Clarissa Harlowe; or the History of a Young Lady* (London, Chapman & Hall, 1902), vol. III, p.57.

21. Hogarth, *Analysis of Beauty*, p.46.

22. Quoted in Arthur B. Chamberlain, *George Romney* (London, Methuen & Co., 1910), p.67.

23. Spence, *Polymetis*, p.59.

24. David Mannings, 'Reynolds, Hogarth and Van Dyck', *Burlington Magazine*, 126 (1984), pp.689-90.

24

Philosophic Light and Gothic Gloom: Landscape and History in Eighteenth-Century Scotland

Michel Baridon

University of Dijon

I

The importance of the role played by Scotland in the intellectual history of eighteenth-century Europe is a fact well known to all the specialists of the period. One has only to name Hutcheson, Hume, Adam Smith, Burns, Millar, Lord Kames, Walter Scott, Raeburn, the Adam brothers, Robertson and several others to make it clear that the Scottish Enlightenment has become famous in all the fields in which it manifested itself. To pay homage to so many distinguished names would be a Herculean task which the present study could never accomplish without transforming itself into a guide book to some Pantheon of the North. It is certainly wiser and more stimulating to assign oneself other aims.

The purpose of this paper is not to glance over marble plates or to ponder over what Johnson, while on his tour of Scotland, called 'mournful memorials';[1] it is to depict, perhaps to resurrect, the intellectual energy everywhere at work in the achievements of those who have just been mentioned. This is the only way to make them come to life again, for if there is one miracle ever performed by Man, it is the recapturing of the mental power by which great creations were achieved and can endure through the centuries. Of this kind of power the Scottish philosophers had an ample share, for intellectual stimuli came to them from many quarters: economics, sociology, politics, history, the visual arts, linguistics and the whole range of the sciences, whether applied or theoretical. But they were also stimulated by the deep contradictions which beset them; and since no philosopher, no thinking being even, can accept prolonged contradictions (unless he drowns his vexation in the reading of guide books), their works grew out of their passionate desire to solve them and to unravel the cluster of issues which constituted the problematics of the age.

Of these contradictions, some examples spring readily to mind. There was national feeling versus cosmopolitanism: we find Hume, for example, providing his readers with a list of Scotticisms at the end of his *History of England* and taking great pride in the achievements of his compatriots:

> Is it not strange that, at a time when we have lost our princes, our Parliaments, our independent government, even the presence of our chief nobility, are unhappy in our accent and pronunciation, speak a very corrupt dialect of the tongue we make use of; is it not strange, I say, that, in these Circumstances, we shou'd really be the people most distinguished for Literature in Europe?[2]

Yet he certainly approved of the elocution classes organised in Edinburgh under Sheridan's father to promote 'the reading and the speaking of the English language'[3] and he tried hard to surpass the French in the difficult art of cutting a fine figure in the Parisian salons. Equally important was the contradiction between the Scottish philosophers who adhered to the cosmopolitanism prevalent in the first phase of the Enlightenment, at the time when Voltaire and Montesquieu dominated the intellectual scene, and those who stood for the new values of cultural nationalism, for the gothic revival, the vogue of Ossian and the general trend towards primitivism. Hume wrote to Gibbon in 1776:

> But among many other marks of decline, the prevalence of superstition in England prognosticates the fall of philosophy and the decay of taste.[4]

This would probably have met with the disapproval of Adam Smith, Ferguson and Monboddo, to say nothing of Millar and Mackenzie. There were dissensions in the Athens of the North. So that, by a strange contradiction, while the philosophers and the historians of Scotland were spreading 'philosophic light' over Europe, her novelists and her poets took delight in popular superstitions and in old songs, in 'ruinated castles' and in the gloom of primitivism. At the same time as Gibbon writes:

> a strong ray of philosophic light has broken from Scotland in our own times; and it is with private as well as public regard that I repeat the names of Hume, Robertson and Adam Smith.[5]

we find Hugh Blair saying that the 'barbarity' of Ossian pleases because:

> trees and forests, heath and grass and flowers, rocks and mountains, music and songs, light and darkness, spirits and ghosts...form the circle within which [his] comparisons generally run.[6]

What I would like to explore is the apparent contradiction existing between 'philosophic light', which tried to clarify all things by promoting the spirit of rational enquiry, and the taste for the gloomy, the dark, the sombre, the irrational, the chaotic, which grew throughout the second half of the eighteenth century and ultimately triumphed in the Romantic age. What I should like to make clear is the fact that far from impeding the progress of the Scottish Enlightenment the contradiction between gothic gloom and philosophic light was central to its development and accounted for some of its outstanding achievements.

II

If we revert to its very beginning, we shall understand why philosophic light and gothic gloom were inseparable in the genesis of the whole movement. Deep rifts existed between the Highlands and the Lowlands, between the rigid, semi-tribal stratification prevailing in the former, and the rapidly changing society of the latter, a society in which landowners, entrepreneurs and the commercial elements of the urban middle classes were determined to take advantage of the union with England. Those were socio-economic rifts, now made larger by the changes introduced by the Glorious Revolution. A revolution is always marked by an acceleration of historical time; it inevitably exaggerates, as if by a sort of foreshortening of the perspective, the antagonisms already in existence. Walter Scott remarked:

> There is no European nation which, within the course of half a century, or little more, has undergone so complete a change as this kingdom of Scotland.[7]

It was not only the socio-economic structures which were more contrasted after the Glorious Revolution, it was also the intellectual scene. While the Highlands clung to tradition, while they romanticised the past to increase its power of seduction, the fast developing Lowlands tended to open themselves more to the influences coming from the Continent, whether they were French, English or Dutch. But this inevitably resulted in other contradictions, for the presbyterianism of the Lowlands had its narrow aspects which antagonised the more liberal elements of the North East, and one could well find opponents of bigotry either among the enlightened élites who fostered the opportunities for change, or among the tradition-loving lairds who considered themselves above the fanaticism of the presbyterians.

The educated laity of the North East read Giannone[8] and this was in no way incompatible with their Scottish patriotism as long as both attitudes were felt to counter the narrow mindedness of the penny-wise entrepreneurs of Glasgow; conversely Hutcheson, who taught the sons of the aspiring merchants of the Lowlands, felt it his duty to open their minds to the currents of thought perceptible in every society where the Enlightenment had a foothold. Hence a feeling, probably shared by many, that a Scottish intellectual was bound to discover very soon that he lived in a land of change and deep loyalties. His was a land divided even by its geography in such a way as to reveal why the winds of change blew sometimes in opposite directions and sometimes in directions which were made parallel by historical contradictions. All this was made perfectly clear by David Daiches in his contribution to the *Scott Bicentenary Essays* when he wrote:

> The Union of 1707 worked in two equal and opposite directions. One response was to cultivate Scotch feeling in song and ballad... The other response...tried to compensate for a loss of cultural independence by cultural means, but through Enlightenment rather than nostalgia.[9]

This was, of course, the main contradiction, the widest gulf. But there were others, extending in an intricate network, over the whole intellectual landscape, a landscape so fascinating however, that it attracted many English eyes. Without going as far as to say, with Franklin, that the Union of 1707 allowed Jonah to swallow the whale, we may nevertheless assume that it had deep repercussions on the south side of the Border. The three creative artists who introduced the greatest and the most lasting innovations (I mean Defoe in fiction, Thomson in poetry and Vanbrugh in the visual arts) were interested in things Scottish shortly before or after the union with England. All three also took a particular interest in the scientific movement or were personally acquainted with some of its leading figures; and, as the scientific movement was studied in the Scottish universities more attentively than anywhere else, it may well be that the three men mentioned above were feeling, with the wonderful instinct of artists and poets, that Scotland was becoming an essential part of the new world picture, the world picture of post Glorious Revolution times. The rifts which cut across Scotland certainly gave rise to an intense intellectual fermentation which was particularly active in the deepest rift of all, the Border.

Thomson was a Border man, popular and widely read in England and in Scotland,[10] and he will detain us for some time because he was the earliest and the most explicit exponent of the contradiction between philosophic light and gothic gloom. In this he proved that he had all the characteristics of a truly great poet who captured the essence of the modernity of his age and who expressed it in a way which still communicates mental elation to the twentieth-century reader. Granted that the formation of a poet is a thing almost as mysterious as poetry itself, one may at least assume that an understanding of his childhood and adolescence is essential for a full appreciation of his originality. And in the case of Thomson, this originality, soon to assert itself in the tempestuous visions of *Winter*, clearly has its source in his ramblings near Jedburgh and in his education as a son of the manse. It was then that his memory was marked for ever by the storms which raged over the mountains of his native country, and it was then also that he associated these visions with the cosmic poetry of the psalms read in the family household.[11] Madame de Stael denied the influence of the Bible in the nature poetry of the eighteenth century, but Coleridge and Victor Hugo thought otherwise and as poets they should be trusted in preference to a critic, however brilliant.[12]

What Thomson had seen and felt as a child, his education was soon to confirm. He was taught Newtonian physics and astronomy as well as Newtonian optics at Edinburgh by no less illustrious a professor than Colin MacLaurin whom Newton himself recommended when he later applied for a professorship in Edinburgh. This was followed by a study of Locke,[13] then not even mentioned at Oxford, if Adam Smith is to be believed. Thomson could thus fuse the new cosmogony—the cosmogony which inspired both the serene world picture of the Boyle lectures and the apocalyptic visions of Burnet's *Sacred Theory of the Earth*—together with the images teeming in his young mind. The flights of his poetic genius fused both these elements together and achieved the unique association of natural science and exalted sublimity which took England by storm when he published his *Winter*. The shock spread over the whole of Europe and we can well understand the sensation made by Thomson's poem, for one has only to compare *Windsor Forest* with the opening lines of *Winter* to understand why the former is an admirably chiselled jewel of neoclassical aesthetics while the latter already displays a breadth of vision and a force of inspiration later to be found in the poems of Wordsworth, the music of Beethoven's *Pastoral Symphony* or the pictures of Turner. This could be illustrated by *Loch Coriskin* in which Turner, himself a great reader of Thomson, has admirably expressed the Burnetian sublimity so often present in *Winter*.

Thomson is also a great poet of light. He paints light in all its aspects; he is indeed the poet of 'philosophic light'. When he celebrated Newton he glorified him as 'the father of light', the scientist who had discovered the mysteries of its power:

> Light itself which everything displays,
> Shone undiscovered, till his brighter mind
> Untwisted all the shining robe of day.[14]

Turner's *Kilchurch Castle*—Turner seems truest to Thomson when he paints the landscapes of his native land—shows this 'untwisting' of the 'shining robe of day' (Plate 5). In Thomson's view, the brightest intellect of the age could only be compared to the sun and, on another occasion, he indeed called him 'our philosophic sun'. But 'philosophic' is an interesting word here; taken in the sense of 'scientific', or, as the *Oxford English Dictionary* says, 'pertaining to or used in the study of natural philosophy or some branch of physical science; physical, scientific', it is used by Thomson in association with 'melancholy' on more than one occasion.[15] So the philosopher is the man who sheds light, as the example of Newton proves; but he can also be the man who takes pleasure in plunging into the darkest abysses of nature and in exploring the gloomy recesses of his own mind. This explains the famous 'Welcome, kindred glooms! Congenial horrors hail!' in the opening lines of *Winter*. The poet can be philosophic by being gloomy or by singing 'light immense'. This was the revelation which brought about the instant success of the *Seasons* because *Winter* met a secret expectation of the reading public.

No original vision can impose itself by the sheer force of surprise, however, and the real explanation of instant success lies often in the slow underground processes which prepare spectacular changes. Among these underground processes, the emergence of 'northern sublimity' seems to have been particularly important. It was the result of a number of factors, all different in

Plate 5. *Kilchurn Castle with the Cruchan Ben Mountains, Scotland: Noon* by J.M.W. Turner, c. 1801, by kind permission of the Plymouth City Museum and Art Gallery.

origin and all contributing to the same general aim. According to Shaftesbury, Britain had never been so powerful as in the early decades of the eighteenth century and she now had to prove that she was able to develop art forms which corresponded to the eminence she had reached. Shaftesbury's impassioned rhapsodies delineated the general characteristics of this national art.[16] It was to mark a complete severance from classicism and from the baroque by resorting to the sublimity of cosmic inspiration and to the dark atmosphere of Rosa's pictures. In a way, what Shaftesbury predicted was achieved by Thomson. But even before the *Seasons* were published, the visual arts were already exploring the possibilities offered by wider landscapes and darker climates of sensibility. Among those who developed trends which were then thoroughly new was Sir John Vanbrugh. And Vanbrugh is important because, like Thomson, he derived his inspiration from the buildings and from the landscapes he discovered when he visited, as he said, 'all the great houses of the north'.

Castle Howard, which was built for Lord Carlisle, was the first great assertion of the architectural modernity of the age. It was the expression of northern sublimity because it made the building inseparable from the dark horizons which surrounded it and it proudly asserted the strength and independence of the nobility whose influence would henceforth play a decisive role in public affairs. Vanbrugh, being associated with the great figures of the Whig party, necessarily adhered to the great political myths that they popularised. And since a myth lives by historical allusions to precedents, the mixed constitution so much praised after the Glorious Revolution was presented as a return to the institutions which had made the greatness of Britain in the days of Alfred, the Saxon king, and in those of the great barons who had compelled John Lackland to concede Magna Carta. This explained why Swift said that he loved parliaments because they were a 'Gothick institution'.[17]

The myth of Gothic liberty became central to Whig propaganda and it could be spread by the visual arts both because of its historical associations and because it could play on the emotions generated by Rosa-esque trends in painting. And what could be more Rosa-esque than a Scottish landscape? As Gray said, using obvious 'Gothick' connotations:

> The mountains are ecstatic and ought to be visited in pilgrimage once a year. None but those monstrous creatures of God know how to join so much beauty with so much horror. A fig for your poets, painters, gardners and clergymen that have not been among them.[18]

The Duke of Argyll, whose importance in British politics need not be discussed here, certainly understood that the proud independence of the nobility and its historical role could be an inspiration to architects interested in reviving the style of gothic times. His Whig convictions were proudly proclaimed in his park at Whitton (Plate 6) and in the castle he rebuilt at Inveraray, a castle with which Vanbrugh and Morris were associated and which later inspired Turner himself (Plate 7). The note of gloom and grandeur

Plate 6. 'The Duke of Argyll's Tower at Whitton' by John Adam, 1748, by kind permission of the Royal Institute of British Architects. Thanks also to Blackie & Son Ltd for permission to reproduce the plate from James Macaulay, *The Gothic Revival* (1975).

Plate 7. *Inverary, Loch Fyne* by J.M.W. Turner, c. 1802-1803, by kind permission of City of Manchester Art Gallery.

which was then sounded in the landscape reverberated through the whole of the eighteenth century, for we find Horace Walpole describing Castle Howard as 'a fortified city' with 'woods worthy each of being a metropolis of the druids'[19] and Reynolds speaking of the delight given by:

> Whatever buildings bring to our remembrance ancient customs and manners, such as the castles of the barons of the ancient chivalry ... Hence it is that towers and battlements are so often selected by the painter and the poet to make part of the composition of their landscape; and it is from hence, in a great degree that in the buildings of Vanbrugh, who was a poet as well as an architect, there is a greater degree of imagination than we shall find perhaps in any other.[20]

III

I should like now to study the formation and diffusion of the new world picture by the contrasted forces of gothic gloom and philosophic light, analysing the role of northern sublimity as a catalyst in the whole process. In this merging together of ideas and forms the Scottish Enlightenment played an important role for which it was prepared by historical factors (the Union of 1707 and the economic developments which ensued) as well as geographical ones (the landscapes and the climate described by Thomson).

There were also social factors: the active intellectual life developing on either side of the rifts which have been described, manifested itself in clubs and in universities which contributed actively to the diffusion of the discoveries of empirical science. This was made necessary by the economic developments of the Lowlands and was greatly facilitated by the emphasis put on practical education by Locke, and by the intellectual tradition of Calvinism. All the conditions combined to promote research in the academic world: great teachers, keen students, job opportunities, either in Scotland or in England, and funds. Apart from Hume, who was privately taught, the names of Beattie, Monboddo and Reid remain associated with the University of Aberdeen, those of Ferguson, Kames and Robertson with the University of Edinburgh and those of Hutcheson, Adam Smith and Millar with the University of Glasgow.

In those famous universities the works of Locke, Newton, Sydenham and Boyle had gained an early reputation. They stood in the forefront; but Continental thinkers were not far behind, as we can judge by the purchases made by university libraries.[21] Yet, although deism tended to spread, the emphasis was not so much on religious speculation as on social sciences and psychology; and quite understandably so, given the general intellectual trends then prevailing in Scottish universities. The Scots were not faced with the same problems as Voltaire. Intolerance came from enthusiasm not from superstition, and with enthusiasm one could at least argue, for even Hume, who had his reasons to dislike it, considered it was a friend to liberty.[22]

So attention was drawn to the other key figure of the Continental Enlightenment, Montesquieu. According to Dugald Stewart, he was the initiator of 'theoretical or conjectural history', that is, a type of historical writing which, 'starting from the changes in the conditions of mankind which take place in the different stages of their progress', tried to account 'for the corresponding alterations which their institutions undergo'.[23] It is in this sense that Millar could say that 'the great Montesquieu pointed out the road'[24] to the Scottish school, for nowhere else in Europe had progress been so evident in some areas and nowhere else had the winds of change blown with such force, bringing great pressure to bear on age-old institutions. Montesquieu was indeed the thinker who had best established what Fontenelle called a 'liaison secrète', a secret link, between all the activities of a given society and the legal framework to which it had given birth. From this point of view the *Considérations* was an invaluable 'conjectural history' of Rome. In the same way as Voltaire had broadened his field of investigation by passing from Louis XIV to the whole planet, Montesquieu had passed from Rome to the rest of Europe, initiating research into what might be called the experimental theory of social statics, the spirit of laws resulting from the nature of the societies whose life they regulated. Scottish readers of Montesquieu might well feel stimulated by a type of conjectural history which provided causes for the changes they could see taking place under their own eyes. All the more so as they were able to use Montesquieu's 'boldness of hypothesis' (Gibbon's phrase) to improve on his system of causal relation.

Among Montesquieu's early disciples Lord Kames occupied a place almost as conspicuous as Hume's. His *Historical Law Tracts*, published in 1758, at a time when Hume was writing his *History of England*, openly acknowledged its debt to the *Esprit des Lois*. What was perhaps more important still to the projection of 'philosophic light' on human history is the fact that the disciples of Hume and of Lord Kames were able to master the workings of an important factor in social change, economics. Montesquieu himself had 'pointed the way' as Millar said, by introducing economic factors in his definition of *l'esprit général*. But Hume carried things a step further in his essays on 'Superstition and enthusiasm' and in his discussion of the feudal system and of the decline of serfdom in Europe.

Smith and Millar took things further still because they were able to put together the contributions made by the English arithmeticians of the Petty school and those made by the French Physiocrats. They kept the 'liaison cachée', the hidden link, but they applied empirical methods with more boldness than Montesquieu. Man was led by passions, and to satisfy his needs he had to be considered not only from the political and legal angle (which is what Montesquieu had done), but also from the economic angle.

The writing of history was regenerated by what present experience revealed and it was made 'philosophic' by the application of scientific methods of investigation to the facts supplied by the study of the past. 'History', said Mackintosh, 'has now become a museum'.[25] In other words, it was the work, the mission of the philosopher, to turn towards the past for documents, and to piece documents together in order to reveal an intelligible whole where nothing but chaos had existed before. The disciples of Montesquieu felt that they had it in their power to achieve such a goal because they could shed light on the inner workings of social organisations, whether they had long been dead or whether they were still active and productive. And, as has already been indicated, few places in Europe could reveal the links between past and present with greater force than Scotland. The study of economics brought the philosopher into contact with a world hitherto unexplored, the world of the anonymous productive masses, the world of the arithmeticians and of the physiocrats, the world of the division of labour. The philosopher found himself confronted with the difficult task of charting the past history of mankind not by enquiring into the successive systems of legal organisation but into its successive systems of production. Hence the various stages of the history of mankind discussed by Hume, Smith, Adam Ferguson and Millar. This step was essential in the history of the Enlightenment. It was also taken by Herder in Germany, Turgot and Condorcet in France, and it changed the nature of the historian's perception of history over a long period of time from one of cycles to one of gradual evolution. 'Grandeur' and 'décadence' had to be replaced by a gradual ascension from primitivism to progress. To Kames who had said:

> Hunting and fishing, in order for sustenance, were the original occupations of man. The shepherd life succeeded; and the next stage was that of agriculture. These progressive changes, in the order now mentioned, may be traced in all nations, so far as we have remains of their original history.[26]

Adam Smith made a substantial addition when he wrote:

> There are four distinct states which mankind passes through. 1st the age of Hunters; 2nd, the age of Shepherds; 3rd, the age of Agriculture; 4th, the age of Commerce.[27]

And Millar could naturally conclude:

> There is thus, in human society, a natural progress from ignorance to knowledge, and from rude to civilized manners, the several stages of which are usually accompanied with peculiar laws and customs.[28]

To the attentive student of the history of ideas, it has always appeared that the marrying of two central ideas, when it is brought about by the evolution of the scientific movement, produces something like a tidal wave in the whole intellectual scene. Such was the case with the Scottish philosophers. Their vision of the long duration in history did not proceed only from their interest in economics. It also had the support of empirical epistemology and of Lockian psychology, itself an offshoot of empirical science. It is by turning to those two disciplines, so essential to the modernity of the eighteenth century, that we shall discover why gothic gloom was as essential to the Scottish Enlightenment as philosophic light.

IV

If the history of man is not ruled only by climates, if, in such concepts as *l'esprit général*, the idea enters that a gradual development of societies is proved by history and can be shown to apply to all models of historical development, then a process of gradual change may be demonstrated. The philosophers of the second phase of the Enlightenment were well equipped to chart this. Locke's emphasis on psychology and language enabled them to show that what a generation acquired was passed on to the next because language was common to all men and taught by the old to the young. It was a sort of repository of common knowledge and it increased the intellectual capacities of all the members of a society by a process of accumulation comparable to Locke's description of the mental life of all individuals from infancy to adulthood. This theory of language was to be found in Turgot, a physiocrat whom Adam Smith had visited while on his visit to Paris; Adam Smith found himself in agreement with this genetic conception of language and developed it in his *Considerations concerning the first Formation of Languages*, a text later translated by the widow of that great apostle of perfectibility, Condorcet.[29]

Once he accepted the idea that a given society was in perpetual evolution, the philosopher must inevitably be attracted to speculations concerning its origins and its further stages of development. On this point, the Scottish *philosophes* found themselves in agreement with the views of Turgot, Rousseau and Herder. The perfectibility of the human race confronted them with issues which were completely outside the scope of the problematics of cycles so central to the *Considérations* and to the *Essai sur les moeurs*. They wished to enquire into the origins of mankind, into the early developments of all the manifestations of man's knowledge; hence the number of essays on the origins of language, of literature, on the distinction of ranks, of man himself. Uncivilised ages revealed in the raw, so to speak, truths essential to the understanding of the later stages of development.

But here again Scotland could meet the challenge. Ever since the days of Ramsay she had treasured the heritage of the past. What Percy was doing in England out of intellectual curiosity had been done here out of patriotic feeling. Alexander Runciman's *St Margaret landing at Dunfermline* or his *Ossian singing* illustrate this interest in national history and they also show that the gothic past could best be represented by the aesthetics of northern sublimity. The two lines of development defined by David Daiches, 'Enlightenment' and 'nostalgia', were thus reconciled by new aesthetic trends. But those new aesthetic trends resulted in their turn from the popularisation of scientific literature. A new world picture was emerging, and this world picture expedited decisive changes as it permeated the collective imagination of the age.

The great figures of experimental science had always made it clear that the spectacular results of their researches were attributable to their method. Their observations were made empirically by way of what they called 'histories': 'histories', they maintained, were far superior to the method used before, either by the schoolmen who merely described phenomena or by the Cartesians who substituted their systems for a thorough observation of nature. 'Histories' were tables of observations carefully compiled without any preconceived ideas; they were unencumbered by metaphysical preoccupations.

In such 'histories' the emphasis was put on details, on 'particulars' which guaranteed the truth and accuracy of the observations which were made, at the very time when they were made. Locke compiled a history of the weather for the year 1692, noting down several times a day the temperature, the state of the sky and the atmospheric pressure. When he wrote his *Essay Concerning Human Understanding* he described it in his introduction as having been composed 'by the historical plain method'. Boyle advised all the correspondents of the Royal Society to write similar histories of the countries they were visiting, emphasising the particular detail in observation. In his *General Heads for a Natural History of a Country Great or Small* he spoke of the need for drawing up 'articles of inquisition into particulars', 'to superstruct in time a solid and useful Philosophy' upon the experimental method.[30] This text was considered so important that Chambers made use of it in his *Encyclopedia* to illustrate the contribution made by the Royal Society to the scientific movement. The experimental philosopher, in order to be true to nature, had to observe the particulars of time as carefully as those of space; it was not so much his ability to frame a system which was important as taking into account the volume of information provided by the history of a given phenomenon. Locke was so careful not to divorce time and space from his description of mental life that he wrote in his *Essay Concerning Human Understanding*:

> Expansion and duration do mutually embrace and comprehend each other, every part of space being in every part of duration, and every part of duration in every part of expansion.[31]

Indeed his psychology abundantly proves that he considered mental life to be governed by the particulars of time and space, for, according to him, sensory impressions had to be stored up in the memory before the child could think; so gradual was this accumulation that his intellect was not to be considered similar to that of an adolescent, let alone to that of an adult. Thought, in Locke's view, was a genetic process in which every age had its particulars and in which sense impressions depended on the conditions and on the place in which they were experienced. This had far reaching consequences in the learned world. To accept Newtonian physics was to accept corpuscular physics; to accept corpuscular physics was to accept Lockian psychology because sense impressions resulted from the impact of particles on sensory organs. It was also to accept the idea that man's intellect was governed by sensibility more than by reason since Locke insisted that:

> Pleasure and pain and that which causes them, good and evil, are the hinges on which our passions turn.[32]

The consequence was that associationism soon became inseparable from sensibility as the works of Hutcheson, Hume and Adam Smith show. But sensibility in its turn led them on to sympathy, and sympathy linked man to man so as to make society a total entity; and not only did sympathy make society a whole composed of sentient beings, but linguistics made it a community of speaking beings whose language constituted the collective memory of the species. One can understand why the moral philosophers of Scotland were so positive when they described the progress of society which consisted, according to Adam Ferguson:

> in the continual succession of one generation to another; in progressive attainments made by different ages; communicated with additions from age to age; and in periods, the farthest advanced, not appearing to have arrived at any necessary limits.[33]

But if such was the case, the past literature of a people conveyed all the 'particulars' necessary for a full understanding of this people. Particulars of place, local accents, peculiarities of speech due to rank and to cultural habits, particulars of time preserved in medieval ballads and primitive art forms, all became necessary to a full understanding of history. Since pain and pleasure accompanied all the manifestations of mental life, the nostalgia of the folk literature lover was not (as is often thought) complacent self-indulgence, it was the best way of understanding the past because sensibility was vital to any true intellectual apprehension. Nostalgia did not merely accompany knowledge. It was knowledge itself.

Besides, folk poetry was the poetry of the anonymous masses with which the philosopher was linked both in time and in space. In space, because he consumed the goods they produced and because he was linked to them by the bonds of sympathy; in time because they had transmitted the language he was speaking. But sympathy, the capacity to feel the emotions of other men, extended to nature itself. Hutcheson had said:

> Inanimate objects often have such positions as resemble those of the human body in various circumstances; these airs and gestures of the body are indications of dispositions in the Mind, so that our passions and affections as well as other Circumstances obtain the Resemblance to inanimate objects. Thus a tempest at sea is an emblem of wrath; a plant or tree drooping under the rain is a person in sorrow; a poppy bending its stalk or a flower withering when cut by the plow resembles the death of a blooming hero; an aged oak in the mountains shall represent an old empire, a flame seizing a wood shall represent a war.[34]

If sensibility enabled man not only to communicate with his fellow beings but also to be emotionally moved by the landscape which echoed the innermost impressions of his sensibility, then nature was given an unprecedented function in the creations of literature and the visual arts. When Thomson made the anonymous poor part of the landscape, he was heralding the day when Gainsborough would fuse them with nature; he was also heralding the day when a landscape would be painted with all the particulars of time and space made requisite by the epistemology of the age. When Alexander Nasmyth painted his views of *West Loch Tarbert* he provided the indications 'looking North' or 'looking South' and the fishermen figuring in the foreground of his *Inveraray from the sea* are real fishermen. The vapours and the gloom of Scotland, the mysterious correspondence between sky and water everywhere visible on the lochs, provided the painters with captivating 'modern' subjects because their finest effects were so transient that they could only be captured by the magic of a single brush stroke (Turner, *Loch Long, Morning*, Plate 8).

All the painters whose works have been mentioned could have said, like Shenstone, that there was not 'a single cloud or Dimness in the Sky, but had its exact Image or Counterpart in [their] Imagination'[35] and they expressed visually the need to catch the particulars of a landscape at a glance. The 'here and now' was the supreme achievement of an artist's virtuosity as we can see by the works of Turner. Perhaps, if one considers that Paul Sandby's career as a landscape painter began in Scotland, if we consider too that Dayes, Girtin and Turner were particularly attracted to the mists and vapours of the north, one may risk the idea that the ever changing colours of the Scottish landscape, the sudden alteration of light and the ever renewed effects provoked by the drifting clouds made it necessary to use water-colour to catch the most subtle changes at the very second they occurred. If such is the case, the 'north' played an important role in the development of the landscape in watercolour, an art form in which, as we have seen, the artistic imagination of the age brought together the philosophic light of the scientist and the gloom so necessary to the artist's gothic vision.

To conclude this study of the relation of history to landscape, the great figure of Walter Scott will show how a man of genius can combine the achievements of other writers and the creations made in the visual arts. In a way, Scott saw himself as a landscape painter *manqué* and as a historian *manqué*. He wrote in his *Journal*:

> I could make no progress either in painting or drawing. Even the humble ambition which I long cherished of making sketches of those places which interested me, from a defect of eye or hand were totally ineffectual. After long study and many efforts...I was obliged to relinquish in despair an art which I was most anxious to practise.[36]

As a novelist, however, Scott managed to provide extraordinary stimulation both to painters and to historians. He was one of those great hybrids very typical of the Romantic age: a poet in the world of fiction, a reviver of dead worlds gifted with extraordinary imaginative powers which he relentlessly applied to the retrieving of the past. The relation that Scott established between fiction and history has been fully explained by Herbert Butterfield:

> There is all the difference in the world between a man who has a story to tell and wishes to set it in past age and to adjust it to the demand of history, and the man who has the past in his head and allows it to come forth in story.[37]

Scott had indeed 'the past in his head' because, as Edgar Johnson said, 'Scott's own approach to the past strangely resembles that of the French philosophes'. Edgar Johnson probably meant that Scott had derived from

Plate 8. *Loch Long, Morning* by J.M.W. Turner, c. 1801, by kind permission of the Trustees of the Tate Gallery.

Montesquieu the historical vision of a given society as a whole; but since he calls him elsewhere 'a rationalist and an empiricist'[38] he might have added that Scott was indebted not to Montesquieu alone, but to the great figures of the Scottish Enlightenment, to Smith, to Dugald Stewart, to Lord Kames, to Hutcheson and indeed to all the philosophers whom we have had occasion to quote in this study. He saw society not only as a body whose life was regulated by laws, but also as a whole which comprised different modes of production, different ranks, and which was nevertheless united by a language common to all. The inner life of such a body could be recaptured by plunging into the past and allowing one's imagination to restore it to life by reconstituting all the 'particulars' of 'expansion and duration' which could still be retrieved. David Daiches, who sees Scott as 'a man of the Scottish Enlightenment', once remarked that 'Many of Scott's novels take the form of a sort of pilgrim's progress'.[39]

But what is a 'pilgrim's progress' if not a 'history' in the empiricist's sense of the word, a perambulation in space and time? The very structure of Scott's novels testifies to his debt to empirical science and to the philosophers of the eighteenth century. He is nevertheless a nineteenth- century man by reason of what Coleridge could have called his 'plastic imagination'. Like Niebuhr, the historian, he could claim that, with the help of a few documents, he could give life to a whole society; like Cuvier, the French biologist, he knew that he could reconstruct the skeleton of a prehistoric monster from a collection of scattered remains. This aspect of Scott's literary personality, his perception of the organic life of the social body, links the Enlightenment to Romanticism. His historical imagination, like that of Niebuhr, was perfectibility turned backwards, a unique capacity to see the past through the present and to hear people speak through the depths of ages.

In many ways he is identifiable with the men of the Enlightenment for he shares their attraction to social studies, and their wish to 'level our bristling prejudices' as Hazlitt remarked. This is the lighter side of his works. But the dark side is no less essential to the dramatisation of the whole. The northern sublimity of the Scottish landscapes to which he was so sensitive (his house was designed in the Gothic style to harmonise with them) enabled him to give his literary creations the 'particulars' of expansion which were no less vital to historical truth than the 'particulars' of duration. This is clearly visible in the following description:

> The meeting of two superb rivers, the Tweed and the Teviot, both renowned in song—the ruins of an ancient abbey—the most distant vestiges of Roxburgh Castle—the modern mansion of Fleurs, which is so situated as to combine the idea of baronial grandeur with those of modern taste, are themselves objects of the first class; yet they are so mixed, united and melted among a thousand other beauties of a less prominent description, that they harmonize into one general picture and please rather by unison than concord.[40]

In a passage like this, it is not only the old and the new which 'harmonise'; it is also the feudal past and the modern 'philosophic' observation of nature.

Landscape and history are fused together by a novelist who made it palpable to millions of readers that philosophic light was never so strong as when it was projected on the 'dark ages'. If the creative imagination was to bring past worlds to light, it must muster all the 'particulars' of expansion and duration that were to be found. Then, and then only, could their vivid colours be retrieved, even from the gloom of primeval times.

From the days when Vanbrugh was discovering the romantic appeal of gothic architecture and when Thomson was singing the 'mists and vapours' of the north, to those in which Walter Scott rode from village to village in order to recapture the life of the past, the contribution of Scotland to the cultural life of the rest of the world appears to have been truly outstanding. This was due not only to historical and geographical conditions; it was also due to the degree of coherence achieved by the Scottish philosophers. Without Hume, Smith and Millar, Montesquieu could never have proved such a source of inspiration to historians. Without Hutcheson, psychology could never have transformed the vision of nature. Without Ramsay and Macpherson, Scott could never have created the historical novel which made Scottish landscapes inseparable from Scottish history.

It is not at all certain whether all the tourists who visit the country are aware of the fact; but those who are lucky enough to have some knowledge of intellectual history cannot fail to be gratified by the thought that the scenic beauties of Scotland are now part of our cultural heritage because the novelists, the poets and the artists who saw them were able to fuse together the two great powers which ruled over the imagination of an enlightened age, gothic gloom and philosophic light.

Notes

1. Quoted by James Macaulay, *The Gothic Revival, 1745-1845* (Glasgow, Blackie, 1975), p.20.
2. Hume, letter to Gilbert Eliot of Minto, quoted by D. Daiches in 'Scott and Scotland', *Scott Bicentenary Essays*, ed. Alan Bell (Edinburgh and London, Scottish Academic Press, 1973), p.51.
3. David Murison, 'The Two languages in Scott', *Scott's Mind and Art*, ed. A.N. Jeffares (Edinburgh, Olwen & Boyd, 1969), p.207.
4. Quoted by Gibbon in his *Memoirs*, ed. G. Bonnard (London, Nelson, 1966), p.168.
5. Edward Gibbon, *Decline and Fall*, 7 vols, ed. J.B. Bury (London, Methuen, 1896-1900), vol VI, p.445.
6. H. Blair, *Critical Dissertation* in *The Poems of Ossian*, 2 vols (Edinburgh, A.Constable, 1805), vol. I, pp.229-30.
7. Scott in *Waverley*, quoted by D.D. Devlin, 'Scott and history', *Scott's Mind and Art*, p.86.
8. Jane Rendall, *The Origins of the Scottish Enlightenment* (London, Macmillan, 1978), p.6.
9. Daiches, 'Scott and Scotland', pp.49-50.
10. The anecdote of Coleridge finding a copy of *The Seasons* in an inn and exclaiming: 'This is fame' is well known. But Thomson was also read and loved in Scotland;

see Alan D. McKillop, *The Background to Thomson's Seasons* (Minnesota, Minnesota U.P., 1942), p.5.
11. 'The true God is here represented as wielding all the Elements of Nature and commanding each part thereof, Light and Darkness, Snow and Vapour, Wind and Storm, fulfilling his word', Thomson, Preface to the *Seasons*.
12. Coleridge's 'Sublimity is Hebrew by birth', *Table Talk and Omniana*, ed. T. Ashe (London, 1884), p.174, is essential to trace the links between Thomson and Wordsworth, or more generally, between eighteenth- and nineteenth-century sublimity.
13. According to Thomson, Locke had made the 'Whole internal world his own', *Seasons*, 'Summer', line 1449.
14. Thomson, *To the Memory of Sir Isaac Newton*, line 1, pp.96-98.
15. *The Seasons*, 'Autumn', line 1005.
16. Earl of Shaftesbury, *Characteristics*, 3 vols, ed. J.M. Robertson (New York, 1900), vol.I, pp.145-47.
17. Molesworth, a Whig, also spoke of parliaments as 'gothick' institutions, see H.T. Dickinson, *Politics and Literature in the Eighteenth Century* (London, J.M. Dent, 1974), p.24.
18. Quoted by C. Hussey, *The Picturesque* (London, Archon, 1927), p.106.
19. *The Yale Edition of Horace Walpole's Correspondence*, ed. W.S. Lewis (New Haven, Yale U.P., 1937-1983), vol.30, p.257.
20. Joshua Reynolds, *Discourses on Art*, ed. Robert E. Wark (New Haven & London, Yale U.P., 1975), pp.241-42.
21. See Alison K. Howard, 'Montesquieu, Voltaire and Rousseau in 18th-Century Scotland', *The Bibliothek*, II (1959).
22. See his Essay 'On Superstition and Enthusiasm'.
23. Quoted by Ian Simpson Ross, *Lord Kames and the Scotland of his Day* (Oxford, Clarendon Press, 1972), p.203.
24. Quoted by William C. Lehmann, *John Millar of Glasgow* (Cambridge, CUP, 1960), p.363.
25. *Ibid.*, p.120.
26. Quoted by Rendall, *The Origin of the Scottish Enlightenment*, pp.140-41.
27. *Ibid.*, p.141.
28. *Ibid.*, p.145.
29. Charles Porset, ed., *Varia Linguistica* (Paris, Ducros, 1970), p.306.
30. *Philosophical Transactions*, 1666, No.13, pp.222-26.
31. Locke, *Essay Concerning Human Understanding*, 2 vols (London, OUP, 1975), vol.II, Section XV, Paragraph 12, p.204.
32. *Ibid.*, vol.II, Section XX, Paragraph 3, p.229.
33. Quoted by Rendall, *The Origins of the Scottish Enlightenment*, p.131.
34. Frances Hutcheson, *An Enquiry into the Origins of our Ideas of Beauty and Virtue*, (1725, New York, Garland, 1971), Section II, article 4.
35. Shenstone, Letter to Lady Luxborough, 25 July 1748. *Letters of William Shenstone*, ed. Marjorie Williams (Oxford, Basil Blackwell, 1939), p.155.
36. Quoted by Marcia Allentuck, 'Scott and the Picturesque: afforestation and history', *Scott Bicentenary Essays*, p.188.
37. Quoted by Devlin, *Scott's Mind and Art*, p.75.
38. Edgar Johnson, *Sir W. Scott, The Great Unknown*, 2 vols (London, Hamish Hamilton, 1970), vol.I, p.1261.
39. Daiches, 'Scott and Scotland', *Scott Bicentenary Essays*, p.40; Daiches, 'Scott's achievement' in *Scott's Mind and Art*, p.25.
40. Quoted by Allentuck, *Scott Bicentenary Essays*, p.189.

SECTION IV

The Language and Bibliography of the Enlightenment

25

James Dunbar and the Enlightenment Debate on Language

Christopher J. Berry

University of Glasgow

James Dunbar was regent at King's College, Aberdeen from 1765 to 1794 and published in 1780 a volume entitled *Essays on the History of Mankind in Rude and Cultivated Ages.*[1] As the title indicates, this work took the form of a number of more or less discrete disquisitions on universal history. This was a favourite Enlightenment theme with Scottish writers. Dunbar's book may thus be compared with Ferguson's *History of Civil Society* (1767), Millar's *Observations concerning the Distinction of Ranks* (1771) and Kames's *Sketches on the History of Man* (1774). Like these, and many other works, Dunbar's *Essays* exhibit methodologically the two key features of what Dugald Stewart called Theoretical or Conjectural History, namely, that when direct factual evidence is unavailable then it is necessary to conjecture how men are 'likely to have proceeded from the principles of their nature and the circumstances of their external situation'.[2] The immediate context of these remarks was Adam Smith's *Considerations concerning the First Formation of Languages* (1761) and one of the special features of Dunbar's own conjectural history of mankind is the attention he pays to language. The object of this paper is to present Dunbar's account not only for its own sake but also for the ways in which it exemplifies certain broader Enlightenment assumptions about human nature, history and society.

Dunbar's own version differs from that of his compatriots by adopting a different periodisation. He identifies three eras in the history of the species:

> First, Man may have subsisted, in some sort, like other animals, in a separate and individual state, before the date of language, or the commencement of any regular intercourse. Secondly, He may be contemplated in a higher stage; a proficient in language, and a member of that artless community which consists with equality, with freedom and independence. Last of all, by slow and imper-

ceptible transitions, he subsists and flourishes under the protection and discipline of civil government.(pp.2-3)

Whereas most Scots, with the exception of Monboddo, are chiefly concerned with the changes within the third of Dunbar's eras (the so-called 'four-stages' theory)[3] Dunbar is concerned in his opening Essay with the change from the first to the second era, and in his Second Essay with the fact that the possession of language is one of the specific differences between the two eras. In addition, Dunbar's own periodisation, as his terminology reveals, is indebted to Rousseau's conjectural history as found in the *Discourse on Inequality* (1754).

To see the history of mankind as in some sense developmental was, of course, an Enlightenment commonplace. This development was underwritten by the attribution to human nature of a principle of progress or improvement (what Rousseau, for example, called Man's *perfectibilité*). While most writers were content with this simple attribution Dunbar provides also a periodisation of development of human nature. He is here exploiting, though with an explicit acknowledgement that the parallels are not exact, a long-standing analogy between the individual human being and the species at large. Hence we find the three eras of the history of the species have as a complement the following periodisation:

> First of all, those of sense appear, grow up spontaneously, or require but little culture. Next in order, the propensities of the heart display their force; a fellow-feeling with others unfolds itself gradually on the appearance of proper objects; for man becomes sociable long before he is a rational being. Last in the train, the powers of intellect begin to blossom, are reared up by culture, and demand an intercourse of minds.(p.16)

It is one of the distinctive characteristics of Dunbar's thought that he makes explicit that the principle underlying this capacity to develop is of Aristotelian provenance. Mankind possesses latent powers which upon the appearance of those above-mentioned 'proper objects' open and expand. Dunbar puts this schema to various uses throughout his book,[4] but here we will examine how he applies it in the particular case of language.

First, it is worth bringing out the significance of what we have already established. We know from the way that Dunbar has set up the question that he postulates a time when Man was without language. This approach enables him to achieve two objectives: one, it permits the origin of language to be conceptually identified and, two, it permits him to clarify the difference between Man and animals. This latter objective had considerable topicality due to Monboddo's publication of the first volume of his *Origin and Progress of Language* in 1773. It was Monboddo's belief that language was not natural to Man and, in his argument to prove that it was rather merely an acquired habit, he cited the behaviour of orang-outangs. According to Monboddo the orang was really a species of *homo sapiens* since although devoid of language it nevertheless practised such other human habits as living communally, building homes, possessing a sense of decorum, using weapons and so on.[5]

Dunbar noted the apparent similarity in the possession of vocal cords (p.67), but later referred to the work of Camper because he had shown in opposition to Monboddo that the orang was organically incapable of speech (p.203).[6] The former of the two above objectives betrays the Enlightenment approach. Overwhelmingly Enlightenment thinkers located the origin of language naturalistically, that is to say, in human nature so that from that locus they were able to conjecture how language developed alongside Man's own development. There is a clear connexion between the two objectives. The conceptual search for the origin of language was simultaneously a search for the special capacity of humans that differentiated them from the brutes.

Openly acknowledging that there is no evidence concerning the 'opening scene of man' (p.2), Dunbar provides a conjectural description of the psychology of Man at that time. These conjectures are underwritten by the belief in the uniformity of human nature (perhaps the key premise of Enlightenment thought)[7] and the similarity of the individual and the species. This permits Dunbar in typical fashion to draw on the evidence of children.[8] And since 'savages' are the children of the human species then, where available, their practices can be used as corroborative evidence. Dunbar provides a striking illustration of this. He declares that the 'South Sea isles' enable us 'to glance at society in some of its earliest forms' (p.26), and then later remarks that Omiah (the celebrated Tahitian) is as 'circumscribed as a child in the number of his ideas' (p.110).

Dunbar depicts this primitive psychology as follows: 'Man we may observe is at first possessed of few ideas, and of still fewer desires, he seldom indulges any train of reflection on the past, and cares not by anxious anticipation to antedate futurity' (p.68). Significantly, as we shall see, this also means that Man 'uses the resources of instinct, rather than the lights of the understanding; is scarce capable of abstraction, and a stranger to all the combinations and connexions of systematic thought' (p.69). The immediate inference Dunbar draws from this picture is that at this time 'there is no need for the details of language'. There is silent communication as the 'feelings of the heart break forth in visible form'. Coeval with this, and equally 'independently of art', there is a 'mechanical connexion between the feelings of the soul and the enunciation of sound' which declares 'the purposes of man to man' and it is these 'accents and exclamations [that] compose the first elements of a rising language' (p.70).

This notion that the origin of language is to be found in natural exclamations or cries was common. Thus views similar to Dunbar's can be found throughout the contemporary literature.[9] An indication of the character of this natural speech is provided by interjections for they have retained 'its primeval character' (p.71). The language of early Man, it can thus be conjectured, was unarticulated or monosyllabic and exempted from arbitrary rules. Similarly, to Priestley, interjections were unarticulated cries of passion;[10] to Blair, they represent as 'passionate exclamations' the 'first elements of speech'; to Harris[11] they are adventitious sounds which arise spontaneously in the human soul[12] and for Monboddo the interjection 'may be considered as remains of the most antient language among men, that by which they expressed their feelings not their ideas'.[13]

These natural cries are thus the first step in Dunbar's account of the development of language. The second step is imitation. Dunbar refers to Man having an 'imitative faculty' (p.78). (The question of 'faculties' will concern us later.) He argues that Man is not alone in possessing a talent for imitation because it is also found in animals; but Man alone can imitate all other animals whilst none can imitate him. More significantly, in Man imitation is performed from 'a love of the effect' and it may 'be justly called the first intellectual amusement congenial with our being' (p.76). That imitation plays a role in the development of language was also an idea found in many writers—in Monboddo,[14] Blair[15] and Condillac[16] to name but a few.

After the imitative faculty Dunbar posits the development of another— the analogical faculty. This faculty in general 'has vast powers in binding the associations of thought in all mental arrangements' (p.79). In the more particular case of language this 'power' is such that there is no object which the mind 'cannot assimilate to something antecedently in its possession. By consequence a term already appropriated, and in use, will, by no violent transition, be shaped and adjusted to the new idea' (p.80). We now witness a decisive move. These analogical connexions 'supply the place of real resemblance' and now 'instinct borrows aid from the imagination' (p.79). This is decisive because it is here that the 'reign of invention' commences and it is also here that 'perhaps we should stop and draw the boundary of art and nature'. The consequence of this is that Man and brutes can be decisively differentiated since it is the 'weakness of this principle [analogical faculty] which imposes the law of silence and excludes all possibility of improvement in the animal world'.

As his schema of the three eras of species-development testifies, there is a social counterpart to this. Dunbar is explicit that 'every effort beyond what is merely animal has reference to a community' (p.5). This communal life, attained in the second era, is the 'prime mover of our *inventive* powers' (p.5: my emphasis) and it is there that 'the springs of ingenuity are put into motion' so that 'the language of nature gradually participates of art' (p.31).

Dunbar's postulated analogical faculty provides a particularly clear exemplification of Aarsleff's observation that the point behind the search for origins was to attempt to get down to basic principles in order to distinguish what was owing to nature and what to art.[17] However Dunbar puts this faculty to greater use.

The vital role which Dunbar allots to the analogical faculty is to account for the development and generation of language and speech in all parts without recourse to powers of abstract reasoning. Such a recourse would be inconsistent with his conjecture that Man in the rudest ages was 'scarce capable of abstraction'. The question of abstraction arose because of the still prevalent conception of language in terms of its grammatical composition— nouns, verbs, adjectives and so on—with the crucial corollary that some of these 'parts', especially particles such as prepositions, expressed abstract or metaphysical relations. Dunbar believes that if language is thought of as invented then it means that these putative inventors 'must have resolved in imagination all the subtleties of logic and entered far into the science of grammar, before its objects had any existence. Profound abstraction and generalisation must have been constantly exercised' (p.93). But thanks to the postulated presence of the analogical faculty the need for this 'constant exercise' can be obviated.

We have already seen that this faculty operates by appropriation and assimilation, and the cumulative effect of these processes is that language develops through 'the laws of analogy [which] by one gentle and uniform effect superseding and alleviating the efforts of abstraction permit language to advance' (p.92). Once again the speech-patterns of children are cited in corroboration (p.80). Since *ex hypothesi* children have not developed their reasoning powers then to attribute the development of language to abstraction is 'by no means compatible with the limited capacity of the human mind' (p.94).

This argument against abstraction was integral to a lively Enlightenment debate on the evolution of the parts of speech. While Dunbar does not himself engage in this debate to any great extent, he explicitly follows Adam Smith's argument that verbs have developed from impersonal to personal without supposing any act of abstraction or metaphysics (p.113).[18] Moreover, when Dunbar remarks in passing that 'though every sound formed not a complete sentence as at the beginning' (p.85) he reveals that he also shares with Smith, and many others,[19] the conception that at the root of linguistic structure lie primal or pre-syntactic utterances and that the development of language is the breaking-down of such utterances (sentences) into their constituent logical parts.[20] Dunbar's point, to repeat, is that the development of the parts of speech is not in itself an exercise of logic or abstraction but the operation of the analogical faculty as it moves 'from object to object in the *concrete*' (p.89: Dunbar's emphasis).

Dunbar's governing assumption, derived ultimately, like all standard Enlightenment accounts, from Locke, is that language and the human mind develop concurrently. He states this key point unequivocally when he observes that 'ideas and language' are 'uniformly in close conjunction' (p.94). While the conceptual and polemical thrust behind this point, and thence behind the postulated analogical faculty, lies in its implications for the *processes* of language there are two further points we can make.

First, though the formal attention Dunbar pays to analogy is greater than that of his contemporaries[21] the postulated presence of an analogical faculty is his version of the prevalent associationist psychology. This is apparent in his explicit avowal of the common link between association, imagination and invention, as seen for example in his fellow Aberdonian, Alexander Gerard.[22] It is because of this link that Dunbar is able to use this faculty to account for the development of the figurativeness of language, whereby, in orthodox fashion, corporeal or material ideas are by analogy taken to encompass 'qualities of the mind' (p.82) (not, he notes, citing D'Alembert, that the reverse is not possible in a 'cultivated language' [p.111]). In a closely related vein this faculty also serves as his explanation for the universally metaphorical quality of early speech (p.112). On this latter point Dunbar essentially shares the views of those who explain the ubiquity of metaphor in early language by the poverty or scarcity of words.[23]

The second point will enable us to relate Dunbar's treatment of language to his wider concerns. Given the conjunction between 'ideas' and 'language' then, according to Dunbar, in that 'artless community', with its equality, freedom and independence, that is, in the second of the three eras identified above, there 'men were not only devoid of the inclination but unfurnished with the means of deceit' (p.70). It was only with the subsequent developments in social life that the 'powers of intellect begin to blossom' and though this was indeed an improvement yet it carried with it the consequence that 'feuds and animosities' were introduced into the world (p.32). The linguistic development that ran *pari passu* with this was that the indissoluble natural tie between sentiment and expression (p.72) was lost so that, along with artificial language, equivocation in due course entered into the scene (compare pp.397, 402). The wider import of this example is that it is indicative of the strategic use to which Dunbar puts his adaptation of Rousseau. He openly acknowledges that Rousseau's view that progress is corrupting is an exaggeration (p.154); nevertheless one of the lynch-pins of Dunbar's entire analysis is that the second of the three eras—a time of unrestricted fellow-feeling and the depiction of which owes much to Rousseau—acts as a normative benchmark for the later period of dependency.

But we have not yet completed our exposition of Dunbar's theory of language because he postulates yet another faculty:

> on a more exact survey, the mind discriminates its objects and breaks the system of analogy by attending to the minute differences of things. As therefore the analogical faculty enlarges the sense of words, the discriminating faculty augments them in number. It breaks speech into smaller divisions and bestows a copiousness on language by a more precise arrangement of the objects.(pp.96-7)

Since Dunbar had earlier observed that it was 'easier for the mind to perceive resemblance than to specify the minute differences of things' (p.89) the operation of this discriminating faculty can be presumed to be a later development. In a subsequent *Essay* Dunbar remarks that one of the advantages of a 'cultivated', in contrast to a 'rude', tongue is its 'copiousness of expression' (p.130)—though in keeping with his moderate Rousseauism the rude tongue is acknowledged to enjoy an advantage when it comes to vivacity.[24] Yet there is here also a clear indication of Dunbar's distance from Rousseau. Rousseau thought that the more primitive a language then the more copious (*étendu*) its dictionary because it takes a long time before similarities rather than differences are perceived.[25]

To Dunbar, therefore, language develops through four stages—from natural cries to imitation to the operation of the analogical faculty and finally to the exertions of the discriminating faculty. He is aware that this four-fold process is an over-simplification. He allows that the analogical faculty is 'allied' to the imitative and that it is 'often undistinguished in its operations' (p.79) and, towards the end of the Second Essay, he admits that in the development of language through its various stages 'the mind has no doubt exerted collectively at all times various powers' (p.99).

These admissions by Dunbar that his scheme is an over-simplification defuse in some measure the obvious criticism that this use of 'faculty psychology' misleadingly atomises human consciousness by implying that it has separate parts of which only some are in operation at any one time.[26] However, Dunbar seems less exempt from other standard objections. His faculties would appear to be little better than occult agencies. The mind, for example, perceives an analogy; 'something', it is posited, must be responsible for this perception. The answer is a specific mental faculty since of what else could the perceived analogy be an effect? A further weakness of faculty psychology, which this assumption of specific agencies engenders, and of which Dunbar provides a clear example, is the tendency to multiply the number of faculties in order to accommodate any new process believed to exist.

Despite its inherent weaknesses, what this recourse to the terminology of faculties indicates is Dunbar's basic commitment to the proposition that the development of language is integral to mental development. We can, in conclusion, pursue a little further this idea of mental development and its bearing on the 'language-question'.

Dunbar himself identifies three schools of thought on the origin of language: 'Is language, it may be asked, derived to us at first from the happy invention of a few, or to be regarded as an original accomplishment and investiture of nature or to be attributed to some succeeding effort of the human mind?' (p.63). With regard to the first of these arguments Dunbar adopted the anti-individualism characteristic of the Scottish Enlightenment and we have seen that the whole thrust behind the idea of the analogical faculty was to explain the development of language without recourse to some imagined 'great projectors in an early age, balancing a regular plan for the conveyance of sentiment and the establishment of general intercourse' (p.93). In contrast it seems undeniable that Dunbar considers language to be 'a succeeding effort of the human mind'. He is explicit that his account was designed to show 'the *gradations* of a simple institution referring to those faculties of the mind which appear principally concerned in conducting its *successive* improvements' (p.99: my emphasis).

There is, however, more to Dunbar's developmental theory than the above. This additional element derives from the Aristotelian nature of his theory—so that language, for Dunbar, is really the actualisation of the potential possessed by each individual. It follows from this that Dunbar in addition to regarding language as a 'succeeding effort' (the third of his schools) could also be said to believe it to be an 'original investiture' (the second of his schools). Indeed at the end of the Second Essay, he pronounces that language has developed as a 'superstructure' constructed 'on the foundation of nature' (p.99). The natural bases of language comprise natural cries and imitation (both common to Man and beast), and the operation of the analogical and discriminating faculties (where 'the boundary of art and nature' is drawn and which are therefore the prerogative of Man alone) represent the super-structure of language.

To believe that language is natural to Man is to acknowledge, with very few exceptions in the eighteenth century, that Man has been given language, like everything else from instincts to a sense of humour, by his Designer. In the case of language, on Dunbar's account, Man has not been given it from 'without' but internally by possessing it *in potentia*. Such a theory in fact runs contrary in its explanatory thrust to a theological explanation of the origin of language—a view still to be found in some of his contemporaries[27]—which invoked the 'super-natural' agency of Divine inspiration. Dunbar, it may be said, believes language is an 'original investiture' but not an 'original accomplishment'.

In fine, Dunbar's theory represents a characteristically Enlightenment attempt at explaining the development of language in terms of the concurrent evolution of Man's mind—language is a distinctively human characteristic and an explanation of its possession must be in human terms and com-mensurate with human abilities. The entire enterprise is admitted to be con-jectural but nevertheless is that which is 'most consonant to the probability of things, to the experience of early life, and to the genius and complexion of the ruder ages' (p.99).

Notes

1. All page references are to the Second Edition with Additions (1781) and are placed in parentheses in the text. For further information on Dunbar's life and career see my 'James Dunbar and the American War of Independence', *Aberdeen University Review*, 45 (1974), pp.255-56.

2. D. Stewart, 'An account of the life and writings of Adam Smith', in A. Smith, *Essays on Philosophical Subjects*, ed. W.P.D. Wightman, Glasgow Edition of Smith's Works (Indianapolis, Liberty Press, 1982), p.293.

3. This theory that societies passed successively through hunting, pastoral, agri-cultural to commercial stages was seminally developed by Adam Smith and has been the subject of extensive commentary. For a recent overview of this see A. Skinner, 'A Scottish contribution to Marxist sociology?', in *Classical and Marxian Political Economy*, eds I. Bradley and M Howard (London, Macmillan, 1982), pp.79-114.

4. For a discussion of its bearing on his account of human social life see my 'James Dunbar and ideas of sociality in eighteenth-century Scotland', *Il Pensiero Politico*, 6 (1973), pp.188-201.

5. See *Origin and Progress of Language* (cited hereafter as *OPL*), vol.1, book 1, chapter 14; book 2, chapters 8,9; *Antient Metaphysics*, vol.3, book 2, chapter 1 etc.

6. Dunbar's relation to Monboddo is interesting because of the Aristotelian elements in their philosophies. Dunbar holds that the orangs need an enlargement of ideas, but he also believes that the ideas of animals are fixed and they have not the potential to progress (p.68). Monboddo himself believes what 'distinguishes human nature from that of the brute is not the actual possession of higher faculties but the greater capacity of acquiring them' (Letter to Harris reprinted

in W. Knight, *Monboddo and some of his Contemporaries* [London, John Murray, 1900], p.73). The crucial difference between the two is that Dunbar excludes the orang from the genus Man, whereas for Monboddo 'the large monkeys or baboons appear to me to stand in the same relation to us, that the ass does to the horse' (Letter to Pringle in Knight, p.85). To Monboddo the orangs are related to Man because they use sticks, desire human females and so on but are not identical since they do not possess language, yet since language is not natural to Man then this absence cannot deny them the 'appellation of men' *OPL*, vol.1, p.176n. For discussion of the debates raised by the orang see several writings by R. Wokler, for example, 'The ape debates in Enlightenment anthropology', *Voltaire Studies*, 192 (1980), pp.1164-75.

7. For further discussion see my *Hume, Hegel and Human Nature* (The Hague, M. Nijhoff, 1982), chapter 1.

8. This heuristic device is used by writers as otherwise diverse as Vico, de Brosses, Priestley and Herder (for references see my 'Adam Smith's "Considerations" on language', in *Journal of the History of Ideas*, 35 (1974), p.136). It played a crucial role in Condillac's *Essai sur l'origine des connaissances humaines* (1746), part 2, section 1 which Aarsleff has argued is the key eighteenth-century text on the question of the origin of language, 'The tradition of Condillac' in *Studies in the History of Linguistics*, ed. H. Hymes (Bloomington, Indiana U.P., 1974), pp.93-156 (this is reprinted in H. Aarsleff, *From Locke to Saussure* [London, Athlone Press, 1982], pp.146-209).

9. See *inter alia* Turgot, 'Autres réflexions sur les langues', in *Oeuvres*, ed. G. Schelle (Paris, 1913), vol.1, p.351; Blackwell, *Enquiry into the Life and Writings of Homer* (London, 1735), p.37; Beauzée, articles 'Interjection' and 'Langue' in *Encyclopédie* (Neuchâtel, 1765), vols 8 and 9; Rousseau, *Discours de l'inégalité parmi les hommes* (1754) (Paris, Garnier, 1962), p.53; Mandeville, *Fable of the Bees* (1714 and later), ed. F. Kaye (Oxford, Clarendon Press, 1957), vol.2, pp.285 and following; Condillac, 'Essai', ed. C. Porset (Auvers-sur-Oise, Editions Galilée, 1973), pp.195 and following.

10. J. Priestley, *Lectures on the Theory of Language* (Warrington, W. Eyres 1762), p.65.

11. H. Blair, *Lectures on Rhetoric and Belles-Lettres* (1783) (London, Chas. Daly, 1838), p.67.

12. James Harris, *Hermes* (London, J. Nourse, P. Vaillant, 1751), p.290.

13. *OPL*, vol.2, p.181.

14. *OPL*, vol.1, p.191 where the term 'imitative faculty' itself is employed.

15. *Lectures*, p.65.

16. 'Essai', p.195.

17. 'Tradition of Condillac' in Hymes, pp.104-5.

18. See Berry, *JHI*, 1974, pp.135 and following for further discussion.

19. See *inter alia* Smith, 'Considerations', in *Lectures on Rhetoric and Belles-Lettres*, ed. J.C. Bryce, Glasgow Edition (Indianapolis, Liberty Press, 1985), p.216; Rousseau, *Discours*, p.54; Monboddo, *OPL*, vol.1, pp.360,395; Blair (who explicitly follows Monboddo), *Lectures*, p.89.

20. For instructive analysis of Smith's position see Stephen K. Land, 'Adam Smith's "Considerations concerning the First Formation of Languages"' in *Journal of the History of Ideas*, 38 (1977), pp.677-90; also the same author's 'Lord Monboddo and the theory of syntax in the late eighteenth century', *JHI*, 37 (1976), pp.423-40.

21. Turgot in his article 'Étymologie' in the *Encyclopédie* (vol.6, p.100), referred in

passing to 'les lois de l'analogie'; Smith, who explicitly said that he had received 'a good deal of entertainment' from the grammatical articles in the *Encyclopédie* (see Letter to Baird in J. Rae, *Life of Adam Smith* [New York, Kelley reprint, 1965], p.160), referred to the 'love of analogy', rather than any act of abstraction, as the source of the rules of grammar—'Considerations' in *Lectures*, p.211; finally, Condillac (whose work Smith possessed) mentions, in a discussion of 'le génie des langues', 'les règles de l'analogie', 'Essai', p.263. (In a later discussion Condillac made analogy the source of all methods of instruction and invention— 'Langue des Calculs', (1798).

22. See his *Essay on Genius* (London, 1774).
23. For a full discussion of this point see my 'Eighteenth-century approaches to the origins of metaphor', in *Neuphilologische Mitteilungen*, 74 (1973), pp.690-713.
24. Thomas Reid had pointed out the superior 'force and energy' of the savage tongue—*Inquiry into the Human Mind* (1764) in *Works*, ed. W. Hamilton (Edinburgh, 1846), p.118. The more general point that early speech had a distinctive tonal quality was widely made, and featured in debates concerning the origin and development of music as well as the relative priority of poetry or prose—see Berry, *Neuphil.Mitt.*, for further discussion.
25. *Discours*, p.54.
26. A thoroughgoing contemporary assault on faculty psychology was mounted by Herder within, significantly, his own prize-winning discussion of language— 'Abhändlung über den Ursprung der Sprache' (1772) in *Werke*, 33 vols, ed. B. Suphan (Berlin, 1891), vol.5, especially pp.29-30.
27. See, for example, W. Warburton, *Divine Legation of Moses Demonstrated*, 4th Edition, 5 vols (London, A. Millar, J.& R. Tonson, 1765), vol.3, p.106 (book 4, section 4); J. Beattie, *Dissertations Moral, Critical and Literary* (London, W. Strahan, T. Cadell, 1783), pp.304 and following; Beauzée, 'Langue'; H. Blair, *Lectures*, p.64. Blair is prompted to invoke a divine original by Rousseau's conundrum (though Blair does not identify his source) that society needs language yet language needs society (*Discours*, p.56). Blair is not alone in this: for comment see Aarsleff, 'Tradition of Condillac' in Hymes, pp.131 and following (on Süssmilch) and D. Droixhe, 'Langage et société dans la grammaire philosophique de Du Marsais à Michaelis', in *Études sur le XVIIIe siècle*, 3 (1976), pp.119-32.

26

James Beattie and the Languages of Scotland

David Hewitt
University of Aberdeen

An ardent nationalist might describe James Beattie, Professor of Moral Philosophy in Marischal College, Aberdeen, from 1760, as a linguistic quisling who assisted the colonisation of Scots by English. It would be a colourful way of representing the position of a man who did say that he was one of those who wished 'to see the English spirit and English manners prevail over the whole island',[1] but it is simplistic. The story of the displacement of Scots by English is very well-known, and little new information is likely to be discovered, but the pattern was not as straightforward as is sometimes suggested. Although Beattie was undoubtedly an angliciser, the recognition and use of Scottish regional dialects for poetic purposes owes not a little to him.

In the Introduction to *The Concise Scots Dictionary* A.J. Aitken restates succinctly the standard interpretation of the language situation in eighteenth-century Scotland:

> The progressive anglicization of writings in manuscript (records, diaries, manuscript histories, and others) proceeded through the seventeenth century and into the eighteenth, until finally virtually every trace of Scottishness had disappeared from Scottish writing. In print, partly or largely as a result of commercial considerations by publishers and printers, the demise of literary Older Scots is far earlier and more sudden. After 1610, except for a few legal texts and one or two comic or satiric *tours-de-force*, all Scots writings in prose, whether printed in Scotland or, as often, in London, are in what can only be called English with an occasional Scots locution only every dozen pages or so.[2]

With the wavering exception of the poetry of Allan Ramsay, the major Scottish achievements of the first half of the eighteenth century are in English—Thomson's *The Seasons*, Hume's *A Treatise of Human Nature*, and Smollett's *Roderick Random*. Thus Hume's well-known attempts to combat Scotticisms in his own works and in those of his friends are not a major innovation, although they are sometimes presented as such, but are merely the polishing of a historical process that had been proceeding with little opposition for nearly two centuries.

The history of the change in speech is somewhat different, and the changes themselves generated more controversy. A.J. Aitken argues that as early as the end of the seventeenth century 'the formal or, in the language of the period, "polite" speech of the social élite of Scotland was ... expected to approximate to the southern English dialect'.[3] The 'Journall of the Easy Club', established in 1712, supports A.J. Aitken's point for it explains that the gentlemen 'who Compose this Society' resolved to meet so that 'by a Mutual improvement in Conversation they may become more adapted for fellowship with the politer part of mankind'.[4] It seems that the 'improvement in Conversation' comprehended both the manner and the matter of the art. However, A.J. Aitken's position must be qualified; the ideal did not correspond with the actuality. No doubt there was a considerable absorption of English lexis and grammatical forms, and a significant modification in pronunciation as a consequence of the increase in the political, business, social and intellectual traffic with England in the early eighteenth century, but until the mid century nearly everyone (excepting only those few educated in England or who became naturalised Englishmen) continued to speak Scots. The point can be humorously illustrated by David Hume who is said to have changed the spelling of his surname from 'Home' because 'thae glaekit English bodies ... could not call him aright'.[5]

Whereas in the earlier part of the century the modifications in the speech of the educated in Scotland were by and large the result of an increasing awareness of English, in the middle period, say 1745-1765, the anglicisation of speech was deliberately promoted. The evidence that is usually cited is in the 'Regulations of the Select Society for promoting the Reading and Speaking of the English Language in Scotland' which were promulgated in 1761 and published in *The Scots Magazine*[6] after Thomas Sheridan had lectured in Edinburgh on 'Elocution' and 'The English Tongue' earlier in the same year. A new Society for Promoting the Reading and Speaking of the English Language in Scotland was formed and it intended to employ teachers of English from England—and to examine the pupils and inspect the teachers regularly. Although the intention never became an actuality, there is no doubt that in the period the pronunciation of the educated changed markedly, and English lexis and idioms displaced Scots. John Ramsay of Ochtertyre, who provides more information about how people talked than any other commentator of the period, describes the new situation:

> Besides the colloquial Scotch spoken in good company, there was likewise the oratorical, which was used by judges, lawyers and clergymen, in their several departments. In this, perhaps, there was even greater variety than in the other; but it may be concluded, that such as wished to excel in their public appearances, strove to bring their speeches or sermons some degrees nearer pure English than their ordinary talk.[7]

Some accounts of the language seem to suggest that in twenty years the upper classes all came to talk English. But of course there was variety; Ramsay criticises Lord Auchinleck, Boswell's father, for doing nothing to improve his speech: 'As he was one of the very few that never endeavoured to form an oratorical language half-way between familiar discourse and their style of writing, so he seems to have thought that dialect and pronunciation mattered very little.'[8] It is also possible to exaggerate the Englishness of the new speech. Ramsay does not say that what Lord Kames uttered when on the bench was English; it was rather something that 'approached to English'.[9] He also comments that 'after all their exertions, strong traces of a provincial dialect would be conspicuous, even in those who had the greatest flexibility of speech and tones'.[10] Thirty years on, Jeffrey talked in a made-up dialect of English compounded with Scots, which was most amusingly described by Thomas Carlyle in his *Reminiscences*:

> His accent was indeed singular, but it was by no means Scotch: at his first going to Oxford (where he did not stay long), he had peremptorily crushed down his Scotch (which he privately had in store, in excellent condition, to the very end of his life, producible with highly ludicrous effect on occasion), and adopted instead a strange swift, sharp-sounding, fitful modulation ... Old Braxie (MacQueen, 'Lord *Braxfield*', a sad old cynic, on whom Jeffrey used to set me laughing often enough) was commonly reported to have said, ... 'The laddie has tint his Scotch, and found nae English!'[11]

It would not have been possible to anglicise thoroughly, but there is evidence that some wanted to modify speech for the sake of being understood, but still wished to indicate their Scottishness in their accent; Boswell is one:

> though it was too late in life for a Caledonian to acquire the genuine English cadence, yet so successful were Mr. Wedderburne's instructors, and his own unabating endeavours, that he got rid of the coarse part of his Scotch accent, retaining only so much of the 'native wood-note wild,' as to mark his country; which, if any Scotchman should affect to forget, I should heartily despise him.[12]

There was some feeling that it was not decorous to 'go overboard' in the pursuit of an English accent, nor to retain a too exaggeratedly Scottish pronunciation. Ramsay says that 'nothing was more possible than for preachers and other public speakers to be *over* or *under* dressed in their pronunciation and accenting'. And he explains that 'the former would endeavour to sound the vowels in the English way, and to put the emphasis on the proper words'.[13] Burns illustrates the point with his ministers in 'The Holy Fair'; of one Burns says:

> Hear how he clears the points o' Faith,
> Wi rattlin an' thumpin!
> Now meekly calm, now wild in wrath,
> He's stampan, an' he's jumpan!

And of another he says:

> What signifies his barren shine,
> Of *moral pow'rs* an' *reason*;
> His English style, an' gesture fine,
> Are a' clean out o' season.[14]

It seems from this evidence that the acceptable norm in formal speech was not southern English but what we would now call Scots English.

Initially Scotsmen found difficulty in speaking English naturally; in the entry for 1748 in his *Anecdotes and Characters of the Times*, for instance, Alexander Carlyle says that it is a gross mistake to think that the Scots are humourless but adds: 'Since we began to affect speaking a foreign language, which the English dialect is to us, humour, it must be confessed, is less apparent in conversation.'[15] But once Scots English became naturalised, it was not a question of possessing two languages, that could be alternated by the operation of fixed-ratio gears, but rather of having a command of both Scots and English and applying them in varying ratios as subject and situation demanded.

The speaking style of the writing classes became the matter of their art. It is obvious that in the poetry of Burns there is at times a confusion between Scots and English that is a consequence of Burns's use of English orthography to render Scots[16] but there is also a deliberate variation. In 'Tam o'Shanter' the narrator, who usually speaks in a familiar manner, seems to speak in English when he tells us that pleasures are like poppies spread; but of course Burns's aim is not to suggest the southern English dialect but to indicate the moralising voice of the minister or the schoolmaster, now conventionally rendered by English. The same argument can be used of the fiction of Scott or Hogg or Galt. The sharp division between the Scots of dialogue and the English of narration is apparent, not real; it is a linguistic way of representing social variety, but is not a phonetic transcription of speech.

The development of a new literary language with a greatly increased social range—one that did not previously exist in either English or Scottish literature—is the most important literary consequence of the advent of English. A second effect, which was probably a response to the *deliberate* promotion of English, and the description of Scots as improper, uncouth, and barbarous in the pages of *The Scots Magazine*, the principal organ of opinion in Scotland, was to provoke poets such as Alexander Ross and Robert Fergusson into using Scots as a poetic medium. I cannot prove that Alexander Ross was irritated by the insistence on English, but the advice given to him by his muse, Scota, in the introduction to his pastoral epic *Helenore* (1768) seems a clear reply to the kinds of argument used to promote English:

> Speak my ain leed, 'tis gueed auld Scots I mean;
> Your Southren gnaps I count not worth a preen.
> We've words a fouth, that we can ca' our ain,
> Tho' frae them now my childer sair refrain,
> An' are to my gueed auld proverb confeerin—
> Neither gueed fish nor flesh, nor yet sa't herrin.[17]

Ross was justified in being confident about the poetic resources of Scots. Although English seemed the victorious literary medium in mid century, Thomas Ruddiman's edition of Douglas's translation of the *Aeneid* (1710) which included the first glossary of Scots words, William Hamilton of Gilbertfield's version of Hary's *Wallace* (1722), and Allan Ramsay's *The Ever Green* (1724) maintained, or perhaps even created, a sense of the previous greatness of Scottish literature. Collections of Scottish songs, music, and proverbs were published, and suggest both a desire to assert Scottishness and a curiosity about the past. Furthermore, the literati, in spite of their promotion of English, themselves created an intellectual environment more favourable to the vernacular. Their ideas on the origins of language and literature were illustrated by works such as Macpherson's *Ossian* (1760, 1761, 1763), Percy's *Reliques* (1765) and Herd's *Ancient and Modern Scottish Songs, Heroic Ballads, &c.* (1769); both the thinking and the models must have helped the writers of imaginative literature in the vernacular, and at the same time modified the taste and sensibility of the readership. But it was the promotion of the speaking of English that was the sand in the oyster, that provoked poets like Ross and Fergusson, perhaps not into using Scots as the language of poetry, but being deliberate in their use of it.[18]

A third development arising from the promotion of English may be associated particularly with James Beattie. His book *Scoticisms*, first issued in 1779 and republished in 1787, is usually cited as one of the best examples of the anglicising tendencies of the Scottish professoriate, but why, when the strongest anglicising thrust was in the fifties and sixties, should Beattie have published his *Scoticisms* so late? His purpose, he says in the Advertisement to the 1787 edition, is 'nothing more, than to put young writers and speakers on their guard against some of those Scotch idioms, which, in this country, are liable to be mistaken for English'.[19] It might be assumed that Aberdeen was a more conservative place than Edinburgh, and therefore slower in taking up fashionable activities such as expurgating Scotticisms, but the most striking feature of the Advertisement is Beattie's concern for the 'purity of the language'. He observes that 'of late, there has been a strange propensity, in too many of our people, to debase the purity of the language, by a mixture of foreign and provincial idioms, and cant phrases'.[20] He explains:

> Our tongue was brought to perfection in the days of Addison and Swift ... Every unauthorised word and idiom, which has of late been, without necessity, introduced into it, tends to its debasement.

In other documents of the same period Beattie makes it clear that he is objecting specifically to the effect of Scots on English; in a letter of 26 November 1785 to his friend Robert Arbuthnot he doubts the propriety of republishing *Scoticisms*, because:

> Our language (I mean the English) is degenerating very fast; and many phrases, which I know to be Scottish idioms, have got into it of late years: so that many

of my strictures are liable to be opposed by authorities which the world accounts unexceptionable.[21]

His concern is unusual; he is not worried about how Scotsmen could approximate their speech to 'the southern English dialect', but how English could resist being contaminated by Scots. In a letter to Sylvester Douglas in 1778, the year before the first edition of *Scoticisms*, Beattie identifies the 'authorities which the world accounts unexceptionable':

> I am convinced the greater part of Scottish authors hurt their style by admiring and imitating one another. At Edinburgh it is currently said by your critical people, that Hume, Robertson, &c. write English better than the English themselves; than which, in my judgment, there cannot be a greater absurdity.[22]

It seems clear that *Scoticisms* had a double purpose, to promote the use of proper English and to attack what might be called the Edinburgh standard of English; in fact the implicit attack is on the whole Edinburgh language settlement for in 1778 he also told John Pinkerton that 'Those who now write Scotch, use an affected, mixed, barbarous dialect, which is neither Scotch nor English, but a strange jumble of both'.[23]

Beattie believed that it was necessary for Scots to study the best English authors to improve their command of the written language. In 1774 he tells one of his former students to attend 'to the phraseology of the best English writers, with a view to correct and improve your English style'.[24] He admits to Sir William Forbes that he himself is not proof against 'provincial improprieties', and adds: 'The longer I study English, the more I am satisfied that Addison's prose is the best model: and if I were to give advice to a young man on the subject of English style, I would desire him to read that author day and night.'[25] He is as thorough in his attitude to spoken English. In the *The Theory of Language* (1783) he observes that 'To speak with the English, or with the Scotch, accent, is no more praiseworthy, or blameable, than to be born in England or Scotland'. He then adds:

> Of accent, as well as of spelling, syntax, and idiom, there is a standard in every polite nation. And, in all these particulars, the example of approved authors, and the practice of those, who, by their rank, education, and way of life, have had the best opportunities to know men and manners, and domestick and foreign literature, ought undoubtedly to give the law. Now it is in the metropolis of a kingdom, and in the most famous schools of learning, where the greatest resort may be expected of persons adorned with all useful and elegant accomplishments. The language, therefore, of the most learned and polite persons in London, and the neighbouring Universities of Oxford and Cambridge, ought to be accounted the standard of the English tongue, especially in accent and pronunciation: syntax, spelling, and idiom, having been ascertained by the practice of good authors, and the consent of former ages.[26]

Beattie clearly rejects the kind of Scots English compromise that emerged in

Edinburgh and which was specifically approved of by such as Boswell and Ramsay of Ochtertyre.

In his comments on Scottish dialect as well, Beattie seems to be resistant to Edinburgh's language settlement. In 1768 he sent Ross's *The Fortunate Shepherdess* (renamed *Helenore* in its second edition) to Dr Blacklock, saying in the accompanying letter that the dialect is 'licentious'; he immediately explains: '(I mean it is so different from that of the south country, which is acknowledged the standard of broad Scotch), that I am afraid that you will be at a loss to understand it in many places.'[27] On the other hand the poem he published to promote *Helenore* shows none of this defensiveness, and is a forthright claim for the value of a regional dialect against the cultural centrism of Edinburgh:

> The Southland chiels indeed hae mettle,
> And brawley at a sang can ettle,
> Yet we right couthily might settle
>   O' this side Forth.
> The devil pay them with a pettle
>   That slight the North.

> Our countra leed is far frae barren,
> It's even right pithy and aulfarren,
> Oursells are neiper-like, I warran,
>   For sense and smergh;
> In kittle times when faes are yarring,
>   We're no thought ergh.[28]

There follow several stanzas in which Beattie talks disparagingly of 'newfangle sparks' and 'critics' and which seem to be directed against the Edinburgh literary establishment, not against London; he is one of the 'Norlans' who are on 'this side Forth'.

A decade later, in the letter to Sylvester Douglas that has already been mentioned, he lists some of the dialects of Scotland, but proposes none as a standard:

> The Scottish dialect is different in almost every province. The common people of Aberdeen speak a language, that would scarce be understood in Fife; and how much the Buchan dialect differs from that of Lothian, may be seen by comparing Ramsay's 'Gentle Shepherd' with 'Ajax's speech to the Grecian Knabbs,' which you will no doubt remember to have seen in your youth. I have attended so much to this matter, that I think I could know by his speech, a native of Banffshire, Buchan, Aberdeen, Dee-side, Mearns, Angus, Lothian, and Fife, as well as of Ross-shire, and Inverness.[29]

Beattie's linguistic arguments, although flavoured by the prejudices of his age, make sense, whether or not one agrees with them. However, it was not through observation and thought alone that he came to hold these views, but through a complex sense of political and social opposition to Edinburgh and what it represented. In his *Essay on Truth* (1770) he attacked Hume and scepticism and found that he was attacking the centre of literary authority in Scotland. The language used by Ramsay of Ochtertyre to describe the disagreement suggests that 'bystanders' felt that Hume and his friends resented the presumption of Beattie's attack as much as his bad philosophy: 'Yet it was, we all remember, exceedingly ill received by the junto at Edinburgh that decided authoritatively upon matters of taste and philosophy.'[30] On the other hand, in 1771, the year after the publication of the *Essay on Truth*, Beattie visited London, and was much lauded and feted because he had vindicated, so they felt, the truth of religion against Edinburgh scepticism. To judge from the documents published in William Forbes's *An Account of the Life and Writings of James Beattie*, the arguments in favour of London English date from after this time; it looks almost as though he were repaying London for what it had done for him. Of course it would require a more thorough analysis of the Beattie papers in Aberdeen University Library to substantiate properly the suggestions made in this paragraph, but the context that has been suggested for his linguistic arguments is important because a writer's choice of language is an indication of his political and social identity.

James Beattie's arguments and affiliations offer a view of the possibilities for Scottish literature different from that prevalent in the south of Scotland. He wants English as written by the best writers, and spoken by the best educated in London, Oxford and Cambridge, to be the one language of Britain, but he promotes a local dialect to express a regional consciousness. He rejects the Edinburgh compromise that Edinburgh, consciously or unconsciously, represented as the national language, and in so doing provides an intellectual basis for Scottish literary regionalism.

The standard interpretation of the literary achievement of Scotland in the eighteenth century is that it produced intellectual masterpieces, but that its imaginative literature was flawed. David Daiches believes that the state of the language was the cause. He observes that writers wrote in English but continued to speak in Scots. 'In these circumstances', he argues, 'there steadily ceased to be a Scots literary language, rooted in the spoken language yet continuously reaching out beyond it, capable of expressing the whole thinking and feeling man.'[31] I believe that Professor Daiches is mistaken; the linguistic and the cultural conflicts were, on the whole, productive, anglicisation facilitating the internationalism of Hume, Smith, and Robertson, reaction facilitating a dialectal poetry, and the two together creating at the end of the century the rhetorical language that Burns and Scott used as their medium. On the other hand the literary dominance of Edinburgh provoked James Beattie into publishing and defending Ross, thus establishing the dialect of the North East as a literary medium in its own right. His example inspired Burns to attempt a regional poetry:

> I am highly flattered by the news you tell me of Coila. I may say to the fair painter who does me so much honour, as Dr. Beattie says to Ross the poet, of his muse Scota, from which, by the by, I took the idea of Coila: ('Tis a poem of Beattie's in the Scottish dialect, which perhaps you have never seen.)

'Ye shak your head, but o' my fegs,
Ye've set auld Scota on her legs:
Lang had she lien wi buffe and flegs,
Bombaz'd and dizzie,
Her fiddle wanted strings and pegs,
Waes me, poor hizzie!'[32]

Notes

1. William Forbes, *An Account of the Life and Writings of James Beattie*, 2 vols (Edinburgh, Constable, 1806),vol.I,p.379.
2. *The Concise Scots Dictionary*, ed. Mairi Robinson (Aberdeen, AUP, 1985), pp.x-xi.
3. *Ibid.*, p.xi.
4. *The Works of Allan Ramsay*, eds Alexander M. Kinghorn and Alexander Law, 6 vols (Edinburgh, Scottish Text Society, 1944-74), vol.V, p.5.
5. Quoted in Ernest Mossner, *The Life of David Hume*, 2nd edition (Oxford, Clarendon Press, 1970), p.90.
6. *The Scots Magazine*, 23 (1761), pp.440-41.
7. John Ramsay of Ochtertyre, *Scotland and Scotsmen in the Eighteenth Century. From the MSS. of John Ramsay, Esq. of Ochtertyre*, ed. Alexander Allardyce, 2 vols (Edinburgh and London, W.Blackwood & Sons, 1888), vol.II, p.544.
8. *Ibid.*, vol.I, pp.168-69.
9. *Ibid.*, vol.I, p.212.
10. *Ibid.*, vol.II, p.545.
11. Thomas Carlyle, *Reminiscences*, ed. Charles Eliot Norton, introduction by Ian Campbell (London, Dent, 1972), pp.333-34.
12. *Boswell's Life of Johnson*, eds George Birkbeck Hill and L.F. Powell, 6 vols (Oxford, Clarendon Press, 1934-50), vol.I, pp.386-87.
13. John Ramsay, *Scotland and Scotsmen*, vol.II, pp.544-45.
14. *The Poems and Songs of Robert Burns*, ed. James Kinsley, 3 vols (Oxford, Clarendon Press, 1968), vol.I, pp.132-33, no. 70, lines 109-112, 127-130.
15. Alexander Carlyle, *Anecdotes and Characters of the Times*, ed. James Kinsley (London, OUP, 1973), p.114.
16. See, for instance, David Hewitt, 'Burns and the argument for standardisation', *Text*, I (1981), pp.217-29.
17. *The Scottish Works of Alexander Ross*, ed. Margaret Wattie (Edinburgh, Scottish Text Society 1938); *Helenore*, lines 56-61.
18. See David Hewitt, 'Scoticisms and Cultural Conflict', paper presented to the conference on the Literature of Region and Nation, Aberdeen, 21 August 1986. To be published.
19. James Beattie, *Scoticisms* (Edinburgh, W.Creech, 1787), p.2.
20. *Ibid.*, pp. 3-5.
21. William Forbes, *James Beattie*, vol.II, p.180.
22. *Ibid.*, vol.II, pp.17-18.
23. *The Literary Correspondence of John Pinkerton, Esq.*, 2 vols (London, H.Colburn etc., 1830), vol.I, p.7.
24. William Forbes, *James Beattie*, vol.I, p.376.
25. *Ibid.*, vol.II, p.5.
26. James Beattie, *The Theory of Language* (London, A.Strachan, 1788), pp.91-92.

27. William Forbes, *James Beattie*, vol.II, p.118.
28. Quoted from *The Oxford Book of Scottish Verse*, eds John MacQueen and Tom Scott (Oxford, Clarendon Press, 1966), p.340.
29. William Forbes, *James Beattie*, vol.I, pp.18-19.
30. John Ramsay, *Scotland and Scotsmen*, vol.I, p.508.
31. David Daiches, *The Paradox of Scottish Culture* (London, OUP, 1964), p.20.
32. *The Letters of Robert Burns*, eds J. De Lancey Ferguson and G. Ross Roy, 2nd edition, 2 vols (Oxford, Clarendon Press, 1985), vol.I, p.256, no. 219. The quotation from Beattie is as quoted by Burns.

27

Language and Genre in Allan Ramsay's 1721 Poems

J. Derrick McClure

University of Aberdeen

In one respect, if in one only, Allan Ramsay is the MacDiarmid of the eighteenth century: he provided a focus for the circumambient revival of interest in Scottish letters, and by his prolific output and strongly emphasised individual personality he exerted a fundamental influence on their subsequent course. In particular, the use which he made of the Scots tongue played a major part in determining not only the use of it made by his successors but also the attitudes to the language and its possible range of functions which their work overtly or implicitly reflects. Ramsay has been seen as permanently associating Scots with comic and satiric poetry, leaving the field of serious literature to be largely monopolised by English. Though this is obviously far too general and simplistic a statement to be of much critical value, it can to some extent be substantiated by facts: it *is* the case that the serious poems in Ramsay's first collection are less Scots in their language than the comic ones; and this seems to belie his vigorous defence of the Scots tongue, in the preface to this volume and elsewhere in his writings. However, a closer look at the language and style of the poems, and at Ramsay's reasons (when these can be ascertained) for the association of language with tone in particular instances, will go a long way towards exonerating him from any charges of incompetence or hypocrisy. A factor which will be found to be highly relevant is his choice of metrical form.

Since it is clear that a simple binary opposition between Scots and English is inadequate for discussion of Ramsay's linguistic patterns, I will adopt a rough-and-ready quadripartite classification of the language of his poems as follows:

English	— containing no marked Scots features at all
Anglicised Scots	— containing rhymes which require a Scots pronunciation—English spellings, per-

	haps, notwithstanding—but no Scots features of grammar or vocabulary
Thin Scots	— containing some, even if only a few, Scots features of grammar as well as phonology and an occasional Scots word
Full Scots	— making frequent, if not necessarily consistent, use of Scots features on all three levels

This schema at once requires some qualifications or reservations. First, it is a categorisation of the language of written texts. Were the poems read aloud in the pronunciation intended by the author, even those classed as 'English' would of course be audibly Scottish. At the very least they would be pronounced with a Scottish accent; and since Ramsay at times used the spelling of an English word to represent its Scots phonological cognate—a practice current among Scottish writers since the seventeenth or even, arguably, the late sixteenth century—it may in some cases be impossible to be certain that the sound in Ramsay's mind was *not* that of a Scots word. Secondly, the fact that these criteria can be mechanically applied, so that the text of a given poem is by the stated definition unequivocally English, Anglicised Scots, Thin Scots or Full Scots, is not offered as evidence that Ramsay himself thought in terms of such a series of categories. He was naturally aware of Scots and English as distinct systems, and (as his preface makes clear at several points) realised that though to some extent mutually opposed, they were not mutually exclusive. But he was never a systematic writer nor one with a clearly-defined theoretical approach to the question of language, and it is quite probable that, particularly in the case of the shorter poems, the fact that one or another fits the criteria for, say, Anglicised Scots rather than Thin Scots may be due as much to accident as to design.

Allan Ramsay's first volume of poetry, published in 1721, contains an index in which the poems are classed under seven headings: serious, comick, satyrick, pastoral, lyrick, epistolary and epigrammatical. The pastoral section contains three poems: *Richy and Sandy*, *Patie and Roger* and *Keitha*. All three are in dialogue form, in heroic couplets, and in Full Scots, though *Patie and Roger* has a dedicatory epistle in the Habbie stanza. This section, however, is the only one which approaches linguistic and stylistic homogeneity; and it is by far the smallest. All the other sections contain poems in a variety of metrical and stanzaic forms—in the case of the 'lyrick' group (the largest) a truly remarkable variety—and in either three or all four of the linguistic categories. Of the six poems in the 'satyrick' class (the next smallest), for example, *The Scriblers Lash'd* and *The Rise and Fall of Stocks* are in octosyllabic couplets, *Wealth or the Woody* and *A Prologue* in heroic couplets, *Lucky Spence's Last Advice* in Habbie stanzas, and *The Satyr's Project* in an eight-line stanza of anapaestic trimeter lines rhyming ABABCDCD. *Lucky Spence* is in Full Scots, *Wealth or the Woody*, *The Rise and Fall of Stocks* and *A Prologue* are in Thin Scots, *The Scriblers Lash'd* is in Anglicised Scots (a few rhymes such as *crew-now, hate them—treat them, crowd-multitude, fashions-nations, nature-creature, mount-affront* are its only visible Scots features), and *The Satyr's Project* is in English. The larger groups show still greater diversity. The 'comick' section contains four poems in Habbie stanzas, three in octosyllabic couplets, one in heroic couplets, and Ramsay's additional cantos of *Christis Kirk on the Green*, which maintain the distinctive stanza of the original poem as Ramsay found it in Watson's *Choice Collection*. Of these, five are in Full Scots, three in Thin Scots, one in Anglicised Scots, and none in English. The 'epistolary' group—omitting from consideration Josiah Burchet's epistle to Ramsay and the six poems in Ramsay's exchange with William Hamilton of Gilbertfield—contains five poems in heroic couplets (two in Full Scots, three in English), two in octosyllabic couplets (both in Thin Scots), two in Habbie stanzas (both in Full Scots), two in ballad stanzas (both in English), and one—the additional Epistle to Lieutenant Hamilton—in what is printed as a ten-line stanza but reads like an eight-line one with internal rhymes in the fifth and seventh (in Full Scots).

Clearly, if the poems in this volume are categorised by genre (at least accepting Ramsay's own categorisation), by metrical form, and by language, there is no clear correspondence between the categories. There are, however, a few general tendencies which may be observed. First, and least surprising, is the fact that poems in the Habbie stanza are invariably in Full Scots. This group includes, from the 'comick' section, the *Elegies* on Maggy Johnston, John Cowper, Lucky Wood and Patie Birnie; from the 'satyrick', *Lucky Spence's Last Advice*; and from the 'epistolary', *To R.H.B.* and the correspondence with Hamilton of Gilbertfield: at least four poems from this set are generally considered to be among Ramsay's best and most characteristic work.

The firm association of the Habbie stanza with Full Scots seems, in retrospect, so predictable as to be uninteresting; but it is not an *a priori* necessity, and would hardly have seemed self-evidently appropriate in 1721. After all, the stanza had originated in Provence, had been used in France and England before making its way to Scotland, and was later to be employed by Burns's friend James Lapraik for an ironic comment, in almost unmixed English, on the fall of the Ayr Bank in 1773, and by Wordsworth for two very worthy poetic tributes to Burns. Ramsay himself in his 1728 volume addressed a *Scots Ode* in Habbie stanzas to the members of the Society of British Antiquaries, which despite its title is in Anglicised Scots.

Ramsay's immediate precedents were the four poems in the stanza in Watson's *Choice Collection*: Robert Sempill's *The Life and Death of the Piper of Kilbarchan* (*Habbie Simpson*), William Hamilton's *The Last Dying Words of Bonny Heck*, and the anonymous *Epitaph on Sanny Briggs* (which is not attributed to Sempill by Watson, nor at all until James Paterson's 1849 edition of *The Poems of the Sempills of Beltrees*) and *William Lithgow, Writer in Edinburgh, His Epitaph*. This quartet was certainly enough to establish an association of the stanza with mock elegies and 'last dying words'; but since only *Habbie Simpson* (on balance) and *Sanny Briggs* (incontestably) are in Full Scots, they hardly make Ramsay's choice of this register inevitable.

(*Bonny Heck* is at best in Thin Scots: the concentration of Scots words increases somewhat towards the end, but the first six stanzas contain not a single word—'bonny' in an eighteenth-century poem does not qualify—which is Scots except in its phonology: and the Scots of *William Lithgow*, which is merely an enfeebled and vulgarised imitation of *Habbie Simpson*, is even thinner.) Probably, in fact, Ramsay in *John Cowper*, *Lucky Wood*, *Lucky Spence* and *Patie Birnie* is simply following a precedent set by himself. *Maggy Johnston* first appeared in 1712 and was evidently very popular: it was copied several times, in manuscript and print, before the publication of the 1712 volume. The other four followed at intervals, the next three appearing in print in 1718 and *Patie Birnie* in 1720. It seems likely that Ramsay was simply endeavouring to recapture the success, by repeating the formula, of *Maggy Johnston*: a comic mock-elegy, in Habbie stanzas, in Full Scots. The combination of this particular mood, linguistic register and stanza form in Ramsay's poems is thus self-perpetuating: the more so, perhaps, as his skill in handling the stanza improved dramatically between *Maggy Johnston* and *John Cowper*.

It is perhaps worth a moment's notice that despite the precedence universally accorded to *Habbie Simpson* in the long line of poems using that celebrated stanza form, Ramsay's elegies, and especially the pace-setter *Maggy Johnston*, are much closer in tone and register to *Sanny Briggs*. *Sanny* is grossly inferior in verbal technique to *Habbie*, so much so that the present writer finds the attribution of both poems to the same author very dubious: its vacuous lines ('It very muckle did me please'or 'Baith to the Field and frae the Field'), its repeated syntactic distortions ('To Board me speed' or 'well me Happ'), the feeble repetition of the lines 'Alake the day! Though kind to me / Yet now he's dead' in two successive stanzas, and the unheralded and bathetic suggestion of a change of mood in the penultimate stanza ('Shou'd I like a Bell'd Wadder bleat, / Since Sanny's dead?'), suggest a far less skilled hand than that of Robert Sempill. But whereas the humour of *Habbie* is gentle, restrained, and suggestive of a real regret behind the jesting, *Sanny* is a piece of boisterous slapstick, opening with an extravagantly exaggerated expression of grief, exploiting the comic possibilities of the topics of food and drink, and abounding in loud noises and violent action. In all these features, *Maggy Johnston* clearly resembles it and not its predecessor. Both poems contain strings of words:

> And glowren fow both reel and rumble
> > And clour their head.
> Now they may gape, and girn, and grumble,
> > Since Sanny's dead.
> > > (*Sanny Briggs*, ll.9-12)
> Fou closs we us'd to drink and rant
> Until we did baith glower and gant,
> > And pish and spew, and yesk and mant...
> > > (*Maggy Johnston*, ll.31-3)

and 'It made me Yelp, and Yeul and Yell,/ And Skirl and Skreed' seems to be echoed in Ramsay's 'Let a' thy Gossies yelp and yell'. Despite Ramsay's choice of 'Standart Habby' as the title for the verse form, and despite also his tribute to *Bonny Heck* in his answer to Hamilton's first Epistle—'Then Emulation did me pierce'—it was evidently neither of these that determined precisely the use he was to make of the stanza.

Ramsay classes *Lucky Spence* as 'satyrick', in contradistinction to the other four which are 'comick'; but it is in fact very much one of a set with them, the main difference being that its eponymous protagonist is not dead and is the persona of the poem. His remaining poems in the Habbie stanza are 'epistolary'. His choice of it for the exchange with Hamilton needs no further explanation than the fact that it was in this form that Hamilton initiated the correspondence; and if reasons have to be sought for the density of the Scots—more marked than Hamilton's, especially in the latter's first Epistle— they may well be found in the other poet's complimentary references to Ramsay's 'dictionary of ancient words' in the first Epistle and 'bonny auld words' in the second, and in the fact that Ramsay in his first Answer is overtly taking a tone of assertive cultural nationalism (though spoiling the effect somewhat with what must surely be the worst-constructed Habbie stanza in literature, his stanza 9). This set too forms a self-perpetuating sequence, though more limited. *To R.H.B.* (i.e. Right Honourable Baron, his mode of address to Sir John Clark) is a rendering of a Horatian ode, and the only Habbie poem in the volume which does not belong to either set.

No poems in Habbie stanzas appear in the 'serious' group. Here, the dominant metrical form is the heroic couplet: the section contains fourteen poems of which ten are in this metre. None of these is in Full Scots, and only one in Thin Scots: this is *The Prospect of Plenty*, a substantial poem of 245 lines and, I would argue, the best 'serious' piece in the collection. Here Ramsay, in an interesting and not unsuccessful attempt to establish a Scots Augustan register, has adopted several familiar devices from contemporary English poetry: rhetorical apostrophes :

> Delytfou' Labour, where the Industrious gains
> Profit surmounting ten times a' his Pains. (ll.41-2)

> Malicious Envy! Root of a' Debates,
> The plague of Government and Bane of States. (ll.145-6)

classical allusions: Thetis, Amphitrite, Thalia, Hymen, Nereus,

> ... dire Pharsalia's plain,
> Where doughty Romans were by Romans slain, (ll.102-3)

phrases on the model of 'finny Thrang' and 'scaly Nations': and combined them with a language which is, except for an occasional false rhyme such as *night* (in Scots pronounced 'nicht')—*delight*, fairly consistently Scots in phonology and grammar and sprinkled with enough Scots words, and the occasional idiom such as 'get the Wistle of their Groat' and Scottish reference such as 'Does Tam the Rhimer spae oughtlins of this?' to make the language of the poem decidedly Scots. Where the tone becomes more satiric the density of the Scots increases, but Scots features are present throughout. In this poem, the forthrightness associated with Scots combines most effectively with the dignity of the Augustan style to give a register well suited to the optimism and patriotic pride with which Ramsay hails the development of the North Sea fisheries; and the result is a very attractive poem. That Ramsay did not experiment more extensively with this Scots Augustan register is greatly to be regretted, the more so as none of the other 'serious' poems in heroic couplets, which have little or nothing Scots in the language, comes near to being as impressive as this one.

Content is one of those poems cited by Ramsay in his Preface, where he claims that 'tho' the words be pure English, the idiom or phraseology is still Scots'. In fact, Content is Scots in nothing more than a few rhymes (head-plead, sweet-invite, retreat-evite; poor-whore (though the English poor, not the Scots puir, must be used here), thought-groat (though thought pronounced 'thoat' must be described as Scotticised English rather than Scots: Scots would be thocht), and one or two others, the use of load, and elevate as past participles, and a tiny handful of Scots words: scrimp, h'auch, vivace and a rare word jum, meaning aloof or taciturn. In a poem of 518 lines, this gives only a very faint Scots flavour to the language, which otherwise is obstinately undistinguished. Somewhat more interesting is Tartana or The Plaid, where at least the theme—the antiquity, beauty and utility of the tartan—is more enterprising than the unexceptionable but thoroughly banal sentiments of Content; but the Scots veneer on the language is, if possible, even thinner: smile rhyming with jail, lost with boast, appear with wear, and the spelling threed constitute virtually the whole of it. Similarly, Edinburgh's Address to the Country contains the words gurly and ding, rhymes of youth with mouth and too with bow, and nothing else that could identify it linguistically as a Scots poem. The remaining heroic couplet poems in this section are in a language which on the printed page is English throughout. Ramsay, of course, could and elsewhere in this volume did write heroic couplets in perfectly good Scots, and the fact that he only once did so in a poem which he classed as 'serious' is certainly striking. However, the implication that he did not naturally make the threefold association of a Scots register, a 'serious' tone and the heroic couplet may not be the correct one. Some of the poems in this group, English language notwithstanding, are assertively Scottish in subject matter, and have the air of being written specifically to bring certain facts about the country and the national life to the admiring attention of the poems' readers. Tartana is a boldly patriotic celebration of the Scottish dress (and one must agree that as a national symbol this is at the very least as worthy as the Scots food and drink that Fergusson and Burns were to promote so memorably in this capacity); Edinburgh's Address is a eulogy of the capital city, extolling its artistic and intellectual delights and the beauty of its ladies and prophesying for it a still more glorious future; Clyde's Welcome to his Prince, though ostensibly a praise poem for the Duke of Hamilton, says much more in praise of the river, finally calling on the Duke to 'slight my rival Thames, and love his Clyde'. The sentiment of these poems—a strong and confident patriotism based on deeply-felt appreciation of what is both distinctive and aesthetically or morally admirable in the land and its traditions—is by any standards worthy of respect. Moreover, the poems on Scottish themes are, apart from *Content*, the most substantial of the ten: those which are Scottish neither in language nor in subject-matter are short occasional pieces. Surely it is likely that Ramsay is using English not because of any conscious or unconscious assumption that Scots is unworthy of such noble sentiments, but to enlighten an English audience regarding the grounds of a Scotsman's patriotic pride.

This ambitious use of the heroic couplet is in accordance with his use of the form in other sections of the anthology. 'Serious' with Ramsay, whatever it implies, does not imply 'gloomy': his claim:

> Then for the Fabrick of my Mind,
> 'Tis mair to Mirth than Grief inclin'd.
> (*An Epistle to Mr Arbuckle*, ll.77-8)

is well borne out by his poems, and the resulting poetic persona is surely one of the most agreeable in Scottish literature. Slapstick and physical comedy, however, are not as a rule associated in his work with the heroic couplet. *Wealth or the Woody*, though classed as 'satyrick' rather than 'serious', is very similar in tone and, though in this respect less inventive, in language, than *The Prospect of Plenty*. The reason for their different classifications appears to be that in *The Prospect of Plenty* the satire, certainly present, is subordinate to the expression of optimistic patriotism. His Epistles in heroic couplets, whether in English or in Full Scots, are mostly straightforward praise poems, lacking the cheerful humour of the Epistles in Habbies; and of the three Pastorals, two are elegies and the third, *Patie and Roger* (which, of course, later developed into *The Gentle Shepherd*) is a romantic dialogue, comic but certainly not farcical in tone.

Only one poem in the 'comick' section, *The Morning Interview*, is in heroic couplets, and it is also unique in this section in being in Anglicised Scots: the group contains no poems in English, all except this one being in Thin or Full Scots. Its humorously cynical portrayal of Edinburgh polite society sits very uneasily in the company of the Elegies and *Christ's Kirk*, and by no amount of imagination or goodwill could it be described as one of Ramsay's best poems. But though a poet who challenges comparison with Pope—as Ramsay, here as elsewhere, does overtly, even bringing in sylphs—must take the consequences, it can at least be argued that the poem, if considered in itself, is not without its felicitous touches: the description of the returning drunkards after the pastoral opening paragraph, an identical linguistic register combining ironically with the discordant change of topic; some neat throw-away lines such as 'Where Aulus oft makes Law for Justice pass'; the immediate debasement of the associations of *gold* following a reference to Cupid's golden arrow. Comedy in the style of *The Rape of the Lock*, however, was a one-time experiment with Ramsay; and this is not a matter for regret.

It is of some interest to note that of the four 'serious' poems which are not in heroic couplets, all are in verse forms with strong Scottish associations. *Edinburgh's Salutation to the Marquis of Carnarvon*, a six-stanza piece in praise of Edinburgh, is in the 'Christ's Kirk' stanza, slightly varied by making the tag-line rhyme in successive pairs of verses. Here, as in *Edinburgh's Address* (and also *The Morning Interview*), a passing expression of regret for the city's loss of its status as a seat of government is counter-balanced by praise of its attractions. Apart from *Christ's Kirk* itself, this is the only poem in the collection to be written in the stanza; and though Ramsay's technical skill is certainly adequate, its choice for a 'serious' poem on this theme is not a happy one: the metre, even apart from its associations, is inherently lacking in the dignity which a poem on this subject seems to demand, and the quadruple rhymes become obtrusive and distracting; this is not necessarily a fault in a humorous poem, but it clearly is in a 'serious' one. The remaining three are in the 'Cherrie and the Slae' stanza, the only instances of it in the 1721 collection. They differ markedly in tone and subject matter. The most memorable of them, *The Author's Address to the Council of Edinburgh*, is a strongly-worded complaint against the pirating of his pastoral *Richie and Sandy* (acted on immediately by the Council). *The Poet's Wish*, a translation from Horace but naturalised by references to the Carse of Gowrie, the Grampians, Tay and Tweed, and to bannocks and lang-kail, is an expression of desire for the simple life as contrasted with wealth and luxury. *The Bill of the Whin-Bush Club* is simply the poet's personal letter of introduction.

These four 'serious' poems are 'serious' in different senses. *Edinburgh's Salutation* expresses, though in a less convincing format, the patriotic pride of other poems in this section, and *The Poet's Wish* reiterates, more succinctly and more decoratively, some of the sentiments of *Content*; the other two, by contrast, are on a much more trivial level, though Ramsay's wish to be admitted to membership of the Whin-Bush Club and, still more, his anger at the unlicensed circulation of inferior versions of his poem were no doubt serious matters to him at the time. It is, however, interesting that his exercises in the Christ's Kirk and Cherrie-and-the-Slae stanzas, both distinctively Scottish and both, especially the latter, calling for considerable technical skill, should have been reserved for what he intended as serious poetry. This may well be taken as another expression of his cultural patriotism: a hypothesis strengthened by the fact that all four of these poems are in Thin or Full Scots. *The Author's Address* in particular draws extensively on the resources of the vernacular for hard-hitting satire:

> They spoil'd my Sense and staw my Cash,
>   My Muses Pride murgully'd,
> And printing it like their vile Trash,
>   The honest lieges whilly'd.
>   Thus undone, to London
>   It gade to my Disgrace,
>   Sae pimpin and limpin
>   In Rags wi' bluther'd Face. (ll.7-14)

A verse form which appears rarely in this collection, though Ramsay's evident aptitude for it comes to fruition in his subsequent work, is the octosyllabic couplet: again, a form for which the Scottish credentials could hardly be more respectable, and which was to remain a potent force in the national literature until much later. This verse form does not appear in the 'serious' section; in the 'lyrick' only for a short translation from Horace into Full Scots; and in the 'epistolary', for two slight pieces, also in Full Scots. His principal exemplars of the couplet are, in the 'satyrick' section, *The Scriblers Lash'd*, a very forceful if not very subtle piece of polemic in Anglicised Scots, and *The Rise and Fall of Stocks*, in Thin Scots; and in the 'comick', his self-introducing *Epistle to James Arbuckle* and his cheerfully complacent *Conclusion*, both in Full Scots. Clearly Ramsay associated the octosyllabic couplet principally with Scots, an association confirmed by, among other things, his excellent series of fables in the 1728 volume. It is in his Scots octosyllabic poems, too, that the potential of the form—its aptness for epigrammatic witticisms decorated with clever and pointed rhymes—is most skilfully exploited. The best of them in this respect, as well as being the most completely Scots in language, is his poetic self-portrait.

Despite his strongly held and vigorously expressed opinions on poetry and its function, and on the Scots language, Ramsay was no scholar or intellectual, and his chosen association of language, metre and subject-matter in a given poem or group of poems is due, one may assume, to nonce decisions based on a somewhat erratic poetic taste rather than to a consciously applied theory. He recognised the availability of both Scots and English as a literary advantage, and certainly did not regard the use of English as cultural treason: as we have seen, some of his proudest expressions of Scottish patriotism are in English verse. And no more than the medieval Makars did he regard English models as beyond the pale in his attempts to contribute to the revival of Scottish letters. If much of his 'serious' poetry is in English or Anglicised Scots this is not because he considered Scots to be unsuitable for serious work—he certainly did not—but because for poems in this vein he had ready models in the works of Dryden and Pope: though unfortunately his talents in that particular direction were no match for theirs. Conversely, if some of his most lively and most linguistically inventive poems are both in Scots and on farcical or satiric themes this is not because Scots was, in his view, good for nothing else, but simply because farce and satire, and—independently— his native vernacular, were congenial to his taste and allowed him to exercise his talents to the full. But the associations established through Ramsay's happening to be the kind of man and poet he was became, in the minds of his successors, assumptions regarding the 'rightful' place of Scots in letters; and they are far from eradicated yet.

28

Thought and Language in George Campbell's *Philosophy of Rhetoric*

H. Lewis Ulman
Ohio State University

In *The Philosophy of Rhetoric* (1776), George Campbell raises rhetorical theory from a state that one reviewer of John Ward's *A System of Oratory* (1959) characterises as 'the disgusting dryness of names and definitions'.[1] By contrast, Campbell links rhetorical theory to the new and vital inquiries of the eighteenth century into the operation of the mind and the nature and power of language. Though Campbell's treatment of thought and language now seems dated, his strictly rhetorical theory remains a useful touchstone for modern discourse theory.

As has every age, the eighteenth century held divergent notions about the relationships among thought, language, and eloquence. On the one hand, the philosophers tend to view language as a hindrance to philosophic inquiry and, therefore, to propose remedies for the abuses of thought occasioned by words. In John Locke's *Essay Concerning Human Understanding* (1690), he blames a fair portion of those abuses on rhetoric:

> All the Art of Rhetorick, besides Order and Clearness, all the artificial and figurative application of Words Eloquence hath invented, are for nothing else but to insinuate wrong *Ideas*, move the Passions, and thereby mislead the Judgment; and so indeed are perfect cheat.[2]

Often the philosophers employ physical metaphors that separate language from thought: for instance, in his *Treatise Concerning the Principles of Human Knowledge* (1710), Berkeley argues that 'we need only draw the curtain of words, to behold the fairest tree of knowledge'.[3] Thomas Reid, too, asserts in his *Essays on the Intellectual Powers of Man* (1785) that 'There is no greater impediment to the advancement of knowledge than the ambiguity of words'.[4] Though their theories of language differ and are certainly more subtle and complex than I suggest here, all three of these philosophers discuss language with a common goal in mind: to clear the smoke of language from the air of philosophical thought.

On the other hand, later eighteenth-century rhetoricians and literary critics understandably attempt to explain and extend the special powers of words, the essential medium of civil and literary discourse. For instance, Hugh Blair's *Lectures on Rhetoric and Belles Lettres* (1783) provides this alternative metaphor for the relationship between thought and language:

> Whether we consider Poetry in particular, and Discourse in general, as Imitative or Descriptive; it is evident, that their whole power, in recalling the impressions of real objects, is derived from the significancy of words. As their excellency flows altogether from this source, we must ... begin at this fountain head.[5]

Clearly, if Campbell were to write a *philosophy of rhetoric*, one that could reconcile these extreme approaches to the relationship between thought and language, he would have to seek some common ground.

Campbell's controlling metaphor for rhetoric represents something of a compromise between the two extremes. He maintains a clear distinction between thought and language but binds them inextricably in a genealogical metaphor, maintaining that the *parent sciences* of thought and language and the corresponding *parent arts* of logic and grammar each contribute essential characteristics to human discourse:

> Now, if it be by the sense or soul of the discourse that rhetoric holds of logic, or the art of thinking and reasoning, it is by the expression or body of the discourse that she holds of grammar, or the art of conveying our thoughts in the words of a particular language.

Extending the metaphor, he establishes an important distinction between the characteristics discourse inherits from each parent:

> As the soul is of heavenly extraction and the body of earthly, so the sense of the discourse ought to have its source in the invariable nature of truth and right, whereas the expression can derive its energy only from the arbitrary conventions of men, sources as unlike, or rather as widely different, as the breath of the Almighty and the dust of the earth.[6]

In spite of these differences, the genealogical metaphor precludes any separation of thought and language in theories of human discourse: to borrow Campbell's metaphor, the breath of the Almighty creates human discourse only when it inspires the dust of the earth. Of course it is possible to study each 'parent' separately, but Campbell implies that you are not then studying discourse, but its parent arts and sciences. He argues that in ideal discourse 'language and thought, like body and soul, are made to correspond, and the qualities of one exactly to co-operate with those of the other' (p.215). This metaphor aptly illustrates the most significant features of Campbell's rhetorical theory—his definition of rhetoric, his evaluative criteria for rhetorical discourse, his rhetorical method, and his ancillary theories of thought and language.

In the opening paragraph of *The Philosophy of Rhetoric*, Campbell defines eloquence 'in its greatest latitude' as 'That art or talent by which the discourse is adapted to its end'(p.1). Unlike most earlier rhetorical theorists, he takes all of discourse as his starting point, focusing on that aspect of all discourse which involves adapting means to ends. Though rhetorical theory has always included a practical concern with effective discourse, earlier rhetorical theory tended to emphasise particular ends of discourse (generally persuasion) or particular means of discourse (style or invention or arguments).

Following from his definition of rhetoric, Campbell's main evaluative criterion for eloquent discourse addresses another standard *topos* of rhetorical theory—distinguishing the provinces of logic, grammar, and eloquence:

> It is not ultimately the justness either of the thought or of the expression, which is the aim of the orator; but it is a certain effect to be produced in the hearers. This effect ... he proposeth to produce in them by means of language (p.215).

Here again we find a distinctly human art, one concerned chiefly with the motives of speakers and the effects of discourse on hearers—the laws of logic and grammar only inform and bound the freedom of speakers and hearers to act and respond.

Campbell's holistic perspective also determines his chief methodological principle for discourse:

> In order to evince the truth considered by itself, conclusive arguments alone are requisite; but in order to convince me by these arguments, it is moreover requisite that they be understood, that they be attended to, that they be remembered by me; and in order to persuade me by them to any particular action or conduct, it is further requisite, that by interesting me in the subject, they may, as it were, be felt. It is not therefore the understanding alone that is here concerned. If the orator would prove successful, it is necessary that he engage in his service all these different powers of the mind, the imagination, the memory, and the passions (pp.71-72).

Again, he emphasises the complete human experience of discourse, rather than pigeon-holing rhetoric with imagination or the passions, as Locke's philosophy would have it.

Having established this grand plan for rhetorical theory, Campbell devotes much of *The Philosophy of Rhetoric* to ancillary treatments of rhetoric's parent sciences and arts—theories of thought and language, doctrines of evidence and grammar. As we have seen, Campbell draws an important distinction between the two parents, arguing that thought follows universal laws while language follows laws particular to human communities. More than any feature of his strictly rhetorical theory, this distinction, and Campbell's ultimate treatment of it, distances his work from modern discourse theory.

His doctrine of evidence reveals his penchant for reconciling opposing theories, a habit of mind in this case consistent with his principle that thought is universal, for then there can be only one correct explanation of its laws. Faced with contemporary epistemologies that emphasised either the reliability of common sense intuitions or the necessity (and impossibility) of proving all propositions rationally, Campbell formulates a pragmatic two-path theory of 'logical truth', one which brings together the opposing camps by claiming that we must ground what he calls deductive reasoning—comparison of related ideas—in immediately accepted intuitions: mathematical axioms, 'the reality of...sensations and passions', (see pp.4,5,7) and common sense intuitions such as our conviction that 'there are other intelligent beings in the universe besides me'(pp.35-49). Both paths, intuitive and intuitive-deductive, should lead to conceptions that conform to 'the nature of things'(p.35). This criterion in particular has drawn fire from recent critics who point out that Campbell neglects to consider that language might *create* human reality as well as refer to or test it. That premise, however, would violate his basic distinction between language and thought, the latter aiming at 'the invariable nature of truth and right'. Campbell notes that different languages offer us different ranges and forms of expression, but he attributes this fact to their relative abilities to reflect the 'delicate differences among things'(p.201). This insistence on the 'invariable nature of truth and right', of course, distances Campbell's doctrine of evidence from modern theories of changing scientific paradigms, informal logics, and the epistemic power of discourse.

Campbell's doctrine of use presents similar problems for the modern reader. On the one hand, he champions use as the sole basis for grammar: he believes, as we do, that only the 'tacit consent of the people of a particular state or country' can establish the meaning of words and the structure of language (p.139). Yet in working out his doctrine of use, Campbell controverts the spirit of this central principle. He argues that three laws determine general use—essentially *universal* laws that *exclude* much of any living language; indeed, he argues at one point that general use cannot reflect that of the generality of people, who 'speak and write very badly'(p.142). Arguing that we should conceive of general use as present, national, and reputable use, he insists on the 'king's highway' of English and the use of 'celebrated' authors, dismissing spoken language in favour of the 'certain, steady, and well-known standard' of print (pp.144-46), and playing down the importance of regional or professional dialects. Obviously, all that follows from his laws of use must reflect very particular eighteenth- century British views of history, literary tradition, and national identity. His linguistic theory would be of little use to the student of Inuktitut, say, or Cherokee. But in spite of such limitations, Campbell's further investigation of language can still be instructive to modern rhetorical theorists.

In particular, his discussion of the nature and power of linguistic signs arrives at some surprisingly modern conclusions. Campbell argues that the meanings of words stem not only from their tacitly agreed-upon references to things, but also from their relationships to one another, i.e., to the semantic and syntactic structures of a given language: 'this connexion among the signs is conceived as analogous to that which subsisteth among their archetypes'(p.260); recall that Campbell's definition of logical truth also refers to 'the conformity of our conceptions to their archetypes in the nature of things'(p.35). These overlapping, analogous structures of things, conceptions, and signs, he argues, allow us to use language much of the time without direct reference to the world of things, or, more specifically, to our ideas of things. On the one hand, absurd propositions appear absurd immediately because the *words* do not go together. On the other hand, we generally use words as we do algebraic variables (an idea he got from Berkeley), attending to their place in a more or less rule-bound system rather than forming distinct impressions of their value or reference at a given moment. Consequently, he argues, 'we really think by signs as well as speak by them'(p.260). In his grand scheme, as in much modern theory, the order of language virtually replaces the order of things and the order of mind.

Here we have the broad outline of Campbell's genealogy: thought and language unite to parent human discourse, the distinct province of rhetoric. This genealogy of discourse presents us with a comprehensive view of logic, grammar, and rhetoric that we do not find equalled in nineteenth-century rhetorical treatises, when logic, linguistics, and psychology became more specialised and drifted away from rhetorical concerns. However, a century of specialised experiment and observation in such fields gave the twentieth century more stable ground upon which to raise comprehensive theories of discourse, and specialists eventually began to broaden their perspectives. In 1929, for example, Edward Sapir issued the following challenge to his fellow linguists:

> It is peculiarly important that linguists, who are often accused, and accused justly, of failure to look beyond the pretty patterns of their subject matter, should become aware of what their science may mean for the interpretation of human conduct in general.[7]

Almost thirty-five years later, George Miller noted that psycholinguists had fairly well explained 'hearing and matching', were making progress with 'accepting and interpreting', but still had far to go toward a linguistic account of human conduct:

> Understanding is still over the horizon, and pragmatic questions involving belief systems are presently so vague as to be hardly worth asking. But the whole range of processes must be included in any adequate definition of psycholinguistics.[8]

Yet George Campbell included this 'whole range of processes' in his *Philosophy of Rhetoric*. Today, most rhetoricians once again conceive of their field as broadly as did Campbell. Kenneth Burke hints at our renewed concern with language and psychology when he defines rhetoric as 'the use of language as a symbolic means of inducing cooperation in beings that by nature respond to symbols'.[9] Whatever new terms and concepts we employ, rhetorical theory will still attempt to better account for and enhance 'that art or talent by which the discourse is adapted to its end'. For all the limitations of his theories of thought and language, Campbell's rhetorical theory still provides us with a measure of scope and direction.

Notes

1. George Campbell, *The Philosophy of Rhetoric*, ed. Lloyd F. Bitzer (Carbondale, Southern Illinois U.P., 1963). John Ward, *A System of Oratory*, 2 vols (London, 1759). *The Critical Review*, 1st series, April 1759, p.367.
2. John Locke, *An Essay Concerning Human Understanding*, eds Peter H. Nidditch (Oxford, Clarendon Press, 1975), p.508.
3. George Berkeley, *A Treatise Concerning the Principles of Human Knowledge*, in *The Works of George Berkeley, Bishop of Cloyne*, eds A.A. Luce and T.E. Jessop, 9 vols (London, Nelson, 1948-57), vol. 2, p.40.
4. Thomas Reid, *Essays on the Intellectual Powers of Man*, in *Thomas Reid's Inquiry and Essays*, ed. Keith Lehrer and Ronald E. Beanblossom, The Library of Liberal Arts, 156 (Indianapolis, Bobbs-Merrill, 1975), p.129.
5. Hugh Blair, *Lectures on Rhetoric and Belles Lettres*, 2nd edition, 1785, 3 vols (New York, Garland, 1970), vol. 1, pp.120-21.
6. Campbell, *The Philosophy of Rhetoric*, p.34.
7. Edward Sapir, 'The Status of Linguistics as a Science', *Language*, 5 (1929), p.214.
8. George A. Miller, 'The Psycholinguists', *Psycholinguistics: A Survey of Theory and Research Problems*, eds Charles E. Osgood and Thomas A. Sebeok (Bloomington, Indiana U.P., 1965), p.295.
9. Kenneth Burke, *A Rhetoric of Motives*, 1950 (Berkeley, California U.P., 1969), p.43.

29

Rhetoric and *Belles Lettres* in the North East

Joan H. Pittock

University of Aberdeen

The part played by Rhetoric and Belles Lettres in the degree courses of King's and Marischal Colleges in eighteenth-century Aberdeen is of special interest not only philosophically but as it illustrates pedagogic priorities in the north east of Scotland. The role of such lectures in the degree syllabus is illustrated by the surviving manuscript notes on the lectures of James Beattie, Professor of Moral Philosophy at Marischal College from 1760 to 1794.

Whereas for Adam Smith perspicuity and cogency were priorities in the use of language, for Hugh Blair they were elegance and taste. The one preferred the style of Swift, the other lauded that of Ossian.[1] Blair's *Lectures on Rhetoric and Belles Lettres* which he began to deliver in Edinburgh in 1758 could hardly fail to be influenced to some extent by the recently published prize-winning *Essay on Taste* by Alexander Gerard of Marischal College. It is interesting that the understanding of the faculty of 'Taste' in the North East has less to do with a concern for the socially refining effect of literature and its artistic effects (as emphasised by Blair) than with its moral influence. While in most centres Rhetoric drifted out of the orbit of Logic into that of Taste, or the capacity to respond to literature, in Aberdeen it is related to the moral development of the individual. In his book *Eighteenth-Century British Logic and Rhetoric*, Wilbur S. Howells remarks of the most notable Aberdeen writer on rhetoric, George Campbell:

> Campbell's theory of eloquence rested upon one great principle: that the human soul is not indifferent to the intellectual and moral quality of its ideas—that it has within itself the disposition to be moved only by those ideas which it accepts as truthful and good.[2]

This Shaftesburian understanding of Taste as an innate moral and aesthetic faculty could be grafted onto the Baconian approach to knowledge advocated by David Fordyce, who had taught both Gerard and Campbell at Marischal College. Gerard heightens the importance of susceptibility:

> We may here take occasion to mention a principle distinct from all the internal senses from which taste will, in many instances, receive assistance. It is such a *sensibility of heart*, as fits a man for being easily moved, and for readily catching, as by infection, any passion that a work is fitted to excite.[3]

Gerard's pupil and successor in the Chair of Moral Philosophy at Marischal, James Beattie, wrote one of the most famous and popular poems of the late eighteenth century, *The Minstrel* (subtitled *The Progress of Genius*), of which the first part was published in 1770 and the second four years later. That Gerard's *Essay on Genius* was also published in 1774 is perhaps another indication of the ways in which the members of the Philosophical Society profited from their deliberations. The hero of Beattie's poem is Edwin, the minstrel:

> But She, who set on fire his infant heart,
> And all his dreams, and all his wanderings shared
> And bless'd, the Muse, and her celestial art,
> Still claim'd th'Enthusiast's fond and first regard.
> From Nature's beauties variously compared
> And variously combined, he learns to frame
> Those forms of bright perfection, which the Bard,
> While boundless hopes and boundless views inflame,
> Enamour'd consecrates to never-dying fame.
>
> Of late, with cumbersome, though pompous show,
> Edwin would oft his flowery rhyme deface,
> Through ardour to adorn; but nature now
> To his experienced eye a modest grace
> Presents, where Ornament the second place
> Holds, to intrinsick worth and just design
> Subservient still, Simplicity apace,
> Tempers his rage; he owns her charm divine,
> And clears th'ambiguous phrase, and lops th'unwieldy line.
>
> (Part I, stanzas lviii, lix)

It is clear that Beattie may not quite practise what he preaches, but it is after all to his credit that he did not share Blair's predilection for the fashionably false primitivism of Ossian. For Edwin, in pre-Wordsworthian fashion, nature inculcates the proper use of rhetoric. Edwin's susceptibility to the language of true poetry is his susceptibility to nature: his sensibility is at once the hall-mark of his genius and his avenue to maturity. The exuberance of his imagination is an inherent element of his genius, and experience enables him to develop a purity of style free from the trappings of conventional rhetorical ornament. One of the questions Beattie put before the Philosophical Society concerned the usefulness of Rhetoric. Beattie does not go as far as Adam Smith who shares the Hudibrastic opinion that:

> for all the Rhetorician's Rules
> are but the naming of his tools.[4]

He sees it as necessary to explain and illustrate the purpose of commonly used stylistic devices; any elaboration of the rules of Rhetoric was to be encouraged chiefly as an aid to composition. This movement of Rhetoric away from Logic to literature and criticism was an uneasy one, but had been given some theoretical base by Gerard in the early 1750s. In his *Plan of Education*, which his colleagues at Marischal ordered to be published in 1755, Gerard argues for the postponement of Logic to the end of the course. Instead of beginning with Logic, he argues, the student should proceed through studies based on his experience and knowledge towards Logic, which:

> can be understood no farther than the several sciences which it reviews and criticises are previously understood...we find, that all the systems of Logic which have not been compiled from a careful review and examination of the several sciences, consist more of ingenious subtleties, than of useful precepts assisting to the mind in the various parts of knowledge... [it] is precisely the same to *Philosophy*, that works of criticism are to *Poetry*. The rules of criticism are formed by an accurate scrutiny and examination of the best works of poetry.

The development of taste is one aspect of education which is best encouraged by an acquaintance with the best literature. Both Rhetoric and Belles Lettres however, are considered incidental in the development of human understanding, a process in which 'phenomena must be not only *narrated*, but likewise, as far as possible, *explained*'.[5]

It is in this context that we can turn now to a group of manuscripts which show modestly, but unmistakably, a preoccupation with conscientious teaching in the work of James Beattie. Beattie's lectures at Marischal to the magistrand or fourth-year class for over thirty years are programmed in his meticulously kept *Journal*. This shows, year by year, Beattie's treatment of the field of Moral Philosophy, concluding, as we would expect from Gerard's *Plan*, with Logic. It is interesting that the coverage of Rhetoric fluctuates: some years it is dealt with alongside Logic, in others subsumed in a discussion of aspects of style to emphasise the potential variety of composition and the importance of the study of language.

We are able to rely on the evidence of the *Journal* for the programming of the lectures because there survive confirmatory sets of notes made by students in different years, checked, as we know from Beattie's letters, by the lecturer himself. So we have one set for 1766: 'A System of Philosophy comprehending Pneumatology, Ethics, Logic. Taught by Mr James Beattie Professor of Moral Philosophy in the Marischal College of Aberdeen. Wrote by William Duncan'; a second manuscript notebook compiled by James Smith covers the session 1773-4; a third by A. Martin 1779-80.[6] From a private collection comes a handsome three-volume version of the whole lecture programme for the magistrand session on Moral Philosophy, Psychology and on Cicero's *De Officiis* by George Mylne, a bajan of 1774-5, who would therefore have been likely to have attended Beattie's lectures in the class of 1777-78.[7] The four sets of notes cover the first six years of Beattie's Marischal lectures, the other three coinciding with Beattie's approach to his subject at the period of his highest reputation—the period which saw the publication of *The Minstrel*, the *Essay on Truth* (1770), his work on Scoticisms, and his *Dissertations Moral and Critical* (1783).

In Duncan's notes of 1766, Rhetoric comes under the general head of Logic, which is heralded by a swinging defence of common sense:

> all Reasoning which attempts to subvert the principles of Common Sense, and all Reasoning which calls in question the Belief of our Senses, tends directly to universal Scepticism... Mr Locke [is] not quite so unfavourable to common sense on the whole...his Abhorrence of innate principles, his account of the secondary qualities of Matter, being only Ideas in the Mind, &c do strike directly at the Root of all Common Sense, and if they prove any thing at all, do prove that we ought not to believe our Senses, and that the human Mind is originally as susceptible of any one perception as of another, than which no doctrine whatever can tend more directly to universal Scepticism.(p.177)

Hume thus countered in distinctive north-east fashion, Beattie proceeds to define Rhetoric as 'that part of Logic which explains everything relating to the Communication of our thoughts to others', and consisting of Universal Grammar and Composition. Of Poetry Beattie merely observes that it 'imitates Nature by means of Language'. As for Eloquence, he ends his series of lectures with some abruptness by recommending his audience to seek information in the work of Cicero and Quintilian as these are 'Books to which every one has very easy access and with which every literary scholar ought to be intimately acquainted'. Six years later the notes of James Smith reflect a totally changed course. Language is lectured on at the beginning, instead of at the end of the series, and Beattie's thoughts have clearly been exercised by Campbell and by Reid. Describing the external senses he comes to hearing and discusses language as its product:

> We speak in order to communicate our thoughts. This is done by means of Signs, for thought itself can never be made obvious to sense. The Signs of thought are naturally significant, such as are all the natural expressions of passions w^c appear in ye Eyes, Face, complexion.., Oyrs are artificial, deriving all their Signification from ye compact and practice of men.(p.21)

Among these are physical signs—signals, body language, and language itself. By embarking on an analysis of phenomena systematically and inclusively Beattie enlarges on the more common principles of communication, those of clear and everyday relevance to his hearers. Rhetoric in this programme is subsumed to Universal Grammar as 'the art of making Sentences, and uniting them in a discourse or Composition'. There follows the most specific listing of tropes and figures to appear anywhere in the lectures, with some references to poetic usage, but with rather less attention paid to Belles Lettres than might normally be expected. Beattie's aim is functional: this is the period of his attempts to improve the communicative powers of his students and countrymen by identifying Scoticisms. He even includes in his lectures what he calls a 'Praxis of Scoticisms' a passage full of Scotch expressions—pled for pleaded, relevant for valid, butter and bread for bread and butter, and the same passage corrected. Taste is important because of the effects of poetry on the feelings. There are echoes of Gerard: 'If...we were destitute of Sympathy, we should be incapable of receiving from Poetry or Oratory those emotions ye Author intended to excite, and consequently we could not judge of ye merit or demerit of such performances.'(pp.240,292)

Criticism then becomes an aid to Taste in the study of Belles Lettres (essays in literature). Essential to all this, however, is that Good Sense which is a gift of nature and which enables man to see in the works of nature the goodness of his Creator. Beattie is concerned with the problems of communication of his students and the needs of their future parishioners and scholars and their communities. He adds to the customary list of Reflex Senses at this time those of Shame and Honour. Conscience reminds us of the duties we owe to God, to our fellow-creatures, to ourselves. Beattie's own sense of his accountability as a teacher is manifest. His comprehension of Rhetoric, functional; of criticism, educational; the operations of the human mind as they emanate in literature are seen not in terms of the elegances and refinements of Belles Lettres as these developed in later centuries but of complexity of discourse. He is very conscious in his *Discourses* of 'plainness of Style' and attributes this to the necessity to be comprehensible to his hearers. Rhetoric is to be approached pragmatically in terms of the common needs and assumptions of teacher and pupil: literature brings students face to face with moral issues.

'Taste', Beattie is recorded by Mylne as asserting:

> is an excellent preservative from those vices that harden and debase the heart; for sensibility, which is an essential part of taste, produces benevolence & kind affection; & a relish for the sublime & beautiful elevates the mind above sensuality & meanness—Taste leads to the study of the works of Nature, & this study, attentively pursued, will lead an intelligent mind to contemplate & adore the power, wisdom & goodness of a Creator.(p.181)

Without this sense of priorities—the cultivation of one's own potentialities for the greater good—in education, not merely literature, but everything is pointless.

Notes

The author gratefully acknowledges permission to publish here part of a paper delivered at the Edinburgh Enlightenment conference, and written while holding an IPSE Fellowship.

1. Adam Smith, *Lectures on Rhetoric and Belles Lettres*, ed. J.C. Bryce (Oxford, Clarendon Press, 1983), p.3. Hugh Blair, *Lectures on Rhetoric and Belles Lettres*,

3 vols (London, A. Strahan, T. Cadell; Edinburgh, W. Creech, 1793), vol.1, Lectures 1 and 2.

2. Wilbur S. Howell, *Eighteenth-Century British Logic and Rhetoric* (Princeton, Princeton U.P., 1971), p.580.

3. Alexander Gerard, *An Essay on Taste* (1758; London, A. Millar; Edinburgh, A. Kincaid and J. Bell, 1759).

4. Alexander Gerard, *An Essay on Taste*, pp.78-9. 'The Edinburgh Society for the encouragement of arts, sciences, manufacturers, and agriculture proposed, in the year 1755, a gold medal to the best essay on Taste; and, not having assigned it that year, repeated the proposal in 1756. This determined the author to enter on the following enquiry into the nature of Taste; the general principles of which only he presented to the Society, suspecting that the whole might exceed the limits which they had fixed, by requiring an essay. The judges appointed for that subject, having been pleased to assign the premium to him, he is encouraged to offer the whole, as it was at first composed, to the public'. (Advertisement to the second edition, Aberdeen, 1758.) 1759 and 1766 editions of the essay on Taste appeared with essays on the same subject by Voltaire, d'Alembert and Montesquieu— evidence of the contemporary European relevance of the topic, and the significance of Gerard's contribution.

5. *Ibid.*, pp.12-13; p.9.

6. AUL, MSS M. 185.3; M. 185 2; M. 185.

7. AUL, MS 1740.18.

30

Wit, Humour and Ridicule: George Campbell's First Discourse for the Aberdeen Philosophical Society

Kathleen Holcomb

Angelo State University

At its official inception in January 1758, the Aberdeen Philosophical Society was a remarkably well organised body. There were six members, seventeen rules (though one of these may have been added later), twelve questions suggested for debate, and complicated procedures for choosing a presiding officer for each meeting. Clearly, the initial meeting was the result of much thought; the rules had been 'previously concerted and agreed to by all the members'.[1]

The members had had experience with similar societies; George Campbell, for example, had organised a Theological Society in 1742, when he was a student of divinity. Two other members of that society, James Trail and Alexander Gerard, eventually found their ways into the Philosophical Society, though Trail's association was largely honorary. John Glennie testified 'all the members esteemed Mr Campbell *as the life and soul of the society*'.[2]

The men in the Theological Society had not intended it to be a social organisation. Its object, Campbell tells his own divinity students:

> was our mutual improvement, both in the knowledge of the theory, and also in whatever might be conductive to qualify us for the practical part or duties of the pastoral function ... Amongst other things discussed in this small society, one was, an inquiry into the nature of sermons and other discourses proper for the pulpit, the different kinds into which they might fitly be distributed, and the rules of composition that suited each. On this subject we had several conversations. When these were over, I had the task assigned me to make out a short sketch or abstract of the whole ... Of this abstract, every one who chose it took a copy.[3]

Campbell's biographer insists that Alexander Gerard, the only member of the original Society to be active in the Philosophical Society, was one of those who had a copy and 'followed the arrangement and adopted many of the same sentiments' as did Campbell, both men using the abstracts.[4]

From the common ground covered by Gerard and Campbell, it is apparent that the definition of rhetoric, or eloquence, that forms the foundation of Campbell's *Philosophy of Rhetoric*, as well as his outline of the ends of rhetoric, is derived from those abstracts. Eloquence is that art or talent by which the discourse is adapted to its end. The ends are reducible to four: to enlighten the understanding, to please the imagination, to move the passions, or to influence the will.[5] Wherever Campbell writes of discourse, he uses this scheme. However, Gerard uses it only in his divinity lectures; elsewhere he imposes quite a different structure on communication. This coincidence would not have grown out of their association at Marischal or their simultaneous holding of the divinity professorships at Marischal and King's, since later in life they apparently 'did not live on a ... friendly footing', and declined to lecture in cooperation.[6]

Even after he left Aberdeen for his first ministry at Banchory Ternan, Campbell continued to develop the ideas about discourse suggested by the Theological Society. By 1750 he had completed what he himself identifies as 'the first two chapters of the first Book [of *The Philosophy of Rhetoric*]. These he intended as a sort of groundwork to the whole ... That first outline he showed soon after to several of his acquaintance.'[7] However, he did not have enough confidence in his system of discourse to discuss it in a sermon preached before the Synod of Aberdeen in 1752 on the character of a minister as teacher; there he presents rhetoric in a very traditional way.[8]

But by 1758, as a minister in Aberdeen, Campbell was ready to test what he had been working out. When the Philosophical Society began its activity, he had appropriate material and offered to give the Society's first Discourse. The Society's record shows he gave the first Discourse on 8 March 1758, intimated in advance as 'the Nature of Eloquence its various Species & their Respective Ends'.[9] The two species are serious and colloquial; their respective ends are to affect the different operations of the mind. Part of the material was derived from the Theological Society's abstracts, but Campbell developed it far beyond a set of simple instructions and made it the cornerstone for the important new system of rhetoric he unfolded before the Society in subsequent years. The rest of the material is, I think, quite new; in the second part of the Discourse he elaborates on the system by considering wit, humour, and ridicule the counterparts of serious eloquence.

After it was read, Campbell's paper circulated among the members of the Society. Thomas Gordon, who was not a member when Campbell read his inaugural Discourse, made a copy of it, as he did most of the rest of the Discourses read during the first two years of the Society's activity. Gordon's copy of this Discourse is unusually full, containing marginalia and the text of notes, an amplitude Gordon otherwise lavished only on his own Discourses.[10] Gordon could have used either Campbell's original copy or the book into which the Discourses were all entered.

Gordon was not the only person to have looked at the material. David

Skene, who was present to hear the Discourse, refers to having *read* some of it, specifically the part on Wit, Humour and Ridicule:

> no words are more universally us'd, & yet are very little acquainted to their nature or Characters—nay, many a Man has been witty all his days, who would have been very much puzzl'd to have said, in what real Wit consisted—In this Discourse these Subjects are consider'd w^t a degree of accuracy, & carried a length I have nowhere else met with. I shall subjoin what particular reflections occur'd to me in reading it.[11]

Skene's reflections show careful consideration of the Discourse. He defines a category of wit for which Campbell has not provided, and notes several examples of that kind. He was able to do so because he, too, had made a copy of Part II. Although Skene's copy is not as fine as Gordon's, he too copies marginalia and the text of notes.[12]

A third person impressed with Campbell's ideas was Thomas Reid. Reid had more than one opportunity to examine Campbell's material carefully. First, he was present when the Discourse was read. But Skene's comment strongly suggests that Part II was not read.[13] In that case, Reid, like Skene, would have had a chance to read it himself if Campbell had circulated a copy. The publishing members sometimes did so, as stylistic criticism was not allowed at the discussion of Discourses, and these men were anxious to write correct English. Even if Reid had not been shown Campbell's original copy, he used the Discourse Book after Campbell (Reid read his first Discourse on 14 June) and could have seen the Discourse Book copy. And it is possible that Reid was one of the 'acquaintance' to whom Campbell showed his outline shortly after 1750. The use Reid made of Campbell's ideas strongly suggests this possibility. Reid is not recorded as a member of the earlier Theological Society, but he might have seen its abstract. It should be noted, however, that Reid's papers do not include an abstract or an outline.

Two other relationships must be mentioned only to be dismissed. James Beattie, who was not a member when Campbell read his Discourse, published his *Essays* almost simultaneously with *Philosophy of Rhetoric*. 'An Essay on Laughter and Ludicrous Composition, Written in the year 1764' notes that Beattie and Campbell were both writing on the same subject, but Beattie claims not to have known about Campbell's work until they exchanged manuscripts just before publication of both books. Campbell makes the same point, but with more grace.[14] There is no similarity in the treatments.

The other relationship is the one suggested and dismissed by Campbell's biographer George Skene Keith. In their divinity lectures, both Campbell and Gerard consider pulpit eloquence as a special case of eloquence in general, and both schematise its ends and means in the same way. This division is of fundamental importance to Campbell's new rhetoric; however, Gerard uses it only in his advice to future preachers. In the *Essay on Genius*, Gerard uses an entirely different analysis, and in his psychology lectures, where he atttends most carefully to mental operations, these four are not associated. He does not consider the relationships of wit, humour, and ridicule. Matching these functions to the mental operations addressed by rhetoric is Campbell's original development from the Theological Society's abstract. Gerard's connexion predates the Philosophical Society Discourse.

Finally, there remains Campbell's debt to himself. The lectures on pulpit eloquence, which he gave from 1771 on, draw heavily upon *The Philosophy of Rhetoric* as well as from the abstracts which Campbell still possessed. On the subject of wit, humour, and ridicule Campbell is quite clear. Ridicule has no place in church (Lecture 3, p. 314 and following).

Skene's and Gordon's admiration for Campbell's Discourse is now apparent only in their faithful copies of Part II, and in Skene's commentary. But Reid found a use for his colleague's work. When Reid moved to Glasgow in 1764 to fill the position vacated by Adam Smith, he felt obliged to offer some lectures on rhetoric, although he was apparently not interested in developing his own system.[15] Therefore, he added to his own customary lectures a separate, new, course of lectures on eloquence. In more than one[16] he mentions or quotes Campbell, but *The Philosophy of Rhetoric* was not published until 1776, over ten years after Reid began delivering his lectures. Reid's habitual lecture-writing practices were accretive. What apparently happened is that Reid composed his new eloquence lecture on wit and the facetious in 1765 or 1766 using what he remembered from either Campbell's outline or his Discourse, and enriched it in 1776 with other material from Campbell's Chapter I.

Reid's lecture owes two debts to Campbell. The first is an outline of correspondences between kinds of serious and facetious discourse, and the second is a large group of examples. After an introduction which justifies the facetious as necessary play (based upon, but not credited to, Cicero, *De Officiis*), Reid proceeds to:

> make some Observations on the Facetious, which I think may be reduced to three [forms] Wit Humour & Ridicule. And first of all I would observe *with the ingenious Dr. Campbell* [my italics] that there is a certain Correspondence between these & the last kinds I mentioned of Serious Eloquence. Wit corresponds to grave Description. Humour to the Pathetick and Ridicule to the Vehement.[17]

'[T]he ingenious Dr. Campbell' is superscribed—a later addition to a finished lecture: the lecture itself has little relationship to Campbell's work. It is an adaptation of Addison's *Spectator* series on wit (*Spectator*, numbers 58-62).

The second debt to Campbell is a series of quotations. All but one of the quotations in this section appear in *Philosophy of Rhetoric*, in exactly the order Reid has copied them, but some are missing from the Discourse.[18] The quotations are almost all from Butler and Pope; Campbell uses them to illustrate his three types of wit. Indeed, Reid's marginal notations fit the quotations squarely into Campbell's divisions of the types of wit. Only one quotation—the first—cannot be found in Campbell; it occurs fairly close to the beginning of Kames's essay on wit in *Elements of Criticism*.[19] Campbell's quotations were also singled out by Skene. They aptly illustrate Campbell's sometimes subtle distinctions.

The Discourse that inaugurated the intellectual work of the Philosophical Society was valued by the members, either because of its intrinsic quality or because it was the first.[20] The new framework enabled Campbell to expand the functions of rhetoric, or eloquence, and to relate it to the introspective method of mental science Reid was developing. But what place did wit, humour, and rhetoric hold in the system? Were they merely part of the scheme, or did his observations open new avenues for other rhetoricians as well as for his colleagues?

Campbell's definition of rhetoric, 'That art or talent by which the discourse is adapted to its end', is derived from Quintilian and Cicero, Campbell claims (*Philosophy of Rhetoric*, p.1, note). The ends of speaking 'are reducible to four; every speech being intended to enlighten the understanding, to please the imagination, to move the passions, or to influence the will' (p.1). This is the same programme adopted by the Theological Society. But Campbell develops the analysis. The standard mode of discourse is declamation; a lighter mode is called colloquial eloquence. Suited to light and trivial matters, colloquial eloquence shares with the eloquence of declamation the first end: to enlighten the understanding. However, whereas the eloquence of declamation pleases the fancy through sublimity and description, colloquial eloquence uses wit to 'excite in the mind an agreeable surprise ... solely from the imagery she employs'. The end directed to the passions uses pathos in its declamatory mode but humour in its colloquial. Declamatory eloquence moves the will through vehemence; colloquial through ridicule. These are the Campbell correspondences noted by Reid in his Eloquence lecture, though not carried through by him.

Wit:

Wit pleases the fancy or imagination by exciting an agreeable surprise, Campbell specifies. Reid incorporates this observation into his abstract of Addison's papers on wit, and it is the basis of Skene's reflections. Campbell divides Wit into three categories: what Skene names Burlesque, mock majestic, and 'ye 3d species or what w^c pleases by the uncommonness of ye imagery'. Skene believes that Campbell's exploration of this species is incomplete, because it fails to include a graver kind of wit. Skene gives as a supplementary example:

> Mr. Hume's Comparison of the Priests with Archimedes—It belongs to none of the Species Mention'd in ye Disc. yet is extremely witty—as it points out a Resemblance in a particular point of view betwixt two ideas, w^c seem to have no manner of Connexion—Such Wit I imagine might be employ'd to the greatest advantage by ye gravest Orator.[21]

However, the bulk of Campbell's discussion of wit contains few surprises. It is his coupling of wit with sublimity or description that is important here: wit is the means by which the orator pleases the imagination of his hearers when he uses colloquial eloquence; sublimity or description when he uses declamatory.

Humour:

Humour is the part of colloquial eloquence directed to the passions. Declamatory eloquence arouses passions of sympathy, or by sympathy, but colloquial eloquence arouses contempt. Campbell warns that the emotion aroused must be neither violent nor durable, for in that case, a well-disposed mind would feel pity rather than contempt (*Philosophy of Rhetoric*, p.16).

On at least two counts, Campbell's discussion of humour is noteworthy. First, its association with contempt is not universally accepted; Kames's biographer, Alexander Fraser Tytler, chides both Kames and Campbell for this attitude:

> in every thing justly called *humourous*, there is a singularity of character, which, as deviating from the general standard, may be termed improper, yet it cannot be so readily admitted, that it is the quality of that character to excite contempt... On the contrary, the displeasing ingredient of meanness... seems to lessen, and derogate from, the purer pleasure we receive from the equally ludicrous characters in which it has no place. To be highly pleased with the expression of any emotion, we must completely sympathise with the person who displays it: but the feeling of contempt is in a great degree hostile to sympathy.[22]

Louis Cazamian, tracing the development of English humour, likewise faults Campbell for associating humour with contempt.[23]

Secondly, Campbell's definition is too closely associatd with 'the Jonsonian idea of "a humor", that is to say, an eccentric person under the control of his or her physiological temper'. This concept had been definitively challenged by Corbyn Morris in 1744, in his *Essay Towards Fixing the True Standards of Wit, Humour, Raillery, Satire and Ridicule*.[24] Kames and later writers move away from the Jonsonian concept, but Campbell continues to use it.

Skene has nothing to say on the subject of humour. However, a passage in Reid's lecture associates him with Campbell rather than with Kames and Morris:

> We shall find that the Witty Person personates some imaginary odd Character who might say in sober earnest what he says for entertainment. The Wit lies in the ready conception of this Oddity, but the lively representation of it is Humor and the Oddity which is ascribed to an Imaginary Person is an object of Ridicule.[25]

Ridicule:

The most striking aspect of Campbell's conception of ridicule is the absence of the controversy over ridicule as a test of truth. Forty years after the publication of Shaftesbury's 'Essay on the Freedom of Wit and Humor' John Brown cogently attacked Shaftesbury's essay and was quickly attacked in turn. Brown's work was published in 1751, and the refutations in 1752 and 1753; the controversy was current just after Campbell was working on the material of the *Discourse*.[26] Nonetheless, he does not mention Shaftesbury or the idea of ridicule as a test of truth.

There are good reasons for Campbell to avoid this controversy. For one, at mid century the controversy had more to do with religion than with rhetoric; ridicule was used both by and against deists in particular.[27] For another, in the context of this controversy ridicule was seldom defined; it bordered on satire on the one hand and amiable comedy on the other. Primarily, however, ridicule in the service of truth is not something that fits Campbell's fundamental purpose, which is to explain eloquence in relation to mental operations. The end of ridicule is to move the will; its declamatory counterpart is vehemence.

Campbell in fact denies that ridicule can establish truth. He saw that ridicule, unlike vehemence, 'is not only confined to questions of less moment, But is fitter for refuting error than supporting truth, for restraining from wrong conduct than exciting to the practice of what is right' (*Philosophy of Rhetoric*, p.20). His additional restrictions make it clear that the power of ridicule is very limited. It cannot be levelled at falsity, only at absurdity. It does not strike vicious or criminal conduct, only silly or foolish action. And it certainly does not belong in religious contexts (p.26).

Neither Reid nor Skene uses Campbell's observations on ridicule to any great extent. When Reid later comes to consider wit and humour, he regards them as qualities of mind, not as means by which the mind can be affected.[28]

Campbell's observations on wit, humour, and ridicule are not particularly new. In fact they are quite conservative. Their attraction to the Philosophical Society members lay in their completion of the new system, not in anything intrinsically novel or valuable in their content. In subsequent Discourses, Campbell was able to overcome the tendency to generate neat schemes and to fill them mechanically, but at this early point he needed to be certain he was correct. His listeners, too, were impressed with the system, as well they might be. Campbell's analysis of rhetoric as a system consistently related discourse—all kinds of discourse—to mental operations. It initiated quite satisfactorily the activity of the Society, whose collegial success was fundamental to the Aberdeen Enlightenment.

Notes

1. Minutes of the Aberdeen Philosophical Society, AUL, MS 539/2; Papers of Thomas Gordon, AUL, MS 3107/1/1; *The Literary Essays of David Skene*, AUL, MS 475; The Birkwood Collection of the manuscripts of Thomas Reid, AUL, MS 2131/8/I/2-8/I/14 (Lectures on Eloquence).
2. Minutes of the Aberdeen Philosophical Society, AUL, MS 539, 539/2, 12 January 1758.
3. George Skene Keith, 'Some Account of the Life and Writings of George Campbell', prefaced to *Lectures on Ecclesiastical History ... by the Late George Campbell, D.D., Principal of Marischal College, Aberdeen* (London, Printed for J. Johnson, St. Paul's Church-yard, and A. Brown, Aberdeen, by Bye and Law, St. John's Square, Clerkenwell, 1808).

4. Campbell, 'Lecture V' [On Pulpit Eloquence], *Lectures on Ecclesiastical History*, pp.348-49.
5. This outline is found in Campbell's fifth lecture on pulpit eloquence (p.350) and in Gerard's *The Pastoral Care by the Late Alexander Gerard... Published by his Son and Successor, Gilbert Gerard, D.D.* (London, Printed for T. Cadell Jun. and W. Davies, in the Strand; and A. Brown, at Aberdeen, 1799), p.241.
6. John Ramsay of Ochtertyre, *Scotland and Scotsmen in the Eighteenth Century. From the MSS. of John Ramsay, Esq. of Ochtertyre*, ed. Alexander Allardyce, 2 vols (Edinburgh and London, William Blackwood and Sons, 1888), vol.I, p.485.
7. *The Philosophy of Rhetoric*, 2 vols (London, Printed for W. Strahan; and T. Cadell, in the Strand, and W. Creech at Edinburgh, 1776), vol.I, 1 [iii]-iv. Subsequent references will cite Lloyd F. Bitzer's edition of *The Philosophy of Rhetoric* (Carbondale, Southern Illinois U.P., 1963).
8. *The Character of a Minister of the Gospel as a Teacher and Pattern. A Sermon Preached before the Synod of Aberdeen at Aberdeen, April 7, 1752, by George Campbell, M.A., Minister at Banchory Ternan* (Aberdeen, Printed by James Chalmers, 1752).
9. Minutes, AUL, MS 539, 25 January 1758.
10. Gordon, AUL, MS 3107/1/1. Gordon's title is 'Eloquence defined, its various species exhibited, with their different end & criteria respectively'.
11. Skene, 'Of Witt & Humour', AUL, MS 475, p.1. This comment is one of the few instances I have found in which one member comments on the work of another.
12. Skene, AUL, MS 475, pp.301-14.
13. The meeting of 8 March was unusually full. The Society balloted for three new members and arranged for them to be notified of their election. Campbell read his Discourse. The Society debated the sixth Question and heard an abstract of the conversation on the first Question. Given this business, it is possible that Campbell read only the first part of his prepared Discourse, making the second part available to those who wanted to read it.
14. James Beattie, *Essays* (Edinburgh, Printed for William Creech, 1776), p.587. (Facsimile, New York, Garland Publishing Inc., 1971). Campbell, *Philosophy of Rhetoric*, p.xii.
15. Dugald Stewart, 'Biographical Memoires', prefaced to *The Works of Thomas Reid*, ed. Sir William Hamilton (Edinburgh, Maclean Stewart, and Co. London, Longman, Brown, Green and Longmans, 1846), p.10.
16. The most important for my purposes is MS 2131/8/I/5, which is primarily on wit. However, 2131/8/I/3 adds a quotation on perspicuity from *Philosophy of Rhetoric* to a loose sheet of notes from Quintilian.
17. Reid, AUL, MS 2131/8/I/5 f.1v.
18. One of Campbell's *Philosophy of Rhetoric* footnotes quotes an objection to Pope's definition of wit from Webb's *Remarks on the Beauties of Poetry*. Reid copies both the objection and the offending lines.
19. Henry Home, Lord Kames, *Elements of Criticism*, 6th edition (Edinburgh, Printed for John Bell and William Creech, 1785), pp. 382-3. (Facsimile, New York, Garland Publishing Inc., 1972). The work was first published in 1762.
20. See especially Vincent M. Bevilacqua, 'Philosophical influences in the development of English rhetorical theory: 1748 to 1783', *Proceedings of the Leeds Philosophical and Literary Society, Literary and Historical Section*, 12, No.6 (1968), pp. 191-215; W.W. Howell, 'George Campbell and the philosophical rhetoric of the New Learning', in *Eighteenth-Century British Logic and Rhetoric* (Princeton, Princeton U.P., 1971),pp.577-612; Lloyd Bitzer, Editor's Introduction to *The Philosophy of Rhetoric*.

21. Skene, AUL, MS 475, p.4.
22. Alexander Fraser Tytler, *Memoirs of the Life and Writings of the Honorable Henry Home of Kames,... Containing Sketches of the Progress of Literature and General Improvement in Scotland During the Greater Part of the Eighteenth Century* (Edinburgh, Printed for William Creech and T. Cadell and W. Davies, London, 1807), p.315.
23. Louis Cazamian, *The Development of English Humor*, Part I, 1930; Part II, 1952 (New York, AMS Press, 1965), p.408.
24. *Ibid.*, p.391, 410.
25. Reid, AUL, MS 2131/8/I/5 f.3v.
26. Anthony Ashley Cooper, third Earl of Shaftesbury, '*Sensus Communis*; an Essay on the Freedom of Wit and Humor', in *Characteristics of Men, Manners, Opinions, Times, etc.*, ed. John M. Robertson, 2 vols (Gloucester, Mass., Peter Smith, 1963), vol.1, pp.43-99. Originally published in 1711. John Brown, 'On Ridicule Considered as a Test of Truth', *Essays on the Characteristics* (1751); *Animadversions on Mr. Brown's Three Essays on the Characteristicks* (1752); [Charles Bulkley], *A Vindication of My Lord Shaftesbury, on the Subject of Ridicule. Being Remarks upon a Book, Intitled, Essays on the Characteristics* (1751); 'T.D. Remarks upon the Late Essays on the Characteristicks', *The London Magazine*, XXI (1751), pp.323-25; [Allan Ramsay], *An Essay on Ridicule* (London, 1753).
27. Thomas B. Gilmore, Jr, *The Eighteenth-Century Controversy Over Ridicule as A Test of Truth: A Reconsideration*, School of Arts and Sciences Research Papers, 25 (Georgia, Georgia State U.P., 1970), pp. 4, 10-13. This pamphlet is the source for the papers mentioned above.
28. AUL, MS 2131/6/I/IV.

31

Ideas of the Origin of Language in the Eighteenth Century: Johnson versus the Philosophers

Nalini Jain

University of Delhi

The question of the origin of language became an important subject for debate in the eighteenth century. Locke, for instance, though among the first to define the goal of eighteenth-century empiricist philosophers as the 'study[of]...the human understanding; not to discover its nature, but to know its operations'[1] felt compelled to give an answer to this vexed question. As he was in no way able to account for the origin of language from mere 'sensation' and 'reflection' which, he had declared, were the source of all human knowledge, he said resignedly, in terminology that is alien to the spirit of his *Essay*:

> God having designed Man for a sociable Creature, made him not only with an inclination, and under a necessity to have fellowship with those of his own kind; but furnished him also with Language, which was to be the great Instrument, and common Tye of Society.[2]

When Condillac wrote his *Essay on the Origin of Human Knowledge* (1746) as a supplement to Locke's *Essay Concerning Human Understanding* his aim was to 'take notice of his [Locke's] neglects and omissions' especially regarding the origin of language or 'concerning the manner of acquiring the habit of the operations of the mind, which indeed was the occasion of this Supplement'.[3] The inclusion of the word 'origin' in Condillac's title indicates the difference in emphasis. But once again, when questioned about the 'nature' of this faculty of 'consciousness' that enables the '*tabula rasa*' to create signs Condillac resignedly remarked:

> But if anyone should ask me how that chain itself [repeated consciousness or habit of the operations in the mind] can be formed by attention, I answer, that the reason thereof is to be found only in the nature of the soul and body.[4]

Later in the *Essay* Condillac quotes approvingly the Biblical account of the origin of language from the second volume of Warburton's *Divine Legation*: 'This whole observation seems to me very judicious'.[5] But he could not with confidence adhere to the Biblical account. He felt compelled to demonstrate the origin of language as a true philosopher according to the course of nature:

> I do not think it sufficient for a philosopher to say a thing was effected by extraordinary means, but judge it to be also incumbent upon him to explain how it could have happened according to the ordinary course of nature.[6]

Of course well before Condillac wrestled with the subject, Bernard de Mandeville, unplagued by doubts, had expressed an 'evolutionist' view of the origin of language in his *Fable of the Bees* (1728). Considered the first explicit account of the halting and indirect evolution of language, Mandeville's statement needs to be quoted in full:

> From what we see in children that are backward with their Tongues, we have reason to think, that a wild Pair would make themselves intelligible to others by Signs and Gestures, before they would attempt it by Sounds: But when they lived together for many years, it is very probable, that for the Things they were most conversant with they would find out Sounds, to stir up in each other the Ideas of such Things, when they were out of Sight; these Sounds they would communicate to their young ones; and the longer they lived together the greater Variety of Sounds they would invent as well for Actions as the Things themselves...It is impossible, but some of these young ones would, either by Accident or Design, make use of this superior Aptitude of the Organs at one time or other; ...and this must have been the Origin of all Languages, and Speech itself.[7]

In broad terms Mandeville's account would have been acceptable to Rousseau, Adam Smith and Monboddo. Finally Condillac too threw himself into the evolutionist camp and pointed to the natural cries of two wandering children, 'one male, and the other female' as the source of language.[8]

The 'naturalistic' evolution of language posits an evolution from the natural cries of pain and pleasure to the artificial signs of which language is composed. Differences among the evolutionists would arise on the question of which parts of speech were first created. There were variations in the 'naturalistic' explanation depending on the view of man held by the individual thinker. Rousseau, for instance, held that the initial cries and gestures would be signs of passion, perhaps even of love.[9] Others with a less elevated view of primitive man accorded to these gestures and cries 'need-fulfilment' as the aim and end. According to whether the thinker saw primitive man as a 'noble savage' or 'fallen Adam' he interpreted these early utterances to be outbursts of love and emotional self-expression, or as sounds that drew attention to, and called for, the fulfilment of physical needs. Despite these differences the evolutionist position dominated the century. It created, however, more problems than it solved. Was society in existence before the medium of communication, that is, language, was realised? If not, how did the medium come to be realised? The generally accepted answer would be that there was some social organisation based on natural cries and gestures. More important was the question, of whether man was 'rational' before language, and further, whether he could have developed language without being rational. Rousseau had posed some of these problems in his *Discourse on Inequality among Men*.[10] But it did not need a philosopher to raise the questions. In 1721, even before Mandeville's writing on the subject, Tamworth Reresby, son of Sir John Reresby of Yorkshire, in *A Miscellany of Ingenious Thoughts and Reflections* had asked 'which way could they, who knew not how to speak, agree amongst themselves about Words, whereby to render themselves intelligible?'[11] Reresby pointed out that 'there is little Appearance of Reason in [the] supposition' that men who 'had...at first no Use of Speech amongst them...Judg'd it...proper to make Use of Signs of Voice and Sound, to explain themselves,...and so by degrees agreed to compose a Language'.[12] As late as 1783 Hugh Blair reiterated these doubts.[13] A major difficulty lay in accounting for the point of transition between language as a response to natural and environmental stimuli, and language as a complex system of signs which offered man a sense of choice and purpose. The blurring of the distinction between man and animal was a source of grave concern to James Harris and James Beattie, amongst others, who both quote Aristotle on the subject.[14] As Herder said with regard to the explanations of Condillac and Rousseau, 'the former turned animals into men and the latter men into animals'.[15]

There is little doubt that Johnson was familiar with the explanations of the evolutionists, and with the difficulties posed by their view. He had been 'a great reader of Mandeville'[16] in his youth and referred to him as his 'old tutor'.[17] He had been impressed with the *Fable of the Bees* which he considered 'the work of a thinking man' though he was always anxious to condemn its morality.[18] Boswell records his familiarity with Rousseau whom he once called a 'rascal'.[19] Adam Smith was known to him. And in a letter to Mrs Thrale he mentioned having met Lord Monboddo and referred to his 'strange book about the origin of Language in which he traces Monkeys upto Men'.[20] It was with an awareness of the thought and writing of all the major figures in a well-worn controversy that Johnson argued against the idea that wandering children created language. Johnson's comment on the question has been strangely neglected, perhaps because of its conversational tone; it is, however, a reasoned statement that takes into account all the half-baked philosophical explanations that followed Locke's calculated evasion of the question. In bold and self-assured contrast to the contemporary philosophers Johnson asserts the divine origin of language. He equates the origin of language with the origin of man and thus makes it central to the human consciousness:

> It must have come by inspiration. A thousand, nay, a million of children could not invent a language. While the organs are pliable there is not understanding enough to form a language; by the time there is understanding enough, the organs are become stiff. ...When I maintain that language must have come by inspiration, I do not mean that inspiration is required for Rhetorick, and all the beauties of language; for when man once has language, we can conceive that he may gradually form modifications of it. I mean only that inspiration seems to

> me to be necessary to give man the faculty of speech; to inform him that he may
> have speech; which I think he could no more find out without inspiration, than
> cows or hogs would think of such a faculty.[21]

Johnson's is a vigorous rebuttal of the evolutionists: he uses the word 'inspiration' four times in a short comment. For Johnson man is not only inherently rational but 'ordained' to be united with his fellow beings. The evolutionists predicted an age when man was a non-rational, non-communicating creature, except perhaps on the level of the sexual instinct; hence their repeated image of two children, 'one male, and the other female'. Johnson does not deny progress in language as in other aspects of human life. But he does not temporalise the birth of language, its original conception: 'I mean only that inspiration seems to me to be necessary to give man the faculty of speech; to inform him that he may have speech'. He offers an imaginative apprehension of the point at which man could 'have' language, a point at which the understanding and the organs of speech were in perfect balance—a perfect and correct balance between body and soul which paralleled the original creation.

Perhaps it is more important to distinguish Johnson's views from those of Herder, for the distinction between them is fine, and with Herder's emphasis on human rationality, easily overlooked. The central difference is that while Herder emphasises rationality Johnson emphasises a moral awareness as the human urge that is coeval with language. Hence, while Herder 'discovers' language inherent in man's rational nature Johnson unequivocally assigns to it a divine origin. In his prize essay of 1769 Herder set out to explain how man was by nature a creature different from animals. Human beings are devoid of sharp concentrated instincts by which animals realise themselves, albeit in a narrow sphere. Thus the bee attains 'beeness' in the construct of its perfect hexagonal cell; the spider attains self-expression in the geometric complexity and perfection of its web. But man:

> since he does not fall blindly in any particular spot and does not lie blind in it,
> he learns to stand free, to find for himself a sphere of self-reflection, and seek his
> reflection in himself. No longer an infallible machine in the hands of nature, he
> himself becomes a purpose and objective of his efforts.[22]

Man, therefore, is his own subject. He realises himself as he grows to understand his relationship with the external world and is able to organise it according to his own inner make-up. This understanding is what Herder calls 'reflection' or the agreement of man's soul with itself:

> Man manifests reflection when the force of his soul acts in such freedom, that,
> in the vast ocean of sensations which permeates it through all the channels of
> the senses, it can, if I may say so, single out one way, arrest it, concentrate its
> attention on it, and be conscious of being attentive.[23]

This complex process involving simultaneously a response to the *sensorium commune*; a selection from it; and a knowing concentration on the selected symbol that is the product of a single sense, but carries with it the complex idea, is the process of human reason:

> For...reason is not a separate and singly acting power but is an orientation of all powers and as such a thing peculiar to his species, then man must have it in the first state in which he is man.[24]

It is the power of reason that enables man to 'see' the whole and to concentrate on the 'distinguishing mark', by way of which he can direct his concentration, and hence it is that man must 'discover' language because he is essentially rational: 'Language would become as essential to man as it is to him that he is man'.[25] Herder internalises language deep into the human psyche: 'A human soul could [not] be what it is and not, by that fact alone...be led to invent language'.[26] At the core of Herder's analysis lies the idea that 'the recognition of a thing' is the same as 'the naming of it: for deep in the soul the two actions are one'.[27] In his prize essay Herder was confident that man's 'ability to invent language for himself had been demonstrated to such an extent that one cannot doubt it for one moment if he does not deny man's reason'.[28] There is, however, an incompleteness about Herder's explanation, which in fact lends itself to both 'human' and 'divine' interpretations. This he recognised when in later life under different stimuli he so reinterpreted himself.[29]

The difference in emphasis between Johnson and Herder is important. The crux of the distinction lies in the difference in their concepts of reason. Herder would have defined man as a 'rational animal'; Burke's phrase 'religious animal' is closer to Johnson's conception. When Herder argues that:

> it is not possible that gaps and wants should be the distinctive trait of the human species; else nature was to man the most cruel step-mother, while to every insect she was the most loving mother. To every insect she gave whatever and however much it needed...In man everything is in the greatest disproportion—his sense and his needs, his powers and the sphere of endeavour awaiting him, his organs and his language. We must be missing a certain intermediate link to calculate such disparate parts in the proportion.[30]

He makes a case for human reason to provide the missing 'intermediate link'. So too Johnson's Rasselas notes the 'difference between man and all the rest of animal creation' and concludes that man, unlike animals 'has surely...some desires distinct from sense which must be satisfied before he can be happy'.[31] But when Johnson elaborates the nature of this essential difference between man and beast he defines human consciousness as essentially moral:

> 'Ye' said he 'are happy, and need not envy me that walk thus among you burthened with myself; nor do I, ye gentle beings, envy your felicity, for it is not the felicity of man. I have many distresses from which ye are free; I fear pain when I do not feel it; I sometimes shrink at evils recollected, and sometimes start at evils anticipated: surely the equity of providence has balanced peculiar sufferings with peculiar enjoyments.[32]

In Johnson's thought the notion of recollection and anticipation is inextricably linked with the moral sense of good and evil. In *Rasselas* the quest for a happiness peculiar to man and the idea of divine justice or the 'equity of providence' is worked up to the moral and religious knowledge of the immortality of the soul. It is thus that Johnson and Herder approach the problem of human nature and language from different points of view.

It becomes apparent, then, that Johnson is separated by a fundamental gulf from the philosophers of his age on the question of the origin of language. His affinities lie, rather, with the men of letters of the day, Reresby, Blair,[33] and especially James Beattie whom he probably influenced:

> [It] is clear...Speech, if invented at all, must have been invented either by children, who were incapable of invention, or by men, who were incapable of speech. And therefore reason, as well as history, intimates that mankind in all ages must have been speaking animals; the young having constantly acquired this art by imitating those who were elder. And we may warrantably suppose, that our first parents must have received it by immediate inspiration.[34]

Notes

1. Etienne Bonnot de Condillac, *An Essay on the Origin of Human Knowledge* (1746) translated by Thomas Nugent (1756; New York, Scholar, 1971), pp.5-6.
2. John Locke, *An Essay Concerning Human Understanding* (1690), ed. P.. Nidditch (Oxford, Clarendon Press, 1975), p.402.
3. Thomas Nugent, 'The Translator's Preface' to Condillac, p.ix.
4. Condillac, p.37.
5. *Ibid*, p.171.
6. *Ibid*.
7. Bernard de Mandeville, *The Fable of the Bees* (1728), ed. F.B. Kaye, 2 vols (Oxford, Clarendon Press, 1924), vol.II, pp.287-88.
8. Jean-Jacques Rousseau, *Essay on the Origin of Languages* (1750?), translated by J. Moran and A. Gode, in *On the Origin of Language* (New York, F.Ungar, 1966), pp.5-6. Adam Smith, *Considerations Concerning the First Formation of Languages* (1761), *The Early Writings of Adam Smith*, ed. J.D. Lindgren (New Jersey, Kelley, 1967), p.225. James Burnet (Lord Monboddo), *Of the Origin and Progress of Language*, 6 vols (Edinburgh, J. Balfour, 1773-92), vol.I, pp.318-19. Condillac, p.169.
9. Rousseau, *Essay on the Origin of Languages*, pp.11-12.
10. Jean-Jacques Rousseau, *Discourse on the Origin and Foundations of Inequality Among Men* (1750), in *The First and Second Discourses*, translated by J.R. Masters, ed. R.D. Masters (reprinted New York, St Martin's Press, 1964), pp.120-22.
11. Tamworth Reresby, *A Miscellany of Ingenious Thoughts and Reflections* (London, S. Chapman, 1721), pp.1-2.
12 *Ibid*, p.1.
13. Hugh Blair, *Lectures on Rhetoric and Belles Lettres*, 3 vols (London, W. Strahan, T. Cadell, 1783), vol.I, p.100.
14. James Harris, *Three Treatises* (1744), p.293. James Beattie, *Dissertations, Moral and Critical*, 2 vols (London, W. Strachan, T. Cadell, 1783), vol.I, p.289.

15. G. Herder, *Essay on the Origin of Language* (1772), in Moran and Gode.
16. *Johnsonian Miscellanies*, ed. G.B. Hill, 2 vols (Oxford, Clarendon Press, 1897), vol.I, p. 207.
17. *Ibid.*, p.268.
18. *Ibid.*
19. James Boswell, *Life of Johnson*, eds G.B. Hill and L.F. Powell, 6 vols (Oxford, Clarendon Press, 1934), vol.II, p.11.
20. Samuel Johnson, *The Letters*, ed. R.W. Chapman (Oxford, Clarendon Press, 1952), vol.I, p.321.
21. Boswell, *Life of Johnson*, vol.IV, p.207.
22. Herder, p.109.
23. *Ibid.*, p.115.
24. *Ibid.*, p.112.
25. *Ibid.*, p.108.
26. *Ibid.*, p.119.
27. *Ibid.*, p.127.
28. *Ibid.*, p.165.
29. H. Stam, *Inquiries into the Origin of Language* (New York, Harper and Row, 1976), p.108.
30. Herder, p.108.
31. Samuel Johnson, *Rasselas*, in *Rasselas and Essays*, ed. Charles Peake (London, Routledge and Kegan Paul, reprinted 1969), pp.4-5.
32. *Ibid.*, p.5.
33. Reresby, pp.3-4. Blair, vol.I, p.101.
34. Beattie, vol.I, pp.379-80.

32

Scholar-Printers of the Scottish Enlightenment, 1740-1800

R.H. Carnie

University of Calgary

In order to examine the assertion that there were in Scotland, during the Enlightenment period, a number of printing and publishing firms to whom the name 'scholar-printers' might be legitimately applied, this paper considers the history and known output of four outstanding Scottish printing and publishing firms of the period 1740 to 1800. Four firms were chosen, one in each of Scotland's university towns—Edinburgh, Glasgow, Aberdeen and St Andrews—both to stress the connexion between scholarly printing and publishing and the academy, and to underline the difficulties that a provincial location created for printers and publishers outside Edinburgh. These self-imposed limitations make it impossible to do justice to the claims of other firms, such as Balfour and Smellie of Edinburgh, or Robert Urie and Co. of Glasgow, to be considered 'scholar-printers', claims which are certainly not invalidated by the decision to concentrate on their chief rivals or successors. The time-limitation, after 1740, also excludes such people as the learned Thomas Ruddiman, who was conjoint University Printer at Edinburgh from 1728 to 1754, who is the only Scottish printer about whom two full-length studies have been written (by George Chalmers and Douglas Duncan), and Robert Freebairn, the Jacobite printer whose spell as Queen's Printer, begun in 1711, was sadly interrupted by the 1715 Rebellion and his brief and inglorious career as the Pretender's Printer.[1] Both of these men could also successfully lay claim to the appellation 'scholar-printer', and are excluded here merely because they pre-date the major period of the Scottish Enlightenment.

The four firms chosen are: Hamilton, Balfour and Neill of Edinburgh; Robert and Andrew Foulis of Glasgow; the Morisons of St Andrews; and the Chalmers family of Aberdeen.

1. Hamilton, Balfour and Neill of Edinburgh's co-partnership was estab-

lished in 1749. Neill was the printer, and Hamilton and Balfour the book-seller/publishers.

The firm was made Printer to the University in 1754, and the partnership lasted until the retirement of Hamilton and Balfour in 1766. The history of this firm underlines the dual roles played by talent on the one hand, and influence and patronage on the other, in commercial and social advancement in eighteenth-century Scotland. John Balfour was a member of an influential family—the Balfours of Pilrig—and learnt early in his career how to play the patronage game.[2] His partner, Gavin Hamilton, also had powerful con-nexions. John Balfour's brother was first Professor of Moral Philosophy, and then Professor of Public Law in the University of Edinburgh for a total of twenty-five years. Gavin Hamilton's father had been both Professor of Div-inity and Principal of the University of Edinburgh before 1732. As Warren McDougall puts it in his excellent unpublished Ph.D. thesis on this firm—a piece of scholarship which deserves to see print:

> The verve and pugnacity of John Balfour proved useful when employed on behalf of family and firm. In 1754, for example, the Hamiltons & Balfours desired several pieces of Town Council patronage, so John Balfour was lobbed into action like a grenade (he was elected a Merchant Councillor) while Gavin Ham-ilton's family marshalled the political forces outside. The strategy worked—the Town Council appointed Robert Hamilton, Professor of Divinity at Edinburgh University, James Balfour Professor of Moral Philosophy, and Hamilton & Balfour Printers to the University and City.[3]

Gavin Hamilton's career was a varied one for a printer and bookseller. He was admitted burgess and guild brother as a cloth-merchant in 1722, and did not turn bookseller until 1729, combining his early bookselling career with matriculation in Adam Watt's humanity class. He married Helen Balfour of Pilrig, and started an extensive career in local politics, was a merchant coun-cillor, and served on numerous occasions as a baillie or city magistrate. A staunch Whig, he was forced to leave Edinburgh during the occupation by Prince Charles, and worked on the government side. He was part of the group that engineered the election of his nephew, William Cleghorn, to the Chair of Moral Philosophy in Edinburgh in the 1740s—the group the defeated candidate, David Hume, called 'a pack of scoundrels'. Hamilton was also the owner, from 1752 onwards, of John's coffee-house on the north-east side of Parliament Close, a haunt of many of the authors published by his firm, whose bookshop was just across the street from the coffee-house. From 1755 onwards, Hamilton owned and ran a papermill at Bogsmill near Colinton, and from 1761 he had a country estate there.[4]

Hamilton's career is about as far from the technicalities of the printing shop as that of any university printing patent holder could possibly be. He was essentially an entrepreneur, and like all good entrepreneurs, he and Balfour brought in professionals, in this case the house of Neill, to handle the technical, printing side of the business.

Patrick Neill, a native of Haddington, had learnt the printing trade in the

shop of Murray and Cochran, printers of the *Scots Magazine*. The agreement
with Neill was for the printing partnership only. Neill had no share in the
profits of the bookselling/publishing business, which was to last from 1749
to 1762.[5]

When Hamilton and Balfour got the city and university printing patent in
1754, succeeding Davidson and Ruddiman, they were required to set up a
separate printing-house within the college, and to supply the college library
with a free copy of each of the classics they printed. The minute of the
Town Council reveals the subtle use made by Hamilton and Balfour, in their
petition, of a combined appeal to nationalism, local pride and economic
gain:[6]

> observing what benefit might arise to the good town and the country if handsome
> editions of books that make a figure in this world were printed in this Burgh,
> [The petitioners] have been at considerable expense for obtaining everything
> proper for that purpose, and have published a variety of standard books in a
> manner they were happy to find had met with commendation even in foreign
> countries where printing has been long in perfection; that the petitioners animated
> with these successes have of late turned their thoughts towards publishing good
> editions of the Greek and Latin Classics, and were sensible that if the Council,
> as patrons of the University, would please bestow on them the office of printers
> to the University, as it has been enjoyed by others, they would be enabled to
> print these classics better, and furnish them at easier rates than they could
> otherwise do, and might save the importations thereof from foreign parts which
> would be of very great service to the country and keep much money at home.[7]

The claims made by the firm in this petition are substantiated by a consideration of their output, most of which is listed in McDougall's substantial
bibliographical list. They showed, like Urie of Glasgow, an early interest both
in selling and publishing French literature, and they published a substantial
number of legal, medical and scientific texts. A select list of their authors
would include Lord Hailes, Robert Wallace, Thomas Blacklock, John Home,
William Wilkie, James Macpherson and Alexander Carlyle—to say nothing
of three historians, William Maitland, David Hume and William Robertson.
When Hamilton & Balfour were made University Printers, medical and
scientific theses approved by the University appeared under their imprint.
They made good their promise to produce handsome editions of the classics
with a Virgil and a Sallust in 1755, a Phaedrus in 1757, and a prize-winning
Terence in 1758, which won the Edinburgh Society silver medal for fine
printing. Of the books printed in English carrying their imprint, one of
the most significant was the Edinburgh Philosophical Society's *Essays and
Observations, Physical and Literary*. They were also the publishers of the first
Edinburgh Review, in 1755.[8]

It is important to stress that the firm's principals were not only the printers
and publishers of these works. They were also an integral part of the intellectual society from which the works arose. Hamilton was Treasurer of the
Royal Infirmary, a director of the Edinburgh Assembly, a director of the
SSPCK; one of the managers of the Edinburgh Society for the Encouragement

of Arts, Sciences, Manufactures and Agriculture, and one of the Commissioners appointed for the improvement of streets and public buildings in Edinburgh. He was as much an Enlightenment figure as either the historian and editor, Lord Hailes, or the influential Principal Robertson. If Hamilton spent much less time in the bookselling shop or the printing-house than his counterparts in Glasgow, Aberdeen or St Andrews, or, for that matter, most bookseller/publishers in Edinburgh, he enhanced the public image of his profession in a very significant way.

    2.   My Glasgow example is, inevitably, the printing and publishing firm of Robert and Andrew Foulis, printers and publishers in Glasgow from 1741 to 1776 and University Printers from 1743 to the same year. The brothers had both been students at Glasgow University, and had received patronage from Francis Hutcheson and other members of the Glasgow professoriate. They had visited Europe in 1738, apparently with a view to qualifying themselves as tutors and teachers. Father Thomas Innes, Head of the Scots College of Paris, and one of their hosts in Paris, wrote about his young Protestant visitors:

> They set off chiefly for the Belles-Lettres, and seem to design to be Professors of that, in the University of Glasgow, or perhaps to be governors or tutors to young noblemen, for which last employment they seem to be very well cut out, in their own way, having very good parts and talents, very moderate, and making morality their chief study and application...taking for their guides, among the antients, Epictetus, Seneca, Cicero's Offices, among the moderns—de Cambray's (Fenelon's) works.[9]

All the authors listed here were later to be printed and published by the Foulis Brothers, who found their true careers as university printers and publishers.

    Andrew Foulis II inherited both the printing skills and the considerable debts of his father and uncle. He managed to hold on to his University appointment from 1778 to 1795 despite considerable hostility in the University Senate.[10] They resented the younger Foulis's indifference to University interests, and mistrusted, perhaps with some reason, his business abilities.[11]

    The Glasgow society which produced these talented printers was similar to that of Edinburgh—although on a smaller scale. Glasgow was the centre of the Virginia Trade, and some of the 'Tobacco Lords' were men of wealth and culture who studied commerce as a science. In the period 1740 to 1750, Provost Cochran of Glasgow had encouraged a club for discussing questions relating to trade and political economy, and it was local interest in the 'dismal science' that encouraged the Foulis brothers to publish a series of works on economics, such as Child's *A New Discourse on Trade*, John Law's *Proposals for a Council of Trade in Scotland*, and William Petty's *Political Arithmetic*— all in 1751.[12] But the abiding passions of the Foulis brothers were literature and the fine arts. With the wholesale authorial and editorial support of the University of Glasgow professoriate, the bulk of the Foulis Press output consisted of accurate and finely printed texts of the classics of Greek, Latin and English literature. Philip Gaskell's recently revised standard bibliography of the Foulis Press shows in its 780 entries the impressive range of the Foulis Press output, both with respect to diversity of subject area, fine paper quality, superior typography, and the occasional use of illustration. These qualities combined to place the Foulis Press in the first rank of British printing and publishing.

In both the Glasgow and the St Andrews text-book printing operations, there was a heavy emphasis on correctness, on the need to use reliable copytexts, and the desirability of stringent proof-correcting and cancellation procedures, leading to published texts which were as immaculate as possible.[13] It was the fame of this range of classics, from Homer down to Foulis's contemporary, Thomas Gray, which encouraged James Boswell, who published two of his own books at the Foulis Press, to dub the Foulis brothers 'The Elzevirs of Glasgow', inviting direct comparison with the Leiden family of scholar-printers of the previous century.

Robert Foulis's 1743 petition to the University of Glasgow[14] is a much more modest document than that of Hamilton, Balfour and Neill to the Edinburgh Town Council. It was addressed to the Rector, to the Principal, to the Dean of Faculty and to the other professors in the University of Glasgow:

> The said Robert Foulis hath provided himself with types both Greek and Latin of such exactness & beauty that he can execute printing work in either Language, in such a manner as will be no Dishonour to one who bears the character of University-Printer, & of this he is ready to exhibit Specimens: He therefore humbly petitions that he may be admitted as printer to the University of Glasgow.

On the same day the University, 'having seen specimens of his printing and found it such as he deserves very well to be encouraged, did chuse the said Robert Foulis into the office of University Printer'. It was a condition of the appointment that Foulis would not use the designation of University Printer in any books 'excepting those of antient authors' without permission from the University.

The Foulis Press was also fortunate in that it had first call on the fine Roman and Greek types cast by the Wilsons in their Glasgow foundry, although these types were soon made available to other printers all over Scotland.[15] Despite the Edinburgh location of the aforementioned Edinburgh Society for the Encouragement of Arts, Sciences, Manufactures and Agriculture, the Foulis Press of Glasgow was to win all the silver medals given for printing by that Society, with the solitary exception of that won by Hamilton and Balfour with their 1758 Terence, produced under the superintendence of their brilliant journeyman, William Smellie.[16] The Foulis prizewinners included a Callimachus in 1755; a Horace in 1756; and the impressive folio Homer in 1756 and 1757.[17]

3. St Andrews has a much less comprehensive history as a source of learned printing and publishing in the Enlightenment period. It had but one printer/publisher in the eighteenth century, and that at the very end. The Morison family were University Printers in St Andrews from 1796 to 1800

only, although the firm's main establishment at Perth prospered from the 1770s to the 1800s.[18] I have been able to trace only slim connexions between this family of Perth printers and the University of St Andrews. Robert Morison, bookseller and postmaster in Perth, the founder of the firm, had married one Margaret Russell, daughter of the minister at Forgan in Fife. Margaret Russell's mother was Elizabeth Tullideph, cousin of that Thomas Tullideph who was first Professor of Divinity at St Andrews, and later Principal of United College from 1747 to 1777.[19] It may be that Robert and James Morison, the talented sons of Robert Morison, postmaster, owed their university appointment entirely to their known merits as printers of English and Scottish literature. I doubt it, however. As Roger Emerson put it in his paper, 'The Scottish professoriate in the eighteenth century': 'In most university appointments, idealism, jobbery, friendship and malice, merit and birth all played a part.' I am sure this applied to university printers as well as to professors.

Despite the Morisons' apparent success as University Printers, it is worth noting that their obvious successor as Printer in St Andrews, Francis Ray, a printer in Edinburgh, St Andrews and Dundee from 1793 to 1811, and a former journeyman employed by the Morisons, preferred to move his own printing shop from St Andrews to the larger, neighbouring town of Dundee. A surviving production from Ray's own press in St Andrews—John Buddo's *Progress of Education and Manners* (1801)—attracted only 26 out of 144 known subscribers for 173 copies, from St Andrews and its university. It is hardly surprising that Alexander Smellie, the son of the erudite William Smellie, is recorded in St Andrews University archives as having turned down an offer of the post of University Printer in St Andrews in 1803. The initial appointment of James Morison as University Printer in St Andrews may well have been 'faute de mieux' arising out of adverse market conditions failing to attract a more prominent printer from Edinburgh or Glasgow. The limited size of the bookselling market, in a provincial burgh whose ancient university was just recovering from a period of acute intellectual and economic depression, combined with the reality of increased delivery costs to other, larger markets, may well explain the short career of James Morison as University Printer.

Other factors are attested by James Morison's unpublished letters to the banker, Sir William Forbes. The House of Morison had seriously over-extended itself financially by attempting to produce in its Perth office, that dream of many scholar-printers—an encyclopedia. The 18-volume *Encyclopedia Perthensis*, issued in parts, was finally finished in 1806, but at the cost of James Morison's physical health, and the ruination of his firm's finances. James Morison wrote to another (unidentified) potential backer on 13 December 1798:

I have the honour of being Printer to the St Andrews University, where I am printing a very elegant set of Classics—cura John Hunter, LL.D...Naturally of an active disposition, I have for near twenty years, bustled through a good deal of business in my line—and not without tolerable success, notwithstanding the present application.[20]

Morison goes on to admit that he had imprudently embarked on several heavy undertakings in addition to the *Encyclopedia Perthensis*, which was itself a constant drain of over £100 a month. The production costs of his 'numbers' edition of Shakespeare had been over £1,000 and the 3000 copies he had produced of a Scottish *Gazeteer* had cost him even more. Morison blames an illness, and his consequent inability to attend to spring sales, for his financial problems, but the core problem was the ambitious over-extension of his publication programme, undertaken from a physical situation in Perth relatively remote from the larger book-buying markets. Nevertheless, the scholarly output of the St Andrews Press was not contemptible. Editions of Virgil, Sallust and Horace, all edited by John Hunter, Professor of Humanity, would surely have challenged the work of the younger Foulis for the Edinburgh silver medals, had that desirable scheme of premiums survived. The attractive illustrated editions of Martine, and Colvil and a presumably pirated edition of Cowper, all produced at the St Andrews printing-office, make an agreeable supplement to the major series of Scottish poets produced by Morison at their main office in Perth.[21] A pamphlet on Perth publishing, produced 25 years ago, accurately summed up the modest achievement of the Morison Press:

> It never pretended to the mass of scholarly work which should issue from a University Press. It never produced anything in folio, and only a few volumes in quarto. Most of the items...are unpretentious little 8vo and 12mo volumes, pleasantly printed in readable type, decorated by the delightful and generous use of ornament in the shape of vignettes and engraved plates.[22]

4.   Aberdeen and its university had a continuous printing and publishing history in the eighteenth century. The Aberdeen University printing appointment was associated with that of the City, which in itself may have induced a higher degree of commercial conservatism in printing and publishing enterprise than in Glasgow or St Andrews. Although its hinterland was greater in size, and the city itself was larger, Aberdeen shared St Andrews's problems of a relatively small local market, and high costs of distribution to the Edinburgh and London booksellers. Aberdeen had, nevertheless, managed to support a continuous line of printer/publishers in both the seventeenth and eighteenth centuries.[23] A complete sequence of minutes relating to appointments as Town and University Printer can be found in the Aberdeen Town Council minute books. When Forbes the younger's widow retired as Town and University Printer in 1710, she was succeeded by her son-in-law, James Nicoll; who was, in his turn, succeeded by the Chalmers dynasty, starting with James Chalmers I, who became printer to the town and university in 1736, (and whose father just happened to be Professor of Divinity in Marischal College). James Chalmers II, a Marischal College graduate, was Town and University Printer until 1810. He had trained in his craft with

printing firms in London and Cambridge, and produced output of excellent technical quality. James Chalmers II was succeeded by his son, David, a student under Beattie at Marischal College in 1794.[24]

Aberdeen, unlike St Andrews, had an active cultural and intellectual life. It was James Chalmers I who brought Andrew Tait, musician, to Aberdeen to help in the establishment of the Aberdeen Musical Society in 1748, a society which consolidated the long-standing pursuit of musical pleasure by the citizens and academics of Aberdeen. James Beattie in his *Day-Book*, describes James Chalmers II as a moral, genial man, proficient in languages.[25]

In a paper delivered in Aberdeen, some knowledge of the Aberdeen Philosophical Society, and its major contribution, through Gerard, Campbell, Reid and Beattie, to the study of aesthetics and to the philosophy of Common Sense, has been taken for granted. Despite this Aberdeen Enlightenment, it is surprising to find, through a study of its output, that the Chalmers Press was not an outstanding scholarly press in the sense that the Edinburgh, Glasgow and St Andrews examples were. In one of the few articles on Aberdeen printing and publishing, William MacDonald noted that the Chalmers Press was recognised as their official printers by the Town Council, the two colleges and the Commissioners of Supply for the County. While not a monopoly, the Chalmers business was in such a flourishing financial condition that its owners apparently saw little need for the kind of innovative enterprise displayed by Robert Foulis and James Morison. When one reviews the solid, well-printed output of the Aberdeen Press from 1740 to 1800, as was done recently in terms of the British Library holdings, (ESTC), some surprising characteristics come to light. Local history and sermons by local authors dominate the lists, which is no great surprise. There are, however, only limited examples of edited versions of the major classics, and these, mostly of Plato, come from the press of Chalmers's short-lived rivals, Douglass and Murray. The Aberdeen University philosophers consistently printed their major works in Edinburgh and/or London. Gerard and Campbell, for example, printed at the Chalmers Press only sermons addressed to Aberdeen audiences, and not their major works. Beattie had Chalmers print his list of Scoticisms, and lecture notes for student use. Beattie paid for the paper, and Chalmers for the printing of Ross's Scottish poems.[26] Where Aberdeen editions of classics of English and Scottish literature existed, they were generally from the presses of Chalmers's chief rivals—Francis Douglass or John Boyle. Books related to the 'improving' movement, and chiefly directed at Aberdeenshire lairds, also tended to come from Chalmers's rivals. There may be a political dimension here, as well as economic and social considerations. Chalmers was a Whig in a society which had strong Episcopalian and Jacobite leanings. Nevertheless, the failure of the Aberdeen philosophers and theologians to use their own university press for their major publications, and to enjoy the obvious convenience of a local press for proof-reading and editorial revision, remains a partial puzzle. The emphasis by Chalmers on newspaper and magazine printing may be one answer; the desire of the Aberdeen philosophers to have their work known outside the local hinterland is obviously another. The contrast with Glasgow is striking.

The four presses I have dealt with have a number of features in common apart from the facts that they operated in university towns, and directed some of their output at scholarly markets. They all participated as well in purely commercial printing and publishing activities, in addition to their university commitments. The Chalmers firm was the owner of a thriving periodical, *The Aberdeen Journal*, ran book auctions, and did a good deal of jobbing printing for the country booksellers and for the chapbook market. The Foulis brothers also had a stake in a Glasgow newspaper until 1760—*The Glasgow Courant*.[27] Although the Foulis name does not appear in the imprint, the *Courant* was printed in their printing shop, and was their chief medium for book advertisements. The Morisons did not have a newspaper, but they published a series of short-lived magazines, which carried advertisements on their covers.[28] They were deeply involved in the 'numbers' trade, printing large books in 4d or 6d parts, or books in series, for the lower end of the book-buying market. The lack of rival printers of any staying power gave the Morisons a near monopoly on local printing in the Perth area. Hamilton, Balfour & Neill, on the other hand, operated their extensive business in the intensely competitive printing and publishing world of metropolitan Edinburgh, which encouraged them actively to seek publishing business. The Foulis brothers' involvement in a Fine Arts Academy, and in a peat moss reclamation scheme, were enterprising, though hardly profitable, extensions of their entrepreneurial spirit.[29]

None of these firms were 'scholar-printers' in the exclusive sense of that name, as decisively and correctly associated with the growth of Renaissance learning in such European cities as Venice, Leipzig, Basle, Paris and Leiden. The Virgilius issued in Venice in 1501, and the Herodotus of 1502, are only two of the long series of octavo editions of Latin and Greek classics, prized both for their accuracy and their sober elegance, to come from the press of the Venetian printer, Aldus Manutius (1495-1519), the first scholar-printer. To take another example from the end of the sixteenth century—1583 to be exact—Louis Elzevir, who had learned his trade with Plantin in Antwerp, set up a bookseller's shop in Leiden. By 1587, he had been given permission to build a shop in the grounds of the university. The Elzevir business continued in Leiden until about 1702; it expanded to The Hague, Amsterdam and Utrecht, and produced over 5,000 books.[30] The most highly praised part of this extra-ordinary output was the series of neat, clearly printed, vellum-bound editions of French and Latin classics of pocket book size (12mo and under). On the evidence of surviving sale catalogues, (e.g. Dumfries House, 7-9) Scottish country house libraries in the first half of the eighteenth century had their due meed of 8vo Aldines and 12mo Elzevirs, and proud parents whose sons were going off to study at the Scottish universities would often make a parting gift of an Elzevir or similar production. The impact of the European scholar-printers on Scottish culture was considerable and their prestige enormous.

In 1817, the Morisons of Perth sold off the books and engravings from the library of William Stewart of Spoutwells, from a 380-page catalogue. The books are listed by short title, and by author and size—but David Morison's scholarly annotations stress the continuity of fine printing and exact scholarship when dealing with the products of both Scottish and European presses. Comments such as that on an Aulus Gellius (Paris, 1521) 'A very rare volume from the celebrated press of Badius' (Spoutwells, 1) are frequent. A copy of Gray's *Poems* (Glasgow, Foulis, 1768) is described as 'one of the most elegant pieces of printing that the Glasgow Press, or any other press has ever produced'. Of his own uncle's 8vo edition of Goldsmith's *History of England* (Perth, 1792), David Morison exults: 'This work is beautifully printed on white wove post, and is considered one of the first productions of the Perth Press.' Morison's head-note on the Elzevir classics in this sale reads as follows: 'The Works published by the Elzevir family have been so long and justly celebrated for accuracy and beauty of typography, that their scarcity and value have become very great.'[31] This can be compared with Morison's head-note for a set of Foulis Press classics in the post-octavo size: 'long and justly celebrated on containing the Text of the Authors IMMACULATE, and printed in a style of neatness and beauty, excelling all other editions, not only in this country, but even those from the most celebrated Presses on the Continent'.[32]

These comparisons suggest that what can be found in the best eighteenth-century Scottish printing is both a conscious emulation of the European tradition of scholar-printers, and an extraordinarily successful imitation and extension of that tradition.

Notes

The present writer's substantial debts to the precise and detailed scholarship of Philip Gaskell, William MacDonald and Warren McDougall, as exhibited in their published and unpublished writings, and in their correspondence and conversation, are gratefully acknowledged.

1. George Chalmers, *The Life of Thomas Ruddiman* (London, 1794); Douglas Duncan, *Thomas Ruddiman: A Study in Scottish Scholarship*, (Edinburgh, Oliver and Boyd, 1965); W.J. Couper, 'The Rebel press at Perth in 1715', *Records of the Glasgow Bibliographical Society*, 7, pp.44-56.
2. C.B. Watson, 'Notes on the Balfours of Pilrig', MS in Edinburgh Public Library.
3. Warren McDougall, 'Gavin Hamilton, John Balfour and Patrick Neill: a study of publishing in Edinburgh in the eighteenth century' (University of Edinburgh, Ph.D thesis, 1974), p.5.
4. *Ibid.*, pp.10-31.
5. *Ibid.*, pp.17-83. Anon, *The History of the Firm of Neill & Company, Ltd.* (Edinburgh, Neill & Co., 1900).
6. A.R. Turnbull, 'Academiae typographus', *University of Edinburgh Gazette* (25 October 1959), pp.34-42. Warren McDougall, pp.150-54.
7. Warren McDougall, p.152.
8. *Ibid.*, pp.133-38 and following; A.K. Howard, 'Montesquieu, Voltaire and Rousseau in eighteenth-century Scotland', *The Bibliotheck*, 2 (2), pp.40-63.
9. David Murray, 'Robert and Andrew Foulis and the Glasgow Press', *Records of the Glasgow Bibliographical Society*, 2, pp.1-144. [NB. separate pagination from other items in volume.]

10. James MacLehose, *The Glasgow University Press, 1638-1931* (Glasgow, Glasgow U.P., 1931), pp.195-203.
11. R.H. Carnie, 'Andrew Foulis the Younger: some illustrative letters', *The Bibliotheck*, 6 (4), p.94. David Murray, 'Robert and Andrew Foulis and the Glasgow Press', pp.116-26.
12. David Murray, 'Robert and Andrew Foulis and the Glasgow Press', pp.27-28.
13. Philip Gaskell, *A Bibliography of the Foulis Press*, 2nd edition (Winchester, St Paul's Bibliographies, 1986), pp.462, 473. James Boswell, *Boswell's Life of Johnson*, ed. G.B. Hill, 5 vols (Oxford, Clarendon Press, 1887), vol.V, p.370.
14. Glasgow University Archives, Foulis file, MS 6307.
15. Philip Gaskell, *A Bibliography of the Foulis Press*, pp.29-49; 'The Early work of the Foulis Press and the Wilson foundry', *The Library*, 5th series, 7, pp.77-116, 149-77.
16. Brian Hillyard, 'The Edinburgh Society's silver medals for printing', *Papers of the Bibliographical Society of America*, 78(3), pp.295-319.
17. *Ibid.*
18. R.. Carnie, *Publishing in Perth before 1807* (Dundee, Abertay Historical Society, 1960), pp.18-20.
19. D.C. Smith, *The Historians of Perth* (Perth, John Christie, 1906), p.87. *Fasti Ecclesiae Scoticanae*, ed. Hew Scott, 8 vols (Edinburgh, Oliver & Boyd, 1915-50), vol.7 (1928), pp.413-14.
20. Durham University Library, Forbes MSS.
21. R.. Carnie, *Publishing in Perth before 1807*, pp.20, 29-38.
22. *Ibid.*, p.22.
23. Alexander Keith, *A Thousand Years of Aberdeen* (Aberdeen, AUP, 1972), pp.212-17, 358-59.
24. William R. MacDonald, 'Some aspects of printing and the book trade in Aberdeen', *The Hero as Printer*, ed. C.A. McLaren (Aberdeen, AUL, 1976). *James Beattie's Day Book*, ed. R.S. Walker (Aberdeen, Third Spalding Club, 1948), p.70.
25. *James Beattie's Day Book* p.20.
26. *Ibid.*, pp.70, 85, 213.
27. Philip Gaskell, *A Bibliography of the Foulis Press*, p.65.
28. R.. Carnie, *Publishing in Perth before 1807*, p.19.
29. James MacLehose, *The Glasgow University Press, 1638-1931*, pp.183-92; David Murray, 'Robert and Andrew Foulis and the Glasgow Press', pp.93-94.
30. A. Willems, *Les Elzevier: Histoire et annales typographiques*, (Brussels, 1880, reprinted Nieuwkhoop, 1962).
31. David Morison, *Catalogue of an extensive and valuable Collection of Books and Prints, chiefly old: Being the Entire Library of the late William Stewart, Esq. of Spoutwells, Perth*, (1817), p.275.
32. *Ibid.*, p.164.

33

Aberdeen, Imprints and the ESTC: Towards a Definitive Bibliography

Donald W. Nichol

Memorial University, St John's, Newfoundland

Printing in Aberdeen began in 1622, when some professors of Marischal College lured Edward Raban from St Andrews, though there had been earlier associations with Andrew Myllar's press in Edinburgh. As Alexander Keith points out in the introduction to his history of Aberdeen University Press:

> Aberdeen's connection with printing goes back a full century beyond [Raban's] time...Of the only two productions of the first Scottish press, that of Andro Myllar established in 1507 in Edinburgh, one is by John Vaus, first professor of humanity in King's College, Aberdeen. The following year in partnership with Walter Chepman, Myllar printed, amongst other books, *The Porteous of Noblenes* by a Burgess of Aberdeen named Andrew Cadiou, MA of Paris, who was an advocate and notary public in the burgh; and *Ane Buke of Gude Counsale to the King* by Bishop Elphinstone, the founder of Aberdeen University. In 1509 Chepman printed the fine *Breviarum Aberdonense*. These three books constitute the whole known output of the Chepman-Myllar press, so that two-thirds of its work was of Aberdeen origin.[1]

Keith goes on to point out that the next Scottish press was founded in 1532 by Thomas Davidson, an Aberdonian. Printers in Scotland were in short supply and much demand. When Raban moved into the Castlegate, he brought with him *Raban's Resolution against Drunkennesse* followed by *Raban's Resolution against Whoredome, the Companion of Drunkennesse*. While he printed the moral code he believed in, Raban also instituted, according to the Aberdeen Borough Accounts, the custom of 'merrymaking' or 'drinksilver', that is to say, a liquid celebration at the end of a job paid for by the city council. Raban's first official publication in 1622 as 'Universitatis Typographus' was a set of theses for King's College.[2] For Marischal College his first duty was to print the funeral oration of its founder, George Keith, fifth Earl Marischal. Raban here signed himself 'Academiae Typographus'. By 1625, Raban's imprints reflect his dual role as 'Printer to the Citie and both Colledges' or, alternately, 'Academiae & Urbis Typographus'. Although his imprint vanishes after 1649, Raban not only established the town and gown pattern for his eighteenth-century successors, he also gave them their most popular perennial item: the almanac.

With the development of the *Eighteenth-Century Short Title Catalogue* (ESTC) scholars are in a better position to assemble book trade statistics.[3] The most frequent item appearing on the ESTC list of Aberdeen imprints is the almanac, usually identified by the keyword phrases 'Aberdeen's new prognostication' and 'a well-wisher of the mathematicks'—the generic author. The first almanac recorded on the ESTC was printed by the successors of John Forbes in 1709, the second in 1710; then comes an intermittent series of thirteen almanacs, 'printed and sold by James Nicol, and in Edinburgh by John Paton', between 1717 and 1736 (with one anonymous duplication for 1729). There is a hiatus until 1759 when the first of many imprints under the authorship of 'Merry Andrew, professor of prediction by stargazing at Tamtallan' appears. By 1773 the 'J. Chalmers & Co.' imprint appeared with the more staid, but official *Aberdeen Almanack*. Perhaps wilting under the competition, the Merry Andrew variety faded after 1777 and in its place sprang up a new hybrid, directed specifically at the agrarian market: *The Aberdeen Farmer's Large Pocket Companion: Or, A New Prognostication.*

A preliminary comparison between the latest off-line ESTC listing and its predecessors will give an idea of how it outstrips other catalogues. On the 1983 ESTC microfiche, which provides an index for places of publication, there are a mere eighteen titles listed between 1701 and 1750 with gaps for 1703-1706, 1709, 1715-1716 and 1718-1729. This microfiche list suggests two possibilities: either that there was very little printing going on in Aberdeen during the first half of the century; or that the list itself, based on British Library holdings, is not fully representative. This list needs to be supplemented by the most up-to-date ESTC citations which fill in many of the gaps and enhance the overall picture. Supplemented by the latest off-line printout, the 1983 figure of eighteen titles up to 1750 now rises to forty. More definite patterns emerge from this new list. Unlike most London imprints where printers' names are only occasionally given on a titlepage—the book-sellers tending to take all the glory or blame—most Aberdeen imprints tend to carry the names of their printers (who doubled as booksellers): John Forbes II (*fl.* 1675-1704 and his successors 1704-1714); James Nicol (*fl.* 1717-1736); James Chalmers I (*fl.* 1737-1764); Francis Douglas (*fl.* 1750-1768); John Boyle (*fl.* 1768-93).[4] The Forbes imprint overlaps from the seventeenth century, dating back to 1656. John Forbes the younger is the fourth link in the Aberdeen chain of printers, preceded by his father (*fl.* 1656-1675), James Brown (*fl.* 1650-1661) and Raban. The first Forbes imprint on the ESTC, Robert Calder's 1701 *Schola Sepulchri*, is a fairly representative product, a slim octavo meditation on death with a titlepage bordered by fleur-de-lis. Calder's ten other known titles were printed elsewhere, mainly in Edinburgh and London.

James Nicol became connected with the Forbes family through marriage and presumably lived in the premises once occupied by Raban. Associate printer from 1710, his press was commandeered by the Jacobites in 1715.[5] According to the latest ESTC figures, between 1717 and 1732 James Nicol printed seventeen titles, thirteen of which were almanacs, all distributed by John Paton in Edinburgh. Aberdeen University Library adds six more titles, but even so, printing books seems to have been more of a sideline than a primary occupation. Although Nicol retired in 1736, thus allowing Chalmers to become the official Printer to the Town and University, he later served as a town magistrate and remained a merchant as late as 1748.[6] No one better exemplifies than Chalmers the tradition of the learned printer. The earliest Chalmers imprint recorded on the ESTC is the 1737 *The A.B.C. with the Shorter Catechism* for the General Assembly; the next item is Robert Barclay's 1740 *Genealogical Account of the Barclays*. Chalmers's is by far the most prolific printing house of the eighteenth century, with 82 titles out of an overall 261 items on the ESTC. By Edinburgh and London standards, his output is relatively small, but the population of Aberdeen—15,730 in 1755, a small percentage of them avid book-buyers—could hardly support an elaborate network of independent printers, booksellers, stationers and book-binders. Chalmers printed John Bissett's *Communion betwixt Christ and his Believers* in 1742 and two more of his sermons in 1749. In 1748 he launched Aberdeen's first weekly newspaper, the *Aberdeen Journal*. Under his son, who succeeded to the business in 1764, the imprint changed to 'J. Chalmers & Co.'. Continuing as a printer-publisher, James Chalmers II attended Marischal College and learned the trade in London alongside Benjamin Franklin in Watts's printing house. The family name spread well into the nineteenth century with George Chalmers's *Biographical Dictionary*.

From about the year 1750, when Francis Douglas's *Collection of the Most Approv'd Receipts for Pastry* appeared, Aberdeen ceased to be a one-printer town. While the quality of his printing never challenges that of the Chalmers Press, Douglas undeniably exerted a healthy influence over the Aberdeen book trade and broke the printing monopoly handed down from Raban once and for all. Originally apprenticed as a baker, Douglas went to London for about five years and returned to Aberdeen in 1743. As soon as his printing and bookselling career got under way, he engaged a fellow church-goer and druggist, William Murray, as a sleeping partner. Until Douglas's arrival, book production was primarily divided between religious works, almanacs and university material. David Foxon's *English Verse* records only two poems printed in Aberdeen between 1701 and 1750: *Alexis, a Pastoral to the Memory of Alexander Innes, P.P. in Marischal-College* and William Meston's *Ad Consulum Aberdonensum*, both printed by Chalmers in 1744. In 1754 Douglas inundated Aberdeen with a new line of poetry: *Chevy Chase* (with Douglas's own inimitable preface touting his namesake); Pope's *Epistles*; Prior's *Poems on Several Occasions*; and Ramsay's *Gentle Shepherd*. In 1756 he published Montesquieu's *The Spirit of the Laws*; the next year, Addison's *Cato* and Sir Archibald Grant's *Farmer's New Year's Gift*. Not only did Douglas offer an alternative outlet to the university book-buyers by publishing the first Greek texts in Aberdeen (Plato in 1759 followed by Epictetus in 1760); he helped revive Henry Scougal's reputation by reprinting his *Life of God in the Soul of Man* (1757) and his *Works* (1759). His pro-Jacobite periodical, the *Aberdeen Intelligencer*, modelled largely on the *Gentleman's Magazine*, ran from 3 October 1752 to 22 February 1757, when it merged with Chalmers's Whig-aligned *Journal*. Douglas's *History of the Rebellion in 1745 and 1746* (garnered from the *Scots Magazine* accounts) attracted attention when it was attacked in the first issue of the *Edinburgh Magazine* in August 1755. The controversy grew with Douglas's defence in the September *Scots Magazine* which no doubt helped boost sales on all sides. Douglas's printing of Beattie's *Original Poems and Translations* might have irritated Chalmers, the 'official' University Printer although the book was first released in London through Andrew Millar in 1760, who had come to Aberdeen on a 'fishing' expedition. Judging by the *Scots Magazine* review of April 1761, Beattie's success was assured before the publication of the Aberdeen edition, which appears to have been composed of sheets identical to those of the London edition, apart from the reset title page. When Douglas left printing to tend a farm in 1768, John Boyle filled the void. While Beattie published his 1778 *Letter to the Reverend Hugh Blair* with Chalmers and had his *List of Two Hundred Scoticisms* printed privately for his classes, he sent most of his other works, like *The Minstrel*, to Creech in Edinburgh or to E. and C. Dilly in London.[7]

How effective is the ESTC when compared with more standard 'hard-copy', microfiche or card catalogues? The following decade-by-decade chart of Aberdeen imprints is compiled from four sources: the 1982 *Index to Eighteenth-Century British Books* (ECBB 1982); 1983 ESTC microfiche (ESTC 1983)); an August 1986 ESTC off-line bibliographic citation (ESTC 1986); and imprints not already recorded on the ESTC in the Special Collections catalogue of Aberdeen University (AUL). The 1982 ECBB is a conflation of British Library, Bodleian and Cambridge University Library catalogues which explains why it contains more imprints than the 1983 ESTC microfiche which is based on British Library holdings alone.[8] Totals are given for ESTC 1986 and AUL imprints still to be logged in the ESTC.

	ECBB 1982	*ESTC 1983*	*ESTC 1986*	*AUL*	*Total*
1701-10	7	6	8	4	12
1711-20	5	3	7	5	12
1721-30	1	1	9	3	12
1731-40	2	2	7	10	17
1741-50	8	6	8	13	21
1751-60	55	41	48	19	67
1761-70	29	17	28	22	50
1771-80	47	26	52	44	96
1781-90	25	14	37	60	97
1791-1800	*51*	*30*	*57*	*72*	*129*
Century Total	*230*	*146*	*261*	*252*	*513*

The AUL eighteenth-century collection yields 252 items not yet recorded on the ESTC. When this is done, there will be at least 513 eighteenth-century Aberdeen imprints. Thus, while Aberdeen's output of printed material has been reckoned to be fairly small over the century, the century total has grown from source to source—from the 146 items in the BL to the 230 items in the BL, Oxford and Cambridge; from the latest total of 261 to a potential century total of well over 500.

In the minute particulars, the ESTC enables us to revise Plomer's and Bushnell's Scottish entries.[9] Robert Carnie and Ronald Doig have done much to extend the professional life-span of various Scottish booksellers, using the Ruddiman MSS, the Edinburgh University Library Account book, a private collection and the records of a public library.[10] Through Ruddiman's account, Carnie found David Angus, a bookbinder and possibly a bookseller who owed Ruddiman money for schoolbooks in 1739. Angus's name first appears in an Aberdonian imprint in a 1740 edition of *The Psalms of David in Metre*. Bushnell dated Alexander Thomson's activity as a bookseller between 1751 and 1755. Carnie added 22 more years to Thomson's business life when he uncovered a 1777 imprint. With the ESTC, we can now add two more years with the 1779 imprint of George Campbell's *Address to the People*. Thomson's name appears twice as a bookseller in 1742 on Alexander Russell's *Dissertatio Medica* and at the tail-end of the imprint to William Hooper's sermon, *Christ the Life of True Believers*, which can lay claim to being one of the first Aberdonian imprints distributed in more than two locations: printed by James Chalmers, and sold by John Trail in Edinburgh, A. and R. Foulis in Glasgow, John Glass in Dundee, James Hunter in Aberbrothock, James Bissett in Montrose, and by D. Angus and A. Thomson in Aberdeen. Thus Thomson flourishes for a new total of 37 years.

Lateral thinking will add more items to the ESTC's list. In his *Day-Book* James Beattie mentions James Riddoch's two-volume *Sermons on Several Subjects* advertised in the *Aberdeen Journal* on 22 April 1782, printed by Chalmers and Co. and sold at 10 shillings; he also notes Alexander Geddes's translation of *Select Satires of Horace*, advertised in the *Aberdeen Journal* on 28 June 1779 as being printed by A. Angus and Son and J. Boyle, although the imprint to the National Library of Scotland's copy reads 'London: printed for the author; and sold by T. Cadell'.[11] Might this be another Aberdonian product stamped with a London imprint; and how many more titles might be added by combing through the book lists in local newspapers?

At the touch of the fingertips, the ESTC can provide the most complete picture of the overall printing and bookselling situation in Scotland, the rest of Britain and beyond. For the first time, we can virtually re-create a printer's or bookseller's lifetime inventory in seconds. The name of Francis Douglas, for example, occurs in 45 imprints, the last of which is Alexander Ross's *The Fortunate Shepherdess* in 1768. Obviously in the case of Aberdeen, local supply could not have met demand. The University and general public would have found more printed matter from Edinburgh, London and the Continent in booksellers' shops than from local presses. In order to gain a fuller impression of bookbuying, we need to consult the available auction and library catalogues. Compare our current ESTC and AUL century total of

513 imprints with the more than 800 books contained in James Beattie's personal library, the 8000 items belonging to Alexander Gerard and others, or the 10,000 volumes in Lord Haddo's collection.[12] One might pore over the university accessions for a better impression of the import and export situation.[13] A study of subscription lists may turn up new items.[14] When the records from all major eighteenth-century collections have been incorporated, the ESTC will enable us to complete the bibliography of the Enlightenment.

Notes

1. Alexander Keith, *Aberdeen University Press: an Account of the Press from its Inception in 1840 until...1963* (Aberdeen, AUP, 1963), pp.10-11.
2. For more background on Raban and his successors, see W.R. MacDonald, 'Some aspects of printing and the book trade in Aberdeen', in *The Hero as Printer*, ed. C.A. McLaren (Aberdeen, AUL, 1976), pp.27-36. The title page of Raban's 1622 *Theses Philosophicae* is reproduced there as plate 5 (a).
3. For a variety of scholarly approaches to the ESTC, see *Searching the Eighteenth Century: Papers presented at the Symposium on the Eighteenth Century Short Title Catalogue in July 1982*, eds M. Crump and M. Harris (The British Library in association with the Department of Extra-Mural Studies, University of London, 1983).
4. Any study of this nature owes an immediate debt to many predecessors, including Harry G. Aldis, *A List of Books Printed in Scotland before 1700* (Edinburgh, Edinburgh Bibliographical Society, 1904, reprinted 1970); J.P. Edmond, *Aberdeen Printers* (Aberdeen, privately printed, 1886), and *Last Notes on Aberdeen Printers* (Aberdeen, privately printed, 1888); R. Dickson and J.P. Edmond, *Annals of Scottish Printing* (Cambridge, CUP, 1890); J.F. Kellas Johnstone and A.W. Robertson, *Bibliographia Aberdonensis*, 2 vols (Aberdeen, 1929). For more information about individual printers and booksellers, see Walter Kendall Watkins, *The Life and Ancestry of Francis Douglass: Bookseller and Author of Aberdeen and Paisley, Scotland* (Boston, Mass., privately printed, 1903), which concentrates more on Douglas's ancestry than his life (which relies on the DNB account); G.M. Fraser, 'Francis Douglas: a notable Aberdeen printer of the eighteenth century', *The Aberdeen Book-Lover*, 2, (1916-18), pp.2-9; Robert Murdoch Lawrance, 'An old bookselling firm: Alexander Angus and Son', *The Aberdeen Book-Lover*, 4, (1922-24), pp.94-101 and 'John Boyle, bookseller and bookbinder, Aberdeen', *The Aberdeen Book-Lover*, 5, (1925-27), pp.35-43.
5. See *Scottish Notes and Queries*, vol.1, 3rd series.
6. G.M. Fraser, 'Local History', *Times Literary Supplement* (1 April 1920), p.213.
7. Everard H. King, *James Beattie* (Boston, Twayne, 1977), p.20.
8. *Eighteenth-Century British Books: an Author Union Catalogue*, eds F.J.G. Robinson, G. Averley, D.R. Esslemont and P.J. Wallis, 5 vols (Folkestone, Dawson, 1981); and *Eighteenth-Century British Books: a Subject Catalogue*, eds G. Averley, A. Flowers, F.J.G. Robinson, E.A. Thompson, R.V. and P.J. Wallis, 4 vols (Folkestone, Dawson, 1979). See E. Rainey's review of ECBB in *British Journal for Eighteenth-Century Studies*, 5, (1982), pp.131-37. While the ECBB has several shortcomings, its *Index* provides some useful statistics. Century tallies of imprints give an overview of Scottish book production: Edinburgh has 8399 printed items; Glasgow 2020; Aberdeen 230; Perth 142; Paisley 87; Stirling 69; Falkirk 66;

Dundee 40; St Andrews 8. Eighteen Scottish locations record one imprint only. For a largely positive assessment of the ESTC with some mild reservations, see Hugh Amory's review in *Papers of the Bibliographical Society of America*, 79, (January 1985), pp.128-33.

9. H.R. Plomer, *A Dictionary of the Printers and Booksellers who were at Work in England, Scotland and Ireland from 1668 to 1725* (The Bibliographical Society, Oxford, OUP, 1922; reprinted 1968); and H.R. Plomer, G.H. Bushnell and E.R. McC. Dix, *A Dictionary of the Printers and Booksellers who were at Work in England, Scotland and Ireland from 1726 to 1775* (The Bibliographical Society, Oxford, OUP, 1932; reprinted 1968).

10. Robert H. Carnie and Ronald P. Doig, 'Scottish printers and booksellers 1668-1775: a supplement', *Studies in Bibliography*, 12 (1959), pp.131-59. See also Carnie's 'Supplements' in *Studies in Bibliography*, 14 (1961), pp.81-96; and *Studies in Bibliography*, 15 (1962), pp.105-20.

11. *James Beattie's Day Book, 1773-1798*, ed. Ralph S. Walker (Aberdeen, Third Spalding Club, 1948), p.116.

12. Figures taken from W.R. MacDonald, 'Some aspects of printing and the book trade in Aberdeen', in *The Hero as Printer*, ed. C.A. McLaren (Aberdeen, AUL, 1976), pp.27-36; 34.

13. Giles Barber uses Customs records to chart the flow of books in and out of Great Britain in 'Book imports and exports in the eighteenth century', *Sale and Distribution of Books from 1700*, eds Robin Myers and Michael Harris (Oxford, Oxford Polytechnic, 1982), pp.102-3.

14. For a model of this kind of research, see P.J. Wallis, 'The MacLaurin 'Circle': the evidence of subscription lists', *The Bibliotheck*, II (2) (1982), pp.38-58. Colin MacLaurin (1698-1746) was a professor of mathematics who introduced the subscription method of publication to Aberdeen, although none apparently derived from an Aberdeen printing press, F.J.G. Robinson and P.J. Wallis *Book subscription lists: a revised guide* (Newcastle, Harold Hill and Son, 1975) offers two eighteenth-century Aberdeen subscriptions: Francis Peacock, *Fifty Scottish airs* (1762); and James Fordyce, *A Collection of Hymns* (1787). James Beattie's activities in this regard should be more fully examined. Although the ESTC challenges previous senses of the 'definitive', I have, in the course of collecting data for this paper, compiled 'A preliminary checklist of books printed in Aberdeen 1701-1800', which will soon be lodged with Special Collections, Aberdeen University Library, whose staff have been more than helpful in my labours. When all the records from Aberdeen, the National Library of Scotland and other likely sources of Aberdonian imprints have been logged on the ESTC, a new and more complete chronological list will be made. I would especially like to acknowledge the assistance of Mrs M.I. Anderson-Smith, Keeper of Special Collections, Aberdeen University Library, and Michael Crump, Manager Editor, ESTC, British Library.

34

Bibliography of the Enlightenment: Some Supplementary Notes on the Aberdeen Booktrade

Iain Beavan

University of Aberdeen

The Enlightenment was not marked by a notable growth of scholarly printing in Aberdeen, and booksellers were as important as printers in distributing scholarly material. Recent research, including that of Professor Carnie and Dr Nichol, is showing us more of the strengths and weaknesses of the local booktrade.

Scholarly printing may be defined in various ways. Account must be taken of the work printed (whether a classical text or a work of contemporary scholarship); of textual reliability; of the quality of typographical layout— or a combination of all three elements. However defined, little of this kind of printing seems to have taken place in Aberdeen during the height of the Scottish Enlightenment from 1740 to 1790. In spite of the printers in Aberdeen, from the introduction of printing in 1622, having been designated as Printers to the Universities, few examples of their printing classical texts are known.[1] Yet neither the size of their market nor problems of distribution need have hindered the Aberdeen printers. Working for a similar market, the Morison family of Perth, and later of St Andrews as well, produced a series of classical texts of high quality, and this series of so-called 'immaculate classics' was continued into the early nineteenth century by the subsequent Printer to the University of St Andrews, Robert Tullis.[2] The editor of these texts was John Hunter, a noted scholar and Professor of Humanity at the University of St Andrews, and it may be that the absence of a similar academic initiative at Aberdeen best accounts for the lack of such printing here. Distribution into the country areas need not have been a problem to the Aberdeen booktrade. As Feather has pointed out, the emergence of the provincial newspaper revolutionised the distribution of books.[3] The proprietors of newspapers were often also jobbing and book printers and could and did use the networks of newspaper distribution to distribute books printed by themselves or others. In Aberdeen, the *Aberdeen Journal*, produced by James Chalmers (father and son), had been in existence since the beginning of 1748, and could have been used for this purpose. Further, if not a positive inducement, at least there was no financial penalty attached to scholarly printing. The Stamp Act of 1712 (10 Anne cap 19, sects 63,64) allowed for any duties paid on paper used for printing works in Latin, Greek, etc for the advancement of learning to be claimed back, and this provision was not repealed during the eighteenth century.

It would not be true to say that there were no texts of interest to, or representative of the Scottish Enlightenment printed in Aberdeen. Some printing of vernacular literature took place, support for which was characteristic of one aspect of the Enlightenment. *The Fortunate Shepherdess, a Pastoral Tale* by Alexander Ross seems to have been first printed and published in Aberdeen by Francis Douglas in 1768. It is not obvious why Douglas was entrusted with this publication, rather than Chalmers, whose firm was likely to have done a superior job. Perhaps the explanatory link is James Beattie, Professor of Moral Philosophy at Marischal College. As R.S. Walker has pointed out in his edition of Beattie's *Day-Book*, Ross was a close and established friend of the Beattie family.[4] Ross offered his poem for evaluation to Beattie, who was sufficiently enthusiastic to want to see it printed. Francis Douglas had printed and published Beattie's *Original Poems and Translations* in 1760/61[5] and continued his connexion with Beattie at least until 1777, when the *Day-Book* entry for 28 August records their having lunch together.

The Fortunate Shepherdess is supposed to be modelled on Allan Ramsay's more famous *The Gentle Shepherd*, an edition of which was printed first in Aberdeen by Douglas and Murray in 1754—not that any great initiative can be claimed for the Aberdeen booktrade in taking on this title. At least fourteen editions had been printed before 1754, some by the well-known printers Thomas Ruddiman, R. & A. Foulis, and Hamilton & Balfour.[6] Beattie's attachment to Ross and his text lasted many years as may be seen from the *Day-Book* entry under 12 April 1780 (which should read 1778) pp. 213-14:

> This day I paid Jas. Chalmers, printer, for eleven Reams of French paper £3.11.6 at 6/6d pr ream, for the Second Edition of Ross's Scotch poems. Mr Chalmers agreed to give the printing, and I to give the paper; and we are to indemnify ourselves out of the sale of the edition:— and if anything more can be made by the sale (which is not very likely) it belongs to Mr Ross.

Beattie's pessimism about the sales seems to have been unfounded as before the end of the century two further Aberdeen editions were printed. Chalmers organised the distribution of the second edition well. The imprint reads:

> Aberdeen: printed by J. Chalmers and Co. Sold by A. Angus and Son, A. Thomson, J. Boyle and J. Taylor, booksellers, Aberdeen; J. Imlach, bookseller, Banff; D. Buchanan, Montrose; J. Dickson, Edinburgh; and by Dunlop and Wilson, Glasgow. M.DCC.LXVIII.

In 1789 John Boyle produced the third edition, and the last known eighteenth-century printing from Aberdeen was by Burnett & Rettie in 1796.

The contrasts between Douglas, who printed the first edition of Ross's poems, and Chalmers, who printed the second are interesting.[7] At first sight Chalmers would seem the better placed to undertake scholarly printing. James Chalmers's father, also James, was Professor of Divinity in Marischal College and his son had obtained the semi-official status of Printer to the Town and the Universities. But Chalmers and Co. clearly preferred their role as printers to the town, to that of printers to the university. Francis Douglas was the more innovative and scholarly printer, yet his background was unorthodox. He began his career in Aberdeen as a baker, later becoming a printer and publisher, newspaper proprietor (the *Aberdeen Intelligencer*, 1752-1757) and writer of miscellaneous works. Over the years 1752-1768 during which he was active as a printer in Aberdeen, either in partnership or on his own account, Douglas produced, *inter alia*: editions of Pope's *An Essay on Man* (1754); two editions of Addison's *Cato* (1754 and 1757); Montesquieu's *The Spirit of the Laws* (2 vols, 1756); Aelianus the rhetorician, *Delectus ex Aeliano, Polyaeno aliisque* (1758); a Greek and Latin text of Plato, *Platonis apologia Socratis* (1759); and a year later a Latin edition of Sallust, *C.Crispi Sallusti belli Catinarii & Jugurthini historiae*. In 1760 he also produced a Greek and Latin edition of the *Enchiridion* of Epictetus, obviously a popular work as no fewer than six classical language editions came from the Foulis press between 1744 and 1775. Few editions of works by significant authors preceded or followed this outburst of activity by Douglas. Some titles can be picked out: an edition of Aesop's *Fables* by Chalmers in 1781; *The Whole Works...of Josephus Flavius* by Bruce and Boyle in 1768; editions of Pope's translations of Homer's *Iliad* and *Odyssey* by Boyle in 1774 and 1778. Perhaps a brave initial move, not to be followed up, was a 1762 edition of George Buchanan's *Rerum Scoticarum Historia*, printed by Chalmers for Alexander Angus: Boyle in 1771, and Burnett and Rettie in 1799 produced English language editions. The standard edition of Buchanan's *Opera omnia* had been produced in Edinburgh as far back as 1715 under the editorship of Thomas Ruddiman. Henry Scougal, the seventeenth-century Professor of Divinity at King's College, fared better. His *Private Reflexions and Occasional Meditations* was printed in 1740 by Chalmers, though again his major work, *The life of God in the Soul of Man*, was printed and published in Edinburgh in the same year by J. Paton, G. Hamilton and J. Balfour. Douglas and Murray were the first Aberdeen printers to produce an edition of this work in 1753. Of the Aberdeen printers of this period, they seem to have taken their publishing activities the most seriously, as being the only ones (so far as can be traced) to have troubled to protect their interests by recording any of their titles in the Stationers' Company Register: Douglas's own composition, *Rural love, a tale* ..., was registered in March 1760, and Ross's *The Fortunate Shepherdess* ..., in May 1768. No entry appears for Beattie's *Original Poems and Translations*.

This pattern of the major works of Enlightenment figures associated with Aberdeen being printed in Edinburgh and/or London can be seen time and again. Apart from some sermons, no eighteenth-century edition of George

Campbell's *The Philosophy of Rhetoric* is known to have come from the Aberdeen presses, and nothing of Thomas Reid. James Beattie's *Essay on the Nature and Immutability of Truth* (1770) was produced and distributed from Edinburgh and London. It is obvious from Beattie's *Day-Book* that he regarded Edinburgh as the natural place for his work to be published—the local trade would print only lesser stuff. Typical is Beattie's *A List of Two Hundred Scoticisms with Remarks* which although it does not give the printer's name was in fact run off by Chalmers in March 1779.[8] It is perhaps slightly surprising that no edition of Robert Fergusson's works was attempted, his *Poems* being first produced by Walter and Thomas Ruddiman in 1773. Certainly the Morison family of Perth undertook an edition in 1788.

What was the size and type of output of the Aberdeen press in the eighteenth century? A recent search in the ESTC revealed some 303 Aberdeen imprints. However, a closer figure would seem to be nearer 440, ignoring magazines, newspapers and other serial titles.[9] The Chalmers family seem to have printed some 170 separate works; followed by James Boyle, in partnership with J. Bruce or on his own account, with circa 75 titles; Douglas, and Douglas & Murray, circa 50 titles; and, later in the century, John Burnett and Rettie together and on their own accounts, circa 30 titles. Some 70 titles are known to have been printed in Aberdeen, of which the names of the printers—as opposed to the sellers or distributors—are not known. The figures in Table I have been taken from the ESTC and the ECBB.[10]

Table I

| | ECBB | | | Edmond & MacDonald | ESTC | |
	Aberdeen	Edinburgh	Glasgow	Aberdeen (1700-1710 inclusive)	Edinburgh	Glasgow
1701-1710	7	756	10	18		
1711-1720	5	549	43	14	1711-1719 585	32
1721-1730	1	490	35	14		
1731-1740	2	520	55	10	1730-1739 603	40
1741-1750	8	585	307	14		
1751-1760	55	669	410	79	1750-1759 745	394
1761-1770	29	941	341	54		
1771-1780	47	1184	286	78	1770-1779 2520	606
1781-1790	25	1127	223	68		
1791-1800	51	1678	310	91		
Totals	230	8499	2020	440	1700-1799 8835	1927

One of the more obvious features in these figures is the jump in output in the decade 1751-60, which coincides broadly with the time Douglas and Murray were at work. Some indication has been given of the type of work they published, and this compares with the general lack of adventure shown by the Chalmers press. The output of the two presses may be compared further (see Table II):

TABLE II

Subjects (expressed as a % of total output)	Douglas (& Murray)	Chalmers
Theology/philosophy		
(inc. psalms, hymn tunes and sermons)	28	54
History	12	6.6
Law/jurisprudence	2	3.3
Literature	35	5.7
Agriculture	4.6	—
Economic history	2	—
Classical studies	16	2.5
(History, language and literature)		
Medicine	—	4
Educational theory	—	3.3
Current affairs (burgh/civic)	—	20

Typical of the last category are *Contract of the Banking Company in Aberdeen* (1769) and *Regulations of the Northern Shooting Club* (1782)

In addition to telling us what was published in Aberdeen, the ESTC also allows us to trace books distributed here. The file was recently searched to find what books, published outside Aberdeen, were explicitly sold by and/or published for the Aberdeen booktrade. Out of the huge number of titles on the ESTC file, only 97 citations were offered, 13 of which were discounted for the present purpose because they were printed in Aberdeen for an Aberdonian seller or distributor. The ESTC figures are as follows:

1700-1755	12
1756-1789	30
1790-1800	42

We know that a few books printed in Aberdeen were explicitly distributed elsewhere (Dundee, Edinburgh) in the seventeenth century, and that James Nicol consistently used John Paton, bookseller in Edinburgh, as distributor for his almanacs from 1717 onwards. Nevertheless, the pattern of Aberdeen output and distribution seen in the ESTC figures shows that there was relatively little activity in the Aberdeen booktrade until the second half of the century, and not an enormous amount then. An interesting point about distribution is that Chalmers seems to have been used as a distributor very little indeed. The ESTC currently yields only one title he distributed: William Cruden, *Nature Spiritualised in a Variety of Poems* (London, printed by J. and W. Oliver...and sold by...J. Chalmers, at Aberdeen...1766). Why Chalmers acted as a distributor so seldom is an unanswerable question. Aberdeen booksellers rather than printers seem to have been the most active distributors, and from the 1780s onwards the names of the Angus family, Alexander Brown, and William Knight appear with the most frequency.

No major Enlightenment text seems to have been explicitly distributed in Aberdeen, not even one by an Aberdeen author. The majority of books distributed here are small tracts, mostly printed in Edinburgh, Glasgow or London. An interest in agricultural improvement is seen in the number of titles printed under the superintendence of William Smellie (co-producer of the first edition of the *Encyclopaedia Britannica*) acting as printer to the Society for the Improvement of British Wool, and which were explicitly distributed by Angus in the early 1790s. The only other systematic distribution arrangement discernible was between John Ogle of Edinburgh and William Knight in the late 1790s, the works being mostly theological in nature. It was Douglas (and Murray) who most immediately seized the opportunity of using wider distribution networks for their books. Typical here is *St. Justin...his Exhortations to the Gentiles* (1757) which bears the imprint:

> Aberdeen: Printed by F. Douglass and W. Murray, sold by C. Hitch and L. Hawes in Pater-Noster-Row, London, Mr Charnly in Newcastle, A. Kincaid and A. Donaldson in Edinburgh, and by the said F. Douglass at Aberdeen.

It would not be true to say that, because titles characteristic of the Enlightenment were to no great extent printed or explicitly distributed in Aberdeen, they were not available here. A glance through the booksellers' advertisements in the *Aberdeen Journal* will show otherwise. Two examples from Beattie's *Day-Book* point in the same direction: 24 January 1775 (p.59) 'Paid R. Chalmers for a copy of *Priestly agt Reid*', 31 December 1779 (p.97) details the purchase from Joseph Taylor, bookseller in Aberdeen, of John Gregory, *Elements of the Practice of Physic*. It is to the booksellers, rather than to the printers, that we must turn for signs of Enlightenment in the Aberdeen booktrade.

Notes

The author would like to express his gratitude to Mrs Carla Leslie for her very considerable help in the analysis and verification of data in the manuscript papers of W.R. MacDonald.

1. The major printers at work in Aberdeen, 1700-1800, were as follows:—

John Forbes, junior	-1704
his successors	1704-1710
James Nicol	1711-1736
James Chalmers, senior	1736-1764
Francis Douglas	
(in partnership with William Murray and on his own)	1752-1768
James Chalmers, junior	1764-
John Boyle	
(in partnership with J.Bruce and on his own)	1768-1794
Andrew Shirrefs	1783-1790
John Burnett and William Rettie	1795-1800

To this list should be added the names of the following, who were major booksellers but not known to be printers:—

Alexander Angus & Son	1742/43-
Joseph Taylor	1776-1785
Alexander Brown	
(initially in partnership with William Paterson)	1785-
William Knight	1782-

These lists are taken from the bibliographical papers of W.R.MacDonald (AUL MS 3167). See also W.R. MacDonald, 'Some aspects of printing and the book trade in Aberdeen' in C.A. McLaren, ed., *The Hero as Printer* (Aberdeen, AUL, 1976), pp.27-36.

2. For Morison see R.. Carnie, *Publishing in Perth before 1807* (Dundee, Abertay Historical Society Publications, 6, 1960). For Tullis see D.W. Doughty, *The Tullis Press, Cupar, 1803-1849* (Dundee, Abertay Historical Society Publications, 12, 1967), with further details in '...a supplement, 1801-1849', *The Bibliotheck*, 11 (2), (1982), pp.108-125.

3. J. Feather, *The Provincial Booktrade in Eighteenth-Century England* (Cambridge, CUP, 1985) Chapter 4.

4. J. Beattie, *James Beattie's Day-Book, 1773-1798*, ed. R.S. Walker (Aberdeen, AUP, Third Spalding Club, 1948).

5. For Francis Douglas generally, and the circumstances surrounding the publication of Beattie's book, see G.M. Fraser, 'Francis Douglas, a notable Aberdeen printer of the eighteenth century', *The Aberdeen Book-Lover*, 2, (1916/18), pp.2-9.

6. B. Martin, 'A bibliography of the writings of Allan Ramsay' *Glasgow Bibliographical Society Records*, 10 (1931), pp.3-114. For Foulis see P. Gaskell, *A Bibliography of the Foulis Press*, 2nd edition (Winchester, St Paul's Bibliographies, 1986).

7. J.P. Edmond, *The Aberdeen Printers, Edward Raban to James Nicol, 1620-1736* (Aberdeen, J. & J.P. Edmond & Spark, 1886), gives Chalmers's submission, pp. lxii-lxiii. For details of the rivalry between the *Aberdeen Journal* and the *Aberdeen Intelligencer* see W.R. MacDonald, 'The *Aberdeen Journal* and the *Aberdeen Intelligencer*', *The Bibliotheck*, 5 (1967/70), pp.204-6.

8. *Day-Book*, p.98.

9. Care has to be taken to check the wording of imprints. To search under 'Aberdeen' may yield an incorrect figure. That a work was printed in Aberdeen usually means that it was printed and published here, but there can be exceptions. For example, it could be held that *The Scots Blackbird, Containing One Hundred and Seven Songs...*, bearing the imprint 'Aberdeen: printed by J. Chalmers: for William Coke, bookseller in Leith MDCCLXCI' was merely printed in Aberdeen, but was published by William Coke in Leith. The ESTC research has recently been undertaken by Dr D.W. Nichol. Supplementary figures are taken from J.P. Edmond, *The Aberdeen Printers*, for the period until the retirement of James Nicol, in 1736, and then from the papers of W.R. McDonald in AUL.

10. For reasons of time and cost the ESTC was only sampled under the dates indicated, though overall figures for the century were also obtained. Because the ECBB is compiled from a limited number of library catalogues, the editors are the first to admit that the figures are not complete, although I believe we can readily accept their point that the overall relative pattern is unlikely to change significantly even if more titles were to be added. We can also note that the pattern continued into the nineteenth century, by comparing figures taken from the NSTC

	Aberdeen	Glasgow	Edinburgh
1801-1810	119	487	1851

Nineteenth-century Short Title Catalogue, ser. I, Phase I, 1801-15, 5 vols (Newcastle-upon-Tyne, AVERO Publications, 1984/85).

SECTION V

Literature of the Enlightenment

35

Beattie's *Minstrel* and the Lessons of Solitude

W. Ruddick
University of Manchester

James Beattie was Professor of Moral Philosophy at Marischal College, Aberdeen, for over forty years. He was a brilliant teacher and a moral and aesthetic theorist whose work enjoyed the highest contemporary repute; Thomas Gray and Samuel Johnson were among his warmest admirers. He was also a poet whose best pieces were read and admired for generations, exerting a significant influence upon some of the most important poems of the English Romantic period.

In the year 1766 Beattie began to write a prose *Essay on Truth*. Probably as a relaxation from this work he also began to compose a largely auto-biographical poem, *The Minstrel: or, The Progress of Genius*, in which memories of his boyhood, which had been spent amid scenes of natural sublimity, are interpreted by, or lead into, passages of speculation on the relationship between environmental circumstances and the development and nature of poetic genius.

The Minstrel is a poem which raises particularly interesting questions for the reader of Romantic poetry, as it did for the Romantic poets themselves. In particular it poses problems concerning possible modes of procedure in autobiographical verse. It explores the possibilities of interpreting the development of mature personality which some of the greatest poems written between the 1790s and 1830 try, with varying degrees of success, to resolve.

Beattie had written part of the first book of *The Minstrel* and planned the rest of the poem in a fairly general fashion by about November 1769, when he sent his material to Thomas Gray for appraisal. He had found 'the first hint' for his poem in Thomas Percy's description of the lofty character of the ancient English minstrels in his preface to the *Reliques of Ancient English Poetry* in 1765. Building on Percy's depiction of 'wild and romantic' genius, Beattie intended to show how in the first part of his life his hero would gain knowledge from 'that part of the book of nature which is open before him' in wild and romantic landscapes. Then would follow his meeting with a wise hermit who would add knowledge of history and philosophy, but would discourage the young man's 'strong attachment to poetry'. At this point Edwin, the hero, would be torn from his influence by 'an irruption of Danes or robbers (I have not as yet determined which)' who would rob him and necessitate his going forth into the world with his harp on his shoulder 'in the character of a Minstrel'.[1]

Thomas Gray commented appreciatively on what he had seen of the poem in July 1770, but rightly noted that Beattie's plan 'seems somehow imperfect at the end'. He wished Beattie to assign some more active role to poetry:

> Why may not young Edwin, when necessity has driven him to take up the harp, and assume the profession of a minstrel, do some great and singular service to his country? (what service I must leave to your invention) such as no general, no statesman, no moralist could do without the aid of music, inspiration, and poetry ... it will be a full answer to all the Hermit has said, when he dissuaded him from cultivating these pleasing arts; it will show their use, and make the best panegyric of our favourite and celestial science. And lastly (what weighs most with me), it will throw more of action, pathos and interest into your design, which already abounds in reflection and sentiment.[2]

If Beattie could follow Gray's plan he would demonstrate the function of actively engaged and heroic poetry in society without landing his hero in a kind of martial impasse in which prophetic fury can find no outlet in patriotic action and the visionary is inevitably driven towards impotent rage and eventual suicide, as happens at the end of Gray's own poem, *The Bard*.

Thomas Gray died before Book I of *The Minstrel* was published in 1771. The second book, in which the Hermit tells Edwin sobering truths about the modern world, followed in 1774; but despite Beattie's later attempts to contrive a conclusion the poem never advanced to a point where Edwin, having learned the lessons of nature and mature human wisdom, could become involved with life and active as a poet of moral truth. As Kathryn Sutherland has pointed out, Gray's comments identify a real problem, for 'Beattie does not know what to do with the Minstrel once he has made him'. No role answering Gray's request for a poet who does what 'no statesman, no moralist could do without the aid of music, inspiration, and poetry' was seemingly to be found. Kathryn Sutherland identifies what proved, in practice, to be the fundamental problem (as Gray's failure to offer a suggestion seems to indicate that it might) when she asserts that 'Beattie's poem fails precisely because its autobiographical basis cannot sustain a narrative action'.[3] Why this may be thought to be structurally inescapable will be a chief concern of the rest of this paper.

Book II of *The Minstrel* ends with Edwin, the projection of Beattie's own early experiences and perceptions, left in an historically earlier period than the poet's own, when the bard could be cast as a romantic and potentially heroic figure, but, in reality, frozen into inactivity by the chilling revelations of modern philosophy. Edwin becomes a totally passive figure, absorbed back into his creator's personality once more as the sad news of a close friend's death stills Beattie's impulse towards creation:

> Here on his recent grave I fix my view,
> And pour my bitter tears. Ye flowery lays, adieu!

The inspiration bestowed by nature has been frozen in the poet's breath by bereavement; but in his representative, Edwin, it has been stilled by his social education. The Hermit's lessons, we are told, result in 'forms of bright perfection', but we are offered none of them. Edwin's education, in fact, brings assertions of chastened genius but no real fruit.

The solipsistic nature of *The Minstrel* did not strike the generation of poets who were born at the time of its first publication and who read it with avidity in their youth. *The Minstrel* had half a century of real popularity. Joan Pittock and Everard H. King[4] have noted how the Romantics identified their youthful selves with Beattie's Edwin. 'Indeed the whole character of Edwin resembles William much' wrote the young Dorothy Wordsworth, and Wordsworth's poetry, both early and late, shows his abiding consciousness of Beattie's poem. Everard King can indeed demonstrate strong echoes of *The Minstrel* in the work of all the major Romantics, even including the second generation poets, Shelley and Keats.

But what everyone identified with was the youthful poet in a landscape experiencing sublimity of Book I. Parts of this book are, indeed, heady stuff:

> Oft when the winter storm had ceased to rave,
> He roam'd the snowy waste at ev'n to view
> The cloud stupendous, from th'Atlantic wave
> High-tow'ring, sail along th'horizon blue:
> Where, 'midst the changeful scenery, ever new,
> Fancy a thousand wondrous forms descries,
> More wildly great than ever pencil drew,
> Rocks, torrents, gulfs, and shapes of giant size,
> And glitt'ring cliffs on cliffs, and fiery ramparts rise.
>
> Thence musing onward to the sounding shore,
> The lone enthusiast oft would take his way,
> Listening, with pleasing dread to the deep roar
> Of the wide-weltering waves. In black array
> When sulphurous clouds roll'd on th'autumnal day,
> Ev'n then he hasten'd from the haunt of man,
> Along the trembling wilderness to stray,
> What time the lightning's fierce career began,
> And o'er Heaven's rending arch the rattling thunder ran.

But though impressive as a proto-Romantic, Beattie still falls far short of adopting what might be described as an Aeolian Harp, or Blithe Spirit, or 'Aetherial Minstrel, Pilgrim of the Sky' conception of the poet. Edwin actually possesses a 'wild harp' and an 'adventurous hand' to strike it with, but his 'infant muse', though 'not mute', is 'artless'. 'Of elegance as yet he took no care' notes Beattie firmly. And in the second book (which the Romantics virtually ignored) the wise Hermit checks Edwin's rhapsodic impulse with 'the Muse of History' and stern reflections on the dangers of Fancy. 'Science' and 'Philosophy' must be his themes. Edwin is 'enraptured by the hermit's strain' and must be supposed to write verse which falls somewhere between Pope's *Essay on Man* and *The Excursion*, but Beattie cannot do so himself. He lacks the philosophical imagination with which he optimistically credits his hero. Kathryn Sutherland declared that:

> in the teachings of the Hermit and the occasional intrusions of the narrator, the distorting burden of the neo-classical present is felt, and the metaphor breaks down into a self-conscious pose. Under these circumstances the description of the career of an eighteenth-century man of letters in terms of the life of a medieval minstrel was bound to fail. It was left to Coleridge and to Wordsworth to renew and redirect the metaphor.[5]

In fact, however, this renewal was far from easy, and the power of *The Minstrel*'s influence caused at least as many problems as it helped to solve. The model for a poem which explores the poet's upbringing close to nature, and shows his education towards poetic creativity being achieved with the help of nature experiences was certainly to be found in the first book of *The Minstrel*. *The Prelude* shows its power. But, like *The Minstrel*, *The Prelude* breaks off when the tale of youthful experience is completed. *The Recluse*, Wordsworth's attempt to fuse 'Science' and 'Philosophy' in verse expressive of the adult's viewpoint, proved impossible to write. The problem which Beattie imposed upon his hero and upon himself, and the problem which Wordsworth, in particular, inherited from his example, is two-fold. First of all, *The Minstrel* splits the poet's consciousness in two: the younger self, growing up under nature's tuition, is both presented as an active participant in the poem and scrutinised by the poet's older self. This can cause problems of focus. Though Wordsworth often copes with these brilliantly in *The Prelude*, Byron, in comparison, can never keep the older and the younger self apart. In *Childe Harold*, which is, in its earlier cantos, very much influenced by Beattie, the young man Harold soon disappears, having his role as a sympathetic observer and commentator on modern European society merged with the essentially similar viewpoint of the older narrator. And in *Don Juan* the naive enthusiast for life and love is only saved from total absorption into the personality of the ever-interjecting older narrator by elaborate Sternean comic devices. A late eighteenth-century poet such as Cowper (who appreciated Beattie's verse, but was scarcely influenced by him) had a much easier time of it when he continued to develop the more structurally straightforward reflective mode, involving the observations of only a single figure, the mature poet in a stable landscape, which derives directly from Thomson's *Seasons*.

The second problem which *The Minstrel* poses relates to the concept of poetry which Beattie's awkwardly well-informed and experienced Hermit insists on in Book II:

> But now let other themes our care engage.
> For lo! with modest yet majestic grace,
> To curb Imagination's lawless rage,
> And from within the cherish'd heart to brace
> Philosophy appears!

'Enraptured by the hermit's strain' Edwin's mind explores 'the path of Science' and is 'expanded to the beam of truth'. Thereafter:

> fix'd in aim, and conscious of her power,
> Aloft from cause to cause [his Fancy] exults to rise,
> Creation's blended stores arranging as she flies.

This is noble, but since Beattie could not imagine the result we never see it. And though the idea of a highly-personal philosophic poem attracted the young Coleridge he soon passed the task of writing it on to Wordsworth: and Wordsworth, having written his equivalent to Book I of *The Minstrel* with *The Prelude*, ground to a halt in his philosophic masterpiece, *The Recluse*, and backtracked into his equivalent to Book II of *The Minstrel* with *The Excursion*. In his poem Beattie's wise hermit is elaborated into two characters, the Pedlar (the account of whose early life is full of echoes of Book I of *The Minstrel*) and the Pastor. Since Wordsworth had already depicted his own Edwin-like youth and growth to maturity in *The Prelude* he now imparts errors of judgement and taste to an older man, who has misread both philosophy and nature to become a solitary. Wordsworth's elaborations carry him no further than Beattie's simpler structure had done: the debating is too one-sided and experience seems to have little to recommend save quietism and acceptance. Once again the endowing of sober wisdom with superior authority to the more spontaneous impulses of the heart and feelings proves a dead end poetically.

Yet there was an alterative to explicit philosophical moralising present in Beattie's poem from the start, and though Beattie himself failed to appreciate its importance Thomas Gray picked up the hint clearly enough. In his youthful wanderings Edwin listens not only to the voice of nature but also to 'old heroic ditties' chanted by beldames at their own firesides. Traditional ballads wake his poetic powers and Beattie praises the 'mighty masters of the lay'. It is, surely, in examples of narrative (in both verse and prose) that *The Minstrel* can be seen exerting a genuinely beneficial and successful influence. Everard King charts Beattie's presence in Scott's *Rokeby*, in *The Eve of Saint Agnes* and other Romantic narrative poems. He is surely right to do so, and to his list may surely be added Wordsworth's *The White Doe of Rylstone* as a generally underrated example of true philosophical narrative in verse. But it is surely also the case that with the extension of Scott's imaginative powers from verse into prose fiction Beattie's influence revealed a new potentiality. The early Scott heroes, in particular Edward Waverley and Frank Osbaldistone, have much that is Edwin-like about them. The structure of the narratives through which their growing to maturity is revealed recalls *The*

Minstrel in several respects. This is particularly true of *Rob Roy*, a novel in which Scott comes as close to solving the problem of the divided consciousness as anyone ever did. The young Frank's education through natural and social experience is explored through the first-person narrative in which wiser perspectives can be offered on occasion by his older narrating self. The philosophical values of his life experience can be incorporated without explicit commentary into the larger shape and colouring of the narrative.

Thomas Gray wanted Edwin to 'assume the profession of a minstrel, [and] do some great and singular service to his country'. In Scott's lays, and more specifically in his fiction, the dead end of philosophical poetry is avoided and Beattie's aims are largely achieved by being incorporated within a developed mode of narrative, rooted in the narrative methods of the folk poets and, like Edwin's youthful verses, modernising and developing the scope and function of their art.

Notes

1. *Correspondence of Thomas Gray*, eds Paget Toynbee and Leonard Whibley, 3 vols (Oxford, Clarendon Press, 1935), vol.3, p.1084.
2. Toynbee and Whibley, vol.3, p.1140.
3. Kathryn Sutherland, 'The native poet: The influence of Percy's minstrel from Beattie to Wordsworth', *Review of English Studies*, NS XXXIII (1982), p.425.
4. Joan H.Pittock, 'James Beattie: a Friend to All', in *Literature of the North*, eds David Hewitt and Michael Spiller (Aberdeen, AUP, 1983), p.56; Everard H.King, 'James Beattie and the growth of Romantic melancholy', *Scottish Literary Journal*, 5, no.1 (May 1978), pp.24-25.
5. Sutherland, p.426.

36

Burns and the Masonic Enlightenment

Marie Roberts
University of Manchester

The subject of this paper, the relationship between Freemasonry and the Enlightenment, has already been explored within the French and German movements. Less attention, however, has been paid to the Scottish Enlightenment which, in many respects, was a stronghold of Freemasonry. According to records held by the Grand Lodge of Scotland, both Edward Gibbon and James Boswell were Freemasons: members prominent in the literary world have included Walter Scott, James Hogg and Robert Burns. Most of my discussion will focus upon the impact of Scottish Freemasonry on the life and work of Burns. But first it is important to draw attention to some of the connexions between the Enlightenment and the Masonic movement before showing how they surfaced in Scotland.

Freemasonry, which was officially established in Scotland in 1736, was nurtured by the ideals of the Enlightenment. To a great extent the fraternal spirit of the Enlightenment was realised within the Masonic lodges. Operating in some respects as a friendly society, the Freemasons were for many 'one closed system of benevolence'. Eighteenth-century aspirations towards the breaking down of social and religious barriers were felt most keenly in the lodge room where the Masonic brethren set out to dismantle the existing social hierarchy. The non-partisanship of Masonry was founded on the ideals of a community of mankind intent upon a universal Enlightenment. The masonic credo rested on a notion of *humanitas* which in terms of orthodox ritual and symbolism virtually excluded Christianity. The craft's first official historian, the Scottish Mason, James Anderson, only mentions Christianity during a passing reference to the historical Christ as the Messiah and the great Architect of the Church who was born during the reign of the Emperor Augustus. Eighteenth-century thinkers identified with this period of Ancient Rome which may be why Anderson claims that the Emperor Augustus was an early Grand Master. Freemasonry drew on the classical characteristics of the Augustan world-picture which developed into the cultural panoply of the

Enlightenment. The Neo-Classical tenor of eighteenth-century Masonry is also evident in its borrowings from Vitruvian architectural theory. Through the reification of aspects of the building trade, the Masons extolled the values of symmetry, balance and harmony. These expressed the prevailing Augustan ideology which had been anchored by the Freemasons to the belief in the 'Great Architect of the Universe'. The image of this Deistic deity measuring out the cosmos with compass and square would also have appealed to the Newtonian mechanistic outlook of the founding fathers. Deism, which attracted Enlightened thinkers, was adopted as the creed of the Freemason. In Anderson's *Constitutions*, the section dealing with the 'Charges of a Free-Mason' begins: 'It is now thought more expedient only to oblige them [the Freemasons] to that religion in which all men agree, leaving their particular opinions to themselves'.[1] Philosophers such as Locke and Voltaire who became Deists made overtures towards Freemasonry as a compatible belief-system which in some respects was a microcosm of the Enlightenment.

The blanket belief in a non-demoninational supreme being was one strategy of uniting the world of Freemasons by enabling them to cross the boundaries of religious and sectarian creeds and national differences. Yet ironically in regard to the French and American Revolutions, Freemasonry was allegedly instrumental in galvanising the new spirit of nationalism through its pursuit of universal liberties. Nevertheless Freemasonry's levelling out of nationality could be seen as antithetical to the emergence of the nation state. Theoretically, by helping to neutralise the forces of devolution, the Masonic lodges were counter-productive in the advance towards Scottish independence. But in practice the lodges were known to harbour Jacobin sympathisers. Though in general Freemasonry may not have contributed greatly to Scottish separatism, it did help mobilise cultural nationalism in generating a sense of national identity by supporting literary figures such as Burns.

Burns became a Mason on 4 July 1781 when, at the age of 23, he joined St David's Lodge No. 174, Tarbolton. According to tradition the ceremony took place in Mason's Tavern, located in what is now known as Burns Street. From then on Burns progressed rapidly through the tripartite system of Masonic degrees. Three months after his initiation as an Entered Apprentice, he advanced to the second degree of Fellowcraftsman and then to the third degree of Master Mason. From here in 1787 he was installed into a fourth Masonic degree, the Royal Arch, which was reserved for Master Masons.

Burns's involvement with Scottish Freemasonry took place during a turbulent period in its history. Ten years earlier, the Grand Lodge of Scotland had been seeking to centralise the craft. The original St James's Kilwinning Lodge, Tarbolton, had resisted this move with the result that twenty malcontent members who had wanted the sanction of Grand Lodge left in protest to form a new lodge called St James, No. 174. Eventually, the former dissenting Tarbolton Lodge agreed to be affiliated with Grand Lodge whereupon it was renamed St James, No. 178. Inevitably, rivalry grew up between the two lodges until the Scottish Grand Lodge authorised them to merge together under the name of St David on 25 June 1781.

Burns's concern for his Masonic brethren during this period of uncertainty was an important factor in his election to Depute-Master of the lodge on 27 July 1784, an office which he commemorated in his poem, 'The Farewell. To the Brethren of St James's Lodge, Tarbolton' (1786). Burns was 'so keen a mason, that he would hold lodges for the admission of new members in his own house'.[2] During one Masonic gathering, Burns even initiated his own brother, Gilbert.

The question now is how to account for Burns's great enthusiasm for Freemasonry. There were a number of attractions for him: first the fellowship of the lodge served a convivial role at a time when social clubs proliferated. Secondly, Freemasonry with its revolutionary connexions would have appealed to Burns's radicalism. The Masonic ideals of liberty, equality and fraternity united his support of the French Revolution with his Scottish patriotism. Thirdly, Burns may have found in Freemasonry a challenge to the domination of the kirk. Even though there must have been an overlapping membership between the lodge and the kirk, Burns's defection to the Masons could be interpreted, in symbolic terms at least, as an act of betrayal in view of the official complaint made against the fraternity by the Presbyterian Church. After a Synod held in 1745, the Presbyterians passed an act of the assembly in 1757 condemning the Masons' oath as a mixture of 'sinful, profane and superstitious devices'.[3] And finally, Freemasonry opened up an alternative form of patronage which could free the artist from the restrictions of the aristocratic patron.

The lodges helped to launch Burns's career as a poet by campaigning for subscribers in order to meet the publishing costs of his volumes of poetry. Gavin Hamilton, a fellow Mason, was influential in getting St James's Lodge to provide funds for the publication of Burns's first book, *Poems Chiefly in the Scottish Dialect* (1786). The book was published in Kilmarnock where the local brethren admitted Burns into St John's Lodge on 26 October 1786. This was the first time in Masonic circles that Burns was acknowledged as a poet since he was described in the lodge minutes as 'Robert Burns, poet, from Mauchline, a member of St James'. The Kilmarnock members accepted 350 copies of the book which became known as the Kilmarnock edition. The Right Worshipful Master subscribed to 35 copies and another brother to 75. Since the majority of Burns's friends and business acquaintances were Freemasons, it is likely that the moral imperative to help a fellow-Mason operated to Burns's advantage. For example, some enthusiastic brothers even bought volumes of his poems to swell book sales. Robert Aiken, mentioned in 'Holy Willie's Prayer', boasted of having read Burns into fame by obtaining 145 subscribers for the Kilmarnock edition. The printer, William Smellie, and the engraver, Alexander Nasmith, were both Masons while the publisher, John Wilson, was a member of the Kilmarnock Lodge.

The publisher of the Edinburgh edition of Burns's *Poems* was William Creech whom Burns had met at a Masonic meeting. Creech became the subject of two of Burns's poems, including a satirical lament for his absence. Burns extended his Masonic contacts by gaining admittance into another lodge, the Canongate Kilwinning, Edinburgh, in 1787. Earlier that year, on 6 February, the Prince of Wales had been initiated into Freemasonry at the

Star and Garter, London. The Canongate Kilwinning Lodge responded by calling a meeting for the purpose of sending him their congratulations. According to popular myth, it was upon this occasion that the Master of the Lodge, Ferguson of Craigdarroch, decided to confer upon Burns the title of 'Poet-Laureate of the Lodge'.

The literary influence of Freemasonry on the Scottish Enlightenment is best demonstrated through the poetry of the Masons' first poet-laureate. The three poems which will be discussed are 'The Master's Apron', 'Farewell. To the Brethren of St James's Lodge, Tarbolton', and 'The Sons of Old Killie'. The first of these, 'The Master's Apron', is an explicitly Masonic poem which has been attributed to Burns:

> Ther's mony a badge that's unco braw;
>   Wi' ribbon, lace and tape on;
> Let kings an' princes wear them a'
>   Gie me the Master's apron!
>
> The honest craftsman's apron,
> The jolly Freemason's apron,
> Be he at hame, or roam afar,
> Before his touch fa's bold and bar,
> The gates of fortune fly ajar,
> 'Gin he but wears the apron!
>
> For wealth and honour, pride and power
>   Are crumbling stanes to base on;
> Fraternity suld rule the hour,
>   And ilka worthy Mason!
>   Each Free Accepted Mason,
>   Each Ancient Crafted Mason.
>
> Then brithers, let a halesome sang
> Arise your friendly ranks alang!
> Guidwives and bairnies blithely sing
> To the ancient badge wi' the apron string
> That is worn by the Master Mason! [4]

The poem is filled with references to Masonic symbolism and craft ritual which would be instantly intelligible to the initiated. Through the secret figurative language of the lodge, Burns venerated the 'badge' of Freemasonry, the Mason's apron. The antiquity of this item of Masonic regalia is evident from the last two lines where Burns refers to 'the ancient badge' worn by the 'Master Mason'. The Mason reader would be reminded here of the apron worn by Hiram Abif, the legendary founder of the brotherhood, who was also the chief architect of King Solomon's Temple. The importance of the apron to Freemasonry had emerged from its use in the operative craft as protective clothing for the 'Ancient Crafted Mason'. From this functional origin the apron, which was traditionally made out of lamb skin, had taken on an emblematic significance which evoked the purity and moral integrity of the craftsman.

As an apprenticed tradesman, Burns would have appreciated the operative purpose of the apron which functioned in the lodge-room to identify a member's rank and duties within the order. This information was communicated by the 'ribbon, lace and tape' which also served to decorate the apron. In the first line of the poem, Burns voices his disapproval of elaborate aprons as 'unco braw'. Yet, towards the end of his life in 1790, Burns modified his ascetic tastes sufficiently to accept a decorative apron from the composer and lyricist, Charles Sharpe.

By appropriating the elaborate apron to kings and princes in line three of the poem, Burns demonstrates his awareness of the link between royalty and the craft. Nevertheless, he acknowedges the egalitarian ideals of Freemasonry by praising the Master and honest craftsman above kings and princes. In doing so he pays homage to the second and third degrees of the brotherhood, that of the Fellowcraftsman and Master Mason. According to Burns, the fraternity was more important than 'wealth and honour, pride and power'. These secular goals are dismissed as crumbling stones which evoke powerful metaphors for Freemasonry whose legendary past had cultivated the skills of the stone-mason. King Solomon's Temple stood at the heart of Masonic mythology, having been transmuted into the spiritual ideal of the temple of 'living stones'. The vitality of the Freemason as a living stone eager to rebuild the temple of mystical Enlightenment contrasted with the false values of wealth, honour, pride, and power which are seen as crumbling stones. The revolutionary message of Freemasonry as a vast edifice which encompassed an alternative system of morality signified a movement intent upon reforming the spiritual destiny of mankind through the central image of the builder. Hence Burns's attempt to arouse his fellow-Masons, their wives and children, to sing a hymn of praise to the uniform of the master-builder, the Mason's apron.

In the second poem 'Farewell. To the Brethren of St James's Lodge, Tarbolton', Burns praises the fraternal spirit and describes his fellow-Masons as 'Companions of my social joy!'. For Burns, Freemasonry was a compound of mysticism and conviviality which he presents in his address to his 'brothers of the *mystic tye*!':

> ADIEU! a heart-warm, fond adieu!
>   Dear brothers of the *mystic tye*!
> Ye favour'd, ye enlighten'd Few
>   Companions of my social joy!
> Tho' I to foreign lands must hie,
>   Pursuing Fortune's slidd'ry ba'
> With melting heart, and brimful eye,
>   I'll mind you still, tho' far awa'.
>
> Oft have I met your social Band,
>   And spent the chearful, festive night;
> Oft, honor'd with supreme command,
>   Presided o'er the *Sons of light*:
> And by that *Hieroglyphic* bright,

Which none but *Craftsmen* ever saw!
Strong Mem'ry on my heart shall write
Those happy scenes when far awa'!

May Freedom, Harmony and Love
   Unite you in the *grand Design*,
Beneath th' Omniscient Eye above
   The glorious ARCHITECT Divine!
That you may keep th' *unerring line*,
   Still rising by the *plummet's law*,
Till *Order* bright, completely shine,
   Shall be my Pray'r when far awa'.

And You, farewell! whose merits claim,
   Justly that *highest badge* to wear!
Heav'n bless your honor'd, noble Name,
   To MASONRY and SCOTIA dear!
A last request, permit me her,
   When yearly ye assemble a',
One *round*, I ask it with a tear,
   To him, *the Bard, that's far awa'*. (I, p.271)

The tone of this poem is sorrowful since it was composed as Burns's valediction to Scottish Freemasonry as he had recently completed all his arrangements for emigration to Jamaica. The poet claims that after his departure he will remember the lodge through the Masonic symbol of the compass and square 'that *Hieroglyphic* bright/Which none but *Craftsmen* ever saw!' Since the Freemasons' code of ethics was symbolised by the craftsman's working tools, Burns urges his fellow-Masons to follow the plummet's '*unerring line*' so that order may reign over the lodge. This symbolism is derived from the Masonic version of the creation myth which described how the Architect of the Universe measured out the cosmos with the craftsman's working tools. Thus Freemasons unite in the grand design of their craft as a tribute to the Creator. In the last stanza, Burns addresses his final farewells to William Wallace, Sheriff of Ayr, the Grand Master-Mason of Scotland and then 'To MASONRY and SCOTIA dear!'.

   Departure is also the key-note of the Masonic song 'The Sons of old Killie' which Burns wrote shortly before leaving Kilmarnock for Edinburgh in 1786. At a lodge meeting held at the Old Commercial Inn, Croft Street, Burns sang this lyric in gratitude to the brethren of Kilmarnock Lodge for making him an honorary member:

Ye sons of old Killie, assembled by Willie,
   To follow the noble vocation;
Your thrifty old mother has scarce such another
   To sit in that honoured station.
I've little to say, but only to pray,
   As praying's the ton of your fashion;
A prayer from the Muse you well may excuse,
   'Tis seldom her favourite passion.

> Ye powers who preside o'er the wind and the tide,
>   Who marked each element's border;
> Who formed this frame with beneficent aim,
>   Whose sovereign statute is order;
> Within this dear mansion may wayward contention
>   Or withered envy ne'er enter;
> May secresy round be the mystical bound,
>   And brotherly love be the centre! (I, pp.299-300)

Burns addresses his brothers of the mystic tie as 'Ye favour'd, ye enlighten'd few' which points to the relationship between mystical initiation and illumination through the light of reason which had already begun to dawn in the lodges. This is expressed in the following couplet from a lodge song:

> Where scepter'd Reason from her Throne,
> Surveys the Lodge and makes us one.[5]

In an analogy of universal Enlightenment, every candidate for Masonic initiation was taken out of the darkness and received into the light of Freemasonry. The metaphor of Enlightenment was realised through ritual illumination since the initiate was blindfolded before being dazzled by brilliant artificial lights. The privileges of Freemasonry were then extended to the neophyte. Ironically the Enlightenment, despite its egalitarian ideals, spawned elitist attitudes and sects. The paradigm of *Aufklärung* built upon the paradox between elitism and egalitarianism was contained within the deeper structures of the secret societies which proliferated during the Golden Age of the Scottish Enlightenment. According to Herbert Grierson and J.C. Smith, Burns encapsulated the development of the democratic spirit, yet he chose to be one of the 'favour'd' and 'enlighten'd' few[6] of a secret society. His social poetry had christened him the poet of the people even though his Masonic verse was addressed to a highly selective audience, his fellow-Masons. While the Masonic network represented an ideological alternative to society, it also intensified and endorsed some of its values such as aristocratic patronage and the existing social hierarchy. Burns's career as a poet reflected the polarised forces of equality and exclusivity contained within Freemasonry which in turn mirrored the culture of the Enlightenment itself.[7] Appropriately, it was a secret society in Germany which had set out to define the term 'Enlightenment' in 1783.

Finally, Burns's connexion with Freemasonry ensured that he would never have to endure the solitary life of the garreted poet who was without friend or patron. The Freemasons also helped cultivate Burns as a poet of the Anglo-Scottish vernacular by encouraging him to continue writing Scots poetry. In this way, the Masons kept Burns in touch with his cultural roots which helped him retain his identity as the ploughman poet. Burns was an active Mason until the end of his life. He became an honorary member of Loudon Kilwinning Lodge at Newmilns and of St John's Kilwinning, Kilmarnock Lodge. On St Andrew's Day (30 November) 1792 he was elected Senior Warden at

St Andrew's Lodge, in Dumfries which he attended up to just three months before his death. Eventually the lodge was named after Burns in recognition of his contribution to Freemasonry.

Notes

1. James Anderson, *Constitutions of the Ancient Fraternity of Free and Accepted Masons* (1723), ed. John Noorthouck (London, J. Rozea, 1748), p.351.
2. *The Life and Work of Robert Burns*, ed. Robert Chambers, revised William Wallace, 4 vols (London, W. and R. Chambers, 1896), p.129.
3. 'Act concerning the Mason-Oath', *Scots Magazine*, XIX (1757), p.433.
4. *A Treasury of Masonic Thought*, ed. C. Glick (London, R. Hale, 1961).
5. James Anderson, *The New Book of Constitutions* (London, T. Payne, 1738).
6. Herbert J.C. Grierson and J.C. Smith, *A Critical History of English Poetry* (London, Chatto and Windus, 1947), p.285.
7. See Marie Roberts, *British Poets and Secret Societies* (London, Croom Helm, 1986), pp.79-80.

37

Henry Fielding's *Tom Jones* as Epic

Masafumi Masubuchi
Miyagi University, Japan

In his Prefaces to *Joseph Andrews* and *Tom Jones* Fielding insists on the distinctive structuring of his work. *Joseph Andrews* is 'a comic Romance...a comic Epic-Poem in Prose'.[1] The description of *Tom Jones* is even more specific: it is a 'Heroic, Historical, Prosaic Poem' or 'a Prosai-comi-epic Writing'.[2] Nor are questions of genre and mode left there. In the second novel Fielding proudly asserts that he is 'the Founder of a new Province of Writing'.[3] With all this his contemporary and editor, Arthur Murphy, concurs, praising *Tom Jones* as a 'more artful epick fable'.[4] All this in contradistinction to Richardson's apparently less sophisticated attitude to matters of artistic tradition and high authorial intention.

It is, of course, the comprehensiveness of approach to the individual in society in Fielding's work, particularly in *Tom Jones*, which has enabled his critics to agree on the term 'epic'. In the twentieth century, for example, the French scholar Aurélion Digeon writes that '*Tom Jones* often gives the impression of an epic. It is a picture of all England that we find there'.[5] F. Homes Dudden comes to the same conclusion: *Tom Jones* could be called epic in the sense that it was a whole picture of the age.[6] In *The Rise of the Novel*, Ian Watt is of the opinion that '*Tom Jones*'s action has epic quality at least in the sense that it presents a sweeping panorama of a whole society'.[7] With such a consensus it is interesting that E.M. Thornbury can write 'We should think of Fielding, not as the first English novelist, but as the last of the Renaissance writers of epic...To call him the 'Father of the English novel' is a little misleading...But he is the father of the English prose epic.'[8] Into this area of uncertainty of defining the novel-epic relationship E.M.W. Tillyard enters with an attack on the unity of *Tom Jones*, not so much as a structure as in terms of the experience it offers the reader:

> *Tom Jones*, then lacks sustained intensity; it does not make the heroic impression; and on that account it fails of the epic effect. And Fielding's claim to be in the

tradition of the comic epic can in no way influence this conclusion. Not that such a conclusion affects the success of *Tom Jones*; it merely warns us what *Tom Jones* is not. Take *Tom Jones* as a comedy in the form of a narrative fiction, reflecting the manners rather than the soul of a generation, and you find its success beyond doubt and its merits worthy of the praise which has greeted it since its birth.[9]

The concept of the epic has become uncertain: for Tillyard it must catch the soul of its subject; this for him seems to be precluded by the comic mode.

Paul Merchant examines various aspects of the epic from the viewpoint of modern man in *The Epic*, but I do not think the scope of the epic is as extensive as he suggests.[10] I would turn instead to the view of epic described by Aristotle and voiced in seventeenth- and eighteenth-century writers on poetics, especially in France, and by Fielding himself.

Elizabethan poetics echoed Horace, 'aut prodesse volunt aut delectare poetae'[11]—so did those of the seventeenth and eighteenth centuries. So did Henry Fielding's poetics. In *Tom Jones* he writes:

> I will therefore endeavour in the remaining Part of this Chapter, to explain the Marks of this Character, and to shew what Criticism I here intend to obviate: For I can never be understood, unless by the very Persons here meant, to insinuate, that there are no proper Judges of Writing, or to endeavour to exclude from the Commonwealth of Literature any of those noble Critics, to whose Labours the learned World are so greatly indebted. Such were *Aristotle*, *Horace* and *Longinus* among the Ancients, *Dacier* and *Bossu* among the French, and some perhaps among us, who have certainly been duly authorized to execute at least a judicial Authority in Foro Literario.[12]

In *Joseph Andrews* we find the following:

> Thus the *Telemachus* of the Arch-Bishop of *Cambray* appears to me of the Epic Kind, as well as the *Odyssey* of *Homer*; indeed, it is much fairer and more reasonable to give it a Name common with that Species from which it differs only in a single Instance, than to confound it with those which it resembles in no other. Such are those voluminous works commonly called *Romances*, namely, *Clelia*, *Cleopatra*, *Astraea*, *Cassandra*, the *Grand Cyrus*, and innumerable others which contain, as I apprehend, very little Instruction or Entertainment.[13]

'Instruction' and 'Entertainment' are the business of Romance: where Epic is concerned Fielding seems to echo Bossu rather than Aristotle or Horace:

> when any kind of Writing contains all its other Parts, such as Fable, Action, Characters, Sentiments and Diction, and is deficient in Metre only; it seems, I think, reasonable to refer it to the Epic.[14]

Let us compare this with Bossu. His *Traité du poème épique* is divided into six books:

I. De la Nature du Poème Epique, & de la Fable; II. De la Matière du Poème

Epique, ou de L'Action; III. De la Forme du Poème Epique, ou de la Narration;
IV. Des Moeurs; V. Des Machines; VI. Des Sentiments et de l'Expression.[15]

'La fable', 'l'action', and 'Sentiments' correspond to Fielding's epic con-
stituents. 'La narration' is an elaboration of the 'action'. Moreover 'Moeurs'
meant 'manners', which at the time involved characterisation. As far as
'machines' are concerned, Fielding only occasionally uses the marvellous in
his comic prose epic. 'Sentiments and expression', the sixth book of Bossu's
treatise, are frequently the theme of Fielding's introductory chapters to the
various books of *Tom Jones* as the basis for the illumination of his more
serious readers. Fielding's reference to *Telemachus* proves he accepted the
notion of the prose epic. Indeed many Renaissance commentators on Aristotle assumed a prose writer to be worthy to be called a poet.[16]

The study of the structure of *Tom Jones* by R.S. Crane and, more recently,
by James J. Lynch in *Henry Fielding and the Heliodoran Novel* are extremely
acute.[17] I have myself analysed *Tom Jones* as an organic structure in a paper
in Japanese, approaching the idea of the epic plot from rather a different
angle from that of Pat Rogers who assumes it to be so well-known that 'it
would be tedious to describe its plot or characters in any detail'.[18]

In *Tom Jones*, as well as in *Joseph Andrews*, Fielding was unable to tolerate
affectation and hypocrisy and he tried to instruct his readers to live without
hypocrisy and with goodness in their eighteenth-century world. The happy
ending he provides for Tom is the result of his having preserved his ingenu-
ousness and honesty in spite of the reverses of fortune with which they might
seem to be connected. In order to convey this Fielding follows the action of
the *Odyssey* which was certainly more appropriate for his purposes than that
of the *Iliad*.

Bossu describes the 'action' as follows:

> Aristotle not only says that the epic action should be one, but adds that it should
> be entire, perfect, and complete, and for this purpose ought to have a beginning,
> a middle, and an end. These three parts of a whole are too generally and
> universally denoted by the words *beginning*, *middle* and *end*; we may interpret
> them more precisely and say that the causes and designs of an action are the
> beginning, that the effects of these causes and the difficulties that are met with
> in the execution of these designs are the middle, and that the unravelling and
> resolution of these difficulties are the end (Book II, Chapter 9).[19]

With these guidelines he analyses Homer's two epics in Book II, Chapter I
On the structure of the *Odyssey* he writes:

> The beginning of this action is that which happens to Ulysses when, upon his
> leaving Troy, he bends his course for Ithaca. The middle comprehends all the
> misfortunes he endured and all the disorders of his own government. The end is
> the reinstating of his hero in the peaceable possession of his kingdom, where he
> was acknowledged by his son, his wife, his father, and several others.[20]

The action of *Tom Jones* may be described in similar fashion. Tom, a foundling, is brought up by Allworthy, a country squire. As he grows up he becomes vulnerable to temptations so that he is finally banished from Allworthy's home, and from his sweetheart, Sophia, who follows him. His adventures bring him into contact with a variety of dangers and mishaps. He and Sophia miss each other on the road to London. When in London, Tom falls into an affair with an older woman and, in prison because of a duel, is led to believe that he has unwittingly committed incest with his mother. From the nadir of misfortune Tom is suddenly rescued when his true identity is revealed. Tom marries Sophia (wisdom) to live happily ever after. Comparing this action of *Tom Jones* with that of the *Odyssey* it may be seen that Tom's birth to his banishment (the first six books) is the 'beginning'; the period of mishaps to Book 18 Chapter 2 is the 'middle' and the unravelling of the mystery of Tom's identity and the happy (comic) dénouement the 'end'. The beginning is Tom's early life, the middle a journey, and the end the consummation of his love and in Sophia's wedlock. Such a design is the orderly structuring of the epic according to Bossu. It is mirrored, of course, in other earlier prose narratives, including that of Cervantes. E.M.W. Tillyard, then, confuses 'a whole picture of the age' with 'the soul of a generation' in his objection to *Tom Jones* as an epic. A distinction between the two must be made.

Tom Jones gives a comprehensive picture of its age and country—of all classes of people, the life of town and country, the reaction to the Jacobite invasion of the '45 and so on. It is significant that Tom's encounter with soldiers is related to the Jacobite incursion only peripherally. According to Fielding it does not affect the life of the country in any fundamental way. In ancient times the epic dealt with the rise and fall of a nation. It is therefore solemn, sublime and bloody, lacking the dimension of heroism that E.M.W. Tillyard describes as essential to the novel as epic. The age of Fielding, however, is an 'age of Enlightenment', an 'age of reason', an 'age of deism'. Although this age also is an age politically under stress, of incessant strife, it is characteristically termed 'the Augustan Age', and, in the time of Walpole, one of domestic peace and national stability.[21] It was not an age in which serious or bloody drama could flourish. So Tate gave Shakespeare's *Lear* a happy ending. Curiously enough both Fielding and Richardson shared the disgust for pure epic virtues which is shown in mock heroic or in the standards of Sir Charles Grandison after Milton has given it Christian perspectives. It must still for Fielding entertain and instruct. Tom is to triumph morally, not heroically in the military sense. So although Fielding uses epic conventions, he describes scenes of battle comically and to excite ridicule, as in Molly's battle in the churchyard, Tom's battle with Thwackum, and so on. No one is killed: we are only entertained and instructed by the ridiculing of inert conventions. This is the 'soul' of the age of Enlightenment.

When he wrote plays, Fielding was persecuted by Walpole's Licensing Act to turn to a different kind of writing, the novel. He studied at Temple Bar and became a magistrate, leaving the theatre for good. It may be suggested, though, that if Ralph Allen, Fielding's patron, is the model for Squire Allworthy, there is something of Walpole about him. His magnanimity and benevolence are undermined by a gullibility which, in contrast to Tom's active generosity of spirit and goodness of heart, might have resulted in a very different and less fortunate outcome to the action.

As George Meredith says, comedy prospers in a peaceful age.[22] The desire to maintain peace and to cement over strife was particularly widespread in the first half of the eighteenth century. Generosity and tolerance are virtues to be cultivated; dissension and civic disturbance to be deplored or minimised. *Tom Jones* has, according to Fielding's intention and in terms of its achievement as a novel, a strong claim to being the only comic epic poem in prose England has ever produced.

Notes

1. *Joseph Andrews*, The Wesleyan Edition of Henry Fielding, ed. Martin C. Battestin (Oxford, OUP, 1967), p.4.
2. *The History of Tom Jones*, The Wesleyan Edition of Henry Fielding, ed. Fredson Bowers (Oxford, OUP, 1974), pp.152, 209.
3. *Ibid.*, p.77.
4. Arthur Murphy, 'Essay on the Life and Genius of Henry Fielding, Esq', *The Works of Henry Fielding, Esq.*, 4 vols (London, A. Millar, 1762), p.180.
5. Aurélion Digeon, *The Novels of Fielding* (1925; reprinted New York, Russell & Russell, 1962), p.180.
6. F. Homes Dudden, *Henry Fielding: His Life, Works, and Times*, 2 vols (1952 reprinted Hamden, Archon Books, 1966), p.330.
7. Ian Watt, *The Rise of the Novel* (London, Chatto & Windus, 1957), p.251.
8. E.M. Thornbury, *Henry Fielding's Theory of the Comic Prose Epic* (1931; reprinted New York, Russell & Russell, 1966), pp.164,166.
9. E.M.W. Tillyard, *The Epic Strain in the English Novel* (London, Chatto & Windus, 1958), p.58.
10. Paul Merchant, *The Epic*, Critical Idiom Series 17 (London, Methuen, 1971).
11. Horace, *Satires, Epistles, Ars Poetica*, The Loeb Classical Library,194 (1926, Cambridge, Mass., Harvard U.P., 1970), p.479.
12. *Tom Jones*, pp.569-70.
13. *Joseph Andrews*, pp.3-4.
14. *Ibid.*, p.3.
15. Thornbury, *Fielding's Theory*, p.58.
16. J.E. Spingarr, *Literary Criticism in the Renaissance* (New York, Columbia U.P., 1963), p.31. Thornbury, *Fielding's Theory*, pp.102, 103, *et passim*.
17. R.S. Crane, ed., *Critics and Criticism, Ancient and Modern* (Chicago, Chicago U.P., 1952), pp.616-47; James J. Lynch, *Henry Fielding and the Heliodoran Novel* (London and Toronto, Associated University Presses, 1986), pp.9-87.
18. Pat Rogers, *Henry Fielding: A Biography* (London, Paul Elek, 1979), p.160.
19. Scott Elledge and Donald Schier, eds, *The Continental Model* (Ithaca and London, Cornell U.P., 1970), p.317.
20. *Ibid.*, p.318.
21. See Claude Rawson, *Henry Fielding and the Augustan Ideal under Stress* (London, Routledge & Kegan Paul, 1972).
22. George Meredith, 'On the Idea of Comedy and of the Uses of the Comic Spirit'. A lecture delivered at the London Institution, 1 February 1877.

38

Ossian: Success or Failure for the Scottish Enlightenment?

Maurice Colgan

University of Bradford

Literary historians do not find it difficult to explain the European-wide interest in James Macpherson's 'translations' from the Gaelic of the ancient bard, Ossian. The Enlightenment, still very interested in the classical world, did not want to be confined to it. Non-classical cultures offered varieties of literary diet and alternative insights into human nature and society: they were part of the expanding consciousness of the age. Primitive cultures appeared to have most to offer, with their imagination and feeling uninhibited by belief in rationality as the essence of humanity, and by classical rules of composition.[1] One of the most influential works taking this viewpoint was Thomas Blackwell's *An Enquiry into the Life and Writings of Homer* (1735). Blackwell lectured at Marischal College, Aberdeen, where Macpherson studied. The question of the relationship between primitive society and genius was one of those discussed at meetings of the Aberdeen Philosophical Society,[2] founded in 1758.

The germination of these theories in Macpherson's mind led him to the belief that in his native Highlands there had existed such a primitive society. Could it have produced a poet of Homeric quality? In 1755, the headmaster of Dunkeld Academy, Jerome Stone, wrote to the *Scots Magazine* to arouse the interest of its readers in the great number of poems which he claimed were available in Gaelic, 'some of them of great antiquity'. To his communication he added as an example a translation of one poem.[3] After Stone's death Macpherson gained access to some of his manuscripts, and also to the Dean of Lismore's collection, in which several of the poems are headed, 'Auctor hujus Ossin'.[4] This was that Ossian whom Macpherson later was to claim flourished in the third century A.D.

Edinburgh Enlightenment circles were aware of the primitivist theories of Blackwell and his followers, but Highland Gaelic culture was a closed book to them. John Home, the minister-playwright, had his interest aroused when he was a prisoner of the Jacobite army after the Battle of Falkirk in 1746. Through a fellow-prisoner, an English officer with whom he became friendly, he later met William Collins. Their reminiscences of the Jacobite Highlanders inspired Collins to write his 'Ode on the Popular Superstitions of the Highlands of Scotland', which was an admonition to Home to leave the metropolitan literary world and delve more deeply into Gaelic culture.[5] Knowing Home's interest, Adam Ferguson, the only Gaelic speaker in Enlightenment circles, gave Macpherson a letter of introduction to him.

Travelling as tutor to a gentleman's son, Macpherson caught up with Home at Moffat, Dumfries, which was then a spa. He had copies of the poems in his possession, which he translated for Home, who was impressed. Alexander Carlyle, who was introduced to Macpherson on the Moffat bowling green a few days later, was 'perfectly astonished at the poetical genius displayed' in the translations. Next to be contacted was the Rev. Hugh Blair, who was just about to become Professor of Rhetoric and Belles Lettres in the University of Edinburgh. Blair found himself in the rare and advantageous situation of being able to announce the discovery of a literature hitherto unknown to the civilized world. Most astonishing of all was that it had been found, not in remotest Tahiti or Ceylon, but almost on Edinburgh's doorstep.[6] The *Fragments of Ancient Poetry Collected in the Highlands of Scotland* was published in 1760, and in the preface Macpherson claimed that the poems were probably part of an epic. Blair organised a subscription to finance an expedition to the Highlands by Macpherson to search for the epic, which was found and published as *Fingal* (1761). A second expedition, on which Home accompanied Macpherson, was partly financed by the Earl of Bute, the King's favourite, who was shortly to become Prime Minister. This resulted in the discovery of another epic, *Temora*, published in 1763.

Translations into Italian, German, French, and other languages excited even greater interest in Ossian in Europe than in Britain, and inspired the recovery and dissemination of other national literatures. Artists and composers throughout the Continent created visual and musical equivalents of ideas and emotions released by reading Ossian, of which Mendelssohn's 'Fingal's Cave' is only the best known.[7] Nationalism, as an ideology, owes much to Macpherson. The great philosopher of nationalism, J.G. Herder, collaborated with Goethe on a work entitled *Von Deutscher Art und Kunst* (1773), to which he contributed an essay, 'On Ossian and the Songs of Ancient Peoples'. This, and another essay on Shakespeare in the same volume, are described by a recent editor as displaying 'a degree of imaginative historical understanding hitherto unprecedented in the German Enlightenment'.[8] It was that expansion of historical understanding, and the new appreciation of non-classical cultures that resulted from it, that marked the success of Ossian.

When the particular effect of Ossian on the appreciation of Gaelic literary culture is studied, however, the story is a different one. Samuel Johnson, who appears to have been immune to the vogue for the primitive, regarded Ossian from the start as a forgery. The Highlanders, as a mainly illiterate people, were, he believed, incapable of an epic, or, indeed, of any worthwhile poetry. They were even incapable of remembering anything:

> In an unwritten speech, nothing that is not very short is transmitted from one generation to another. Few have opportunities of hearing a long composition often enough to learn it, or have inclination to repeat it so often as is necessary to retain it; and what is once forgotten is lost forever.[9]

But most preferred to believe Hugh Blair, whose *A Critical Dissertation on the Poems of Ossian, the Son of Fingal,* often reprinted with the poems, guaranteed both the authenticity of Ossian and the superlative moral and aesthetic qualities of primitive Highland society. *Critical Observations on the Poems of Ossian* by another formidable scholar, Lord Kames, added weight to the cause.[10] When pressed to show his originals, Macpherson said that they had already been displayed in his publisher's window, but his critics had not bothered to look there.[11] After his death, the Highland Society of Scotland set up a Committee of Inquiry into Ossian. After eight years of investigation, the committee reported in 1805 that Ossianic poetry existed in the Highlands in great abundance; that Macpherson had added and suppressed passages and changed the general tone; and that it was unable to find any one poem 'the same in title and tenor with the poems published by him'.[12] Stated thus baldly, these conclusions sound damning, but in the body of the report, hedged about with qualifications, and preceded by the evidence of witnesses who believed in Macpherson's authenticity, they appear much less emphatic. During his lifetime, Highlanders in the service of the East India Company raised a thousand pounds to publish the original Gaelic poems of Ossian. Such a gesture by well-wishers could not be rejected, and Macpherson himself wrote that no excuse, 'but want of leisure', could prevent him from commencing the work in 'a very few months'. That was in 1784.

At the time of his death in 1796, the supposed preparation of the originals was still incomplete, but in 1805 the Highland Society of London was able to publish the Gaelic Ossian in three volumes, with a Latin translation on facing pages. This helped to bolster Macpherson's reputation in the nineteenth century, but modern scholarship has demonstrated that the Gaelic is a translation of Macpherson's *English* Ossian.[13]

The appearance of the 'Gaelic' Ossian was the finishing touch to an episode that must be regarded as the most successful forgery in literary history. Macpherson's audacious mode of operation was to take poems which he sometimes imperfectly understood, and alter them radically in 'translations' tailored to meet the demands of those eager to read the compositions of a bard of ancient times. When the originals, which he himself had used, were presented as evidence of his inaccuracy, he denounced them as spurious fifteenth-century Irish versions of his third-century poems. A minister in Argyll and Mull, the Rev. Archibald MacArthur, stopped collecting Gaelic poems because he came to believe that those he was finding were of the kind Macpherson had denounced as spurious. Even before the publication of Macpherson's *Fragments*, Archibald Fletcher of Glenorchy, who was illiterate, had recited Ossianic poems to neighbours, who wrote them down. The manuscript eventually found its way to the Advocates' Library in Edinburgh, where the cover was marked 'Corrupt copies'—corrupt because they did not tally with Macpherson's versions![14] It took John Francis Campbell, the great nineteenth-century collector of folklore, thirty years to convince himself that Macpherson was a forger. His *Leabhar na Feinne* (1872) printed all known Ossianic poems in Gaelic, but included nothing by Macpherson. Macpherson's supporters—and he still had many—ignored Campbell's work. Others had become so sceptical that *any* Ossianic poetry was associated with the bogus, and, like the work of another famous Scot, *Leabhar na Feinne* fell still-born from the press. Because of lack of interest the second volume, which was to have given the English translations, was never published.

Some of the texts Campbell used were from Ireland, the original homeland of Gaelic culture, and one of these was Charlotte Brooke's *Reliques of Irish Poetry* (1789). Aware of the controversy surrounding Macpherson, Miss Brooke was careful to give the sources of her translations. A later development in Ireland was the bringing together of a small group of Gaelic scholars between 1834 and 1837 to work on the historical and topographical aspects of the Irish Ordnance Survey. One of them, Eugene or Eoin O'Curry, devoted the rest of his life to the listing and study of ancient Irish manuscripts both literary and historical, some of which had been discovered during the survey.[15] An Irish Ossianic Society was founded in Dublin in 1853 to publish these manuscripts, but the language was often so archaic that many words and even sentences could not be understood. Enough, however, was revealed to inspire the Irish Literary Renaissance at the turn of the century. W.B. Yeats and the other writers involved used Standish James O'Grady's *History of Ireland*, published between 1878 and 1880. As his title implies, O'Grady believed that the literature was recounting historical facts. Because his sources were still fragmentary, he made major additions and revisions, but at least he knew that the Ossianic and Ulster epic cycles, which Macpherson had confused, were different.

The breakthrough which enabled the old manuscripts to be understood and assessed came neither in Scotland nor in Ireland. A German philologist, Johann Caspar Zeuss, was looking at some early medieval Irish manuscripts in the monastery of Würzburg when he was struck by the number of root-words similar to some in Sanskrit, and by the archaic nature of the language. He decided to study old Gaelic and the result was the publication in 1853 of *Grammatica Celtica*, a landmark in Indo-European philology. He was followed by several generations of scholars who had come to the conclusion that the language was Western Europe's oldest vernacular. One of them, Kuno Meyer, asked himself, if the language were so archaic, would not the literature be so, too? In the introduction to his *Selections from Ancient Irish Poetry* (1911) he wrote:

> Slowly ... the fact is becoming recognised ... that the vernacular literature of ancient Ireland is the most primitive ... among the literatures of Western Europe

... its importance as the earliest voice from the dawn of West European civilisation cannot be denied.[16]

This point was taken up by Kenneth Jackson when he delivered a public lecture in Cambridge in 1964 on the earlier of the two Gaelic epic cycles, the *Táin Bó Cuailnge* ('The Cattle Raid of Cooley') to which he gave the sub-title, 'A Window on the Iron Age'. His point was that the *Táin*, believed by some scholars to date as far back as the first century B.C., is our only literary evidence for the culture of Iron Age Europe, which is otherwise known only from archaeology.[17] Publication in 1969 of an English translation of the *Táin* by Thomas Kinsella has demonstrated to the world that it is also great literature.[18] These developments, from Zeuss to Kinsella, have passed Scotland by. Apart from a handful of Celtic scholars, everyone's vision is still blinkered by Macpherson. In a work entitled *History of Scottish Literature*, which typically ignores any Gaelic writing, Maurice Lindsay says, 'No amount of high-toned purist condemnation gets over the fact that Macpherson's influence in Europe was immense'. There is no mention that the same Macpherson frustrated for nearly 150 years the recovery of an indigenous literary culture of greater antiquity and quality than even he had claimed![19] If, as his nineteenth-century biographer, Bailey Saunders, and the more recent writer, Richard Sher, have claimed, Macpherson was led into the path of deception by the demands of the Edinburgh literati of the time, the failure is as much theirs as his.[20]

Notes

1. Perhaps its source was the quarrel of the 'ancients' and 'moderns'. It is significant that Voltaire, who was one of the 'moderns', took an unfavourable view of both Homer and Ossian. See Kirsti Simonsuuri, *Homer's Original Genius* (Cambridge, CUP, 1979), pp.65-73 and 116.
2. William Duff, *An Essay on Original Genius* (London, E. and C. Dilly, 1767), and Alexander Gerard, *An Essay on Genius* (London, W. Strahan, T. Cadell, 1774) reflect Blackwell's influence. See Simonsuuri, p.122.
3. For a brief account of Stone, see J. Butt and G. Carnall, *The Mid-Eighteenth Century* (Oxford, Clarendon Press, 1979), pp.106-7.
4. The *Book of the Dean of Lismore* dates from 1512. See Derick S. Thomson, *The Gaelic Sources of Macpherson's Ossian* (Aberdeen, AUP, 1952; reprinted Edinburgh, Edinburgh U.P., 1973), p.80.
5. Arthur Johnston, *Selected Poems of Thomas Gray and William Collins* (London, Athlone Press, 1967), pp.210-11.
6. Richard Sher, *Church and University in the Scottish Enlightenment* (Edinburgh, Edinburgh U.P., 1985), pp.242-61, emphasises the role of those mentioned, whom he calls the 'Edinburgh Moderate literati', in encouraging Macpherson for their immediate cultural and political purposes, but there can be no doubt that the general enthusiasm for the primitive was the main factor.
7. A concert by the Scottish National Orchestra and the Edinburgh International Festival Chorus at the Usher Hall, Edinburgh, on 17 August 1986, included Niels Gade's *Echoes of Ossian, opus 1*, 'Ossian's Dream', from Lesueur's opera *Les*

Bardes, which was commissioned by Napoleon, and a concert version of Mehul's opera, *Uthal*, as well as the famous 'Fingal's Cave' overture.

8. H.B. Nisbet, ed., *German Aesthetic and Literary Criticism: Winckelmann, Lessing, Hamann, Herder, Schiller, Goethe* (Cambridge, CUP, 1985), p.153.

9. *A Journey to the Western Islands of Scotland*, ed. R.W. Chapman (Oxford, Clarendon Press, 1930), p.106.

10. See, for example, *The Poems of Ossian*, 2 vols, translated by James Macpherson (Edinburgh, J. Elder & T. Brown, 1797), vol.2, pp.175 and 285.

11. J.S. Smart, *James Macpherson* (London, D. Nutt, 1905), pp.140-41.

12. Smart, *James Macpherson*, p.164.

13. Thomson, *The Gaelic Sources*, appendix II, 'The Gaelic Ossian of 1807', pp.85-90.

14. Smart, *James Macpherson*, pp.43, 49-51.

15. See Patricia Boyne, 'Thank you, Eoin O'Curry', *Studies*, LXXII, 1983, pp.76-83. It was John Henry Newman, who, as Rector of the Catholic University of Ireland, insisted that O'Curry's lectures should be published as *Manuscript Materials of Ancient Irish History* (1861). Newman had attended the lectures and was astonished to learn of the 'unrivalled treasures' of Gaelic literature and learning available in libraries and monasteries throughout Europe. He was aware that a lot of hard work would be required to understand and assess the treasures. Of the manuscripts, he wrote: 'Few know what they contain; few can decipher their contents.' This contribution by Newman to the cause of Gaelic scholarship deserves to be as well-known as that of Matthew Arnold, whose *On the Study of Celtic Literature* was published in 1867.

16. Their work is often listed in bibliographies, but usually without any reference to its vital significance. Frank O'Connor, *The Backward Look* (London, Macmillan, 1967), pp.156-57, is an exception.

17. Kenneth Jackson, *The Oldest Irish Tradition: a Window on the Iron Age* (Cambridge, CUP, 1964).

18. Thomas Kinsella, *The Tain* (Oxford, OUP, 1970).

19. Maurice Lindsay, *History of Scottish Literature* (London, Hale, 1977), p.245. Roderick Watson, *The Literature of Scotland* (London, Macmillan, 1984), does cover Gaelic as well as English writing in Scotland. Watson hails the eighteenth-century Gaelic poets, Rob Donn Mackay, Alexander MacDonald and Duncan Ban MacIntyre, as the creators of a Scottish vernacular poetry, but he is dismissive of Ossianic poetry and does not mention the *Táin* at all (the influence of Macpherson's forgeries at work again?).

20. Bailey Saunders, *The Life and Letters of James Macpherson* (London, Swan Sonneschein, 1894), pp.72-94, and Richard Sher, note 6 above.

39

The Influence of James Macpherson's *Ossian* on Johan Ludvig Runeberg's *Kung Fjalar*: Some Notes

Josef Bysveen

Sweden

In his dissertation, *Ossian i den svenska dikten och litteraturen*, Theodor Hasselqvist points out that:

> the poems meant a deeper understanding of the sublime and the wild, of what is essentially untouched, and when Ossianic scenery was strangely and erroneously transferred to the Highlands of Scotland, the result was that only now did men become aware of the beauty of mountain scenery.[1]

Besides, the poetry painting Ossianic scenery filled it with life of its own. Nature becomes animate and strongly affects man's sensibility with a love of freedom and a deep sense of sincerity, simplicity and generosity.[2] Thus, when the poems were circulated in France and Germany, it was this spirit of *Ossian* which caused the sentimental release that the social and political restraint prevailing in these states had held back for so long.[3] In Sweden and Finland, however, the spread of the poems had no such initial effect.[4] It is rather the resemblance of Scandinavian scenery to *Ossian*'s and the number of Scandinavian themes in the poems which best account for the great popularity of *Ossian* in these two countries.[5]

The position of *Ossian* in Swedish literature is definitely a consequence of the interchange of ideas in the European world of learning and literature after the Enlightenment. The very first mention of *Ossian* is in a note written by Gjörwell and printed in April 1765.[6] Of famous poets of the time who were actually concerned with *Ossian*, at least to some extent, the following should be remembered : J.H. Kellgren (1751-1795); Thomas Thorild (1759-1808); Benkt Lidner (1757-1793); C.G. af Leopold (1756-1829): P.D.A. Atterbom (1790-1855); E.G. Gejer (1783-1847).

Johan Ludvig Runeberg (1804-1877), who wrote the national anthem of

350

Finland, was not only an eminent poet but also a classical scholar and a penetrating critic.[7] As a distinguished man of letters he was keenly alive to the European literary tradition; the use he made of Macpherson's *Ossian* clearly testifies to this. It was at Christmas 1842 that Runeberg laid his hand on the first part of Nils Arfwidsson, *Ossians sånger efter gaeliska originalet*.[8] It is true that he had already some knowledge of the poems before 1842: his fiancée had clarified parts of the English *Ossian* to him before he read Arfwidsson's translation and as a young poet he had actually translated Darthula's lament (from Herder). But none of this provided him with so deep and comprehensive a knowledge of *Ossian* as did Arfwidsson's translation. Critics agree that when Runeberg wrote *Kung Fjalar*, *Ossian*'s influence on him was indeed considerable. How great this influence was I shall show in the following summary of *Kung Fjalar*:[9]

The first lines of the poem introduce Fjalar, king of Gauthiod, seated in his royal chair. His eyes are clear and young while his hair is silver grey. Torches light up the hall where the king's warriors, young and old, are assembled for the Youle feast. The king then rises with the drinking-horn held firmly in his hand. He wants to speak, that is to swear a solemn oath, for now the right moment has come for the king to make a vow. King Fjalar then declares that from now on he wants peace and prosperity to obtain in his kingdom, since he has had enough of heroic deeds and battles. The king sits down. Then a stranger unannounced comes before him. He is Dargar the seer. He knows of King Fjalar's oath and now comes to warn the king because 'Fjalar has forgotten that gods make men's lot; he proudly believes in the law of his own will, wanting to arrange for the future with earthly might'.[10] To atone for this pride the king shall live to know that his only son has embraced his own sister in marriage. With subdued emotions the king sends for his children, Hjalmar and Gerda. To prevent the seer's prophecy from coming true the king finally lets Sjolf, an old warrior, take Gerda, whom he throws into the waves of the ocean from a steep rock nearby.

'Witness to Fjalar's grief', he says, 'the fight is on, hear the word of your king: Woe to him who does not bury in the grave of silence what he has now seen. Shame shall cover him and my vengeance shall trace his steps even if the storm took him to the end of the world.'[11] So, at the end of Song I Fjalar's resolve to keep the peace in the kingdom and guard his lineage in defiance of Dargar's prophecy remains unbroken.

In Song II the setting is Finjal's former hall in Shelma, Morven. Here live old king Morannal and his three sons Gall, Rurmar and Clesamor. In Finjal's and Ossian's times both song and harp-music enlivened Morven's men. The minds of the three brothers, however, are full of mutual suspicion, because they all want the same girl, Oihonna. Knowing that they might try to kill each other to have the girl, the brothers together ask their father to reconcile them. He then tells them that the ocean gave her to him. 'Freedom she saw in the fields of the waves. Unconstrained, as in a mirror she could see her childhood here in the calmness of rivers.'[12] He finally asks Gall to propose to her first. But her answer is no. Rurmar and Clesamor in their turn also get the same answer.

The setting of Song III is the valley of Lora. Oihonna, who has killed a deer with one of her arrows, is sitting in the heather beside the deer with her dog. Without Oihonna noticing it another huntress has followed her. She is Gylnandyne,

Hidjallan's daughter, renowned for her songs. The two meet and Oihonna asks her to sing to her. Glynandyne does so, following the only cloud in the sky with her eyes.[13] The spirit of Le speaks to her from the cloud. In reply she tells the spirit to look down from the edge of it to see that Oihonna is there as well. Gylnandyne then relates that Le thought much of them both and eventually mentions Le's premature death which is why a woman and not a bard laments him. The question is further asked why Morven no longer has any heroes as in the past: 'To Finjal's race his shield is too heavy and feebly does a pining poet touch the strings of Ossian's harp'.[14] Oihonna has become impatient with the sighs and tears of Morven's doleful heroes and wants to meet the warrior whose heart she has already kindled through the fame of her beauty and by being present in his dreams. The following events then take place in Gauthoid. Oihonna relates: In defiance of Fjalar's will never to wage war against anyone any more Hjalmar, his son, has built a warship and manned it with the best warriors in the land and is ready to set sail for foreign coasts. Eventually Hjalmar comes before his father to be punished by death for his disobedience. The weak blow of the king's sword, however, does not hurt Hjalmar at all. His heavy yellow locks, it seems, saved him. Now he is free to go.

Song IV opens with Morannal calling for Oihonna from a window in his tower. He is blind and needs her help. At last she comes. The king then tells her that Hjalmar and a fleet of Lochliners have arrived in Innishonna. From there he has sent the king of Morven a declaration of war. The reason for this is that he wants to take Oihonna for his bride, whose beauty he has heard of everywhere. The old king further tells Oihonna how a lonesome sea marauder of Lochlin, called Darg, had to jump into the sea from his ship in a thunderstorm, holding a child in his arms. Morannal saved them both. The child was Oihonna. Morannal also tells Oihonna that Darg found her in the sea outside Fjalar's castle in Lochlin, near a cliff. The Lochliners come and during the fight Hjalmar meets Gall, Rurmar and Clesamor in single combat. After fighting courageously and fiercely they all fall one by one at Hjalmar's sword. When the fighting is over the king of Morven expires.

Lochlin is the setting of Song V. The old king, who spends most of his time in the hall, asks to be taken to Telmar, a mountain nearby, from which he can overlook his whole kingdom. He does so and says he has kept the oath he swore once, seeing houses and tilled fertile fields of which there were none in his youth. Sjolf, however, rebukes him for his self-sufficiency. Fjalar says he wants to die and mentions Dargar, who comes beside him there on the top of the mountain. The king reminds Dargar that the divine threat he had pronounced over his lineage has not come true. Then Hjalmar comes before his father and discloses to him that Fjalar's only son had come to marry his own sister. Previously Hjalmar had killed Oihonna with blood-stained sword in his hand. Before father and son die simultaneously Fjalar humbles himself before the gods: 'I do know you now. I am not ashamed of bending to you. I have had enough of life and earthly greatness is worth little to me. I go to you.'[15]

As has been shown, the poem opens in Gauthiod. But in his youth, the king points out in his first speech, he made war on Morven. This reference signals, so to speak, the total setting of Song II: Morven. Its opening lines have a rare, simple beauty: 'Gloriously Shelma of the heroes mirrors its gleaming towers in Crona's wave. The sun empties from the east a flood of light over Morven'.[16] Finjal's former hall is in itself an inviting place. Now, however harp-music and mirth have fled from it because of Gall's, Rurmar's and Clesamor's ill-feeling against each other. Here too live king Morannal and Oihonna. The marriage talks which Gall, Rurmar and Clesamor have in turn with Oihonna, contain many references to physical nature and animal life or weapons, which are also in *Ossian*: *cave, rustling leaves, deer, arrow, bow, the blood of the deer, dark clouds*. Runeberg also mentions the *top of Mallmor* (the poet's spelling) and bardic song.[17]

The setting of Song III, too, is Morven and the hunting scene with which it opens is indeed typical of *Ossian*. Gylnandyne's elegy and Oihonna's forceful lines touch on common themes of Ossianic balladry.

The action of Song IV is also set in Morven. Morannal calls Oihonna 'you beam of light in Shelma's misty night' and goes on to mention evening clouds turned pale sailing in the starlit sky.[18] The moon shedding 'its stream of quivering light on its hills' is there, too.[19] The following description of a rock is very beautiful: 'The sky is overcast, the ocean more and more is covered with darkness and steel grey Garmalla's rock towers shaking from its crown the white foam of the surf'.[20] As the last part of this Song is a battle description, weapons like *the sword, the spear* and *the shield* are mentioned. So are fallen heroes at rest 'on the bed of sand', 'a tombstone in the land of harps', and *the grave* Morannal asks Oihonna to bury him in.[21] It should be noted that Runeberg introduces an equivalent of the *of genitive* into a number of his epithets.

The action of Song V, finally, only evolves at and near King Fjalar's castle. Here the two most interesting points with reference to setting are the mountain top of Telmar and the Gauthiod the king sees from its top. Does it differ from Morven at all in a physical sense? The following comments on the setting of the poem will throw some light on this question and on Runeberg's method of integrating elements from *Ossian* in his poem. The setting in *Kung Fjalar* has its precedent in *Ossian*. Runeberg integrated elements from *Ossian* into his poem and did so exactly where they became natural and necessary in accordance with his own plan for *Kung Fjalar*. Gauthiod and Morven resemble each other, having rocky coasts, mountains and valleys. While farming is not mentioned with respect to Morven, Fjalar refers to it seeing Gauthiod from Telmar. This is a remarkable difference in the living conditions of peoples belonging to the same heroic age. It probably is an inconsistency of the poet's. Runeberg even changed the tenor of a passage in *Ossian* when he dovetailed it into his own poem. Thus the deer at Crona's stream mentioned in Comala leapt away, while in *Kung Fjalar* Oihonna's arrow has killed it.[22] Macpherson's Oithona, and Runeberg's Oihonna, live very different lives though both are truly heroic characters. Oihonna helping old Morannal in his blindness in Runeberg's poem again shows that she has actually taken on the duties which Malvina, Oscar's bride, carried out according to Macpherson's poems. (See for instance *Carthon* and *Croma*.) In *Carthon* there is an invocation to the sun.[23] There may be an echo from this in Morannal's words to his sons before the war with Hjalmar. Subsequently, however, he says something which definitely goes back to the ending of *Croma*: 'Happy is he whom years do not break, who is allowed, still young, to fall among heroes'. In comparison Macpherson's text in *Croma* runs: 'Happy are they who die in youth, when their renown is around them'.[24] Also note that in *Kung Fjalar* Gall, Rurmar and Clesamor are brothers, but not in Macpherson's *Ossian*.

With regard to heroic character it should be noted that Fjalar and Hjalmar have never been beaten in battle. Therefore they represent invincible heroic strength. To ideals of conduct like theirs Oihonna also adheres. In Morven, however, a heroic second generation afterglow prevails after Finjal's death. Still Morannal's three sons fight against Hjalmar with the utmost bravery before they die. Morven's men fell with honour, as worthy adversaries to Hjalmar. It is possible that Runeberg depicted Gauthiod strong and Morven weaker because the dramatic action of the poem as a whole needed this. Other explanations, however, exist. In the first place it is reasonable to contend that the idea of the successive ages of man actually influenced him. Other sources from which he could have derived the concept of Morven were Montesquieu's *L'Esprit des lois* and Edward Gibbon's *Decline and Fall of the Roman Empire*.[25] The doctrine of the superiority of the North, prevalent in European thought ever since Montesquieu, evidently underlies Runeberg's heroic picture of Gauthiod.[26]

Fingal's peace follows on full reconciliation. Though it is the victor's peace, it leaves no resentment since he also used to give it under the pledge and seal of friendship. As Fingal's heroic greatness is always beyond dispute, the peace which he dispenses is genuinely generous. He does not demand it. Heaven simply gives it to him as a blessing for others. Fjalar on his side wants to give lasting peace to realms both near and far. He wants to do so because continuous warfare will impoverish his country and others. But a curse, a threat from the gods, lies over Fjalar's peace. Here is no doubt the big difference between Fingal's and Fjalar's peace. Fjalar, further, proclaims his peace while Fingal's is a natural outflow of his own generous personality. Reconciliation is vital to Fingal, the peacemaker, as *Fingal* shows. King Fjalar, however, does not mention it.[27]

Dargar is a messenger of the gods to men. When he first approaches the king 'his figure appeared taller at every step he took and stood before Fjalar like a giant'.[28] He speaks firmly and acts calmly and has existed in the land for a century. Who is this seer, hearing the words of men from afar? Söderhjelm says that Dargar is modelled on the figure of Tiresias.[29] If he is right it is quite surprising to find Dargar sitting 'at the top of a cliff in the calm, quietly listening to sounds from the brim of a mighty cloud' which clearly reminds the reader of *Ossian*. Dargar is moreover a spirit appearing in the full shape of a man. Therefore it is possible that the writer has got this figure from ideas of the happy Celtic otherworld or from the Bible.[30] Oihonna for her part points out that it is in dreams that she has appeared to the hero she admires but whom she has not yet met. Still her presence in his dreams has enflamed his heart for her as a preparation for their fateful encounter. This is a convention of *Ossian*'s which Runeberg benefitted from when knitting parts of his poem closely together.[31]

Why did Runeberg work into his poem so many details of setting and character from *Ossian*? Like many writers of epic poetry Runeberg felt a need for attaching *Kung Fjalar* to the epic tradition, which he found in *Ossian*.

Runeberg had not only a deep sense of the dramatic element in narrative writing but he was also possessed of a strong, lyrical vein. He must have found it difficult to use this gift in times when the social novel attracted greater interest than poetry.[32] For these two main reasons I hold that the Celtic material Runeberg met with in the process of writing *Kung Fjalar* became an incentive to use this kind of poetry widely.

The action is closely held together. A reference in one part is regularly given to prepare the reader for coming events in another. The extremely clear delineation of the action may, to some extent, depend on the relative shortness of the poem, even compared to *Fingal*, but also on the strongly dramatic progress of the action. In composing the action of *Kung Fjalar* Runeberg may have used a story in the *Didrik Saga*, he certainly used *Ossian*, Sophocles's *Antigone* and in particular *Oedipus Rex*.[33] Oihonna's encounter with Gylnandyne is clearly an episode. So are retrospective parts of King Fjalar's speeches.

The poem has one regular battle. There is bloodshed too, when Hjalmar kills his bride (sister) and when father and son die, but the interior conflict dominates. There is therefore little scope for the display of skill in the use of arms, common in epic poetry. Thus heroic virtues bear more on the interior conflict in the poem than on the epic battle. This exists, but it is unimportant as a description. This is so because the poet uses few of Macpherson's battle conventions and merely hints at some of them. Runeberg refers to bards singing to the harp, but this does not happen within the action proper as in *Fingal*. In the *Iliad* and in *Fingal* they celebrate the epic feast, which also King Fjalar's warriors do. Is *Kung Fjalar*, then, an epic poem in the strictest sense? My contention is that it is rather a dramatic poem than an epic. Still, however, this is poetry of a master's making. It is a pity that very few will ever be able to understand Runeberg's poetry in its original language.

Notes

The author is responsible for all translations in this paper. Ossian refers to Macpherson's *Ossian*. When Runeberg's poem is concerned I follow his spelling of names.

1. Theodor Hasselqvist, *"Ossian" i den svenska dikten och litteraturen jämte inledning*, akademisk afhandling (Malmö, Förlags-Aktiebolagets Boktryckeri, 1885), p.7, cited hereafter as Hasselqvist.
2. Hasselqvist, pp.6-7, 43.
3. *Ibid.*, p.43.
4. *Ibid.*, p.43.
5. Paul van Tieghem, *Le Préromantisme: études d'histoire littéraire européenne* (Paris, SFELT, 1948), vol.I, p.22.
6. Hasselqvist, p.41.
7. Johan Ludvig Runeberg, *Samlade Aberten* Normaluppluga, 8 vols (Helsingfors,

G.W. Edlunds Förlag, 1899-1902), vol.V, pp.5-87. These pages are subsequently referred to as *Kung Fjalar*. Werner Söderhjelm, *Johan Ludvig Runeberg* Senare Delen (Stockholm, Holger Schildts Förlag, Helsingfors, 1929). This work is cited hereafter as Söderhjelm.

8. Söderhjelm, pp.132-33. *Ossians Sånger* Förra delen, translated by Nils Arfwidsson (Stockholm, Tryckta pâ C.A. Bagges Förlag Hos P.A. Norstedt & Söner, Kongl. Boktryckare, 1842).

9. *Kung Fjalar*, for page reference see n.7.

10. *Ibid.*, translated from p.11.

11. *Ibid.*, translated from p.15.

12. *Ibid.*, translated from p.23.

13. *The Poems of Ossian In the Original Gaelic with a literal translation into English and a dissertation on the authenticity of the poems by the Rev. Archibald Clerk together with the English translation by Macpherson*, 2 vols (Edinburgh and London, William Blackwood and Sons, 1860), vol.I, pp.259-79: *Golnandona*.

14. *Kung Fjalar*, translated from p.39.

15. *Ibid.*, translated from p.87.

16. *Ibid.*, translated from p.19.

17. *Ibid.*, pp.24-30, 'grottans svalka' (p.24), 'darrande löf' (p.24), 'hjorten' (p.25), 'hjortens blod' (p.26), 'pilen' (p.26), 'min bâge' (p.26), 'dunkla skyarnas irrande fält' (p.30).

18. *Ibid.*, translated from p.53: 'du strimma / I Shelmas dimmiga natt'.

19. *Ibid.*, translated from p.53. 'pâ dess kullar / Sin ström av darrandeljus'.

20. *Ibid.*, translated from pp.58-59.

21. *Ibid.*, pp.64-69,, 'svärdets blixt' (p.64), 'sin ungdoms sköld (p.65), 'pê sandens bädd' (p.69), 'En vârd i harpornas land' (p.69).

22. James Macpherson, *Poems of Ossian*, ed. Malcolm Laing (Edinburgh, 1805), facsimile of the 1805 edition, 2 vols (Edinburgh, James Thin, 1971), vol.I, p.216. Hereafter cited as Laing.

23. Laing, vol.I, pp.342-45.

24. *Kung Fjalar*, translated from p.58: 'Säll den som af âr ej bryts, / Som ung fâr falla i hjeltars rund'. Laing, vol.I, p.549, *Croma*.

25. A complete Swedish translation of Gibbon's work was published 1820-34.

26. In my thesis, *Epic Tradition and Innovation in James Macpherson's Fingal*, Acta Universitatis Upsaliensis Studia Anglistica Upsaliensia 44 (Uppsala, Distributor Almqvist & Wiksell International, Stockholm, 1982), pp.51, 66, there are references to Mallet, whose ideas are also of importance on this point. My dissertation will be quoted hereafter as *Epic Tradition and Innovation*. P.v. Tieghem, *Ossian et l'Ossianisme dans la littérature européenne au 18e siècle* (Den Haag, Groningen, 1920), pp.41 45.

27. *Epic Tradition and Innovation*, pp.92, 112-13.

28. *Kung Fjalar*, translated from p.10: 'Högre dock varje steg hans skepnad Gjorde och jättelik han för Fjalar stod'.

29. Södderhjelm, p.133.

30. *Kung Fjalar*, translated from p.10: 'pâ klippans spets i lugnet / Lyssnade tyst till ljud frân ett nattmolns rand'.

31. James Macpherson's *Ossian, herausgegeben von Otto L. Jiriczek, Faksimile-Neudruck der Erstausgabe von 1762/63 mit Gleitband; Die Varianten, in drei Bänden* (Heidelberg, Carl Winters Universitätsbuchhandlung, 1940), vol.I, p.52 (*Fingal*).

32. Johan Ludvig Runeberg, *Kung Fjalar*, ed. Algot Werin (Lund, Gleerups Förlag, 1966), p.3.

33. Söderhjelm, pp.134, 133.

40

The Effects of Ossian in Lowland Scotland

Leah Leneman
University of Edinburgh

In the first half of the eighteenth century the Highlands held no appeal for Lowland Scots. The scenery had no attraction, as evidenced by descriptions such as Daniel Defoe's 'frightful country full of hidious desart mountains'.[1] The language was considered barbarous and the people were seen as superstitious and incorrigibly idle. Indeed, their whole way of life seemed an offence against the Calvinist work ethic.

The only attraction which the Highlands had at this time was *potential*. If the Highlanders could be remade in the image of Lowlanders—learn to speak English, become honest, hardworking, and industrious, discover the delights of true religion, and become imbued with the principles of the Glorious Revolution—then the area might become peaceful and prosperous instead of warlike and poor.

As far as the reformers were concerned there was nothing to be weighed in the balance against these benefits. If someone had suggested to them (no one did) that perhaps there was much joy to be gained from singing songs and reciting poetry in a language rich in such productions; that a conviction of kinship with the chief of the clan might give a feeling of worth to every man however poor and lowly; that hospitality, generosity and loyalty were virtues not to be despised; and that hardiness, endurance and the ability to withstand extremes of cold and hunger were in any way admirable, the response would have been utter incomprehension. The Highlanders were 'savages'; no one in the early eighteenth century was interested in observing them or in learning more about them.[2] The aim was to 'civilise' them.

After the '45 it became necessary to get to grips with the Highlands. The strand of thought which dominated the pre-1745 attitude toward the Highlands—that the whole of the *Gaidhealtachd* should be refashioned in the image of the Lowlands—can be found in the aftermath of the rising, particularly in the debate which took place within the pages of the *Scots Magazine* in 1746.[3] One writer enjoined compassion on the 'poor ignorant

357

men, whose whole way of life rendered them incapable of enjoying the benefit, and insensible of the blessing of a mild and gracious government, and so more liable to be drawn into the snare by the subtle insinuations of their chiefs'. The notion of the common people as slaves who could be redeemed and rendered respectable citizens if only they were removed from the sway of their chiefs is one which recurs frequently in this period.

The idea of 'civilising' the Highlands could be illustrated from many other sources,[4] but the theme of this paper is the very different stream of thought which became prevalent after the publication of James Macpherson's 'Ossianic' poems in the early 1760s. This stream of thought also started from the premise that the Highlanders were 'savage', but it came to a different conclusion, because the primitivist ideas which were so intrinsic to Enlightenment thinking saw virtue in 'savage' societies. Important seeds were sown by the publication of Jerome Stone's translation (or, rather, adaptation) of a fine old Gaelic elegy in the *Scots Magazine* in January 1756, for it made it feasible to consider the possibility of more fine ancient poetry emanating from the 'savage' Highlands. Clearly it was this belief that made John Home, and later Hugh Blair and others, so eager to accept the fragments and then the 'epic' which James Macpherson presented to them. Similarly, the belief already in existence, that primitive societies were not just braver and bolder than modern societies but also somehow more refined and nobler of spirit, made it easy for the literati to accept the type of society which Macpherson pictured for them in the Ossianic poems. The frequency with which Ossian was subsequently invoked to 'prove' such theories is evidence enough of this.

A great deal of attention has been given to the effect of Ossian on Germany and other Continental countries but very little to how it affected Lowland Scots. The effects were threefold, but they coalesced to form a new image of the Highlands.

First of all, Ossian provided a new way of looking at wild and desolate scenery. 'Sublimity' is the key concept here. Hugh Blair's writing enlarged the theme considerably and his ideas gained wide credence. A sublime object, according to Blair, 'produces a sort of internal elevation and expansion; it raises the mind much above its ordinary state; and fills it with a degree of wonder and astonishment'. Flowery fields were not conducive to sublimity, 'but the hoary mountain, and the solitary lake; the aged forest, and the torrent falling over the rock'.[5] The way in which so much of the scenery of the Highlands conforms to these ideas of the sublime is an important element in the impact of Ossian.

The question of whether Blair's ideas about sublimity preceded or postdated Ossian is an interesting one and can probably best be answered by saying, 'both'. Blair's published material appeared after *Fingal* and *Temora*, and he used Ossianic examples to illustrate his points. Blair's biographer summed up the situation: 'Macpherson's stuff was meat for Blair's theories, and Blair's theories were, one suspects, the food on which Macpherson's poetical efforts throve and flourished.'[6]

The new way of looking at Highland scenery may be illustrated by the following passage from a book entitled *Observations relative chiefly to Pic-*

*turesque Beauty made in the year 1776, on several parts of Great Britain;
particularly the High-Lands of Scotland* by William Gilpin. Referring to
remarks made by Samuel Johnson about his tour of the Highlands, Gilpin
writes:

> It is true indeed, that an eye, like Dr Johnson's, which is accustomed to see the
> beauties of landscape *only in flowery pastures, and waving harvests*, cannot be
> attracted to the great, and sublime in nature...Dr.Johnson says, the Scotch
> mountain has the appearance of matter *incapable of form, or usefulness...as for
> it's being incapable of form*, he can mean only that it cannot be formed into
> cornfields, and meadows. Its form as a mountain is unquestionably grand and
> sublime in the highest degree. For that poverty in objects, or *simplicity*, as it may
> be called, which no doubt injures the beauty of a Scottish landscape; is certainly
> at the same time the *source of sublimity*.[7]

Not everyone was able to respond to Highland scenery in this way, but in
the post-Ossianic era every visitor knew how he or she was expected to
respond. This is beautifully captured in the following remarks by Mrs Anne
Grant of Laggan, who was born in the Highlands but spent most of her
childhood in America, before returning in 1773:

> When I came...to Scotland, Ossian obtained a complete ascendant over my
> imagination...Thus determined to like the Highlands; a most unexpected occur-
> rence carried me, in my seventeenth year, to reside there, and that at Abertarfe,
> the most beautiful place in it; yet it is not easy to say how much I was repelled
> and disappointed. In vain I tried to raise my mind to the tone of sublimity. The
> rocky divisions that rose with so much majesty in description, seemed like
> enormous prison walls, confining caitiffs in the narrow glen. These, too, seemed
> like the dreary abode of solitude and silence. These feelings, however, I did not
> even whisper to the rushes.[8]

After she had lived there for some time, Anne Grant became a passionate
advocate of the Highlands and Highlanders, but her initial reaction is certainly revealing.

Apart from the supposed appeal of the sublime in general, the enormous
success of Ossian also gave the Highlands specific associations. When Charles
Cordiner, a minister from Banff who was asked by Thomas Pennant to draw
some picturesque scenes of Highland Scotland, visited a locality connected
with Ossian, he not only described the scene at length, with appropriate
quotations from *Temora*, he also included a blind harper in the foreground
of his picture of the waterfall.[9]

Robert Burns certainly fell under the Ossianic spell. In September 1786,
when he returned to Edinburgh after a tour which included Highland
Perthshire, he wrote to his brother Gilbert, hardly mentioning the last stages
of his journey for, as he put it, '[wa]rm as I was from Ossian's country
where I had seen his very grave, what cared I for fisher-towns and fertile
carses?'[10]

In Tobias Smollett's novel, *Humphry Clinker*, the character of Jery, who is depicted as a very ordinary, down-to-earth young man, writes to a friend from the Highlands: 'I feel an enthusiastic pleasure when I survey the brown heath that Ossian wont to tread; and hear the wind whistle through the bending grass—When I enter our landlord's hall, I look for the suspended harp of that divine poet, and listen in hopes of hearing the aerial sound of his respected spirit.'[11]

However, for Lowland visitors to the Highlands it was not simply a question of losing themselves in associations with a literary past; they also saw present-day Highlanders in a new light. The surroundings in which they lived were said to have had a profound effect on the Ossianic heroes, and those surroundings had not changed significantly over the centuries, so it followed that eighteenth-century Highlanders possessed many of the same qualities as their noble ancestors. Anne Grant writes of 'the hold which long-descended habits of thinking, heightened by wild poetry and wilder scenery, took of even the more powerful intellect, giving to the whole national character a cast of "dreary sublimity" as an elegant critic has happily expressed it, altogether unique and peculiar'. [12]

This new perception made Highlanders acceptable in a way which would hitherto have been unimaginable. It is significant to note that one of Anne Grant's books was entitled *Essays on the Superstitions of the Highlanders*, for in the Romantic era superstitions were not to be despised; they added to the mystical aura of primitive societies. It is fascinating to recall that Anne Grant actually lived among Highlanders, and her books do reveal a good deal of perception about them. For example, she writes of the Highlander that 'he perfectly comprehends that we know many things of which he is ignorant; but then he thinks, first, that in his situation, none of those things would make him better or happier, though he did know them; and, next, that he possesses abilities to acquire all that is valuable in knowledge, if accident had thrown him in the way of culture'.[13] This is all very commonsensical, yet at the same time she can turn them into living exemplars of the primitivist idea, as in the following extract:

> The importance and necessity, in a country thus enervated by luxury, thus lost in frivolous pursuits and vain speculations, to cherish in whatsoever remote obscurity they exist, a hardy manly Race, inured to Suffering, fearless of Danger, and careless of Poverty, to invigorate Society by their Spirit, to defend it by their Courage, and to adorn it with those Virtues that bloom in the shade, but are ready to wither away in the sunshine of prosperity.[14]

It seems to me that Anne Grant is inhabiting two worlds simultaneously, a real one and a mythological or idealised one. She did in fact become proficient enough at the Gaelic language to translate some old poems, and her translations, while versified to suit current taste, are close enough to the originals to be recognisable. However, when she switched to writing her own poetry it became full of sentimental clichés. Here are just three lines from *The Highlanders*:

Where ancient Chieftains rul'd those green retreats,
And faithful Clans delighted to obey
The kind behests of patriarchal sway.[15]

It is noteworthy that in the course of half a century clan chiefs have been transformed from ruthless oppressors to kindly patriarchs.

Anne Grant was by no means the only person capable of inhabiting the two worlds simultaneously. Patrick Graham, who contributed one of the century's numerous essays on the 'authenticity' of Ossian, observed that 'the prospect which perpetually engages the eye of the Highlander, of barren heath, lofty mountains, rugged precipices, and wide stretched lakes, has a natural tendency to call forth sentiments of sublimity, which are unfavourable to frivolousness of thought'.[16] Now Patrick Graham was in fact minister at Aberfoyle, and one can scarcely credit that he did not come into contact with some 'frivolousness of thought' in his daily contact with parishioners. Indeed, in the same publication quoted above he wrote: 'to such scenery as the Trossachs exhibit, the natives attribute no beauty. They consider such scenes as horrible; and however attached they may be to their native soil, they sigh after an exchange of such abodes, for the rich and level plains of the low-country. To enjoy these scenes, the culture of taste is requisite'.[17] If the 'culture of taste' is necessary, then what becomes of the natural tendency of the scenery to call forth sentiments of sublimity?

A final quotation—from Francis Jeffrey's review of *The Lady of the Lake*—seems to me to encapsulate the new view of the Highlands. It will be noted that all the things which everyone wanted to destroy before, and immediately after, the '45 are the very things which are here being lauded:

There are few persons, we believe, of any degree of poetical susceptibility, who have wandered among the secluded vallies of the Highlands, and contemplated the singular people by whom they are still tenanted—with their love of music and of song—their hardy and irregular life, so unlike the unvarying toils of the Saxon mechanic—their devotion to their chiefs—their wild and lofty traditions—their national enthusiasm—the melancholy grandeur of the scenes they inhabit—and the multiplied superstitions which still linger among them,—without feeling, that there is no existing people so well adapted for the purposes of poetry, or so capable of furnishing the occasions of new and striking inventions.[18]

I am certainly not arguing that Ossian led to a greater understanding of Gaelic culture on the part of Lowlanders. The eighteenth century was the era of some of the finest Gaelic poetry ever composed, but this genuine poetry was largely ignored by the Lowlanders who lapped up Ossian. Ossian was eagerly accepted because it chimed in so well with Enlightenment ideas about primitive societies, and because it fulfilled a genuine need by transforming a hitherto unacceptable section of the Scottish population into one which was universally admired.

Notes

1. Daniel Defoe, *A Tour Through the Whole Island of Great Britain*, 2 vols (London, J.M. Dent, 1959), vol.2, p.420.
2. There are some exceptions to this statement, e.g. Martin Martin in the seventeenth century and the Englishman, Edwart Burt, in the 1720s. But their works only gained a readership in the second half of the eighteenth century.
3. *Scots Magazine*, 8 (1746), pp.469-82.
4. E.g. *The Albemarle Papers* (Aberdeen, New Spalding Club, 1902), vol.1, pp.306-11; vol.2, pp.480-91; *Culloden Papers* (London, 1815), pp.299-300; *More Culloden Papers* (Inverness, 1930), vol.5, p.71; A. Lang, ed., *The Highlands of Scotland in 1750* (Edinburgh & London, W. Blackwood & Sons, 1898).
5. Hugh Blair, *Lectures on Rhetoric and Belles Lettres*, 3 vols (Edinburgh, 1806), vol.1, pp.53 and 55.
6. R.N. Schmitz, *Hugh Blair* (New York, 1948), p.45.
7. William Gilpin, *Observations relative chiefly to Picturesque Beauty made in the year 1776, on several Parts of Great Britain; particularly the High-Lands of Scotland*, 2 vols (London, R. Blamire, 1789).
8. Anne Grant of Laggan, *Essays on the Superstitions of the Highlanders of Scotland* (hereafter *Essays*), 2 vols (London, Longman, etc., 1811), vol.II, pp.335-36.
9. Charles Cordiner, *Antiquities and Scenery of the North of Scotland in a Series of Letters to Thomas Pennant Esquire* (London, 1774), p.76. This in spite of Cordiner's own scepticism about the supposed authenticity of the poem.
10. Quoted in F.B.Snyder, *The Life of Robert Burns* (New York, King's Crown Press, 1932), p.249.
11. Thomas Smollett, *The Expeditions of Humphry Clinker* (London, OUP, 1966), p.240.
12. Grant, *Essays*, vol.I, p.256. I have no idea who the elegant critic might be.
13. Grant, *Essays*, vol.I, pp.30-31.
14. Anne Grant, *The Highlanders and Other Poems*, 3rd edition (Edinburgh, Longman, etc., 1810), pp.73-74.
15. *Ibid.*, p.32.
16. Patrick Graham, *Sketches Descriptive of Picturesque Scenery on the Southern Confines of Perthshire* (Edinburgh, P. Hill and W. Hunter, 1806), p.23.
17. *Ibid.*, p.23.
18. *Edinburgh Review* (August 1810), p.280.

41

Ossianic Imagination and the History of India: James and John Macpherson as Propagandists and Intriguers

George McElroy

Indiana University Northwest

Notoriously, James Macpherson invented an epic by a third-century bard hymning the repulse of an eighth-century Scandinavian invasion, turning Ireland's legendary Finn MacCumhal into Fingal, a Scottish king. Less known are Macpherson's historical and political writings, equally rich in imagination and prevarication. Those concerning India, some in collaboration with John Macpherson were, literally, devastating.

As merely a translator of *Fingal* James forwent the title of 'poet', but bid for a scholarly reputation with pseudo-learned notes and dissertations, attempting to wrest from Ireland not merely Finn but all Scots. Many of his arguments, he acknowledged, originated with Dr John Macpherson, minister of Sleat, whom he had met during his 'researches'. He had also met the minister's son, John Macpherson—handsome, tall, ballad-singing, convivial, verbose and enterprising.

John studied at Edinburgh, then tutored the Earl of Warwick's sons, forming a useful (perhaps homosexual) connexion.[1] In 1767 he went to Madras as purser of a ship commanded by his uncle. There he impressed the Nabob of Arcot, the India Company's sponsored ruler of the Carnatic (the province surrounding Madras) not only with his important English contacts, electrical experiments, and a magic lantern, but also his own ingenious invention—that George III had been the Nabob's ally and guarantor since the Treaty of Paris of 1763, in which France and England had recognised 'Mahomed Ally Khan for lawful Nabob of the Carnatic, and Salabat Jang for Lawful Subah of the Deckan'.[2]

The Deckan (South) was the southernmost Suba (province) of the Mughal empire. The Carnatic[3] was its southernmost division, governed by a subordinate Faujdar (loosely, 'Nabob') at Arcot, sixty miles from Madras.

363

Mughal Subadars (or Nizams) and Faujdars were appointed and often changed. But in the mid eighteenth century, with imperial authority collapsing, officers of this military bureaucracy tried to freeze themselves into their jobs; rivals tried to oust them. The French and English companies backed rival Subadars and Nabobs, fighting even when their nations were at peace as 'allies' of these claimants. Thus the final defeat of the French during the Seven Years' War was acknowledged in the treaty by recognising the English-backed rulers. That Salabat Jang proved to have been overthrown by his brother, Nizam Ali, was no matter; France was still eliminated. But now John transformed that elimination into an alliance between George III and Mohammed Ali, and a French-British guarantee of the latter's dominions.

John came home commissioned to represent the Nabob's interests to his royal ally.[4] Warwick introduced him to Grafton, the Premier, after John had smoothed his way by joining James as the chief ministerial propagandists. From then on they were a classic bad guy-good guy team of manipulators: James threatened, John placated. Trevor-Roper rightly calls James a 'sensual bully whose aim ... was wealth and power'.[5] John was everybody's friend until their interests clashed.

James's tri-weekly *Public Advertiser* letters, over various signatures, attributed to Grafton the Ossianic virtues of firmness and manly, vigorous, decisive action; he was guiltless of that worst of ministerial—or epic—sins, timidity. John, in verse and prose, abused Opposition writers as feeble, seditious, ungrammatical, poor, hungry, and Irish, particularly Burke, whom they took to be Junius.[6]

Grafton gladly heard from this valuable supporter that Company servants oppressed the Nabob. The Premier had a quarrel with the India Company, but knew nothing of India. John enlightened him, even while—ever ingratiating—he made friends at India House and influenced dispatches, particularly, I believe, a paragraph in the Directors' letter to the Madras Select Committee of March 1769 concerning Tanjore: from this came decades of trouble.

Tanjore, wealthiest of the Hindu-ruled states south of the Mughal dominions, lay on the coast just south of the Carnatic, small but fertile. Aurengzebe had forced it to pay a tribute, through the Faujdar of Arcot, but it had remained independent. During the long French-English war Raja Pretaub Sing had sometimes wavered with the two powers' fluctuating fortunes, but at several critical times had supported the English, never the French. Consequently when, after the French defeat, the Nabob looked for revenues to pay the Company's bill for war expenses, and suggested borrowing their army to force great sums from Tanjore, Governor Pigot insisted, instead, on mediating a treaty, guaranteed by the Company, settling claims and fixing a moderate tribute. One of the Nabob's grievances against the Company was their not allowing him to squeeze or seize Tanjore.

In 1767-1768 Madras and the Nabob picked a quarrel with Haidar Ali of Mysore, hoping to add his newly-acquired dominions to the Nabob's. The Nabob wrote to Governor Bourchier that Tanjore should contribute to his war; Bourchier noted that the 1762 treaty did not oblige it to, but did ask aid from Raja Tuljaji, who had succeeded his father in 1764 and who sent some troops.

In the fateful March 1769 dispatch, the Directors of the East India Company ordered Madras to stop waging wars to aggrandise Mohammed Ali. But in the paragraph which I think John suggested, they proposed assuaging the Nabob's disappointment by making Tanjore contribute to his war costs, since it was sheltered by his territory. Should the Raja refuse, Madras should take such measures 'as the Nabob may think consistent with the justice and dignity of his government'.[7] That vague grandiloquence was quoted by John and James incessantly for fifteen years.

Tanjore had not been sheltered. Haidar invaded the Carnatic and forced Tanjore to buy its safety. Then he camped before Madras and made the Presidency sign a peace, mutually restoring all conquests. He insisted Tanjore be included, to protect it against reprisals for having ransomed itself. Directors, reading this, sourly told Madras to suspend their orders against Tanjore.

India stock plummeted on news of Haidar's invasion, and a three-man commission was proposed, to go to India with sweeping powers of re-organisation. The Ministry, perhaps at John's suggestion, demanded to share in it; John supported the demand with an imitation of Ossianic horror tales, plus aristocratic scorn of merchants who lacked an Aberdeen or Edinburgh education. In a field 'too great for the narrow and interested Politics of a commercial society', John asserted, Company servants committed 'Cruelties, oppressions, and breaches of Faith' unknown even to the unprincipled despotisms of Asia. One prince, poisoned, 'expired in horrid convulsions ... at the same table with our greatest heroes'. Another was, 'for a paultry Bribe, invited to a Feast, in order to deliver him upon his return to the Dagger of the Assassin'.[8] Under commercial conquerors, with minds 'not opened by education and contracted by avarice' treaties were broken and murders committed to 'fill the pockets of clerks, scriveners, pitiful factors'; hence the Supervisory Commission should include a governmental appointee to add 'weight and permanence to treaties'. Should the Company refuse, Commodore Lindsay, commanding a squadron going to India, should be made Royal Plenipotentiary to negotiate treaties.[9] The Ministry did so but (timorously) kept that commission secret from the Company.

John publicised the Nabob by getting James's friend, Alexander Dow to insert a laudatory account into the second edition of his *History of Hindustan*; that portion was printed in red in copies sent to ministers, then puffed in the press.[10] (Later, Dow also wrote the *History of England, 1660-1715* which James published as his.)[11]

Grafton arranged for the Company to send John back to Madras in their service, and recommended him to Governor Dupré, who made him his private secretary; he also made friends with the second in Council, Warren Hastings. The Supervisory Commission was lost at sea, but Lindsay arrived and produced his plenipotentiary powers. The Council, uninstructed, would not admit him to their records or deliberations, so he dealt with the Nabob, adopting and reporting his views, as did his successor, Admiral Harland.

Both urged Madras to conquer Tanjore for the Nabob, who obligingly supplied the pretexts.

The Madras Select Committee considered that an independent Tanjore, 'in the heart of the Carnatic', was 'contrary to the natural rights of government' because, as in the late war, its ruler might buy off an invader instead of contributing to the common defence. The 1769 paragraph (despite the order 'suspending' it) they took as authority for the attack. But, reluctant to hand Tanjore to the Nabob, they left its destiny ambiguous.[12]

In 1771 an invasion ended in a harsh compromise which forced the Raja into ruinous extortions on his country, while vainly appealing in all directions for help against an expected new invasion. In 1773 it came. Again the Nabob provided pretexts, this time even flimsier. The Select Committee reasoned that, since the pro-Nabob stance of the Company and the Royal Pleni-potentiary kept them from doing justice to the Raja, he would join any invader, and therefore 'reducing' him was self-defence. The country was conquered and handed to the Nabob, John Macpherson profiting as paymaster. He was corresponding with Hastings, now Governor of Bengal, and working to combine his interests with the Nabob's,[13] (although Hastings, while at Madras, had frequently joined Dupré in opposing the Nabob). At home, so did James, whom Hastings thought one of the only two men he could call 'wise',[14] together with Laughlin Macleane, prime mover in a stock-speculation combine ruined by the 1769 collapse. Macleane had owed so much to Laurence Sulivan, Shelburne, and other powerful losers that a Bengal job had been invented for him so that he could repay them. There, he had been prime confidant to Hastings, himself a Sulivan protégé. In 1775, when the new Ministerial Council majority refused to raise Macleane's income to the necessary level, he went home as Hastings's agent, stopping at Madras to pick up an additional, more remunerative, agency from the Nabob.

But Pigot, indignant at the destruction of his Tanjore settlement, had himself again appointed Governor of Madras and sailed with orders to restore the Raja. Forewarned, the Nabob gave orders on the Tanjore rice crop to his many creditors, including, no doubt, bribes on credit to important Company figures.[15] These gave all Madras an interest in his keeping Tanjore; all avail-able capital was sunk in high-interest loans to the Nabob and his officers; private trade was dead.

Pigot's orders were too peremptory to be opposed, but he wanted his old friend, the Nabob, to avoid public humiliation by himself restoring the Raja. Macpherson, in midnight visits, persuaded Mohammed Ali to hold out and appeal to London for revocation of the orders. Angrily, Pigot had John dismissed from the service.[16] The Nabob signed a plea to the Directors, and a copy went to Macleane and James.

James slandered Pigot in the newspapers, then called on himself to produce the hard facts and cool dispassionate reasoning he always advocated and seldom supplied.[17] In answer, he published the Nabob's plea (probably largely John's creation) as *Letter from Mohammed Allee Chan*, with an imaginative 'State of Facts about Tanjore', by which the Nabob, his father, and grand-father had all, unaccountably, loved and aided the English. The Nabob's father had, he said, fallen in their battle (actually, Madras had had no part in that battle); the Nabob had paid for the Company's wars and loaded the English with favours, while the Rajas of Tanjore had been vicious, usurping tyrants who hated the English and helped the French.

James replaced the Maghal military bureaucracy with his own freshly invented Indian feudal system, by which the Nabob was the 'liege lord' of the Raja, a 'Zemindar ... holding of the Carnatic' and removable for any failure to perform 'feudal duties'. Thus the 1762 treaty had been 'ruinous to the just rights of Mohammed Allee'. James called the present Raja an 'inveterate enemy' to the English, who had helped Haidar 'carry war to the gates of Madras', thus annihilating the 1762 treaty which, in any case, had expired when Pretaub Sing died. By the 'nature of the feudal system in India' it could not extend to the son, whose 'election' must depend on 'the favour of the feudal superior'. (James was as great an expert on Indian feudalism as he had been on pre-historic British and Scottish civilisation.) Therefore, when the Raja failed in his 'feudal obligations' the Nabob lawfully deposed him, though he had been so forbearing as to end the 1771 invasion with a compromise. But the 1773 conquest became imperative because the Raja had been gathering allies to carry fire and sword through the Nabob's dominions, and it had been a blessing to Tanjore, which the Raja had 'laid waste' with 'tyranny, cruelty, oppression', squandering treasures on bramins and fakirs while violating 'every principle of religion'; drunkenly talking of driving the English from India, yet a coward in danger—James, in epic tradition, regularly derided opponents as cowards. Private vices were 'veiled' for 'the honour of human nature—supply your own vice. The only truth in all this was that the Raja, made desperate by the first invasion, had farmed his lands for ready cash, borrowed from the Dutch, and sounded out possible allies for assistance in defending his territory. To restore this man, James concluded, was imprudent and contrary to the feudal rights of the Nabob, who might sue! Copies went to all Proprietors, MPs and London coffee-houses; others were distributed by penny post.[18] John Robinson, North's Secretary to the Treasury, and friend of the Macphersons, sent one to the King.[19]

At Madras, Pigot finally restored the Raja. The Nabob's men carried off all movables, and the Nabob—or John Macpherson for him—sent to Council a flow of exaggerated complaints over incidents inevitable in a sudden transfer. These were pretexts for a growing opposition to Pigot by Councillors who wanted to make the Raja honour the Nabob's orders on the Tanjore rice crop, particularly those in the name of Paul Benfield, principal creditor and frontman for those who did not want their names to appear. That crop was Tanjore's only source of revenue. Pigot would not make a mockery of the restoration, and heatedly objected to more midnight consultations between Councillors and the Nabob or his sons.

A bundle of the Nabob's complaints and coloured versions of Pigot's outbursts was shipped to Macleane, with the Nabob's proposal, evidently written by John, that the Tanjore revenues be deposited with the Company until his rights could be determined by a three-man commission, one named by him, one by the Raja, one by the Bengal Council (who, for various reasons, all supported the Nabob against Pigot). Macleane gave these papers to James, who published them, with comments, as *Original Papers Relative to Tanjore*.[20]

Reiterating the 'facts' of his first pamphlet, James went on to 'dispassionate reasoning'. The Treaty of Paris, in declaring Mohammed Ali 'lawful Nabob of the Carnatic', had *ipso facto* declared him 'sovereign and feudal Lord of Tanjore', since Tanjore depended on that province. So the Nabob, should the Company reject his proposal, would petition the King, his guarantor, and Parliament to take him out of their hands. For the Company, being merchants, had no right, of itself, to wage war. It had only, in virtue of that 1769 paragraph, properly supported the Nabob's just claims, as his auxiliaries and allies. By the Law of Nations (references to Plato, Aristotle, Grotius, and others) a conqueror acquires the property of the conquered; auxiliaries do not. *Ergo*, the Company, in restoring the Raja, had taken the Nabob's property, and was liable for damages.

This, too, went to the Proprietors and the King.[21] The proposal was near acceptance when news came that in Madras a hostile Council majority and the military commander had arrested and confined Pigot and expelled his supporters. John Macpherson had audaciously penned a 'Proclamation' in 'The Name of his Majesty, and the English Nation, from whom are derived the Authority and power of the honorable the East India Company',[22] which steadied wavering troops. James and Macleane filled the papers with paid-for anti-Pigot letters,[23] but the India Proprietors voted to restore the Governor and his supporters and recall his opponents. However, Pigot's leading deposers were Sandwich's protégés, and the Ministry had taken John's dismissal as rank political opposition;[24] it could not let Opposition triumph. Robinson arranged for the Proprietors also to recall Pigot and his supporters.

John, too, came home, as did Benfield, recalled on the justified suspicion of having engineered the coup. John and James continued propagandists for and advisers to the Ministry, promoting the Nabob and Hastings, the first officially supported, the latter opposed. The Madras coup had harmed the Nabob's cause, but in 1779 the Macphersons still hoped ministers would support the Nabob's petition to Parliament. To assist in this they collaborated on a pamphlet, *Considerations on the Conquest of Tanjore*.[25] John, the nominal author, hoped for a Company post and described the Directors and even Pigot as acting well *except* for restoring the Raja. As to that, he enhanced Macphersonian 'facts' with imaginative *non sequiturs*. The 1762 treaty ascertained the Raja's tribute; *ergo* it obligated him to support any war with 'his quota of men, money, stores, and provisions'. When the Company included the Raja as an ally in the 1769 peace treaty they thereby annulled the 1762 treaty.

James finished the pamphlet, loftily refusing to answer opponents' works as 'mere complicated arrogance and fallacy' (p.30). Throughout his life James never replied specifically to the arguments of his antagonists. He unleashed his imagination, proving the Raja dangerous by alleged misdeeds attributable only to his father (p.53), while also sneering that he had been left powerless (p.40). Consistency is not an epic virtue. James proved the Nabob faithful by imagining how a powerful sovereign prince with a disciplined army, forewarned of dismemberment of his dominions, might have drenched the Carnatic with blood and endangered the Company—yet this good old unalterable friend of the English had merely pled for mercy (pp.51-52). Actually, his ill-paid troops were useless.

Simultaneously, James resumed his historian's guise with *The History and Management of the East-India Company*, Volume I 'The affairs of the Carnatic'.[26] (Bullyingly, he threatened a second volume on misdeeds in Bengal.) Unlike John, he pronounced the Company's history mere swindling at home, corruption and tyranny abroad, inevitable among grasping merchants. All this was ammunition for the Ministry; the charter would expire the following year. As usual, he disdains specifics: 'instances of rapacity and injustice ... are too mean for the pen of a historian'; too numerous for brevity. He recounts Indian history less fancifully than in his 'State of Facts', drawing selectively on Orme's *History of the Military Transactions of the British Nation in Indostan*. A map, adapted from Orme, omits a whole mountain range, the Eastern Ghats, and changes type-faces to make CARNATIC embrace the territories of Haidar and the Nabob, making more plausible the latter's claim to the former's territories, now the natural barrier is removed. Many references are broad: 'Universal History, Vol. X'; 'Jesuits Epistles, passim'. Others are untraceable: 'Authentic accounts of Tanjore ... in the hands of the Author'; 'Private information, passim'. One quotation is footnoted to three works.

James purports to counter two books confuting *State of Facts* and *Original Papers*. George Rous's *The Restoration of the King of Tanjore Considered*, with a voluminous appendix of pertinent Company documents, had been commissioned by the Directors. A *Defence of Lord Pigot* had been commissioned by Admiral Hugh Pigot from John Lind, like Rous a barrister and writer. As usual, James avoids their arguments—he disdains pillorying 'fallacies' of men merely doing what they were paid for (assailing Lind, often a co-worker for the Ministry, could have been awkward). He derides the size of Rous's Appendix, as designed to confuse readers, but will use it to condemn the Directors from their own Defence. Most of his specific references are to pages of the Appendix: crucial ones turn out to be in letters from the Nabob, or from Admirals Lindsay and Harland, who knew only what he told them; those to Company proceedings sometimes contain the facts alluded to, but in contexts showing the Nabob's alleged 'rights' were much disputed, for the Macphersons argued 'rights' where Madras frankly argued power.

Leaving two-thirds of Tanjore's revenue to the Raja's disposal, he asserts, is pure waste; Ossianic governments function without money. One footnote is to the point: the 'distress' of the Nabob's creditors extends through Great Britain; it follows that they will act (p.268). The principal creditor, Benfield, was working with the Macphersons.[27]

Benfield got his way, but not immediately, and not about Tanjore. The Macphersons admitted that the Raja's cause, urged by his agent, William Burke, was more popular than the Nabob's.[28] North would not add India debates to his parliamentary problems. But in April 1780, the Macphersons mediated an agreement between the ministers and Laurence Sulivan,[29] who could hope to get out of his financial morass only with the help of the Nabob and Hastings. Ministers abandoned Francis and Wheler, their men on the Bengal Council, signalling support for Hastings by countenancing John's nomination to that Council. Benfield was whitewashed and returned to Madras, recommended by North and Robinson to Lord Macartney, a career civil servant who, though previously not connected with the Company, was made Governor of Madras in order to keep out Pigot's adherents.[30]

Edmund Burke summarised the Macphersons' services to the Nabob:

> They have been indefatigable in their intrigues and publications. They have filled the world with many new topics of argument, and new narratives of fact. They have even been at the pains of correcting and amending history in order to accomodate it to his views ... He had great objects in view, which were not to be compassed but by the arms of the English.

Therefore, nothing was omitted to gain the Nabob British authority to use British power. But, said Burke, the Macphersons argue 'solely about Princes and the rights of Princes. The wretched *people* are no part whatsoever of their consideration'.[31] True: what epic hero ever worried about the peasants?

Burke and his supporters helped keep the Nabob's hands off Tanjore and its people. They could not, though Edmund tried mightily, keep the Nabob's people from the hands of Benfield and the Macphersons. Macartney soon turned against Benfield, but as James (now the Nabob's agent) had written, Benfield could trust to the exertions of his friends at home.[32] When Macpherson and Benfield's supporters helped Pitt defeat Fox, Pitt had all the Nabob's alleged debts authenticated and charged on the Carnatic. Benfield cleared nearly half a million.[33] When Hastings left Bengal before a successor arrived, John became an accidental and incompetent Governor-General, until Cornwallis arrived. He and James teased the Nabob with non-existent prospects of Tanjore, keeping James's agent's fee coming. When the Nabob died John billed the new Nabob for sums he said Mohammed Ali had promised him; he obtained a bond for £100,000,[34] later traded to the Company for a £1,000 a year pension. James's imagination and what Hastings called John's 'elegant and unceasing flow of words'[35] had been a golden fount.

Notes

1. The late Dr James Macleane (who, regrettably, died before completing his projected translation and edition of James Macpherson's papers, largely written, he said, in 'Putney Green gaelic') told me—on what evidence, I do not know—that John was homosexual and that James, having caught him *in flagrante* with Charles Greville, told him he was, thenceforth, in James's power. John never married, nor left such a crop of bastards as proved James's normality. John and Charles Greville, who also never married, were always on cordial terms.

2. In a memorial recounting his services which John sent the Nabob in 1771, he claimed his was the first 'public mention' of the Treaty of Paris 'guarantee'. Or, as the Macphersons later put it, Madras officials had 'industriously concealed'

from the Nabob the implication of that clause. This memo. is the fullest record of John's pro-Nabob actions in 1768-1770. It is printed in [John Lind], *Defence of Lord Pigot* (London, T.Cadell, 1777), Appendix, pp.49-51, and in the Appendix of the Third Report of the Select Committee (1782), *Reports from Committees of the House of Commons, re-printed by Order of the House*, V, 641-43. (Hereafter, *Reports*.) Admiral Harland sent a copy of this memo., with a contemptuous description of Macpherson's dealings with the Nabob, to Lord Rochford, September 1772. India Office Library, *Home Miscellaneous*, 110, fols 495 ff.

3. This is the eighteenth-century British sense of the name. The ancient 'Karnataka' was divided into 'Ballaghat' (above the Ghats—the Eastern Mountain range), roughly, Mysore, and 'Payenghat' (below the Ghats), the coastal province.

4. Harland, in the letter cited in n. 2, said John was paid 1,000 pagodas (about £400) and promised another 3,000 if he succeeded; he was given £3,000 worth of jewels to secure admittance to those in power in England. But, said Harland, the 'credentials' John displayed were really a memorandum of a private transaction he had with the Nabob's dubash (translator), sealed by the latter. That is, John enlarged a commission to deliver letters to Chatham and Shelburne, and urge them to countenance certain requests, into an appointment as Nabob's *vakil*, authorised to negotiate in his name, by displaying a document, with seal, no-one could read. Back in Madras, John was paid his additional 3,000 pagodas, but wanted more; the Nabob wondered what had happened to the jewels, which neither Grafton nor his secretary would accept.

5. 'The Highland Tradition of Scotland' in *The Invention of Tradition*, eds Eric Hobsbawm and Terence Ranger (Cambridge, CUP, 1984), p.41.

6. John is identified as 'Poetikastos', author of an anti-Junius 'Monody' (*Public Advertiser*, 10 April 1769), in *Junius, including Letters by the Same Writer, under other Signatures*, 2nd edition (London, G. Woodfall, 1814), vol. III, pp.201-2. For other identifications of newspaper letters by both Macphersons, I rely primarily on my own stylometric analysis, considering (a) sentence and paragraph lengths, (b) proportions of various grammatical constructions, particularly dividing sentences into 'unified' (simple, or complex with only noun and restrictive clauses) and 'disunified' (complex with non-restrictive clauses; compound complex; compound). My system will be more fully explained in the appendix to my forthcoming article, 'Reflections on the Nabob's debts', in the *Bodleian Record* (1988).

In a letter of John's, he boasts that two Macphersons, under a score of signatures, maintained, unaided, the Ministry's battle against Junius and the Opposition throughout 1769. I have counted at least 21 signatures they used; as with other writing teams, *noms de plume* were passed back and forth.

7. Directors to Madras Select Committee, 17 March 1769, in *Reports*, III, p.188.

8. 'Sallust', *Public Advertiser*, 16 August 1769.

9. 'Vindex', *ibid.*, 19 August 1769.

10. *The History of Hindostan ... Translated from the Persian of Mahummad Casim Ferishta ... with an Appendix containing the History of the Mogul Empire from its Decline in the Reign of Mahummed Shaw, to the present Times*, 2nd edition (London, 1770), pp.396-98. The *Public Advertiser*, 1 March 1770, was 'favoured' with a 'picture of Mahomed Ali Khan' by a correspondent who, having a 'perfect knowledge' of the Nabob, had been so pleased by the 'delineation' of his virtues in Dow's history he had been moved to make his own 'attempt', from 'gratitude and admiration'. Actually, he writes almost a verbatim transcript of the insert in Dow. It was re-printed in the *General Evening Post*, 3 March, the same day the

Public Advertiser had John's versified response to himself—'On reading the Character of Mahommed Ally Kawn, in the *Public Advertiser*':

> Such is the graceful Presence Millions find
> Blest with that Sway despotic they revere.
> Enrich'd with every treasure of the mind,
> Calm in distress, magnificent, sincere.
>
> * * * * * * *
>
> Remotest souls' congenial Virtues blend,
> And George esteems in Asia Britain's Friend.

Whether this implies that Britons, too, would revere a 'sway despotic' is a nice question. Opponents certainly contended that the Macphersons thought so.

11. There are numerous indications of the close relations between Dow and the Macphersons. E.g. in 1768 Dow and James 'kept house together' and went to the King of Denmark's masquerade as a pair of Turks. John Macdonald, *Travels in Various Parts of Europe, Asia, and Africa* (London, Printed for the author and sold by J. Forbes, 1790), p.150. In February 1775, William Forbes wrote (to the Hon. John Forbes) that Macpherson was about to publish 'four huge historical quartos' but had executed them 'in so short a space, that it is wonderful how he has been able to copy it over, besides to compose it; that people do not seem to augur much instruction from it'. NLS, MS 3112, f.27. The wonder ceases on examining the volumes. Two were *Original Papers Containing the Secret History of Great Britain from the Restoration to the Accession of the House of Hanover*, papers admittedly collected by others from the archives of the exiled Stuarts and those of Hanover; James admitted that a 'friend', probably Dow, helped with the translation, and he called himself merely the 'arranger'. A glance will show that, though he claimed authorship of the other two volumes, *The History of Great Britain from the Restoration to the Accession of the House of Hanover* (London, T. Cadell, 1775), in all but the introduction, the sentences are too short, the paragraphs too long, for him. Dow seems far the likeliest 'ghost' for James. He sailed for India about this time to become Commissary-General to Clavering in Bengal, the post first invented for Laughlin Macleane. Perhaps James pulled strings to get him this coveted post; he might have given James the *History* as *quid pro quo*.

12. The Madras Select Committee's recorded reasonings and negotiations, over several months, go through some evolution, but are all based on power and strategy. They had told the Nabob that, should they conquer Tanjore, all arrangements must be provisional, pending the Company's decision. The Nabob outmanoeuvred them by professing reluctance at the last moment. They had no pretext to attack Tanjore on their own account, so they ostentatiously agreed to hand it to the Nabob with no stipulations, reasoning that thus the Company was not bound to anything, though the Nabob assumed everything had been yielded to him. The minutes are printed in George Rous, *The Restoration of the King of Tanjore Considered* ([Printed by order of the Directors of the East India Company] London, 1777), vol. II, pp.569-731.

13. Macpherson to Hastings, 27 September 1774. BL, Add. MSS 29, 135, f.236. Keith Feiling, *Warren Hastings* (London, Macmillan & Co., 1966), p.213.

14. Hastings to John Macpherson, [July 1782]; 27 January 1784. *Warren Hastings' Letters to Sir John Macpherson*, ed. Henry Dodwell (London, 1927), pp.146; 192.

15. The *tankas*, as calculated by William Ross, Marathi translator to Pigot, amounted to 1,407,226 star pagodas, or over £560,000, three fourths to Europeans. In

addition, *taujis*, for services, added 700,000 pagodas, or £280,000. *Defence of Lord Pigot*, Appendix, pp.64-5. Appendix XXX to Rous's *Restoration* documents the Nabob's debts and attendant controversies from Company records. The fullest study, using Macpherson's private papers and the Nabob's Persian records, is John Gurney, *The Debts of the Nabob of Arcot*, (Oxford, D. Phil. thesis, d.4406).

16. Formally, Pigot brought to the Board a copy of Macpherson's memorial of services rendered to the Nabob (see note 2 above), and his dismissal was grounded on the principles, inimical to the Company, displayed in it, and the presumption he still held them. Four Councillors signed a minute adding that they thought he had been 'concerned in the intrigues which ... have lately been carried on at the Nabob's Durbar to the detriment of the Company's service, and which may have impeded the execution of their late orders'. *Defence of Lord Pigot*, Appendix, p.56. *Reports*, vol. V, p.681 and following. 'Chocapah' to Robert Palk, 10 February 1776. HMC, *Palk MSS*, p.264.

17. Paragraphs in *Public Advertiser*, 11 and 14 December 1776. 'An Enemy to Opression', *ibid.*, 17 December. 'Asiaticus', *ibid.*, 18 December. 'An Old Stager on the Coast' (calling for 'facts'), *ibid.*, 19 December. 'INDIA AFFAIRS' (same day): 'a detail of Peculations on the Coast is preparing in the Press'. Another letter calling on Pigot's accusers to provide 'facts', *ibid.*, 14 January 1777. 'An Enemy to Injustice and Oppression', announcing in answer that the *Letter from Mahomed Ali Chan* and *State of Facts* has already been sent, *gratis*, to all MPs and India Company Proprietors, *ibid.*, 17 January.

18. *Morning Chronicle*, 29 March; 31 March 1777.

19. Robinson to the King, 21 March 1777. BL, Add. MSS 33,833, ff.80-82.

20. (London, 1777).

21. See n. 19.

22. *Defence of Lord Pigot*, Appendix, pp.69-72.

23. E.g. four letters in the *Public Advertiser*, 31 March, the day of the Proprietors' ballot to restore Pigot and recall his opponents. The *Public Advertiser* repeatedly specified that *all* letters on India must be paid for as advertisements. More frankly, the *Gazetteer*, the same day, printed as advertisements over two columns of anti-Pigot letters, many identical with those in the *Public Advertiser*. One moderate one complained that Macpherson's 'proclamation' had been taken as the whole of the case for the Madras usurpers. Hugh Boyd, an old friend of Macleane's, was hired to write for the *Gazetteer* and to report debates in India House (for which a Proprietor's stock qualification was temporarily made over to him) and in Parliament. He was notable for his memory in reporting debates, and the identical accounts of these debates which appeared in most papers are presumably his. 'Verax', *True Briton*, 19 December 1799. George Chalmers, *The Author of Junius Ascertained* (London, T. Egerton, 1819), pp.34-36. *The Miscellaneous Works of Hugh Boyd*, ed. Lawrence Dundas Campbell (London, T. Cadell, Jr and W. Boyd, 1800), vol.I, p.276. For weeks almost the only notable newspaper letters disapproving of the Madras coup were from 'Regulus' (probably the virulently anti-Scot, the Rev. Thomas Northcote), a paid regular contributor to the *Gazetteer*.

24. Macleane to Hastings, 4 January 1777. BL, Add. MSS 29,138, f.98.

25. (London, 1779). I believe John wrote the first half, through the first twelve lines of p.29, and that James wrote the rest, beginning, 'We have now gone through the first and second topics originally proposed for discussion'. Note the 'we'.

26. (London, T. Cadell, 1779).

27. Lucy S. Sutherland, *The East India Company in Eighteenth-Century Politics* (Oxford, Clarendon Press, 1952), p.336.
28. *History and Management*, p.268. John Macpherson to Hastings, 13 February 1779. BL, Add. MSS, 29,143, f.79. John, however, hopes that the 'stream which has run against' the Nabob will 'soon turn in his favour'.
29. Feiling, *Hastings*, p.212.
30. North to Macartney, 31 January 1781. Macartney Collection, Deccan College, Poona, d.1013 C. (I owe a xerox of this letter to Professor Regina Janes.) Macartney to Robinson, 12 January 1781. *The Private Correspondence of Lord Macartney*, ed. C. Collin Davies (Camden 3rd series, vol. LXVII, London, the Royal Historical Society, 1950), p.177.
31. *An Enquiry into the Policy of Making Conquests for the Mahometans in India, by the British Arms* (London, 1779), pp. 2, 116. This pamphlet is nominally by William Burke, and he did write about half of it, but both quotations are from portions I believe Edmund wrote. The pamphlet is re-printed in vol. V, *India: Madras and Bengal, 1774-1785*, of the new Oxford edition of *The Writings and Speeches of Edmund Burke*, ed. P.J. Marshall, (Oxford, Clarendon Press, 1981), but from the second edition which was, I believe, revised by William.
32. To Benfield, 19 February 1781. Pierpont Morgan Library.
33. He told Walter Boyd, his partner in a later, disastrous, speculation, that when he left India in 1788, his property there, exclusive of what he had in England, was 14 lacks of pagodas, or about £560,000. By October 1796 he had estates and investments in England worth £247,000; eight lacks (about £320,000) were still in India. Even if he exaggerated somewhat, his assets were more than substantial. It was no consolation to peasants in Southern India that he lost everything by betting mistakenly on the course of funds in revolutionary France. *Letter to the Creditors of the House of Boyd, Benfield and Company* (London, 1800).
34. Memorial by John Macpherson, 7 April 1800. Printed in *Documents Explanatory of the Claim of Sir John Macpherson* (n.p.n.d., printed for Macpherson). Hansard, *Parliamentary Debates*, VII, pp.284-88.
35. To Major Scott, 4 January 1784. G.R. Gleig, *Memoirs of the Life of the Right Hon. Warren Hastings* (London, R. Bentley, 1841), vol. III, p.145.

42

Johnson's Last Word on Ossian: Ghostwriting for William Shaw

Thomas M. Curley

Bridgewater State College, Massachusetts

One of the famous minor episodes in British literary history, Samuel Johnson's debunking of James Macpherson's bogus Ossian poetry, has a direct bearing on Aberdeen and the Enlightenment. Macpherson matriculated at both King's College and Marischal College, Aberdeen, in the 1750s shortly before his spectacular Gaelic forgeries appeared and dazzled Europeans into an awed credulity for more than a century. At Aberdeen too his chief antagonist, Johnson, honoured with the freedom of the city on his only visit in 1773, hoped that the academic community would uncover Macpherson's fraud decisively:

> If the poems were really translated, they were certainly first written down. Let Mr. Macpherson deposit the manuscript in one of the colleges at Aberdeen, where there are people who can judge; and, if the professors certify the authenticity, then there will be an end of the controversy. If he does not take this obvious and easy method, he gives the best reason to doubt; considering too, how much is against it *a priori*.[1]

Johnson himself, however, exposed Macpherson in his memorable *Journey to the Western Islands of Scotland* of 1775. Far less well known was his continuing involvement in the controversy almost to the end of his life through his patronage of the Gaelic scholarship of a young Scottish minister, William Shaw (1743-1831). Their forgotten friendship resulted in a noteworthy pamphlet against a defender of Ossian, entitled *A Reply to Mr. Clark*, that was substantially ghostwritten by Johnson for Shaw in 1782. This neglected and fascinating essay represents, in fact, his last long prose work to be printed in his lifetime. The pamphlet is analysed in the light of his ten year association with Shaw and fully reproduced in these pages for the first time.

Macpherson's forgeries and their exposure by Johnson and Shaw reflected the spirit of the Enlightenment equally, though from opposite angles. The success of the Ossian poems owed much to their anticipation of Romantic literary ideals springing from the cultural upheaval of the European Enlightenment. These publications supposedly comprised a body of primitive epic poetry by a third-century bard who was thought to rival, nay to surpass, Homer himself. Macpherson took advantage of changing tastes by cultivating a sentimental melancholy and a rhapsodic style wholly unlike anything in genuine Scots-Gaelic verse. Johnson, very much a man of the Enlightenment who respected reason (as well as imagination and emotion) in pursuit of truth, attacked what seemed to him an obvious antiquarian hoax. He did not denounce Ossian, as commonly conjectured, because he disliked Scotland or rejected any aesthetic norms other than the traditional Renaissance-Christian classicism in contemporary literary theory. On the contrary, this true-blue patriot of English civilisation was actually a sympathetic observer of north Britain in both its ancient and its modern state. Often as sceptical and historically sophisticated as Hume or Voltaire, Johnson wanted his Highland tour to serve as a time-tunnel into Britain's primitive past for an accurate glimpse of the island's cultural legacy. Yet, obscuring that historical vision of a bygone Celtic Scotland was, as he explained in the *Journey*, a seductive pseudo-history fabricated around Ossian, 'in which the giants of antiquated romance have been exhibited as realities. If we know little of the ancient Highlanders, let us not fill the vacuity with *Ossian*'.[2]

Strict standards of historical truth, far more than national or literary prejudices, ultimately accounted for his antipathy to Macpherson's poems. Johnson had a personal reason to be sensitive about literary fraud; to his later regret he had not only fabricated parliamentary reports ('Debates in the Senate of Lilliput', 1741-44) but had also become entangled in William Lauder's forgery to discredit *Paradise Lost* and found himself forced to pen a retraction for the dishonest Scotsman in 1751. Predisposed to detecting literary lies, Johnson was by no means ill-disposed towards literature of the type that Ossianic poetry purported to be. As early as 1757, he encouraged Charles O'Conor to study Irish Gaelic; nine years later he exhorted the Society for the Propagation of Christian Knowledge to preserve Scottish Gaelic by sponsoring an Erse translation of the Bible: 'I am not very willing that any language should be totally extinguished. The similitude and derivation of languages afford the most indubitable proof of the traduction of nations, and the genealogy of mankind.'[3] Evan Evans's *Some Specimens of the Antient Welsh Bards* (1764) won Johnson's praise; Thomas Percy's *Reliques of Ancient English Poetry* (1765) went forth with Johnson's blessing and ghostwritten dedication; and Thomas Chatterton's bogus Rowley poems provoked Johnson's investigation and grudging appreciation of their precocious beauty. Finally but foremost, all of William Shaw's publications on Gaelic language and literature could boast Johnson's personal supervision and support. To be sure, any genuine linguistic specimen from antiquity was of serious intellectual interest to an author whose international reputation derived from publishing the first genuine English dictionary. Macpherson's poetry was not genuine and, therefore, had no merit: 'Had it been really an ancient work, a true specimen of how men thought at that time, it would have been a curiosity of the first rate. As a modern production, it is nothing.'[4]

Although subsequent studies have shown the fundamental correctness of the case made by Johnson and Shaw against Ossian, Macpherson is still at times forgiven, even commended, for a hoax considered responsible for stimulating popular and scholarly interest in Scottish Gaelic literature. If Johnson could ever have foreseen this inclination to whitewash his disreputable adversary, he surely would have answered that good is never finally promoted by evil. Scottish Gaelic scholarship hardly benefited from the commission of successive literary cheats that would not be fully unmasked until more than a century later when Gaelic studies started to have a respectable historical footing. Self-aggrandisement, rather than a love of Highland lore, motivated Macpherson's literary schemes from the outset. His *Fragments of Ancient Poetry Collected in the Highlands* (1760) contains 'translations' that are much more dependent upon his own imagination than upon authentic Gaelic verse: fourteen of the sixteen published poems were primarily his own creation.[5] Nevertheless, the preface promises a greater discovery by outlining the plot of *Fingal*, a complete epic poem of about nine thousand lines supposedly preserved in the Highlands.

A six-week Highland tour in search of this Gaelic masterpiece, funded by the Scottish literati, including young James Boswell, in 1761, became the pretext for publishing in 1762 an even bolder Ossianic forgery, *Fingal*, in six books. The introduction to this epic insists on its exact translation from *the* (implying a single) Gaelic original, to be made public separately in the future: 'All that can be said of the translation, is that it is literal, and that simplicity is studied. The arrangement of the words in the original is imitated, and the inversions of the style observed.'[6] Macpherson was never to print the Gaelic original of *Fingal* because none existed. The English *Fingal* was its own original, with only a tangential relationship to genuine Ossianic Gaelic sources. Macpherson had concocted it by combining for the first time two distinct ballad traditions about Cuchullin and Finn with fragments of other tales to produce an imaginary narration of Highland heroism found nowhere in ancient Scottish verse. Cashing in on the popularity of *Fingal*, he compounded his literary crimes by publishing in 1763 an 'easy and free translation' from 'broken fragments' of a Highland epic, *Temora*, which is longer by two books and even less related to actual Ossianic Gaelic sources than its bogus predecessor.[7] Incredibly enough, the ruse continued with an attempt at rewriting British history by falsely claiming Scotland, rather than Ireland, as the mother country of Celtic culture in order to lend credence to the Ossianic forgeries. Thus, there appeared John Macpherson's highly unreliable *Critical Dissertations on the Origin, Antiquities, &c. of the Ancient Caledonians* (1768), which did not please either Johnson or Boswell. James Macpherson followed suit with a potpourri of antiquarian nonsense in *An Introduction to the History of Great Britain and Ireland* (1771).

If Macpherson's poems were not literal translations of ancient Gaelic manuscripts, how did he compose them? Johnson succinctly provided the answer during a conversation at Skye in 1773: Macpherson 'found names, and stories, and phrases, nay passages in old songs, and with them has blended his own compositions, and so made what he gives to the world as the translation of an ancient poem'.[8] Johnson's perception was right on the mark. The modern Gaelic scholar, Derick S. Thomson, basically elaborates on this Johnsonian insight in a more sympathetic summing up of Macpherson's methods:

> He collected a considerable quantity of Gaelic Ossianic ballads from oral and manuscript sources, and used characters and stories, related traditions and history, as and when it suited him; sometimes following the gist and sequence of the ballads but more often altering these, always adding ideas and incidents which have no Gaelic counterpart, and imposing on the whole a style which bears very little resemblance to anything in Gaelic literature.[9]

As for the allegation by Macpherson's publisher, Thomas Becket, that Gaelic manuscripts of *Fingal* lay in his shop for public inspection in 1762, Thomson conjectures that these documents refer to the *Book of the Dean of Lismore*, an early sixteenth-century source of authentic Ossianic poems. William Shaw regarded these alleged manuscripts as written in Irish Gaelic without any Ossianic matter. Both Gaelic scholars corroborate Johnson's insistence that no ancient manuscripts (from the third century, according to Macpherson) of entire Scottish Gaelic epic poems existed to validate the pretended English translations. The translator was the author; Macpherson was Ossian.

At first much of the British public lacked Johnson's wariness. Boswell himself started as a believer, on the lookout in London for the 'Sublime Savage' Macpherson, who seemed very much a 'man of great genius and an honest Scottish Highlander' in 1762.[10] As the wave of enthusiasm for *Fingal* crested, Boswell arranged eight recorded meetings with the supposed translator, who treated his fellow Scot to at least one reading of Ossianic poems purporting to be part of the Gaelic original. It was at this very time that Johnson first entered Boswell's life, and the topic of Macpherson inevitably came up in their conversation. Reacting to Boswell's report of Macpherson's avowed disregard of morality, Johnson intuitively sized up his future antagonist already by 14 July 1763: 'He wants to make himself conspicuous... But if he does really think that there is no distinction between virtue and vice, why, Sir, when he leaves our houses, let us count our spoons.'[11] An actual interview with Macpherson, who evaded direct questioning about the genuineness of Ossian, only confirmed Johnson's early doubts about the Highlander's integrity. Aggravating these unfavourable first impressions were extravagant estimates of the literary merit of Macpherson's epics in Hugh Blair's *Critical Dissertations on the Poems of Ossian* (1763). This bulky and foolish treatise, which Johnson read and criticised by 1768, ultimately recorded a critical judgement likely to have offended him, namely, that the primitive poetry of Ossian excelled even Homer's epics in overall greatness. Such a grandiose evaluation violated classical canons of literary taste as well as common sense. A sensible reader like Johnson was quick to experience the downright tediousness of wading through *Fingal*, which he found 'a mere unconnected rhapsody, a tiresome repetition of the same images. In vain shall we look for the *lucidus ordo*, where there is neither end or object, design or moral, *nec certa recurrit imago*'.[12]

Therefore, because Macpherson's poems were unhistorical and mediocre forgeries, Johnson set himself against them unwaveringly. Although he was not the first to question their authenticity, since the controversy had erupted already by 1762, he was doubtless the major and most effective spokesman against them. Not surprisingly, in 1773 when a new edition of the counterfeit poems appeared, Johnson would not forget to make ancient Scottish poetry a special topic of inquiry on his famous tour of the Highlands with Boswell. His repeated, if casual, investigations turned up little evidence of a robust tradition of Highland verse and, consequently, did nothing to moderate his memorably contemptuous attack against Ossian at the end of his summary survey of Skye on *A Journey to the Western Islands of Scotland*, published on 18 January 1775. Mistakes do, unfortunately, mar his reflections on Scottish Gaelic—or 'Earse'—literature in the travel book. He, like Shaw, was probably wrong in making such a sharp distinction between Irish and Erse (or Scottish) Gaelic. He also erred in supposing that bards and senachies were illiterate and virtually extinct, and that oral tradition was a weak and unreliable conveyer of old verse when, in fact, the recoverable bardic poetry of Scotland, excluding heroic ballads, consists of approximately 160 items (some over 200 lines in length), dating from 1450 to the post-1700 period.[13] Again, he incorrectly conceived Erse to be a formerly unwritten language without letters and, therefore, without manuscripts older than a hundred years old. As Shaw himself discovered, Erse manuscript collections of heroic ballads survive from the fifteenth century and even earlier. One of these collections with Ossianic matter, the *Book of the Dean of Lismore* (*circa* 1512), was perhaps what Macpherson palmed off as his alleged Gaelic source for *Fingal*, which he characterised as being written in Saxon (actually a peculiar Irish) script.

However, despite these inaccuracies, Johnson's principal charge against Macpherson's forgeries in the *Journey* is indisputable:

> I believe they never existed in any other form than that which we have seen. The editor, or author, never could shew the original; nor can it be shewn by any other; to revenge reasonable incredulity, by refusing evidence, is a degree of insolence, with which the world is not yet acquainted; and stubborn audacity is the last refuge of guilt.[14]

Macpherson, who by this time in London had become the chief ministerial propagandist, 1768-1782, inveigled William Strahan, printer of the *Journey*, into letting him preview the text on the eve of its public appearance. In a fury Macpherson fired off letters to Johnson, at first politely demanding emendations or a printed apology and then threatening physical retaliation. Johnson, arming himself with a stout six-foot truncheon, fearlessly penned his famous reply of 20 January 1775, promising further defiance of Macpherson, unless this lying poetaster could satisfactorily prove his claims. Thus it was that the best known phase of the controversy concluded, with neither antagonist ever again to participate publicly in the literary fray, although each did so behind the scenes. Johnson would continue the attack until the end of his life through his new-found friendship with William Shaw.

The timing of their first encounter, 'About Christmas, 1774' was auspicious, since the imminent publication of the *Journey* with its blast against Ossian made conversation with a neutral Gaelic scholar like Shaw most welcome to Johnson.[15] An ambitious Highlander born on the Isle of Arran on 3 February 1749, Shaw had matriculated at the University of Glasgow in 1766, eventually to receive his M.A. degree there, before he arrived in London living poorly and obscurely as a tutor and a Scottish dissenting minister. At the first meeting arranged by James Elphinston, an acquaintance of both men, Johnson questioned Shaw about the existence of *Fingal* in Erse. But at this point Shaw could not answer that query and preferred a neutral posture because he was simultaneously enlisting Macpherson's assistance in preparing an Erse grammar for publication. According to Shaw:

> Instead of *introducing myself* to Mr. Macpherson, I was made acquainted with him in 1774-5, as a 'man who had studied Galic'... With Mr. Macpherson I have had many conversations on Galic; he saw my MSS. of the grammar, and when I advised with him concerning some particulars relative to the structure of the Earse, our opinions not altogether coinciding, he recommended to me to do it in the easiest manner to myself, 'as there were no judges of Galic.' From the same motives he thought his Fingalian fraud could never be detected.[16]

Johnson would also see and promote the Erse grammar in manuscript. Boswell, whose former fondness for Ossian had cooled considerably, looked over this manuscript with qualified approval at the London residence of the Scottish Earl of Eglinton in April 1776 and then forwarded it to Johnson, who by the following March requested Boswell's patronage for its publication, despite its excessive price: 'One Shaw, who seems a modest and decent man, has written an Erse Grammar, which a very learned Highlander, Macbean [Johnson's former amanuensis for the *Dictionary*], has, at my request examined and approved.'[17] Enclosed with this letter were receipts for subscriptions as well as proposals for publication, which Boswell instantly recognised as having been written 'by *the hand of a* MASTER'.[18] Boswell may well have talked directly with 'Erse-grammar Shaw' about this first of Johnson's ghostwritten contributions to the Highlander's Gaelic scholarship in May of 1777 during a meeting at Edinburgh. These 'Proposals' attest to the importance that Johnson, a premier lexicographer, attached to philological inquiry, to Gaelic studies, and ultimately to the detection of the truth about Ossian:

> Though the Earse dialect of the Celtic language has, from the earliest times, been spoken in Britain, and still subsists in the northern parts and adjacent islands, yet by the negligence of a people rather warlike than lettered, it has hitherto been left to the caprice and judgement of every speaker, and has floated in the living voice, without the steadiness of analogy or direction of rules. An Earse Grammar

is an addition to the stores of literature, and its author hopes for the indulgence always shewn to those that attempt to do what was never done before. If his work shall be found defective, it is at least all his own; he is not like other grammarians a compiler or transcriber; what he delivers, he has learned by attentive observation among his countrymen, who perhaps will be themselves surprized to see that speech reduced to principles, which they have used only by imitation.

The use of this book will however not be confined to mountains and islands; it will afford a pleasing and important subject of speculation, to those whose studies lead them to trace the affinity of languages, and the migrations of the ancient races of mankind.[19]

Though of questionable philological value, *An Analysis of the Galic Language* (London, W. & A. Strahan, 1778) owed much to Johnson for its public appearance, since it was he who introduced Shaw to his publisher and to influential subscribers through Boswell. Shaw's preface acknowledges the debt:

> Mr. Boswell, ...hearing from his Lordship [Eglinton] of the existence of these sheets, obtained a perusal of them, which he afterwards left with Dr. Samuel Johnson. To the advice and encouragement of Dr. Johnson, the friend of letters and humanity, the Public is indebted for these sheets.[20]

When presented with a copy for his private library, Johnson was understandably grateful for the glowing compliment: 'Sir, you have treated me handsomely; *you are an honour to your country.*'[21] Dedicated to Eglinton, this flawed grammar boasts celebrated subscribers besides Boswell, including Gibbon, Adam Smith, Henry Dundas, Thomas Pennant, and, of immediate interest, James Macpherson and his henchman, John Mackenzie, secretary of the newly formed Highland Society in London. Shaw's introduction straddles the fence between conflicting loyalties to Macpherson and to Johnson. On the one hand, there is praise for Macpherson's phony historical estimate of Scotland's cultural preeminence over Ireland for possessing the Gaelic 'mother-tongue'. *Fingal* is even plundered for grammatical illustrations of the language! On the other hand, there are fine remarks about the Highland heritage that echo Johnson's own in the *Journey*, in the 'Proposals' for Shaw's *Analysis*, and in a letter of 13 August 1766, urging William Drummond to promote an Erse translation of the Bible. Despite early indications of Johnson's looming intellectual influence, Shaw was not yet able to deny Ossian or to take sides publicly in the quarrel.

The neutrality persisted when, to complement his grammar, Shaw decided in 1778 to undertake a Gaelic dictionary and solicited the new Highland Society, of which he was a charter member, for financial support for a research expedition through north Britain. Shaw's petition was refused, he claimed, because of the disapproval by Macpherson's partisans of his connexion with Johnson, although the rejection probably owed more to the reservations of members about Shaw's arrogance and linguistic abilities and to a prior promise of promoting a rival Erse dictionary in progress, if never completed.[22]

Professing still his impartiality in the matter of Ossian, the snubbed Gaelic lexicographer, nevertheless, depended increasingly upon 'Dictionary' Johnson for a sympathetic ear and professional advice about collecting and arranging a Gaelic vocabulary before his trip to Scotland. Johnson's exhortation was heady stuff for this young and virtually unknown author: '*Sir, if you give the world a Vocabulary of that language, while the island of Great-Britain stands in the Atlantic Ocean, your name will be mentioned.*'[23] Fired by the compliment, Shaw invested from two to three hundred pounds of his own meagre resources for a three thousand mile tour of the Highlands and part of Ireland from early in 1778 to February 1779. His own description of the trip indicates his twofold aim of gathering Gaelic words and, if possible, of finding the Gaelic originals of Macpherson's Ossian poems:

> In spring 1778, I set out from London, for the Highlands and Hebrides, to collect from songs, old sayings, the voice of the people, and manuscripts, if there should be any, vocables for the dictionary, which I have since published. I knew well the state of the country. It was my resolution, in order to satisfy myself at least, to leave no stone unturned, and be in possession of these poems, if they existed. Not above 17 years had elapsed, since Mr. Macpherson had performed his first expedition thither. All the Highlanders who repeated poetry, I believed had not migrated, nor died; and we have been told that some manuscripts there were in the possession of some individuals. I was elated with anticipated success; and it was my intention to have superseded Mr. Macpherson, by publishing an original, could it be had. I had resolved, had I met with any convincing evidence, to say something on the other side, to convert not only Dr. Johnson, but the public, by taking the affidavits of those who recited the poetry, and those who witnessed it taken down by me in writing, and to have these facts properly vouched by the ministers of the parishes, and neighbouring justices, where such transactions might happen; and in this manner publish them. Nay, the original signatures of the ministers and justices I intended to have had recognized at Edinburgh, and certified there by people of consideration, whose vouchers of it could not be doubted at London. And I am confident, notwithstanding the epithets of 'stubborn infidelity', 'hatred of the Scotch', 'refusing credit to Highland narration', so commonly bestowed on him by the illiberal, Dr. Johnson would believe me, and be converted.
>
> Many mountains I traversed, many vallies I explored, and into many humble cottages I crept on all four to interrogate their inhabitants. I wandered from island to island, wet, fatigued, and uncomfortable. No labour I thought too much, no expense too great, whilst I flattered myself with converting the disbelieving Doctor Johnson, recovering some of the poetry of Ossian, and stripping Mr.Macpherson's brow of what I then used to call them, 'stolen bays'; for I then believed there might be an original, and that he rather wished to appear the *author* than the *translator*.[24]

Shaw proceeds to report the considerable cost of searching for oral and written proof of Ossianic poetry from venal Highlanders, but all to no avail:

> Thus I...found myself not a little mortified, when all they could repeat was nothing but a few fabulous and marvellous verses; or stories concerning Fionn MacCumhal, alias Fingal, and his Fiona or followers chasing each other from

island to island, striding from mountain to mountain, or crossing a frith at a hop, with the help of his spear. There was much of inchantments, fairies, goblins, incantation rhimes, and the second sight. When I heard those of one country, I heard all, for they all repeated the same stories, and when I had the narration of a few, I had every thing. This, however, did not relax my enquiries. I believed these to be the *compositions of the 15th century*; and beyond the next mountain, in the next valley, or the neighbouring island, something of the *genuine Ossian's* poetry might have remained. I therefore traversed and pervaded the whole for near six months, but to no purpose, as to Ossian's poetry; and, like every other person who attempts to prove or procure evidence for the genuineness of these poems, only discovered, that, by a certain 'intellectual retrogradation, knew less, the more I heard of it'.[25]

Shaw's tendency to pepper his own account with quotations from Johnson's *Journey* serves to remind readers that the later search on behalf of a Gaelic dictionary basically repeated and confirmed his friend's more celebrated investigations of 1773:

In the mean time I did not forget MSS.—Since I could not find the poems in the mouths of the people, I concluded, if they existed at all, that Mr. Macpherson must have found them in MSS.; but as I knew the Earse was never written, I began to despair and to doubt. Some told me such a person had a MS. who, upon interrogation, sent me to another, and he to a third, and so on in a circle, until at length one told me that Mr. Macpherson had carried them all to London... Having made this fruitless enquiry after the *genuine Ossian's* poetry, from which I only learned that there never had been any, I passed over to Ireland, there also to pursue Ossian, and other enquiries. I rummaged, with the consent of Dr. Leland, Trinity College library—examined manuscripts—had different persons, who understood the character and language, in pay—conversed with all who might know any thing of the matter—and, after all, could discover no such poetry as Macpherson's.[26]

The immediate result of the trip was *A Galic and English Dictionary. Containing all the Words in the Scotch and Irish Dialects of the Celtic, that could be collected from the Voice, and Old Books and MSS.*, in two octavo volumes, launched in the spring of 1780. Once again, a publication by Shaw benefited from the support of Johnson, who subscribed to it, helped to inspire 'Proposals' for its printing, afterwards corrected proof, and kept a copy in his library. If the work is one of the first of its kind, its usefulness is unfortunately minimal in offering nothing more than a confused list of Erse and Irish words, of obsolete and contemporary vintage, with English equivalents. It consequently never lived up to the advance billing in the 'Proposals' for a truly Johnsonian type of dictionary, with a generous sampling of a complete Gaelic library for illustrating shades of meaning and with a glossary of Scottish personages and lore. The rudimentary compilation foisted on the public caused some disappointed readers (whom Shaw considered allied to Macpherson) not to honour their promises of paying for subscriptions to the two-guinea Gaelic dictionary. A suit against this group in 1783 carried the

Ossian controversy into the Scottish Court of Session, whose judges vindicated Shaw's claims against his subscribers three years later.

Johnson's participation in the first stage of Shaw's writing career went beyond intellectual and editorial assistance to include active support of Shaw's quest for a secure religious livelihood. At the end of 1777 Johnson appealed to Boswell for help in obtaining a military chaplaincy in the gift of Lord Eglinton. Nothing came of this bid for patronage, and two years later Shaw started a troubled tenure as minister of the parish of Ardilach in the presbytery of Nairn. The congregation disliked him and impugned his accent, his morals, and his piety; absenteeism in London for the purpose of publishing his Gaelic dictionary led finally to his forced resignation of the Scottish post in August 1780. About this time, by his own account, he left the Church of Scotland to join the Anglican communion and become a curate in Kent directly through Johnson's mediation: 'So far was the Doctor interested in the success and fortunes of his coadjutor in this business, that he addressed him to take orders in the Church of England.'[27] Corroborating this depiction of Johnson as spiritual adviser is his letter of 1780, asking a vicar of Rochester to extend a warm welcome to Shaw, 'a studious and literary man' who 'is my friend'.[28] Whether or not Shaw deserved his bad reputation when a minister of the Church of Scotland, Johnson evidently considered him a worthy candidate for the Anglican priesthood, in which capacity as rector of Chelvey, Somerset, Shaw was to serve from 1795 until his death on 16 September 1831.

A secondary consequence of Shaw's trip through north Britain for the Gaelic dictionary was his comprehensive critique of the Ossianic controversy, which also represented an authoritative vindication of Johnson's stand in the quarrel. Elected a fellow of the Society of Antiquaries on 17 May 1781, Shaw displayed his credentials as an historian and at last made public his disbelief in Ossian in *An Enquiry into the Authenticity of the Poems Ascribed to Ossian* (London, J.M. Murray, 1781) consisting of eighty-seven octavo pages. No better exposé of the literary fraud would appear until the end of the next century when Gaelic studies became a sophisticated discipline. Almost all of its charges against Macpherson and other forgers of Highland poetry, including its indictment of their methods of fabrication and its prophecy of more literary trickery, proved correct. Enhancing the significance of the work is the possibility that Johnson helped in some of the marshalling of evidence and took enough pleasure in the publication to read the whole over to his blind lodger, Anna Williams: 'He gave his advice and assistance in conducting the argument, and often told Shaw: "*We shall prevail in this controversy*"', despite some apprehension over reviving the debate over Ossian.[29] The pamphlet warfare which burst forth justified Johnson's presentiment of nasty literary bickering.

A review of Shaw's pamphlet suggests that Johnson did lend some advice in its formulation. The *Enquiry* appropriately begins by stressing Johnson's prominence in the history of the controversy in opposing Macpherson and supporters like Hugh Blair:

The ingenious and learned Dr. Johnson first started objections, and those arose from the internal evidence of the poems against their authenticity, and other facts, which served to confirm the Doctor in his infidelity... Dr. Johnson was too sincere a friend to truth, to accept of an elegant criticism by a professor of rhetoric as internal evidence, and letters and ipse dixits from the Highlands, for a demonstration of authenticity. He knew the poems were every where read, and that Caledonians, naturally partial to their country and its antiquities, were not 'sturdy enough moralists' to disown an honour politically done them by a politically cunning *translator*. (pp.1-2)

The complimentary references to Johnson reverberate throughout the exposition, as Shaw hammers home his friend's favourite accusation, that no originals of the poems existed. In a letter to Boswell in 1775 Johnson had noted that Macpherson should have appealed to oral tradition as the groundwork of his poems but instead made the mistake of indicating the survival of ancient written Erse sources behind his supposedly faithful English translations:

The state of the question is this. He, and Dr. Blair, whom I consider as deceived, say, that he copied the poems from old manuscripts. His copies, if he had them, and I believe him to have none, are nothing. Where are the manuscripts? [30]

Six years later, Shaw's possible consultation with Johnson may help to explain the repetition of this question in the *Enquiry* with greater force:

Where is the evidence? Is it what it ought to be? Where is the original?—When the controversy was new, and the poems but just published, one would think the Editor, from views of interest, regard to his country and truth, and from respect to the public, would shew the original; yet none of these considerations had weight with him. (p.39)

As further evidence of Johnson's indirect influence upon the controversy, there are frequent quotations from the *Journey* and a curtailed version of his famous reply to Macpherson's threat of physical retaliation for attacking Ossian in print. The letter included in the *Enquiry* seems a positive indication of Johnson's assistance and probably varies from the original because he had to dictate it from memory for Shaw's immediate use. He may also have furnished Shaw with subsequent information about rare examples of printed Gaelic religious works, books that Boswell had sent to Johnson seven years previously for use in the *Journey*.[31] One of Shaw's final attacks against Macpherson's integrity rests on Charles Vallancey's doubts about forged Gaelic specimens of *Temora* in *A Grammar of the Irish Language* (1773), a treatise found in Johnson's library.

The focus of criticism in the *Enquiry* eventually shifts from Macpherson to his chief supporters beginning with Hugh Blair, whom Johnson had already judged to be a victim of both Macpherson's duplicity and nationalistic self-deception. Echoing Johnson's remarks in the *Journey*, Shaw explains the psychology of the belief in Ossian among the Scots:

They were glad of this new and unknown honour; and many of the names of the heroes in the poems being familiar to their ears, of which they had often heard mention made in the tales and fables of the Highlands in their youthful years, and, in some degree, at this day, could be easily led, by a little *"Caledonian* bigotry", not only to believe, but to vouch for their being a "literal translation of the poems of Ossian, with which they had been familiar in their infancy". From this complexion and disposition, though I agree with Dr. Johnson, that they had not a "settled purpose to deceive", the persons whom Dr. Blair produceth as vouchers of the truth of Ossian, have been led to give in their names, not doubting but Mr. Macpherson would perform his promise to the public of printing them, or depositing the Galic originals in some library: but both the Doctor, who has published the names and those who have permitted him, have been handsomely treated by the *translator*... But what Dr. Johnson says is true: "The people of the Low Countries know as little of the Highlands as the English themselves". (pp.39-40, 41)

In the process of reaffirming the objections of the *Journey*, Shaw devoted far more attention than Johnson ever did to debunking the false historiography undertaken by Macpherson and his partisans to popularise the erroneous notion of a Scottish origin for Gaelic culture and Ossianic heroes. The *Enquiry* correctly argues that ancient Ireland was the root Gaelic source of the language and lore inspiring the counterfeit *Fingal* and *Temora*. Internal historical evidence also demonstrates the falsity of these poems. Macpherson's Ossian, after all, fails to mention wolves and bears, animals that flourished in the alleged era of the Highland epics. Thomas Percy, who is cited by Shaw as the authority for this objection, had made the same point in Johnson's company in 1775.[32]

As part of the rebuttal, Shaw indicts a Scottish acquaintance, John Clark, who had the dubious distinction of being the first to follow Macpherson in forging Highland poems. Clark's *Works of Caledonian Bards. Translated from the Galic* (1778), although it contains some genuine pieces, is largely a jumble of spurious Gaelic poems. Shaw in his *Enquiry* claimed that Clark had brazenly confessed in private to publishing a fraud. It was this particular disclosure that shortly provoked Clark to publish a counter-attack which, in turn, drew Johnson into collaborating with Shaw on *A Reply to Mr. Clark* in 1782. Another literary forgery uncovered in the *Enquiry* is John Smith's *Galic Antiquities* (1780), which not only defended Macpherson's Ossian but also made public more false specimens of ancient Highland verse. Smith went so far as to claim support from Thomas Percy, one of Johnson's own circle, who, as the *Enquiry* makes clear, actually came to doubt Ossian but heartily disliked any embroilment in the controversy. The last antagonist to be answered in Shaw's pamphlet is Donald M'Nicol, author of a scurrilous book, *Remarks on Dr. Samuel Johnson's Journey to the Hebrides* (1779-80), which included some abusive passages anonymously added by Macpherson. Johnson would have enjoyed reading the closing critique of the *Remarks*, in which Shaw detects Macpherson's assistance and recounts visiting John Mackenzie of the Highland Society on Johnson's behalf to refute M'Nicol's assertion that Gaelic originals of Ossian existed:[33]

Being impatient to see them, I accordingly lost no time in waiting on Mr.
Mackenzie; and, having looked over these volumes in manuscript, found no
composition of Ossian therein! They are manuscripts written in the Irish dialect
and character, on the subject of Irish and Highland genealogy.—We have every
reason to believe that this is the very manuscript, if any, that was left at Becket's
by Mr. Macpherson some time ago, with a view to impose it as that of Ossian;
for I am credibly informed, this very piece was sent to Mr. Mackenzie by him.
(pp.46-57)

Shaw fearlessly, if immodestly, characterises himself in the *Enquiry* as
Johnson's champion and as a lone Scottish advocate of truth against a
Scottish conspiracy to support a literary cheat that Macpherson himself had
come close to divulging in private:

I can shew Dr. Johnson that there is *one* Scotchman who loves *truth* better than
his country, and that I am a *sturdy* enough *moralist* to declare it, though it should
mortify my Caledonian vanity. I would therefore wish to be considered as a
person who, though I have as much *amor patriae* as I think is a virtue, and
though I have the honour to mention the immortal name of Doctor Johnson
amongst my friends, and have no quarrel with Mr. Macpherson, [am] unbiassed
and uninfluenced. Besides, I am sure Mr. Macpherson no longer wishes the world
should think the poems any thing but his own manufacture; for to me he has
oftener than once observed, "it was more creditable to be an author than a
translator". (p.21)

Shaw seldom lets the reader forget what Johnson himself regarded as the
principal weakness of the opposition, that no one could produce the original
Erse source of Macpherson's Ossian in manuscript. In the absence of such
conclusive evidence, Shaw shared his friend's foreboding that Gaelic verse
would be fabricated to correspond to the English translations and then be
palmed off as the Erse originals of Ossian:

It is very singular, that nobody in the Highlands has attempted a complete Galic
translation of Macpherson's *Fingal* and *Temora*... In my tour of the Highlands,
a respectable minister begged I would set about a translation of *Fingal*, and that
he and others would undertake to prove it the composition of Ossian, and
procure affidavits for that purpose. (p.45)

The suspicions of Shaw and Johnson proved all too true. Under the auspices
of the Highland Society with the early complicity of Macpherson, a bogus
Gaelic translation of his epic poetry did appear in 1807 to complete the
cumulative deception of *Ossian*.[34] A closing reference in the *Enquiry* to the
William Lauder controversy, perhaps inspired by Johnson who participated
in it, serves to remind readers of the need for caution in literary dealings
with Scotsmen like Macpherson. Shaw ends his pamphlet with the familiar
Johnsonian demand that the partisans of Ossian produce an authenticated
Gaelic source for Macpherson's poetry 'for nothing but the original can
persuade'. (p.48)

The *Enquiry* was too impressive a document to remain unchallenged for long. The rebuttal took the form of *An Answer to Mr. Shaw's Inquiry into the Authenticity of the Poems ascribed to Ossian* (Edinburgh and London, 1781) by John Clark, who arraigned his opponent's low origins, character, and motives for taking Johnson's side in the controversy. Mocking Shaw's Gaelic scholarship and changing opinions about Ossian, Clark merely asserts the genuineness of his own forged *Works of Caledonian Bards* as well as *Fingal* and *Temora*, although he concedes the impossibility of ancient Erse manuscripts surviving and argues for a vital oral tradition of Ossianic poetry in Scottish Gaelic. He denies a Scottish attempt to deceive Thomas Percy into a belief in Macpherson's Ossian and, hoping to placate Johnson, suggests that Shaw played on the Englishman's notorious prejudices against Scotland for self-serving ends:

> I would not be ready to suspect that the Author of the Rambler could support a falsehood, knowing it to be such. But the sturdiest moralist is seldom possessed of fortitude totally to reject what he earnestly wishes to be true. Had your averments in this pamphlet really been supported by truth, the Doctor would have had great merit in protecting one whose love of truth had gained a victory over the *amor patriae*. He, however, perhaps thought them so; the integrity of his intentions in that case was equally laudable. The Doctor's great learning and genius are sufficient to cover a multitude of little foibles. I cannot therefore help expressing my astonishment at your insolence, in making him the butt of your buffoonry; and imposing on him under the mask of friendship, on purpose to induce him to provide for you. Such being avowedly your intentions, I hope to acquire some merit with the Doctor for opening his eyes to the imposture.[35]

Clark's oily condescension would have had little conciliatory effect, especially when later passages chastise Johnson's ignorance about Erse manuscripts, insolence toward Macpherson, and patronage of Shaw. Johnson, therefore, was favourably disposed to help his protégé pen a response to Clark, and Shaw knew that the self-confident, *ad hominem* argumentation in the pamphlet required a rejoinder for the sake of his own reputation. Accordingly, a second 'corrected' edition of the *Enquiry* (London, J. Murray, 1782) appeared in eighty-eight octavo pages, primarily to make public an effective apologia in the form of a twenty-nine page *Appendix, containing A Reply to Mr. Clark* with eight more pages of correspondence bearing on Thomas Percy's part in the controversy. This *Reply to Mr. Clark* (pp.51-80) is a noteworthy example of Johnson's intensified assistance on Shaw's behalf, because Johnson not only supervised its entire argumentation but also largely composed half of it and polished portions of the rest. It deserves recognition on its own merits and for preserving the last sustained prose of the great English writer to be published before his death in 1784.

The proof of his considerable contributions to the *Reply* is compelling. There is the primary evidence of Johnson's diary entries: on 18 March 1782, 'I corrected Shaw'; a day later, 'To morrow Shaw comes'; on 20 March, 'Shaw came. I...ended with Shaw'; and on 23 March, 'Corrected proofs for Shaw'.[36] These cryptic temporal references to proofreading by no means encompass the total duration or extent of Johnson's help. Edmond Malone, for example, received a letter dated 2 March 1782, indicating that Johnson's mind was already on the 'obstinate defence of Ossian. For Ossian there is national pride, which may be forgiven though it cannot be applauded'.[37] Furthermore, Shaw's circumstantial account of their partnership in the controversy, in which he terms himself Johnson's 'coadjutor in this business', confirms the likelihood of Johnson's substantial services during the composition of the *Reply*.[38] The secondary evidence is equally persuasive. Boswell, who met Shaw and followed the debate closely, ascribed the 'greatest part, if not the whole' of the *Reply* to Johnson and quoted five paragraphs in the *Life of Johnson* to illustrate the attribution.[39] A note by the learned Samuel Parr in his copy of 'Dr.' Shaw's *Galic and English Dictionary* affirms Johnson's direct collaboration in the second edition of the *Enquiry*:

> Dr. Parr met Dr. Shaw at Bristol, when Sir S. Romilly was invited thither as a candidate to represent that city. He was pleased with the acuteness and vivacity of Dr. Shaw. The Doctor published two books against the authenticity of Ossian. His style, in the first, is clumsy and obscure, but in the second, it was much improved, by the assistance of Dr. Johnson.[40]

In addition to these contemporary witnesses, the *Johnson Bibliography* (1915) accepts the attribution for 'several complete paragraphs' without specifying them, and no modern scholar has denied this vague estimate.[41] Finally, the internal evidence of Johnson's style and sentiments permits a reasonably reliable appraisal of his specific contributions to the *Reply*. Shaw was a plain writer, occasionally though not ordinarily exhibiting Johnsonian balance and antithesis, and capable of awkwardness and obscurity in his choice, arrangement, and accumulation of words. If his combative style is comparable to a blunt dagger hacking away at antagonists, then Johnson's prose is like a mighty broadsword, or better, a two-fisted claymore for mowing down the Scottish opposition with a controlled energy, precision, and epic sweep that reigns supreme over the jarring complexities of literary debate.

Because Johnson seems to have smoothed the underlying coarseness of a first-person narrative, their collaboration probably depended upon a rough draft of an autobiographical vindication prepared by Shaw in the winter months after Clark's pamphlet appeared. Johnson, despite sickness, then discussed the unfinished work, added considerably to the original content mainly at the beginning and the end, and elsewhere refined Shaw's writing. The Johnsonian contributions are most pronounced in the following pages of the *Reply*: the opening pages 51 to the middle of page 57 (except for the authorial footnote on page 52); pages 59-63 and 66-67 (much of the writing outside the quotation marks); and considerable portions of the final pages 74-80 (beginning 'I lament my negligence' and excluding the authorial footnote on page 75). Following the catalogue of Clark's charges, the *Reply* successfully counters them all and emphasises again the principal Johnsonian objection that there was no corresponding written original of Ossian in Erse— either a third-century manuscript or even a reliable later copy of the same— to authenticate Macpherson's so-called translations. Complete Erse epics could not have been transmitted intact by uncertain oral tradition. At best there existed only fifteenth-century fragments of Highland poetry used by Macpherson and imitators like Clark and John Smith 'as common place helps' (p.71) for constructing literary forgeries of negligible indebtedness to genuine Gaelic poetry of Scottish or Irish antiquity. To make matters worse, there were rumours of a Gaelic translation of Macpherson's English Ossian in progress to deceive the public into believing that there was an Erse original. Let readers beware of this final imposture.

The magnificent exordium of the *Reply*, bearing witness to the bond of friendship between the collaborators, is clearly Johnson's handiwork with distinct echoes of his former writings bearing on the William Lauder controversy, as well as his letters dealing with Macpherson:

> Whoever undertakes to oppose the prejudices of the public, or counteract the interest of individuals, must expect to find many keen and acrimonious adversaries. Of this danger I had notice when I proposed to detect the counterfeit Ossian; but considering myself as supported by the strong defence of a good conscience and invigorated with the power of resistless truth, I have ventured to bring the question to a trial, and to give that opinion which I still maintain against menaces and calumny, and which nothing but conviction shall force me to retract.
>
> For impressing this conviction very slight endeavours have hitherto been used. My adversaries, instead of proving the genuineness of Fingal, have contented themselves with insulting me; as if it were a consequence, that because Shaw is weak and wicked, Fingal is genuine.—My business is to keep the main question full in sight—Is Fingal found in the Galic language? Their business is to hide it behind remote considerations, in hopes that while the public is busied in enquiries into my family and fortune, they will let Fingal pass unexamined, and not reproach its defenders with their hardiness of assertion and penury of evidence. (p.51)

In reply to the personal attack launched by Clark under the auspices of Macpherson's partisans, Shaw pleads his integrity and abilities as one of the earliest authors of a Gaelic grammar and dictionary. Undeservedly sharing the enmity of Ossian's defenders were the truth-seeking Johnson and honest Thomas Percy, whom the extracts of correspondence at the end of the Appendix show to be an unfortunate victim of imposture. Although there is no denying the reality of Highland poetry or even a viable tradition of Ossianic ballads, the burden of proof rests with the opposition to produce the written Erse sources from which *Fingal* and other Highland epics were literally translated into English. But such proof is non-existent because, as Charles Vallancey and Johnson maintained, the Erse language was unwritten until recently and oral tradition could never preserve entire ancient epics as published in English. Shaw never could recover the Erse originals in the Highlands or from John Mackenzie of the Highland Society in London or, indeed, from Macpherson who, instead, seemed on the verge of admitting his authorship of the fabrications.

Therefore, with Johnson's secret assistance, Shaw has fulfilled a threat formerly made before Macpherson to expose the literary fraud. Polishing Shaw's narrative at the conclusion of the *Reply*, Johnson summed up the refusal by defenders of Ossian to supply decisive evidence and did so apparently with the following conversation with Dr Henry Mayo in 1778 in mind: ' "Pray, Sir, are Ganganelli's letters authentick?" Johnson. "No, Sir. Voltaire put the same question to the editor of them, that I did to Macpherson— Where are the originals?" '[42] The question is raised for the final time at the end of the *Reply*, without any expectation of an answer that could prove *Fingal* to be authentic:

> Surely there is a time when a question like this must have an end. If Fingal exists in Galic, let the MSS. be shown—When Nodot pretended to have discovered a complete Petronius at Belgrade, the general cry of the learned was "shew us the manuscript". When very lately some letters were printed under the name of the Pope Ganganelli, the reasons, however specious, that were offered for the authenticity, were effectually silenced by one demand, "shew the originals".
>
> If the originals of Fingal can ever be shown, opposition may be silenced, but till then its defenders may justly be considered as sharing the fate of other liars,in being reduced to the necessity of accumulating falsehood upon falsehood, and supporting one imposture by another. (pp.79-80)

With the public appearance of *A Reply to Mr. Clark* in the early spring of 1782, Johnson concluded his active connexion not only with the Ossian controversy but also with literary publication generally. An anonymous newspaper advertisement signed 'Anti-Ossian'—probably Shaw—did appeal to Johnson in December of 1782 for yet another, even fuller refutation of Ossian. If, as Shaw alleged, his friend seriously planned such a publication in the last six months of his life, then the ravages of advanced old age halted the undertaking.[43] In any case Johnson did manage to utter his last word on Ossian in print through Shaw's polemic and linguistic writings. On the occasion of this formal restoration of *A Reply to Mr. Clark* to Johnson's canon as a collaborative venture with Shaw, it is appropriate to note that this last specimen of Johnson's argumentative prose, despite some misconceptions about the oral and written legacy of Erse poetry, was entirely worthy of an author who revered truth in literary, historical, and moral matters. As an apologia for Shaw, it is also a fitting finale for their fruitful association, which Shaw valued for the rest of his long life. In gratitude Shaw would publish the first genuine biography of the great writer, *Memoirs of the Life and Writings of the Late Dr. Samuel Johnson* (1785), a solid and sympathetic study that furnishes this essay with its final words on Johnson: 'He was the friend and advocate of whatever enlarges, heightens, refines, or perfects the happiness of humanity. To this great and prevailing object all his labours had an immediate reference, and his whole life in public and private was consecrated to the welfare and honour of the species.'[44]

Notes

1. James Boswell, *Boswell's Life of Johnson, Together with Boswell's Journal of a Tour to the Hebrides and Johnson's Diary of a Journey into North Wales*, ed.

George Birkbeck Hill, revised L.F. Powell, 6 vols (Oxford, Clarendon Press, 1934-50), vol.5, p.95.

2. Samuel Johnson, *A Journey to the Western Islands of Scotland*, ed. J.D. Fleeman (Oxford, Clarendon Press, 1985), p.99. Macpherson's unannotated copy of the *Journey* is in the Aberdeen University Library.

3. Samuel Johnson, *The Letters of Samuel Johnson, with Mrs. Thrale's Genuine Letters to Him*, ed. R.W. Chapman, 3 vols (Oxford, Clarendon Press, 1952), vol.1, p.188 (no.184).

4. *Boswell's Life of Johnson*, vol.5, p.241.

5. See J.S. Smart, *James Macpherson, An Episode in Literature* (London, David Nutt, 1905), p.50. For a list of publications by Macpherson, his defenders, and detractors, see George F. Black, *Macpherson's Ossian and the Ossianic Controversy: A Contribution Towards a Bibliography* (New York, New York Public Library, 1926). The standard, if too sympathetic, biography is by Bailey Saunders, *The Life and Letters of James Macpherson* (1894; reprinted New York, Haskell House Publishers, 1968).

6. James Macpherson, 'A Dissertation Concerning the Antiquity, &c. of the Poems of Ossian the Son of Fingal', reprinted in *Fingal, an Ancient Epic Poem. In Six Books* (Dublin, Peter Wilson, 1763), p.xvi.

7. See Smart, pp.52-53, and Derick S. Thomson, *The Gaelic Sources of Macpherson's 'Ossian'* (Edinburgh, Oliver and Boyd, 1952), pp.14-16, 59-60. The false historiography surrounding the Ossian forgeries is discussed by Hugh Trevor-Roper, 'The invention of tradition: The Highland tradition of Scotland', in *The Invention of Tradition*, eds Eric Hobsbawm and Terence Ranger (Cambridge, C.U.P., 1983), pp.15-18.

8. *Boswell's Life of Johnson*, vol.5, p.242.

9. Derick S. Thomson, "Ossian", Macpherson and the World of the Eighteenth Century', *Aberdeen University Review*, 40 (1963), p.14.

10. Boswell, *Boswell's London Journal: 1762-1763*, ed. Frederick A. Pottle (New York, McGraw-Hill, 1950), pp.73, 264-66.

11. *Boswell's Life of Johnson*, vol.1, p.432. See also vol.2, p.513.

12. *Boswell's Life of Johnson*, vol.2, p.126.

13. Derick S. Thomson, *An Introduction to Gaelic Poetry* (London, Victor Gollancz Ltd, 1974), p.20.

14. Johnson, *A Journey to the Western Islands of Scotland*, p.98.

15. William Shaw, *Memoirs of the Life and Writings of the Late Dr. Samuel Johnson; Containing Many Valuable Original Letters, and Several Interesting Anecdotes both of his Literary and Social Connections. The Whole Authenticated by Living Evidence* (1785) in *The Early Biographies of Samuel Johnson*, eds O.M. Brack, Jr, and Robert E. Kelley (Iowa City, Iowa U.P., 1974), p.174. Another very useful edition of Shaw's biography included with Hester Lynch Piozzi's *Anecdotes* is by Arthur Sherbo (New York, London, OUP, 1974), pp.5-56. For Shaw's life, see also the DNB and N & Q, 7th series, vol.IX (1890), pp.391-92, 498.

16. William Shaw, *An Enquiry into the Authenticity of the Poems Ascribed to Ossian with a Reply to Mr. Clark's Answer* (London, J. Murray, 2nd 'corrected' edition 1782), pp.68-69.

17. Johnson, *Letters of Samuel Johnson*, vol.2, p.164 (no.510).

18. Boswell, *Boswell's Life of Johnson*, vol.3, p.107. For Boswell's first (28 May 1777) of three (also on 8 April 1779, and 17 July 1785) meetings with Shaw, see *Boswell in Extremes: 1776-1778*, eds Charles McC. Weis and Frederick A. Pottle (New York, McGraw-Hill, 1970), p.128.

19. *Boswell's Life of Johnson*, vol.3, p.107. For the correct punctuation of the original 'Proposals' cited here, I am indebted to J.D. Fleeman, whose bibliographical information appears in 'Johnsonian prospectuses and proposals', *Augustan Studies: Essays in Honor of Irvin Ehrenpreis*, eds Douglas Lane Patney and Timothy Keegan (Newark, Delaware U.P. 1985), p.237.

20. William Shaw, *An Analysis of the Galic Language* (London, W. & A. Strahan, 1778), p.xxii.

21. Shaw, *Memoirs*, p.175.

22. Kenneth D. Macdonald, 'The Rev. William Shaw—pioneer Gaelic lexicographer', *Transactions of the Gaelic Society of Inverness*, 8 (1979), pp.7-10.

23. Shaw, *Memoirs*, p.175.

24. Shaw, *Enquiry*, pp.30-31.

25. Shaw, *Enquiry*, p.32.

26. Shaw, *Enquiry*, pp.32-33. All future references to this work are to the second 'corrected' London edition of 1782, containing the Johnsonian *Reply to Mr. Clark*.

27. Shaw, *Memoirs*, p.176.

28. Johnson, *Letters of Samuel Johnson*, vol.2, p.408 (no. 711.1). See also Macdonald, pp.10-13.

29. Shaw, *Memoirs*, p.176.

30. Johnson, *Letters of Samuel Johnson*, vol.2, p.8 (no. 378).

31. See *Boswell's Life of Johnson*, vol.2, pp.279 and 508, for Boswell's conveyance of some Gaelic books which, according to the *Letters of Samuel Johnson*, vol.1, p.413 (no.360), Johnson gave to the Bodleian Library in 1775 and suggested adding metrical Gaelic psalms to the gift. For bibliographical information, see *A Preliminary Handlist of Copies of Books associated with Dr. Samuel Johnson*, ed. J.D. Fleeman (Oxford, Oxford Bibliographical Society, 1984), p.2 (no.7), p.62 (no.257). Johnson refers to the books in the *Journey*, pp.95, 97, 215-16, 217, and Shaw in the *Enquiry*, pp.8, 36-37, similarly cites Richard Baxter, *Call to the Unconverted*, the *Psalms*, the *Confession of Faith*, and the *Common Catechism* as some of the few printed works in Scottish Gaelic.

32. Shaw's *Enquiry*, pp.14-15, and *Boswell's Life of Johnson*, vol.2, pp.347, 455. See also Cleanth Brooks, Jr, 'Percy's history of the wolf in Great Britain', *Journal of English and Germanic Philology*, 34 (1935), pp.101-3.

33. Robert F. Metzdorf also claims Macpherson's occasional contributions to M'Nicol's *Remarks* in 'M'Nicol, Macpherson, and Johnson', in *Eighteenth-Century Studies in Honor of Donald F. Hyde*, ed. W.H. Bond (New York, The Grolier Club, 1970), pp.45-61, despite M'Nicol's denial of joint authorship with Macpherson in a letter found in John Clark's *Answer to Mr. Shaw's Inquiry* (1781), pp.52-58. For the literary forgeries of Clark and Smith, see also Edward D. Snyder, *The Celtic Revival in English Literature* (1923; reprinted Gloucester, Mass., Peter Smith, 1965).

34. Smart, pp.186-95; Thomson, *The Gaelic Sources of Macpherson's 'Ossian'*, Appendix II; and Saunders, p.290.

35. John Clark, *An Answer to Mr. Shaw's Inquiry into the Authenticity of the Poems Ascribed to Ossian* (Edinburgh and London, C. Elliot, T. Longman, and T. Cadell, 1781), pp.10-11.

36. Johnson, *Diaries, Prayers, and Annals*, ed. E.L. McAdam, Jr, with Donald and Mary Hyde, vol.1 (1958) of the Yale Edition of *The Works of Samuel Johnson* (New Haven, Yale U.P.1958-), pp.313, 315, 317.

37. *Letters of Samuel Johnson*, vol.2, p.464 (no.766).

38. Shaw, *Memoirs*, pp.173-78.
39. Boswell, *Boswell's Life of Johnson*, vol.1, pp.23-24, vol.4, pp.252-53.
40. For this reference in *Bibliotheca Parriana. A Catalogue of the Library of the late reverend and learned Samuel Parr, LL.D.* (London, John Bohn, 1827), p.700, I am indebted to Dr J.D. Fleeman of Pembroke College, Oxford.
41. William Prideaux Courtney and David Nichol Smith, eds, *Johnson Bibliography* (Oxford, Clarendon Press, 1915), p.153.
42. Boswell, *Boswell's Life of Johnson*, vol.3, p.286 and n.2, pp.522-23.
43. Shaw, *Memoirs*, p.178.
44. Shaw, *Memoirs*, p.186.

AN

ENQUIRY

INTO THE

AUTHENTICITY

OF THE

POEMS ASCRIBED TO OSSIAN.

WITH A

REPLY to Mr. CLARK's ANSWER.

The SECOND EDITION corrected

BY

W. SHAW, A.M, F.S.A.

Author of the GALIC DICTIONARY and GRAMMAR.

LONDON.

PRINTED FOR J. MURRAY, N° 32, FLEET STREET.

MDCCLXXXII

A P P E N D I X.

WHOEVER undertakes to oppofe the prejudices of the public, or counteract the
intereft of individuals, muft expect to find many
keen and acrimonious adverfaries.   Of this danger I had notice when I propofed to detect the
counterfeit Offian; but confidering myfelf as
fupported by the ftrong defence of a good con-
fcience and invigorated with the power of réfiftlefs
truth, I have ventured to bring the queftion to a
trial, and to give that opinion which I ftill maintain againft menaces and calumny, and which nothing but conviction fhall force me to retract. 1

For impreffing this conviction very flight endeavours have hitherto been ufed.   My adverfaries, inftead of proving the genuinenefs of Fingal, have contented themfelves with infulting
me ; as if it were a confequence, that becaufe
Shaw is weak and wicked, Fingal is genuine.—
My bufinefs is to keep the main queftion full in
fight—Is Fingal found in the Galic language?
Their bufinefs is to hide it behind remote confi-
derations, in hopes that while the public is bufi-
ed in enquiries into my family and fortune, they
will let Fingal pafs unexamined, and not reproach its defenders with their hardinefs of affertion and penury of evidence.

I am indeed not afraid of prefenting myfelf
before the public with all my accufers clamour-
ing againft me, and doubt not but that when

G 2   the

[52]

the charges of artful and intereſted men ſhall have been diligently diſcuſſed, and the clamours of a prejudiced rabble ſhall have ſubſided, I ſhall be found a man whom his anceſtors * do not diſgrace, and who does not diſgrace his anceſtors, a man whoſe morals deſerve no blame, and whoſe induſtry deſerves praiſe, who has at leaſt this merit, that he firſt regulated his native language by grammar and arranged it by alphabet; but let the reader always bear in mind that the genuineneſs of Fingal does not depend upon the character of Shaw.[2]

My aſſertions are for the moſt part purely negative; I deny the exiſtence of Fingal, becauſe in a long and curious peregrination through the

* As amongſt other curious arguments Mr. Clark has adduced a new one, which I ſhall call, the *Argument from Genealogy*, it has been thought proper to give the following account of my family——When Robert, ſon of Robert Bruce king of Scotland had been defeated, and had fled to the Iſlands until his followers ſhould be able to collect a ſufficient force to bring againſt the king of England, my anceſtor by the mother's ſide Cook, of whom my uncle Capt. Cook, often in London is the repreſentative, and Shaw my progenitor, of whom my father is the lineal deſcendant, attended the Prince, the latter as his temporary cupbearer, while on the Iſland of Arran, and adminiſtered to his neceſſities. They attended him with a company of men to Bannockburn, where fifty thouſand Engliſh are ſaid to have been ſlain, after which the king granted by a military tenure to Cook, the lands called at this day *Glenri* in Arran, or the valley of the king, and to Shaw thoſe of Lettir in Arran and Sornbeg on the continent, but which are now ſwallowed up by the nobles.——It is well known from the hiſtory of Scotland, that eſtates in Arran were commonly given to the favourites of the crown.——The arms of the Sornbeg and Lettir family to this day are three covered cups, &c. vide Niſbet's Heraldry. The late family of Greenock, of which the preſent Lord Cathcart is a lateral repreſentative, I believe to have been a branch of this family.

[53]

Galic regions I have never been able to find it.
What I could not fee myfelf I fufpect to be
equally invifible to others, and I fufpect with
the more reafon, as among all thofe who have
feen it no man can fhew it.[3]

What the defenders of Fingal have been able to
collect, imagine, or invent, has been accumulat-
ed, as I have reafon to fufpect, by their united labour in a pamphlet entitled, *An Anfwer to Mr.
Shaw's Inquiry*, by Mr. Clark of Edinburgh,
which, whatever other qualities it may want, muft
be admitted to have a claim to all the notice due
to difingenuity, impudence, and falfehood.

Of his difingenuity the firft page affords a
fpecimen, where he reprefents the Englifh as denying the exiftence of poetry among the Highlanders. That the Highlanders had poetry was
never doubted, for perhaps no people has been
ever found without it. The exiftence even of
Fingal is not abfolutely denied, but is doubted
with that degree of diftruft which falls properly
and juftly upon thofe who fay what they do not
prove, when the proof would be eafy, if what
they faid were true, and their intereft would
prompt them to produce it, if they had it.[4]

There is however a refource behind, he that
can fay nothing for his caufe can ftill vilify and
calumniate his adverfary. The genuinenefs of
Fingal it is indeed impoffible to maintain, but
there are hopes that I who have queftioned it
may be made contemptible. For this purpofe
my private conduct had been examined; a dif-
contented fervant had been excited to accufe me,
and one fiory at leaft has been told of which I
cannot guefs the author or the occafion.—It is
faid that when I was preaching upon the uncertainty of life, I played a trick to alarm my au-
ditory

[54]

ditory by finking down as lifelefs in the pulpit. The fact is fo humoroufly related, that if any man defires to laugh, I would recommend it to his perufal. But let him not fuppofe that he is laughing at me, who think myfelf obliged to declare upon fuch provocation, that the whole narrative is a lie; that it is a lie malicious and premeditated ; and as this is true, or fallc, I call upon mankind to judge of my veracity and that of my opponents.

Mr. Clark compares the obftinacy of thofe who difbelieve the genuinenefs of Offian to a blind man, who fhould difpute the reality of colours, and deny that the Britifh troops are cloathed in red : —The blind man's doubt would be rational if he did not know by experience that others have a power which he himfelf wants; but what perfpicacity has Mr. Clark which nature has withheld from me or the reft of mankind ?

The true ftate of the parallel muft be this. Suppofe a man, with eyes like his neighbours, was told by a boafting corporal, that the troops indeed wore red cloaths for their ordinary drefs, but that every foldier had likewife a fuit of black velvet, which he put on when the king reviews them. This he thinks ftrange, and defires to fee the fine cloaths, but finds nobody in forty thoufand men that can produce either coat or waiftcoat. One indeed has left them in his cheft at Port Mahon, another has always heard that he ought to have velvet cloaths fomewhere, and a third thinks that he has heard fomebody fay that foldiers ought to wear velvet. Can the enquirer be blamed if he goes away believing that a foldier's red coat is all that he has ?

But the moft obdurate incredulity may be fhamed or filenced by facts. To overpower contradictions,

[55]

tions, let the foldier fhew his velvet coat, and the Fingalift the original of Offian. [5]

The difference between us and the blind man is this.—The blind man is unconvinced becaufe 'he cannot fee, and we, becaufe though we can fee, we find that nothing can be fhown.

I am accufed of inconfiftency, in having fpoken at different times with greater and lefs refpect of the Galic language and writers; but if I am inconfiftent, is Fingal, therefore, genuine? Of the Galic language I always fpoke and wrote in the fame manner; I always mentioned it as an antient tongue, ennobled by the bravery of thofe who fpoke it; but I always declared it not to be a written language till within thefe fifty years that the Highland minifters publifhed fome little tracts for the inftruction of the people.— Of their authors, for writers they had none, I perhaps once believed more than I believe at prefent; but my belief was part of the general ftream of national credulity, a conformity to opinions of which I could give no proof, and of which I now find the proof to be impoffible. From fuch changes of mind no deductions can be drawn, but that I once had the Scotchman's prejudices, and that I have been able to facrifice prejudice to truth. [6]

My fkill in the Galic has been called in queftion.—This charge indeed my vanity did not fuffer me to expect. I thought that when to the opportunities of a native I had added the diligence of a ftudent, when of a tongue fo little cultivated I had compiled the firft grammar and dictionary, my zeal would be praifed, and my fkill not depreciated. But alas! I am now reprefented as decrying that language which I have cultivated with fo much labour, and with
                                                        being

[56]

being ignorant of that which I valued myfelf upon teaching others. I am at laft the native of an Ifland where the worft dialect of the
Galic is fpoken, and in my dictionary a dozen
of blunders, real or imaginary, have been noticed by malicious penetration. [7]

Of an unwritten language it is not eafy to
afcertain the preference of dialects. Let it
however be admitted, that one dialect my excel
another by the regularity of its terminations and
the conftancy of its analogy, yet he who knows
one may quickly learn the reft, and that I have
learned them, my grammar and dictionary will
I hope fufficiently evince.

He that imagines that by noticing a few
faults he can depreciate a dictionary, only expo-
fes his own ignorance.—There is, I fuppofe, no
dictionary without innumerable faults both of
redundancy, deficiency, and miftakes; and for
mine it will be fufficient apology to fay, that it
is the firft; and that it was collected not from
MSS. of *Fingal* or the *Caledonian Bards*, but
from the rude converfation of cottagers and
fhepherds.

If MSS. had been fhewn me, of which it was a
queftion in what age or what country they had
been written, thofe who did not approve of my opinion might with fome reafon have pretended to
doubt my fkill. But to determine nothing not
to be fomething, a very little knowledge is fufficient. He who cannot tell whether a book be
elegant, can at leaft tell whether there be a book.
If I could not know whether a Galic copy of
Fingal were antient, I can at leaft be confident
that no man within my reach of enquiry pretended to fhew a copy. A man may be fome-

[57]

times defrauded by falfe money, but no man can think himfelf paid with no money at all. [8]

I cannot, indeed, charge the admirers of Fingal with many endeavours to deceive me, it was a fufficient crime with them to demand proof, and when I ventured to 'confefs my doubts,' I was put to filence with violent outcries as an abettor of Johnfon and an enemy to my country.

To incite the rabble of the north againft me is the apparent defign of Mr. Clark. My mention of the Highland cottages, into which I was obliged to créep, is reprefented as a national infult, as if it were not already known by the reft of Britain that the Highlanders were poor. My defign was, not to reproach their poverty, but to recommend my own diligence, and to fhew I fpared no labour by which information would be gained.

In return, however, for my infolence, one of the meaneft of the Highland houfes was my father's. Let us mark how this relates to the queftion. In a logical enthymeme it ftands thus: *Mr. Shaw's father lives in a mean houfe, therefore no man can deny Fingal is genuine.*

This, however, fhews the impertinence of Mr. Clark's remark, that I ought to prefer the cottage of the bard to the palace of the chief, for I left no cottage untried where there was any hope of intelligence.

When I came back difappointed, I had at Edinburgh fome converfation with Mr. Clark which in itfelf proves nothing, the circumftance of " Mr. Macpherfon's carrying to London all " the valuable poetry," only is true.

It is true likewife, that Mr. Clark introduced Cameron the taylor, a native of Lochaber, to my knowledge—I certainly paid him for two or

H   three

[58]

three hours of three or four days that he sat with
me, and took down in writing some songs which I
wished to be able to sing at the Highland club. He
can repeat nothing pretended to be written by Of-
sian, except some of the marvellous tales which I
believe to be of the 15th century. Should Mr.
Clark again affert it, I afk if there was not pen, ink,
and paper, to be had at Edinburgh; and if " his
" mind be such a library of Celtic poetry,"
why do they not take copies? Will Mr. Clark,
like a Gothic Barbarian, allow this *Library* to
die without making him heir to what has been
tranfmitted by his anceftors? I call upon the
public to attend particularly to this fact, and to
exact in a particular manner the originals of his
own poems. But alas! Mr. Clark will tell us
that " other avocations" prevented, and before
he had had leifure poor Cameron died! To defend the genuinenefs of Offian feems not be Mr.
Clark's original defign, for what he fays may
moft of it be true, and yet Fingal may be a
forgery.

The attention with which I heard and copied
the recitations of Cameron is, I think, a proof of
my willingnefs to receive information; but how
does it fhew that I took what he recited for the
works of Offian? That in my journey I did
not vifit Mr. Macnicol is undoubtedly true, but
if I fhunned him as an adverfary of Dr. Johnfon, I muft have done it by the fecond fight;
for his book was not then publifhed, and the
firft notice I had of him was from Dr. Robert-
fon on my return to Edinburgh.

Among other falfhoods, it is told by Mr.
Clark that I declared to him my refolution of
denying on my return to London the authenti-

[59]

city of Ossian's poems, and of abusing the Scotch. " *This, says he, as I imagined, was with a view to humm the good people of England by propo∫ing to gratify their prejudice again∫t the Scotch at the expence of their own pockets.*" Let the probability of the assertion be considered.—The people of England are very indifferent about the question. To *hum* or to be *hummed* upon this occasion is peculiar to the Scotch. These mountains of English gold were to rise only from an eighteen penny pamphlet, in which there was as much chance of loss as profit, and of which the profit could not be much.

The history of my grammar and dictionary, of my hopes and disappointments, is nothing to the purpose. The only evidence of Mr. Clark is contained in the following paragraph: " The
" epic poems of Fingal and Temora I have ne-
" ver heard rehearsed by any *single* Highlander,
" in the same arrangement in which Mr. Mac-
" pherson has published them. By *different* per-
" sons I have frequently heard almost every pas-
" sage in those two poems, with no more diffe-
" rence from the translation than what the ge-
" nius of the language required, and not near so
" much as there is between the different editions
" of those poems in the different parts of the
" Highlands."

To this confident assertion I am not afraid to reply that I do not believe it. This is not the only part of the pamphlet in which his fury has over-powered his veracity. I do not believe he has heard them, because with as good ears and more opportunities I could never hear them. I do not believe him, because in the next page he charged me with saying to him what I never said, that the *translator* of Ossian had curtailed the poems

H 2   which

[60]

which he hath introduced as epifodes. I could
not fay it, for I could never know it, having
never feen nor heard the poems. 9

It is true, that, upon a fuppofition which
I then thought probable, I encouraged Mr.
Clark to offer to the public a genuine collection
of Highland poetry; for I was yet willing to believe that much Highland poetry was fomewhere
to be found. But I am now convinced it is only
in the moon, for on earth I could never fee it.
The MSS. of Mr. Clark, like thofe of Mr. Macpherfon, were always invifible; of the Maid of
Creca I never faw a line; of the Earfe poetry I
never heard him repeat more than a fingle ftan-
za; nor has any been found in his poffeffion excepting twenty lines which he once gave to Sir
James Foulis. As to Malvina's dream, which is
produced againft me as a piece of Earfe poetry
acknowledged by myfelf, I allow that I printed
it, but I do not confider it as antient poetry;
for I never heard nor faw it in the Highlands.—
I have been told that was firft fhown in Englifh,
by Mr. Macpherfon, to one of the Lords of Sef-
fion, who was pleafed fo much that he required
the original. It was then given in Earfe, but
Mr. Macpherfon only knows by whom it was
compofed.

I am charged with difingenuous policy in
making ufe of the term Earfe inftead of Galic.
—It is my bufinefs to diftinguifh; it is that of
my adverfaries to perplex. The term Galic is
indeed ufed by the Highlanders both for the
language of Ireland and their own. The Irifh
was the learned and the written dialect; the
Earfe Galic was merely vocal, and therefore often
corrupt. In the Irifh Galic were many MSS. in
the Earfe Galic there were none. It is therefore

[61]

the artifice of my opponents to talk of Galic
poetry and Galic MSS. by which they mean, if
they mean any thing, MSS. in the Irish Galic.
These they shew, and of these they boast; and say
that the Earse and Irish Galic had the same characters and the same contractions, when the truth
is, that the Scotch Galic had till very lately no
character at all. Thus with the term Galic they
play fast and loose. When they talk of the poetry
of the Highlands, they would be thought to
mean the Scotch Galic; but they dismiss us to
the Irish Galic when they talk of MSS. 10

" Our enquirer, however, has fixed upon one
" thing that will satisfy him effectually : if we will
" produce the originals in Ossian's own hand
" writing with proper vouchers that there is no
" collusion, he will then condescend to be con-
" verted. What answer does the reader ima-
" gine I should give to a man who demands ori-
" ginals in the hand writing of a man who had ne-
" ver heard of letters? He would think me highly
" reprehensible did I honour those demands
" with any other notice than a contemptuous
" silence." Mr. C. quotes falsly, then tri-
umphs over his own knavery and folly. I look
not for Ossian's own hand writing, but I look
for a transcript of a transcript; for some copy
however distant.

But Mr. Clark's Ossian never heard of letters.
If Ossian lived in the third century, being an
Irishman, he must have heard of letters and
known them. If he had been a Highlander, as
Mr. Macpherson endeavours to make him, even
of a later age, I could not expect much knowledge of letters from him. " The most antient
" grammar of the Irish (says the learned Col.
" Valancey, on the same page with whose name
" that

[62]

" that of Shaw is unworthy to be written !) is the
" *Uiraceachd nan eigas*, or primer of the bards,
" written by Forchern some few years before our
" vulgar æra, transcribed and illustrated by
" *Ceann faolidh nam foghlama*, an author of the
" 7th century. A copy of this *Uiraceachd* is in
" the Colonel's possession, and there is another in
" Trinity College Library." [11]

The Col. p. 28, preface to his grammar says,
" It appears very extraordinary that the great
" and learned Ossian should have been ignorant
" of the radical construction of his mother
" tongue in the 2d century, and that it should
" be recovered by the Synod of Argile in the
" 17th century; probably the Earse owes this
" refinement to the Iberno Celtic; we know no
" other way to account for it. It was the mis-
" fortune of North-Britain, says Dr. John Mac-
" pherson in the preface to his critical disserta-
" tions, to have been almost totally destitute of
" letters, at a time when Monkish learning, and
" those religious virtues which arose from as-
" cetic austerities, greatly flourished in Ireland
" and England. This was the case in the 7th
" and 8th centuries."

" Again p. 10. We have reason to believe from
" the unfavourable climate, and steril nature of
" the soil, in that part of Scotland which lies to
" the west of Drumalbin, that the ancestors
" of the Scots lived long in an uncultivated
" state; as destitute of great national events as
" of letters to transmit them to posterity: And
" p. 12. It does not appear that letters were any
" part of the booty which they (the Scots) car-
" ried home with them from the deserted Ro-
" man provinces." Contrary, therefore, to what
is asserted in Mr. Clark's pamphlet, letters were
not

[63]

not received by the Irifh from the Romans, but
from the Phœnicians. Such authority the author of the *Bards* and of *Fingal*, I believe,
cannot overturn, by their own unfupported
affertion. If Offian knew letters, he muft have
committed the poems to writing, and tranfcripts
of what is faid to be fo much admired, would
have ftill exifted. If he *did not* write, it is im-
probable, notwithftanding Mr. Clark's conjectures about the mode of tranfmitting them, that
fo much poetry could be orally preferved. Mr.
Macpherfon talked of manufcripts and he is now
required to fhew them. Mr. Clark, if he can,
may now be " contemptuoufly filent," for he
furely has nothing reafonable to fay. [12]

" To prove beyond the power of contradiction,
" the difingenuity as well as the grofs igno-
" rance of Mr. Shaw, on a fubject which he
" pretends to underftand better (" as well as")
" than any man living, I will lay before the rea-
" der the following facts--Mr. Mackenzie has au-
" thorized me to fay, that Mr. Shaw had feen the
" MSS. in his poffeffion before the publication
" of his pamphlet, had looked at them, and
" turned over the leaves; but at that time had
" read only a few words in different places.
" That fince the publication he has again feen
" thofe MSS. and again read fingle words in dif-
" ferent places; but on being preffed by Mr.
" Mackenzie in prefence of *another gentleman*,
" to read a few fentences, he applied to one
" page of a MSS. in verfe; and after poring
" about a quarter of an hour he made out three
" lines, which related, as read aloud by Mr.
" Shaw himfelf, to Ofcar the fon of Oilian : up-
" on being afked how thefe lines agree with the
" doctrines of his pamphlet, Mr. Shaw an-
" fwered,

[64]

" fwered, that he believed they were the com-
" pofitions of the 15th century, and not of Of-
" fian." Mr. Mackenzie, if he has faid this,
has faid more than is true. The fact is, that
foon after the appearance of Mr. Macnicol's fcur-
rility againft Dr. Johnfon, I afked a fight of thefe
MSS. and after examining them, Mr. Mackenzie afked me whether there was not fome of Offian's poetry? I replied, none of the originals
of the *tranflations* Mr. Macpherfon had publifhed; that a few pages, the only poetry in thofe
MSS. were of far inferior merit to any thing Mr.
Macpherfon had given as a fpecimen of Offian—
to oblige him I read one or more fentences of it.
—Laft fummer, after the publication of my *in-*
quiry, having occafion to wait on Mr. Mackenzie, by appointment, but not on fubjects of Galic, I was fhewn into a room until Mr. Mackenzie fhould return, who was gone out a little
before. From the window I faw Mr. Mackenzie
coming, followed at a little diftance by a young
lad, who appeared like the apprentice of fome mechanic, on whom Mr. Mackenzie looked back,
every now and then, as if he were afraid of
lofing him. The circumftance ftruck me—Both
came up ftairs, and this young man ftanding at a
refpectful diftance at the other end of the room,
after I had talked over the fubject of my vifit,
Mr. Mackenzie introduced the MSS. and looking behind him at the young man, as if he defired
him to attend, requefted me to read pieces of
the MSS.—I perceived that there was fome defign to entrap me, and that this young Highlander, " another gentleman," had been brought
for that purpofe, and therefore I pofitively re-
fufed.

[65]

All the truth contained in Mr. Mackenzie's narration is, that I faw in his poffeffion fome pages of poetry; but it was not Earfe, it was not Fingal. Mr. Mackenzie feems to have no great delight in the controverfy, for I have received a very formal meffage forbidding any further ufe of his name.

" Thefe MSS. fays Mr. Clark, were intended " to prove that Mr. Macnicol had fhewn to the " public that there ftill exift Galic MSS. written " many centuries ago, in contradiction to Dr. " Johnfon, who precipitately averred, that " there is not a MS. in the Highlands a hun- " dred years old." Here is a trick played, in which the term Galic is of fovereign virtue. Dr. Johnfon never denied the exiftence of Galic MSS. for the term Galic, perhaps, he did not know; he only faid there were no Earfe MSS. and fo far as yet appears he was right in faying fo; for the MSS. yet produced are not Earfe; they are Galic, but not Scotch Galic.

Mr. Clark affirms, that thefe MSS. were not fhown as containing any of the poems of Offian; but Mr. Macnicol, to whofe page he refers, will fufficiently refute him; " among thefe are con- " tained fome of the poems of Offian."

Mr. Clark's weapons of controverfy are fome-times falfehoods fo audacious, that he affumes a kind of infernal dignity, and fometimes difin-genuity fo mean as would difgrace a pickpocket on his trial—Mr. Shaw's words, fays Mr. C. are thefe:

" I believe I may fay it *without vanity*, I un-" derftand the Galic as well as any man living. " The fame high ftrain of encomium is repeat-" edly pronounced on his own fuperior know-" ledge;—yet the truth at laft comes out, and " he acknowledges his ignorance. Says he, I

I   " rum-

[66].

" rummaged Trinity College Library, had diffe-
" rent perfons in pay who underftood the cha-
" racters and contractions."—Very mortifying!
to be obliged to hire perfons for information in
a language of which he had written a grammar
and dictionary, [the dictionary was not then writ-
ten] and which a few pages back, he himfelf
knew as well as any man living.

In this place every reader but himfelf will find
that here is nothing to do with ignorance or
knowledge; but a complaint that I wanted time,
and a little boaft, that to fupply that want I procured the help of able men.

His next pages about St. Columbe and Galic
literature, and the manners of the Highlands
have little relation to the prefent queftion. I will
allow him that hiftorical fongs are fometimes the
amufement of the common people, as the ftories of Robin Hood are fung in Englifh villages;
but that long poems are learned, retained, or
tranfmitted, neither my own obfervation has
informed me, nor can I gather it from what I can
learn of other countries.—I never heard a Highlander repeat more than fifty lines together of
continued narrative, or coherent fentiment. In
Wales, where the people are idle and paftoral
like the Highlanders, the learned Mr. Evan Evans,
who has lately publifhed a collection of antient
Welfh poems, does not appear to have exhibited
any traditional or tranfmiffive legends. He copied what he had from books, and judging very
rationally of other countries by his own, lets
his reader know that he gives Mr. Macpherfon
very little credit. [13]

What I have faid of Dr. Blair and Mr. Fergu-
fon, when I fhall be convinced of their innocence I fhall willingly retract; but whether that
time

[67]

time is yet come, the readers when they will pe-
rufe the appendix will candidly determine. 14

Of my interview with Mr. Macpherfon the
account is altogether falfe; it is thus related :

"Similar to it, is what Shaw alledges con-
"cerning his interview with Mr. Macpher-
"fon on the fubject of the poems of Offian.
"The diftance of my place of refidence from
"that gentleman prevented me from apply-
"ing to him in perfon; I chofe therefore to
"requeft a friend to wait on him in London,
"rather than write to him; that friend ac-
"cordingly waited upon him in my name; and
"he gave in fubftance the following detail——
"That feveral years ago Mr. Shaw called at his
"houfe and *introduced himfelf*, without either re-
"commendation, or prior acquaintance whatfo-
"ever, but merely as a native of one of the Scotch
"Ifles, and a man who had ftudied the Galic
"language.   That the avowed object of his
"calling was, to folicit Mr. Macpherfon's intereft
"to promote a fubfcription for a grammar of the
"Galic language which he had written or had
"in contemplation to write.   That as a fpecimen
"of his knowledge of the Galic, he left for Mr.
"Macpherfon's perufal and judgment, a tranf-
"lation of Mr. Pope's Meffiah, which has been
"fince printed and annexed by Mr. Shaw to his
"grammar.   That Mr. Macpherfon upon peru-
"fal of this fpecimen, conceived a very indiffe-
"rent opinion, both of Mr. Shaw's poetical ta-
"lents and knowledge of the Galic, being that
"fpoken in the Ifle of Arran, and the words
"throughout mif-fpelt, and fcarcely intelligible.
"That Mr. S. called repeatedly, but at long in-
"tervals, upon Mr. Macpherfon; by whom he
"was received only with a cold and diftant ci-

I 2   "vility.

[63]

" vility. That he does not recollect that Mr.
" Shaw ever prefumed to afk a fight of his
" MSS. and that even if he had, Mr. Macpher-
" fon fhould not have indulged his curiofity, as
". he both difliked the manners of the man and
" knew that he was not capable of forming any
" juft judgment upon the matter. That what-
" ever farther than what is ftated above, has
" been written or faid by Mr. Shaw, relative to
" perfonal interviews with Mr. Macpherfon, is
" mere exaggeration, or a fiction meant to de-
" ceive and miflead the public."—We fhall foon
fee who has formed ftories to " miflead and de-
" ceive the public!"

I am forry that Mr. Macpherfon, who *now*
lives among gentlemen, fhould thus expofe
himfelf to be convicted publickly of a palpable,
wilful, and premeditated fafehood, and from the
bafeft motives too, to injure a young man's
reputation, who wifheth honeftly to go through
life, and who never offered any injury to him
excepting a declaration of his difbelief of Offian.
—But as it is in defence of my own reputation,
I muft and will tell the truth. Inftead of *introducing myfelf* to Mr. Macpherfon, I was made acquainted with him in 1774-5, as a " man who
had ftudied Galic," by a letter from a gentleman, whofe name, if I am called upon, I am able
to produce. Some years afterwards Mr. Macpherfon faw my tranflation of Pope's Meffiah,
and was pleafed *then* to fay civil things of it—
As to his now declared opinion of my talents, I
am perfectly indifferent. His intereft is to depreciate me as much as is poffible, and of his intereft he will never lofe fight, being the only principle that actuates him. With Mr. Macpherfon
I have had many converfations on Galic; he faw

my

[69]

my MSS. of the grammar, and when I advifed
with him concerning fome particulars relafive to
the ftructure of the Earfe, our opinions not altogether coinciding, he recommended to me to
do it in the eafieft manner to myfelf, " as there
were no judges of Galic." From the fame motives he thought his Fingalian fraud could never
be detected.

Within thefe two years, Mr. Macpherfon has
afked me to his houfe.

When the grammar was going to prefs, I requefted of Mr. Macpherfon to furnifh me with
fpecimens of Offian's poetry to ferve as examples,
and to illuftrate the profody.—In my account of
Galic profody, I intended to take whatever I
could get of Offian, together with the beft fongs,
as my text and guide, and to form rules of Earfe
profody from them. Mr. Macpherfon civilly
promifed to give me different pieces of Fingal
and Temora for that purpofe, becaufe he had
told in his notes and preface, that the " verfifi-
" cation was various ;" but put me off exactly
in the manner I have related in the *inquiry*.—
" The MSS. were in the country, the key loft,
—or I fhould fee them fome other time." Having by thefe fruitlefs applications defpaired of
feeing any of Offian's pieces, I took the 7th book
of Temora and Malvina's dream, and from thefe
lines, and fome printed fongs, was enabled to
give fome account of Earfe profody.—The critical reader may prove the truth of this by applying my rules to the feventh book of Temora,
vide Grammar—Yet Mr. Clark moft unfairly
takes advantage, and mifreprefents this profody,
by oppofing thefe rules to what I have faid
in my *inquiry*, and thence concludes, I then be-
                                                    lieved

[70]

lieved in Offian, and knew that these poems were
authentic. If I thought fo, I did not know it—
I had not *then* the opportunities of knowing I
have fince had by travelling in the Highlands,
and other circumftances; and a man may change
his opinion when he has fufficient reafon fo to
do, with great propriety.

The perfonal interviews that I have faid I had
with Mr. Macpherfon he denies, and gives his
kinfman, Mr. Clark, authority to fay I never
" *prefumed* forfooth, *prefumed* to afk a fight of
" *his* MSS."—Now I fhall publickly convict him
here again of another grofs and wilful falfehood:
In 1778-9, on my return from my tour in the
Highlands, and Ireland, having one morning
waited upon Mr. Macpherfon, after enquiring
what fuccefs I had in collecting vocables, I anfwered, very great fuccefs, but that I now, more
than ever, wondered whence he had the originals of his Fingal and Temora, as I could find
no poetry of fuch merit in that language, the
compofitions of the 15th century being far inferior to what was afcribed to Offian. I told him
that fome day I fhould publickly make him the
author of Fingal. He anfwered, " it is more
" honourable to be an author than a tranflator
" at any time; and " I expect to be treated like
" a gentleman." I replied, that one gentleman
had always a right to expect that from another.
But, continued I, " will you be fo kind as to
" repeat to me a few lines of Offian that have not
" yet been publifhed?" After fome meditation,
and biting his pen, he wrote three ftanzas, which
he faid were the originals of fuch and fuch pages
of fuch and fuch books of Fingal, as marked by
himfelf.—Thefe couplets I have ftill in my cuf-
tody in his own hand writing; they are now to

[71]

be feen in the hands of Mr. Murray, my bookfeller, whenever they are required, as a proof
that I have *prefumed* to afk a fight of fome of his
poetry, and alfo that he gave me fome couplets. It is a true faying, and particularly in the
affair of Offian, that to defend one falfehood many
more muft be invented. It is worthy of notice,
that one of thefe ftanzas is the original of a fen-
tence of Fingal, but it is taken from a piece
of the 15th century; and the piece is in the
poffeffion of feveral Highlanders at this hour.—
It confifts of about twenty couplets, and the beft
of them Mr. Macpherfon has ufed as common
place helps—This is a plain proof of what I have
before advanced, that thefe compofitions are entirely made up.—I can prove that this is a modern
piece by Mr. Macpherfon's own preface and introduction to his Fingal, where he fays, that " in
" Offian's time, neither the Chriftian Religion
" was introduced into the Hebrides, nor into
" Ireland," and that " firnames were not then
" known." Now this piece is called a Laoidh, or
hymn, *Laoidh Ghairbh Mac Starno,* or the hymn
of *Garv Mac Starno*; *Mac Starno* being a firname.
The two other ftanzas are one of the feventh
book of Temora already publifhed, and the other
from Malvina's dream, alfo publifhed, fo that
though at this time willing to oblige me, he could
not favour me with any thing new.

" Mr. Macpherfon alfo authorized my friend
" to declare to me that the allegation of Mr.
" Shaw, that the MSS. in the hands of Mr.
" Mackenzie are the fame that were depofited
" with his bookfeller, by Mr. Macpherfon, for
" the infpection of the public, is an *abfolute*
" *falfehood.*" I had no other authority for the
above allegation than that of Mr. Mackenzie, who
the

[72]

the firſt time he ſhewed me theſe MSS. ſignified that they came to him from Mr. Macpherſon.

Mr. C. proceeds to tell the public that I examined his MSS. and criticiſed his tranſlations. if by MSS. he means Galic MSS. I declare with great ſolemnity, that Galic MS. in Mr. Clark's poſſeſſion I never ſaw. The ſix lines which he has triumphantly inſerted, I have heard him repeat again and again with great emphaſis; but by printing them as a ſpecimen of a greater number, I am afraid he means to deceive the public. I do not know him to be in poſſeſſion of more than theſe ſix, and about a dozen more he has given to Sir James Foulis, and which I have ſeen in his hands.—In my private converſation with Mr. Clark theſe ſix are all that I have heard, and more than I have ſeen.

What he ſays concerning *Iwrram na Truaidhe*, I believe is true, I had miſtaken one ſong for another, and what I have advanced concerning it is an error of my memory.

In an argument with Mr. Clark on the authenticity of the poems, I aſked him how it could happen, that neither I nor any body elſe could meet with any poetry concerning theſe ancient heroes, Fingal and Offian, but the hyperbolic compoſitions of the 15th century, and that the 7th book of Temora, and Malvina's dream, were not repeated by thoſe who commonly repeated Highland poetry.—He replied with emphaſis, that this argument ſhould not long ſtand, for that he himſelf would take the trouble to read it to a Cady until he got it by heart. At another time he offered to produce a Cady (or porter) who could repeat the 7th book of Temora, but the man could not get beyond a dozen of lines! If Mr. Clark is ſure of a *thouſand*,

why

[73]

why did he not mention one or more of them, that could repeat this book? This circumstance is a confirmation of what I have said; he chose the man in question, because he knew no others; but if the controverfy continue, he may, perhaps, bring another, and be bufy in the mean time in teaching him to recite it.

After this the reader is led aftray by another digreffion, relating to Mr. Smith, which I fhall pafs over flightly, becaufe it has no relation to the genuinenefs of Fingal. Mr. Smith has one advantage over fome of his competitors for the Celtic laurels, he gives his reader reafon to believe, that fome fpecimens of Galic poetry are really in his hand: but I am at the utmoft diftance from believing that any part of them were compofed by Offian.

With refpect to Mr. Macleod, I now fay again what I have faid before, that I offered him half crown a line for any part of Offian that he would repeat—Such offers at a jovial table are not very ferious—My intention was to provoke him to repeat fomething, but the provocation had no effect. What he has heard Mr. Macpherfon read, he has not diftinctly told us; and the paffages which he has received from Mr. Macpherfon, he does not tell us the length of, nor confequently whether they are not fuch as might be occafionally fabricated.

As the anecdote of the fcolloped fhell hath been fo particularly noticed, I think it neceffary to explain that matter.——The reader is to obferve, that I never made mention of the gentleman's name—The fact is fimply thus—— That anecdote I fet down on a blank page, at fome diftance from the *finis* of the MS. of the Inquiry, for the fake of my own memory, as a

K laughable

[74]

laughable circumſtance, without any intention of publiſhing it. When I delivered the MS. to Mr. Murray, to be printed for him, for I live at ſome diſtance from town, I drew my pen acroſs that anecdote; and was myſelf diſpleaſed and ſurprized, when I ſaw that the printer, or Mr. Murray, had brought it forward to the place where it ſtands in print—The very ſituation being at the *finis* of the pamphlet, as a confirmation of this account.

I lament my negligence, and aſk pardon for the imputation, and hope that the ingenuity of this confeſſion will give me a right to credit in what I ſhall affirm, and what I ſhall deny. [15]

With regard to the Highland Clergyman who adviſed me to tranſlate Fingal, I do not know that he ſeriouſly intended to have the experiment tried; for it was not at all likely that I ſhould embrace ſuch a propoſal. Yet I am of opinion that the event would be what he ſaid; and that many would aver, and very innocently aver, that they had heard from their childhood what was then recited. [16]

I make no doubt that if I were to read Fingal in the Highlands, multitudes who never heard the original, would believe that they had heard it; and deliver their belief upon oath, without conſciouſneſs of falſehood.—Such is the uncertainty of memory, ſuch the groſſneſs of vulgar apprehenſion, and ſuch the violence of national prejudice, that a few names to which their ears had been accuſtomed, a few images to which their eyes were familiar, and a few incidents which may be ſuppoſed to occur in all their ſtories, joined to the obſcurity of a new language, would eaſily gain credit to a new compoſition.

I do not mean by this to reproach the High-

landers

[75]

landers, the fame trick might, I believe, be played in any rude nation where knowledge is traditional.

I have not in any part of my difquifition afked
thefe admirers of Celtic literature, how they
knew any poem to be Offian's. Offian, according to Mr. Clark, * never heard of letters, his
poems could therefore only float along the ftream
of tradition, in which they might be mutilated,
corrupted, and confounded with a thoufand
others; and a traditionary error, once admitted,
cannot be corrected.—I have not afked them
whether the poems be Offian's, for there is yet a
previous queftion to be decided, whether they
have any poems at all—Let the reader keep the
main queftion in view; does Fingal exift in the
Earfe language ? 17 *

In return for my contemptuous mention of
MSS. to which Dr. Johnfon was referred, in the
hands of the fecretary to the Highland Society,
which were *Galic* indeed, but *Irifh Galic;* and
where inftead of the works of Offian, I found a
little Irifh poetry, and enough of Irifh and Highland genealogies, the reader is drawn off again
by a tale of Lauder ; but ftill the great queftion is
laid afleep, and poor Fingal fhifts for itfelf.

My character is next attaked by a furious letter from Mr. Macnicol, whofe acrimony and pe-
tulance will not add much to his credit. What

* That the reader may know who Mr. Clark my oftenfible
opponent is, he himfelf informed me that he had ferved an
apprenticefhip to, I think, a lapidary at Edinburgh ; but
now lives by land furveying. He told me alfo, that he was
nearly related to Mr. Macpherfon, was his pupil when he
taught a parifh fchool in Badenoch for twenty pounds a
year ; he is therefore interefted greatly in this controverfy :
and being a *Tranflator without Originals* will meet with all
the credit that he deferves.

K 2   he

[76]

he fays merely contumelious is below an anfwer; what facts he has advanced I will endeavour to difcufs—The converfation which he relates between Mr. Seton and me, I fincerely profefs myfelf not to remember. If Mr. Seton affirms it, I will not difpute the exactnefs of his memory, and ftill lefs that of his veracity. The report, be it true or falfe, is of little confequence.

The public is particularly required to remark the underhand diligence of Mr. Macpherfon and his party, to ruin the character of his opponent, and inftead of producing his MSS. to obftruct enquiry. The following fact, for the truth of which I refer to Mr. Murray, is a proof of it—Having on the publication of Mr. Clark's pamphlet fent up a letter to Mr. Murray to be publifhed, after looking about a month for the appearance of it, I received for anfwer, " That he had met with " fome difficulty in getting my fhort letter pub-" lifhed, as my opponents had carried their in-" fluence againft me, even into the papers ; but, " fays he, I fhall try again." 18

His next charge is, that I have changed fides, *and the world is afked what can be expected from the confident affertions of one fo wavering in his difpofition.* The world will furely expect more veracity from a man who has changed fides by conviction than from one who refolves to ftay for ever where he happens to ftand. How do we grow wifer but by changing our opinions? He is then in doubt whether I am yet come to a final refolution. Though I am afraid inftruction will do him little good, I will refolve his doubts. When he or any other man fhall prove my prefent opinions to be erroneous, it is my purpofe to retract them.

[77]

But hear, reader, the tragical history of Macintyre of Glenoe, from whom I borrowed about
two sheets of paper folded in octavo, containing
a collection of Earse words, with liberty to
transcribe them; for without that liberty of what
use had been the loan? These papers I did not
immediately return. By keeping what I had the
liberty to transcribe, I could gratify no vicious
disposition but idleness. *Yet this shameful and glar-
ing breach of confidence was instantly made public
over the whole neighbourhood. And as the complaint
came from a person of Glenoe's known modesty and
integrity, Mr. Shaw's character was immediately
blasted, and marked with the proper stigma. At
that very time it was thought prudent, as a ca-
veat to the community, to send a note relative to
the above mentioned fraud to the publishers of the
Weekly Magazine; but they did not think proper
to interfere with private characters.*

These important papers have since been returned, but they let it be supposed that I never
had returned them. To detain by negligence,
for there could be no other cause, a paper lent
to be transcribed, and of which the transcript is to
be printed, can be no *gross* violation of social duties—When once printed, it was worth nothing
to Glenoe. Yet let it be remarked, that this offence, which would have been very venial in any
body else, was to have *blasted* me in the public
papers. If malice could have discovered any thing
worse in my conduct, the worst had certainly
been told. I can only say, I am afraid that it is
beyond the hopes of man to live long without some greater crime. But so bad was now my
character, that few, says Mr. Macnicol, would
entrust me with MSS. my intention was now
publickly known; *and if I saw any thing in them*
that

[78]

that reflected honour on the country, they were con-
fident I would deftroy them. This can only be
anfwered with derifion.

He hints likewife a change of more importance, that I have left the Scotch for the Englifh communion; but he would have it believed
that what I have done was not by choice but
by compulfion. I was prefented to the living of
Ardilach by the Duke of Gordon; but when I
vifited the place I found the prefentation was
difputed, and that the right remained to be
tried; I therefore by a voluntary deed, demitted,
and determined to unite myfelf to a church,
whofe doctrines were more fuitable to my own
private opinions. This is the true ftate of the
tranfaction, and therefore Mr. Clark's narrative
is impudently falfe.

The following pages, deftined to my complete
and irrecoverable confufion, in which I am fhown,
Shaw contra Shaw, and at variance with myfelf
if they even contained all the contradictions,
pretended to be found, would prove only what I
very willingly confefs, that with refpect to the
abundance of Earfe literature I have changed
my mind. I once certainly believed too much;
I perhaps now believe too little; but when my
prefent belief fhall be overpowered by conviction, I have already promifed to change my mind
again.

It may be very reafonably afked, what would
give me the conviction I require. I fhould have
been convinced if I had heard Temora and Fingal in any confiderable parts, repeated in the
Highlands or Hebrides. I fhould be convinced
if I faw them now in any antient MS. But a
few paffages or fragments pretended to be
tranfcribed or antient MSS. will not convince
me; I wonder more fuch have not been already
fabricated.] 19   Dr.

[79]

Dr. Johnfon hinted, that he fhould not admit any thing as an original that was not after his challenge fpeedily produced; for he fufpeded that what was wanting in evidence might be fupplied by zealous induftry; and I have lately received information that Fingal is now diftributed among fome zealous Highlanders, to be tranflated into Earfe. When it fhall come out, I fhall be apt to fay, *Hic niger eft, hunc tu, Romane, caveto.* [20]

The pamphlet concludes with a hiftory of my journey, and a ridiculous account of my manner of travelling, with another grofs and impudent falfehood, that I confeffed myfelf ranging the Highlands at the expence of fome perfons in England to colled proofs againft the authenticity of Fingal. It is falfe that I made any fuch declaration. It is falfe that I travelled at any man's expence but my own.——Where are the Englifhmen that care whether Fingal was of Scotland or Ireland; whether Offian be genuine or fuppofitious? My undertaking was to enlarge my knowledge of the Earfe language and literature, and the refult of my enquiry was, that Fingal cannot be found in the Highlands, either written or recited.

Surely there is a time when a queftion like this muft have an end. If Fingal exifts in Galic, let the MSS. be fhown—When Nodot pretended to have difcovered a complete Petronius at Belgrade, the general cry of the learned was, " fhew us the manufcript." When very lately fome letters were printed under the name of the Pope Ganganelli, the reafons, however fpecious, that were offered for the authenticity, were effectually filenced by one demand, " fhew the originals." [21]

If

[80]

If the originals of Fingal can ever be fhown, oppofition may be filenced, but till then its defenders may juftly be confidered as fharing the fate of other liars, in being reduced to the neceffity of accumulating falfehood upon falfehood, and fupporting one impofture by another.

A P P E N D I X,

Notes to the Appendix

Except for a few emendations of misprints and the deletion of a final anecdotal paragraph in the first edition (1781) of the *Enquiry*, the only consequential change in the second 'corrected' edition of 1782 is the inclusion of the twenty-nine page *Appendix, containing A Reply to Mr. Clark* with eight more pages of extracts of letters bearing on Thomas Percy's part in the Ossian controversy.

Johnson's contributions are most pronounced in the following pages of the *Reply*: opening pages 51 to the middle of page 57 (except for authorial footnote on page 52); pages 59-63 and 66-67 (much of the writing outside quotation marks); and considerable portions of final pages 74-80 (beginning with 'I lament my negligence' and excluding authorial footnote on page 75).

Note numbers have been added to the reproduced text of the *Reply* to signal the inclusion of editorial endnotes with internal evidence of Johnsonian contributions in the form of parallel passages from Johnson's writings and conversations.

1. Compare this and the following paragraph with Johnson's letter to James Macpherson, 20 January 1775, in *The Letters of Samuel Johnson*, ed. R.W. Chapman (Oxford, Clarendon Press, 1952), vol.2, p.3 (number 373): 'Whatever insult is offered me I will do my best to repel. ...I will not desist from detecting what I think a cheat, from any fear of the menaces of a Ruffian. You want me to retract. What shall I retract? I thought your book an imposture from the beginning, I think it upon surer reasons an imposture still. For this opinion I give the publick my reasons which I here dare you to refute. But...I reverence truth and if you can prove the genuineness of the work I will confess it.' See also Johnson's *Preface to William Lauder's Essay on Milton* (1747) in *Samuel Johnson's Prefaces & Dedications*, ed. Allen T. Hazen (1937; reprinted Port Washington, N.Y., Kennikat Press, 1973), p.81: 'Any of these conjectures may possibly be true, but as they stand without sufficient proof, it must be granted likewise, that...they cannot preclude any other opinion, which...may perhaps be [shown] by resistless evidence to be better founded.' See also Johnson on culpably defending a known mistake in *Rambler*, 31 (3 July 1750), eds W.J. Bate and Albrecht B. Strauss, vol.3 (1969) of the Yale Edition of *The Works of Samuel Johnson* (New Haven, Yale U.P., 1958-), pp.169, 172: 'the observation of every day will give new proofs with how much industry subterfuges and evasions are sought to decline the pressure of resistless argument...[H]e may impose on his audience by...intricate deducations of remote causes...that he may sometimes puzzle the weak and well-meaning.'
2. Compare with Johnson's 'Proposals' (1777) for the printing of William Shaw's *Analysis of the Galic Language* (1778), as quoted by James Boswell in *Boswell's Life of Johnson*, ed. George Birkbeck Hill, revised L.F. Powell (Oxford, Clarendon Press, 1934-50), vol.3, p.107: 'An Erse Grammar is an addition to the stores of literature; and its authour hopes for the indulgence always shewn to those that attempt to do what was never done before. If his work shall be found defective, it is at least all his own: he is not like other grammarians, a compiler or transcriber; what he delivers, he has learned by attentive observation among his countrymen, who perhaps will be themselves surprized to see that speech reduced to principles, which they have used only by imitation.'
3. Boswell attributes this and the following four paragraphs to Johnson in *Boswell's Life of Johnson*, vol.4, pp.252-53. Compare this paragraph with Johnson's *A Journey to the Western Islands of Scotland* (1775), ed. J.D. Fleeman (Oxford, Clarendon Press, 1985), p.98: 'I suppose my opinion of the poems of Ossian is already discovered. I believe they never existed in any other form than that which

we have seen. The editor, or author, never could shew the original; nor can it be shewn by any other.' See also Johnson's letter to Boswell, 7 February 1775, in *The Letters of Samuel Johnson*, vol.2, p.8 (no.378): 'Where are the manuscripts? They can be shown if they exist, but they were never shown. *De non existentibus et non apparentibus*, says our law, *eadem est ratio*.'

4. Compare with Johnson's very last, if short, prose writing, his Dedication to the King, for Charles Burney's *Commemoration of Handel* (1785), in *Samuel Johnson's Prefaces & Dedications*, p.32: 'The delight which Music affords seems to be one of the first attainments of rational nature; wherever there is humanity, there is modulated sound.' See also the following passages in *Boswell's Life of Johnson*, vol.5, p.240: 'I am not disputing that you have poetry of great merit; but that M'Pherson's is not a translation from ancient poetry'; in the *Journey*, p.98, on the nonexistent original of Ossian, 'It would be easy to shew it if he had it; but whence could it be had?'; and in Johnson's letter to Boswell on Macpherson, no.378: 'No man has a claim to credit upon his own word, when better evidence, if he had it, may be easily produced.'

5. Compare this and the next paragraph with the attack against Macpherson in the *Journey*, p.98: 'The editor, or author, never could shew the original; nor can it be shewn by any other; to revenge reasonable incredulity, by refusing evidence, is a degree of insolence, with which the world is not yet acquainted; and stubborn audacity is the last refuge of guilt.' See also Johnson's conversational remark about the lack of old Erse manuscripts on 21 March 1775 in *Boswell: The Ominous Years, 1774-1776*, eds Charles Ryskamp and Frederick A. Pottle (New York, McGraw-Hill, 1963), p.89: 'We have seen none; and we have no reason to believe that there are not men with three heads, but that we have seen none.'

6. Compare with the *Journey*, pp.95, 99: 'After what has been lately talked of Highland Bards, and Highland genius, many will startle when they are told, that the *Earse* never was a written language...and that the sounds of the Highlanders were never expressed by letters, till some little books of piety were translated, and a metrical version of the Psalms was made by the Synod of Argyle... A Scotchman must be a very sturdy moralist, who does not love *Scotland* better than truth: he will always love it better than inquiry; and if falsehood flatters his vanity, will not be very diligent to detect it.' See also Johnson's letter on Macpherson, no.378: 'But...the Erse language was never written till very lately for the purposes of religion... If old manuscripts should now be mentioned, I should...suppose them another proof of Scotch conspiracy in national falsehood.'

7. Compare this and the following two paragraphs on Shaw's Gaelic scholarship with these passages by Johnson: (1) in the *Journey*, pp.96-97, 'The *Earse* has many dialects, and the words used in some Islands are not always known in others'; (2) in the ghostwritten 'Proposals' for Shaw's *Analysis* in *Boswell's Life of Johnson*, vol.3, p.107, quoted in my article at note 19; (3) in *The Preface to the English Dictionary* (1755) in *The Works of Samuel Johnson, L.L.D.*, 9 vols (Oxford, Talboys and Wheeler, 1825), vol.5, pp.24-25, 50:

   As language was at its beginning merely oral, all words of necessary or common use were spoken, before they were written; and...must have been spoken with great diversity... From this uncertain pronunciation, arise in a great part, the various dialects of the same country, ...and from this arbitrary representation of sounds by letters proceeds that diversity of spelling...which perplexes or destroys analogy, and produces anomalous formations... That it will immediately become popular, I have not promised to myself: a few wild blunders, from which no work of such multiplicity was ever free, may...harden ignorance into contempt; but useful diligence will at last prevail, and there never can be wanting some who...will consider that no dictionary of a living tongue ever can be perfect.

(4) in the 'Advertisement to the Fourth Edition of the English Dictionary' (1773) in *The Works of Samuel Johnson, L.L.D.*, vol.5, p.52: 'He that undertakes to compile a dictionary, undertakes that, which...he knows himself unable to perform. Yet his labours, though deficient, may be useful... Many faults I have corrected, some superfluities I have taken away, and some deficiencies I have supplied... For negligence or deficience, I have, perhaps, not need of more apology than the nature of the work will furnish.'

8. Compare with Johnson's letter on Macpherson, no.378: 'A nation that cannot write, or a language that was never written, has no manuscripts. But whatever he has, he never offered to show.'

9. Compare with Johnson's conversation on 22 September 1773 with the Rev. Donald Macqueen in *Boswell's Life of Johnson*, vol.5, pp.240-41: 'You do not believe it. I say before you, you do not believe it... I look upon M'Pherson's *Fingal* to be as gross an imposition as ever the world was troubled with.' See also Johnson on lying in *The Adventurer*, 50 (28 April 1753), eds W.J. Bate and others, vol.2 (1965) of the Yale Edition of *The Works of Samuel Johnson*, p.363: 'Yet so it is, that in defiance of censure and contempt, truth is frequently violated...even where the subject of conversation could not have been expected...to have excited...zeal or malignity, sufficient...to overpower the love of truth.'

10. Compare with the *Journey*, pp.95,96,97-98: 'many will startle when they are told, that the *Earse* never was a written language; that there is not in the world an Earse manuscript a hundred years old... The *Welsh* and the *Irish* are cultivated tongues...while the *Earse* merely floated in the breath of the people, and could receive little improvement... But diction, merely vocal, is always in its childhood... We were told, that they had an old translation of the scriptures... Yet...we found, that the translation meant, if any meaning there were, was nothing else than the *Irish* Bible...Martin mentions Irish, but never any Earse manuscripts, to be found in his time.' According to the *Journey*, p.98, n.8, Johnson's distinction between Irish and Earse is false.

11. Charles Vallancey's *A Grammar of the Iberno-Celtic, or Irish Language* (1773) was among Johnson's holdings, according to *Samuel Johnson's Library: An Annotated Guide*, ed. Donald Greene (Victoria B.C., Victoria U.P., 1975), p.112.

12. Compare with the *Journey*, pp.96, 97: 'That the Bards could not read more than the rest of their countrymen, it is reasonable to suppose; because, if they had read, they could probably have written... In an unwritten speech, nothing that is not very short is transmitted from one generation to another... Yet I hear that the father of Ossian boasts of two chests more of ancient poetry, which he suppresses, because they are too good for the *English*.'

13. Compare with Johnson's conversation about the credulity of the common people regarding primitive poetry in Boswell's *Life of Johnson*, vol.5, p.389: 'He would undertake...to write an epick poem on the story of *Robin Hood*, and half England, to whom the names and places he should mention in it are familiar, would believe and declare they had heard it from their earliest years.' For oral tradition and Macpherson's creation of Ossian's poetry, see the *Journey*, p.98: 'It is too long to be remembered, and the language formerly had nothing written. He has doubtless inserted names that circulate in popular stories, and may have translated some wandering ballads, if any can be found... It is said, that some men...heard parts of it, but...it was never said that any of them could recite six

lines.' See also *Boswell's Life of Johnson*, vol.2, p.347: 'Supposing the Irish and Erse languages to be the same, which I do not believe, yet as there is no reason to suppose that the inhabitants of the Highlands and Hebrides ever wrote their native language, it is not to be credited that a long poem was preserved among them.' Again, see *Boswell's Life of Johnson*, vol.2, p.513, for evidence that Johnson read Evan Evans's *Some Specimens of the Ancient Welsh Bards* (1764) but with some disapproval of the credit given by Evans to the 'Pretensions of McPherson and his erse Poetry'.

14. Compare with Johnson's letter to Macpherson, no.373: 'You want me to retract. What shall I retract?... But I reverence truth and if you can prove the genuineness of the work I will confess it.' Johnson considered Hugh Blair a victim of the Ossian deception. The Appendix closes with five extracts of letters by Shaw, Thomas Percy, and Adam Ferguson, the last of whom keenly defends his innocence against a charge of having participated in a staged recital of Ossianic verse by a Highlander in order to make a believer out of Percy, who later doubted Ossian but wanted no part of the quarrel.

15. The anecdotal paragraph below the *FINIS* of the first edition of the *Enquiry*, deleted from the second 'corrected' edition of 1782 containing the Johnsonian *Reply*, is as follows: 'A gentleman promised to ornament a scolloped shell with silver, if I should bring him one from the Highlands, and to swear it was the identical shell out of which Fingal used to drink!' John Clark's *Answer to Mr Shaw's Inquiry into the Authenticity of the Poems ascribed to Ossian* (1781) charged Shaw with ingratitude for mocking the unidentified gentleman of the anecdote who was a very 'respectable baronet' and evidently a patron of Shaw. The circumstantial answer here suggests that Clark's charge hit home and should be compared with Johnson's apology for William Lauder's forgery, *A Letter to the Reverend Mr. Douglas, occasioned by his Vindication of Milton* (London, W. Owen, 1751), p.4: 'On the Sincerity and Punctuality of this Confession, I am willing to depend for all the future Regard of Mankind, and cannot but indulge some Hopes, that they whom my Offence has alienated from me, may, by this Instance of Ingenuity and Repentance, be propitiated and reconciled.'

16. For this and the next paragraph, see note 13 above, and compare with Johnson on Erse and Scottish credulity about Ossian in the *Journey*, pp.95, 97, 98: 'It is the rude speech of a barbarous people who, ...were content, as they conceived grossly, to be grossly understood...I do not say that they deliberately speak studied falsehood, or have a settled purpose to deceive...He has doubtless inserted names that circulate in popular stories, and may have translated some wandering ballads,...and the names, and some of the images being recollected, make an inaccurate auditor imagine by the help of Caledonian bigotry, that he has formerly heard the whole... It is said, that some men of integrity...heard them when they were boys... They remember names, and perhaps some proverbial sentiments; and, having no distinct ideas, coin a resemblance without an original.'

17. Compare with Johnson's 'Proposals' for Shaw's *Analysis*: 'Though the Erse...still subsists in the northern...islands, yet...it...has floated in the living voice,' and with the *Journey*, pp.96, 97, 98: '*Earse* merely floated in the breath of the people... In an unwritten speech, nothing that is not very short is transmitted from one generation to another... He has doubtless...translated some wandering ballads, if any can be found.'

18. Shaw complained about the 'underhand dealings of Macpherson and his party' behind the failure of funding from the Highland Society for his tour of north Britain in his *Memoirs of Johnson* (1785), eds O.M. Brack, Jr, and Robert E.

Kelley, in *The Early Biographies of Samuel Johnson* (Iowa City, University of Iowa, 1974), p.175.

19. Compare this paragraph and the next with the *Journey*, p.98: 'I am far from certainty, that some translations have not been lately made, that may now be obtruded as parts of the original work' and with *The Letters of Samuel Johnson*, vol.2, pp.8-9, 12 (nos.378 and 380): 'Macpherson never in his life offered me the sight of any original or of any evidence of any kind... His copies, if he had them, and I believe him to have none, are nothing. Where are the manuscripts?... If old manuscripts should now be mentioned, I should, unless there were more evidence than can be easily had, suppose them another proof of...national falsehood... If there are manuscripts, let them be shewn, with some proof that they are not forged for the occasion. You say many can remember parts of Ossian. I believe all those parts are versions of the English; at least there is no proof of their antiquity.'

20. Compare with Shaw, *The life of Hannah More with a Critical Review of her Writings by the Rev. Sir Archibald Mac Sarcasm, Bart.* (London, T. Hurst, 1802), p.62: 'Of this the proof ought not to be brought forward in books, but in a court of law. *Hunc tu Romane caveto.*' See also Shaw, *Suggestions Respecting a Plan of National Education, with Conjectures on the Probable Consequences of Non-Descript Methodism and Sunday-Schools* (London, R. Cruttwell, 1801), p.17: 'As therefore, my Lord, "Hic niger est, hunc tu, Romane, caveto".'

21. For this and the final paragraph, see note 19 above and the *Journey*, p.98: 'The editor, or author, never could shew the original; nor can it be shewn by any other. ...I have yet supposed no imposture but in the publisher.' See also *The Adventurer*, 50, pp.364-65: 'A liar of this kind...is often the oracle of an obscure club, and till time discovers his imposture, dictates to his hearers with uncontrouled authority; ...if a new performance of literature draws the attention of the public, he...has seen the work in manuscript... [B]ut the prosperity of the liar is of short duration; the reception of one story, is always an incitement to the forgery of another less probable.' Finally, compare especially with *Boswell's Life of Johnson*, vol.3, p.286 and n.2, p.522: 'Dr. Mayo. "Pray, Sir, are Ganganelli's letters authentick?" Johnson. "No, Sir. Voltaire put the same question to the editor of them, that I did to Macpherson—Where are the originals?"' Johnson's comment of 15 April 1778 to Henry Mayo refers to Giovanni Vincenzi Ganganelli (1705-74), Pope Clement XIV, purported author of *Lettres intéressantes du Pape Clément XIV* (1775; English translation 1776), although actually written by Louis Antoine de Caraccioli (1721-1803). In the *Annual Register* for 1776 (vol.xlvi, p.563) there appeared a letter by Voltaire attacking the authenticity of the work. The passage quoted by Johnson is the following: 'On est en droit de lui dire ce qu'on dit autrefois à l'abbé Nodot: "Montrez-nous votre manuscrit de Pétrone, trouvé à Belgrade, ou consentez à n'être cru de personne."' François Nodot (died c. 1708) was an editor of Petronius.

Index